걸프 사태

국제원유 수급 동향 1

걸프 사태

국제원유 수급 동향 1

한국학술정보

| 머리말

걸프 전쟁은 미국의 주도하에 34개국 연합군 병력이 수행한 전쟁으로, 1990년 8월 이라크의 쿠웨이트 침공 및 합병에 반대하며 발발했다. 미국은 초기부터 파병 외교에 나섰고, 1990년 9월 서울 등에 고위 관리를 파견하며 한국의 동참을 요청했다. 88올림픽 이후 동구권 국교 수립과 유엔 가입 추진 등 적극적인 외교 활동을 펼치는 당시 한국에 있어 이는 미국과 국제 사회의 지지를 얻기 위해서라도 피할 수 없는 일이었다. 결국 정부는 91년 1월부터 약 3개월에 걸쳐 국군의료지원단과 공군수송단을 사우디아라비아 및 아랍 에미리트 연합 등에 파병하였고, 군 · 민간 의료 활동, 병력 수송 임무를 수행했다. 동시에 당시 걸프 지역 8개국에 살던 5천여 명의 교민에게 방독면 등 물자를 제공하고, 특별기 파견 등으로 비상시 대피할 수 있도록 지원했다. 비록 전쟁 부담금과 유가 상승 등 어려움도 있었지만, 걸프전 파병과 군사 외교를 통해 한국은 유엔 가입에 박차를 가할 수 있었고 미국 등 선진 우방국, 아랍권 국가 등과 밀접한 외교 관계를 유지하며 여러 국익을 창출할 수 있었다.

본 총서는 외교부에서 작성하여 30여 년간 유지한 걸프 사태 관련 자료를 담고 있다. 미국을 비롯한 여러 국가와의 군사 외교 과정, 일일 보고 자료와 기타 정부의 대응 및 조치, 재외동포 철수와 보호, 의료지원단과 수송단 파견 및 지원 과정, 유엔을 포함해 세계 각국에서 수집한 관련 동향 자료, 주변국 지원과 전후복구사업 참여 등 총 48권으로 구성되었다. 전체 분량은 약 2만 4천여 쪽에 이른다.

2024년 3월

한국학술정보(주)

| 일러두기

· 본 총서에 실린 자료는 2022년 4월과 2023년 4월에 각각 공개한 외교문서 4,827권, 76만 여 쪽 가운데 일부를 발췌한 것이다.

· 각 권의 제목과 순서는 공개된 원본을 최대한 반영하였으나, 주제에 따라 일부는 적절히 변경하였다.

· 원본 자료는 A4 판형에 맞게 축소하거나 원본 비율을 유지한 채 A4 페이지 안에 삽입하였다. 또한 현재 시점에선 공개되지 않아 '공란'이란 표기만 있는 페이지 역시 그대로 실었다.

· 외교부가 공개한 문서 각 권의 첫 페이지에는 '정리 보존 문서 목록'이란 이름으로 기록물 종류, 일자, 명칭, 간단한 내용 등의 정보가 수록되어 있으며, 이를 기준으로 0001번부터 번호가 매겨져 있다. 이는 삭제하지 않고 총서에 그대로 수록하였다.

· 보고서 내용에 관한 더 자세한 정보가 필요하다면, 외교부가 온라인상에 제공하는 『대한민국 외교사료요약집』 1991년과 1992년 자료를 참조할 수 있다.

| 차례

머리말 4

일러두기 5

걸프사태 : 국제원유 수급 동향, 1990-91. 전6권 (V.1 1990.8.6-17) 7

걸프사태 : 국제원유 수급 동향, 1990-91. 전6권 (V.2 1990.8.18-31) 159

걸프사태 : 국제원유 수급 동향, 1990-91. 전6권 (V.3 1990.9-12월) 335

정 리 보 존 문 서 목 록

기록물종류	일반공문서철	등록번호	2021010194	등록일자	2021-01-27
분류번호	763.5	국가코드	XF	보존기간	영구
명 칭	걸프사태 : 국제원유 수급 동향, 1990-91. 전6권				
생 산 과	기술협력과	생산년도	1990~1991	담당그룹	
권 차 명	V.1 1990.8.6-17				
내용목차	* 국제원유 수급 및 유가전망, 원유 안정확보를 위한 대산유국 외교활동 강화 등				

0001

외 무 부

종 별 :

번 호 : ECW-0554 일 시 : 90 0806 1630

수 신 : 장 관 (중근동,구일,기협,통이,동자부,재무부,상공부)

발 신 : 주 EC 대사대리

제 목 : 이락의 쿠웨이트 침공 (자료응신 제 67호)

연: ECW-0552

1. EC 12 개국은 이태리 요청으로 8.4. 로마에서 긴급소집된 EPC 정무총국장 회의에서 이락의 쿠웨이트 침공에대한 제재조치로서 하기사항을 결정하고, 이락에 의해설립된 쿠웨이트 임시정부를 불승인하는 입장을 밝힘 (관련성명내용 별도 FAX 송부)

- 이락및 쿠웨이트로부터의 석유 금수
- EC 회원국내 이락 자산동결
- 이락에 대한 무기및 기타 군사장비 판매금지
- 군사분야에 있어 이락과의 여하한 협력중지
- 이락과의 과학기술협력 중지
- 이락에 대한 GSP 공여 중지

2. EC 집행위측은 EC 12 개국의 쿠웨이트및 이락으로부터의 원유수입이 EC 전체원유수입의 약 10.9 프로에 달하는 것으로 추산하고 하기사항을 고려할때 금번 석유금수 조치가 EC 회원국의 원유조달에 심각한 지장을 초래하지 않을 것으로 분석함

- EC 회원국들의 현 원유비축량은 130백만톤으로서 105 일분의 소비에 상당
- 1970년대 원유파동시 서구국가간에 구축된 상호지원및 결속 메카니즘이 계속 유효하며 석유공급위기시 IEA 및 EC 차원에서 재가동 가능성

3. 당지 언론및 석유전문가들은 금번사태로 최근유가가 북해산 BRENT 유 기준, 배럴당 24불이상으로 상승하였으며, 이러한 강세기조는 서방측의 제재조치 확산으로 당분간 지속될 것으로 전망 (일부에서는 배럴당 30불까지 상승전망) 하고 있으나, 동사태가 어떤 형식으로든 진정되면 유가는 다시 배럴당 21-22불수준으로 안정될 것으로 예상하고 있음

중아국 1차보 구주국 경제국 통상국 정문국 안기부 재무부 상공부
동자부 2차보

PAGE 1 90.08.07 06:36 FC

외신 1과 통제관

0002

4. 이러한 전망의 근거는

1) 이락경제가 서방측의 제재조치에 장기간 버틸수 있을 만큼 좋지 못하기 때문에 금번사태가 장기간 지속될 것으로는 보지 않으며,

2) 금번 사태 이전에는 일산 2백만배럴정도 원유공급 초과현상을 시현하였으며,

3) 현재 OECD 국가들은 약 100일 정도의 석유를 비축하고 있기 때문임

5. 다만 당지 전문가들은 앞으로 비 OPEC회원국들의 신규 유전개발 가능성이 적기때문에 이번 사건을 계기로 OPEC회원국들이 재결속시 1990년대중 제3의 원유위기 도래 가능성을 우려하고 있음. 끝

(대사대리 신장범-국장)

관리번호	90-546

외 무 부

종 별 :

번 호 : JAW-4856 일 시 : 90 0806 1659

수 신 : 장 관(중근동,아일,기협,경일,통이)

발 신 : 주 일 대사(경제)

제 목 : 대 이라크 제재조치

연 : JAW-4829

당지를 방문중인 김종호 의원등 보이스카웃 의원연맹 대표단이 8.6. 오전 하시모또 대장상을 예방, 환담하는중에, 동 대장상은 일정부의 대 이라크 제재조치 결정에 관해 언급하였는바, 동 요지 아래 보고함.

(당관 이한춘 공사배석)

0 8.5. 저녁 카이후 수상과 외무성, 대장성, 통산성등 관계 각료가 회합, 이라크에 대한 일본의 대응방침을 논의하였는바, 제재조치 관련 가장 어려웠던 문제는 일본이 전시를 상정하여 (전쟁 당사국에 대해) 수출입 금지등을 규정한 분명한 법률적 근거가 없다는 것이었음.

0 그러나 UN 안보리가 강제력을 수반하는 대응조치를 취할수 있을지 등이 불확실한 상황이고, 그대로 방치하면 혼란이 더 확대될 우려도 있어, 여러모로 검토한 끝에 제재조치를 취하기로 결정하였음.

- 대장성은 8.3. 일본 국내의 쿠웨이트 자산을 동결하도록 행정지도를 실시하였는바, 현재 쿠웨이트의 해외자산을 조사하는 움직임이 대두되고 있어 대장성의 한발 앞선 행정지도가 잘된 조치였다고 생각함.

0 8.5 밤 결정된 제재조치는 8.7 각료회의에서 정식 승인을 받게 될것인바, 세관등 관계기관을 통해 금주내로 실제효과가 발생하게 될것으로 보고있음.

0 한편, 일정부가 현재 가장 우려하고 있는것은 기술원조들을 위해 이라크 및 쿠웨이트에 체류하고 있는 일본인들의 신변안전 문제로서 이들은 공항폐쇄로 인해 호텔등에 사실상 연금되어 있는 상태임.끝

(공사 이한춘-국장)

예고:90.12.31. 까지

중아국 장관 차관 1차보 2차보 아주국 경제국 경제국 통상국
정문국 청와대 안기부

PAGE 1

90.08.06 18:25

외신 2과 통제관 DL

0004

관리번호 90-548

외 무 부

종 별 : 지 급

번 호 : USW-3596 일 시 : 90 0806 1804

수 신 : 장관(중근동,미북,기협,항만청)

발 신 : 주 미 대사

제 목 : 이락,쿠웨이트 사태

대 WUS-2579

1. 금 8.6 당관 신정승 서기관및 김성수 해무관은 국무부 WAJDA 해운.육운 담당과장을 면담, 대호에 따라 미국측의 항만 봉쇄등 작전 수행시 아국 선박의 안전이 확보되도록 사전 협조를 요청하였음.

2.WAJDA 과장은 항만 봉쇄등의 작전 가능성에 대해서는 아는바 없다고 하면서, 미국은 현재 이락 및 쿠웨이트에 대해 경제 제재 조치를 취하고 있으며 일본, EC 등 주요 서방국들도 이에 동참하고 있는 상황이기 때문에 자신으로서는 미국이 우선 동 경제 제재 조치의 효과를 기다려 볼것으로 본다고 하면서 항만 봉쇄등에 대한 한국측의 관심 사항에 대해서는 유의하겠다고 답변하였음.

3. 참고로 미국의 대 이락, 쿠웨이트 경제 조치에 따라 미 선박에 의한 동지역 화물 수송 은 사실상 금지된 상태라함.

(대사 박동진-국장)

예고:90.12.31 까지

중아국	차관	1차보	미주국	경제국	정문국	청와대	안기부	해항청

PAGE 1

90.08.07 08:04

외신 2과 통제관 DH

0005

관리 번호 90-551

분류번호 | 보존기간

발 신 전 보

번 호 : WUS-2608 900807 종별 : 지급

수 신 : 주 수신처참조 대사. 총영사 1849

발 신 : 장 관 (기협)

제 목 : 이라크·쿠웨이트 사태

1. 아국은 이라크·쿠웨이트 및 중립지역으로부터 아국 원유 총 도입량(928천B/D)의 15.8% 를 도입하고 있으나, 표제사태로 사실상 동 도입이 중단된 상태임.

2. 이라크·쿠웨이트의 총 원유 생산량이 약 450만 B/D (자유 세계 총 생산량의 약 10% 차지)임을 감안할 시, 금번 사태가 장기화될 경우 또는 인근 지역으로 확산될 경우에는 국제원유수급 및 유가에 크게 영향을 미칠 것으로 판단됨

3. 금번사태 관련 아국의 원유수급대책 수립등에 참고코자 하니 귀 주재국 관련부서 및 전문가가 분석하는 아래 사항에 대해 지급 보고 바람.

- 금번사태에 대한 전망
- 금번사태의 장기화시 국제수급 및 유가전망
- 광역전쟁등 인근지역으로 확산시 국제수급 및 유가전망
- 주재국의 대책등. 끝.

90. 12. 31. 일반문서로 재분류

(국제경제국장대리 김 삼훈)

수신처 : 미국, 일본, 영국, 불란서, 서독, 카나다, 이태리, EC, 오지리, 스위스, 호주, 브라질, 이란, 아랍에미리트, 사우디, 카타르, 말련, 브루나이, 인니, 멕시코, 이집트, 알제리, 베네수엘라, 에콰도르.

보안 통제

앙고재	90년 8월 7일	기술협력과	기안자 성명		과 장		국 장		차 관	장 관
			홍성화				전결			

외신과통제

중동아프리카국장: 제2차관보:

0006

WUS-2608 외 발지급조

WUS-2608 900807 1849 ER

WJA -3334 WUK -1309 WFR -1505 WGE -1127 WCN -0806

WIT -0713 WEC -0470 WAV -0794 WAU -0548 WBR -0350

WIR -0254 WAE -0148 WSB -0287 WQT -0079 WMA -0546

WBU -0102 WDJ -0613 WMX -0693 WCA -0265 WAG -0103

WVZ -0255 WEQ -0181

0007

외 무 부

암호수신

종 별 :
번 호 : BRW-0466 일 시 : 90 0807 2000
수 신 : 장 관(중근동,기협,미남,정일,국방,기정동문)
발 신 : 주 브라질 대사
제 목 : 이라크-쿠웨이트 사태(자료응신 90-37호)

연: BRW-0457

대: WBR-0350

1. 주재국 정부는 무기 수출국으로서의 이라크의 중요성및 대이락 원유의존도로 인해 제재조치가 어려울것이라는 예상에도 불구하고 90.8.6. 외무, 경제, 기간산업부등 관계부처 회의를 열고 유엔안보리의 대이라크 통상제재 결의를 존중, 이라크 및 쿠웨이트와 통상관계를 단절하기로 결정하였음. 이와관련 주재국 외무부 대변인은 주재국 정부가 유엔안보리 결의를 즉각적이고 완전하게 준수할것이라고 발표하였으며, 최근까지도 주재국이 대이락 무기수출을 계속하고 있다는일부 외국 언론보도를 부인하였음.

2. 주재국 정부는 대이라크및 쿠웨이트 통상금지조치를 위한 대통령령을 조만간 공포할 예정이며, 이미 8.6. 부터 양국가 교역을 금지하고 있다함.

3. 브라질은 이라크-쿠웨이트 양국으로부터 일일 원유도입량 55 만배럴의 35프로에 해당하는 19 만배럴(이라크 16 만 배럴(89 년도 25.2 만 배럴), 쿠웨이트 3 만배럴)을 수입하고 있는바, 대 이라크및 쿠웨이트 통상금지 결정에 따라브라질 석유공사가 원유수입 협정이 체결된 10 개국과 원유추가 도입 교섭을 개시할것이라 하며, 주재국의 일일 원유도입 현황은 다음과 같음.

- 이라크 : 16 만 배럴
- 쿠웨이트: 3 만 배럴
- 사우디: 14 만 배럴
- 이란: 10 만 배럴
- 현물시장: 6 만 배럴
- 기타국가: 6 만 배럴

중아국	차관	1차보	2차보	미주국	경제국	정문국	청와대	안기부
국방부								

PAGE 1 90.08.08 08:37

외신 2과 통제관 CW

0008

계: 55 만 배럴

끝

(대사 김기수-국장)

관리 번호 90-556

원 본

외 무 부

종 별 : 지 급

번 호 : USW-3619 일 시 : 90 0807 1840

수 신 : 장관(기협,중동,미북)

발 신 : 주 미 대사

제 목 : 이락.쿠웨이트사태

대 WUS-2608

연 USW-3558,3571

1. 금 8.7 당관 오갑렬 서기관은 미 에너지부 국제과 PUMPHREY 계장을 면담,금번 중동 사태에 대한 미측 견해및 대책을 문의한바, 동 계장의 언급 내용을 아래 보고함.

가. 금번 사태 평가

-금번 경제 제재 조치는 당초 예상보다 더욱 효과적인것으로 보이는바, 경제 제재의 효과가 클수록 군사 조치의 필요성은 줄어들것으로 생각함.

-그간 이라크는 약 250 만 B/D, 쿠웨이트는 150 만 B/D 를 생산, 총 약 400 만 B/D 를 공급하여왔는바, 이라크의 원유 판매가(터키경유 30 만내지 40 만 B/D,사우디경유 40 만 내지 50 만 B/D)금번 사태로 100 만 B/D 정도로 감소함으로서 국제 시장에서 현재 원유 공급 부족분은 약 300 만 B/D 임.

-현재 국제 원유 재고는 약 1 억 8 천만 배럴로 정상보다 매우 많으며, 주로 산유국들이 보유하고 있음(예컨대 사우디가 5 천만 배럴 보유)

-이라크와 쿠웨이트의 원유 공급이 완전히 봉쇄되면 국제 원유 공급 부족은약 400 만 B/D 가 될것이나, 베네주엘라와 나이지리아의 공급 증가가 50 만 내지 75 만 B/D 로 예상되며, 사우디 및 UAE 는 이라크의 후세인 대통령을 자극시키지 않기 위하여 공급량 증가를 하지 않을것으로 예상되어 향후 국제 원유 공급 부족분은 약 300 만 내지 350 만 B/D 가 될것임.

나. 미국의 대책

-미국은 8.9 파리 개최 예정인 INTERNATIONAL ENERGY AGENCY 회의(미측 대표 에너지부 EAST 차관보, 국무부 BILL RAMSEY 부차관보등)에서 국제유가의 안정을 위하여 전략 비축 원유의 사용 개시를 제안할 예정임.

경제국	차관	1차보	2차보	미주국	중아국	정문국	청와대	안기부
동자부								

PAGE 1

90.08.08 09:59

외신 2과 통제관 CW

0010

긴급시 상호공동,

-현재 전략 비축분으로 미국은 5 억 9 천만 배럴, 일본은 2 억 8 백만 배럴, 독일은 5 천 3 백만배럴을 각각 보유하고 있는바, IEA 는 SHARING 체제로 운영하므로 동 전략 비축 원유 사용을 개시할 경우 현재 상태가 지속되고 심리적 변수만 없다면 향후 3 개월 내지 6 개월은 원유 공급 부족분을 감당할수 있을것으로 생각함.

다. 기타 관련 사항

-미국의 경우 원유 관련 물가 통제를 위한 제도적 장치로는 대통령 비상 조치밖에 없으나 미국 정부는 금번 사태와 관련 국민 및 업체들의 심리를 안정시키도록 노력하고 있음. 시중 휘발유 가격은 언론 보도와는 달리 갤론당 4-5 센트 정도로 약간 상승한것으로 파악되고 있음.

-미국 국내 원유 생산은 4-5 년전부터 감소하고 있는바, (금년에도 40-50 만 B/D 감소 전망)수개월내의 단기간에 국내 생산 증가를 기대할수 없으며, 충분한 수요와 높은 유가 수준일경우에도(예컨데 배럴당 40 불 정도로도 불충분할것이라고 함)국내 생산의 증가는 2-3 년 이후에나 가능하게될것임.

2.8.7 당지 주요 언론에 보도된 중동 사태 관련 사항을 아래 보고함.

가. 이라크, 쿠웨이트 원유 공급 중단으로 인한 원유 부족분의 충당 가능 요소

-세계 원유 재고의 사용

-각국의 전략 비축분 사용

-원유 추가 생산 능력 활용 사우디 250 만 B/D, UAE 100 만 B/D, 나이지리아및 베네주엘라 각각 수십만 B/D 등 도합 약 550 만 B/D.

나. 원유등 가격 인상

-8.6 현재 NEW YORK MERCANTILE EXCHANGE 에서 BENCH-MARK 원유 가격은 28.05 불로 몇주전 16 불에서 크게 상승함.

-미국의 PA, NW 등 항공사들은 항공 요금을 인상함.

-미국 시중 휘발류 가격은 지난 금요일 이후 갤론당 4-15 센트 인상됨.

다. 미 행정부의 조치

-교통부는 각종 운송 회사들에게 금번 사태 관련 가격 인상에 대하여 과잉 반응을 보이지 않도록 촉구함.

-법무부는 휘발유 가격 인상의 반독점법 위반 여부를 감시중임.

3. 미국 원유 공급 현황을 참고로 아래보고함.

(단위 천 B/D, 90.1-5 월 평균)

-국내 생산 7,393 (46.9 프로)

-해외 도입 8,381(53.1 프로)

. 아랍 OPEC 2,323(사우디 1,255, 이락 610, 알제리아 297, 쿠웨이트 121, UAE 31, 카타르 9)

. 여타 OPEC 2,184(베네주엘라 1,002, 나이지리아 941, 인니 138, 가봉 63,에쿠아도르 40)

. 비 OPEC 3,874

-총 공급량 15,774

-이라크 및 쿠웨이트로부터 도입분은 전체 해외 도입분의 8.7 프로임.끝

(대사 박동진-국장)

예고:90.12.31 까지

PAGE 3

0012

외 무 부

종 별 :

번 호 : MXW-0960 일 시 : 90 0806 1900

수 신 : 장 관(미중)

발 신 : 주 멕대사

제 목 : 원유수출 동향

1. 이락의 쿠웨이트 침공결과로 인한 최근 국제유가의 상승은 멕시코 원유 수출상 일일 1천만불 상당의 추가 수익을 가능하게 하고있음.즉 멕산 원유 3종류(ISTHMUS, OLMECA, MAYA) 는 지난주 배럴당 8불이 인상된 가격으로 거래되었음.(지난 6월중은 배럴당 9.35-14.57불로거래)

2. 그러나 멕시코 석유산업 전문가들은 PEMEX 의 생산능력상의 제약과 외국과 체결한 장기원유공급 계약으로 인하여 멕시코의 유가 단기급등으로 인한 수익향유에 한계가 있는것으로 지적하고 있음.

3. 최근 수년간 멕시코의 석유 개발분야에 대한 시설투자가 현격히 감소되어(PEMEX 예산은 81년60억불에서 현재 10억불로 삭감) 생산량증대에는 적어도 18개월 이상이 소요될 뿐만아니라 현재 일일 생산량 250만 배럴중 반은 국내 수요에 충당되며일일 수출 총량은 120만배럴에 머물고 있는 실정임.

4. 또한 외국원유 구매국과 체결한 장기원유공급 계약은 멕시코 원유수출 가격을매월평균 단일 유가에의거 결제하도록 규정되어있어 국제유가의 단기급등 효과를 향유치 못하고 있음.(대사이복형-국장)

미주국 2차보 통상국 경제국 동자부

PAGE 1

90.08.07 10:58 WH

외신 1과 통제관

0013

④
1박

외 무 부

암호수신

종 별 :

번 호 : JAW-4887　　　　일 시 : 90 0808 0952

수 신 : 장관(통이,경일,기협,아일,중근동)

발 신 : 주 일 대사(경제)

제 목 : 일 정부의 대 이라크 제재조치

연 : JAW-4829

8.6. 일정부가 취한 대이라크 경제제재 조치가 일본 경제에 미치는 영향 및동 제재조치 장기화에 대비한 일정부의 대책등을 언론보도 중심으로 아래 종합보고함.

1. 전반적 영향 평가 및 전망

0 금번 이라크에 대한 경제제재 조치가 석유수급 핍박 및 석유가 인상에 따른 물가상승을 통해 경제전반에 어떤 영향을 미칠것인가에 일정부 당국, 업계 및전문가들은 당분간은 44 개월동안 지속되어온 대형경기를 감속시키는 일은 거의 없을것으로 전망

- 수급면에서는 현재는 석유 비수요기이고 석유 비축량이 142 일분(1 차 오일쇼크시는 58 일분)에 달해, 당분간은 수입 감소분을 비축량 방출로 보충가능하는 점

- 또한 1,2 차 오일쇼크후 에너지 절약대책 및 기술혁신 진전으로 원유 수입가격이 물가에 미치는 영향은 20% 정도로 2 차 오일쇼크에 비해 매우 적게 되었다는 점

0 다만, 최근 국내물가가 상승기조에 있어 원유가 상승이 이러한 물가상승기를 부채질할 우려가 있다는 관측이 대두되고 있는바, 대장성은 공정금리 인상을 고려할 상황은 아니라고 하면서도 물가동향에 대해 경계심을 표시하고, 석유업계의 편승 인상행위를 감시할 방침을 밝히고 있음.

- 석유가에 대해서는 투기적 매입이 활발해져 당분간은 상승이 불가피한 것으로 보는 견해가 유력하나, 상승폭에 대해서는 견해가 다양

- OPEC 세계 석유 전문가들은 중장기적 관점에서 배럴당 25 달러 이상이 되면 에너지 절약화 및 석탄등 대체 에너지에의 전환으로 석유수요가 감퇴되므로, 25달러 수준이 한계라고 전망

통상국　차관　2차보　아주국　중아국　경제국　경제국　동자부

PAGE 1　　90.08.08　13:24

외신 2과　통제관 BN

0014

0 한편, 금번 사태가 장기화되면 원유가 상승 및 석유수급 핍박을 통해 적지않은 영향이 있을것으로 전망

- 대쿠웨이트 석유제품 수입 의존도가 약 14% 정도로, 공급면에서의 영향이서서히 나타날것으로 예측

- 대 쿠웨이트 및 이라크 원유 수입 의존도가 12% 정도인바, 과거 원유수입량의 3.4%가 감소한 정도로 제 1,2 차 오일쇼크가 발생했던 점으로 미루어 낙관 불허

2. 제재조치에 대한 업계의 반응 및 영향 평가

0 일본 산업계는 전반적으로 정부의 제재조치를 불가피한 조치로 받아들이고 있으나, 동 조치의 장기화에는 경계감을 표시하고 있는바, 특히 석유업계 및 플랜트 수출업계는 적지않은 영향을 받게될 것으로 우려

0 석유업계는 금년 상반기 쿠웨이트 및 이라크 양국으로부터의 원유 수입량이 일일 평균 40 만 베럴에 달하고 있어 정부의 원유 수입금지 조치에 대한 심각한 반응

0 이란, 이라크 전후 부흥계획 참여를 대이라크 무역 및 경제교류를 확대해온 상사 및 메이커등 수출업체는 대형 프로젝트 추진에 큰 타격이 있을것으로 우려하고, 대이라크 채권회수가 동국의 석유수입 감소로 어려워질 것으로 전망

- 89 년 대형 종합상사의 대이라크 계약건수는 총 7 건 430 억엥, 미쯔이 물산등에 의한 대쿠웨이트 담수화 플랜트는 1 건 50 억엥에 달하고, 그외에 대이라크 엥차관 제공을 겨냥한 민간업계간 대형 상담이 추진중

- 일본기업 약 100 개사의 대이라크 채권은 현재 7,000 억엥으로 이중 통산성 소관 무역보험 대상은 4,300 억엥 정도인바, 이라크는 88 년 말부터 대일 석유 수출대금의 약 25%, 90.2 부터는 45%가 주로 이자분으로 지불해 왔으나, 원금은 거의 그대로인 상태

0 여타 업계는 제재조치로 직접적 영향은 거의 없다고 평가

- TV, 비디오등 전기기계 부문의 대이라크 수출은 89 년도 100 억엥(수출구성비 1%)에 불과

- 철강의 대이라크 수출량은 90.1-5 간 4.4 만톤으로 전체수출의 0.7%

- 89 년 자동차의 수출은 이라크에 2,183 대, 쿠웨이트에 22,897 대에 불과

3. 일정부 및 업계의 제재조치 장기화 대비책

가. 일정부의 대책

0 대 업계 석유수입선 다변화등 요청

- 8.6. 통산성은 석유업계에 대해 원유, 가솔린등 석유제품, 액화석유가스(LPG)의 수입선을 여타국으로 다변화하도록 요청하여, 각 석유회사는 여타 산유국에 대해 대일 공급 계약량의 증량교섭에 착수

0 원유의 대 쿠웨이트 및 이라크 수입의존도 12%

. 석유제품의 대쿠웨이트 수입의존도 14%

. LPG 의 대쿠웨이트 수입의존도 12.7%

- 이와 더불어 석유업계가 고가의 원유를 구입치 않도록 지도하고, 석유가의 편승인상을 자숙하도록 요청(주유소등 판매업자에 대한 가격조사 강화방침)

0 석유 비축분(현재 142 일분) 방출

- 8.6. 통산성은 석유판매 회사등에 대한 민간 비축의무를 경감하여 민간 비축분을 방출할수 있도록 결정한데 이어, 석유 수요기인 9 월부터 국가 비축분을 방출한다는 방침하에 방출가격 산출등 구체방안 검토 착수

- 여타 산유국의 증량에는 어느정도 한계가 있을것으로 보고 원유 수입감소분의 보충을 통해 가격인상을 억제하는 것이 목적

0 원유처리 한도량증대

- 8.6. 통산성은 가솔린등 석유제품을 생산하는 원유의 처리한도량을 증대하는 방침을 결정, 관련 업계에 전달

- 89 년 대쿠웨이트 석유제품 수입 비중이 전체의 14%에 달하고 있어 제재조치 장기화시 제품수급에 악영향이 발생할것에 대비, 석유제품 수입 감소분을 국내생산으로 보충하는 것이 목적

0 업계 지원

- 일정부는 제재기간이 장기화될 경우, 민간기업의 보험청구 증가로 통산성의 무역보험 지불이 급증할 것에 대비, 무역보험 특별회계의 운용자금 확보조치 강구

. 현재 민간기업의 무역보험 채권은 이락크관련 채권 4,300 억엥, 쿠웨이트관련 채권 900 억엥 정도로 90 년도내 지불기한을 맞는 무역보험 채권은 약 800억엥 정도로 추산

- 한편, 통산성은 대쿠웨이트 및 이라크 수출 의존도가 높은 중소기업을 대상으로 금수조치가 기업경영에 미치는 영향을 조사, 피해가 광범할 경우 자금을 대부하는 긴급융자 제도 검토 착수

0 종합적 에너지 절약 대책 검토

PAGE 3

0016

- 자원에너지청은 1,2 차 오일쇼크와 같은 위기적 상황이 아니라고 보고, 석유 사용량 규제등 강경대책은 당분간 취할 생각이 없다고 하면서도 제재조치가장기화할 것에 대비, 사우디등에 증산을 요청함과 동시에 석유 수요. 공급면에대책 수립검토 예정

- 73 년, 79 년의 오일쇼크때는 석유사용절감, 주유소 영업시간 단축, 네온싸인 및 냉난방 사용억제등의 종합에너지 절약대책을 작성, 실시한바 있음.

나. 민간업계 반응

0 이라크 및 쿠웨이트 진출업체들은 현지사원의 안전확보에 전력을 기울이고 있으며, 일부에서는 제재조치 장기화에 대비, 현지 인원 감소 또는 폐쇄등 대책 검토

0 특히 대형 종합상사들은 정부의 제재조치가 장기화될 경우, 원유가격 및 상사활동등에 영향이 클것으로 보고, 현지사원 안전대책, 석유정세 및 금후 사업전망등을 분석, 대응책 강구.끝

(공사 이한춘-국장)

PAGE 4

0017

관리번호	90-550

원 본

외 무 부

종 별 : 지 급

번 호 : DJW-1126 일 시 : 90 08081300

수 신 : 장관(기협,경이,정이,동자부)

발 신 : 주 인니 대사

제 목 : 이락.쿠에이트 사태

대: WDJ-0613

이락의 쿠웨이트 침공관련 국제원유 동향에 관한 주재국 관계전문가 논평을하기 보고함

1. 주재국 원유생산및 수출

최대 생산능력: 일산 1.6 백만베럴

OPEC 쿼타량: 일산 1.374 백만베럴

현 생산량: 일산 70 만바렐(일본 50 프로, 미국 30 프로, 중국 13 프로, 대만 5 프로, 기타 2 프로)

수입: 알비안 정유류 10 만바렐(사우디, 이락, 이란등)

국내소비: 수입정유 10 만바렐 프러스 국내상산 70 만바렐(총 80 만바렐)

2. 주재국은 원유자원의 효과적인 활용을 위하여 최대 생산능력에 따른 생산억제, OPEC 쿼타량 이하 생산, 일부 값싼 원유및 정유를 수시수입, 유가의 안정과 원유자원의 장기확보를 기하고저함

3. 주재국 관계전문가 논평

가. 광업에너지성 MARZUAN 오일가스청장 보좌관은 긴급한 사항일지라도 인니가 추가 생산하는데는 어려움이 많고 현 수출량을 조정할수는 있으나 장기계약을 체결한 국가에 대해 적기적량을 공급하지 못할경우 배상문제가 따를것이라고 함. 세계원유정세와 관련, 이락이 쿠웨이트에 망명왕정의 복귀를 저지하고 친이락군정 또는 민간정부 수립을 지원함으로써 세계여론이 이락과 쿠웨이트 원유 불매운동을 벌여 이락과 쿠웨이트로부터 원유를 대량 수입하던 국가는 원유공급선 확보에 어려움이 예상되며, 국제원유가격도 상당한 기간 상승세를 보일것이라고 함

나. 국제전략문제 연구소 SIMANJUNTAK 박사는 쿠웨이트에 왕정이 복귀하기는

경제국 1차보 2차보 경제국 정문국 청와대 안기부 동자부

PAGE 1

90.08.08 16:38

외신 2과 통제관 BT

0018

불가능하다고 예측하면서, 세계유가는 충격요인 매문에 일시 상승할것이나, 유가가 30 불선을 넘을경우 세계경제에 미치는 영향이 심각하므로 비산유국은 물론, OPEC 의 온건회원국들이 유가 안정대책을 마련할것이며, 이락, 쿼이트가 필요한 자금조달을 위해 SPOT MARKET 에 저렴한 가격으로 원유를 판매하게 됨으로써국제유가는 30 불선을 크게 넘지 않을것이라고 함. 다만, 이락, 쿠웨이트 사태가 장기화될경우 OPEC 및 비 OPEC 산유국간의 협상, 산유국과 비산유국간 협상이활발해질 것이라고 전망함.

4. 본건 계속 추보예정임.끝

(대사 김재춘-국장)

예고:90.12.31 일반

PAGE 2

0019

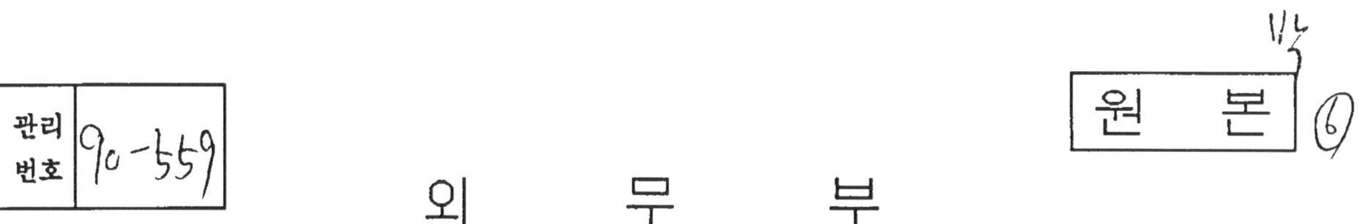

외 무 부

종 별 :

번 호 : MAW-1014 일 시 : 90 0808 1800

수 신 : 장관(기협,아동)

발 신 : 주 말련 대사

제 목 : 이라크,쿠웨이트 사태

대:WMA-0546

1. 대호관련 아래 1 차 보고함

가. 주재국은 이락의 전격적인 쿠웨이트 점령에 경악하고 있으며, 이의 근본적인 이유를 규명하고 사태 발전을 전망하기 위하여 중동지역 및 유엔 대표부등 주요자국 공관과 긴밀히 연락하고 있으나 마하털 수상과 아부하산 외무장관 (베네주엘라 출장중), 압둘라 파질 외무 부장관과 담당국장(OIC 회의 참석)이 모두 외유중이므로 금번사태의 장기화 또는 확산 여부등에 관한 주재국 나름의 전망과 대책수립에는 상당 시간이 소요될것으로 내다보고 있음.(외무부 서아시아과장 언급)

나. 주재국 정부가 카이로 OIC 정상회의에서 금번 사태에대한 중재 용의를 표명하였다는 8.8. 자 당지보도에 대하여, 동 과장은 본부로부터의 훈령에 의한 것이 아님으로 확실치 않다는 반응임

다. 금번 사태가 계속 될시 단기적으로는 원유의 국제수급및 유가면에서 심각한 상황을 야기할 것이나, 이란, 이락전의 경험으로 미루어 볼때 종국적으로는 고 유가가 장기간 지속되거나 상승 일로에 있을 것으로는 보지않는다고 전망하고 있음 (수상실 동자부서및 언론분석)

라. 한편 주요원유 수요국들이원유구입선을 비 OPEC 회원국으로 전환할 것으로 내다 보면서, 세계경제의 지속적 성장에 필수적인 원유시장의 안전을 위하여는 금번 사태가 여하히 발전하든간에 OPEC, 비 OPEC 간 유가 통제합의에 도달해야할 것이라고 분석하고 있음(MIDA 관계관 언급)

마. 경제적 측면에서 주재국은 대이락 경제제재 조치에따라 기존의 대 이락팜오일 수출이 중지되어 다소간의 불이익을 받는 이외에는 원유가 및 LNG.LPG등 부산품가의 상승과 생산 증대로 전반적으로는 경제적이득이 적지 않을것으로 언론은 보도하고있음

경제국 차관 1차보 아주국 정문국 청와대 안기부 동자부

PAGE 1 90.08.08 22:38

외신 2과 통제관 DH

0020

2. 본직은 당지 PETRONAS 회장을 금주중 면담예정인 바, 주재국의 움직임을 주시, 진전 상황 추보하겠음. 끝

(대사 홍순영-국장)

예고문:90.12.31 일반

관리번호	90-560

원 본

외 무 부

종 별 : 지 급

번 호 : SBW-0600 일 시 : 90 0808 1540

수 신 : 장관(기협,중근동,동자부,재무부,기정)

발 신 : 주 사우디 대사

제 목 : 이라크-쿠웨이트 사태

대:WSB-0287

1. 표제관련, 미 대사관 석유담당관등 당지 전문가들의 의견을 하기 보고함.

가. 금번 사태에 대사 전망

-이락의 사우디 침공 가능성을 전혀 배재할수는 없으나, 국제여론 및 미국의 군사개입등을 고려할때 그가능성은 크지않음.

-이라크가 쿠웨이트 철수의사를 전혀 보이지 않고있어, 단시일내의 사태수습 전망은 보이지않음.

나. 금번사태 장기화시 국제수급 및 유가 전망.

-현재 원유시장의 재고분, 각국의 비축분, 사우디, 베네주엘라, 이란등 OPEC회원국들의 증산등을 고려할때, 유가상승 추세는 곧 멈출것으로 봄.

(브랜트 기준 베럴당 30 불을 넘지않은 수준에서 머물것으로 보는 견해가 많음.)

-이라크, 쿠웨이트산 원유의 국제시장에서의 물량은 세계원유시장이 어느정도 감당할수있음.

다. 광역전쟁등 인근지역으로 확산시 국제 수급 및 유가전망

-사우디 원유시설 파괴등이 있을 경우, 그여파는 누구도 예측할수 없을 정도로 심각할것임.

라. 주재국의 대책등

-곧 산유량의 증대에 나설것으로 보임 (주재국의 현보유량은 일산 530 만베럴정도이나, 일산 800 만베럴의 산유능력을 갖추고있음.)

-상금 주재국은 사우디내 이라크 송유관 (일산 160 만베럴 수송용량) 의 봉쇄 문제에 대하여 구체적 조치를 취하지 않고 있으나, 홍해안의 이라크 비축설비에 여유가 없게된면 송유관 봉쇄와 같은 효과를 거두게 됨.

경제국 차관 1차보 2차보 중아국 정문국 청와대 안기부 재무부
동자부

PAGE 1 90.08.08 23:02

외신 2과 통제관 DH

0022

2. 사태진전 추이 추보위계임.

(대사 주병국-국장)

예고:90.12.31 일반

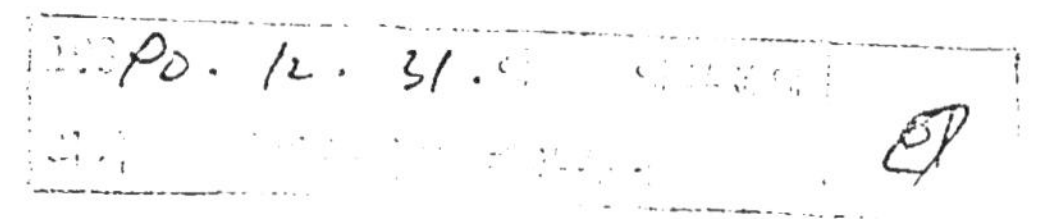

PAGE 2

0023

외 무 부

종 별 :
번 호 : VZW-0434 일 시 : 90 0807 1700
수 신 : 장 관 (미남,중동,경일,기정,국방부)
발 신 : 주 베네수엘라 대사
제 목 : 베네수엘라 석유정책 (자응 제 38호)

1. 주재국 정부가 이라크의 쿠웨이트 침공사태로 예상되고 있는 원유파동에 대한 대응책 마련을 위해 부심하고 있는 가운데, 8.6 ARMAS 동자부장관은 베네수엘라는 OPEC 협정을 준수, 현행 OPEC 쿼타 (194만5천 B/D) 이상으로 생산량을 증대시키는등 독자적 행동을 취하지 않을 것이라고 밝힘.

2. 그러나 동자부 장관의 상기 천명에도 불구, 베네수엘라의 공식입장은 OPEC 쿼타를 준수하는 것이나, 생산증대가 국가 이익에 합당하다고 대통령이 결정할 경우 동 입장은 변경될수도 있다고 동자부 고위관리들이 언급함.

3. 8.4 ROBERTO POCATERRA 재무장관은 이라크, 쿠웨이트 사태로 유가가 배럴당 3미불이상으로 인상될 경우 베네수엘라는 90년도 약 10억불의 추가수입을 올릴 것이라고 언급한 바 있음.

4. 동 관련, 주재국 정계는 미국이 주도한 이라크및 쿠웨이트 원유불매를 지원하기 위하여 원유생산량을 증대, 이라크와 쿠웨이트로부터 원유수입을 중단한 국가들의 수요를 충족시켜 주어야 한다고 주장하고 있음.

5. 한편, 야당인 기독교사회당은 '전시에 안정되고 신뢰할 수 있는 원유 공급자로서의 베네수엘라의 위치'를 확인하기 위하여 동자부내의 대외 원유정책 자문위원회의 개최를 대통령에게 요청하였음.끝.

(대사 김재훈-국장)

미주국 1차보 중아국 경제국 정문국 안기부 국방부

PAGE 1 90.08.09 07:36 FC
외신 1과 통제관

0024

관리번호	90-563

원 본

외 무 부

종 별 :

번 호 : AUW-0597　　　　일 시 : 90 0809 1530

수 신 : 장관(기협,중근동,아동,기정)

발 신 : 주 호주 대사

제 목 : 이라크.쿠웨이트 사태

대:WAU-0548

연:AUW-0588

대호관련, 주재국 전문가(일간지, TV 등)의 사태전망 분석 내용 및 외무 무역성, 1차산업성등이 발표한 주요대책을 다음과 같이 보고함.

1. 금번 사태에 대한 전망

0 유엔 및 미국의 대이라크 경제제재 조치로 이라크 경제는 큰 타격을 받을것으로 전망, 그러나 이라크가 미국의 요구조전(쿠웨이트로부터 완전, 무조건 철수, 쿠웨이트 국왕 복구등)을 쉽게 수락할 가능성은 희박한것으로 분석

- 전례없는 국제적 호응으로 강경한 경제 제재 이행 예상

- 대외무역 동결 등으로 이라크의 경제침체 불가피

0 동 경제조치가 장기화될시 미국, 서방선진국의 경우에도 경제 침체를 초래, 자국및 및 관련사업계의 지지기반 상실 가능성 대두로 인해 정책 딜렘마 현상 야기 가능, 금번 사태는 이라크의 야망과 관련, 미국의 제 3 세계에서의 영향력 쇠태 및 미군사력의 무력감에 대한 시험대로 작용, CREDIBILITY 및 자존심의 대결 양상으로 발전가능

- 경제제재 조치의 비능률성 및 사태해결의 한계

- 피제재국 뿐 아니라 제재국도 타격 감수

- 동조치의 효과가 적을시 미국의 NAVAL BLOCADE 등 추가조치 예상

- 미국의 공세적인 군사작전은 위협부담(이라크의 화학전 대응및 여타 파급영향등)이 많아 가능성이 적은것으로 예측되나, 미국의 대이라크 요구사항 관련,사태해결을 위한 하나의 전략 OPTION 으로서의 군사적인 압력가중 가능성.

0 경제적 측면에서, 단기적으로는 유가인상으로 인하여 국제경제의 침체현상이

경제국　차관　1차보　2차보　아주국　중아국　청와대　안기부

PAGE 1　　　　90.08.09 15:57

외신 2과 통제관 CF

0025

예상

- 인프레 압력, 환율불안, 주식시장 급변, 국제무역 감소, 경제성장 둔화등

0 장기적으로는 각국정부(특히 미국)들의 충격의 단기 및 최소화를 위한 노력으로 국제경제 전반의 흐름을 되찾을 가능성도 많음.

- 국제경제의 대이라크, 쿠웨이트 원유에의 의존도가 낮은점.

- OPEC 의 가격결정시 이라크의 영향력 확대가능성이 희박한점.

- 미국, 원유수급 부족을 없애기 위한 사우디와의 협조등으로, 금번사태의 국제경제에 미치는 영향 최소화 노력계속.

이하 AUW-0596 호로 계속

PAGE 2

0026

관리번호	90-564

원 본

외 무 부

종 별 :

번 호 : AUW-0598 일 시 : 90 0809 1530

수 신 : 장관

발 신 : 대사

제 목 : AUW-0597 PART 2

2. 금번사태의 장기화시 국제수급 및 유가전망

0 이라크, 쿠웨이트의 원유 수급중단시, 유가는 현수준(지난주보다 배럴당 3불 이상 인상)보다 25-50 %선 까지 인상예상

- 앞으로 배럴당 25-35 %까지 인상 추측

- 인상추세가 어느정도 지속될지는 의문

0 원유가격 인상으로 생산 증가요인 발생, OPEC 회원국및 비회원국이 일당 450 만 바렐을 증산, 충당할 가능성이 많다고 전망(이경우 유가안정에 기여)

- 사우디(일당 2 백만바렐 증산 보도), 멕시코 등(단, 시설부자 기간 소요)

- 주재국의 경우, 시추.개발회사에 대한 정부의 혜택 부여 문제 대두

3. 광역 전쟁등 확산시 국제수급 및 유가전망

0 중동은 물론 국제정세 전반에 불안요인으로 등장, 원유의 국제수급은 많은 차질을 받게될것으로 우려

- OPEC 의 원유생산량 및 가격설정, 통제기능이 사실상 어려울것으로 전망.

0 따라서, 유가인상에 대한 예측 불허 실정

4. 주재국의 대책

0 대 이라크. 쿠웨이트 경제제재 조치 참여

- 원칙적으로 무역 및 자금 송금 동결(상세 연호 참조)

- 주재국은 약 10 억호주불(수출판매 미수대금 7 억 및 수출품에 대한 수주액등)손실감소 예상(주재국의 연간 대이라크. 쿠웨이트 수출(소맥, 육류)은 4 억2 천만 호주불, 수입(원유)은 쿠웨이트로부터 1 억 호주불 규모임.원유소비는 일 66 만 바렐 규모로서 이중 40%를 사우디, UAE, 인니등으로부터 수입하고 있음)

0 인프레 억제를 위한 대내적 조치 강구

PAGE 1 90.08.09 16:01

외신 2과 통제관 CF

0027

- 유가인상 억제를 위한 에너지 소비세 인하 추진
- 정부예산 수입감소에 따른 예산지출규모 축소화
-노조와의 임금 인상협상 정책 재고
- 주재국내 석유시추, 개발회사들에 대한 혜택 고려등. 끝.

(대사 이창수-국장)

예고:90.12.31. 까지.

PAGE 2

0028

관리번호	90-562

원 본

외 무 부

종 별 : 지 급

번 호 : JAW-4934　　　　일 시 : 90 0809 1513

수 신 : 장관(기협,경일,통일,중근동,동자부)

발 신 : 주 일 대사(경제)

제 목 : 이라크.쿠웨이트 사태

대 : WJA-3334

연 : JAW-4887

대호관련 일본 통산성 국제자원과 관계관등 접촉 및 전문가의 언론인터뷰 내용을 중심으로 아래 종합 보고함.

1. 금번 사태에 대한 전망

0 통산성 관계자는 금번 사태의 장기화 및 확산여부에 대해서는 이라크, 미국, 사우디의 태도가 주요 변수가 될것이라는 것 이외에 자신있는 전망을 할수 없어, 석유수급대책에 고심하고 있는바, 현재로서는 장기화될것을 상정, 정세변화에 따른 단계적 수급대책을 검토하고 있다고함.

0 한편 중동 경제연구소 관계자는 미국의 사우디 파병 및 사우디의 동 파병수용 결정 관련 이러한 상황전개가 분쟁을 확대시켜 해결이 장기화될 것으로 관측하고 있는바, 이는 교섭에 의한 해결을 시도할 경우 이라크의 교섭 대상국이될수 있었던 사우디를 대이라크 포위망에 참여시킴으로써 교섭을 어렵게 하고 이라크를 힘으로 굴복시키는 길밖에 남지 않게 될 것이기 때문이라고 설명하고 있음.

0 경제 기획청은 대이라크 경제조치가 일본의 경기 및 물가에 미치는 영향을 분석하기 위해, 동청내 관계부서간 연락회의를 설치키로 하였는바, 이는 미국의 사우디 파병으로 분쟁이 장기화될 가능성이 커졌다는 인식에 따른것으로 관측됨.

2. 국제 석유수급 및 유가 전망

가. 국제수급전망(통산성 관계자 발언요지)

0 이라크는 세계 석유소비량의 3.5%, 쿠웨이트는 2.2%를 생산하고 있어서 양국의 생산이 세계 석유수급에 미치는 영향을 무시할수 없는바, 금번 사태가 장기화되면 국제적 석유수급 핍박으로 인한 큰 영향이 있을것임.

경제국	장관	차관	1차보	2차보	중아국	경제국	통상국	청와대
안기부	동자부							

PAGE 1

90.08.09 16:29

외신 2과 통제관 CF

0029

0 다만 OECD 가맹국의 비축량이 현재 4 억 6,800 만톤으로서 81 년 이래 최고수준에 달하고 있고, 여타 산유국에 생산능력이 있으며, 현재는 석유 비수요기임을 감안할때, 단기적으로는 국제수급에의 영향이 적을것으로 봄.

0 사우디로 사태가 확산되어 사우디로부터의 공급이 단절될 경우에는, 국제석유수급에 미칠 영향은 심대할 것인바, IEA(국제에너지기관) 주관하에 석유 비축량 방출 등 국제수급 대책이 검토.협의될 것으로 봄.

- 현재 IEA 가입국의 석유 비축의무는 90 일분임.

0 국제 석유수급 전망을 위해서는 산유국의 생산동향 및 소비국의 수요동향을 지켜볼 필요가 있는바, 8.9. 개최될 IEA 긴급회의에서 정세판단, 대처 및 각국간 대책조정등이 협의될 것임.

- 석유수급핍밥 정도는 수요의 억제 및 산유국의 공급증가에 달려 있는바, 현재 OPEC 국의 증산 움직임은 보이지 않고 있는 실정임.

나. 국제 유가 전망

0 통산성 관계자는 쿠웨이트 및 이라크산 석유 수입금지가 석유가를 앙등시킬 우려가 있으나, 상승폭에 대해서는 예측하기 힘들며, 유가상승이 단기적으로 진정되지 않으면 IEA 에서 대책을 강구하게 될 것으로 본다고 말함.

0 석유 및 종합상사등 업계에서는 국제 석유가는 IEA 각국 협조에 의한 비축 방출 및 사우디등의 증산에 의해 영향을 받을 것인바, 가령 사우디가 증산을 결정할 경우 8.8. 현재 두바이산 원유의 현물가격 24.15($/1B)보다 2-3 달러 하락할 것이라는 견해가 강하며, 사태가 사우디로 확산될 경우는 배럴당 30 달러까지 앙등할 것이라는 견해도 있음.

- 석유업계는 증산 여력이 있는 산유국은 14 개국 정도로 증산에 기대를 걸수있는 산유국은 사우디(일일 증산여력 200 만 배럴) 베네주엘라(동 100 만배럴), UAW(동 80 만 배럴)등 3 개국이라고 보고있음.

- 한편 최근 사우디의 증산 결정 보도에 대해 사실여부 확인은 석유회사 및 상사의 공급희망량 제시에 대해 사우디측이 공급량을 통보해 올 8 월 중순경이 될 것으로 보고있음.

0 한편 석유전문가들은 연호 1 항과 같이 중장기적 관점에서는 배럴당 25 달러가 석유가의 한계라고 보고 있음.

3. 일정부 대책

PAGE 2

0030

0 통산성 관계관에 의하면 일 정부는 금번 사태가 사우디로 확산될 것에 대비하는 대책은 아직 검토하고 있지 않다고 함.

0 현재로서는 석유공급선 대체, 석유소비량 감축, 석유비축방출을 기본으로하여 연호 3 항과 같은 대책을 검토하고 있으며, 대 이라크 경제조치의 효과 및 중동사태 추이에 따라 단계적으로 실시할 예정인바, 우선은 수요면에서의 억제에 중점을 두고 실시할 것이라함.

0 한편 금번 사태에 의한 영향은 일 정부뿐만 아니라 모든 소비국이 함께 받는 것이므로, 일본만이 두드러진 대 산유국 공급증가 교섭을 비난의 대상이 될 우려도 있으므로 IEA, OECD 등과의 협조를 긴밀히 하고자 한다고 말함. 끝

(공사 이한춘-국장)

예고:90.12.31.일반

0031

관리번호 90-570 | 원 본

외 무 부

종 별 :

번 호 : FRW-1434 일 시 : 90 0809 0920

수 신 : 장관(기협)

발 신 : 주 붙 대사

제 목 : 이라크.쿠웨이트 사태

대: WFR-1505

대호, 주재국 전문가의 분석내용 아래 보고함.

1. 사태 장기화및 확산시 원유수급 및 유가 전망

0 장기적으로 하기 사항 감안시 제 3 차 OIL SHOCK 는 쉽게 도래하지 않을 것으로 전망됨.

-소비국의 원유비축량 적정수준(190 만 배럴)

-대체에너지 개발및 원유소비 절약

-OPEC 점유비율 감소(1,2 차 파동시 50 프로-현재 30 프로)

-각국의 세제 감면혜택 부여등

0 중.단기적으로 EMBARGO 및 BLOCKADE 효과, 인플레 기대 심리에 따라 유가가 상승(최고 30-35 불) 할것이나, 이같은 상승세가 6-12 개월을 초과하지는 않을 것임.사우디의 증산등으로 유가상승 요인을 상쇄할 수도 있으나, 정치적으로 실효성이 의문시됨.

0 제반 사정 감안시, OIL SHOCK 여부는 궁극적으로 소비국의 대응여하에 달려있음.(1,2 차 OIL SHOCK 당시에도 공급부족 보다는 원유비축량 부족이 유가 상승의 주요 원인이었음.)

2. 주재국의 대책(8.7 BEREGOVOY 경제. 재무상 발표)

0 유가 동결(1 차시한:9.15 까지)

0 당분간 유통마진을 허용하지 않고 세제혜택을 주는 행정령으로 통제

3. 참고사항

. 주재국은 이락및 쿠웨이트산 원유의존도가 7 프로 선이므로 현재는 직접적인 타격은 적으나, 서방의 대이락 제재가 장기화될 경우 이락의 원유 판매수입으로

경제국 차관 1차보 2차보 구주국 청와대 안기부 동자부

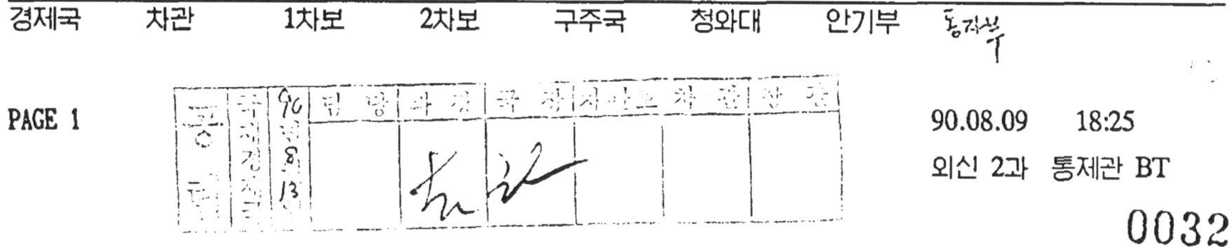

PAGE 1

90.08.09 18:25

외신 2과 통제관 BT

0032

변제되는 대불 부채상환(주로 무기대금)이 원활치 못할것이므로 이에대해 우려를 갖고있음.

4. 본건 수시 추보함. 끝.

(대사 노영찬-국장)

예고:90.12.31. 까지

PAGE 2

0033

관리번호 90-572

원 본

외 무 부

종 별 :

번 호 : BUW-0173 일 시 : 90 0809 1655

수 신 : 장관(기협)

발 신 : 주 브루나이 대사대리

제 목 : 이라크,쿠웨이트사태

대:WBU-102

소직은 8.8. HAMID JAFAR 외무성 경제국장 대리. 8.9. DAVID LAMB 브루나이쉘회사 석유국장과 각각 접촉 대호 문의한바 아래 보고함.

1. 금번 사태는 예기치 않았던 갑작스런 일이며 중동지역내의 복잡한 문제로서 현재로서는 사태 전망은 예측키 어렵다는 신중한 반응을 보임

2. 이락및 쿠웨이트가 OPEC 산유국 생산량의 20% 이상을 점하고있어 금번사태로 인해 국제유가가 당분간 인상될 것으로 보이나 일부 보도에 의하면 사우디,베네주엘라, 인도네시아, 이란, UAE 등 산유국이 생산량을 증대할 움직임도 있어 이경우 국제수급에 큰차질은 없을 것으로 보며 어느정도 유가인상세도 완화될것으로봄

3. 주재국 외무성은 동사태에 대해 지대한 관심을 갖고 있는바 제19 차 OIC 회의 참석중인 MOHAMED 주재국 외무장관은 8.2. 및 8.4. 동회의 개막및 폐막연설에서 동사태에 대해 심각한 우려를 표명하고 양국가에 대해 협상을 통한 평화적인 사태 해결을 촉구한바 있으며 이락을 비난하고 이락군의 무조건 철수를촉구한 OIC 채택 결의안에 전폭적 지지와 동의를 한바있음. 끝.

(대사대리김영준-국장대리)

예고:90.12.31 일반

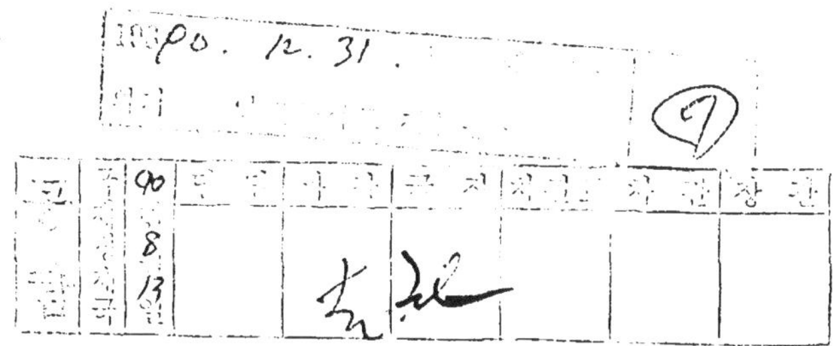

경제국 1차보 2차보 아주국 청와대 안기부 동자부

PAGE 1 90.08.09 19:24

외신 2과 통제관 BT

0034

원 본

외 무 부

종 별 :

번 호 : DJW-1144 일 시 : 90 0809 1430

수 신 : 장 관(기협,동자부)

발 신 : 주 인니 대사

제 목 : 이락.쿠웨이트 사태(자응67호)

주재국 GINANDJAR 광업에너지성 장관은 최근 이락.쿠웨이트 사태와 관련, 주재국입장에 관해 하기와 같이 언급함

1.인니는 이락으로부터 3-4만 베럴의 원유를 수입하고 있으며, 유엔결의에 따른 이락과의 무역중단문제는 외무성과 신중히 협의중임. 이락원유수입을 중지하더라도 국제원유 시장및 예비 비축량으로 충당할수 있어 원유수급에는 차질이 없을것임

2.OPEC 사무총장, 사우디, UAE, 이란, 베네주엘라 석유상과 긴급접촉결과 지난 7.28.합의한 OPEC쿼타는 준수하기로 하고 충격요인으로 인한 국제원유가 상승에 대해OPEC 공시가격인 21불선을 유지하도록 협력키로 함. 그러나 OPEC회원국이 원유가 안정을 위한 개별행동은 취하지 않기로 합의함

3. OPEC 회원국이 현시점에서 쿼타를 준수하지 않을경우, OPEC 의 결속에 심각한 영향을 주게 될것임.끝

(대사 김재춘-국장)

공람	국제경제국	담당	과장	국장	차관보	차관	장관

경제국 동자부 안기부 1차보 2차보 동자부

PAGE 1

90.08.09 21:18 EY

외신 1과 통제관

0035

관리번호	90-576

원 본

외 무 부

종 별 :

번 호 : AEW-0217 일 시 : 90 0809 1430

수 신 : 장 관(기협,중근동,기정)

발 신 : 주 UAE 대사

제 목 : 이락-쿠웨이트사태

대 WAE-148

연 AEW-0214

1. 대호 이락, 쿠웨이트 사태에 관한 당지의 언론 외교관및 관계자등의 의견을 아래와 같이 보고함.

가. 금 8.9 아랍 정상회담에서 이락이 철수할수 있는 명분과 쿠웨이트가 납득할만한 결과가 나오지 않는다면 동 사태의 해결 실마리가 불투명함.

나. 현재 유가가 $32 까지 폭등하고 있으나 일시적 현상이며 시장기능은 회복 조만간 진정될것임.

다. 주재국으로 까지 전쟁이 확산될 가능성은 희박하나 사담 후세인의 비정상적 돌발적 성격및 행위도 배제 못하며 만약 사태발생시 원유의 국제수급에 막대한 차질과 유가앙등을 피할수 없음.

2. 주재국 대통령은 이란대통령의 특사를 접견하고 금일 카이로로 정상회담차 향발하였으며 동사태에 조심스러이 사우디와 공동보조로 대처해 나가고 있음.

(대사 박종기-국장)

예고: 90.12.31 까지

90.12.31	고	국	90.8.13	담 당	과 장	국 장	차관보	차 관	장 관
					(서명)	✓			

경제국 장관 차관 1차보 2차보 중아국 청와대 안기부 동자부

PAGE 1

90.08.09 22:03

외신 2과 통제관 DL

0036

관리 번호	90-568

원 본

외 무 부

종 별 : 지 급

번 호 : IRW-0437 일 시 : 90 0809 1730

수 신 : 장 관(기협,중근동,기정,상공부,건설부장관)

발 신 : 주 이란 대사

제 목 : 이락,쿠웨이트사태

대:WIR-0254

대호건 주재국 시각에서 보는 아래 사항을 보고함. 단 석유수급및 유가전망에 관하여는 8.11 주재국 아가자데 장관을 면담할 예정이므로 동면담후 별도 상세 보고 하겠음. (면담 인사: 외무부 아주국장, 심의관, 연구원 중동연구부장, 주이란,쿠웨이트, UAE 대사, 언론인, 석유부 OPEC 담당관)

1. 전망

앞으로의 사태발전은 다음세가지 방향에서 예측될수있음.

가. 무력사용확대(가능성희박)

1)미국의 확고한 대사우디 지원의지표명

2)장기전화될경우 이락의고립

나. 원상회복(현실적으로 불가능)

1)전세계가 원상회복요구의 성명을 발표하고있으나 강제이행의지 결여

2)아랍권내에서의 쿠웨이트 사바왕조 신임저조

3)서방경제봉쇄의 지속적 실효성의문

가) 쿠웨이트 침공으로 이락은 220 억불의 현금 구매능력 보유, 장기간 생필품 구입 가능

나)금번 사태로 유가가 인상될 경우, 제제 결의에도 불구 국제가 이하의 이락산 원유가 어떤 형태로 든지 거래 될것임.

다. 현상황을 기초로한 타협(가능)

1)쿠웨이트 국경존중

2)현사바왕정체제를 수식, 또는 변화하는 체제수용

2. 사태장기화시 국제원유 수급및 가격

경제국 차관 1차보 2차보 중아국 안기부 상공부 건설부 동자부

PAGE 1

공람	국제경제국	90년8월13일	담 당	과 장	국 장	차관보	차 관	장 관

90.08.10 03:02

외신 2과 통제관 DL

0037

가. 현상을 기초로한 타협은 필연적으로 시간을 요하는 문제이므로 사태는 단기간에 매듭지어 지지는 않을것임.

나. 원유수급

1)OPEC 에서의 이락, 쿠웨이트 할당분, 감량은 이론상 사우디 (최고일산 1400만 베럴능력을 갖고 있으나 1100 만 배럴로 증산)및 이란의 증량 (시설 부족으로 최고 400 만 배럴)으로 충당될수있음.

2)근간 이러한 문제의 협의를 위하여 OPEC 회의가 개최되어야함.

다. 가격

1)금번 사태로 인한 심리적 요인과 OPEC 전체 생산량의 감소 예상 (400 만배럴)으로 유가 인상은 불가피 하다고 봄

2) 앞으로의 OPEC 회의시 현가격보다 2-3 불이 인상된 가격에서 합의점이 이루어질 것으로 보임 (따라서 23-24 불)

3. 주재국 대책

가. 이란이 걸프지역 안정의 중추세력 이라는점을 페만 아랍소국들에게 인식 시키므로써, 종래의 아랍권대 이란의 이원적 대립적 구조 (아랍만의 GCC) 를 PGCC 로 전환 시키려고 함.

나. 이러한 새로운 구조를 배경으로 OPEC 에서의 이란 발언권을 사우디와 동일한선으로 부각시킴.

다. 금번 사태는 모든면에서 이란에 유리한 여건을 조성한다는 인식하에 문제의 장기적 해결 방안을 선호함. 끝

(대사 정경일-국장)

예고:90.12.31 까지

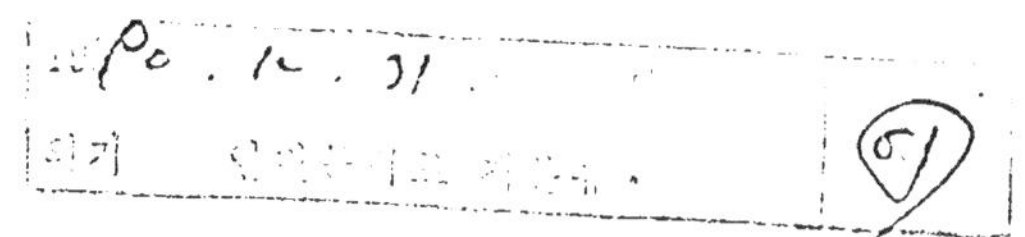

PAGE 2

0038

報告畢

長官報告事項

1990. 8 . 9 .
國際經濟局
(技協 -)

題目 : 이라크·쿠웨이트 사태가 原油需給 및 油價에 미치는 影響

I. 現況

1. 아국의 原油導入 現況

가. 쿠웨이트·이라크 原油導入 : 146천B/D (90년 상반기)

o 90 상반기 總 導入物量 928천B/D의 15.8%

- 이라크 39천 B/D (7.6%), 쿠웨이트 70천B/D (4.2%),

중립지대 37천 B/D (4%)

o 導入物量中 長期契約에 의한 導入量 : 75천 B/D

- 이라크 20천 B/D, 쿠웨이트 55천 B/D

※ 其他地域으로부터의 原油導入 : 782천 B/D (84.2%)

오만(22.7%), 이란(11.2%), UAE(17.6%), 사우디(5.3%), 카타르(2.6%),

말련(8.9%), 브루나이(3.6%), 중국(3.3%), 인니(4.7%), 카나다(1.4%),

기타(3%)

나. 90년 原油導入 計劃 : 총 309,000천배럴

o 長期契約導入 : 517천 B/D (년 188,705천배럴, 61%)

o 現物市場導入 : 330천 B/D (년 120,295천배럴, 39%)

2. 이라크·쿠웨이트의 原油供給量 : 약 450만배럴 (자유세계 총 공급량의 약10%, OPEC의 약 20%)

o 이라크: 약 300만B/D

- 供給經路 : 페르시아만 油槽船 약 40만B/D, 터키 키르쿠크 送油管 약170만B/D

사우디얀부 送油管 약 80만 B/D

o 쿠웨이트 : 약 150만 B/D (페르시아만 油槽船 供給)

0039

3. 現物市場 油價變動 推移

22.71(8.10)

o Dubai 유 : 18.27(8.1)→19.45(8.2)→19.80(8.3)→23.70(8.6)→25.40(8.7)→22.00(8.8)

o Brent 유 : 20.58(8.1)→22.20(8.2)→22.75(8.3)→27.75(8.6)→29.40(8.7)→25.85(8.8)

※ 事態發生 前日인 8.1 價格에 비해 Dubai유의 경우 3.73불, Brent유의 경우 5.27불 上昇

Ⅱ. 分析 및 展望

o OPEC 總會를 계기로 일기 시작한 油價上昇 趨勢에 戰爭勃發이라는 心理的 要因作用으로 急騰 현상 발생

- OPEC 總會는 90.7.27 基準油價 (reference price)를 18불에서 21달러로 引上 決定

o 이라크, 쿠웨이트의 供給量 약 450만 B/D가 전면 封鎖될 경우에 대비 油價는 短期間 急騰現狀을 보였으나, 餘他 原油生産國들의 增産動向에 따라 急騰勢는 일단 停止되는 現狀.
금후 사우디등 剩餘生産能力을 가진 國家等의 增産與否에 따라 油價上昇幅이 결정될 것으로 展望

- 여타 産油國 약 350만 B/D 追加供給 가능 예상
(사우디 200만, 베네주엘라 60만, UAE 40-50만, 나이지리아 20-30만)
※ 따라서 여타 産油國 追加供給時 약 100만 B/D 不足 예상

o 금번 사태가 隣近地域으로 擴散되어 廣域化되지 않는한, 油價上昇에 따른 追加負擔은 불가피하나 世界 原油需給에는 크게 차질이 없을 것으로 전망됨

- 서방 先進工業國 備蓄量 : 약 1백일분
  - 미국 : 5.9억 배럴
  - 일본 : 2.1억 배럴
  - EC 12개국 : 1.3억 배럴

※ 世界一日 平均消費量 : 5,300만 B/D
世界 原油 在庫量 : 1.8억 배럴

0040

Ⅲ. 我國에 대한 影響

o 短期的으로는 政府備蓄物量, 精油社 在庫, 現物市場 확보등으로 需給대처가능

- 政府備蓄量 : 약 4천만 배럴
- 精油社 在庫量 : 약 3천5백만 배럴
- 현재 輸送中 物量 : 약 2천만 배럴

※ 國內 一日 平均消費量 (848천B/D)을 감안할시 아국 導入 全體 物量 3개월이상 充當 가능

※ 이라크·쿠웨이트 양국으로부터의 導入이 완전 中斷되더라도 동 不足分을 備蓄物量으로 약 1년이상 供給 가능

o 금번사태로 國際油價가 引上되더라도 石油事業基金 및 關稅率 調整등을 통해 년내 國內 油價 引上없이 대처가능

- 石油事業基金 : 1조6천억
- 현재 關稅率 : 10%

o 그러나 사태가 隣近地域으로 확산될 경우, 原油需給蹉跌 및 油價急騰으로 인한 經濟에 대한 심각한 打擊 불가피

Ⅳ. 對策

o 이라크·쿠웨이트 原油導入 不足物量 (長期契約分 75천 B/D) 代替確保 가능

- 海外油田開發에 의한 原油導入 : 24,500 B/D
  - 북예멘 마리브 : 21,500 B/D
  - 이집트 칼다 : 3,000 B/D
- 政策原油 早期導入推進 : 25,000 B/D
  - 리비아 15,000 B/D, 멕시코 10,000 B/D
- 나머지 不足分 25,500 B/D은 現物市場에서 구입

※ 政府備蓄物量 (약 4천만 배럴)의 放出時期 및 放出量은 國際油價시세 및 原油需給推移에 따라 결정

0041

o 國産 石油製品輸出中斷 : 경유, 벙커C유등 국산석유제품의 수출을 당분간 중단 (년말까지 수출계획량 : 1,100만배럴)

o 原油導入線 多邊化 : 소련산 원유등 도입추진

o 長期契約 導入擴大 : 현 총 도입물량의 60% 수준에서 70% 수준으로 확대

o 에너지 消費節約

o 原油 및 가스開發 参與 擴大

o 備蓄物量 擴大

o 代替 에너지 開發등을 통한 石油依存度 緩和

0042

〈참고자료〉

1. 아국의 원유 도입현황

(단위 : 천배럴, $/B, 천$)

구분	'88 (1-12월)				'89 (1-12월)				'90 (1-6월)			
	물량	%	단가	금액	물량	%	단가	금액	물량	%	단가	금액
오 만	51.30	19.6	13.79	707,431	66.490	22.4	15.98	1,062,807	38,084	22.7	16.59	631,719
이 란	35.763	13.7	13.63	487,287	38.599	13.0	15.15	584,768	18,777	11.2	15.60	292,859
U A E	40.566	15.5	13.78	559,187	48.170	16.3	15.46	744,607	29,502	17.6	17.15	505,867
북예멘	8.873	3.4	14.88	132,051	8.458	2.9	16.90	142,969				
사우디	7.841	3.0	13.72	107,582	14.974	5.1	15.33	229,502	8,953	5.3	15.46	138,370
쿠웨이트	9.465	3.6	13.47	127,455	15.096	5.1	14.83	223,897	12,683	7.6	15.61	198,030
이라크	12.458	4.8	12.92	160,937	5.750	1.9	13.78	79,224	7,082	4.2	14.74	104,426
카타르	1.276	0.5	14.91	19,025	3,470	1.2	16.54	57,387	4,380	2.6	16.39	71,787
중립지대					14.526	4.9	14.97	217,524	6,730	4.0	15.85	106,645
말 련	22.623	8.7	14.99	339,226	26.974	9.1	17.75	478,685	15,022	8.9	19.03	276,016
브루나이	11.476	4.4	15.15	173,825	12.786	4.3	17.96	229,683	5,985	3.6	19.19	114,863
중 국	3.444	1.3	11.42	39,325	8.100	2.7	14.09	114,151	5,508	3.3	15.52	85,493
인 니	12.680	4.9	15.09	191,330	12.362	4.2	16.90	208,922	7,838	4.7	18.45	138,152
호 주	1.695	0.6	15.05	25,512	1.881	0.6	18.09	34,036	689	0.4	18.07	12,457
에콰돌	18,771	7.2	13.12	246,209	2.996	1.0	13.77	41,245	1,056	0.6	12.77	13,487
멕시코	4.954	1.9	13.40	66,372					551	0.3	13.67	7,532
카나다	120	0.1	10.30	1,236	830	0.3	12.94	10,741	2,317	1.4	13.58	31,482
이집트	9.656	3.7	12.76	123,223	6.199	2.1	13.50	83,694	1,334	0.8	10.77	14,361
알제리	3.709	1.4	16.19	60,045	4.759	1.6	15.28	72.709	1,457	0.9	17.50	25,496
가 봉	1.644	0.6	12.58	20,676	998	3.4	14.81	14,785				
카메룬	630	0.2	13.59	8,562	2.992	1.0	15.68	46,911				
앙골라	700	0.3	13.98	9,787								
콩 고	1.437	0.6	13.65	19,613								
합 계	261.079	100	13.89	3,625,898	296.410	100	15.81	4,685,530	167,951	100	16.49	2,769,045

0043

2. 아국의 석유도입 현황

(단위 :천배럴)

년도	'85	'86	'87	'88	'89	'90 (1-5월)
원유 (Crude Oil)	198.313	230.063	216.163	261.079	296.410	146.435
제품 (Product)	24.095	31.543	48.336	41.947	49.270	38.284
계	222.408	261.606	264.499	303.026	345.680	184.719

※ 제품 : 원유를 정제한 상태 (B-C 유, LPG, 납사등)로 수입되는 것을 의미.

3. 아국의 석유 소비량

(단위 :천배럴)

년도	'85	'86	'87	'88	'89
소 비 량	189.191	200.591	210.511	250.558	287.146

※ 90년도 예상 일일 평균 소비량 : 848천 B/D

4. 아국의 원유도입 계획 ('90) : 309,000천배럴

- 쿠웨이트산 원유도입 예정량
  - ·장기계약분 55천B/D (년 약 20,075천 배럴) : 총도입 계획량의 약 5.1%
- 이라크산 원유도입 예정량
  - ·장기계약분 20천 B/D (년 약 7,300천 배럴) : 총도입 계획량의 약 2.4%

5. 아국의 석유 비축량 (90.7.13 현재)

- 원유 : 38,000천 배럴
- 제품 : 1,800천 배럴

6. 전세계 석유 확인 매장량 (88년말 현재) : 9,166억 배럴

- 중동 : 5,716 (62.3%)
- 아프리카 : 562 (6.1%)
- 아시아 태평양 : 215 (2.3%)
- 서유럽 : 177 (1.9%)
- 북미 : 436 (4.8%)
- 중남미 : 1,221 (4.8%)
- 공산권 : 839 (9.2%)

※ OPEC : 6,761억 배럴 (73.8%)

0044

7. 지역별 석유 생산량

년도	'85	'86	'87	'88	
				생산량 (천B/D)	점유율 (%)
북미	12.360	12.070	11.640	11.525	18.5
중남미	6.685	6.615	6.630	6.860	11.0
서유럽	3.960	4.075	4.090	4.050	6.5
중동	10.900	13.105	13.150	15.065	24.2
아프리카	5.290	5.310	5.205	5.460	8.8
아시아.남양주	3.270	3.470	3.310	3.360	5.4
공산권 (쏘련.중국등)	14.665	15.190	15.420	15.875	25.6
전세계	57.595	60.305	59.895	62.195	100
OPEC	17.215	19.555	19.030	21.145	34.1
쿠웨이트	920	1.250	1.075	1.340	2.2
이라크	1.440	1.745	2.090	2.600	4.2

8. OPEC회원국별 90년 하반기 원유 생산쿼타 (90.7.27 OPEC총회결정)

국 가	쿼다 (단위:천B/D)	점유율(%)
알 제 리	827	3.7
에쿠아도르	273	1.2
가 봉	197	0.8
인 니	1.374	6.1
이 란	3.140	14
이 라 크	3.140	14
쿠 웨 이 트	1.500	6.7
리 비 아	1.233	5.5

0045

국 가	쿼타 (단위 : 천B/D)	점유율(%)
나이지리아	1.611	7.2
카 타 르	371	1.6
사 우 디	5.380	24
U. A. E.	1.495	6.6
베네수엘라	1.945	8.6
계	22.486	100

9. 정유사별 장기계약 현황 ('90.7월 현재)

(단위 : 천B/D)

사 별	도 입 선	계약당사자	계약기간	물량
유 공	쿠웨이트	유공- KPC	'90. 4-'91. 3	30
	북예멘	유공- HUNT	'87.12-2007.12	20
	UAE	유공- ADNOC	'90. 1-'90.12	20
	중국	선경- SINOCHEM	'90. 4-'91. 3	7.6
	카타르	유공- QGPC	'89. 7-'90. 6	10
	브르네이	유공- BSP	'90. 1-'92.12	15
	말레지아	유공- SHELL	'90. 1-'90.12	5
	오만	유공- C.ITOH	'90. 1-'90.12	10
	오만	유공- TOTAL	'90. 1-'90.12	11
	오만	유공- SHELL	'90. 1-'90.12	11
	오만	유공- Neste	'90. 1-'90.12	6.7
	UAE	유공- MITSUBISHI	'90. 4-'91. 3	5.6
	UAE	유공- MARUBENI	'89. 8-'90. 7	15
	계			166.9

0046

사 별	도 입 선	계약당사자	계약기간	물량
호 유	말련	호유- PETRONAS	'89.10-'90. 9	12
	UAE	럭키금성- ADNOC	'89.10-'90. 9	25.1
	에콰돌	럭키금성- CEPE	'90. 4-'90. 7	4
	중동동남아	호유- CALTEX	'86. 7-'91. 6	139.4
	브루네이	럭키금성- BSP	'90. 1-'90.12	3
	브루네이	럭키금성- BSP	'89. 9-'90.12	12
	계			195.5
경 인	오만	경인- MPM	'90. 1-'90.12	10
	말련	경인- PETRONAS	'89.10-'90. 9	11
	카타르	골든벨- QGPC	'90. 1-'90.12	8
	오만	경인- TOTAL	'90. 1-'90.12	5.5
	오만	경인- SHELL	'90. 1-'90.12	5.5
	계			40
쌍 용	이란	쌍용- NIOC	'90. 4-'90. 6	60
극 동	UAE	극동- ADNOC	'89.10-'90. 9	10
	쿠웨이트	극동- KPC	'90. 1-'90.12	25
	계			35
정책원유	이라크	경인- SCMO	'90. 1-'90.12	20
총계	┌ 직접계약 : 272.7 └ 간접계약 : 244.7			517.4

0047

관리번호	90-578

원 본

외 무 부

종 별 :

번 호 : ECW-0556 일 시 : 90 0809 1600

수 신 : 장 관 (기협)

발 신 : 주 EC 대사대리

제 목 : 이라크,쿠웨이트 사태

연: ECW-0554

1. 대호 관련, 당관 윤종곤 서기관은 8.8. EC 집행위 에너지총국 LEYDON 분석과장과 접촉한바, 동과장은 표제사태와 관련 하기와 같이 언급하였음

0 금번 사태 이전, 이락및 쿠웨이트로 부터의 원유 도입량은 EC 전체 원유수입의 약 10 % 를 차지 하였으며, 특히 덴마크 (50%) 및 희랍(18%) 의 경우는 상기 양국으로 부터의 원유수입 의존도가 높음

0 전반적으로 EC 회원국들의 원유 비축량은 약 100 일분의 소비를 초과, 당분간 원유 수급에서는 커다란 지장이 없을것으로 전망하고 다만 금번사태가 장기화될 경우에는 문제가 심각해 질것으로 보고, EC 측으로서는 금번사태를 예의 주시하고 있으며, 특히 이락, 쿠웨이트 원유공급 차질을 보충하기 위해 여타 공급원으로 부터의 수입을 늘려가기 시작하고 있음

0 최근 현물시장에서의 원유가 인상은 수요와 공급의 경제적 측면보다는 심리적 영향에 따른것으로서 1 베럴당 28 불선 까지는 서방경제가 견딜수 있을것이나 그 이상으로 상승할 경우에는 심각한 경제적 위기를 초래할 것으로 전망함

2. 동 과장은 금 8.9. 파리에서 긴급 소집되는 IEA 집행위 회의에서 금번사태에 대한 전망과 서방측의 대응방안이 구체적으로 검토될 것이라고 언급하고 동회의 종료후 재차 접촉키로 하였음. 끝

(대사대리 신장범-국장)

예고: 90.12.31 까지

공람	국제경제국	90.8.13	담 당	과 장	국 장	차관보	차 관	장 관

경제국 차관 2차보 동자부

PAGE 1 90.08.10 03:05

90.12.31.

외신 2과 통제관 DL

0048

관리 번호 90-574

원 본

외 무 부

종 별 :

번 호 : MXW-0969 일 시 : 90 0808 2300

수 신 : 장 관(기협,미중,기정동문,국방)

발 신 : 주 멕시코 대사

제 목 : 이라크-쿠웨이트사태

대 WMX-0693

연 MXW-0960

1. 대호 주재국 외무성 및 국영 석유회사 PEMEX 관계관 접촉, 확인 사항 아래 보고함.

가. 표제사태에 대한 전망

- 이라크에 대한 유엔의 경제제재조치 및 미국을 위시한 각국의 경제봉쇄가 이라크의 조기철군에 영향력을 행사할수는 있겠으나 HUSSEIN 이라크 대통령의 개인적 성격에 비추어 동대통령의 FACE SVAVING 을 위한 어떤 조치가 취해지지 않는한 금번 사태는 다소 장기화될 가능성이 있는것으로 분석

- 한편 8.9. 파리에서 개최될 INT'L ENERGY AGENCY 회의결과는 금번 사태의 귀추에 큰영향을 줄것으로 평가

나. 표제사태의 장기화 및 인근지역 확산시 국제수급 및 유가 전망

- 금번사태의 장기화시 국제원유수급은 이라크, 쿠웨이트 양국의 원유공급 공백을 주 재국을 위시한 베네수엘라, 카나다, 소련, 나이지리아등 여타 생산국의 생산증대로 대체하려는 노력이 기대되나 이들제국의 원유생산량의 현저한 증대는 각국 사정상 어려울 것으로 판단

- 특히 OPEC 제국이 이라크의 군사적 위협을 받지않는 베네수엘라나 나이지리아의 원유생산 증대를 반대하고 있지않다 하더라도 동국들의 급격한 생산증대에는 한계가 있는 것으로봄.

- 더구나 비록 이라크, 쿠웨이트 사태가 종식될 경우 유가가 다소 안정화 될수는 있으나 이미 급등한 유가가 사태발발 이전 상태로는 되돌아가지 않을 것이라는 것이 일반적 견해

경제국 차관 1차보 2차보 미주국 안기부 국방부 동자부

PAGE 1

공람	국제경제국	90년 8월 13일	담 당	과 장	국 장	차관보	차 관	장 관

90.08.10 04:37

외신 2과 통제관 DL

0049

다. 주재국의 대책등

- 최근의 유가 인상은 주재국 원유수출세입의 증대를 야기, 주재국의 경상수지 적자 (금년도 32 억불 예상) 해소에 크게기여할 것으로 전망

- 그러나 주재국의 원유 판매정책은 현재 20 여 외국 원유구매국과 원유 공급계약을 기체결하고 있음에 비추어 동계약 이행을 우선 고려하여 원유수급을 검토 예정이라하며 유가인상에 불구 89 년초 비 OPEC 회원국과 합의한 EXPORT CEILING 을 고수할 방침 (금년초 체결된 멕시코 원유공급 계약에 의하면 일본, 스페인, 이스라엘등이 각각 일일 13 만,15 만,2 만 배럴 상당 구매토록 되어있음)

- 82 년 외채위기 이후 주재국은 국영 석유회사인 PEMEX 에 대한 부자를 75프로 삭감한바 있어 원유생산의 급격한 증대는 현실적으로 기대곤란

- 주재국 SALINAS 정부는 PEMEX 의 생산능력 향상을 위하여 석유 산업분야의 부정부패 일소, PEMEX 생산성 향상을 위한 민간자본 참여 유도 및 PEMEX 기구정비등 적극적인 정책을 펴고있으나 원유생산시설의 장기간에 걸친 관리소홀 및 신규 석유화학 공단건설에 필요한 재정부족등으로 실효를 거두고 있지 못하고있음.

2. 한편 PEMEX 측에 의하면 8 월 중순경 주재국 유조선이 60 만 배럴상당의 원유를 적재, 아국 극동정유와 원유매매 교섭차 방한 예정이라하니 참고바람.

(대사 이복형-국장)

예고 90.12.31. 까지

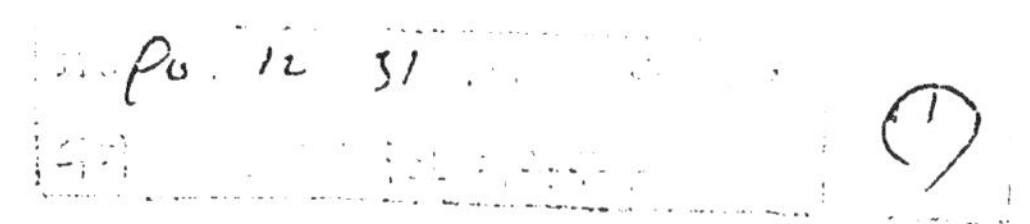

PAGE 2

0050

원 본

외 무 부

종 별 :

번 호 : MXW-0977　　　　일 시 : 90 0809 1800

수 신 : 장 관(기협,미중)

발 신 : 주 멕대사

제 목 : 이-쿠웨이트 사태

1. 주재국 F. ROJAS 국영석유회사(PEMEX)사장은 작 8.8. 기자회견을 통하여 표제사태로 야기된 국제원유 수급상의 부족분 보충을 위하여 향후 60일 동안 멕산 원유를 10 만 바렐 증산키로 하였다고 발표함. 동 증산분은 미.일 및 유럽에 추가공급될 것이라함.

2. 동인은 멕시코가 원유판매로 부터 가능한한 최대한의 수익을 얻기를 바라지만 이러한 수익이 안정적이고 지속적으로 이루어질 것을 희망한다면서 최근 이-쿠웨이트 사태로 야기한 국제 원유부족의 결과 각국의 원유증산 개시로 국제유가의 하락가능성에 대하여 우려를 표시함. 이와관련 동인은 멕시코가 국제무대에서 안정적이고견고 한국제 석유정책이 채택되어질 것을 계속 추구해나갈 방침임을 밝힘.

3. 멕시코 석유는 현재 배럴당 20.5불로 거래되고 있으며 동유가 인상으로 주재국은 월 약375백만불상당 추가수익을 얻을것으로 기대되고있음.(대사이복형-국장)

공람	국제경제국	년 월 일	담 당	과 장	국 장	차관보	차 관	장 관

경제국　1차보　미주국　안기부　정문국 동자부

PAGE 1　　　　90.08.10　10:03 WH

외신 1과 통제관

0051

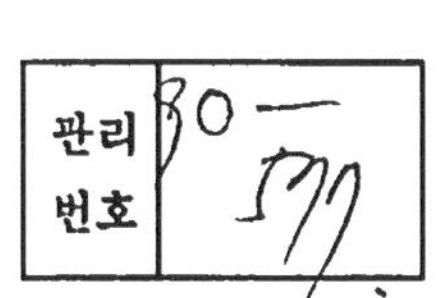

원 본

외 무 부

종 별 : 지 급

번 호 : CNW-1193 일 시 : 90 0809 1830

수 신 : 장 관(기협,미북,중근동,상공부,동자부)

발 신 : 주 카나 다 대사

제 목 : 이락.쿠웨이트 사태

대 : WCN-0806

연 : CNW-1183,1188

표제 사태 관련 국제 원유 수급 및 유가 전망에 대한 당지 평가를 아래와 같이 보고함.

1. 국제 석유 수급 및 유가 전망

가. 이락, 쿠웨이트산 원유에 대한 금수조치에도 불구하고 90. 3/4 분기까지는 현상태의 국제석유 수급 균형이 대체로 유지될 것이고, 이에 따라 석유가도현 수준을 능가하지는 않을 것으로 당지에서는 전망되고 있는바, 그 주요 이유는 아래와 같음.

0 금번 금수조치로 이락, 쿠웨이트산 석유생산이 일산 440 - 450 만 바렐 (B/D) 감소될 것으로 예상되나 사우디, UAE, 베네주엘라등 기타 OPEC 국가의 추가공급 능력 보유로 동 감소분의 대부분 충당 가능

- 사우디 : 240 B/D 추가 생산 가능

- UAE : 20 만 B/D 추가생산가능

- 베네주얼라 : 60 만 B/D 추가 생산 가능

0 그동안 OPEC 초과 생산으로 인해 OECD 국가의 충분한 재고 보유

- 90.7.1. 현재 평균 99 - 100 일분에 대한 재고 수준 유지(90. 3/4 분기중OECD 제국의 원유 소비증가율이 1.5 프로에 달해 1 일 평균 소비량이 37.3 백만에 이를 경우를 전제로 할때)

. 석유회사 재고 보유분 : 약 70 일

. 정부 및 공공기관 보유분 : 약 30 일

- 1 년 전보다 3 일간 연장

- 미국의 경우 90.8.4. 현재 560 백만 바렐의 예비 재고 보유

경제국 2차보 미주국 중아국 상공부 동자부

PAGE 1

공람	국제경제국	년 월 일	담 당	과 장	국 장	차관보	차 관	장 관

90.08.10 11:23

외신 2과 통제관 BN

0052

. 원유 : 334 백만 바렐

. 개소린 : 226 백만 바렐

0 90. 3/4 분기중 OECD 국가의 OPEC 석유 수요는 2180 만 B/D 로 전망되나 이는 이락, 쿠웨이트를 제외한 OPEC 산유량(2210 B/D) 에 미달

나. 그러나 금번의 제재조치가 금년 4/4 분기까지 지속되는 경우, 세계 석유 공급면에서의 애로 현상이 노정될 것으로 보이며 이는 국제석유가 추가 인상 압력 요인으로 작용할 것으로 분석됨.

0 4/4 분기 난방등 계절 요인으로 OECD 의 OPEC 산 석유 수요가 2440 만 B/D 로 증가할 것으로 예상되는바, 이는 현 OPEC 생산량을 상회하는 수준임.

2. 주재국의 대책

가. 주재국은 160 만 B/D 의 석유를 생산, 이중 60 만 B/D 을 주로 미국에 수출하는 반면, 50 만 B/D 의 북해산 석유를 수입하고 있음.(북해산 석유 수입은퀘벡주 및 동해안 지역 소요 충당분으로서 카나다 서부지역 생산 원유의 동지역 운송에 비해 수입하는 편이 운송비 면에서 유리함)

나. 따라서 주재국은 약 10 만 B/D 의 원유 출조입장에 있으, 금번 사태로 인한 석유 수급및 유가문제에 대해 크게 우려하지 않으며 다만 현재로서는 사태추이를 모니터링 하고 있는 단계라고 함. 끝

(대사 - 국장)

예고문 : 90.12.31. 까지

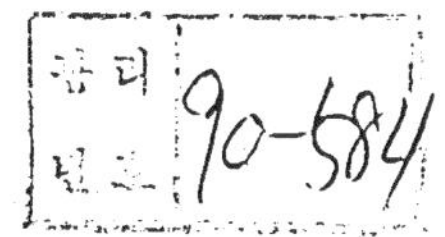
분류번호 90-584

"에너지는 나라의 힘 아껴쓰고 비축하자"

동 력 자 원 부

원유 29210-41 503-9627 1990. 8. 9.

수신 외무부 장관

제목 원유 안정확보를 위한 대산유국 외교활동 강화협조

1. 당부는 제 1,2차 석유파동 이후 석유수요 전량을 해외에 의존하고 있는 우리 여건상 산유국들의 일방적 공급감축에 대비하고 국제 석유시장의 불안시 대국민 경제에 미치는 영향을 최소화하기 위하여 원유도입선의 다변화 및 장기계약 물량의 확보로 국내 석유류 수급안정 도모에 힘쓰고 있습니다.

2. 그러나, 최근 이라크.쿠웨이트 분쟁이후 국제유가가 30$/바렐대로 급등하는등 국제 석유시장의 불안이 야기되어 아국의 기존 도입선의 안정공급을 저해할 것이 예상되므로,

o 귀부에서는 "아래" 대상국가에 외교활동을 강화하여 최근의 사태로 인하여 아국의 원유 안정공급에 차질이 없도록 최소한 기존 계약물량의 현수준 유지 및 증량협조 등을 통하여 적기공급될 수 있도록 현지 아국대사관에 협조요청하여 주시기 바라며,

- 원유의 안정확보가 경제발전 및 국가안보에 미치는 영향이 지대한 점을 충분히 감안, 적극적인 산유국외교를 전개하여 주시기 바랍니다.

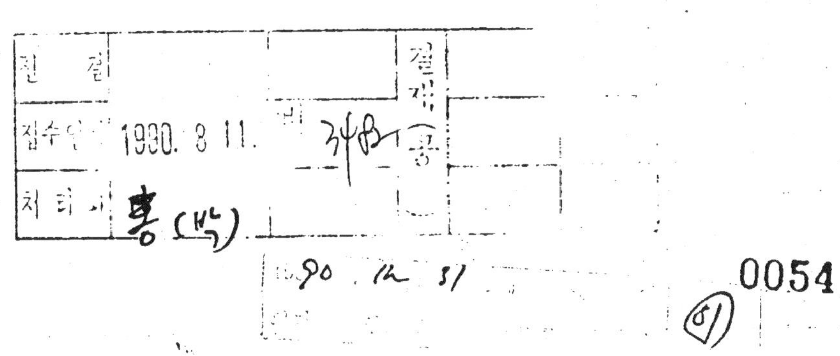

접 결		결재
접수일시	1990. 8. 11.	34801
처리과	홍 (박)	

1990. 12. 31

0054

(61)

원유 29210-　　　　　　　　　　　　　　　　1990. 8. 9.

"아　　　　래"

o 아국과 장기계약을 기체결한 국가 (8개국)

- UAE, 이란, 오만, 브루네이, 말레지아, 카타르, 에콰돌, 멕시코

o 아국이 장기계약을 체결 추진중이거나 희망국가 (3개국)

- 사우디, 인니, 리비아. 끝.

동 력 자 원 부 장 관

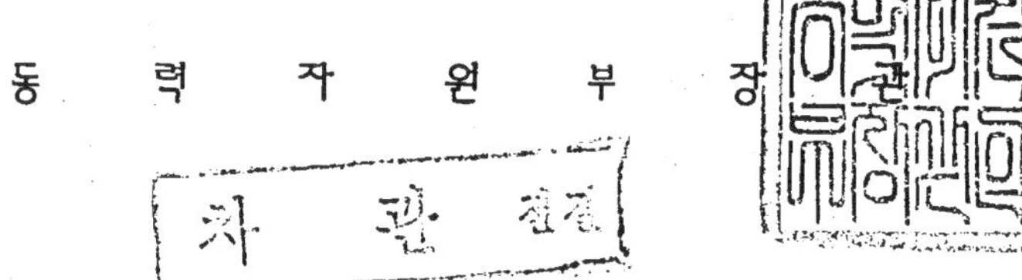

0055

61

주 리비아 대사관

리(건)-90-236　　　　　　　　　　1990. 8. 9.

수신 : 장 관 (건설부 장관)

참조 : 중동 아프리카 국장

제목 : 유가 인상에 따른 주재국 건설 시장 전망

최근 유가 인상 및 쿠웨이트 사태에 따른 당지 건설시장 전망을 별첨과 같이 보고 합니다.

첨부 : 유가 인상과 리비아 건설시장 전망 1부.　끝.

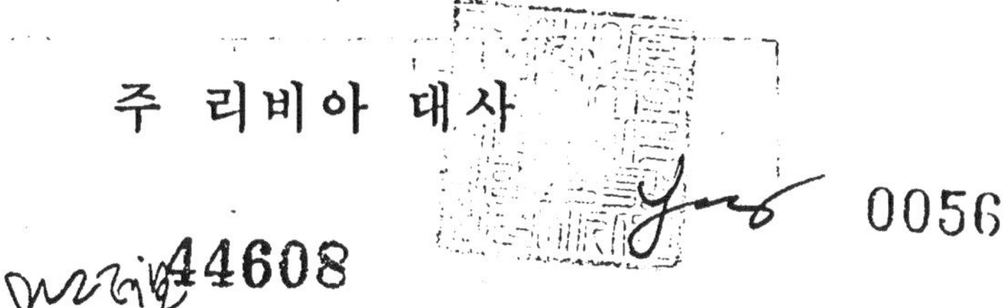

주 리비아 대사

44608

0056

유가 인상에 따른 주재국 건설시장 전망

1. 유가 현황 및 전망

- OPEC 총회에서의 공시유가 인상 및 이라크의 쿠웨이트 침공 및 합병에 따라 그동안 배럴당 14-16불 수준에 머물렀던 국제 석유 가격이 배럴당 20불 이상으로 급등하고 있으나 이는 유가 상승 분위기의 확산과 전쟁에 따른 심리적인 효과에 기인한 바가 매우큼.

- 종래 산유국들이 쿼타를 지키지 않아 발생했던 석유의 공급 과잉 현상은 쿠웨이트의 감산 및 이라크의 석유 수출 봉쇄에 따라 일시적으로는 공급 부족현상으로 반전 될 것으로 예상됨.

- 그러나 이러한 단기적인 공급 부족현상은 사우디 등 기타 OPEC 국가의 증산으로 해소될 것으로 보여 현재의 이상반등 현상은 점차 진정세를 보일 것으로 예상됨.

- 앞으로 유가는 점진적인 상승세를 보여 연말 경에는 배럴당 21-23불 수준을 유지 할 것으로 전문가 들은 전망하고 있음.

2. 유가 인상과 리비아 건설 시장의 변화 전망

가. 건설 시장 규모

- 리비아 정부의 건설투자 규모(개발예산)는 '89까지 감소 추세를 보여 왔으나 '90의 개발 예산은 약 38억불(11,7억 디나)로 '89대비 30% 증가 하였음.

단위: 백만불

구 분	'86	'87	'88	'89	'90
계	14,771	-	-	11,091	10,692
경상 예산	4,501	-	4,102	3,878	4,851
개발 예산	5,610	4,785	4,785	2,970	3,861
수입 예산	4,660	4,528	-	4,243	1,980

* 90년 예산은 수입예산이 폐지되고 국방예산으로 대체되었음.

0057

o '90 예산 중 개발예산은 전체 예산의 36.1%를 차지하고 있으나, 이중 대수로 공사예산은 8.9억불(2.7억 디나)이 포함되어 있어 실질적인 건설투자 규모는 29.7억불(9억 디나)로 전년도 수준임.

나. 유가 인상과 건설시장의 변화

o 리비아의 OPEC 석유 쿼타량은 일 123,3만 배럴로 '90석유 수입은 85억불로 예상되고 있어(EIU 추정) '89의 75억불에 비해 13%증대 될 것으로 보임.

o 그러나 OPEC 총회에서 공시가격을 배럴당 18불에서 21불로 인상하였고, 최근 쿠웨이트 사태로 현물시장 가격이 폭등하고 있어 리비아의 원유 판매 수입은 증대 될 것으로 전망 되는바, 리비아의 석유 쿼타량에 비추어 볼때 석유 가격이 배럴당 1불 상승하면 석유 판매 수입은 년 4억불 정도 증대 될 것으로 보여, 연말경 유가가 OPEC 공시 가격을 유지하는 경우 리비아의 '90 석유 수입은 4-5억불, 배럴당 23불 수준인 경우 7-8억불 증대 될 것으로 예상 됨.

3. 당지 진출 아국업체에 대한 영향

o 긍정적인면

* 단기적으로 발주처의 예산부족 등 사유로 발생하고 있는 미수금의 부분적인 해소가 가능할 것으로 보이며, 외화 수입의 증대에 따라 신규 공사의 계약시에는 대금 지급 조건이 개선 될 것으로 예상 됨.

o 부정적인면

* 유가 인상에 따라 자재비가 상승하고, 한국내의 물가 상승에 따른 근로자의 임금 인상을 유발하게 되어 공사 단가가 상승할 것으로 예상 됨.

* 시공중인 공사는 수익성이 악화 될 것으로 우려되며, 특히 기성금을 원유로 수령하는 공사의 경우 리비아측이 공사대금의 원유 지급을 기피 할 것으로 예상 되어 신규 미수금의 발생이 우려 됨.

* 신규 공사 입찰시에도 공사 단가의 상승에 따른 가격 경쟁력의 약화가 우려되나 자재비의 상승은 외국업체에도 해당되므로 아국근로자의 임금인상 정도에 따라 경쟁력은 영향을 받을 것으로 보임.

0058

o 현재 리비아 건설시장에서의 아국업체 점유율은 30-35%에 달하고 있어 최근 유가 인상은 당지에서의 아국업체 활동에 전반적으로 긍정적인 영향을 미칠 것으로 사료되나, 구체적인 내용은 리비아 정부의 증산여부, 증대된 석유수입의 배분등에 따라 달라질 것으로 전망 됨.

0059

08/09/90 17:41 ☎202 797 0595 EMBASSY OF KOREA →→→ WOI 013/

번호 : USW(F)- 1766

수신 : 장 관 (중근동, 기협) 발신 : 주미대사

제목 : 유가 동향 (1 매)

OIL MARKETS EASE; STOCK PRICES RISE

Outlook Remains Uncertain, Awaiting Mideast Moves

By ROBERT D. HERSHEY Jr.

Oil prices fell and financial markets around the world steadied yesterday after the United States decision to send troops to Saudi Arabia and reports that the oil-rich kingdom would increase its production.

But the easing in oil markets and a leveling off in share prices seemed tentative, with the economic outlook hinging entirely on the uncertain prospect of developments in the Middle East.

Despite a decline in the price of oil of more than $2 a barrel yesterday, to just under $26, the price remains about 50 percent higher than it was in July, with much of that increase coming after Iraq invaded Kuwait last week. The oil-price run-up has been quickly — and controversially — translated into higher fuel costs for businesses and higher gasoline prices for motorists. Higher energy prices have made it seem increasingly likely that an already-weak economy will slip into recession.

In his televised address yesterday, President Bush called on the oil industry to avoid taking advantage of political turmoil in the Persian Gulf to maximize profits.

"I'm asking the oil companies to do their fair share," the President said in a broadcast to the nation yesterday morning. "They should show restraint and not abuse today's uncertainties to raise prices."

Mr. Bush also said, "I will explore whether we and our allies should draw down our strategic petroleum reserves."

Most stock markets steadied yesterday. In New York, the Dow Jones industrial average rose 24.26 points, to 2,734.90, after falling day after day since the Iraqi invasion last week. Similarly, the Tokyo market rallied on the news that oil prices were no longer climbing for the moment. In Europe, the performance was mixed, with the Frankfurt market falling and the London market inching ahead.

ARCO's Commitment

In response to President Bush's urging to restrain oil and gasoline price increases, the American Petroleum Institute, the industry's largest trade association, pledged its "complete cooperation" and ARCO, a big marketer in five Western states, said it would freeze wholesale prices for one week.

No other companies, however, gave any immediate indication that they would follow the lead of ARCO, whose foregone profits for the week were thought likely to amount to tens of millions of dollars.

"We hope the market will stabilize during this time," George Babikian, head of the Los Angeles-based company's refining and marketing division, said in a statement, "but if at the end of the week our position is out of line with world market prices, we will have to recognize that fact."

Telegram to Bush From Mobil

A spokesman for the Mobil Corporation said he could not comment on any pending price moves but supplied a copy of a telegram that the company's chairman, Allen E. Murray, sent to the White House after the President's plea.

"I can assure you that we will continue to show restraint in the face of escalating prices for crude oil," Mr. Murray stated. "While we have raised prices, to date we have recovered only a fraction of the higher costs incurred. Please be assured that in this time of crisis Mobil will do its fair share."

But with retail gasoline prices having already climbed by an average of more than 12 cents a gallon since Iraq's invasion of Kuwait — and twice as much in some cases — the industry was once again smarting from a public-image black eye.

Threat by Senator Dole

No less a friend than the Senate Republican leader, Bob Dole of Kansas, whose state ranks among the top 10 oil producers, complained of "irresponsible and arbitrary" price increases and said these invited punitive Government action.

"Sometimes the oil companies never learn," Senator Dole declared. "They're just asking for some kind of excess-profits or windfall-profits tax."

Congressional Democrats, meanwhile, kept up their barrage of criticism of the oil industry, with the Senate majority leader, George J. Mitchell of Maine, insisting that Attorney General Dick Thornburgh conduct an investigation of possible conspiratorial pricing.

The episode recalled for some the 1962 confrontation between President John F. Kennedy and the steel industry, whose effort to raise prices an average of $6 a ton was held by the President to be "a wholly unjustifiable and irresponsible defiance of the public interest."

The industry cited mounting costs of production but capitulated and withdrew the increase within four days of Mr. Kennedy's direct, public challenge in which he spoke of "this serious hour in our nation's history when we are confronted with grave crises in Berlin and Southeast Asia, when we are devoting our energies to economic recovery and stability, when we are asking reservists to leave their homes and families months on end and servicemen to risk their lives."

John H. Sununu, President Bush's chief of staff, convened a meeting of Government policy makers yesterday afternoon to discuss oil prices, but no industry officials were invited, an official said. Nor did President Bush, a former oilman himself, make any private telephone calls to urge price restraint.

The President did, however, phone ARCO to express pleasure at the company's price freeze.

Another development welcomed by the Administration was a decision by Mexico to raise production by 100,000 barrels a day, a modest amount but a supply addition that had not been formally requested or counted upon. Treasury Secretary Nicholas F. Brady called the increase a gesture of good will.

The outlook for oil remains uncertain, but most analysts said prices were unlikely to fall much further soon because the embargo against Iraqi and Kuwaiti output has been effective so far.

"Right now the embargo appears to be working well," said Theodore R. Eck, chief economist for the Amoco Corporation. "They are having trouble selling oil because they have lost their traditional customers. But that may not be true a month from now."

Mr. Eck said the pipeline through Turkey appeared to be closed down, but that Saudi Arabia had been silent on the pipeline that passes through its territory to the Red Sea port of Yanbu.

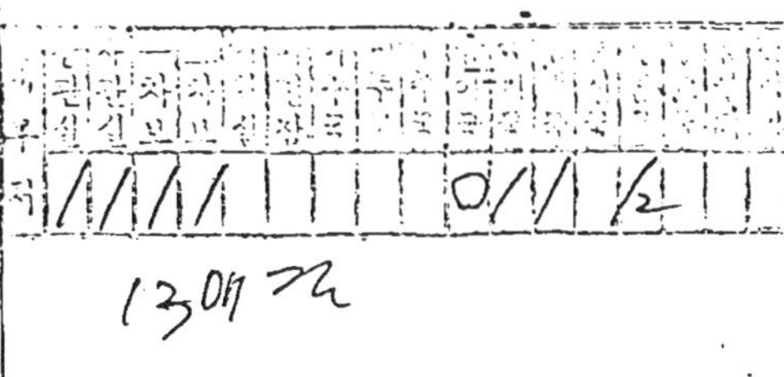

1304 22

기협

August 9, 1990 NYT

0060

관리번호	90-565

분류번호	보존기간

발 신 전 보

WFR-1526 900810 1147 ER

번 호 :

종별 :

수 신 : 주 불 대사. 총영사

발 신 : 장 관 (기협)

제 목 : 이라크.쿠웨이트 사태

연 : WFR - 1505

1. 연호 관련, 8.9. 귀지에서 개최된 IEA 긴급 대책회의 결과를 지급 보고 바람.

2. 아울러 IEA 각 회원국들이 보유하고 있는 원유 비축물량을 파악 보고 바람.

끝.

(국제경제국장 최대화)

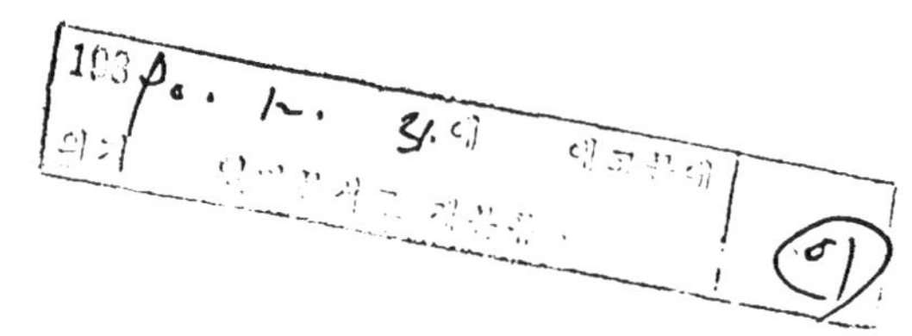

보안통제	

앙고재	90년 8월 10일	기술협력과	기안자 성명		과 장	심의관	국 장		차 관	장 관
			홍성화				전결			

외신과통제

0061

관리번호	90-579

원 본

외 무 부

종 별 :

번 호 : QTW-0097　　일 시 : 90 0810 0900

수 신 : 장관(기협)

발 신 : 주 카타르 대사

제 목 : 이락.쿠웨이트사태

대:WQT-0079

1. 대호관련 산유국동향에 관한 첩보를 우선보고함.

가. 이란주재 일본상사의 일본대사관 보고에 의하면 ,8.6 AGHAZADEH 이란석유상이 기자회견을 통해 OPEC 의 생산쿼터를 준수하겠다고 언명하면서도 내용적으로는 일본을 포함한 동아시아 지역에 대한 원유수출량을 증량하기로 결정하였다함.314 만 B/D 의 쿼터를 지키면서 현재의 생산여력을 할애하고 유럽에 대한 배분을 삭감해서라도 동 지역수요 충당한다안 방침밝힘.

일본 각 회사는 원유수출 여력이 큰 이란에 대하여 집중적인 교섭전개중이며 이에따라 8 월분 대 일본수출양은 약간증가 ,9 월분 대폭증량 (40 만 내지 50만) 될 예정이라함.

NIOC 는 현재 각 회사에 9 월이후 연말 까지의 소요량 신청토록 통보하고 있으며 그 집계에 따라 각사에 대한 배당과 이란국내생산계획을 수립할 것임. 가격은 그달 SPOT 가격에 따라 설정하며 , 9 월분은 사우디 9 월가격에 따라 결정 예정이나 종전의 가격 FOMULA 는 변경될 예정임.

나. 일본측의 각 산유국 원유 증산능력 및 가격추세 전망

1)원유수급 전망

0 비 OPEC 산유국은 현재까지 FULL CAPACITY 로 생산해 왔기 때문에 금번 사태로 인한 5 백만 B/D 의 GAP 을 메울수는 없음. (JAMES SCHLESINGER 전 미 에너지장관)

0 유럽각국은 종전부터 석유수입선을 중동에서 북해, 아프리카, 중남미로전환시켜 왔으므로 금번 경제제재조치에 따르는 수입선변경 검토 불요. 원유수급에 미치는 영향은 한달후 부터 일 것이며 시장동향 주시중.(8.7 불 석유공사TOTAL 의 부우리니에 동반구 담당 부장)

경제국

PAGE 1

공람	국제경제국	90년8월13일	담당	과장	국장	차관보	차관	장관

90.08.10　18:17

외신 2과　통제관 DH

0062

0 오만은 금번 사태 이전부터 FULL 생산을 계속, 전량을 각국에 배정완료하고 있으며 원유재고량도 없기때문에 증가배정 여력없음.(8.7 증배요청 일본측에 대한 오만석유성 바르와니 원유판매국장)

0 말련 마하달 수상은 8.8 원유 증산검토 용의 있으나 한계가 있다고 하고 동국 석유공사 (PETRONAS)의 생산담당 DR. AZIZ MAHMUD 수석 부총재는 증산에대한 기술적인 검토 중이나 증량폭은 3 만 B/D 가 한계일 것이며 현재 필리핀 의 증배요청함. 전향적으로 검토중 임을 밝힘

0 인니의 증산 능력은 현재한계에 달한 것으로 (12 월까지 OPEC 합의 쿼 터선 137.4 만 B/D) 판단되나 증산여부에 대하여는 8.11 이후 SUHARTO 대통령의재가를 얻게될 것이라함.

0 UAE 는 일본이 현 비축량으로 감당불가시 대비 증배 선처요망한 요네야마 일본대사 에 OPEC 합의 쿼터등 제약은 있으나 양국의 특수관계를 고려 최대한의 협력확약하였다함.

2)원유가격전망

0 세계석유시장의 충분한 비축여유로 향후 3 개월 간은 석유부족사태는 일어 나지 않을 것이며 OPEC 각국이 3 개월간 생사쿼터를 준수한다면 적정원유가 형성가능 (8.6 이란 AGAZADEH 석유상)

0 유렵각국은 충분한 석유를 비축하고 있으며 불도 현재 법정일수 (90 일) 분을 초과하고 있는 현상태에서 시장에 긴박감은 없음. 금후 원유가는 30 불 이하선에서 추이할 것으로 예상되는데, 심리적 벽이라 생각되는 30 불선은 이락이 사우디를 침공않는한 무너지지 않을 것임. (8.7 불 석유공사 TOTAL 의 부우르니에 동반구 담당부장)

0 에콰돌 의 타마리스 광산성장관은 8.3 이락. 쿠웨이트 사태의 영향에 대해 최근 수일간의 유가상승은 2/4 분기 에 발생한 하락을 상쇄한것이 될것이나 그 리스크는 매우크다. 왜냐하면 상승후의 급격한 하락이 발생할 가는성이 있기 때문이다. 이것은 아무에게도 이익이 되지 못할 것이라고 논평함.

0 유가의 지나친 상승은 바람지하지 않으며 지속가능한 OPEC 기준가격인 21불 선 유지가 바람직함 (8.8 말련 마하딜 수상)

2. 주재국의 관측 및 대책등에 관하여는 추보 위계임.

(대사 유내형 -국장)

예고 :90.12.31 일반

PAGE 3

0064

외 무 부

종 별 :

번 호 : ECW-0558 일 시 : 90 0810 1000

수 신 : 장관 (통이,기협,재무부)

발 신 : 주 EC 대사

제 목 : 최근의 유가동향과 전망

1. 이라크, 쿠웨이트 사태와 관련한 유가동향및 전망에 대한 EC 국가의 보도내용 요지를 아래 보고함

가. 유가및 자본시장 동향

0 UN 의 이라크산 원유수입 금지 결의안 채택이후 원유 현물시세는 북해산 BRENT 유기준 8.6. 현재 배럴당 28.65 불까지 급등 하였으나, GULF 만 위기가 군사조치보다는 경제적인 측면에서 해결될수 있을것이라는 분위기 고조와 함께 베네주엘라가 유가안정을 위해 50만 B/D을 추가 공급할 용의가 있다는 보도에 따라 BRENT 유가가 8.7. 26.15 불, 8.8. 24.75불로 하락하여 전반적인 하향 안정 추세를 보이고있음

0 국제 자본시장에서도 8.6. 까지는 주식및 BOND 가격이 급락 하였으나, 8.7.이후 점진적인 회복세를 보이고 있음

나. OPEC 의 입장

0 OPEC 가 3.7백만 B/D 의 추가 공급능력을 보유하고 있는것으로 추정되고 있기때문에 이라크및 쿠웨이트 원유 (4백만 B/D) 에 대한 EMBARGO 조치가 상당기간 계속되더라도 OPEC 의 태도여하에 따라서는 원유의 공급부족 현상은 심각하지 않을것으로 예상하고 있음

0 다만, OPEC 국가들은 최근의 유가급등 현상은 공급부족 현상에서 초래된 것이아니고 심리적인 현상으로 보고 있으며, OPEC 가 원유를 추가 공급할 경우 중장기적으로 오히려 유가하락을 촉진할 가능성을 우려하여 추가공급을 주저하고 있는 실정임

0 이문제는 결국 사우디의 입장에 달려 있는것으로 평가하고 있으며, 이곳 전문가들은 사우디가 안보문제를 미국에 의존하고 있는한 미국의 요청에따라 추가공급에

통상국 2차보 경제국 재무부 동자부

PAGE 1

공람	국제경제국	담당	과장	국장	차관보	차관	장관

90.08.10 20:31 DA

외신 1과 통제관 0065

응할수 밖에 없을것으로 예상하고 있음

다. IEA 가맹국 보유 전략원유 비축량 사용문제

0 THE INT'L ENERGY AGENCY 가맹국의 전략원유 비축량은 약 10억 배럴로 추정되고 있으며, 동비축량은 세계석유 소비량의 약 30일분에 상당하는 수준으로 평가됨

0 미국은 IEA 가맹국에 대해 전략 원유비축량의 사용문제를 협의할 것을 요청한바 있으며, 이와관련, 8.9. 파리에서 개최 예정인 IEA 긴급 이사회에서 필요시 전략원유 비축량을 무제한 공급하겠다는 원칙적인 입장을 밝힐것으로 예상하고 있음

- 다만 IEA 관계자에 의하면 GULF 만 위기에 따른 4백만 B/D 수준의 공급축소는원유 공급량의 약 7 수준에 불과하기 매문에 전략원유 비축량의 의무적인 공급할당은 현 상태로서는 필요하지 않다는 입장을 보임

라. 향후 유가전망

0 유렵 전문가들의 일반적인 견해는 GULF 만 위기가 더이상 악화되지 않을 경우최근의 유가급등 현상은 조만간 진정되어 배럴당 20-21불 수준으로 회복될 것으로전망하고 있음

- 이러한 전망의 근거는

첫째, GULF 만 위기 이전에 약 2백만 B/D수준의 공급초과 현상이 존재하고 있었으며

둘째, OPEC 가 3.7백만 B/D 의 추가 공급능력이 있으며, 또한 7-8 억배럴 수준의원유 재고를 보유하고 있는것으로 추정되고 있음

세째, IEA 가맹국은 약 10억 배럴 수준의 전략원유 비축량을 보유하고 있으며,아울러 민간 재고량을 합할 경우 약 30억 배럴 수준을 보유하고 있는것으로 평가되기 때문임

0 다만, 이라크에 대한 무기및 식량공급의 중단조치에도 불구하고, 이곳 전문가들은 이라크가 약 6개월분의 식량과 무기 재고를 보유하고 있을것으로 추정하고 있기 때문에 GULF 만 위기가 장기간 계속될 가능성을 우려하고 있으며 한편으로는이라크의 또다른 도발 가능성을 우려하고 있음

0 따라서 향후 유가는 원유의 수요공급 측면보다는 오히려 GULF 만의 정치상황의 변화에 따라 움직일 것으로 예상하고 있음

2. 이곳 전문가들의 의견을 종합하면 유가 급등현상은 조만간 진정될 것으로 전망하고 있으나, 일부 전문가들은 그동안 비 OPEC 국가에서 대규모 유전을 개발하지

못하고 있기 매문에 OPEC 국가가 재단결하면 2-3년내 제 3의 석유위기 가능성을예견하고 있음. 끝

(대사 권동만-국장)

원 본

외 무 부

종 별 :

번 호 : ECW-0560 일 시 : 90 0810 1530

수 신 : 장 관 (기협,중근동,통일,통이)

발 신 : 주 EC 대사대리

제 목 : 이락.쿠웨이트 사태

연: ECW-0554

1. 작 8.9. 파리에서 개최된 IEA 집행위 긴급회의에서 미,유럽,일등 21개 석유소비국들은 이락.쿠웨이트 원유공급 중단에도 불구하고 현재 전세계적으로 원유공급량은 충분하다고 판단하고 금번사태로 각국이 당장 전략비축 석유를 사용하거나 특별에너지 절약계획을 시행하는등 긴급조치를 취할 위기상황은 아니라는데 의견의 일치를 봄

2. IEA 회원국들은 또한 최근 유가인상은 즉각적인 원유공급 부족사태에 기인하기 보다는 전반적인 불확실에 대한 심리적 반응으로서 평가하고 유가인상 억제와 원유공급의 안정을 기하기 위하여 국제 석유회사들에게 현재 충분한 상업적 비축을 활용할것과 현물시장에서 과도한 원유구입을 자제할 것을 촉구하였음

3. IEA 측은 금번사태에 따른 선진공업국들의 석유공급 상황은 지난 2차례 석유파동시보다 훨씬 나은것으로 분석하고 그이유로서 하기사항을 듬

- 각국정부의 전략비축 석유는 현재 8년만에 최고수준인 총 10억 배럴로서 서방공업국들의 순원유수입 150일분에 상당

- 사우디, 베네주엘라등 여타 산유국들이 이락,쿠웨이트의 원유공급 중단을 보충할 원유생산량 증가 가능성

4. IEA 측은 또한 금번사태가 원유공급 부족사태로 발전할 가능성을 배제하지 않으면서도 기존 원유부존량 개발및 여타 에너지원 전환등 대응방안을 고려할때 원유수급의 심각한 불균형이 재발될 가능성은 적은것으로 전망함.

5. 한편, 당지 원유 전문가들은 막대한 상업적, 전략적 원유 비축량을 감안할때중.단기적 원유부족사태는 없을것으로 보고, 걸프지역의 긴장이 완화될 경우 유가는배럴당 25불선 이하로 하락할 것이며, 향후 수주이내 20-22불선을 유지할 것으로 전망함. 끝

경제국 중아국 통상국 통상국 1차보 2차보 동자부

PAGE 1

90.08.10 23:56 FC

외신 1과 통제관

0068

관리번호 90-571

원 본

외 무 부

종 별 : 지 급

번 호 : FRW-1455 일 시 : 90 0810 1810

수 신 : 장관(기협)

발 신 : 주 불 대사

제 목 : 이라크.쿠웨이트 사태

대:WFR-1526

연:FRW-1434

대호 IEA 회의결과 및 회원국 원유 비축 물량 아래 보고함.

1. 회의결과(이사회 CONCLUSION)

가. 주요 검토내용

0 수요 제한조치(에너지 절약 포함)

0STOCK 감축

0GAS 및 기타 에너지에 의한 원유 단기 대체

0 원유 증산

나. 주요결론

0 원유 매장량, STOCK (원유회사 및 정부 차원), 증산 가능성등을 감안시, 원유 공급이 충분하므로, IEA 의 비상 대응 체제 전환은 불필요

0 원유회사의 지난친 현물구매 자제

0 소비자의 건전한 원유 구매 유도

0IEA 회원국은 하기 방법으로 원유 공급 추이 MONITORING

-사태 진전및 GULF 원유 공급의 불확실성 감안, 필요시 이사회 소집(STOCKDRAW, 수요 자제등 검토)

-회원국은 이사회 결의에 따른 상설 GROUP 설치, 공동 대응 방안 수립

0 회원국의 대응조치는 개별국가 또는 전체회원국의 공급 부족을 해결할 수있도록 추진

0 이사회는 81 년의 이사회 결정(설문지 A 및 B 제출)에 근거한 사무총장의결정을 재확인

경제국 차관 1차보 2차보 중아국 청와대 동자부

PAGE 1

공람	국제경제국	90.8.11	담 당	과 장	국 장	차관보	차 관	장 관

90.08.11 01:36

외신 2과 통제관 CF

2.IEA 회원국 비축물량(단위:100 (836)톤,90.7.1 현재:IEA 전체:437.3)

가. 북미:215.9

-미국:200.1, 카나다:15.8

나. 유럽:137.5

-오지리:2.6, 벨지움:4.9, 덴막:4.7, 독일:39.1

-희랍:4.5, 아일랜드:1.1, 이태리:21.4, 룩셈부르크:0.3

-화란:9.3, 놀웨이:4.5, 폴투갈:2.8, 스페인:9.7

-스웨덴:6.4, 스위스:5.6, 터키:3.6, 영국:17.0

다. 태평양 연안국:83.9

-일본:77.1, 호주:5.8, 뉴질랜드:1.0

라.IEA 비회원국

-핀랜드:3.4

-프랑스:18.5

마.OECD 전체:469.6

3. 상기 IEA 문서 차파편 송부함. 끝.

(대사-국장)

예고:90.12.31. 까지

PAGE 2

0070

관리번호	90-580

원 본

외 무 부

종 별 :

번 호 : CAW-0505 일 시 : 90 0810 1830

수 신 : 장관(기협,마그)

발 신 : 주 카이로 총영사

제 목 : 이라크,쿠웨이트 사태

대:WCA-0265

대호 주재국 석유성, 내각사무처 정보센타 및 기타 석유공사등 관련 기관의종합된 의견을 아래 보고함.

1. 전망

이락이 8.2 쿠웨이트 참공이래 아랍각국을 비롯 UN 및 세계 여러나라의 압력에도 불구하고 계속 무력을 증강, 8.8. 쿠웨이트와의 합방을 선언하고 이에 반대하는 각국과 대결 자세를 취하고 있으며 현재 당지에서 개최하고 있는 아랍긴급정상회담의 결과에 관계없이 이락이 쿠웨이트철수를 거부할것이라고 추정되는경우 외부세력의 개입등 이락의 쿠웨이트 침공으로 야기된 사태는 장기화 될것으로 전망됨.

2. 현상태 장기 고찰시

8.2. 이락의 쿠웨이트 침공이후 국제 원유가는 사소의 상승세를 보이고 있으나, 사우디가 이락 및 쿠웨이트 양국의 하루 총생산량의 약 절반에 해당하는 2백만 배럴을 증산 할것으로 보도되고 있으며, UAE, 베네주엘라, 나이지리아 등기타 산유국들도 다소 증산 능력이 있으므로 제 1 및 제 2 차 오일 쇼크때와 같은 급격한 유가 상승은 없을것이라는것이고 당지 전문가들은 보고있음

3. 광역 전쟁으로 확산시

사우디아라비아 반도로 확전될시 사우디 산유량의 격감내지 수출불능 상태로 세계적인 원유 공급부족은 불가피할 것이며 이경우 사태가 호전될때까지 각국가별로 비상 에너지 대책을 발동, 원유확보 및 유류 배급제등 원유 소비를 축소화 할 수 있는 조치를 위해야 할 것이라고 당지 전문가들은 보고있음.

4. 주재국 대책

주재국은 일산 약 87 만 배럴을 생산 약 55-60 만 배럴을 소비하고 20-27 만

경제국 차관 1차보 2차보 중아국 청와대 동자부

PAGE 1

공람	국제경제국	90년8월13일	담당	과장	국장	차관보	차관	장관

90.08.11 05:37

외신 2과 통제관 CF

0071

배런을 수출하고 있으므로 금번 사태관련 특별 유류 대책을 수립해 놓고 있지는 않음. 끝.

(총영사 박동순-국장)

예고:90.12.31. 까지

PAGE 2

0072

관리 번호	90-585

외 무 부

종 별 :

번 호 : MAW-1035　　　　일 시 : 90 0810 2040

수 신 : 장 관(통일,기협,중근동,아동)

발 신 : 주 말련 대사

제 목 : 이라크,쿠웨이트사태

대:WMA-0546

연:MAW-1014

본직은 금 8.10. 국책석유회사인 PETRONAS 회장 BASIR 박사를 면담, 대호에 관해 의견을 청취한바, 요지 아래 보고함

1. 이락의 쿠웨이트 침공은 단기적으로는 (수개월간) 유가앙등 등으로 인하여 국제적 불안을 야기 시킬것이나 그이상의 위기로 발전됨이 없이 조만간 진정될것으로 전망함

2. 이락에 대한 미쏘의 공동보조 계속및 아랍권의 반이락 입장등이 확고해지고 경제제재 조치가 유효히 이행된다면 이락은 식량 및 무기 수입등에 있어 심각한 난관에 봉착하여 조만간 후퇴하거나 후세인이 실각되는 사태로 발전될 것으로 봄

3. 주재국은 이같은 전망과 일단 증산을 시작하면 감산하기가 어렵다는 점에서 현재로서는 원유의 증산을 고려하고 있지 않다 함. 끝

(대사 홍순영-국장)

예고:90.12.31.까지

공람	국제경제국	90 8 13	담 당	과 장	국 장	차관보	차 관	장 관
				(서명)	(서명)			

통상국　차관　1차보　2차보　아주국　중아국　경제국　정와대　안기부

PAGE 1　　　　90.08.11　12:07

외신 2과　통제관 DL

0073

관리번호	90-586

외 무 부

종 별 :

번 호 : EQW-0318 일 시 : 90 0810 2100

수 신 : 장 관(통일,기협)

발 신 : 주 에쿠아돌 대사

제 목 : 이락.쿠에이트 사태

대:WEQ-0181

대호 지시에 의거 주재국 에너지성 및 전문가 의견을 아래 보고함.

1. 금번 사태에 대한 전망

- 사우디 국경에 많은 병력을 유지, 이를 바탕으로 쿠웨이트에 대한 지배권을 유지하고자 할것으로 예상

- 이락이 쿠웨이트를 지배할시 이락의 원유매장량은 총 1,950 억 배럴 (이락 950 억 배럴, 쿠웨이트 1,000 억 배럴)로 세계 원유매장량의 20%를 보유, 유가 결정력 증대

2. 금번 사태의 장기화시 국제수급 및 유가전망

가. 국제 수급

- 비중동지역 OPEC 회원국은 생산증대에 힘쓸것이나 생산설비, 매장량, 여타 회원국과의 과계등을 감안하면 단시간내에 쿼타량 10-20% 이상의 증산은 어려울 것으로 판단됨

- 단기간내의 국제원유수급 불균형은 비 OPEC 회원국 (멕시코, 영국, 소련등)의 원유생산 증대와 원유가 상승에 따른 수요국의 수요감축, 대체에너지 사용등으로 대처될것임.

- 쿠웨이트 및 이락의 원유는 미국등 서방제국이 EMBARGO 조치를 취하고 있음으로 실제적으로 대이락 원유수입국은 당분간 없을 것임.

나. 유가 전망

- OPEC 은 이미 기준유가를 21 불로 상향조정한바 있음으로 금번사태는 기준유가 또는 그 이상가격 유지의 촉매작용을 할것으로 전망됨.

- 그러나 산유국들도 2 차 원유파동때 겪은 경제적인 어려움 및 외환수급상의

통상국 차관 1차보 2차보 미주국 경제국 동자부

PAGE 1

공람	국제경제국	90 년 8월 13일	담 당	과 장	국 장	차관보	차 관	장 관

90.08.11 12:48

외신 2과 통제관 DL

0074

문제점등을 인식하고 있기 때문에 급격한 원유가의 상승보다는 배럴당 미화 21불선을 상회하는 수준에서 점진적이고 안정적인 원유가의 상승을 희구할것임.

3. 과역전쟁등 인근지역으로 확산시 국제수급 및 유가전망

가. 국제수급

- 예상할수 있는 광역전쟁이라함은 사우디 및 입접아랍국등 페르시아만 연안국으로 전쟁이 확대될 경우인데, 미.소가 현상황에서 일치된 견해를 보이고 있음을 감안, 광역전쟁의 발발 가능성은 희박한 것으로 보고 있음

나. 유가전망

- 광역전쟁의 발발시에는 대처에너지등의 개발에 필요한 시간및 소비국들의 유류소비 패턴이 변경되는 시기까지는 2 차 원유파동시와 같이 가격상승이 예상되나, 세계경제의 침체로 인한 수요감소로 시장원리에 의하여 배럴당 30 불대에서 형성될 것으로 전망하고 있음.

4. 에쿠아돌의 현황

가. 현황

- OPEC 의 쿼타는 24 만 배럴이며, 일일 원유생산량은 28 만배럴, 일일 수출량은 15 만배럴 수준임.

- 단기적인 생산증가량은 30 만배럴에 이를 것이며, 최대 생산 가능량은 31 만배럴 수준임.

- 원유수출가는 7.31 배럴당 15.61 불이였으나, 금번사태로 8 월 첫주초 18.23 불, 주말 20.30 불, 금주는 23.66 불 까지 치솟고 있음.

- 이러한 급격한 가격 상승에 대하여 에너지성 장관등은 환영할만한 현상은 아니라고 우려를 표하고 있음

나. 현사태가 에쿠아돌에 미치는 영향

- 금번사태로 인한 국제시장의 원유가 상승으로 만성적인 외환 부족상태에 있는 주재국에는 플러스 효과가 발생함

- 그러나 서방제국이 원유공급 부족사태에 대한 대응책을 강구할 것이므로 현상황에 따른 과도한 기대는 않고 있음.

- 최근까지 주재국이 겪고있는 장기공급 계약자의 발군난에서 벗어나 향후 1-2 년간은 안정적인 수출선 확보가 용이하리라고 보고있음. 끝.

(대사 정해웅 - 국장)

90 12 31

PAGE 2

0075

예고:1990.12.31. 일반

PAGE 3

0076

관리 번호 90-588

원 본

외 무 부

종 별 : 지 급

번 호 : IRW-0438　　　　일 시 : 90 0811 1100

수 신 : 장관(기협,중근동,기정,상공부,건설부,동자부)

발 신 : 주 이란대사

제 목 : 이락,쿠웨이트사태

연:IRW-0437

1. 본직은 금 8.11(토) 0830 주재국 아가자데 석유장관을 면담하였는바, 동인의 언급 요지 아래보고함(전참사관배석)

가. 사태전망

-현재로서는 현재상황의 상당기간 계속될것으로 예상

-사태가 이락의 사우디침공으로 확대될경우, 사우디의 산유시설이 파괴되어 국제원유시장의 혼란우려

나. 원유가격전망

-각국의 생산능력감안시, 사우디가 170 만 BD, UAE 50-60 만 BD, 베네주엘라 30-40 만 BD, 기타 OPEC 국가 20-30 만 BD 이란 50 만 BD 등 합계 약 350-400 만 BD 의 원유 수출증대가 가능한바, 이는 장기적으로 볼때 이락, 쿠웨이트의 감량분을 거의 상쇄할수 있는 물량임.

-단기적으로볼때 국제원유시장에 공급부족현상은 없을것이나, 주요 소비국이 비축분을 사용하기 보다는 우선 국제시장에서 구입을 선호할것이므로 원유가는 다소간 상승예상

-이란은 원유시장의 급작스런 변동을 원하지않으며 질서있는 원유수급의 확보와 장기적인 시장안정을위해서는 OPEC 생산국및 소비국들의 협의가 있어야된다고 봄.

-(본직의 OPEC 각료회의 재소집가능성 문의에대해)

동회의의 소집필요성은 검토해야 할것이나 현재로서는 결정할수없음 또한 쿠웨이트에 2 등의 석유상이 있는등 기술적으로도 회의소집이 불가능함. 그러나 OPEC 각국은 전화를 통한 대화등으로 화속 협의하고있음.

다. 대아국 석유공급

경제국 장관 차관 1차보 2차보 중아국 청와대 안기부 상공부
동자부 건설부

PAGE 1

공람	국제경제국	90 년 월 일	담 당	과 장	국 장	차관보	차 관	장 관

90.08.11 18:21
외신 2과 통제관 DO
0077

-금번사태로 아국이 원유공급에 문제가 발생시, 이란은 양국간 우호관계를 고려, 필요한 협조를할 용의가 있음(아국이 이락, 쿠웨이트에서 공급받아왔던 물량을 이란이 공급할수 있음)

-일본은 이미 이란으로부터의 원유구매 계약관련, 계약기간을 6 개월 이상의 장기계약으로하고 구입물량도 증대하여줄것을 요청하여왔음

-(본직이 90.2 양국간 공동위 개최시 양국간 원유의 장기공급계약문제가 협의된바 있음을 지적한바)

-아국의 우려를 이해하며, 차기 공동위개최 이전이라도 한국및 이란의 관계전문가가 상호방문, 원유의 장기계약등 필요사항을 사전 협의할것을 제의하며 동협의를 기초로 최종안을 공동위에서 확정하는것이 바람직함. 끝

(대사정경일-국장)

예고:90.12.31 까지

PAGE 2

0078

관리번호	90-589

원 본

외 무 부

종 별 :

번 호 : IRW-0440 일 시 : 90 0811 1200

수 신 : 장관(기협,중근동,기정,상공,건설,동자)

발 신 : 주 이란 대사

제 목 : 이락,쿠웨이트사태

연:IRW-0438

연호 주재국 아가자데 석유장관 면담관련, 당관의 관찰및 의견 아래보고함.

1. 석유장관은 일본이 금반 사태와관련 이란으로부터의 장기원유 공급을 요청하고 있음에도 불구, 아국으로부터는 아무런 움직임이 없는것에 대해 호의적인 주의를 환기시키면서, 아국과 시무레벨에서의 협의를 제의한점등에 비추어 아국의 관련 부처의 실무자가 당지를 방문, 협의를 하도록 하는것이 필요하다고봄.

2. 동장관은 타브리즈 석유화학단지 프로젝트에 한국, 일본, 불란서등이 경합하고 있으나, 한국업체(대림)가 어떤 형태로든지 참여할수 있도록 하겠다고 약속하고 일반적인 문제로서 특히 대우, 현대가 좀더 적극적인 수주활동을 하였으면하는 개인적인 의견을 표시하였음. 한편 BIPC(전 IJPC) 에 한국기업이 UC(UNIT CONTRECTOR)로 참여할수있도록 호의적인 고려를 하여 달라는 본직의 요망에 대하여 BIPC 는 매우 중요한 사업이기 때문에 한국기업에 한 파트를 틀림없이 할애하겠다고 확약하였음(ONE PART WILL DEFINITELY BE LEFT TO YOU-SIC-) 이러한 장관의 발언에 비추어 앞으로 BIPC 와 관련 주재국과의 연락, 정보수집등 많은 업무를 당관이 담당하여야 할것으로 예상됨. 따라서 해외건설협회에서 아국기업의 BIPC 참여 계획등에 관하여 어떤 계획이나 추진중인 사항이 있다면 이를 당관에도 계속 알려주도록 협조요청하여 주기바람.

(대사정경일-국장)

예고:90.12.31 까지

공람	국제경제국	90.8.13	담당	과장	국장	차관보	차관	장관

경제국	장관	차관	1차보	2차보	중아국	청와대	안기부	상공부
동자부	건설부							

PAGE 1 90.08.11 18:27

외신 2과 통제관 DO

0079

관리번호	90-587

원 본

외 무 부

종 별 :

번 호 : QTW-0100　　　　　일 시 : 90 0811 1315

수 신 : 장 관(기협)

발 신 : 주 카타르 대사

제 목 : 이락.쿠웨이트 사태

대:WQT-0079

연:QTW-0097

1. 카타르 석유공사 (QGPC)의 IBRAHIM MOTAWAH 원유판매부장이 8.11 언급한바에 의하면

0 주재국은 7,8 양월간 OPEC 쿼터인 37.1 만 B/D 선을 초과하는 38 만 B/D 를 생산중에 있는바 이것이 동사의 생산능력의 상한선이며 그이상 증산은 불가능함.

0 더우기 9 월말 부터 11 월까지는 정기시설 정비를 위해 약 30 프로 감산이 불가피하나 금년도 연수단 총생산양은 OPEC 쿼터선에 도달할 것임.

0 이락, 쿠웨이트 산유량 400 만 B/D 의 GOP 을 여하히 메우는 가에 대해서는 판단하기 어려 우나 주요 소비국에 약 100 일분의 비축량이 있기 때문에 당분간 현재 이상으로 유가가 상승할것으로는 보지 않음.

(대사 유내형-국장)

예고:90.12.31 일반)

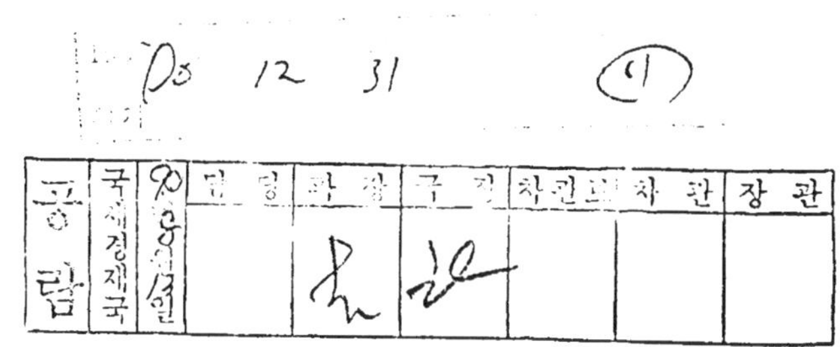

경제국　차관　1차보　2차보　중아국　통상국

PAGE 1　　　　　90.08.12 13:14

외신 2과 통제관 DL

0080

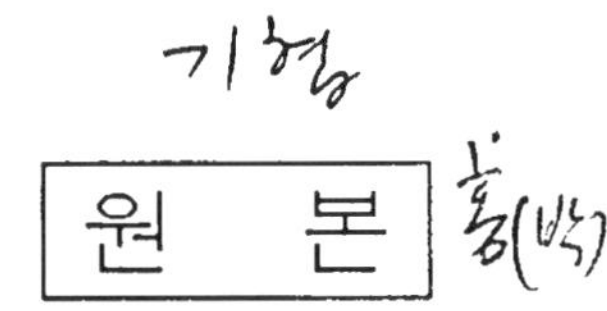

관리번호	90-591

원 본

외 무 부

종 별 :

번 호 : IRW-0444　　　　일 시 : 90 0812 1100

수 신 : 장 관(경이,중근동,건설부,노동부)

발 신 : 주 이란 대사

제 목 : 이락,쿠웨이트사태 관련대책

1. 대:WIR-0263(8.10)

2. 주재국 건설시장에 미치는 영향및 대책

가. 건설시장에 미치는영향

-90.8.2 자 산유관련 이락의 쿠웨이트 침공 여파로 이란산 유가가 오르고 있는 실정이고 (8.6 자 수출가: 23 불 PB) 동 사태악화가 지속될 경우 국제 원유수급에 차질이 예상 되는바 OPEC 의 할당량및 유가 재조정이 불가피 할것으로 보며 이에 따라 이란 원유 생산량이 증가 될것으로 예상되나 (현할당량 3,140 천 BD) 원유 생산시설의 부족으로 인해 대폭적인 증산은 어려울 것으로 보여짐.

-원유증산및 유가상승이 이란 건설시장에 즉각적인 반응 (호황)이 있을 것으로 보여지지 않으나 90.7.27 자 오펙의 기준유가인상 (21 불 PB)과 더불어 이락, 쿠웨이트 사태가 장기화될 경우 이란건설시장 활성화 예상됨.

나. 대책

-단기적으로 진출 아국건설업체의 수주활동 강화

-장기적으로 사태진전 추이를 관망하면서 현지여건 (할당량 증량, 생산량 증가, 유가 상승등)을 감안, 건설업체의 추가 진출 모색

3. 이락, 쿠웨이트 진출 아국건설업체 지원가능성및 방안

-이락 진출건설업체 근로자의 이란내에로의 긴급 대피 문제는 양국간의 국교 관계로 보아 곤란할것으로 보나 쿠웨이트 진출건설업체 근로자의 긴급대피는 주재국 정부에서 비자발급이 가능한것으로 확인 되었음.

-현재 이들 근로자의 이란내 대피 적정지를 물색중에 있은 본부의 대피계획이 수립되었을 경우 회보바람. 끝

(대사 정경일-국장)

90. 12. 31

(61)

경제국 장관 차관 1차보 2차보 중아국 통상국 청와대 안기부
건설부 노동부

PAGE 1

공람	국제경제국	년 월 일	담 당	과 장	국 장	차관보	차 관	장 관

90.08.12　17:13

외신 2과　통제관 DL

0081

예고:90.12.31 까지

PAGE 2

0082

외 무 부

종 별 : 지 급

번 호 : NDW-1083 일 시 : 90 0812 1500

수 신 : 장 관(중근동,아서,통일) 기협

발 신 : 주 인도 대사

제 목 : 이락의 쿠웨이트 침공과 관련한 인도의 반응(5)

1. 작 8.11 인도 외무부대변인은 이락의 쿠웨이트침공 이후 이락 및 쿠웨이트에잔류중이던 인도여행자문제 및 주이락 대사관 인원보강에 대해 다음과 같이 밝힘.

가. 약 700명의 인도인이 HAJ 순례후 이락의 KARBALA 순례지를 방문중 이락의 쿠웨이트 침공으로 이락을 떠나지 못하고 있었는 바, 인도정부는 이들을 요르단까지 육로로 이동시킨 후 특별기편으로 인도로 수송할 계획이며 이를 위한 이락정부의 허가를 주이락 대사를 통해 득하였음.

나. 또한 주쿠웨이트 대사는 이락당국의 허가를 받아, 이락군의 쿠웨이트공항 점거로 묶여 있던 BRITISH AIRWAYS(인도 마드라스 향발 예정)편에 탑승중인 120명의인도 승객을 면회하였는 바,동 승객은 전원 무사하며 건강상태도 양호하다고함.

다. 인도정부는 이락 및 쿠웨이트에 거주하는 인도인에 대한 영사보호업무의 효율적 수행을 위해 주이락 대사관의 인력을 보강 조치중임.

2. 한편, H.K.SINGH 인도 외무담당 국무장관은 페루,베네주엘라 및 콜롬비아를 방문후 귀로에 뉴욕에서 케야르 유엔 사무총장과 면담,.대이락 경제제재조치 관련문제를 협의한 것으로 당지 언론(8.12자 HINDUSTAN TIMES) 은 다음 요지 보도함.

가. SINGH 국무장관이 케야르 사무총장에게 전달한 인도입장은 다음과 같음.

1) 유엔 안보리 결의에 따른 대이락 경제제재조치로 영향을 받게 될 인도 및 여타 개발도상국에 대해 유엔이 산하기관 등을 통해 원조를 제공해야 할 것임.

2) 유엔의 제재조치로 인해 경제적 어려움을 받게되는 경우에 대한 원조제공은 유엔헌장에도 규정되어 있음.

3) 금번 제재조치로 이락내의 많은 프로젝트, 특히 건설프로젝트가 지연되거나 중

중아국	1차보	아주국	경제국	정문국	안기부	통상국	공보실	그차관	장관

차관

PAGE 1

90.08.12 21:55 ND

외신 1과 통제관

0083

지될 것이며, 이락에 대한 수출도 중단될 것인 바, 인도와 여타국가들이 심각한 영향을 받게 될 것이 확실하므로 유엔은 이러한 국가들을 지원할 의무가 있음.

나. 동 국무장관은 자신의 상기 입장 표명에 대해 유엔 사무총장이 매우 동정적인 반응을 보였다고 밝힘.

다. 또한, 동 국무장관은 인도의 대이락 대응이 너무 미온적이지 않느냐는 기자의 질문에 대해서는 다음과 같이 답변함.

1) 쿠웨이트와 이락은 모두 인도에 우호적인 국가이며 우리는 그들 자신이 그들간의 문제를 해결하기를 희망함.

2) 직설적인 규탄으로 문제가 해결되는 것은아니며, 인도가 이야기한 것이 약하게 들릴지 모르나,인도의 의도는 매우 강한 것임. 우리는 이락의 행동에 동의하지 아니하며 가능한 조속한 시일내에 이러한 이락의 행동이 철회되기를 희망함.

3. 당지에서는 인도 원유수입의 40 프로 이상을 점유하는 이락 및 쿠웨이트(특히 이락)로부터의 수입이 막힐 경우에 대한 우려가 점차 높아지고 있으며, 당지 언론관측통은 인도 정부가 원유부족분을 사우디, UAE 및 이란 등으로부터 도입하려고 노력중이나 외환부족으로 큰 어려움을 겪을 것으로 분석하고 있음.

(대사 김태지-국장)

PAGE 2

0084

08/13/90 18:41 ☎202 797 0595 EMBASSY OF KOREA →→→ WOI 016/0

번호 : USW(F) - 1802

수신 : 장 관 (중근동, 미북, 동력, 기정) 발신 : 주미대사

제목 :

(3 매)

Oil Crisis Like 1973's? It's Not Necessarily So

By STEPHEN GREENHOUSE

Special to The New York Times

PARIS, Aug. 12 — The jump in oil prices and drop in supplies stemming from Iraq's invasion of Kuwait will do far less damage to the world's economy than did the 1973 and 1979 oil shocks, economists and energy experts say.

Economists say that barring an escalation of the gulf crisis, the global economy will adapt to the higher oil prices, both because they are less than in the previous oil shocks and because many countries have systematically reduced their reliance on petroleum.

Nevertheless, if the gulf crisis worsens dramatically and disrupts a substantially larger part of the Middle East's oil exports, through the bombing, for instance, of Saudi oilfields, then world oil prices could skyrocket well above $50 a barrel, sending the world economy into a tailspin.

The industrial countries' oil bill will rise about $90 billion a year if oil goes to $30 a barrel. That sounds immense, but it will be far easier to handle than the increased oil bills of the 1970's because it represents just six-tenths of 1 percent of the industrial world's economic output.

The additional oil bills from the 1970's shocks represented 2 percent of economic output.

The United States, Europe and Japan have established large emergency stocks of oil and have set up a system of cooperative procedures, including potential measures to cut demand.

"We have been able to learn lessons from the previous crises," said Joseph Stanislaw, managing director of Cambridge Energy Research Associates in England. "The potential for governments to have coordinated actions is now much better than 10 years ago."

The governments of the industrial world have about a billion barrels of oil in their emergency reserves, which represents 250 days of Iraqi and Kuwaiti exports.

What is more, the ability of the industrial world's governments to draw on their emergency reserves, which are far larger than in the 1970's, can help prevent astronomical price leaps.

"It is not necessary to let the price rush upward if we very quickly adopt a policy of releasing stocks in a gradual manner," said Robert Mabro, director of the Oxford Institute for Energy Research in England.

Lessons From Earlier Crises

Another factor that could mitigate the damage from an oil price increase, economists say, is the lesson that finance officials and central bankers learned from previous oil shocks. This could help them prevent an oil price rise from producing an unmanageable inflationary spiral.

In many countries, after governments did not move in time to prevent the 1973 and 1979 shocks from causing inflationary spirals, they clamped down on prices and pushed their nations into deep recessions.

"The simple lesson is that if you have an energy price hike, you have to limit the inflationary damage to the rest of the economy as best you can," said Michél Develle, chief economist for Banque Paribas in Paris.

World oil demand is rising only slowly nowadays, and this will make it easier for nations to absorb a shortage. Demand is climbing 2 percent a year, compared with 5 percent in 1979, when economic growth was strong. "The softer is demand, the less likely that oil price increases will stick," said Allen Sinai, an economic adviser to the Boston Company.

Many economists and petroleum experts predict oil prices will stay in the $22 to $28 range over the next few months, assuming that other producers make up for much of the Iraqi and Kuwaiti oil, as they have promised to do, and assuming that the gulf crisis does not intensify.

If the projected shortage of four million barrels a day is not significantly reduced, then prices could rise to $30 or more per barrel, many oil analysts say.

Although most economists say the industrial world is less vulnerable to oil shocks, the recent oil price increase is expected to help push the already-weak United States economy into recession.

"A $5 increase will bring the U.S. very close to a recession if not into a brief recession," said Roger Brinner, chief economist for DRI, an economic consulting company. "A $10-a-barrel increase would certainly bring the U.S. into a classic recession."

The International Energy Agency, a Paris-based group of oil-importing nations, has coordinated the West's efforts to react to an oil shock and to keep demand for balance in balance with supply. For example, it has encouraged countries to build power plants that use other fuels as well as plants that can switch from oil to other fuels.

Mr. Stanislaw, the Cambridge Energy Research Associates official, says that the industrial world could cut demand for oil by 700,000 barrels a day

1802-1

0085

번호 : USW(F)-
수신 : 장 관 발신 : 주미대사 보안 통제
제목 : (매)

Showdown: Facing Up to Saddam—and Our Oil Habit

By Jimmy Carter

FOR ALMOST half a century, every president has had to confront a complex and dangerous threat emanating from the Middle East and to decide whether American forces would be dispatched to that region in the midst of a crisis. No other part of the world has so frequently forced us to face the prospect of massive and potentially devastating conflict.

President Bush now joins an unbroken line of his predecessors stretching back to President Truman. I, like all Americans, wish him well as he wrestles with this recurring threat. Once the Iraqi invasion was launched, a firm response was his only option. He has our prayers and our support.

As difficult and dangerous as this task will be, we can take comfort in at least one advantage of tremendous significance: For the first time, our strategy and tactics can be devised and implemented without an overriding concern for their impact on the Cold War. The additional flexibility thus provided to the president is almost impossible to overestimate. For the first time, neither we nor the leaders of the Soviet Union labor under the possibility, if not the probability, that any action taken by either side will be misinterpreted and/or exploited by the other. Though the dangers of miscalculation in the present crisis are numerous and severe, neither a major shift in the geo-strategic balance between Moscow and Washington nor nuclear holocaust are among them. For that we can all be thankful.

It is also encouraging to note the relatively rapid and positive response of other industrialized nations on both the diplomatic and economic fronts. This has seldom occurred in the past even when we were faced with behavior no less egregious and as threatening to their interests as to ours. Credit should be given to the diplomatic skills of our political leaders and also, perhaps, to an increased international recognition that half-hearted measures and the pursuit of shortsighted interests only serve to increase the ultimate danger to us all. Of course, we have every reason to watch carefully to determine if sustained actions conform to promises.

If the ending of the Cold War and a greater willingness to act in concert provide us with substantial advantages compared to previous crises, there are at least two other factors that plague President Bush as they did each of his predecessors: namely, the Arab-Israeli conflict, particularly the Palestinian question, and the dismal failure of our own country to acknowledge and deal with its energy vulnerability.

Unlike some other crises in the area, the Iraqi aggression is not the direct result of the inability to find a lasting and just compromise between the rights of Israelis and Palestinians. However, it is undeniably true that the absence of a viable peace process strengthens the hands of radicals, exacerbates tensions, encourages military adventurism and complicates the solution of existing problems. A persistent and believable peace effort has been absent from the region for more than a decade. The serious consequences have been made repeatedly obvious.

It would be a mistake to believe that Saddam Hussein is only supported by those who fear him. As our friends in the region are only too well aware, he has enjoyed considerable support from Arabs who have not shared in oil wealth, from those who admire a Nasser-like Arab strongman, from those who see the United States and other Western nations as enemies because of our sup-

See CARTER, C2, Col. 1

Former president Jimmy Carter is the founder of the Carter Center in Atlanta and serves as distinguished professor at Emory University.

port for Israel, and particularly from many Palestinians who resent what they see as a lack of support for their cause from some of the oil-rich kingdoms, especially Kuwait.

Saddam has now lost this appeal to many potential Arab supporters in the region, however, by overplaying his hand. With wise diplomacy after the invasion of Kuwait, he might have been able to consolidate some of his gains, but his subsequent military maneuvers and belligerent statements have cost him greatly. There can be little doubt that this loss of his previous backing is now well understood by Saddam. One has only to review the text of his Wednesday and Friday speeches, more an appeal for support from the Palestinians and other Arabs than a justification of his actions to the world, to understand that he still seeks to exploit his appeal to the frustrated as well as military power to reach his goals.

If the peace process has been allowed to languish, our efforts to deal with our dangerous, embarrassing, and growing dependence on imported oil have been left to wither and die. If it is true that Providence punishes the foolish, then we face some difficult days indeed.

We learned in 1973 that we could no longer depend upon reliable supplies of cheap oil. We were reminded again in 1979. We are now in the early stages of lesson No. 3, and our dependence is, for all practical purposes, as great as it was when

1802-2
W
August 12 1990

0086

번호 : USW(F)-

수신 : 장 관 발신 : 주미대사

보안 통제

제목 : (매)

those two shocks produced a virulent combination of recession and inflation, which dashed the dreams of millions of American families.

It would not be much of an exaggeration to say that we have wasted the 17 years since oil prices more than quadrupled in 1973, or the 11 years since the Iran-Iraq war doubled prices in less than a year. The hard fact, known quite well by President Bush and only too well by Arab oil suppliers, is that we now have no effective national energy policy, nor any commitment to adopt one.

No plan will totally free us from a significant dependence on imported oil. We can never completely insulate ourselves from the vagaries of the international petroleum market any more than we can from the twists and turns of other sectors of an increasingly interdependent global economy. We can, however, with a modicum of forethought and creativity, greatly increase our ability to weather future crises.

But we must do it ourselves, for ourselves. No one and no thing, including the free market, will do it for us—as events of the past decade have amply demonstrated.

We did, it is true, take some action in the late 1970s that mandated an increase in automobile efficiency, improved home insulation, and discouraged the waste of electric power. We initiated a strategic petroleum reserve, which now holds some 590 million barrels of oil, equivalent to 80 days of imports. This limited supply has already helped to hold down the price of oil, but it also underscores our shortsightedness. We reduced our planned purchases for the reserve out of a misguided belief that this was a cheap and painless way to reduce escalating budget deficits. (The reductions would have been much worse had Congress not intervened.) To make matters worse, these reductions came at a time when the cost of oil was at rock bottom, less than half what it is today. The net result is that the strategic reserve is now smaller relative to our level of imports than it was five years ago.

Almost all the other measures that could have helped us now, some established by law, have been ignored and virtually abandoned. Alternative energy sources such as solar power, clean coal, synthetic fuels and the recycling of trash to energy are testimonies to unrealized potential.

Conservation of energy, which I have always believed to be the cornerstone of a workable plan and which other industrialized nations have made a continuing focus of national policy and public education, has become an afterthought in the United States.

A tax on imported oil which would have promoted conservation, reduced the federal deficit, stimulated domestic production and discouraged imports was shot down in a political cross fire before it got off the ground.

Domestic production, which requires some degree of price stability, a measure of carefully targeted government support and active promotion of reasonable compromises with conflicting interests, is now significantly lower than it ought to be. More than 4,000 drilling rigs were operating in this country at the beginning of the decade. Last week the total was less than 1,000. We are now *importing one half* the oil we consume.

Not only are we no better off now than we were 10 years ago in terms of our ability to weather a disruption in oil supplies, but we are much worse off in comparison to our economic competitors.

Abandoned mills and factories, vanished jobs, and the prolonged erosion of the economic well-being of American workers are eloquent testimony to the fact that we are, if not losing the battle for international competitiveness, at least sustaining heavy losses. This oil crisis will add to that casualty list and will leave us even less able to compete effectively. This will happen, not because of unfair laws and practices in Germany and Japan, but because those countries learned their lesson years ago and acted upon it, and we did not.

Recently reported figures underscore the point: each $1 increase in the price of a barrel of oil will cut $1.2 billion a year from Japan's massive trade surplus, but it will add more than twice that amount to our already dangerous trade deficit. The impact of increasing oil prices on the production costs of Japanese goods will be only one-third the impact on American products. We use 2.5 times more energy per person for commercial purposes than Japan and 1.5 times more than West Germany. Japan's oil reserves, measured in terms of days of supply, are 75 percent greater than ours.

Few people know better than I the difficulty involved in devising a workable energy policy for a nation as large and complex as ours, particularly in a year like 1977 when oil supplies were adequate and many argued that there would be no crisis in the foreseeable future. Certainly, some of those difficulties were caused by try
do too much too fast and others by nc
understanding the interplay of the co
interests involved.

I hope the next effort will be free
those shortcomings. Whether it is o
my message at its simplest is that
must be a next effort.

I was pleased to hear President Bu
for conservation in his speech last W
day. Indeed, there are a few steps th
bring *immediate* results. But the mo
portant elements of an effective energ
icy will require some long-term chan
our societal attitudes and priorities.
issues are involved, success is not as
There will be inevitable dissension a
consumers, producers and the myriad
sure groups involved. No truly compr
sive proposal will be totally accepta
every interest, perhaps not to any.
short-term politics of the issue are n
tractive for the White House or Capit

In short, we will once again be face
the necessity of paying a near-term
economically and politically for much
or long-term gain. We will have a
between accepting the many reasons
nothing and looking for ways to get t
done. How we choose will depend
whether we have learned any more
our third lesson than we did from th
two.

I remember that in my first of ma
tempts to mobilize support for a na
energy policy I spoke of the "moral e
alent of war." It was, perhaps, a rhet
excess in an administration often desc
as somewhat deficient in rhetoric, exc
or otherwise. In any case, I also reca
there were those who were amused. I
now watch our carriers steaming to
the Straits of Hormuz and our young m
battle gear embarking for the Arabia
insula, I hope that our national respon
be more sober.

1802-3

Aug 12 1990 1110

0087

관리번호 90-590

외 무 부

종 별 :

번 호 : IRW-0450　　　　　일 시 : 90 0813 1430

수 신 : 장관(중근동,통일,기정,상공부,건설부)

발 신 : 주 이란 대사

제 목 : 이락,쿠웨이트사태

연:IRW-0438

본직은 금 8.13(월) 외무부 BURJERDI 아시아, 대양주담당 차관을면담한바, 표제관련 동인의 언급요지 아래보고함.

1. 이락 사담대통령이 8.12 연설을통하여 금번사태 해결과 관련 이락군의 철수조건으로 이스라엘의 팔레스타인지역, 시리아, 레바논등으로부터의 즉각적인무조건철군을 요구함으로써, 사태가 장기화될것으로 전망됨.

2. 쿠웨이트로부터 이라크의 철군을 요구하는 이란의 입장은 확고한것임.이란은 군사적 방법이외에 모든방법을동원, 쿠웨이트의 원상회복을위해 노력할것임.

3. 서방및 아랍제국의 대이락금수조치는, 바그다드내에 생필품부족현상이 생기는등 상당한 효과가 있는것으로 평가됨(이란의 대이락 제재조치로써 아랍정상회의결의나 서방국가의 예에따라 군사적 조치를 취할가능성문의에대해)현재로서 동가능성은 없음(이락의 쿠웨이트 무력점령이 묵인될경우, 향후 전례가되어 걸프지역내 정세불안 요인이되어 장기적 석유수급에 불안정요인이 될것임)

4.(본직이 아국의 대이락 관련조치를 설명한바), 이락과 경제, 정치관계가 단절된 이란과달리, 중동 원유 등에 의존하고있는 상황에서 그같은 조치를 취한 아국에 경의를표명하고, 이란의 대아국 경제관계 강화가능성등을 시사함. 끝

(대사정경일-국장)

예고:90.12.31 까지

기협

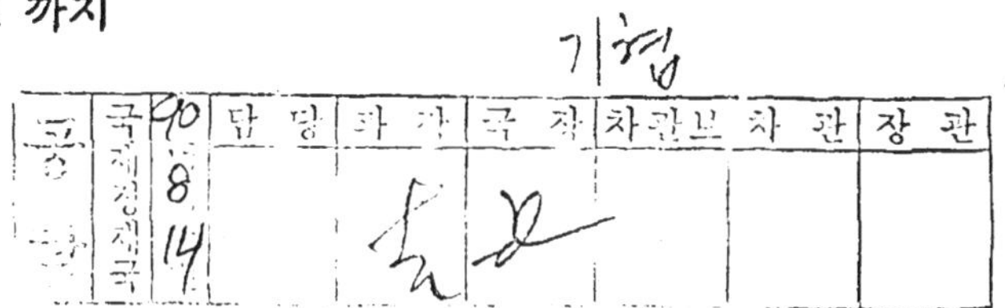

중아국	장관	차관	1차보	2차보	경제국	통상국	상황실	청와대
안기부	상공부	동자부	건설부					

PAGE 1　　　90 12 31　　　90.08.13 21:18

외신 2과 통제관 FE

0088

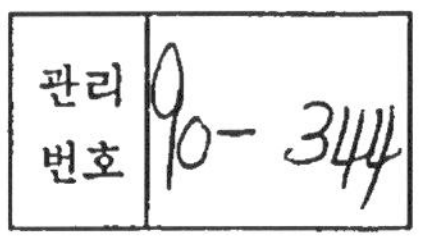

외 무 부

종 별 : 지 급

번 호 : GEW-1376 일 시 : 90 0813 1930

수 신 : 장관(기협,통일,미북,구일)

발 신 : 주 독 대사

제 목 : 이락-쿠웨이트 사태

대:WGE-1127, 1161

대호 당관 이상완 참사관은 8.13. 외무부 원유담당관 DOMASCH 를 면담 아래보고함

1. 금번 사태의 전망

가. 이락의 대사우디 공격은 그시기를 이미 잃은 것으로 보아 실행은 어려울것이고 사우디내의 반왕정, 사회주의 노선 세력의 대내적 봉기 분위기를 고조시키면서 기회를 포착하려 할것임. 이락으로서는 사우디내에서 수년간 멕카에서 있었던 이러한 반정부운동의 재등장을 기대할 것임. 이락은 현재및 중동사태 진정후에도 사우디내에서 파레스타인 계열등 사우디 부의 혜택을 받지 못하고 왕정에 반대하는 세력이 증가함을 기대하면서 수년전 멕카에서 있었던 이러한 반왕정운동의 재등장을 기대하여 그어떠한 구실을 포착하려할 것임.

나. 이락은 쿠웨이트에 대하여는 원래부터 이락영토에 속하였음을 후세인이수차 언급한것으로 보아 쿠웨이트의 예속을 기정사실화 할려할것이고, 또한 이락은 팔레스타인등 사회 빈곤계층과 왕정반대세력을 종용 쿠웨이트 지배를 지속하려 할것임

2. 원유수급및 유가전망

가. 사태이전인 8.1. 은 바렐당 20 불, 발발일 이후 수일간은 발렐당 30 불로 앙등하였으나, 금 8.13. 은 바렐당 26.7 불로 하락하는등 단기간에는 가격변동의 폭이 크게 작용할것이나, 중기(3 개월 정도)로볼때 바렐당 약 23 불선으로 유지될것으로 전망됨.

나. 일부 산유국의 증산계획 언급및 움직임(사우디 2 백만 바렐, UAE 1 백만 바렐, 베네주엘라, 멕시코등 산유국의 증산언급)및 북해유전의 증산 가능성이이락및 쿠웨이트의 산유량 감소를 COMPENSATE 할것임으로 중장기로보아 유가는안정적 방향으로 갈것으로 전망됨

경제국	장관	차관	1차보	2차보	미주국	구주국	통상국	청와대
안기부	대책반	동자부						

PAGE 1 국제경제국	90.8.14	담 당	과 장	국 장	차관보	차 관	장 관

CONFIDENTIAL

90.08.14 03:24

외신 2과 통제관 FE

0089

다. 주재국의 대이락 쿠웨이트 원유수입량및 전체의 비율은 아래와 같음

89 년도

-대쿠웨이트 수입 657 천 MT(1 프로)

-대이락 수입 863 천 MT(1.3 프로)

-이락, 쿠웨이트로부터의 수입비율: 2.3 프로

90 년도(상반기)

-대쿠웨이트 수입 168 천 MT(0.8 프로)

-대이락 수입 151 천 MT(0.4 프로)

-이락, 쿠웨이트로부터의 수입비율: 1.2 프로

라.89 년도 쿠웨이트, 이락 산유량은 아래와 같음을 참고 바람(단위 백만톤)

쿠웨이트 91 백만

이락 138 백만

(대사 신동원-차관)

예고:90.12.31. 까지

0090

관리번호	90-593

분류번호	보존기간

발 신 전 보

WAE-0160 900813 1900 DY

번 호 :

종별 : 지 급

수 신 : 주 수신처참조 대사. 총영사

발 신 : 장 관 (기협)

제 목 : 원유안정확보를 위한 대 산유국 외교활동 강화

WQT -0083 WOM -0116
WIR -0266 WMA -0559
WBU -0104 WEQ -0188
WMX -0714 WSB -0310
WDJ -0635 WLY -0294

연 : WIR-0254, WAE-0148, WSB-0287, WQT-0079, WMA-0546, WBU-0102, WDJ-0613, WMX-0693, WVZ-0255, WEQ-0181

1. 연호 이라크. 쿠웨이트 사태에 따른 국제유가의 급등 및 국제 석유 시장의 불안으로 아국의 기존원유 도입선으로부터의 안정공급 및 이라크, 쿠웨이트산 원유부족분의 현물시장 구입등에 어려움이 예상되는 바, 귀 주재국 관련부서 및 기관과의 접촉을 통하여 기존 계약 물량이 정상적으로 공급되고, 가능한한 증량공급이 이루어질 수 있도록 협조요청하고 결과보고 바람. 정유사들이 원하는 경우

2. 특히, 아국 ~~원유~~ 정유사들이 귀 주재국 석유회사등과 증량교섭등을 전개할 경우 귀관에 대한 지원협조 요청이 있을 것인 바, 적극 측면 지원 바람.

3. 귀 주재국과 아국 정유회사간 장기계약 현황은 다음과 같음

가. 기장기계약 (직접계약) 체결국

- UAE (ADNOC): 유공 (20천B/D), 호유 (25천 B/D) 극동 (10천 B/D)

- 카타르 (QGPC) : 유공 (10천 B/D), 경인 (8천B/D)

/계속...

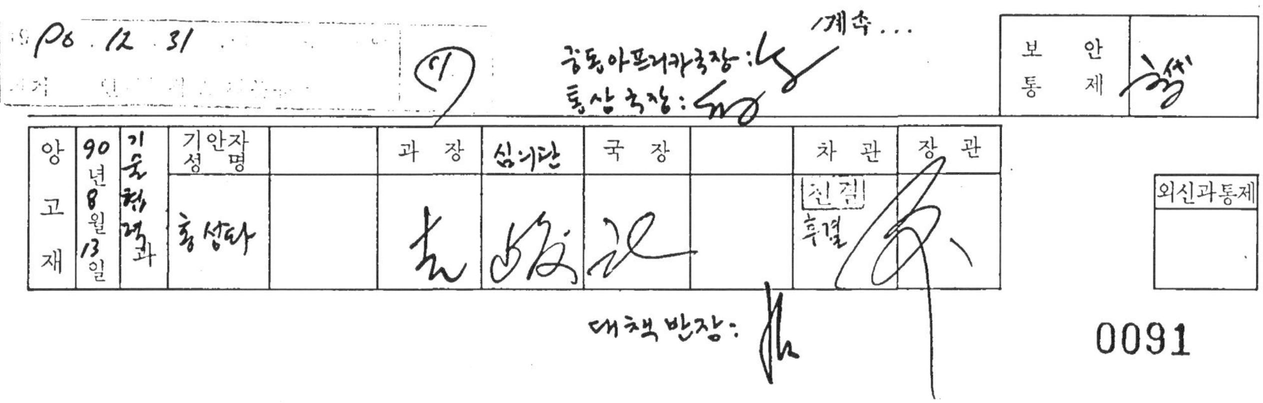

'06. 12. 31

공동아프리카국장, 통상국장, 대책반장 (서명)

보안통제	(서명)

앙고재	90년 8월 13일	기술협력과	기안자 성명: 홍성화	과장	심의관	국장	차관	장관
				(서명)	(서명)	(서명)	전결 후결	(서명)

외신과통제

0091

- 오만 (MPM) : 경인 (10천B/D)

- 이란 (NIOC) : 쌍용 (60천 B/D)

- 말련 (PETRONAS) : 유공 (12천 B/D), 호유 (12천B/D)
  경인 (11천 B/D)

- 브르네이(BSP): 유공 (15천 B/D), 호유 (15천 B/D)

- 에쿠아돌 (CEPE) : 호유 (4천B/D)

- 멕시코(PMI) : 호유 (10천 B/D)

나. 장기계약 체결 추진중 국가

- 사우디 (ARAMCO) : 선경 (유공) (35천 B/D)

- 인니 (PERTAMINA) : 유공 (15천 B/D)

- 리비아 (BIMC) : 유공 (15천 B/D)

(차관 유 종하)

수신처 : UAE, 카타르, 오만, 이란, 말련, 브르네이, 에쿠아돌, 멕시코,
사우디, 인니, 리비아.

0092

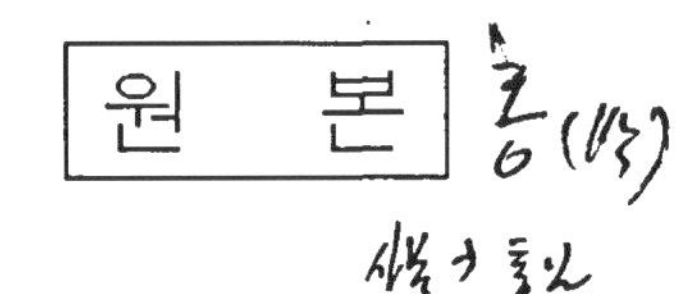

외 무 부

종 별 : 지 급

번 호 : SBW-0633　　　　　　　　일 시 : 90 0813 1400

수 신 : 장 관(기협,중근동,재무부,한은(참조:기획담당이사),국방부

발 신 : 주 사우디 대사

제 목 : 중동사태관련 현지 동향

1.중동사태 이후 주재국의 각은행은 미달러화의수요급증으로 인한 현찰부족으로고객의교환요구에 응하지 못하고 있음, 특히 지난 8.8-9양일간 일부은행 및 환전상들이 공정환율보다높게 고객에게 교환해준 사실이 중앙은행에의하여 적발되어 제제조치를 받은 바 있음. 현재각은행은 1인당 5천불한도 T/C 를 발급하고있으며 중앙은행에대하여 보유외화의 매각을건의중에 있음.

2.주재국 정부는 긴급사태에 따른 일반적인우려와 달리 건설업체에 대한 공사대금을종전과 다름없이 지급하고 있음.

3.중동지역에 근무하는 각은행지점요원 및자금관리주재원의 동정은 아래와같음.

가.쿠웨이주재원은 8.3이후 통신두절로 상황파악이불가능함.

나.이락 주재원(2명)은 각은행본점의 지시에따라현재 귀국준비중임.

다.기타(사우디,바레인)주재원중외환은행(10명)은 가족을 런던에한일은행(6명)은가족을 서울로 철수중에 있고기타 은행주재원(6명)은 현재 사태를 관망하며본점과 협의중에 있음.끝

(대사 주병국-국장)

공람	국제경제국	90년 8월 14일	담당	과장	국장	차관보	차관	장관
				(서명)	(서명)			

경제국　중아국　국방부　재무부　한은　안기부(?)　1차보　2차보　청와대(?)　안기부

PAGE 1　　　　90.08.13　21:29 CT

외신 1과 통제관

0093

원 본

외 무 부

종 별 :

번 호 : NJW-0628 일 시 : 90 0813 1630

수 신 : 장 관 (기협,아프일)

발 신 : 주 나이제리아 대사

제 목 : 석유정보(자료응신 67호)

1.8.13자 당지 신문들은 주재국 AMINU석유장관의 원유관련 발언을 요지 다음과같이보도함.

-국제원유시장의 현 호경기는 다분히 인위적이고일시적인 것이며,원유 생산국에대하여도 해로운현상임.

-최근 제네바의 OPEC 회의에서 원유가를배럴당 18불에서 21불로 상향시킨것은국제경제의 인플레 추세와 달라화 가치의하락추세를 감안할때 매우 합리적임. OPEC국가의 제네바 합의내용 침해는 용납될수없음.

-중동위기가 장기화될 경우 공백을 메꾸기위하여 원유를 일산 24만 내지 28만 배럴증산할수 있을것임.(나이제리아는 일산 2백만배럴까지 생산)

2.8.13.자 당지 보도에 의하면 8.7.런던시장에서나이제리아산 BONNY LIGHT 가 배럴당 28.20불까지상승했으나 8.10에는 25.40으로 하락했다함.

(대사 오채기-국장)

공람	국제경제국	90 8 14	담 당	과 장	국 장	차관보	차 관	장 관

경제국 중아국

PAGE 1

90.08.14 00:36 CT

외신 1과 통제관

0094

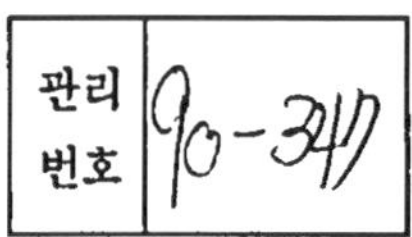

외 무 부

종 별 : 긴 급

번 호 : USW-3731 일 시 : 90 0813 2002

수 신 : 장관(미북,기협, 중근동, 통일,기정)

발 신 : 주 미 대사

제 목 : 이락-쿠웨이트 사태 전망

대:WUS-2677

대호관련, 이락-쿠웨이트 사태에 관해 현재의 상황을 아래 요지 종합 보고함(경제 정세 전망은 별전 보고)

기타 상세에 대해서는 그간의 당관 보고를 참조 바람.

1. 현 중동 사태의 배경

가. 이락의 후세인 대통령이 쿠웨이트를 전격 침공, 합병선을 하게된 직접적 동기는 다음과 같은것으로 보임.

-쿠웨이트를 합병함으로써 원유수출에 절대 필요한 항만 시설 확보(이락의기존 해안선은 약 30KM 미만)

-쿠웨이트의 풍부한 유전지대확보(역사적 연고권 주장 및 실현)

-아랍권 지도국으로서의 위상확립

나. 그러나 금번 사태의 근저에는 아랍권의 전통적인 반이스라엘 , 반외세 감정, 일부 산유국 집권층의 "부" 의 독점 및 친서방 태도에 대한 비판 심리등도작용한것으로 보임.

다. 또한 전쟁을 자신의 정치적 목표 달성을 위한 하나의 수단으로 간주하는 후세인 대통령의 호전적 태도도 금번 쿠웨이트 침공을 일으킨 가장 직접적인 동기로 볼수 있음.

다만 후세인 대통령 자신도 이락의 쿠웨이트 침공이 현재와 같은 범세계적 차원의 규탄과 경제제재, 그리고 미군의 사우디 파병과 같은 엄청난 반향을 불러일으킬 것으로 예기치 못했을 가능성이 큰바, 이러한 점에서 후세인 대통령이 오판을 범한것으로 분석하는 당지 중동 전문가들도 많이 있음.

2. 미국의 기본전략

미주국 장관 차관 1차보 2차보 중아국 경제국 통상국 정문국
청와대 안기부

PAGE 1 90.08.14 10:11
외신 2과 통제관 CW

0095

가. 미국은 금번 쿠웨이트를 침공한 이락군의 사우디 침공 가능성을 중점 부각시킴으로써 사우디측으로 부터 미군 주둔 허가를 얻고, 즉각 파병 조치를 실시한바 우선 이락의 대사우디 진격을 억지하는 전략적 성과를 거두었음.

즉, 현상황하에서 이락의 사우디 침공은 곧 대미 선전 포고를 의미한다는 점을 이락측에 중점 인식시킴으로써 TRIP-WIRE 효과에 의한 억지 전략을 구사하고 있음.

나. 한편, 외교적으로 유엔을 통한 이락의 쿠웨이트 침공 규탄 결의안 및 쿠웨이트 합병 무효선언 결의안 채택등을 통해 이락의 국제적 고립화를 추구하고있고, 경제적으로는 유엔 안보리의 대이락 경제제재 결의 및 소련을 포함하는 범세계적 차원의 경제제재 동참을 유도함으로써 소위 대이락 질식(CHOKE) 전략을구사하고 있음.

(미국은 이락이 여사한 질식 전략의 고통을 느끼기 시작하는데에는 약 1 개월이 소요될것으로 예상하고 있으며 3-4 개월이 경과하게 되면 심각한 정도의 고통을 받게될 것으로 기대하고 있음)

다. 전술한 바와같은 군사적 억지 전략, 외교적 고립화 전략 및 경제적 질식 전략을 통해, 미국은 이락을 상대로 일종의 지구전(WAITIN GAME) 을 전개하고있는바, 미국 자신도 사우디 파병의 기본 성격이 방어적이라는 점을 수차에 걸쳐 분명히 밝힘으로써 여사한 지구전 태세를 갖추고 있다는 점을 간접적으로 시인한바 있음.

라. 미국으로서는 여사한 전략이 이락을 무력화 시킴으로써, 궁극적으로 이락군의 무조건적이고 전면적인 쿠웨이트로 부터의 철수를 통한 전전 상태의 회복이 이루어질것으로 기대하고 있으며, 한편으로는 이락지도층 내부의 반란이나 민중 봉기에 의한 훗세인 정권의 전복도 기대하고 있는것으로 보임.

마. 이러한 미국의 전략 수행에 긍정적 기여를 하고 있는 환경적 요인으로는 다음의 세가지를 지적할수 있음.

1)미소 관계가 소위 탈 냉전 시대에 접어들게 됨에 따라, 제 3 세계에서의 지역분쟁 발발시 통상 미국이 느껴오던 소련과의 경쟁적 부담을 지지 않아도 되는점.

2)이집트 주도하에 개최된 아랍 정상회담이 범 아랍군의 사우디 파병을 결정한점(따라서, 미국으로서는 자국의 사우디 파병이 아랍제국에 심어줄수도 있는 소위 "제국주의자" 적 인상을 어느정도는 탈색할수 있게 되었으며, 또한 금번사태를 미국 대이락의 대결 뿐만이 아닌 아랍권 내부의 분열로도 인식시키는 효과를 거두게 되었음.)

3) NATO , 일본, 한국등 기존 우방국들 뿐 아니라 중공도 대이락 제재조치

시행등에 있어 거의 완전히 보조를 맞추고 있는점.

이하 USW-3733 으로 계속됨.

PAGE 3

0097

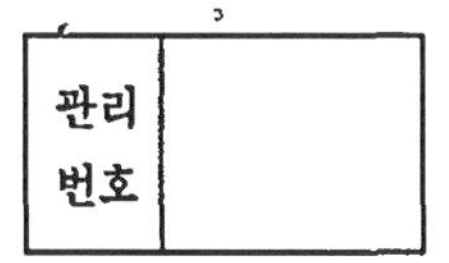

외 무 부

종 별 : 긴 급

번 호 : USW-3733 일 시 : 90 0813 2002

수 신 : 장관(미북)

발 신 : 주미대사

제 목 : USW-3731 계속분

바. 그러나 여사한 미국의 지구전 전략은 이락과의 군사적 대결이 교착된 상태하에서 시간이 지나면 지날수록 그결과가 점점 더 미국이 불리한 방향으로 전개될수 있으며, 이점 미측드 잘인식하고 있는것으로 보임.

즉, 지금 당장은 미국민들이 정치적 성향에 관계없이 미군의 사우디 파병을지지하고 부쉬 대통령의 대응 방안을 높이 평가하는 입장을 견지하고 있으나, 11 월 중간선거, 12 월 크리스마스등이 다가옴에따라 소위 "BRING OUR BOYS HOEM"을 주장하는 철군론이 대두할 가능성도 크며, 또한 미국을 제국주의자로, 사우디를 아랍 내부에 외세를 끌어 들인 시온주의자로 규정짓는 이락의 심리전 전술이 소기의 성과를 거두는 경우 아랍 민족주의를 바탕으로 하는 외세 배제론이 아랍권내에서 강력히 주창될 가능성도 배제키 어려움.

이러한 경우 부쉬 대통령은 문자 그대로 진퇴양난에 빠질 것임.

3. 이락의 기본 전략

가. 미국이 사우디 파병 미군 병력을 TRIP-WIRE 로 이용, 이락의 군사행동 확대를 억지하고 있는반면, 이락은 이락과 쿠웨이트에 억류된 것과 다름없는 약 3,500 명의 미국인들을 사실상의 볼모로 잡고, 파나마나 그레나다 에서와 같은 미군의 전격 기습 전략이나 리비아에서와 같은 공중 폭격 가능성을 억지하고 있다고 볼수 있음.

따라서, 미국내 일각에서는 전기 미국인들의 출국이 실현되기 까지는 상당시간이 소요될것으로 조심스러운 예측을 하고 있기도 함.

(미국 행정부에서 이들 미국인을 "볼모"로 호칭하지 않기 위해 노력하고 있다는 사실 자체가, 역설적이기는 하나 이들이 실질적인 볼모임을 입증하고 있음)

나. 또한 이락군은 공공연히 미국의 관찰이 가능하도록 대 이란전 및 쿠르드족 살상시에 사용된 화학 무기 배치를 실시하고 있는바, 미측은 여사한 화학전에

미주국 장관 차관 1차보 2차보 중아국 경제국 통상국 정문국 청와대 안기부

PAGE 1 공람 국제경제국 90.8.14 담당 과장 국장 차관보 차관 장관 90.08.14 10:21

외신 2과 통제관 CW

0098

완벽하게 대비하고 있다고 하기는 하나, 이락측의 화학무기 사용가능성 불배제도 어느 정도의 대미 억지 효과를 거두고 있는것으로 봄.

4. 정세 전망

가. 요약컨데, 현재의 중동정세는 미국과 이락 양국간의 상호 억지 전략을 통한 군사적 교착상태로 요약할수 있음.

나. 또한, 이러한 군사적 교착상태는 일종의 소모전 성격을 띄면서, 미국이지구전 전략을 계속 이행하고 이락이 체면을 지키면서 후퇴를 할수 있는 방안이 없는한 상당기간 지속될 것으로 전망됨.

다. 미 행정부의 입장에서는 적어도 11 월 중간선거 까지는 현재의 전략을 계속 추구할 가능성이 큰 것으로 예측되는바, 동 전략을 수행해 나가면서 후세인대통령 전복 가능성등 이락의 국내 정세를 예의 주시할것으로 전망됨.

라. 현재 미측이 요구하고 있는 이락군의 즉각적이고 무조건적인 쿠웨이트로 부터의 철수가 훗세인 대통령의 입장에서 볼때 국내정치요인등을 감안시 절대수용할수 없는 조건인것 처럼, 이락측이 쿠웨이트로 부터의 철군 조건으로 내세우고 있는 WEST BANK 및 GAZA 지구로부터의 이스라엘군 철수도 미측으로서는받아들일수 없는 조건인바, 이처럼 현 상황이 ZERO- SUM GAME 의 성격을 띄고 있기 때문에 당분간은 타협의 여지가 있는 중도적 해결 방안을 모색하기 어려울것으로 봄.

마. 한편 전술한 미국의 대이락 억지 전략은 서구적인 기준에서볼때 이락도RATIONAL ACTOR 라는 대전제하에서 수립된 전략인바, 만약 이락이 이미 선전 포고한 "성전(JIHAD)" 을 실행으로 옮겨서 이스라엘에 대한 군사적 도발을 할경우 사태는 더욱 심각한 국면에 빠질 가능성도 희박하나마 배제할수는 없음.

바. 현재까지의 중동사태 관련 미 행정부의 대응은 미리 준비된 계획에 따른 단계적 전략 이행이라기 보다는, 주어진 여건에 대한 상황 대응의 성격이 강한바, 조만간 미 행정부는 경제제재 조치의 효과를 극대화 시키기 위해 보다 더 구체적인 MANEUVER 방안을 천명 할것으로 봄.

(대사 박동진-차관)

예고:90.12.31. 일반

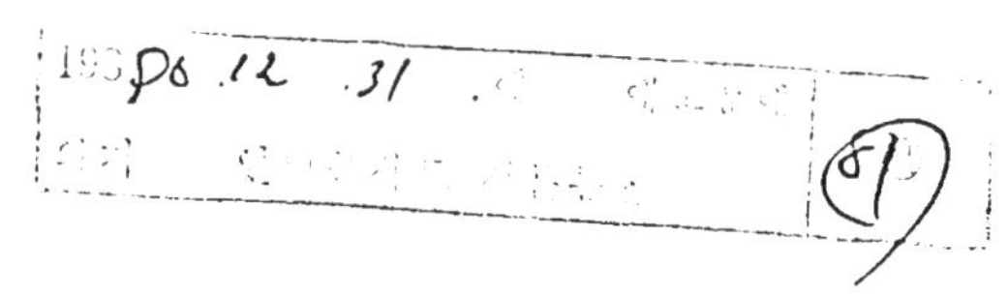

PAGE 2

0099

원 본

외 무 부

종 별 :

번 호 : ITW-0944 일 시 : 90 0813 1600

수 신 : 장 관(기협)

발 신 : 주 이태리 대사

제 목 : 이라크,쿠웨이트사태

대: WIT-0713

대호사항 아래 보고함.

1.금번사태전망

0 정치적 평가는 불확실시되며 현재로서는 전망키 어려움

0 경제적으로는 최근 IAEA 회의(8.9)에서 현사태를 비상사태로 보고 있지 않은점 감안시 과거 오일쇼크와는 달리 평가되며 유가경우 최근수준보다 높은 수준을 보일 것으로 전망되어 세계경제에 인플레 압박등 어느정도 부정적효과는 예상됨.

2.사태장기화시 국제수급및 유가전망

0 각국 에너지 의존구조가 과거 오일쇼크때와 다른데다 현재 각국이 충분한 비축량을 보유하고 있으며 (OECD 각국 100일분 이상 보유)생산국의 재고량도 많아 앞으로 2-3개월간은 국제수급에 차질이 예상되지 않으며 유가도 2-3개월간은 배럴당 21-22불선을 유지하고 그이후에도 25불선 정도가 될것으로 봄.

3.광역전쟁등 인근지역으로 확산시 국제수급및 유가전망

0 광역전쟁으로 사우디 생산량이 감소하는 경우는 비상사태에 돌입 국제수급이나 유가에 부정적 영향이 큰 오일쇼크재현을 상상갈수 있음.

4.주재국의 대책

0 현재로선 비상대책을 사용치 않고 있으나 항상준비된 상태임.비상대책으로 소비감소, 비상비축량 활용 및 79년 합의된 OECD간 공동대책적용등이 있음.

(대사 김석규-국장).

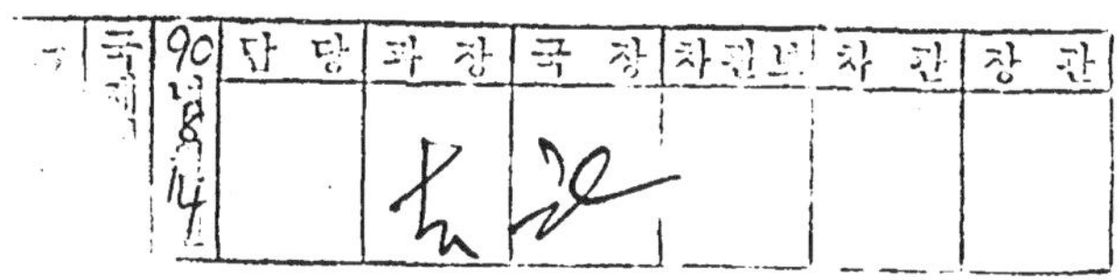

경제국 통상국 구주국 정문국 대책반 1차보 2차보 차관 동자부

PAGE 1

90.08.14 11:31 CT

외신 1과 통제관

0100

관리번호	90-596

원 본

외 무 부

종 별 :

번 호 : OMW-0235 일 시 : 90 0814 0950

수 신 : 장관(기협)

발 신 : 주 오만 대사

제 목 : 원유안정 확보 활동 강화

대:WOM-0116

대호 1 항에 언급된 "연호" 내용을 당관에도 통보 바람. 끝

(대사 강종원-국장)

예고:90.12.31. 까지

국	국제경제국					차관보	차 관	장 관

경제국

PAGE 1

90.08.14 15:40

외신 2과 통제관 CD

0101

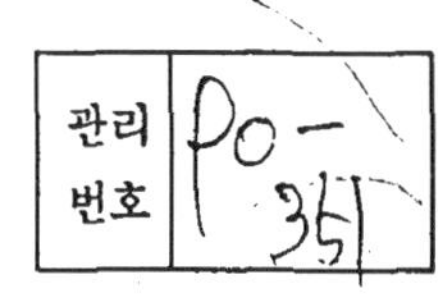

외 무 부

종 별 : 지 급

번 호 : JAW-5014 일 시 : 90 0814 1806

수 신 : 장관(통일,경일)

발 신 : 주 일 대사(경제)

제 목 : 대 이라크 경제제재

대: WJA-3410

대호 관련 주재국 통산성 수입과 담당관에 탐문한 결과를 아래 보고함.

1. 대 쿠웨이트산 유류도입분 지불

0 쿠웨이트 및 이라크에 대한 무역결재는 90.8.15. 부터 허가제로 이행하게 되어있는바, 수입금지조치 (8.9) 전에 쿠웨이트에서 선적된 원유분에 대해서는 수입업자가 수입승인을 요청한 경우, 동 도입원유 통관에 대한 조건부가 여부와 동시에 대금지불 루트가 어떻게 되어있는가에 따라 지불허가 여부를 결정할 예정임.

0 일본 회사들은 쿠웨이트 석유공사로부터 석유를 도입하고있고, 동 석유대금은 대부분 미국등의 제 3 국 은행구좌에 입금하도록 되어있는바, 동 대금 지불 허가 여부를 결정함에 있어서 고려할 사항으로 검토하고 있는것은 다음과 같음.

-일본회사들의 대금지불에 사용토록 되어있는 쿠웨이트석유공사 구좌는 대체로 미국내에 있는바, 미국이 동 구좌를 BLOCK 하고 있는지 여부 (현재 이에관해 조사, 확인중)

-미국 이외의 국가에 지정된 구좌가 있는 경우는 동 국가가 당해 구좌를 BLOCK 하고 있는지 여부외에 UN 결의를 준수하고 있는지 여부.

-석유대금 지불은 정통 쿠웨이트 정부의 구좌인가가 확인되어야 할것인바, 이라크의 쿠웨이트 침공이후 선적된 석유는 사실상 없으므로 현 잠정정부에 대한 수입석유 대금 지불문제는 없음.

0 석유대금 지불은 수입업자가 신청을 했을경우에 정부가 허가여부를 결정하는 것으로서, 수입업자의 신청여부 및 정부의 지불불허에 따른 동 대금 처리여부는 수입업자가 상거래 관점에서 조치하지 않을까 생각함. (현재로서는 지불이 불허된 대금에 대한 정부조치는 특별히 검토되고 있는것이 없음).

통상국	장관	차관	1차보	2차보	경제국	청와대	안기부	동자부

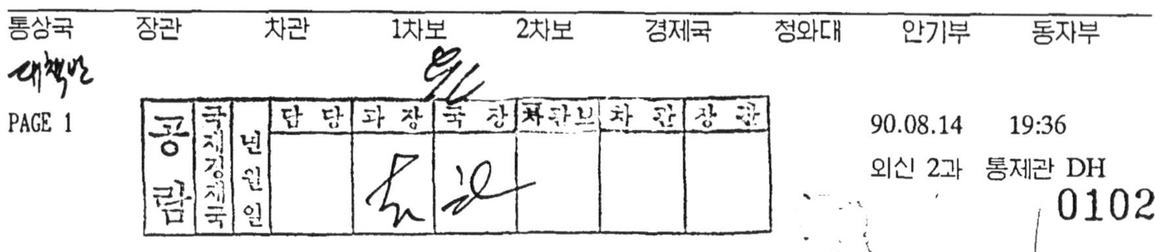

PAGE 1

90.08.14 19:36

외신 2과 통제관 DH

0102

2. 대 이라크산 유류도입분

0 경제제재 조치 이전에 선적된 이라크산 원유가 아직 일본에 도착하지 않고있는 상황이며, 동 원유수입업자가 통관승인 신청과 더불어 대금지불 허가신청을 해올지는 아직 미지수임.

0 동 신청을 해올 경우 어떻게 대처해야 할것인지는 지금부터 검토해야할 문제로서 아직 구체적 방침이 정해지지 않고있음. 끝

(공사이한춘-국장)

예고:90.12.31. 일반

PAGE 2

0103

관리번호	90-598

원 본

외 무 부

종 별 :

번 호 : MAW-1045 일 시 : 90 0814 1630

수 신 : 장관(기협,아동)

발 신 : 주 말련 대사

제 목 : 원유 안정 확보

대:WMA-0559

1. 당관 이준규 서기관은 금 8.14 주재국 수상실 ANWAR AJI 석유개발 과장을 면담, 대호관련 의견 교환한바, 요지 아래보고함.

가. 주재국 정부는 금 8.14 각의에서 쿠웨이트 사태에 관해 종합검토할 예정이며, 원유 증산 여부도 여기서 논의될 가능성이 많음.

나. 단기적으로는 별도의 유정 개발없이도 3-5 프로(2-3 만 BPD)증산 가능하며, 이는 장기 계약이 아닌 1 회 계약 방식으로 공급될수 있을 것임. 아국이 증량 공급을 요청할 경우 당연히 호의적으로 검토될 것으로 생각함. 장기 계약을 위한 증산은 별도로 검토되어야 할 문제임.

다. 현재 체결되어 있는 장기 계약 물량의 정상적 공급에는 아무런 문제가 없음.

2. 본직은 금명간 수상실 SULAIMANN 장관(에너지 담당), 국영석유 공사(PETRONAS) AZIZAN 사장등을 면담, 대호관련 협조 요청할 예정임.끝

(대사 홍순영-국장)

예고:90.12.31 까지

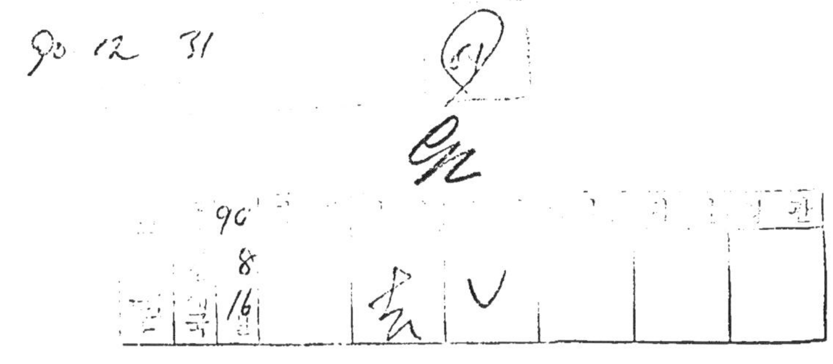

경제국 차관 1차보 2차보 아주국 동자부 ✓

PAGE 1

90.08.14 21:11

외신 2과 통제관 CN

0104

관리번호	90-597

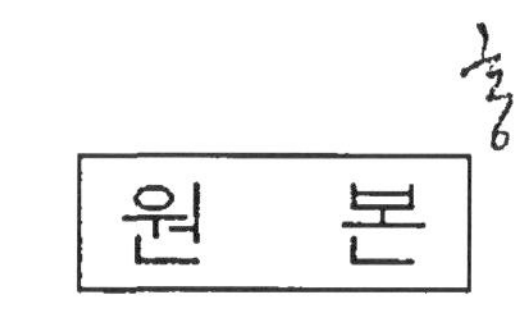

외 무 부

종 별 :

번 호 : IRW-0457 일 시 : 90 0814 1600

수 신 : 장관(기협)

발 신 : 주 이란 대사

제 목 : 원유안정확보

대:WIR-0266, 연:IRW-0438

대호관련, 연호로보고한바와같이 주재국 아가자데 장관은 아국의 원유수급상 문제가 발생할경우, 필요협조를할 용의를 표명한바있는바 추가공급가능성등 구체적인 사항등 확인되는대로 추보하겠음. 끝

(대사정경일-국장)

예고:90.12.31 까지

90 12 31

공람	국제경제국	90년8월16일	담 당	과 장	국 장	차관보	차 관	장 관
					√			

경제국

PAGE 1

90.08.14 22:27

외신 2과 통제관 CN

0105

관리번호 90-350

외 무 부

종 별 : 지 급

번 호 : ECW-0563 일 시 : 90 0814 1730

수 신 : 장관 (통일,중근동,기협)

발 신 : 주 EC 대사

제 목 : 대이라크 제재

대: WECM-0020, AM-0145

연: ECW-0554

1. 대호관련, 당관 윤종곤서기관이 8.13. 및 8.14. BECHET EC 집행위 대외관계총국 GULF 지역담당관및 CUNHA EC 집행위 사무총장실 정무협력 담당관과 각각 면담하여 파악한 EC 측의 대이라크 제재조치 관련사항 아래보고함

가. 대이라크 추가 제재조치

0 EC 측은 유엔안보리 결의채택에 따라 연호 제재조치에 이어 8.9. 이락및 쿠웨이트와의 모든 상품교역및 무역관련 써비스 교역(보험, 운송등) 을 금지키로 결정

0 단, 건설업등 순수 써비스업은 EC 집행위 권한외의 사항으로서 유엔안보리 결의에 의거, 각 회원국이 별도로 필요한 조치 강구

나. EC 의 대이라크및 쿠웨이트 교역량

1) 대이라크 교역 (89 년 기준, 1 ECU - 1.10 미불)

0 수입: 33 억 25 백만 ECU (그중 96.7% 가 원유및 석유관련 제품)

- EC 의 총 역외수입중 차지비중: 0.7%

0 수출: 30 억 11 백만 ECU

- EC 의 총 역외수출중 차지비중: 0.7%

2) 대쿠웨이트 교역 (89 년 기준)

0 수입: 26 억 54 백만 ECU (그중 95.1% 가 원유및 석유관련 제품)

- EC 의 총 역외수입중 차지비중: 0.6%

0 수출: 16 억 29 백만 ECU

- EC 의 총 역외수출중 차지비중: 0.4%

다. 이라크및 쿠웨이트내 EC 체류국민 현황

통상국 안기부	장관	차관	1차보	2차보	중아국	경제국	정문국	청와대

PAGE 1 | 공람 | 국제경제국 | 90.8.16 | 담 당 | 과 장 | 국 장 | 차관보 | 차 관 | 장 관 |

90.08.15 04:20

외신 2과 통제관 CN

0106

1) 쿠웨이트 (총 5,580 명)

영국 4,000 명, 아일랜드 500, 불란서 300, 서독 270 (동독 16), 희랍 130,이태리 125, 스페인 100, 화란 70, 덴마크 60, 벨지움 24 명

2) 이라크 (총 2,671 명)

0 영국 800 명, 서독 500-600, 아일랜드 350, 이태리 340, 불란서 209, 화란 150, 스페인 55, 폴투갈 50, 덴마크 40, 벨지움 38, 희랍 35, 룩셈부르그 4 명

라. EC 의 대이라크및 쿠웨이트 부자현황및 채무내역

0 EC 집행위측은 상기관련 통계를 파악치 못하고 있는바, 관련정보 입수되는대로 추보하겠음

마. EC 의 대이라크 제재조치 영향

0 BECHET EC 집행위 GULF 담당관에 따르면, 이라크및 쿠웨이트와의 교역이 EC 의 총 역외교역중 차지하는 비중이 미미하며, 또한 EC 수입의 대부분은 원유및 석유관련 제품으로서 다소의 유가인상외에는 커다란 경제적 영향이 없을것으로 보고있음

0 또한 원유수급 측면에 있어서도 덴마크및 희랍의 대이라크및 쿠웨이트 의존도가 높기는 하지만 EC 전체로 보아서는 11% 정도이며, 금번 사태가 일부 GULF 지역에만 국한되어 있어 전세계적 원유부족 사태는 상정되기 어렵기 때문에 커다란 문제는 없을것이라는 반응임

0 동 담당관은 또한 국제사회의 대이라크 제재조치가 현재와 같이 효과적이고 강력히 계속 시행될 경우, 이라크 당국이 장기간 (6 개월 정도) 버티기에는 어려울 것으로 보고, 이락측이 도발적 행동을 취함으로써 사태를 ESCALATE 할 가능성을 배제치 않고 있으나 이 경우에도 국제 원유수급 상황에는 커다란 변화가 없을 것으로 전망함

바. EC 측의 대이라크 조치사항

0 바그다드 주재 12 개 EC 회원국 대사들은 8.9. 이라크 당국에 이라크및 쿠웨이트 체류 EC 국민뿐만 아니라 모든 외국인의 안전에 필요한 조치를 취할것과 행방불명자의 소재에 관한 정보를 제공할 것을 요청하는 강력한 DEMARCHE 를 행하였음

- 호주, 오지리, 카나다, 핀랜드, 동독, 일본, 뉴질랜드, 놀웨이, 스웨덴, 스위스, 터키, 미국이 동 DEMARCHE 를 전폭적으로 지지하는 입장을 표명한바 있음

0 EC 12 개 회원국 외무장관들은 8.10. 브랏셀 EPC 특별 각료회의에서 금번사태 관련 성명발표 (동 전문 별도 FAX 송부)

- 이라크의 쿠웨이트 합병무효

- 쿠웨이트 주재 외국공관 철수요청 거부

- 이라크및 쿠웨이트 체류 EC 국민의 이동 자유보장및 신변안전을 위해 적극노력

- 걸프지역 긴장완화와 국제적 합법성 회복위한 아랍국가의 노력에 지원제공

0 상기 성명에 따라 EC TROIKA 외무장관들은 금번사태 관련, 아랍국가들과의 협력방안및 역내 EC 회원국 국민들의 신변안전 문제등 협의를위해 명 8.15. 사우디, 요르단, 이집트등 3 개국 방문예정

0 또한 EC 12 개국은 금 8.14. 브랏셀에서 EPC 특별회의를 갖고, 당분간 EC12 개국 외교공관을 쿠웨이트내에 계속 유지키로 할것과 향후 1-2 일 내에 이라크및 쿠웨이트 당국에 외국인 신변안전 보호에관한 DEMARCHE 를 재차 수행할것을 결정하고 모든 관련국가의 동참을 촉구하였음

2. CUNHA EC 집행위 정무협력 담당관은 동 DEMARCHE 에 한국이 참여를 희망할 경우에는 주이라크 이태리대사및 주유엔 이태리대사에 아측의 참여의사를 전달, 상호 협력하는 방안도 모색할수 있을것이라고 말함

3. BECHET 담당관은 EC 집행위측이 아국을 포함, 주요 관계국들과 대이라크 경제제재조치 시행에 관한 상호 정보교환을 위해 브랏셀에서 실무회의를 개최할 것을 추진중이며 이에관한 EC 측 공한을 금명간 당관에 송부하게 될것이라고 말함. 동 공한 접수즉시 추보위계임. 이와관련, 8.14. EC 집행위 DG I 의 한국담당관실도 상기관련, EC 측 공한 발송예정 사실을 당관에 알려온바 있음. 끝

(대사 권동만-국장)

예고: 90.12.31 일반

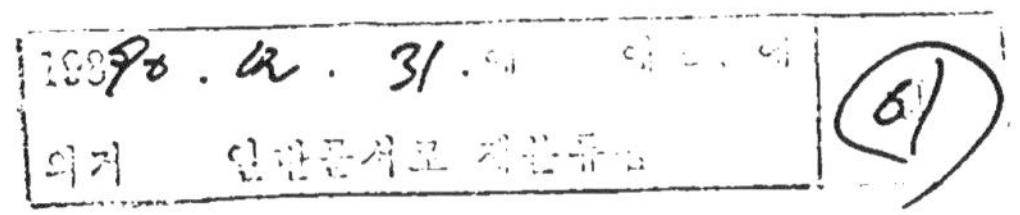

PAGE 3

0108

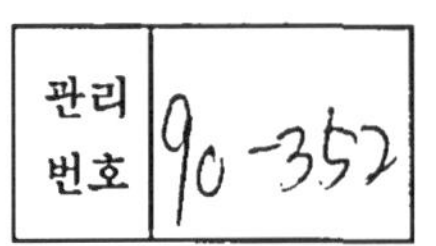
관리 번호 90-352

외 무 부

종 별 :

번 호 : BRW-0482 일 시 : 90 0814 2100

수 신 : 장 관(중근동,기협,미북,미남,정일,기정동문)

발 신 : 주 브라질 대사

제 목 : 이라크-쿠웨이트 사태(자료응신 90-40)

연: BRW-0480

주재국 REZEK 외무장관이 작(8.13)일 당지 CORREIO BRAZILIENSE 지와 가진 인터뷰에서 이라크-쿠웨이트 사태에 대한 주재국 입장등 외교현안에 대한 견해를표명하였는바, 동 언급내용중 표제관련 부분을 발췌 보고함.

1. 동사태는 국제사회가 냉전시대를 극복하고 국제관계의 장래에 대한 낙관적 분위기속에서도 국지적 분쟁가능성이 우려되던 시기에 발생한 예상치 않은 사태로서 국제관계에 있어 매우 중대한 사건임.

2. 브라질 정부는 동사태 발발직후 타국의 반응과 관계없이 무력침공을 비난하는 공식입장을 발표하였으며, 이라크측으로 부터 무력침공을 정당화하는 설명이 있었으나 이라크의 주장이 옳다하더라도 분쟁을 무력으로 해결하는 것은 국제법 원칙에 반한다는 입장임. 브라질은 유엔의 성실한 회원국으로서 안보리의 결의를 기다렸으며 안보리 결의에 따른 회원국으로서의 의무를 수행하는 조치를 취하였는바, 브라질 정부가 동사태와 관련 취한 입장은 사태의 성격과 전개과정을 감안할때 적절한 것이었음.

3. 이라크를 위요한 현 국제정세가 지속하는한 대이라크 무기수출 관련 브라질이 과거의 정책으로 복구할수 없음. 브라질은 18 개월전부터 정치적 이유아닌 경제적 이유(이라크, 대 브라질 부채 5 억불 상당 미지불)로 대 이라크 무기수출을 중단하고 있었는바 사태발발 이후 무기 인도 연기등 조치를 취할 필요는 없었음.

4. 일부 외국언론이 브라질의 대 이라크 무기수출을 비난하고 있는 것은 부당함. 브라질 뿐만 아니라 서구제국도 이라크에 대해 무기를 판매하였으며 무기수출 당시에 공급된 무기들이 방위목적에 사용되지 않으리라고 추측할 이유가 없음. 끝.

(대사 김기수-국장)

중아국 장관 차관 1차보 2차보 미주국 미주국 경제국 통상국
정문국 청와대 안기부

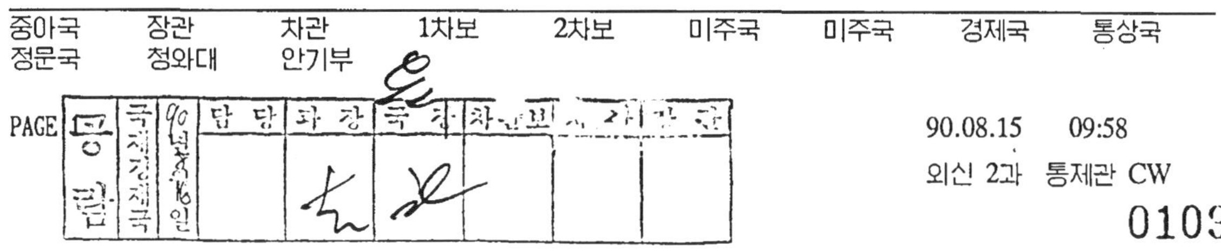

PAGE 1

90.08.15 09:58

외신 2과 통제관 CW

0109

예고: 90.12.31. 일반

19 90 . 12 . 31 .에 예고문에
의거 일반문서로 재분류됨.

PAGE 2

0110

관리 번호 90-348

원 본

외 무 부

종 별 : 지 급

번 호 : USW-3757　　일 시 : 90 0814 2045

수 신 : 장관(기협,미북)

발 신 : 주 미 대사

제 목 : 이락,쿠웨이트 사태

대 WUS-2677

연 USW-3731

대호 이락-쿠웨이트 사태가 세계 경제에 미치는 영향에 대해 아래 보고함.

1. 개관

0 금번 사태에 따른 국제 원유가의 상승으로 미국, 서구 제국, 일본및 다수개도국등 비산유국은 물가 상승및 경제 성장 후퇴라는 2 중의 어려움을 겪게 될것임.

0 그러나 당지 전문가들은 금번 사태로 인한 유가 상승은 과거 1,2 차 석유위기에 비해 소폭에 그칠것이며, 비산유국 경제의 석유의존도도 과거에 비해 낮어졌기 때문에 금번 사태가 전쟁으로 확산되지 않는한, 심각한 제 3 의 석유위기발생 가능성은 적으며, 현재의 전반적인 세계 경제의 추이도 금번 사태로 인해결정적으로 변화되지 않을것으로 관측하고 있음.

2. 유가 상승 전망

0 당지 석유 전문가들은 쿠웨이트에서의 현 교착상태에 큰 변화가 없는한 국제 유가는 향후 수개월간 배럴당 22-28 불선을 유지할것으로 전망하고있는바, 그 이유는 아래임.

가. 세계 원유 수급 동향

0 세계 원유 수요는 최근 세계 경제 성장 둔화를 반영, 연 평균 2 프로 내외의 낮은 증가율을 보여 온데 비해 산유국들은 재정 문제로 다량 생산을 계속, 금년도 2/4 분기의 경우 수요 대비 세계 원유 공급 초과량은 1 일 280 만 배럴에 달했는바, 이러한 세계 석유 수급 사정에 비추어 배럴당 30 불 이상의 원유가가 지속되기는 어려움.

경제국	장관	차관	1차보	2차보	미주국	중아국	통상국	정문국
청와대	안기부							

PAGE 1

90.08.15 11:05

외신 2과 통제관 CW

0111

나. 여타 산유국의 추가 생산

0 이락 및 쿠웨이트로부터의 원유 수입 금지로 발생하는 공급 부족량은 1 일 약 400 만배럴에 달하나, 사우디, 베네주엘라, 나이지리아등의 증산 능력을 감안할때 부족량의 상당부분이 충당 가능함.

다. 비축 원유

0 현재 OECD 국가 전체의 전략 비축 원유는 35 억 배럴에 달하는것으로 집계되고 있는바, 이는 해당국들의 100 일간 원유 수요량에 달함.

3. 금번 유가 인상이 세계 경제에 미치는 영향

0 금번 유가 인상은 석유 관련 제품의 가격 인상을 비롯한 전반적인 물가 인상 외에 비산유국의 실질 소득 감소에 기인한 수요 감퇴를 초래, 경제 성장을 위축시킬것임.

0 그러나 당지 전문가들은 유가 인상의 소폭 외에 하기 이유로 인해 금번의유가 인상에 따른 세계 경제의 위축 정도는 소규모에 그칠 가능성이 큰것으로 예상하고 있음.

가. 세계 경제의 석유 의존도 감소

0 에너지 사용의 효율 제고 및 원자력등 대체 에너지 개발을 통해 OECD 국의 경우 GNP 1 불을 생산하기 위한 석유 소모량은 73 년에 비해 40 프로가 감소했음.

0 그결과 원유가가 배럴당 30 불인 경우 OECD 국의 산유국에 대한 석유 대금 추가 지불액은 연 900 억불에 달하나 이는 OECD 국 전체 GNP 의 0.6 프로에 불과함(1,2 차 석유 위기의 경우 2 프로 초과)

나. 인플레이션 압력 완화

0 1,2 차 석유 위기시는 석유의 원자재 가격의 급격한 상승, 각국의 방만한통화, 재정 정책 실시로 인해 급격한 인플레이션 현상을 초래하였으나, 현재는국제 원자재 가격이 안정세를 보이고 있으며 주요 선진국 정부는 인플레이션 억제를 위한 안정적인 통화및 이자율 정책을 실시하고 있어 평균 인플레이션율이4 프로에 불과함.

0 유가가 배럴당 30 불인 경우 OECD 국의 91 년 물가 상승율은 당초 예측에비해 2 프로가 높아질것이나 이자율 인상등 효과적인 통화 긴축 정책 실시를 통해 92 년 말까지는 추가 물가 상승율을 0.5 프로로 억제할수 있으며, OECD 국의 경제 성장율도 당초 예측에 비해 91 년 0.5 프로, 92 년 0.3 프로 정도만 감소할것으로 전망되고 있음.

PAGE 2

0112

다. 산유국 석유 수출 대금의 원할한 유통

0 1,2 차 석유 위기의 경우 산유국들은 유가 인상전 이미 경상 수지 흑자를갖고 있었으며, 세계 경제에의 통합 정도가 낮아 누적된 석유 수출 대금의 RECYCLING 에 많은 시일이 소요되어 세계 경제의 위축을 심화 시켰으나, 현재 대부분의 산유국들은 재정적자및 무역 적자를 갖고 있어 석유 수출 대금의 RECYCLING이 단기간내 실현될수 있음.

라.80 년대 선진국 경제의 자율화

0 70 년대 석유 가격 및 임금 통제정책의 실패 이후 주요 선진국은 경제 전반에 걸쳐 시장 자율화 정책을 실시, 외부 충격에 효과적으로 대응할수 있는 능력을 배양해 왔음.

4. 주요국 경제에 대한 유가 인상의 영향

가. 미국

0 경제 성장

-당지 전문가들은 미국 경제가 금번 유가 인상전 이미 경제 성장 둔화(90 년 2/4 분기 경제 성장율 1.2 프로)), 실업율 상승등 경기 후퇴 국면에 들어선것으로 평가하고 있으며, 유가 인상은 이러한 경기 후퇴를 심화시킬것이나, 미국의비교적 낮은 해외 원유 의존도(50 프로)를 감안, 91 년 경제 성장율은 당초 예측에 비해 0.2 프로 감소될것으로 관측하고 있음.

0 이자율

-유가 인상으로 인한 경기 후퇴의 심화 가능성에 따라 행정부 및 업계는 연방 준비은행(FRB)에 대해 이자율을 인하할것을 강력히 요구하고 있으나, 연준 은유가 인상에 따른 인프레 상승을 의식 이자율 인상을 꺼려하고 있는바 연준 은가중되는 정치적 압력을 의식, 조만간 소폭(0.25 프로 내외)의 이자율 인하를 실시하되 금번 사태 악화로 인한 급격한 경기 후퇴가 없는한 인플레율을 현재의 4프로 내외에서 유지할수 있도록 통화 긴축 정책을 실시하기 위해 계속 노력해 나갈것으로 관측되고 있음.

0 재정적자

-행정부 및 의회는 그간 재정 적자 축소를 위해 에너지 세금 신설 및 국방 예산 삭감등 방안을 협의해왔으나 금번 사태로 인해 에너지 세금 신설및 국방 예산의 대폭 삭감이 어려워짐으로서 재정적자의 축소 규모도 당초 목표보다 크게 후퇴된 선에서

합의될것으로 전망됨.

0 무역 적자

-원유 수입을 위한 추가 부담액 발생과 세계 경제 둔화에 따른 미국 상품에대한 수요 감퇴로 미국의 무역 적자는 당초 예상 보다 200-300 억불 정도 증가할것으로 전망됨.

나. 서구 제국

0 92 년 시장 단일화 계획 추진에 따른 부자 증대, 동서독 통일및 동구권 경제 재건등 경제 성장에 유리한 요인들이 많아 유가 인상에 따른 경제 성장율 감소가 91 년의 경우 0.5 프로 내외에 그칠것으로 인플레이션 추가 상승률은 금년말까지 0.5-1.0 프로 내외로 억제될수 있을것으로 전망됨.

다. 일본

0 그간 경제성장의 석유 의존도를 줄이기 위한 노력을 집중적으로 기울여온 결과(유가가 10 프로 인상될 경우 소비자 물가 0.1 프로 상승) 91 년 경제 성장율은 당초 예측 보다 0.5 프로 감소할것으로 전망됨.

0 당분간 인플 억제를 위해 이자율 인상등 통화 긴축 정책 계속할것으로 관측됨.

라. 소련

0 유가 인상으로 경화 수입이 대폭 증대될것으로 전망

-유가 1 불 상승시 수출 대금 5 억불 증가

마. 개도국

0 교역 조건 악화에 따른 실질 소득 감소 외에 선진국 경제 성장 둔화로 인한 개도국 원자재 수요 감퇴로 큰 타격을 받을것으로 관측

0 특히 막대한 규모의 오 채를 갖고 있는 일부국의 경우 세계 금융 시장에서의 자금 조달이 더욱 어려워질것임.

0 한편 동구권 국가의 경우 91 년부터 소련산 원유를 경화로 수입해야할뿐 아니라, 산업 구조가 중공업등 에너지 소비 산업에 집중되어 있어 가장 큰 타격을 받을것으로 관측됨.

(대사 박동진-차관)

예고:90.12.31 일반

PAGE 4

0114

번호 : USW(F) - 1822
수신 : 장 관 (중근동, 미북, 통일, 기협) 발신 : 주미대사
제목 : 이락-쿠웨이트 사태 (오일 문제) (2 - 매)

보안 통제

No Quick Increase In Oil Production By OPEC Expected

Some Members Said to Balk at Call for Talks

By Mark Potts
Washington Post Staff Writer

The Organization of Petroleum Exporting Countries appears to be having trouble agreeing to increase production to make up for oil lost in the cutoff of supplies from Iraq and Kuwait—despite indications last week that a production increase was imminent.

Meanwhile, Iraq threatened to retaliate against Venezuela and other OPEC nations if they increase their oil output to replace blocked supplies from Iraq and occupied Kuwait, the Associated Press reported.

While most experts believe production eventually will be increased, growing doubts that the rise will come as quickly as originally expected are putting new upward pressures on crude oil prices. The price of a benchmark barrel of crude oil rose 19 cents on the New York Mercantile Exchange yesterday to $26.42, the second trading session that the benchmark price has increased since it tumbled more than $3 from a peak of $29.20 a barrel last week.

Analysts and industry sources said yesterday it appears that several members of the oil cartel are balking at Saudi Arabia's desire to hold a special meeting of OPEC to approve a production increase by amending production quotas agreed to by the members of the cartel last month, before Iraq invaded Kuwait.

The dissenting members apparently want to maintain OPEC solidarity and protect the recent run-up in oil prices, which likely would be reduced by additional output. Most of those dissenting are nations that would be unable to increase oil production much beyond current levels and thus could only lose revenue in an overall production increase because of declining prices.

President Bush said yesterday that he was confident that several OPEC nations would increase their oil production. "I think the Saudis will do their part in helping out along the way. I'm confident of that," the president said at his news conference. "I also would say . . . that I am also confident that other countries will make up the shortfall in production that comes about from Iraqi oil and Kuwaiti oil not going to market. And I can't give you the details on that, but I've had enough conversations with people around the world . . . to feel that things are moving in the right direction there."

But industry sources said yesterday it appears that no OPEC members have raised their output so far, at least not significantly enough to make a major dent in the 4.5 million-barrel-a-day shortfall caused by the shutdown of Kuwaiti oil fields and the embargo on Iraqi oil exports.

Analysts believe that individual OPEC members will not increase their production significantly without a group decision that would protect them politically. "If no one is going to increase production before they can get an OPEC meeting, then it might be a while," said John Redpath, an oil analyst at Energy Security Analysis Inc. in Washington.

Venezuela and Iran both said yesterday that they would not increase production unilaterally. Iran is believed to have become an important swing vote in the negotiations over an OPEC accord, torn between its desire for higher oil prices and its animosity toward longtime enemy Iraq.

In Caracas, Iraq's ambassador to Venezuela, Majid A. Al Samarra'i, said his nation viewed raising oil production by OPEC members "an act against the Iraqi government," adding that "those who take action against us will suffer damage." He did not say what sort of retaliation Iraq had in mind.

Samarra'i spoke at a news conference and said he was relaying a communique from his government.

A spokesman for the Department of Energy said the agency had been unable to confirm that Saudi Arabia, OPEC's largest and most important member, so far had increased production, as had been expected in return for American military protection. Saudi production had been expected to increase by 2 million barrels a day, enough to cover almost half the oil lost from Iraq and Kuwait. Venezuela and the United Arab Emirates also had been expected to raise production significantly.

"Some of the countries that would like to produce more are looking to do it under the protection of OPEC," said Lawrence J. Goldstein, president of Petroleum Industry Research Foundation, a New York think tank partly funded by the oil industry. "While there are still a lot of promises out there, so far all there are are promises."

"I think right now Saudi Arabia, Venezuela, Nigeria would like to have [OPEC] officially make an announcement that would sanction raising output beyond their quotas," said Vahan Zanoyan, an OPEC expert who is senior director at Petroleum Finance Co., a Washington consulting firm. "It's a matter of the internal politics now of convincing enough countries to hold a meeting."

Zanoyan said Saudi Arabia's apparent reluctance to unilaterally call for an OPEC meeting to approve the higher production levels seems to indicate that the Saudis don't feel they have enough support yet for the proposal. "Saudi Arabia can call a meeting, but they don't like calling a meeting unless they can get their own way," he said. "If Saudi Arabia does call a meeting, you can almost be sure that they've got it together."

W. P24
8/15/90

과 장	국 장	차관보	차 관	장 관
	✓ 1822			

0115

W(F)-

관

발신 : 주미대사

보안 통제	

(매)

Joseph Story, president of Gulf Consulting Services, a McLean-based Middle East analysis firm, described the tug of war among the OPEC members as "sort of a division between the haves and have nots." Members such as Algeria and Iran, already producing at full capacity, don't want overall production raised because the resulting price decrease would cut into their revenue.

Similarly, Zanoyan said, "They're enjoying this price increase. They don't want to mess it up."

Iran is in a particular quandary, experts said, because it has benefited from the sharp increase in oil prices, which at their peak last week were nearly double their levels of a month earlier. Sources say Iran last week sold 30 million barrels of oil it had in storage in Europe, and Zanoyan said: "The windfall has been humongous for Iran. . . . They made a killing."

However, Iran also would like to hurt Iraq by encouraging the world boycott that is attempting to economically isolate the nation led by Saddam Hussein, and supporting an increase in OPEC oil production to make up for the lost Iraqi and Kuwaiti crude would endorse that boycott. So Iran is believed to be under considerable pressure from the Saudis to vote for increased production. "If Iran were to change sides on this issue, then the group that wants [increased output] would win," Zanoyan said.

The longer OPEC's internal bickering drags on, the more jittery world oil markets will become, analysts and oil traders said yesterday.

W.P4
8/15/90

1822-2

0116

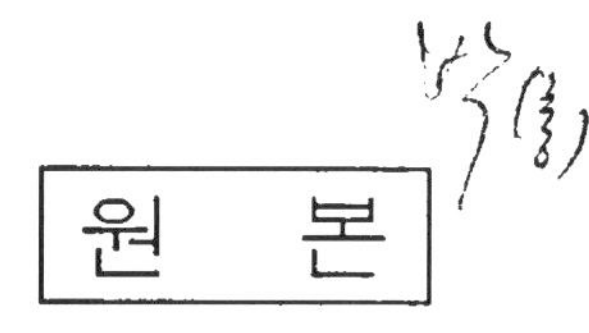

관리 번호 90-600

원 본

외 무 부

종 별 :

번 호 : VZW-0441　　　　일 시 : 90 0814 2000

수 신 : 장관(기협,미남,중동,기정)

발 신 : 주 베네수엘라 대사

제 목 : 이라크-쿠웨이트 사태

대: WVZ-0255

대호 관련, 당관 온중열 참사관이 주재국 동자부 SEDWICKS 국제 협력국장및 석유공사 SPORN 국제협력부장과 접촉한 결과를 아래 보고함.

1. 금번 사태에 대한 전망

- 이라크 쿠웨이트 침공사태는 표면상으로는 쿠웨이트가 이라크 영내의 유전을 도굴하는 동 OPEC 쿼타 이상의 원유를 생산함으로써 국제 유가를 하락시켜왔다는 것에 기인하고 있으나, 기실은 이란-이라크 전쟁시 쿠웨이트가 이라크에 제공한 약 200 억불 상당의 채무 변제를 강력히 요구한데서 발생한것임.

- 이라크는 금번 군사행동을 통해서 상기 부채를 청산한 것으로 보이는 바, 사우디가 전쟁중 이라크측에 제공한 약 400 억불의 부채를 막후 교섭을 통해서 포기할 경우 동 사태는 진정될 것으로 보임.

- 그러나 이라크는 1961 년 쿠웨이트 독립당시 쿠웨이트에 대한 영유권을 주장해 왔고, 금번 사태를 통해 이를 장악한 만큼 미국등 서방의 봉쇄 조치가 매우 효과적으로 지속되지 않는한 쉽게 포기할 것으로 보이지 않음.

2. 사태 장기화시 국제 수급및 유가전망

- 미국등의 이라크 및 쿠웨이트산 원유에 대한 금제 (INTERDICTION) 조치가 성공적으로 이루어질 경우 국제 원유시장에서 약 460 만 B/D 정도가 탈루되는 것임.

베네수엘라(60 만), 사우디(200 만), 멕시코(10 만), UAE(30 만)의 증산계획 을 감안할때 약 160 만 배럴의 공급 부족이 예상되나, 베네수엘라는 사태의 장기화 경우에도 베럴당 21 미불 선에서 국제원유가 안정되는 것이 베네수엘라 이익에 합당한 것으로 판단하고 있음.

- FIGUEREDO 외상이 여타 OPEC 회원국을 순방, 증산 교섭중인바, 사태의 장기화

경제국 차관 1차보 2차보 미주국 중아국 통상국 안기부 동자부

PAGE 1　　공람 국제경제국 90년 8월 16일 | 담당 | 과장 | 국장 | 차관보 | 차관 | 장관　　90.08.15 22:10 외신 2과 통제관 DH

0117

경우에도 유가는 현 수준에서 안정될 것으로 보임.

3. 확정시 국제 수급및 유가전망

- OPEC 회원국 전체는 국제 원유가의 안정이 자국이익에 부합되는 것으로 판단하고 있는바, 이라크가 자포자기의 심정으로 사우디의 주요 유전을 파괴할 경우 가공할 사태가 야기될 것이나, 이라크 지도층이 이러한 무책임한 행동은 삼갈 것으로 보임.

4. 주재국 대책

-베네수엘라는 전기 언급대로 원유의 안정 공급과 이에 따른 가격안정을 희망하고 있음으로 이라크, 쿠웨이트 사태의 장기화가 국제 원유시장의 불안을 초래할 것으로 판단될 경우 국내 생산 가능시설 (280 만 B/D) 을 최대한으로 가동하는 한편 NON-OPEC 회원국과도 접촉, 이들이 증산을 강력히 권유할 계획임.끝.

(대사 김재훈-국장)

예고: 90.12.31 일반

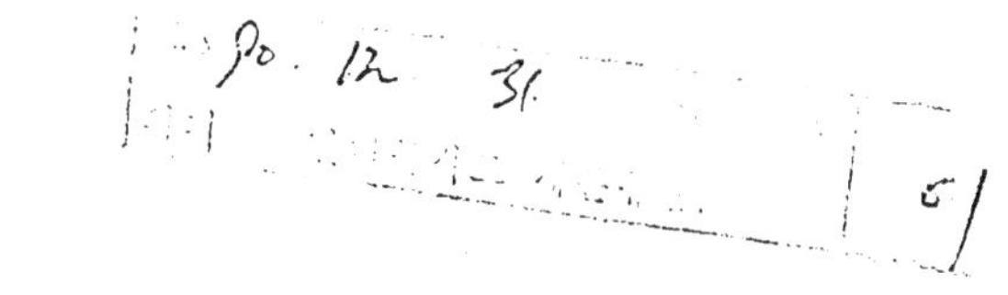

PAGE 2

0118

외 무 부

종 별 :

번 호 : USW-3765 일 시 : 90 0815 1249

수 신 : 장 관 (중근동,미북,통일,기협)

발 신 : 주 미 대사

제 목 : 중동 사태

이락-쿠웨이트 사태관련 금 8.15 당지 언론보도 요지 아래 보고함 (기사 전문은 별전 FAX송부함)

1. CNN 방송은 09:00 뉴스를 통해 사담후세인 이락 대통령이 이란에 대해 군대철수, 전쟁포로 교환, 국경조약 체결등 전면화해를 제의했다고 보도했는바, 이는 시리아의 대이락 제재동참에 따라 고립상태에 빠진 이락이 이란과의 화해를 통해 현재 이란-이락전에 개입되어 있는 이락군을 이동시켜 쿠웨이트내 점령군을 증강시킬수 있는 전술로 평가되고 있음.

2. 미국 정부는 요르단의 AQABA 항구가 이락에 대한 물품반입에 이용되고 있다고비난하면서 동항구의 봉쇄가능성을 시사했으며, 또한 사우디내 미군증강을 위해 20만명 규모의 예비군의 동원계획을 검토중인 것으로 알려졌음.

한편 금일 아침 워싱턴에 도착한 후세인 요르단국왕은 명일 부쉬 대통령과 메인주 휴가소 (캐니벙커포트)에서 회담할 예정임.

3. 대이락 제재조치에 대한 아랍국가들의 동참과 관련, 미국정부는 이집트에 1억불 이상의 무기판매를 결정했으며, 요르단이 동 제재에 동참할 경우 요르단에 대한경제지원도 고려하고 있다고 알려졌음. 또한 사우디, 오만, 바레인, UAE, 모르코등에 대한 무기판매 확대문제도 검토중인 것으로 보임.

4. NYT, WP 는 금일자 사설을 통해 미국이 취한 일방적인 해상단속이 유엔헌장의규정에 따른 적법한 조치라 할지라도, 안보리 상임 이사국인 소,불 등의 반대에 유의, 유엔안보리등에서 강대국과의 긴밀한 협의를 통해 실시할것을 촉구했음.

5. 한편 당지 전문가들의 분석에 따르면 미국은 금번사태가 장기화될 경우 제반상황이 미국측에 불리하게 전개될 것으로 판단, 대규모병력 파견을 통해 대 이락 압력을 강화함으로서 이락이 스스로 협상에 응해오던지, 아니면 이락의 대 사우디

중아국 1차보 미주국 경제국 통상국 정문국 안기부 그차보 차관 대책반

PAGE 1

공람	국제경제국	년 월 일	담 당	과 장	국 장	차관보	차 관	장 관

90.08.16 07:23 FC

외신 1과 통제관

0119

침공 또는 이락군 내부의 반란에 의한 후세인의 몰락을 예상하고 있다함.

(대사 박동진-국장)

PAGE 2

0120

외 무 부

종 별 :
번 호 : USW-3788 일 시 : 90 0816 1934
수 신 : 장 관(미북,중근동,통일,기협)
발 신 : 주 미 대사
제 목 : 요르단 국왕 방미

연: USW(F)-1843,(2)USW(F)-1842

1.부쉬 대통령은 현재 방미중인 요르단의 훗쎄인 왕과 금 8.16 메인주 KENNEBUNKPORT에서 정상 회담을 가졌는바, 동 정상 회담후가진 기자회견에서 부쉬 대통령 주요 언급 요지 하기보고함 (기자 회견 전문은 연호 (1)송부)

가.금일 회담을 통해 금번 중동 사태 관련 미-요르단간의 이견이 좁혀졌는바, 특히 훗쎄인 왕은 대이락 경제 제재 조치에의 동참 입장을 재천명하였음.

나.훗쎄인 왕은 AQABA 항을 통한 대이락 수출입의 금지를 약속하였음 (단, 요르단측은 식량등 인도적 상품도 경제 제재 대상 품목인지에 대해 유엔측의 의견을구하고 있는 상태임)

다.또한 금일 회담시 후세인 왕의 최근 이락 방문 결과에 관해서는 언급이 없었는바, 이락측이 쿠웨이트로 부터 철수 하리라는 느낌은 받지 못했음.

라.한편 후쎄인 왕은 현재 미-이락간에 여하한 중개자 역할도 하고 있지 않음.

마.미국으로서는 이락 골비화 정책을 계속 추구할것이며, 자국만의 경제적 이익을 위해 전 세계적차원의 경제 제재 조치를 위배하는 CHEATERS를 계속 경계할것임.

2.또한 전기 정상 회담후 후쎄인왕은 기자들과 간단한 질의 응답을 가졌는바 동인 주요 언급 요지하기 보고함 (기자 회견 전문 연호(2) 송부)

가. 요르단 정부는 유엔 안보리의 대이락 경제 제재결의를 존중해 왔음.다만 SANCTION 의 구체적 의미에 관해서는 유엔측의 의견을 구하고 있는중임.

나.금번 방미시 이락측으로부터 여하한 MESSAGE 도 가지고 오지 않았음.

다.현재 AQABA 항을 통한 대이락 수출입 상품은 없음.

(대사 박동진-국장)

미주국 1차보 중아국 경제국 통상국 안기부 대책반 그차관 차관

PAGE 1

국	담 당	과 장	국 장	차관보	차 관	장 관

90.08.17 10:23 WG
외신 1과 통제관

0121

08/16/90 18:50 ☎202 797 0595 EMBASSY OF KOREA --- WOI ⊠001/009

번 호 : USW(F)- 1842

수 신 : 장 관 (미북, 중근동, 통일, 기협) 발신 : 주미대사

제 목 : 후세인 王 기자회견 (미-요르단 정상회담) (8 매)

REMARKS OF KING HUSSEIN I

FOLLOWING MEETING WITH PRESIDENT BUSH

KENNEBUNKPORT, MAINE

THURSDAY, AUGUST 16, 1990

.STX

Q King Hussein, did you make any progress towards a solution?

Q Your majesty --

Q Any progress towards a solution?

KING HUSSEIN: First of all, let me clarify a few points. I came to the United States with the purpose of seeing and meeting personally an old friend of mine, President Bush. I've had the opportunity to do so today. We have had a very frank, open, candid discussion. I believe we understand where we both stand. And at the same time, I am leaving with a clearer idea of what the President's thinking is, and I feel very happy with the warmth with which I was received, and also, at the same, with the opportunity that I had to have this meeting at this very, very crucial time.

Q Your Majesty, did --

Q Sir, will you now stop supplies going through the port of Aqaba to the Iraqis? Will -- are you -- will you abide by the UN sanctions now against the Iraqis?

KING HUSSEIN: We -- I am not suggesting that we have altered our position at all in this regard. The government of Jordan stated very clearly at the very outset following the Security Council resolution that it regarded these mandatory sanctions and measures as ones that the government of Jordan would respect, and this has been the case. So this is nothing new to talk about, now.

(Cross talk.)

Q Your Majesty, did you bring a message from Saddam Husayn? And, if so, what did it say?

KING HUSSEIN: I did not bring any message. I am not talking on behalf of anyone in the area, but for myself as a person who has been in a position of responsibility over the last 38 years and with the interest and concern that this crisis hopefully will begin to de-escalate and we might find solutions to the many problems that are there now. I am concerned as any within the area. I have tried my utmost to see what could be done initially within an Arab context. And I'll continue to do my best to obtain a resolution of this problem.

1842-1

0122

Q Is a diplomatic solution --

Q Your Majesty, why --

Q What gives you such hope?

Q -- any closer as a result of this meeting? Did you make any progress or hear anything from the President that suggested a diplomatic solution might be closer?

KING HUSSEIN: I just had a chance to hear the President and have his point of view, which I appreciate very much indeed. It wasn't possible to communicate otherwise.

Q Any agreements at all?

KING HUSSEIN: No. I mean just -- there is nothing more that I can say.

Q Why is food getting through port of Aqaba?

KING HUSSEIN: I beg your pardon?

Q If you are in favor of mandatory sanctions, why is food getting through the port?

KING HUSSEIN: We are reaching the United Nations to find out exactly what these sanctions mean. This is what the government is doing at this stage, and I believe that there are certain categories or areas where the situation is unclear. But --

Q And you --

KING HUSSEIN: -- we are appealing to these --

Q -- consider food to be one of them then?

KING HUSSEIN: I beg your pardon?

Q And you consider food to be one of those exemptions then?

KING HUSSEIN: This is something we are trying to clarify with the --

Q Sir --

KING HUSSEIN: -- (inaudible).

Q Do you have any reason for hope at all, sir?

KING HUSSEIN: I suppose one has to have hope. Without hope, you can't get anywhere. And the dangers are such that it's unthinkable to contemplate the idea of giving up and not trying one's best to resolve this problem to the satisfaction of all and hopefully for a better future for all.

Q Sir, will you visit Baghdad now?

Q Did anything happen at this meeting that gives --

1842-2

0123

Q Will you go back to Baghdad?

Q -- you hope, sir

KING HUSSEIN: I don't know. I have no plans in the immediate future.

Q Where will you go from here?

KING HUSSEIN: Back to my country.

Q So, Your Majesty, you acknowledge that there are some shipments now passing through the port of Aqaba --

KING HUSSEIN: There are no shipments --

Q There are no shipments?

KING HUSSEIN: -- at the moment as far as I know. No.

Q Might you close that port altogether, sir, if --

KING HUSSEIN: It's our only outlet to the sea -- to the sea, and it's our only outlet to the sea and to the rest of the world. And it's what we will -- our port. We receive everything that we import into Jordan. We export a lot of our own phosphates and other things.

Q Might you close it to shipments to Iraq or from Iraq?

KING HUSSEIN: What?

Q Might you close the port to Iraqi commerce?

KING HUSSEIN: Sir, this is a question of detail; the government is dealing with it. I told you that we are adhering to this UN Security Council sanctions. And we regret very much indeed that the situation has happened --

Q Your Majesty, you said that the President has --

Q Did the President offer American help if Iran --

Q You said you have a better understanding now of what the President's viewpoint is. Did you express your viewpoint? Did you ask for any understanding about the kind of economic situation, political situation, you're in? And what did --

KING HUSSEIN: Very frankly and honestly, the -- we are passing through a very difficult economic and -- situation in Jordan, and we are affected probably much more than any in this regard. But this, as I expressed to the President before I arrived here, was the least of my worries at the moment. I was concerned with the problem that all of us are worried about, both in my part of the world and here and everywhere in the world, and that is what I wanted to talk about and I have done.

1842-3

0124

Q Did an offer emerge in help --

Q (Did the President ?) offer any help?

Q -- for Jordan by the --

KING HUSSEIN: We didn't -- I didn't discuss this.

Q Any specific agreement --

KING HUSSEIN: Thank you very much indeed.

END

0125

08/16/90 18:53 ☎202 797 0595 EMBASSY OF KOREA --- WOI

USW(F)- 1843
장 관(미북,중근동,통일,기획) 발신 : 주미대사
Bush 대통령 기자회견 (이-요르단 정상회담) (5 매)

REMARKS BY PRESIDENT BUSH
AND
SECRETARY OF STATE BAKER

FOLLOWING MEETINGS WITH

KING HUSSEIN OF JORDAN
AND
FOREIGN MINISTER PRINCE SAUD
OF SAUDI ARABIA

KENNEBUNKPORT, MAINE

THURSDAY, AUGUST 16, 1990

.STX

PRESIDENT BUSH: Well, we've had some good meetings here today, two good meetings. One with King Hussein of Jordan, the other with the Foreign Minister, His Highness Prince Saud of Saudi Arabia. In addition, I was on the phone earlier to President Ozál of Turkey. He reported in on some conversations he's had and I must say was somewhat optimistic about the effectiveness of these international sanctions in which most countries around the world have joined. And so it's been a very illuminating day.

I, of course, was very pleased that King Hussein, who previously had announced his support for sanctions, his willingness to go with sanctions, reiterated that to me, making clear that this was a decision that Jordan had taken some time ago. But, nevertheless, I put this under the heading of very encouraging -- encouraging developments and in terms of the Saudis I -- Prince Saud very kindly thanked me for the strong support from the United States and I told him that we were determined and wanted to do everything in our power to enforce the United Nations resolution which calls for Iraq to get out of Kuwait, and the -- calls for the restoration of the rulers to Kuwait.

So, we're in sync with the Saudis. I feel that the differences that possibly existed with Jordan have been narrowed, and I cited one extremely important point there, but I was pleased to see them both here at our home.

I'll be glad to take some questions. Yeah, Terry, and then Jeff.

Q Mr. President, what kind of report did King Hussein give you on his trip to Baghdad? And did he offer any kind of hope that Saddam Husayn would pull his troops out of Kuwait and let the Emir return to power?

1843-

0126

PRESIDENT BUSH: I got -- he didn't go into any details of his trip to Baghdad, and I did not come away from that conversation with a feeling of hope that Saddam Husayn would do that which he's been called upon to do by international -- under international law.

Q Mr. President, what can you tell us about reports, or what do you know about reports that foreign nationals in both Iraq and Kuwait have been ordered segregated and been reported to report to one place, including some 2,500 Americans? Are you concerned that their lives may be in danger at this point?

PRESIDENT BUSH: I'm concerned that any coercion on foreign nationals in some other country is a violation of international norms and I must say that I did see a report. We've discussed it. They checked with one of the hotels to which people were encouraged to go, and the hotel had no knowledge of an influx of people coming there. So it's a little vague right now, Jim. But anything that compels individuals to do something against their will would of course concern me. And I don't want to overstate it, because we continue to get statements out of these various representatives of Iraq, the ambassador to the UN for example, that these people will -- all countries will be permitted free passage or will not be harrassed. But I saw the report and thus I must say I was concerned. Yeah, Anne (sp)?

Q Following up on that. The Americans who are in Baghdad I believe are the ones who were taken from Kuwait. And today the American Embassy personnel were for the first time not allowed to go in and see them and newspeople were thrown out. Isn't it getting more dangerous for those Americans? And would there be anything --

PRESIDENT BUSH: It gets more dangerous, I think, if I heighten the conern that I've already expressed. And I said that the other day
and I'll repeat it here. On the other hand, when you get reports of this nature, of course you're concerned about them.

Q Mr. President, what -- may I ask your reaction to the rather bellicose speech we heard today from Saddam Husayn in which, as you probably know, he called you a liar and vowed to send Americans home in body bags?

PRESIDENT BUSH: Well, I really haven't seen the speech. I've seen some excerpts or the open letter I think it was. And I think it's clear that what we need to do at this point is to enforce the international law; the statements at the United Nations from many countries really say it all. And so there's no point in me responding to the letter. I didn't see any -- or nobody's at least presented so far to me from that letter any concrete proposals to which I feel a necessity to respond.

Yeah?

Q Mr. President, what is the situation on the ground in Iraq and Kuwait? What's going on with the sanctions? How are they working today compared to how they were working two days ago say?

PRESIDENT BUSH: The sanctions against Iraq in Kuwait? I get the feeling that the sanctions just put into effect and just being put into effect are beginning to take hold. And I would cite a very

(8 43 - 7.

upbeat statement from President Ozal of Turkey in this regard. And so, there doesn't appear [illegible] any shipments of oil c[illegible]ng out of Iraq and that is very positive because I think 90 per[illegible]t of their foreign exchange looking for help here is based on petroleum. And so, I'd say that is a very encouraging step. And the other part of it has to be arms being interdicted and everything all across the board -- foodstuffs, whatever it is. They have been penalized by the United Nations. Chapter VII is seldom used, but it has been used now to call these people -- to bring these people to do what's right. And I'm -- I must say I'm encouraged with this concept of the world staying together and making these sanctions fully effective. So --

Q Is there evidence that they're feeling it, though?

PRESIDENT BUSH: I can't cite specific evidence. There was one little tidbit that we saw, saying that -- and again, I probably shouldn't even go into the details of it at all -- but anyway, it was a report that some of the bakers had been ordered to stop making confections, confectionary goods, whatever it is -- sweets and these things -- and concentrate on the fundamentals, the staples.

But I think there's -- knowing that -- the economic situation in Iraq -- I don't think one can sustain true international isolation for long, especially when you depend on the outside world for a lot of your -- a lot of your goods.

Yes, Ann?

Q If you call up -- or sign the order calling up -- the reserves, then is that something you think you may have to call upon?

PRESIDENT BUSH: I've not signed up anything on that -- there's some consideration. We have a ready reserve, we have a reserve that, I've been told by a couple of proponents of the reserves, are very eager to do their part but no decision has been made in that regard.

Yes?

Q Mr. President, your feeling now of the situation -- do you think the situation is stabilizing or do you think the United States and Iraq are getting closer to war?

PRESIDENT BUSH: I don't know that I can choose between the two options, but I do know that there is a determination on the part of so many countries to do something about redressing the grievances that I think it's going to work. But I can't say that it's stablized totally. I hope that the American presence and the presence of Arab forces and the presence of others -- many others in Saudi Arabia, and in that -- those areas, has lessened the risk of further adventure on the part of Saddam Husayn.

Yeah?

Q Is Saddam making the -- King Hussein of Jordan in any way a go-between, between the United States and Iraq?

(847-3

0128

PRESIDENT BUSH: I ≡n't get the feeling. I _d some reports and now I'm wondering where they all came from, because I'd read some previous reports indicating that a man was coming with a letter from Saddam Husayn, some -- maybe printed it here, which I'd find hard to believe without any evidence. And so I wondering where all this is coming from, and I think I addressed myself to that question at the press conference -- when was it? -- yesterday or the day before, where I said I didn't know of that and that I -- I -- and I have felt to myself, and whether I said it is, I think he might have mentioned to me if there was such a letter, but back to your question, there was no intermediary mission that I detected at all.

I think he'd like to find some way to be helpful and he reiterated his interest of making everything in an Arab context, but I had an opportunity to tell him my views on the situation and to tell him that in spite of the differences that may have appeared to be grievous, a few -- a week or so ago, that on the part of this President, and I think of the United States entirely, we'd like to see better relations, and I do think that his express willingness -- again, expressed before he came here and then reiterated -- to go forward on these international sanctions is something that will be widely appreciated here in the United States and, indeed, around the world.

Yeah?

Q Mr. President, did King Hussein give you assurances that Jordan would not allow Iraqi goods in and out of the port of Aqaba?

PRESIDENT BUSH: Yes.

Jim?

Q Mr. President, Iraq made some pretty significant peace overtures to Iran. Were you surprised by that? What do you know by it? How do you think it'll affect the overall equation there? Are you concerned by it?

PRESIDENT BUSH: No, I'm not concerned at all by it, and I'm surprised only in the fact that it seems to be acquiescing to all of Iran's terms, something that Saddam Husayn has been unwilling to accept -- not all -- totally -- all of them. But I don't know the effect of it, and I do know that Iran has expressed their indignation about the takeover to -- of Kuwait by Iraq. And I see nothing that has changed that. I don't know of any statement that leads me to be concerned that they're going to reverse their position on that point.

Q You're not concerned that Iran may throw in with Iraq? Or what does it tell you about Saddam Husayn's position right now?

PRESIDENT BUSH: Well, I'm not concerned about the former, and I would simply let the facts and the evolution of events answer this -- the last part, because, you see, I don't know that there's been an agreement on all these points.

1843-4

0129

I don't think there [illegible] that I know of. I don't think it's been fully finally agreed, has it?

... Yeah, Terry?

Q (In view of that ?), don't you think he's desperate, sir?

PRESIDENT BUSH: Well, that's what you think. I'm -- I'd rather just not speculate on that and just keep my eye on the ball, which is to isolate -- in conjunction with others, to isolate Iraq.

Q Back to King Hussein, Mr. President. You said that he agreed to cut off shipments to Iraq through the port of Aqaba. But he told us that he's exploring with the United Nations what the sanctions mean. Did he tell you that everything would be cut off, including food?

PRESIDENT BUSH: Let me ask Jim, because I think he -- let me ask the Secretary, lawyer -- fine lawyer that he is in addition to being a good Secretary of State, to answer that, because he was the one that engaged the King in that particular discussion.

SEC. BAKER: Yeah. I think what the King meant was that there is a provision in the sanctions that permits food for humanitarian purposes, or some such language. And there's really been no definition of exactly when that triggers and what that means. And the government of Jordan is seeking some guidance from the United Nations on the subject.

Q Is that a loophole?

SEC. BAKER: No. It's not a loophole. It's the way the sanctions were written by the United Nations when they voted 13 to nothing to impose them.

PRESIDENT BUSH: Last one.

Q Are you satisfied that goods will no longer go through Jordan to Iraq? Are you --

PRESIDENT BUSH: I'm not satisfied to total satisfaction on any point regarding the sanctions. I'm very encouraged that they look like they'll be effective. We've got to guard against cheaters. You've got to guard against people who, for economic gain, will try to violate these sanctions, from whatever part of the world they come from, whatever country they come from. So I can't say I am satisfied, but what I am is encouraged that Jordan, prior to the King's coming here, took this position, and I think that is something that is encouraging, and I think it might send a message to some who have been around the world who need a little leadership in that regard.

Thank you all very much. I know you have a deadline. It's been a full day. Thank you.

END

18435

0130

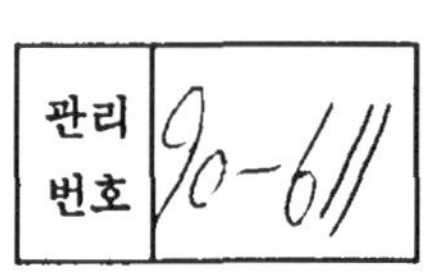

원 본

외 무 부

종 별 :

번 호 : MAW-1051 일 시 : 90 0816 1200

수 신 : 장관(기협,아동)

발 신 : 주 말련 대사

제 목 : 원유 안정 확보

대: WMA-0559

연: MAW-1045

1. 주재국 정부는 8.15 각의에서 국영석유공사(PETRONAS)의 산유량을 일산 1만 배럴 늘리기로 결정하였음.

2. 동 증산은 이라. 쿠웨이트에서 원유를 공급 받아온 국가들의 추가 수요에 부응키위한 것이며, 5 천 바렐은 아세안 국가들에, 잔여 5 천 바렐은 기타 비산유국에 공급할 예정이라함.

3. 표제관련 대 주재국 교섭에 참고코자 하니 아국 정유사들의 대 말련 원유 증량공급 요청현황을 당관에 통보바람. 끝

(대사 홍순영-국장)

예고: 90.12.31 까지

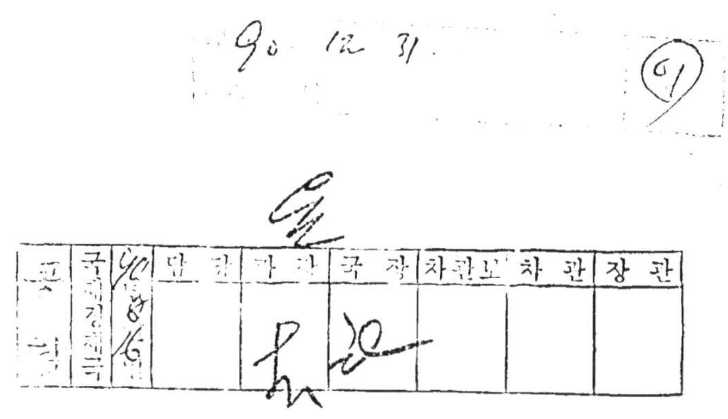

경제국 차관 1차보 2차보 아주국 동자부

PAGE 1 90.08.16 14:00

외신 2과 통제관 EZ

0131

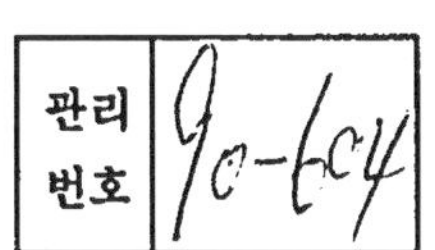

원 본

외 무 부

종 별 :

번 호 : BUW-0180 일 시 : 90 0816 2110

수 신 : 장 관(기협)

발 신 : 주 브루나이 대사

제 목 : 원유안정 확보위한 대 산유국 외교활동 강화

대:WBU-104

1. 본직은 8.16. RAHMAN 산업자원성 장관에게 유공과 호남정유가 브루나이쉘로부터 도입하는 원유의 기존 계약물량이 정상적으로 공급되도록 협조해 줄것을 요청함

2. 동장관에 의하면 현재로서는 주재국의 원유 생산량(일 15 만 배럴)을 증량생산할 계획이 없다함. 끝

(대사 허세린-국장)

예고:90.12.31. 까지

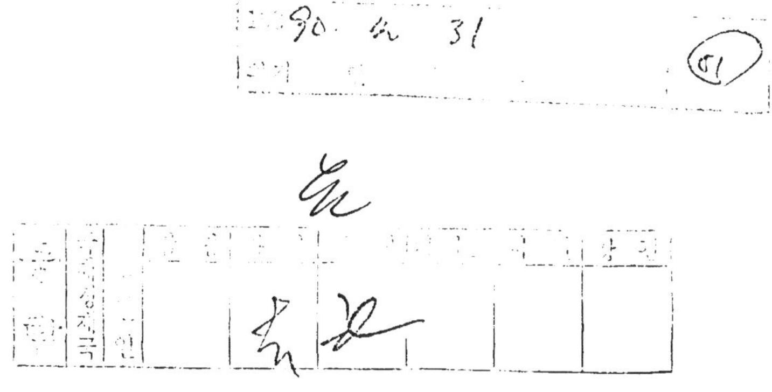

경제국 아주국

PAGE 1 90.08.16 23:51

외신 2과 통제관 DL

0132

관리 번호 90-605

외 무 부

종 별 :

번 호 : LYW-0500 일 시 : 90 0816 1600

수 신 : 장 관(마그)

발 신 : 주 리비아 대사

제 목 : 리비아산 원유 도입

연:LYW-0493

1. 주재국 정책 원유 일 15 천 배럴의 도입을 위한 주재국 정부와의 협의는 계속 추진할 것이나 당사자가 서울에서 더욱 적극적으로 교섭토록 하기 바람

2. 주재국 원유의 국내 도입과 관련, 당지 진출 아국 건설업체들이 그동안 건설공사 대금으로 수령한 원유가 1.5 억배럴 32 억불에 달하고 있으나 국내 도입이 곤란하여 전량을 유럽지역에서 처분하여 왔음. 국제 원유 공급이 불안한 현시점에서도 아국 업체의 공사 대전 원유 수령은 큰 지장이 없을 것으로 사료되는바, 국내 소요 원유의 안정적 확보를 위하여 향후 아국 건설 업체들이 수령하는 원유를 반입한다면 원유공급 부족분을 해결 할수 있을 것으로 사료됨. 끝

(대사 최필립-국장)

예고 90.12.31. 까지

90 12 31

공람	국제경제국	년 월 일	담 당	과 장	국 장	차관보	차 관	장 관

중아국 경제국 통상국 동자부

PAGE 1

90.08.17 04:43

외신 2과 통제관 DL

0133

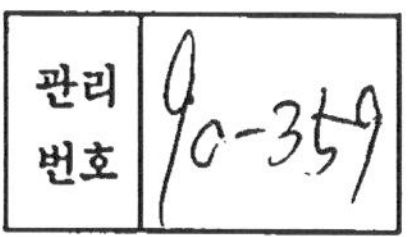
관리번호 90-359

홍

외 무 부

종 별 :

번 호 : GEW-1389 일 시 : 90 0816 1630

수 신 : 장관(중근동,미북,구일,기협)

발 신 : 주 독 대사

제 목 : 이락,쿠웨이트 사태

당관 이양 참사관이 금 8.16. 주재국 외무부 DASSEL 중동국장을 면담, 표제사태에 관하여 문의한바, 동인의 반응 다음과 같음

1. 표제사태는 연일 악화되어가고 있는것으로 보며, 전반적인 상황으로보아 열전화 가능성이 평화적해결 가능성보다 더욱 큰것으로 전망됨

2. 주재국 정부로서는 이락, 쿠웨이트 지역에 거류하는 교민들을 철수시키기 위하여 양자및 다자관계의 모든 CHANNEL 을 동원, 노력하여 왔으나 현재까지 아무성과가 없어 안타까운 실정임

실질적으로 외국인 특히 서방외국인들은 이라크의 볼모가 된셈임.

3. 이라크측의 주쿠웨이트 외교공관 폐쇄및 바그다드 이전 요청에 대하여 주재국측의 일차적인 반응이 있었으나 이문제는 EPC 테두리 내에서 동요청을 거부하는 공동보조를 취하게 될것으로 예상됨.(EPC 는 아직까지 이에대한 공식입장을 결정하지는 않았음)

주쿠웨이트 서독대사관은 교민보호등 정상적인 업무수행을 계속하고 있음

4. 서독 소해정 (MINESWEEPERS)의 걸프만 파견문제는 아직 결정된것은 없으며, 8.21. 개최될 WEU(서구연맹) 각료회의 결과를 보아 주재국정부의 입장이 수립될 것으로 보임.

실제로 이문제는 서독군을 NATO 해당지역 이원지역으로 파견하는 것이 기본법에 저촉되는 것이 아니냐는 법률적문제와 소해정이 걸프만사태 대응에 적합한 장비를 갖추지 못하고 있는 기술적문제(방공가능장비 결여)가 연결되어 있음

(대사 신동원-국장)

예고:90.12.31. 일반

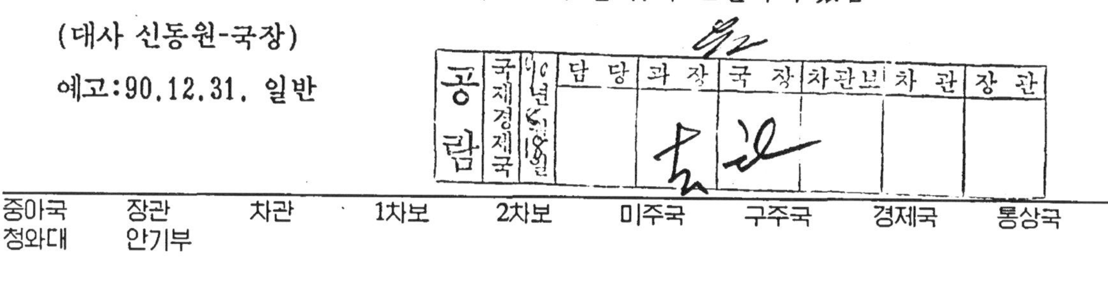

공람	국제경제국	90년 8월 18일	담 당	과 장	국 장	차관보	차 관	장 관

중아국 장관 차관 1차보 2차보 미주국 구주국 경제국 통상국
청와대 안기부

PAGE 1

90.08.17 11:21

외신 2과 통제관 FE

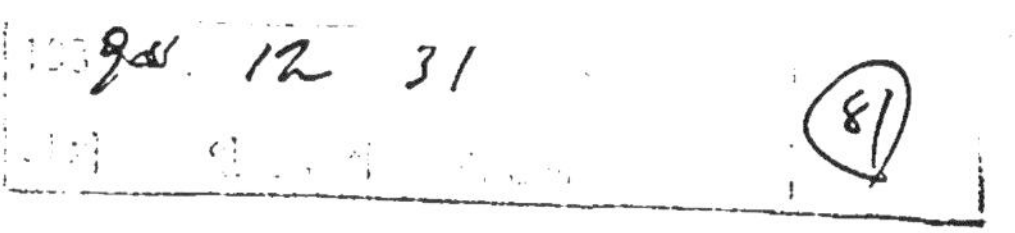

90. 12. 31

0134

관리 번호	90-620

분류번호	보존기간

발 신 전 보

WOM-0120 900817 1532 DY

번 호 :　　　　종별 :

수 신 : 주 오만 대사. 총영사

발 신 : 장 관 (기협)

제 목 : 이라크·쿠웨이트 사태

대 : OMW - 0235

대호로 요청한 "연호" 내용은 다음과 같음

1. 아국은 이라크·쿠웨이트 및 중립지역으로부터 아국 원유 총 도입량 (928천B/D)의 15.8%를 도입하고 있으나, 표제사태로 사실상 동 도입이 중단된 상태임

2. 이라크·쿠웨이트의 총 원유생산량이 약 450만B/D (자유 세계 총 생산량의 약 10%차지)입을 감안할 시, 금번 사태가 장기화될 경우 또는 인근 지역으로 확산될 경우에는 국제원유수급 및 유가에 크게 영향을 미칠 것으로 판단됨

3. 금번사태 관련 아국의 원유수급대책 수립등에 참고코자 하니 귀 주재국 관련부서 및 전문가가 분석하는 아래사항에 대해 지급 보고 바람.

- 금번사태에 대한 전망
- 금번사태의 장기화시 국제수급 및 유가전망
- 광역전쟁등 인근지역으로 확산시 국제수급 및 유가전망
- 주재국의 대책등. 끝.

(국제경제국장 최대화)

90 12 31 일반문서로 재분류

보안 통제	

앙 고 재	90년 8월 17일	기협과	기안자 성명	과 장	국 장	차 관	장 관
			박홍경		전결		

외신과통제

0135

08/17/90 17:14 ☎202 797 0595 EMBASSY OF KOREA --- WOI 001/002

주 미 대 사 관

통제 | 21

번 호 : USW(F) - 1855

수 신 : 장 관 (기협)

발 신 : 주미대사

제 목 : 원유가격 상승 (8.17. NYT - 2매)

Oil Prices Resume Rise as Tensions Grow

By MATTHEW L. WALD

Oil prices resumed their climb yesterday, as a nervous market contemplated the continuing loss of Iraqi and Kuwaiti crude, the heightened tensions in the Middle East and a delay by OPEC members in increasing their oil production.

In trading on the New York Mercantile Exchange, oil for September delivery closed at $27.36 a barrel yesterday, up 90 cents from Wednesday.

Traders said the market also rose on confusing news about the level of Saudi output. The Japanese Foreign Ministry said early yesterday in Tokyo that Saudi Arabia had notified American, European and Japanese oil companies of a 15 to 20 percent supply cutback in September, but the Saudis later denied making such a notification. Industry experts said oil jargon might have created the confusion.

Reassessing the tightening embargo on Iraq and Kuwait, oil company executives and other experts are also concluding that more than the loss of crude is involved; the United States Navy is now also blocking the output of three sophisticated Kuwaiti refineries, which could create further tightness in the market for refined products, especially gasoline. Gasoline may be due for further increases anyway because prices thus far do not fully reflect increased crude costs, oil company executives say.

The oil price rise yesterday seemed to indicate a changing mood among traders. Last week and earlier this week, analysts said the absence of major developments in the Persian Gulf turmoil contributed to price stability. But now the mood is changing about who would benefit from a status quo, especially since Saudi Arabia has called for, thus far unsuc-

Continued From First Business Page

cessfully, a meeting of the Organization of Petroleum Exporting Countries to permit higher production. Saudia Arabia can produce far more oil, and Venezuela promised to do so, but they want an OPEC agreement first.

Analysts think an OPEC meeting would be exceptionally difficult because it would produce a dispute over who would represent Kuwait, among other problems. The organization met during the eight-year war between Iran and Iraq, but was not able to accomplish much, experts say.

Iran had some extra oil in storage and has been able to move it to market, experts say, but little if any oil is reaching the market because of increased production, the news that traders have been anxiously awaiting.

"Last week people thought that no news was O.K. news, because there would be good news forthcoming," said Cheryl J. Trench of the Petroleum Industry Research Foundation in New York. "Now, not only have we not had good news, but we've had little negative pieces that are troubling."

Oil Prices Turn Upward

The price for a barrel of crude oil for September delivery on the New York Mercantile Exchange since the start of July.

Aug. 2: Iraq invades Kuwait

July 27: OPEC oil summit ends

Aug. 16: $27.36, up $0.90

$30, 28, 26, 24, 22, 20, 18, 16

7/2, 7/9, 7/16, 7/23

Source: Knight-Ridder Financial

The New York Times

Traders try to decide who gains if the Mideast standoff continues.

1855-1

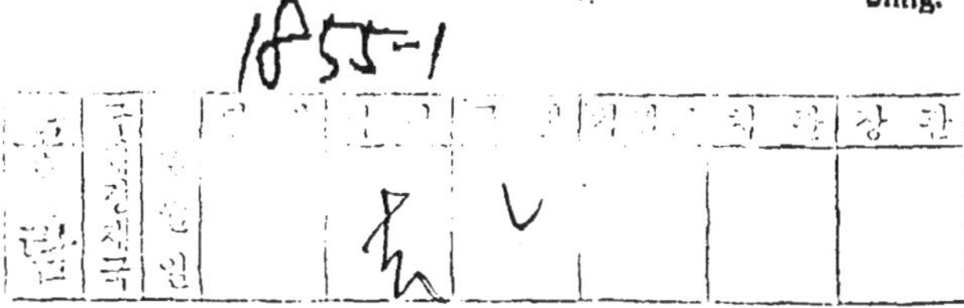

0136

Saudi Request

Two such pieces of news today were a Saudi request for an emergency OPEC meeting, without a date or time being established, and the report of lower Saudi production next month.

Vahan Zanoyan of the Petroleum Finance Company a consulting firm in Washington, said the Saudis appeared to have cut "nominations," but not deliveries. Nominations are orders from oil buyers, and they may have risen sharply in recent weeks. Even if the Saudis cut the nominations, the volume of deliveries could still rise from previous levels, he said.

But "what's dominating the market, [illegible] up," Mr. Zanoyan said.

Shahrokh Nikkhah, an oil specialist at Prudential-Bache, said: "The market obviously believes the only way out of this is a military solution.

Fighting Expected

"The market is anticipating, if not an all-out military conflict, certainly the potential for some skirmishes, which could lead to acts of terrorism against Saudi facilities, Kuwaiti facilities or even Iraqi facilities."

While prices may already incorporate the fear of more fighting, however, they do not approach the levels that would be reached if that fighting occurs, or even if no new production comes into the market, analysts say.

"We are very bullish on this market," Mr. Nikkhah said. "The probability of it going to $32 to $35 a barrel is very, very good." With military action, he said, "the market could spike up substantially higher than $35."

Lacy H. Hunt, an economist who specializes in oil at Carroll McEntee & McGinley, a government securities dealer, said: "The longer this drags on, the more it serves to constrict oil supplies. At some point in time, it will be necessary to gradually release [illegible] leum Reserve, in order to prevent prices from going a lot higher."

The Bush Administration has thus far resisted that move.

Five Billion Barrels a Day

Mr. Hunt said that with the current crisis, five million barrels of oil a day had been removed from the world market. That compares with the four million barrels at the time of the Arab oil embargo of 1973-74, and about two million barrels at the time of the Iranian revolution, in 1979.

In addition, he said, the shortfall will be felt more this time because the United States now imports half its oil, up from about 45 percent in 1979, and 35 percent during the Arab embargo.

The American Petroleum Institute, the industry's main trade association, reported yesterday that imports accounted for 51.3 percent of the oil used in this country in July.

The institute reported deliveries of imported oil had been 6.5 percent higher than the previous year, but that consumption had probably not grown that much, indicating that users at various levels were accumulating inventory, probably because prices were rising or expected to rise further. The report covers the period before the Iraqi invasion of Kuwait on Aug. 2.

Refining at Capacity

The United States imports about 20 percent of its refined products, and domestic refineries are running at virtually full capacity. Experts say that relatively few foreign refineries can make gasoline for export to this country; only half make unleaded fuel, for example, which accounts for about 94 percent of the American market. In addition, wide areas of the United States now require the use of specially formulated fuel with low butane content, to cut air pollution.

Apart from the rise in crude price, many analysts are predicting that the price of gasoline will rise. A top executive of a leading oil company said yesterday that while his company was selling gasoline for about 10 cents a gallon more in the last six weeks, the cost of its crude oil had gone up about 25 cents a gallon.

1855 —2. 끝.

0137

원 본

홍

외 무 부

종 별 : 지 급

번 호 : SBW-0667 일 시 : 90 0817 1000

수 신 : 장 관(기협,중근동,동자부,기정)

발 신 : 주 사우디 대사

제 목 : 비상 OPEC 회의 소집

1.8.16 NAZER 주재국 석유장관은 이라크.쿠웨이트 위기관련, 원유수급 문제를 협의하기위한 비상 OPEC 회의 소집을 요구함.

2.동장관은 동 OPEC 회의 소집 요청을 발표하면서, 일부 외국 언론이 보도한 주재국의 산유량 감축설을 공식 부인하고 향후 산유량을 감축하는 일은 결코 없을 것이라고 강조함.

(대사 주병국-국장)

경제국 2차보 중아국 안기부 동자부 대책반 총무국

PAGE 1 90.08.17 17:28 WG

외신 1과 통제관

0138

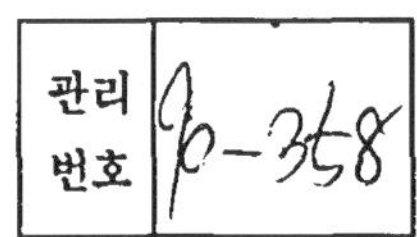
관리 번호 90-358

외 무 부

종 별 : 지 급

번 호 : BGW-0521 일 시 : 90 0817 1130

수 신 : 장관(중근동,영재,정일,기협,건설부,노동부)

발 신 : 주 이라크 대사

제 목 : 전황보고

당지외교단 OECD 모임(카나다, 호주, EC 제국, 일본, 한국등 17 개국 20 명참석)이 8.15 이태리대사관에서 긴급 소집되어 유엔안보리의 대이라크 경제제조치의 효율성및 이라크경제에 미칠영향등에 대해 논의하였는바, 토의내용 아래보고함. 당관에서는 권찬공사가 참석, 아국입장 설명하였음

1. 대이라크경제제재 조치는 상금 100 프로 완벽하지는 못하나 1 개월내에 군사조치에 상응한 효과가 나타날것임.즉, 이라크가 내핍생활을 통해 1 개월은 견딜수 있을것이나 그후 아주 어려운 상황에 처할것이라는 전망

2. 동 제재조치는 이라크경제에 큰타격을 줄것임

참가국 전체가 8.10 이전 대이라크 수출입을 전면중단하고 석유수입을 금지함. 현재사우디및 터키통과 송유관이 완전 폐쇄되었음. 주재국은 국가세입 95 프로를 원유수출에 의존하고있음

3. 호주를 제외한 모든 참가국들은 경제제재 품목중 식량과 식품을 인도적인 고려에서 제외하고 농산물전면 금수조치함. 단, 호주는 아직도 식량수출만은 계속중임.

4. 주재국의 쌀재고량은 현재 70 일분, 설탕은 17 일분 밖에 없는것으로 분석함

동수치는 주재국의 수입통계, 자체생산량을 합해서 인구비로 환산한것이며 영국대표의 발표숫자임. 이라크는 쌀소비량의 25 프로를 자체생산하고있음

5. 쇠고기및 양고기 재고량은 주재국정부가 연말까지 재고가있는것으로 발표하고있으나 수입선이 전면 동결되어 벌써 시중에 품귀현상이 나타나고 닭고기는 전혀 구할수 없음

6. 주재국내 시공중인 외국인 건설공사현장은 대부분 작업을 중단했음. 인도, 방글라데쉬등 아세아 및 유고등 동구 노동자들은 8.13 부터 대량 철수하고있음.

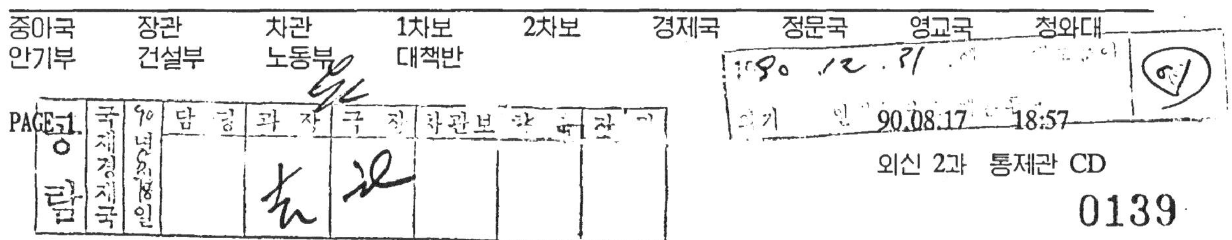

중아국	장관	차관	1차보	2차보	경제국	정문국	영교국	청와대
안기부	건설부	노동부	대책반					

PAGE 1

1990.12.31

90.08.17 18:57

외신 2과 통제관 CD

0139

7. 일본인 업체근로자들도 공사중단하고 8.14 부터 선별적으로 출국허가되고 있으나, 외교관및 가족들은 영, 미 등과함께 출국금지 조치당하고있음. 또한 일본은 공관및 개인은행구좌가 전부 폐쇄되었으며 서독등 이라크 자산을 동결한 국가들도 이 카테고리에 포함시키고있음. 끝

(대사 최봉름-국장)

예고:90.12.31

관리 번호	90-601

원 본

외 무 부

종 별 :

번 호 : MAW-1072 일 시 : 90 0817 1830

수 신 : 장관(기협,아동,사본:동자부장관)

발 신 : 주 말련 대사

제 목 : 이라크,쿠웨이트 사태: 원유 안정확보

연:MAW-1045,1051

대:WMA-0559

1. 본직은 금 8.17 주재국 수상실 SULAIMAN 장관(에너지 담당)을 면담, 이라크. 쿠웨이트 사태 전반에 관해 의견을 교환하였음.

2. 말련 정부는 현사태의 장기화및 유가의 급상승이 산유국, 비산유국 모두에게 바람직하지 않은 영향을 초래할것으로 보며, 사태의 조속한 진정을 희망하고 있다함. 동 장관은 사우디등 일부 OPEC 산유국이 원유를 증산하여 대 이라크 봉쇄조치를 측면 지원할 가능성이 큰 것으로 본다함. 그러나 이란, 베네주엘라등일부국가는 금번 사태를 자국의 이익을 위해 EXPLOIT 한다는 인상을 주지 않기위해 원유 증산에 매우 소극적이라함. 말련은 전체의 생산능력(현재 일산 595,000배럴)도 별로 크지않고, 자원 보존정책에 의한 증산 제한 원칙이 있기때문에 급속한 증산은 기대할수 없으나, 연호와 같이 우선 인근 ASEAN 국가들의 긴급한 수요에 부응키 위해 일단 10,000 배럴의 증산을 결정하였함.

3. 본직은 아국의 원유 수급현황을 설명하고, 아국 정유사로부터의 구체적 증량 공급 요청이 있을 경우 호의적 고려를 요청하였음. 동 장관은 현재 일본, 인도, 불란서 등으로부터 증량공급 요청이 접수돼 있다하고, 아국으로부터 그러한 요청이 있을경우 양국간의 긴밀한 관계에 비추어 최대한 호의적으로 검토하겠다함. 끝

(대사 홍순영-국장)

예고:90.12.31 까지

경제국	장관	차관	1차보	2차보	아주국	통상국	청와대	안기부
동자부√	대책반							

PAGE 1

90.08.17 21:54

외신 2과 통제관 CW

0141

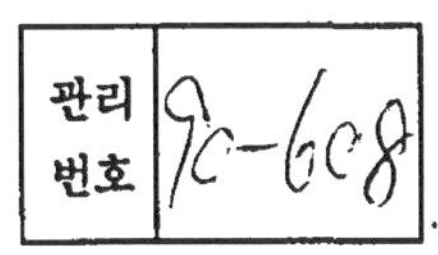

원 본

외 무 부

종 별 :

번 호 : NJW-0653 일 시 : 90 0817 1730

수 신 : 장 관(기협,아프일)

발 신 : 주 나이제리아 대사

제 목 : 나이제리아의 원유생산(자료응신 71호)

연:NJW-0628

1. 나이제리아 정부는 표면적으로는 중동사태로 인한 국제적 원유부족상황에도 불구하고 OPEC 할당량 초과생산하지 않을 뜻을 거듭밝히고 있으나, 당지의 국제석유회사들에 의하면, 나이제리아는 중동사태전 일산 123 만 배럴생산하던 것을 현재 170 만 배럴 생산하고 있으며, 앞으로 1 주일후에는 190 만, 2 주일후에는 200 만 배럴을 생산예정이며, 초과생산분은 현재 SPOT MARKET 에서 판매중이라함.

3. 이와같은 예기치 않은 국고 수입증가는 경제적으로는 물론 4 월의 쿠데타기도후 정치적으로 불안정한 현 정권에 큰 도움이 될것으로 보임.

(대사 오채기-국장)

예고:90.12.31 까지

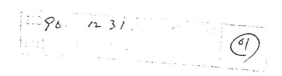

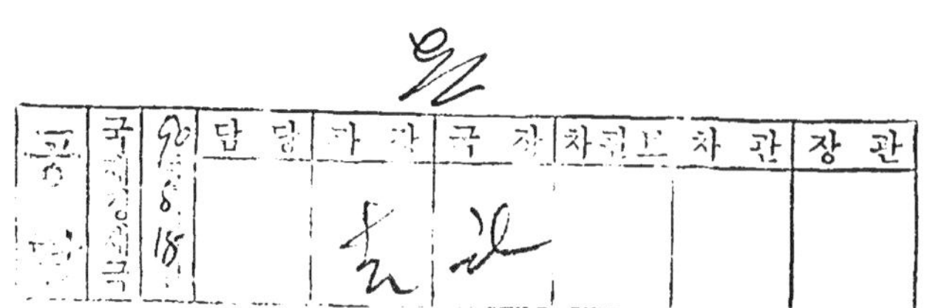

경제국	차관	1차보	2차보	중아국	중아국	통상국	정문국	청와대
안기부	동자부 ✓	대책반						

PAGE 1

90.08.18 06:41

외신 2과 통제관 CW

0142

원 본

관리번호	90-609

외 무 부

종 별 :

번 호 : EQW-0327 일 시 : 90 0817 1800

수 신 : 장관(기협,통일)

발 신 : 주 에쿠아돌 대사

제 목 : 원유안정 확보를 위한 대산유국 외교활동

대:WEQ-0188

1. 대호 지시에 의거, 당관 배 1 등서기관은 금 8.17.(금) 주재국 석유공사(PETROECUADOR) BISMARCK W. ANDRADE 원유 판매담당 이사를 예방하여, 아국 호남정유와의 계약물량(18 천 BD)이 정상적으로 공급되도록 협조를 요청하였는바, 동인은 계약물량을 차질없이 공급하겠다고 하면서, 금년 11 월말경 12 천 BD 에 대한 입찰이 있을 예정인데, 동입찰에 아국업체의 참가를 요청하였음.

2. 주재국은 8.16.(목) 부터 배럴당 원유 수출가격 산정기준을 아래와 같이변경하였음을 참고로 보고함.

가. 미국 서안 및 한국등 태평양 국가로 수출할 경우:

최근 5 일의 ALASKA NORTH SLOP(ANS) 평균가격 - $ 1.11

나. 미국 GULF 지역 및 여타국가:

최근 5 일의 ANS 평균가격의 60% 미 TEXAS 서부 중질유의 40% - $ 1.63. 끝.

(대사 정해웅 - 국장)

예고:1990. 12. 31. 일반

90 12 31

공람	국제경제국	90 8 18	담 당	과 장	국 장	차관보	차 관	장 관
				[signature]	[signature]			

경제국 차관 1차보 2차보 통상국 동자부

PAGE 1

90.08.18 08:58

외신 2과 통제관 FE

0143

이라크·쿠웨이트 사태에 따른 석유 수급 및 유가 전망

(공관 보고 요약)

미국

o 이라크·쿠웨이트 원유공급 완전봉쇄시 400만B/D 공급 부족 발생

o 미국, 국내생산 46.9%, 해외도입 53.1% (이중 이라크·쿠웨이트로부터 도입분이 8.7% 차지)

o 미국, 단기간내 국내생산 기대 불가

o 이라크·쿠웨이트 원유공급 중단에 따른 원유 부족분의 충당 가능요소

- 세계 원유재고 사용 (1.8억배럴)
- 각국의 전략 비축분 사용 (미국5.9%, 일본2.1억, 서독 0.53억 배럴등)
- 원유추가 생산능력 활용 (사우디, UAE, 나이지리아, 베네주엘라등) 약 550만B/D

o 교통부, 각종 운수회사에게 가격인상에 대한 과잉반응 자제 촉구
법무부, 휘발유 가격인상의 반독점법 위반 여부 감시중

인니

o 인니 원유생산 및 수출 :

- 최대 생산능력 (1.6백만B/D), OPEC 쿼타량 (1.4백만B/D)
- 현 생산량 : 70만 B/D
- 수입 : 사우디, 이라크, 이란등로부터 10만B/D

o 유가 일시 상승하나, 30불선 넘지 않을 전망

o 유가의 안정과 원유자원의 장기확보를 위해 OPEC 쿼타량 이하 생산, 저가 원유 및 정유 수시 수입등 실시

- 이라크 원유수입 (3-4만B/D) 중지하더라도 원유수급 차질 없을 것으로 예상

0144

브라질

o 이라크·쿠웨이트에서 19만B/D 도입 : 총 도입량 55만B/D의 35%

o 석유공사, 원유수입 10개국과 추가도입 교섭 개시 예정

멕시코

o 국영석유회사 (PEMEX) 사장, 향후 60동안 10만B/D 증산 발표 (8.8)
  - '82년 외채위기 이후, PEMEX 에 대한 투자 75% 삭감, 원유생산의 급격한 증대는 현실적으로 기대 곤란

o 여타 산유국의 현저한 증산도 각국 사정상 어려울 것이며, 이라크·쿠웨이트 사태가 종식될 경우 유가가 다소 안정화 될 수 있으나, 이미 급등한 유가가 사태발발이전 상태로 되돌아가지 않을 것이라는 것이 일반적 견해

이란

o 현재상황 상당기간 계속 예상
  - 사우디로 확대시, 국제원유시장 혼란 우려

o 단기적으로 국제원유시장에 공급부족현상 없을 것이나, 주요 소비국이 비축분 사용보다 우선 국제시장구입을 선호할 것이므로 원유가 다소 상승 예상

o 이란은 원유시장의 급작스런 변동을 원하지 않으며, 질서있는 원유수급의 확보와 장기적 시장 안정을 위해서는 OPEC 생산국 및 소비국간 협의가 있어야 한다고 봄

o 금번사태로 아국이 원유공급에 문제가 발생시, 이란은 양국간 우호관계를 고려, 필요한 협조를 할 용의 표명

0145

불란서

o 중·단기적으로 embargo 및 blockade효과, 인플레 기대심리에 따라 유가 상승 (최고 30-35불)할 것이나, 이같은 상승세 6-12개월 초과하지 않을것임

o 장기적으로 하기사항 감안시 제 3차 oil shock 도래 용이하지 않음

- 원유비축량, 대체에너지개발 및 원유소비절약, OPEC 점유 비율감소 각국의 세제감면 혜택등

o 불란서 대책 : 유가동결 (1차 시한 : 9.15까지), 당분간 유통 마진불허용 및 세재 혜택으로 통제

일본

[석유수급]

o 이라크·쿠웨이트 각각 세계 석유소비량의 3.5%, 2.2% 생산

- 사태 장기화시, 국제적 석유수급 핍박으로 인한 영향 지대 예상

- 단기적으로는, OECD 가맹국의 비축량, 여타 산유국의 생산능력, 현재 석유비수요기등 감안 국제수급에 대한 영향 적을 것으로 예상

※ 석유수급은 산유국의 생산동향 및 소비국의 수요동향에 달려 있음

[유가 전망]

o 국제 석유가는 IEA 비축량 방출 및 사우디등의 증산에 의해 영향을 받을 것임

o 중장기적 관점에서 배럴당 25달러 이상이 되면 에너지 절약화 및 대체 에너지로의 전환으로 석유수요가 감퇴하므로 25달러 수준이 한계

[대책]

o 석유소비량 감축, 석유공급선 대체, 석유비축방출을 기본으로 하여 중동 사태후 이에따라 단계적 실시 예정

0146

사우디

o 원유시장의 재고분, 각국의 비축분, OPEC 회원국들의 증산등 고려시, 유가 상승추세 곧 진정예상

- 브렌트기준 배럴당 30불 수준을 넘지 않을 것이라는 다수 견해

o 사우디, 곧 산유량 증대 예상 : 현 보유량 일산 530B/D이나 일산 800만B/D 산유능력 보유

말련

o 금번 사태 계속될 시, 단기적으로 원유의 국제수급 및 유가에 대한 심각한 상황 예상

- 그러나 이·이전 경험에 비추어 종국적으로는 고유가의 장기간 지속이 있을 것으로 보지 않음

베네주엘라 | 동자부 SEDWICKS 국제협력국장 및 석유공사 SPORN 국제협력부장 접촉결과

o 베네주엘라는 사태의 장기화 경우에도 배럴당 21불선에서 국제원유가 안정되는 것이 베네주엘라 이익에 합당

o Figueredo 외상, 여타 OPEC 회원국 순방, 증산고섭중

- 사태 장기화 경우에도 유가는 현수준 안정 예상

o 베네주엘라는 사태의 장기화가 국제원유시장 불안을 초래할 것으로 판단될 경우, 국내생산가능시설(280만B/D)을 최대한 가동하는 한편, 비OPEC 회원국과도 접촉, 증산 권유 계획

0147

호주

o 단기적으로 유가인상에 의한 국제경제 침체현상 예상

o 장기적으로 유가는 현수준보다 25-50% 까지 인상 예상
(인상추세의 지속기간은 의문)

- 유가인상으로 생산증가요인 발생, 여타 산유국 450만B/D 증산으로 부족분 충당 가능 전망

o 대책 : 인플레 억제 위한 대내적 조치 강구, 유가인상억제 위한 에너지 소비세 인하, 예산지출규모축소, 석유시추 및 개발회사에 대한 혜택 고려등

브루나이

o 국제유가가 당분간 인상될 것으로 보이나, 여타 산유국의 증산 움직임 보도 등도 있어 국제수급에는 큰 차질 없을 것이며, 유가인상세도 완화 예상

UAE

o 현재 유가가 배럴당 32불까지 폭등하고 있으나 일시적 현상이며, 시장기능은 회복, 조만간 진정 예상

카나다

o 이라크·쿠웨이트산 원유에 대한 금수조치 불구, 90.3/4분기까지는 현상태의 국제석유수급 균형이 대체로 유지될 것이고, 유가도 현 수준을 능가하지 않을 것으로 전망 (8.9)

- 여타 산유국의 추가공급능력보유, 그동안 OPEC 초과생산으로 OECD 국가의 충분한 재고보유, OECD국가의 OPEC는 석유수요 (2,180만 B/D)의 쿠웨이트 이라크제외 OPEC 산유량 (2,210B/D) 미달

0148

o 금번 제재조치가 4/4분기까지 지속되는 경우, 석유수급차질 및 유가추가 인상 압력 예상

- 4/4분기 난방등 계절요인 작용

o 카나다는 약 10만B/D의 원유 출초로 현재로서는 사태추이 모니터링 단계

EC (8.10)

o IEA 집행위 8.9 긴급 총회 개최

- 이라크·쿠웨이트 원유공급중단 불구, 전세계적으로 원유공급량 충분 판단, 당장 전략비축석유 사용이나 특별에너지 절약계획시행등 긴급조치 상황 아님

- 최근 유가인상은 즉각적인 원유공급부족사태에 기인하기보다는 불확실에 대한 심리적 반응으로 평가

  · 국제 석유회사들에게 현재 충분한 상업적비축활용과 현물시장에서의 과도한 원유구입 자제 촉구

o Gulf만 위기가 더이상 악화되지 않을 경우, 최근의 유가급등 현상은 조만간 진정되어 배럴당 20-21불 수준 회복 전망

- Gulf만 위기 이전 약 2백만B/D의 공급초과 현상 존재

- OPEC, 약 3.7백만B/D의 추가공급능력

- IEA 가맹국, 약 10억 배럴의 전략 비축량 보유

o 향후 유가는 원유의 수요공급측면보다 오히려 Gulf만의 정치 상황변화에 따라 움직일 것으로 전망

카타르 (8.10)

o 세계 석유시장의 충분한 비축여유로 향후 3개월간은 석유부족사태가 일어나지 않을 것이며 OPEC 각국이 3개월간 생산쿼타를 준수한다면 적정 원유가 형성 가능 (8.6 이란 석유상)

0149

o 심리적벽이라 생각되는 유가 30불선은 이라크가 사우디를 침공하지 않는 한 무너지지 않을 것임. (8.7 불란서 석유공사 TOTAL의 동반구 담당부장)

o 카타르 1만B/D 이상 증산 불가능

o 주요 소비국에 약 1백일분의 비축량이 있기 때문에 당분간 현재의 유가상승 없을 것임(8.11 카타르 석유공사 원유 판매부장)

카이로 (8.10)

o 여타 산유국의 증산능력으로 1.2차 오일 쇼크때와 같은 급격한 유가상승은 없을 것임

o 사태가 사우디 반도로 확전될 시, 원유공급 부족 불가피 사태 호전시까지 각국별 비상에너지 대책 발동 필요

에쿠아돌 (8.10)

o 비중동 OPEC 회원국, 생산설비, 매장량, 여타 회원국과의 관계 감안시, 단시간내 쿼타량의 10-20% 이상의 증산은 난망

- 단기간내 국제원유수급 불균형은 비 OPEC 회원국 (멕시코, 영국, 소련등)의 증산과 소비국의 수요감축, 대체에너지 사용등으로 대체 전망

o OPEC은 이미 기준유가를 21불로 상향 조정한 바 있으므로 금번 사태는 기준유가 또는 그 이상 가격유지의 촉매 작용 전망

- 그러나 산유국들도 급격한 원유가 상승보다 배럴당 미화 21불선을 상회하는 수준에서 점진적이고 안정적인 원유가 상승 희구

나이지리아 (8.17)

o 석유회사들에 의하면, 중동사태전 123만B/D 생산에서 현재 170만B/D 생산하고 있으며, 앞으로 1주일후에는 190만B/D, 2주일후에는 200만B/D 생산 예정이며, 초과생산분은 현재 SPOT MARKET 에서 판매중

0150

서독 (8.13) 외무부 원유담당관 언급 요지

o 단기간에는 가격변동의 폭이 크게 작용할 것이나, 중기 (3개월)로 볼때 배럴당 약 23불선 유지 전망
o 일부 산유국의 증산계획 언급 및 움직임, 북해 유전의 증산 가능성이 이라크 쿠웨이트 산유량 감소를 보전할 것이므로 중장기로 보아 유가는 안정적 방향으로 갈 것으로 전망

이태리 (8.13)

o 과거 오일 쇼크와는 달리 평가되며, 유가는 최근 수준보다 높은 수준 전망되어 세계경제에 인플레 압박등 어느정도 부정적 효과 예상
o 각국의 충분한 비축량, 생산국 재고량등으로 앞으로 2-3개월간 국제수급에 차질이 예상되지 않으며, 유가도 2-3개월간은 배럴당 21-22불선을 유지하고 그이후에도 25불선 정도 예상

0151

정 리 보 존 문 서 목 록					
기록물종류	일반공문서철	등록번호	2021010195	등록일자	2021-01-27
분류번호	763.5	국가코드	XF	보존기간	영구
명 칭	걸프사태 : 국제원유 수급 동향, 1990-91. 전6권				
생 산 과	기술협력과	생산년도	1990~1991	담당그룹	
권 차 명	V.2 1990.8.18-31				
내용목차	* 국제원유 수급 및 유가전망, 원유 안정확보를 위한 대산유국 외교활동 강화 등				

0001

지급

동 력 자 원 부

원유 29210-5748　　503-9627　　1990. 8.18.

수신 외무부장관
참조 경제국장
　　이.쿠사태대책반장

제목 『이.쿠』 사태와 관련한 각국의 동향파악 협조요청

1. 최근의 이라크.쿠웨이트 사태와 관련하여 당부는 민생유류의 소요 물량 확보와 가격안정을 위하여 다각적인 방안을 강구하여 추진중에 있읍니다.

2. 이에 우리나라의 원유확보 및 석유수급안정대책 수립에 참고코자 현지대사관으로 하여금 아래사항에 대하여 협조요청하오니 당부로 회시하여 주시기 바랍니다.

아 래

1) 산유국

- 대상국가 :사우디,이란,UAE,오만,베네주엘라,에쿠아돌,리비아,페루, 가봉,인도네시아,말레이지아,멕시코,이집트,브르네이,소련, 미국,케나다,영국

- 조사사항
  - 산유능력, 최근의 생산량, 석유소비량, 수출량 및 수출국별 현황, 수출시 기간계약 현황
  - 이.쿠사태에 따른 증산실시 여부(증산시 예상물량)

0002

원유 29210-5148

- 향후 국제원유시장에 대한 수급 및 가격전망(OPEC회원국인 경우 OPEC임시회의 개최 가능성 및 이에 대한 주재국 반응 포함)

- 기타 주재국의 산유정책 관련사항

2)소비국

ㅇ 대상국가 :미국,캐나다,영국,프랑스,독일,이태리,일본,대만,스페인, 소련

ㅇ 조사사항

- 석유소비량,도입국별 물량,사태전이라크.쿠웨이트로부터의 도입물량 (기간계약 및 현물시장 구분)

- 원유 및 석유제품 비축현황(물량,지속일수등),비축유 방출여부 및 향후계획

- 이라크.쿠웨이트로부터의 수입물량 감소에 대한 확보대책 및 대응 방안(에너지절약대책 포함)

- 이.쿠사태와 관련한 주재국의 유류가격 동향

- 향후 국제원유시장에 대한 수급 및 가격전망

- 기타 우리나라 원유확보와 석유수급안정대책 수립시 참고사항. 끝.

동 력 자 원 부 장

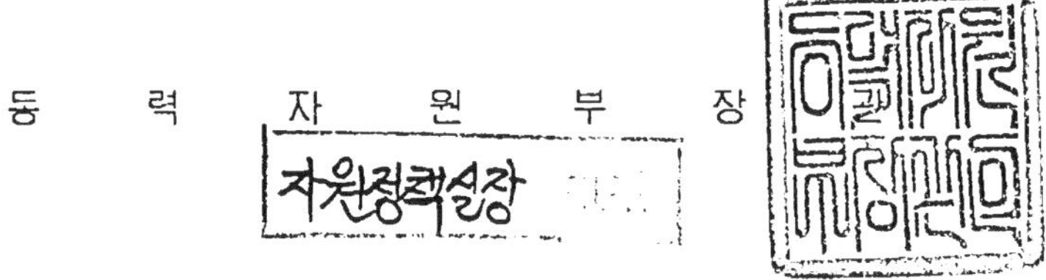

0003

장관 (기협) ~~(통제)~~

수신처 참조 900819 1218 지급.

석유 수급 및 유가 동향 등 파악

최근의 이라크·쿠웨이트 사태와 관련, 아국의 원유 확보 및 석유수급 안정대책 수립에 참고코자 하니 아래 사항 파악, 지급 보고 바람.

(우선) ~~(외교)~~ 리포트리 로

1. 산유국 관련 사항
   - 산유 능력, 최근의 생산량, 석유 소비량, 수출량 및 수출국별 현황, 수출시 기간계약 현황
   - 이·쿠 사태에 따른 증산 실시 여부 (증산시 예상 물량)
2. 이라크·쿠웨이트로 부터의 수입물량 감소에 대한 확보대책 및 대응 방안 (에너지 절약대책 포함)
3. 주재국의 유류 가격 동향
4. 향후 국제원유 시장에 대한 수급 및 가격 전망
5. 기타 아국의 원유확보와 석유수급 안정 대책 수립시 참고 사항. 끝. (국제경제국장 최대화)

수신처: 주 사우디, 이란, UAE, 오만, 베네수엘라, 에콰도르, 리비아, 페루, 가봉, 인도네시아, 말레이시아, 멕시코, 부르나이, 미국, 카나다, 영국 대사
주 카이로 총영사
주 쏘 영사처장

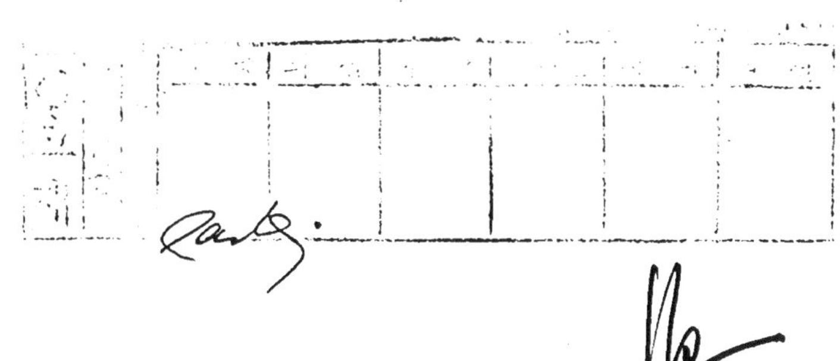

0004

WSB-0336 외 별지참조

WSB-0336 900319 1218 CT

WIR -0276 WAE -0169 WOM -0122 WVZ -0267 WEQ -0193
WLY -0302 WPU -0353 WGA -0124 WDJ -0650 WMA -0582
WMX -0732 WBU -0112 WUS -2739 WCN -0850 WUK -1379
WCA -0297 WSV -0598

0005

이라크·쿠웨이트 사태가 아국경제에 미치는 영향

8. 20

국제경제국

1. 원유수급 및 유가문제
   - o 이라크·쿠웨이트로부터의 장기계약 물량 75천B/D (이라크20천B/D, 쿠웨이트55천B/D)의 도입중단
     - 동 부족분 대체 확보 필요
   - o 유가상승으로 인한 국내물가 및 국제수지등에 대한 부정적 영향
     - 국제원유가 1$/B 상승시 국내유가 5% 인상 및 도매물가 0.44%, 소비자물가 0.07% 상승요인
     - 국제원유가 1$ 상승시 원유수입 대전은 년간 330백만불 증대
     - 선진국의 수입수요감소및 일본엔화의 약세에 따른 아국상품의 수출환경 악화
2. 해외건설수지의 악화
   - o 이라크·쿠웨이트지역의 신규수주 중단
   - o 이라크·쿠웨이트 진출 건설사업의 차질 예상
     - 공사대금등 992백만불의 결제 불투명

(단위 :천불)

구분	계	기성미수	유보금	어음	기타
이라크	927,466	32,454	124,813	601,616	168,583
쿠웨이트	65,000	32,000	33,000	-	-
합 계	992,466	64,454	157,813	601,616	168,583

     - 858백만불 상당의 잔여공사 계속도 차질 예상

(단위 : 백만불)

구 분	계약 금액	시공 잔액
이라크	1,208	776
쿠웨이트	211	82
합 계	1,419	858

   - o 기타 중동지역에서의 건설사업도 사태진전에 따라서는 영향 받을 것으로 예상
3. 일반상품 수출 중단
   - o 90년 상반기 아국수출: 이라크 82,481천불, 쿠웨이트 98,757천불 수출 (아국전체수출의 0.4%)

0006

관리번호	90-618

원 본

외 무 부

종 별 : 지 급

번 호 : MAW-1082　　　　일 시 : 90 0820 1800

수 신 : 장관(기협,아동,사본:동자부장관)

발 신 : 주 말련 대사

제 목 : 석유 수급및 유가 동향 파악

대: WMA-0582

연: MAW-1072

1. 대호 아래 보고함.

가. 산유국 관련사항

0 산유능력: 일산 약 60 만 배럴

0 최근의 생산량: 일산 595,000 배럴

0 석유 소비량: 일산 약 13 만 배럴

0 수출현황(89 년 년간 수출 통계, 단위 천톤)

싱가폴: 6,184, 29.0 프로

한국: 3,902, 18.3 프로

일본: 3,689, 17.3 프로

미국: 1,429, 6.7 프로

태국: 1,365, 6.4 프로

필리핀: 1,130, 5.3 프로

기타: 3,624, 17.0 프로

0 이, 쿠 사태에 따른 증산: 일산 10,000 배럴 증산 결정

나. 주재국의 유류가격 동향

이.쿠 사태 이후의 국제 원유가격 상승을 고려하여 9.1 부터 유가 인상을 예정하고 있으며, 인상률은 약 5 프로가 될것으로 예측되고 있음.

다. 향후 국제 원유 시장에 대한 수급및 가격 전망

연호 보고한 바와 같이 주재국 현 상태의 장기화및 유가의 급속한 상승이 산유국, 비산유국 모두에게 바람직하지 않은 영향을 초래할 것으로 보며, 유가 안정을 위한

경제국 1차보 2차보 아주국 통상국 동자부 대책반

PAGE 1

90.08.20 19:24

외신 2과 통제관 BT

0007

노력이 꾸준히 전개될 것으로 예측함. 따라서 금번 사태로 인한 다소간의 유가 인상은 피할수 없다 하더라도, 지난 2 차에 걸친 유류파동과 같은 급속한 가격 상승이나 수급 분균형은 방지될수 있을 것으로 보고있음.

라. 기타 참고 사항: 주재국의 원유 생산량은 타국에 비해 소량이며, 금번 증산분도 1 만 배럴에 지나지 않아 아국이 추가로 도입할수 있는 물량은 제한적일 것으로 보임. 금번 사태를 계기로 LNG 도입의 조기 추진 검토가 필요하다고 보며, 이때 수입선 다변화의 관점에서 동일한 조건이라면 말련산 LNG 도입에 호의적 고려를 함이 바람직하다고 판단됨.

2. 관련 사항 파악되는 대로 수시 보고하겠음. 끝

(대사 홍순영-국장)

90.12.31 까지

원 본

외 무 부

종 별 :

번 호 : DJW-1202 일 시 : 90 0820 1540

수 신 : 장관(기협,정일)

발 신 : 주 인니대사

제 목 : 석유수급및 유가동향등 파악 (자응 72호)

대: WDJ-0650

대호관련 주재국 상황을에 관해 광업에너지성 대외협력국장 대리와 긴급 면담한 내용 하기 보고함

1.산유국 관련동향

가.산유능력: 1,600,000베럴

나.최근생산량: 1,290,000베럴

다.석유소비량: 800,000베럴

라.수출량및 수출국별 현황: 700,000베럴

일본:55.7프로,미국 24.7프로, 대만 3.9프로, 한국 3.8프로, 싱가폴 3.4프로, 호주 3,0프로, 뉴질랜드 1.1프로, 이태리 0.2프로, 기타 0.9프로

마.수출시 기간계약 현황: 10년 내외의 장기판매계약 체결

바.증산실시 여부: 산유능력은 있으나, 주재국의 장기 원유자원 확보정책 때문에 어떠한 경우도 증산은 고려할수 없음

2.수입물량 감소에 대한 확보대책및 방안

이락으로부터 아리비안나잇 CRUDE 3 만베럴 수입선을 사우디로 기전환하고, 이란으로부터 수입량을 증가시키고 있음

3.유류가격 동향

국내 유류가격 인상은 고려하지 않고 있으며 수출가격은 MARKET PRICE 를 적용함

4.국제원유 시장에 대한 수급및 가격전망

OPEC 의 단합을 통해 가격안정및 쿼타 준수노력을 계속할것이며 지난 7월 OPEC이 합의한 공시가격 21분선에서 안정되도록 다각적인 협력을 모색중임

5.기타

경제국 정문국 동자부 안기부 2차보

PAGE 1

90.08.20 22:05 DA

외신 1과 통제관

0003

가.사우디와 베네주엘라가 요청하는 긴급 OPEC회의 소집은 시기적으로 불적합하며 세계원유 재고량을 파악한후 8월말 또는 9월초 임시회의 소집 가능성을 타진중임

나. GINANDJAR 장관은 세계원유 비축량이 300만 베럴이 가장 적절하나 현 비축량은 500만 베럴 이상이므로 국제유가 안정을 위해 OPEC 이 증산하기보다 소비국의비축량을 소비토록 유도해 나갈것이라고 함

6.관계기관과 계속 접촉 위계임. 끝

(대사 김재춘-국장)

원 본

외 무 부

종 별 :

번 호 : LYW-0512 일 시 : 90 0820 1400

수 신 : 장관(기협,마그)

발 신 : 주 리비아 대사

제 목 : 석유 수급및 유가 동향등 파악

대: WLY-0302

1. 사유 관련 사항

가.산유능력은 160-200만 정도이나

나.오펙식 쿼타 123만 이하를 생산하면서 3/4부터 160만 생산 계획중에 있었음.그러나 이.쿠 사태로 증산 계획을 보류하고 있는 것으로 보임

다.최근 생산량:110만

라.자체 소비량:14만

마.수출량:32만(독일,이태리,불란서및 동구제국으로 GG 및 SPOT 혼용)

바.제품 상태 46만(해외 정유능력 이태리에 55만, 자체 31만)

사.물물 교환및 부채 상환: 20만 7천(건설 대전및 부책 15만)

부채및건설: 토이기: 6만, 소련: 3만, 이태리: 4만, 희랍: 1만5천, 유고: 1만2천, 기타: 5만(현대,삼성,비정기적 대우는 상당량)

아.수출 계약 기간: 1년 단위

자.이.쿠 사태 이후 증산하지 않고 있음. 증산하는 경우 160-200만 가능함

2.이미 건의한바와 같이 건설 업체의 공사대전으로 지불되는 원유를 국내용으로확보 하는것이 바람직함. 진출 3사중 삼성과 현대는 비정기적으로 받으나 대우는거의 정기적으로 지급받고 있음을 유의 바람

-이.쿠 사태전 원유 가격은 아래와 같음

명칭, GSP, SPORT PRICE(BRENT 대비),의 순서임 (단위: 미불)

BREGA, 18.67, 18.67

ZUEITINA, 18.67, -0.05

ESLSIDIR, 18.52, -0.50

경제국 중아국 동자부 그차관 1차보 통상국 대책반 안기부

PAGE 1

90.08.20 22:28 DA

외신 1과 통제관

0011

SIRTICA, 18.60, -0.35

SARIR, 18.05, -1.25

AMNA, 17.80, -1.35

3. 수출 가격은 GSP 와 SPOT 가격임. 바타및 부채 공사 대전은 GSP 와 넷백으로혼용됨. 증산을할 경우 가격 상승의 이득을 위해 수출량을 늘릴 것으로 전망됨.

4. 산유국들이 증산을 시작한다 해도 이.쿠 생산량에 가늠하는 양의 증산은 불가능 할것으로 보임. 설사 가능하더라도 상당한 시일이 걸릴것임. 뿐만 아니라 이.쿠 사태 당사자 격인 걸프만 제국을 제외한 여타 산유국은 이번 사태로 인한 유가앙등의 절호의 기회를 이용할 것은 틀림없음

5. 해외건설 공사가 많은 우리나라로서는 저유가 시대에 공사 대전을 원유로 지급 받어 국내 반입이 불가능하여 SPOT 에 처분 하므로서 막대한 손실이 있었음.이는 거대한 공사를 하고 있는 건설회사가 국내 정유 사업과 연관이 없기 때문임. 안정적 확보와 수급을 위해서는 건설회사가 직접 정유사업에 참가하든가, 유개공이건설 대전 원유를 무조건 인수하도록 하는 장기적 대책이 필요할 것임. 끝

(대사 최필립-국장)

PAGE 2

0012

관리 번호 90-619 | 원 본

외 무 부

종 별 :

번 호 : SBW-0694 일 시 : 90 0820 1700

수 신 : 장 관(기협,중근동,동자부,기정)

발 신 : 주 사우디 대사

제 목 : 주재국 석유동향

연:SBW-336

8.19 주재국 석유광물부는 연호 2 항 관련 UPI 보도(NAZER 장관이 일산 200 만 베럴증산위협) 내용을 국영통신을 통해 공식 부인하고, NAZER 장관 언급 내용은 현 OPEC CEILING 보다 200 만 베럴이상 여유가 있다고 말한것이 와전된것 이라고 해명함.

(대사 주병국-국장)

예고:90.12.31 까지

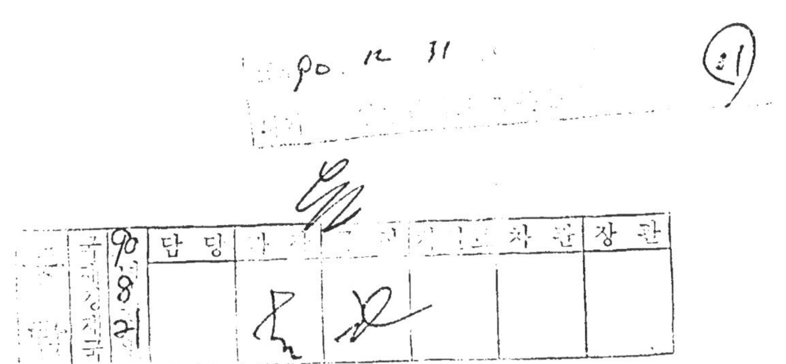

경제국 차관 1차보 2차보 중아국 안기부 동자부

PAGE 1

90.08.21 00:40

외신 2과 통제관 DO

0013

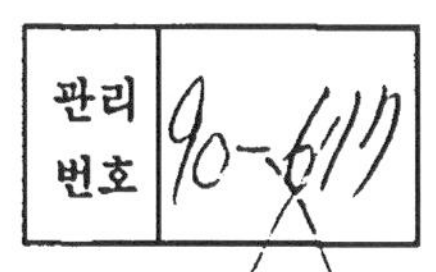

원 본

외 무 부

종 별 :

번 호 : SBW-0695 일 시 : 90 0820 1710

수 신 : 장관(기협,중근동,동자부)

발 신 : 주 사우디 대사

제 목 : 원유안정확보

대:WSB-310,336

연:SBW-667

1. 8.19 정우성 참사관은 DAHRAN 소재 사우디 국영 석유회사의 HANSARD 원유 판매부장을 방문, 당초 금년 9 월 또는 10 월 예정되어 있던 선경(유공)과 ARAMCO 간의 장기공급 계약 서명 및 사우디산 원유의 증량 공급문제에 대한 협조를 요청한바, 동인 언급내용을 하기보고함.

가. 선경과의 계약은 최근 사태에도 불구하고 9 월에 서명토록 준비중임.

나. 최근 선경측이 상기계약상 인도시기(90.2)를 앞당겨 9 월부터계약 물량(일산 35,000 베럴)을 인도하는 가능성을 타진하여 왔으나, 동문제는 불원 개최될 긴급 OPEC 회의 이후 검토될수있을것임.

다. 계약물량 증대 문제도 나항과 같은 시기에 검토될수 있을것이나 ARAMCO 측은 계약상의 공급물량 변경 보다는 사우디측 물량에 여유가 있을 경우 계약과는 별도로 수시로 증량 판매하는 방안을 선호하고 있음.(계약내용 변경의 경우에는 공급량을 감축할수 있도록 명기)

2. 한편 연호 사우디의 연호 긴급 OPEC 회의 소집요구 관련, 8.18 NAZER 석유장관은 기자회견을 통해 OPEC 회의 개최의 급박성을 재강조하고 만약동 회의가 개최되지 못하거나 동회의시 산유량 증대에 대한 합의가 이루어 지지 않는다면 주재국은 독자적으로 증산을 단행 할것이며, 수일내에 일산 200 만 베럴까지는추가 생산할수 있다고 말한바, 이와 관련 상기면담시 원유판매부장의 설명내용은 아래와 같음.

가.8.19 오전 현재 OPEC 13 개회원국중 과반수인 7 개국이 긴급 OPEC 회의 소집에 찬성하는 의사표시를 한바 있어, 동회의는 불원 개최될것으로 봄.

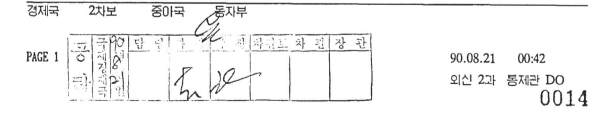

경제국 2차보 중아국 동자부

PAGE 1

공람	국제경제국	90년 8월 21일	담당	과장	심의관	국장	차관보	차관	장관

90.08.21 00:42

외신 2과 통제관 DO

0014

나.NAZER 석유장관 언급내용과 같이 금번 OPEC 회의에서의 합의 여부와 관계없이 동회의만 끝나면 사우디는 증산에 들어갈것이나 일산 200 만 베럴까지 증산할것으로는 보지않음(사우디의 생산능력상 일산 200 만 증산은 이론적으로는 가능하나, 이경우 수요가 크지않은 중질유의 생산량이 크게늘게되어 판매에 어려움이 있음)

3. 상기와 같이 주재국의 산유량 증대 방침이 확실하고, 늦어도 9 월경에는 증산분의 대고객 배분 결정이 있을 것으로 보여지는바, 선경측이 보다 구체적인 조건등을 마련하여 ARAMCO 측과 적극적으로 (776)촉하는것이 필요할것으로 사료됨. 끝

(대사 주병국-국장)

예고:90.12.31 까지

PAGE 2

0015

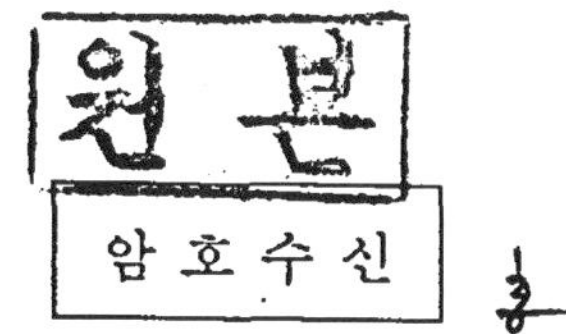

외 무 부

종 별 : 지 급

번 호 : EQW-0330 일 시 : 90 0820 1610

수 신 : 장관(기협)

발 신 : 주 에쿠아돌 대사대리

제 목 : 석유 수급 및 유가 동향 파악

대:WEQ-0193

연:EQW-0327

대호 관련, 지시사항 아래 보고함.

1. 산유국 관련 사항

- 산유능력: 최대생산 가능량은 31 만 BD

- 최근 생산량: 28 만 BD

- 석유 소비량: 11 만 BD

- 수출 량: 17 만 BD

- 수출국별 현황(단위:BD), 한국:18 천, 일본:12 천, 대만:15 천, 칠레:12 천, 브라질:7.5 천, 미국:105.5 천

- 수출 계약 기간: 1 년

2. 주재국의 유류가격 동향

- 연호 2 항 보고와 같이 미국서안 및 한국등 태평양 국가로 수출할 경우는 ANS 가격에 따라 결정되며, 8.17. 수출가격은 배럴당 23.88 불임.

- 국내 시판 가격: 이락. 쿠웨이트 사태 발발 이전과 동일

3. 향후 국제 원유 시장에 대한 수급 및 가격 전망: 급격한 원유가 인상보다는 OPEC 기준가 21 불을 조금 상회하는 선에서 결정될 것으로 전망하고 있음.

4. 아국 원유 확보 대책시 참고 사항: 연호 1 항 보고와 같이 주재국은 금년 11 월말 12 천 BD 에 대한 국제 입찰이 있을 예정임, 끝.

(대사 대리 - 국장)

공람	국제경제국 90.8.21	담 당	과 장	국 장	차관보	차 관	장 관
			(서명)	(서명)			

경제국 차관 1차보 2차보 통상국 동자부

PAGE 1 90.08.21 07:10

외신 2과 통제관 EZ

0016

원 본

외 무 부

종 별 :

번 호 : CNW-1250 일 시 : 90 0820 1830

수 신 : 장 관(기협,미북,중동,정일,동자부)

발 신 : 주 카나다 대사

제 목 : 석유수급 및 유가동향 파악(자료응신 제 88 호)

대 : WCN-0850

주재국 에너지 광물자원부로 부터 파악한 카나다 석유수급 관련 사항을 우선 아래와 같이 보고함.

1. 산유능력, 최근 생산량

- 88 년 172 만 B/D 의 원유 (경질유, SYNTHETIC및 중질유)을 생산한 카나다는 경질유 생산감소로 89 년에는 167 만 B/D 생산함.

- 90.1/4 분기 산유량은 162 만 B/D 로서 전년동기대비 4 프로 감소 하였으며, 주로 기존의 알버타 유전 산유량 감소에 기인함. 이중 경질류는 90.5 만 B/ D 이며, SYNTHETIC 유 16.5 만 B/D,PENTANES 유 11.5 만 B/D, HYPHKPUVKR 43.5 MEF B/D임.

- 90 년도 평균 생산량은 164 만 B/D 로 전망되며, 최대 생산 능력은 현 수준보도 3.1 만 B/D 추가된 167 만 B/D 로 평가됨.

2. 석유 소비량

- 90 년 1/4 분기중 석유 생산물 총 소비는 147 만 B/D 로서 금년 소비량은 146만 - 148 만 B/D 로추정됨 (상기 소비량에는 정유공장 자체 소비량 7.5만 - 9.5 만 B/D 포함안되었는바, 동 소비량포함시 153.5 만 - 157.5 만 B/D KUH)

3. 수출 및 수입량

가. 수출

- 89 년도에 약 66.6 만 B/D 를 수출하였으며, 이중 미국에 약 65.4 만 B/D, 기타 한국을 포함 대만, 일본등 태평양 지역 국가에 약 1.2 만 B/D를 수출함.

- 90 년 1/4 분기에는 약 60.8 만 B/D 를 수출, 미국에 약 59 만 B/D, 태평양 국가에 약 1.8 만 B/D 수출함.

나. 수입

경제국 2차보 미주국 중아국 정문국 안기부 동자부

PAGE 1

90.08.21 09:35 WG

외신 1과 통제관

0017

- 89 년도에 약 48.4 만 B/D 를 수입함. 이중 영국.놀웨이산 북해 원유가 58 프로인 약 28.3 만 B/D, OPEC 산 원유가 36 프로인 약 17.6 만 B/D (나이지리아 : 6.9 만 B/D, 사우디 3.1만 B/D, 베네주엘라(중질유): 3.1 만 B/D), 멕시코산 6천 B/D 등임.

- 90. 1/4 분기에는 전년동기 대비 20 프로 증가된 약 57.2 만 B/D 를 수입하였는바, 북해 원유가 34.6 만 B/D (퀘벡주 수입량의 90 프로, 대서양각주 수입량의 45 프로 해당), OPEC 산원유 18.9만 B/D, 미국산 3.1 만 B/D (전량 온타리오주에 공급), 멕시코산 6 천 B/D 수준임.

4. 수출시 기간 계약 현황

- 천연가스 수출의 경우에는 장기계약에의하나 원유수출경우 대부분 미국으로 수출되며 1 - 2 개월 단위의 단기 공급 계약이며 가격은 WTI 기준현물 시장 가격으로 결정됨.

5. 이.쿠 사태에 따른 증산 실시여부

- 카나다는 현재 최대 산유능력에 근접하게 생산중인바, 필요시 현 생산량보다 최대 약 3.1만 B/D 증산이 가능함.

- 이.쿠 사태가 불과 1 - 주일전에 발생 아직구체적으로 파악치 못하고 있으나, 장기적으로 고유가 상태가 지속될 경우 추가증산 및 신규 유전개발여부가 결정될것임.

6. 이락크. 쿠웨이트로 부터의 수입물량 감소대책

- 기본적으로 카나다는 원유 수출국이며 이.쿠로부터 원유를 수입치 않고 있으나, 사우디가 증산하지않을 경우 유럽국가의 북해원유 수요가 증대될 것으로 전망됨에 따라 총 수입량의 1/2 이상을 북해로부터 수입해온 카나다로서는 나이지리아, 이란등으로의 수입선 전환이 불가피하며 북해원유를 주로 사용한 대서양 각주에 대한 공급에 다소 영향을 미칠 가능성이 있음.

- 현재 카나다의 원유 및 석유 생산물 비축량은 65 일분으로서 전량 사기업이 비축하고 있음.

7. 주재국 유류가격 동향

- 카나다는 원유소비시 선입 선출법 (FIFO SYSTEM:FIRST-IN FIRST-OUT) 을 채택하고 있어 아직 휘발유.난방용 유류 가격 상승은 없으나 원유비축량이 2 개월여에 불과, 현 사태가 지속될경우 약 2 개월후에는 상향조정이 불가피할 것으로 전망됨.끝

(대사 - 국장)

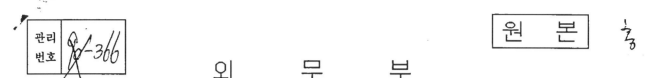

관리번호	90-366

원 본

외 무 부

종 별 :

번 호 : AEW-0237 일 시 : 90 0821 1430

수 신 : 장관(기협,중근동,정일)

발 신 : 주 UAE 대사

제 목 : 이라크-쿠웨이트 사태(8)(자료응신 13호)

대:WAE-0169

1. 대호, 소직은 8.21 주재국 국영회사인 ADNOC 대표 AL MAZROUI 를 면담(오참사관 배석) 하였는바, 동인 반응 아래와 같음.

가.UAE 는 단기적 유가폭등을 반대하며 국제유가의 안정을 목표로 삼고 있으며, 따라서 한국등 기존 원유 도입선에 대하여는 지속적 공급에 차질이 없을것임

나. 또한 UAE 는 현재는 이라크. 쿠웨이트사태 직전 결정된 OPEC 쿼타 150 만 B/D 생산을 고수하고 있으나, 동사태로 인한 이라크. 쿠웨이트의 감산물량만큼은 반드시 보충생산되어야 한다고 생각하고 있음. 현재 OPEC 는 보충물량 협의를 모색코자하나 알제리, 리비아등의 반대로 지연되고 있으며, 만일 OPEC 에서의협의가 이루어지지 않는경우 사우디를 포함 몇개국의 증산에 의해 해결될것으로 생각함

다. 유가는 현재 비정상적으로 폭등하고 있으나 전술한 보충물량등에 의거 시장기능을 회복 21 불에서 2-3 불 정도 오른 가격으로 유지될것으로 전망됨

2. 동인은 UAE 의 산유능력을 약 3.5 백만 B/D 로 말한바 있으나 실제 2.1 백만 B/D 가 최대 산유능력인 것으로 당지 전문가들은 보고 있으며 동사태 추이에 따라 증산은 확실시 될것으로 관측됨. 끝.

(대사 박종기-국장)

예고:90.12.31 일반

90.12.31

공람	국제경제국	90년 8월 22일	담 당	과 장	국 장	차관보	차 관	장 관
				(서명)	(서명)			

경제국 차관 1차보 2차보 중아국 통상국 정문국 청와대 안기부
동자부 대책반

PAGE 1 90.08.21 21:39

외신 2과 통제관 CW

0019

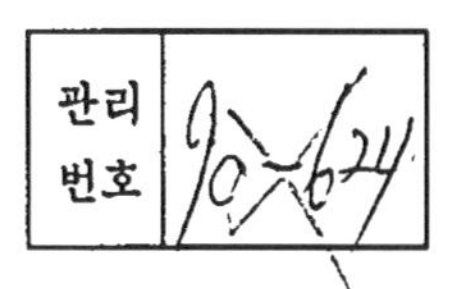

원 본

외 무 부

종 별 :

번 호 : SBW-0701 일 시 : 90 0821 1540

수 신 : 장 관(기협,동자부)

발 신 : 주사우디대사

제 목 : 석유수급 및 유가동향등 파악

대:WSB-336

연:SBW-695

대호 관련사항 하기 보고함.

1. 주재국 관련사항

0 산유능력: 일산 750 만

0 최근산유량:540 만정도(기준 OPEC 쿼타준수)

0 석유소비량:일산 80 만정도

0 원유수출량:일산 380 만내외(정유등 포함시는 450 만정도)

0 수출국별 현황 및 수출시 기간계약 현황:최근 관련자료 미공개로 상세파악 곤란(북미 30 프로, 아주 30 프로, 유럽 25 프로정도 추정)

0 이.쿠 사태에 따는 증산실시 여부:현재까지는 증산을 실시하지 않았으나 긴급 OPEC 회의 개최가 무산됨에 따라 조만간 증산실시가 예상되며, 증산물량은 100-150 만정도 예상.

2. 주재국의 유류가격 동향:변동없음.

3. 향후 국제원유시장에 대한 수급및 가격

0 금번사태로 인하여 약 400 만베럴의 이.쿠산 원유의 공급이 감소되었으나, OECD 회원국들의 비축물량(IEA 통계:4 억 6,800 만톤, 99 일분)및 곧개시될것으로 예상되는 일부 OPEC 회원국(사우디외에 UAE 가 일산 50 만, 베네주엘라가 일산 70 만 까지 증산가능)및 멕시코, 이집트, 북해산 원유의 증산을 감안하면 중기적(MEDIUM-TERM)으로 원유수급자체는 커다란 문제점 없음.

0 그러나 현재 국제원유시장에서의 유가형성은 중기적 원유수급 전망보다 걸프만 전쟁발발 가능성이 가격등락의 주요원인으로 작용하여, 비교적높은 유가를

경제국 장관 차관 1차보 2차보 중아국 통상국 청와대 안기부
동자부 대책반

PAGE 1

공람	국제경제국	90 8 22 인	담 당	과 장	국 장	차관보	차 관	장 관

90.08.22 00:23

외신 2과 통제관 CW

0020

보이고있으나, OPEC 원유의 증산이 가시화되고 현교착상태가 계속되는 경우 10월이후의 계절적 원유수요 증대를 감안하더라도 OPEC 산 원유의 평균가격은 베럴당 25 불이내에서 안정을 유지할것으로 예상됨.

0 현걸프만 위기가 종식되면 일시적인 공급과잉 현상이 발생 유가는 상당수준 하락하다가 종전 쿼터수준으로 공급량이 감소할 경우 현기준가인 21 불 전후에서 안정예상

4. 기타사항 연호 참조.끝

(대사 주병국-국장)

예고:90.12.31 일반

PAGE 2

0021

원 본

외 무 부

종 별 :

번 호 : OMW-0242 일 시 : 90 0821 1700

수 신 : 장관(기협)

발 신 : 주오만대사

제 목 : 주재국 석유수급 및 유가동향

대: OMW-0122

대호, 원유수급 관련사항 아래 보고함.

1. 산유능력및 생산량: 주재국은 최근 65만 BPD를 생산하였으나, 금년도말까지 70만 BPD 로 증량 추진중임.

2. 생산량및 수출량(89년)

0 총생산량: 233.8백만배럴

0 총수출량: 215.9백만 배럴

0 주요국별 수출량(백만배럴)및 점유율( ):

일본:83.8(38.8) 한국:69.3(32.1) 대만:21.0(9.7)싱가폴:12.1(5.6) 미국:5.8(2.7) 태국:2.7(1.3)

3. 유가동향: 석유.광물부 관계자에 의하면,주재국 원유가격은 현재 배럴당 26.7불이나, 향후 상승할 것으로 전망함.

4. 주재국 원유 안정적 도입 방안:

가. 직도입량 증대

-기존 1만 BPD 를 직도입하고 있는 경인에너지측의 증량교섭이 요망됨.

-연이나 주재국 금년도 증산량이 5만 BPD 에 불과하며 직도입량 대량증대는 기대키 어려움.

나. 주재국 원유생산에 직접참여(장기적 대책)

주재국은 현재 매장량을 43억 배럴로 보고있으나향후 탐사에 따라 계속 증대될것으로 전망하고 생산량을 100만 BPD 까지 증량을 목표로 하고있는바, 주재국으로부터 안정적 도입을 위해서는 아국의 직접 참여가 바람직함.

주재국내 각국의 석유생산 참여 현황:

경제국 2차보 동자부 통상국 대책반

PAGE 1

90.08.22 00:25 CG

외신 1과 통제관

0022

- PETROLEUM DEVELOPMENT OMAN(정부지분 60 ,SHELL지분 40):60 만 BPD
- ELF AQUITANCE OMAN(불란서계):1만 BPD
- OCCIDENTAL OF OMAN (미국계):2만 BPD
- JAPAX(일본계): 84년 참여 금년부터 1만 BPD생산(전량 일본에 수출)
- 호주계 회사(BHP) 가 금년 9월부터 탐사에 착수예정.끝

(대사 강종원-국장)

원 본

외 무 부

종 별 :

번 호 : GAW-0203 일 시 : 90 0821 2000

수 신 : 장관(기협,아프일)

발 신 : 주 가봉 대사

제 목 : 석유 수급및 유가동향등 파악

대: WGA-0124

대호건,아래와 같이보고함.

1.주재국은 OPEC 회원국중 최소산유국임.

가. OPEC 쿼타:191천 B/D

나.산유능력:350천 B/D

다.최근의 생산량:270천B/D(OPEC 쿼타 초과)

라.석유소비량:생산량의 6PERCENT

마.수출량및 수출국별 현황:1989년8,595천톤,1990년 12,595천톤 예상.주요수출국은 프랑스,미국,브라질등

바.수출시 기간계약현황:석유생산량의 25 PERCENT 는 가봉정부지분,나머지는 ELF와 SHELL 의지분으로서 각각 독자적으로 판매하는바,장기계약에 의한 판매보다는 주로 현물시장에서판매함.(아국은 1989년 현물시장에서 약17백만불에 달하는 주재국원유수입)

사.이.쿠사태에 따른증산실시여부:주재국은 상금 증산계획없음.

2.주재국 유류 가격동향주재국은산유국임에도 불구, 시중 유류가격이 높은편임.현재 고급휘발유는 리터당 131센트,디젤유는리터당 약 79센트로서 1989년과 같은 수준이며현재로서는 인상계획이 없다고함.

3.향후국제원유시장의 수급및 가격전망

가.이라크및쿠웨이트산 원유에 대한 금수조치로 4,000천 B/D의 부족분이 발생함으로써 8.24현재 OPEC공시가인 불 21를 훨씬 초과하는 불28로매매되고 있음.

나.그러나 산유량증가문제를검토하기위한 OPEC 임시회의의 소집이무산되었음에도불구,사우디와 베네주엘라등이각각2,000천 B/D 와 500천 내지

경제국 중아국 동자부 2차보 대책반

PAGE 1

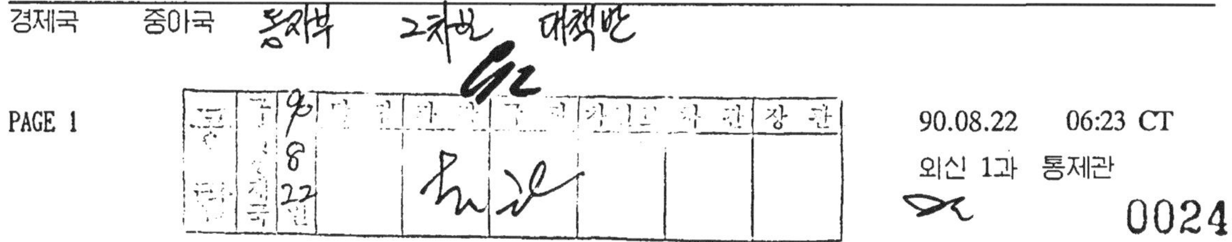

90.08.22 06:23 CT

외신 1과 통제관

0024

700천 B/D 의원유를 증산할 계획이어서 원유가가 불28이상으로인상되지는 않을 것이며 이를 고비로 하락세로반전할 것으로 전망됨. 끝.

(대사박창일-국제경제국장)

주 미 대 사 관

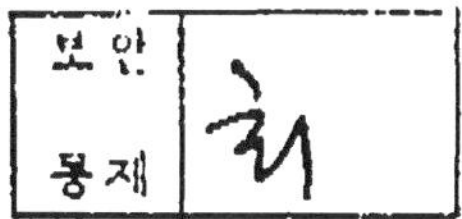

번 호 : USW(F) - 1890
수 신 : 장 관 (기협, 동일, 경일)
발 신 : 주미대사
제 목 : 원유가격 관련 기사 (2매)

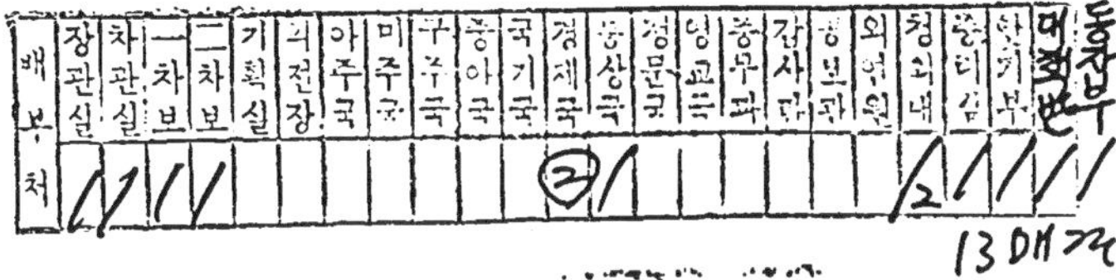

Fighting 'could push oil price up to $40'

By Anthony Robinson

Financial Times 8/21

A MAJOR military conflict in the Gulf, with fighting around the oilfields, could see oil prices rise to $40 a barrel initially and push up world inflation to 8 per cent by 1991, according to a study by the chief economic adviser to the Confederation of British Industry (CBI) and the journal Petroleum Economist.

This would be the most immediately painful of four scenarios examined in the study and lead to higher interest rates and world economic growth slowing to a halt, to squeeze inflation out of the system.

But if military intervention were over by the end of 1991, the world economy would [illegible] would fall back to about $20 per barrel at 1990 prices by 1996. "Instead of being threatened by Iraqi pressures to keep oil prices high, Gulf producers will be conscious of western military power and unlikely to limit production aggressively to boost prices artificially," the report says.

Although outlining four scenarios – an Iraqi climbdown, a protracted economic and military stalemate, a large military conflict or a climbdown by the west – the most likely outcome was that the present crisis would lead to stalemate or military conflict. In none of the scenarios does the world economy suffer as badly as in the previous two oil crises.

On the worst case of a western backdown allowing Iraq to control Gulf oil supplies (currently 30.1 per cent of world output), the study estimates a cumulative 4 per cent loss of world gross national product in aggregate during the 1990s, against a 7 per cent cumulative loss in the mid-1970s and one of 5 per cent for 1979-82.

In a lengthy military and economic stalemate, oil prices would rise for three or four years, with world growth slowing to about 2 per cent from an 1990.

Prof Douglas McWilliams, CBI chief adviser, and the report's main author, notes that the UK, as an oil producer, is likely to be less affected by higher oil prices than its EC partners and other heavy importers, like the US and Japan. UK inflation was already too high and higher oil prices would make the battle against it "all the harder. But the economy is slowing down and a further interest rate rise is probably unnecessary".

공람	국제경제국	담당	과장	국장	차관보	차관	장관
			서명	✓			

1890-1

0026

Energy Imports Could Reverse US Trade Gains

By WILLIAM ARMBRUSTER
Journal of Commerce Staff

Rising oil prices and the United States' growing dependence on imported oil could undo efforts to reduce the trade deficit, energy experts and economists say.

They see this possibility despite U.S. progress in conserving energy and the improvement in the nation's trade balance so far this year, partly because of the long-term decline of the dollar since 1985.

Alarmed by a trade deficit that was blasting through the roof, the Reagan administration in 1985 launched a major push to control the trade imbalance. It devalued the dollar and began putting intense pressure on other countries, most notably Japan, to open their markets to American exports.

Those efforts, continued by the Bush administration, have achieved substantial results, although the merchandise trade deficit actually widened for two more years before it started narrowing. But by 1989, the deficit fell to $109 billion, down from a peak of $152 billion in 1987.

Both administrations, however, took a hands-off approach to energy policy, abandoning government conservation programs and efforts to develop alternative sources such as solar and wind power. "Let the markets decide" was the guiding philosophy, one that was easy to adopt in a period of sliding oil prices.

That approach, largely shared by a Congress that thundered against the Japanese for not opening their markets wide enough but said little about energy conservation, now threatens to undo efforts to reduce the trade deficit, which reached its lowest level in seven years in June.

U.S. oil imports last year, when the Organization of Petroleum Exporting Countries maintained a price ceiling of $10 a barrel, totaled $50.9 billion. If prices, which soared above $28 a barrel in the wake of Iraq's Aug. 2 invasion of Kuwait, hold at that level or go even higher, the nation's energy trade deficit undoubtedly will jump by billions of dollars, especially as the United States becomes ever more dependent on imported oil.

[illegible] Bosworth, now a senior fellow at the Washington-based Brookings Institution, noted that an average price of $25 a barrel alone could lead to a $25 billion jump in the U.S. trade deficit.

In June alone, despite prices that averaged just $14.64 a barrel, the United States paid $3.7 billion for imported oil, according to figures released Friday by the Commerce Department. This contributed to its total trade deficit of $5.1 billion for the month.

For the first six months of this year, the total oil import bill was $27.8 billion, and the total deficit was $45.1 billion. Oil imports were $22.4 billion in the first six months of last year.

"It will get worse as the price goes up and our import dependence gets worse," said Ray Piccini, a senior economist at the Washington-based American Petroleum Institute.

The United States now imports exactly half the oil it uses. In the first seven months of this year, imports averaged 8.6 million barrels a day, while the nation consumed 17 million barrels daily, according to the API. In July, imports represented 51.3% of consumption, the institute said.

That dependence will become much more substantial over the next few years. Henry Schuler, director of the energy security program at the Washington-based Center for Strategic and International Studies, noted that the Energy Information Administration, a unit of the U.S. Department of Energy, forecasts that average daily consumption will reach 12.3 million barrels by 2010, up from 7.2 million barrels last year.

Mr. Schuler, who described that forecast as "very conservative," did not offer any estimates of his own, but Mr. Piccini of the API said many experts believe oil imports will reach two-thirds of consumption by 2000.

To some, however, it would be wrong to emphasize the energy deficit too much. R.K. Morris, director of international trade at the National Association of Manufacturers, noted that the country has a huge deficit in manufactured goods. "This country shouldn't have a manufacturing deficit. It can't avoid having an oil deficit," he said.

The prospects for a higher oil tab demonstrate the need to improve the manufacturing sector's performance, Mr. Morris said.

In fact, higher oil prices could [illegible] tured goods by pushing the value of the dollar down, thus making those goods cheaper on foreign markets, said Mr. Bosworth of Brookings. He was director of the Council on Wage and Price Stability under President Carter. Of course, he added, manufacturers that use a lot of oil would be hurt.

Often overlooked in the debate over energy policy is the fact that the United States does export both petroleum and petroleum products, as well as coal. Last year, for example, exports of petroleum and petroleum products totaled $5.6 billion. Coal exports totaled $4.2 billion.

Even so, that left an energy trade deficit of some $41 billion, again accounting for much of the total trade deficit.

The petroleum exports consist mainly of petroleum coke, which when calcified can yield almost pure carbon and graphite. It can then be used to make electrode dry cells for various electronic products. Japan is the largest market.

Prospects for reducing the energy trade deficit by increasing coal exports are limited, with European utilities that still burn oil offering the biggest potential market, said John Grasser, director of media relations for the National Coal Association. Coal now accounts for 60% of the utility fuel mix in the United States, while oil represents only 5%. Natural gas, nuclear power and hydropower account for the remaining 35%.

The record for U.S. coal exports was set in 1981, when shipments totaled 112.5 million short tons, valued at $5.8 billion. Exports in 1982 fell to 106.3 million tons, although they rose slightly in dollar terms to $5.9 billion. Coal exports last year amounted to 100.8 million tons.

JoC 8/20/90

1890-2

0027

원 본

외 무 부

종 별 : 지 급

번 호 : USW-3828 일 시 : 90 0821 1532

수 신 : 장관(기협)

발 신 : 주미대사

제 목 : 석유 수급 및 유가 동향 파악

대: WUS-2739

대호, 8.20(월) 당관 최경림 서기관의 에너지부 국제과 PUMPHREY 예측 담당관면담 결과및 당지 언론 보도등을 종합, 아래 보고함.

1.산유국 관련 사항

가.국별 산유 능력 및 최근 생산량

0 별첨 1: ESTIMATED OIL PRODUCTION CAPACITY ANDEXCESS CAPACITY (90.8.2.의회 예산처 작성) 참조

나.수출량 및 수출국별 현황

0 별첨 2 NET OIL IMPORTS INTO OECD COUNTRIES (미 에너지부 발간 INT'L PETROLEUM STATISTICS REPORT,90년7월) 참조

다. 수출시 계약 기간 현황

0 70년대말-80년대 초까지는 2-3년 단위의 장기계약이 대부분 이었으나 80년대의석유 공급과잉및 유가하락에 따라 평균 계약기간이 꾸준히 단축되어 왔는바,현재는 2/3 이상이 수개월내의 단기계약이며,계약시에는 기준 물량 및 가격만 설정한후 실제거래물량및 가격은 도입당시의 현물시장 수급 사정및 가격변동 상황을 반영하여 결정하는 FLEXIBLE PACKAGE 형태를 취하는것으로 알려지고 있음.(수출국 및 석유회사는 구체적인 계약내용을 공개하지 않기 때문에 정확한 계약기간 현황의 파악은 어려움)

0 과거 석유위기시에는 단기간내의 급속한 가격인상으로 인해 산유국이 계약 기간을 단축하는 경향을 보였는바, 금번에도 일단 사태가 진정되기까지는 금번에도 계약기간이 단축될 것으로전망됨.

라. 이라-쿠웨이트 사태에 따른 증산 실시 여부

경제국

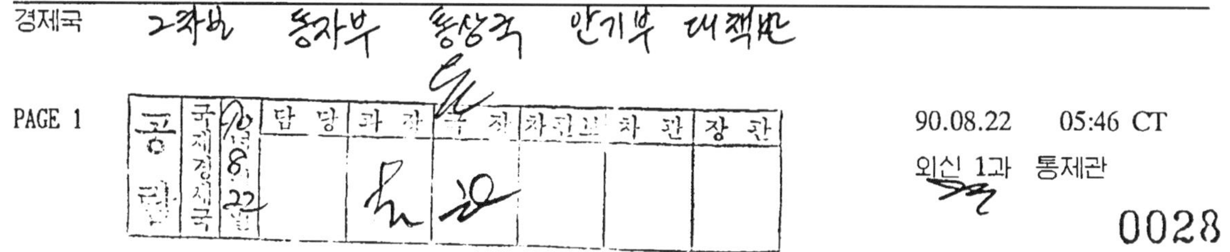

PAGE 1

90.08.22 05:46 CT

외신 1과 통제관

0028

0 금번 사태 발발이후 가봉등 일부 국가가 증산을실시하고 있는것으로 알려지고있으나, 세계 총생산량에 비해 극히 미미한 양에 불과함.

0 사우디는 그간 이락.쿠웨이트 석유 수입 금지에 따른 부족분 충당을 위해 여타 OPEC 회원국의증산이 필요함을 주장하고,이문제의 협의를 위한 OPEC 회의 소집을요구하면서 OPEC 회의가소집되지 않을 경우 일일 2백만 배럴을 증산할것임을 공언해왔으나, OPEC 일부국이 현재세계 석유 시장이 공급 과잉 현상을 보이고 있으므로(전략 비축분을 제외한 비축분이 5억 배럴에 달함) 수급균형을 위해 증산에 반대하는 입장을취함에 따라 OPEC 회의 소집 가능성은 희박해 졌으며,이에 따라 사우디는향후 1주일내에 증산을 실시,일일 총 700-750만 배럴을 생산할 것으로알려졌음.

0 한편 사우디가 증산을 실시할 경우 베네수엘라, UAE ,나이제리아등도 이에 동조,각각 50만 배럴,50 만배럴, 30 만 배럴을 증산 할것으로 알려지고있음.(산유국별 증산능력은 별첨 1 참조)

2. 수입 물량 감소에 대한 확보 대책 및 대응방안

0 미국정부는 일일 60-70만 배럴에 달하는 이락.쿠웨이트로부터의 수입 금지로 인한 공급 부족분은국내 증산,추가 유정 개발,천연개소등 대체에너지사용 증대및 석유소비자제 등을 통해 연말까지40만 배럴정도 충당할수 있으며, 멕시코 사우디등으로부터도 부족분 추가 도입이 가능한 것으로 추산하고 있음.

0 WATKINS 미 에너지 장관은 8.17 기자회견에서금번 사태에 대한 에너지부 대책으로 국내 석유증산 권유,대체 에너지 사용증대,국민들에 대한에너지 절약요청등을발표하였으나,동 대책은 주로권고적인 사항만을 포함하고 있어 가까운 시일내에 뚜렷한 성과를 거두기는 어려운 것으로 평가되고 있음.(별첨 3 참조)

0 기본적으로 미국 정부는 현재까지 세계 석유상황 및 유가 인상폭에 비추어 볼때 비상 대책이 필요한 위기 상황에도 도달하지 않았다고 판단하고 있으며, 이에 따라석유,확보를 위한 별도의정부 조치보다는 시장 기능에 따른 수요.공급의 자동조절에의존하고 있음.

0 다만 미 정부내에서는 유가 안정을 위해 5.9 억배럴에 달하는 전략비축 석유를 방출하는 문제를 둘러싸고 활발한 토론이 벌어지고 있는바,금번사태가 장기화되거나 사우디까지 확산될 가능성에대한 우려,산유국 증산 가능성 및 아직은 전략비축 석유 방출에 필요한 SEVERE ENERGY SHORTAGE 에 도달하지 않았다는 점을 감안,

결정을유보한채 사태 진전을 예의 주시하고 있는 형편임.

3. 미국의 유류 가격 동향

0 사태 발생 직후 주요 석유 회사들이 휘발유가격등을 일시적으로 인상한바 있으나 미정부의석유회사들에 대한 가격 추가인상 자제요청 및비판적인 국민여론에 따라전반적인 유류 가격은더이상의 급등세를 보이지 않고 안정을 되찾고있는것으로 관측됨.(별첨 4 참조)

4. 향후 국제 원유 수급 및 가격 전망

0 향후 원유 수급및 가격은 국제 원유 시장 내의경제적 요인보다는 이락-쿠웨이트 사태의 진전상황이라는 정치.군사적 요인과 이에 대한 원유시장의 비합리적 심리적반응에 따라 좌우될것이므로,정확한 예측이 거의 불가능하다고 할수있음.

0 당지 소수 일부 전문가들은 만약 금번 사태가페르시아만 지역에서의 전쟁으로확산될 경우이지역으로부터의 원유 공급의 일부 중단과 함께국제 시장에서의 PANICBUYING 으로 유가가 배럴당 40-50불 이상 으로 폭등,세계 경제에 큰 충격을 가져올것으로 예측하고 있음.

0 대부분의 전문가들은 금번 사태가 당분간 현상태로 지속될 경우 원유수급 및 가격에 대해서는 아래와같이 전망하고 있음.

가. 수급 전망

0 금번 사태로 인한 세계 석유 공급 감소분은 일일4.3 백만 배럴이나, 기타 산유국의 최대 증산 가능규모는 일일 4.0 백만 배럴로 추정됨.

0 따라서 기타 산유국들이 최대한 증산을 실시할경우 금번 사태로 인한 공급 감소량은 일일 30만 배럴에 불과하고 80년대의 공급과잉으로 현재까지 세계 시장의 석유비축량(전략 비축량 제외)이 5억배럴에 달하므로,금번 사태가 급격히 확산되지 않는한 당분간 심각한 석유공급 부족현상이 나타나리라고는 예상되지 않음.

0 한편 금번 사태 이전의 국제 원유 가격은 세계석유 수급 사정을 감안한 정상저긴 가격보다 낮게책정된 가격이며, 70년대말 -80년대 초의 원유가격과 비교해 볼때도 실질가격은 오히려 하락하였으므로 금번 가격 인상에 따른 직접적인 수요 감소효과는 총 수요량의 0.5-1.0 퍼센트에 불과할 것으로예상되나, 유가 인상으로 향후 세계경제 성장이현저히 둔화될 경우 석유 수요도 상당량 감퇴할것임.

나.가격 전망

0 당분간 원유 가격은 금번 사태가 더 이상 확대되지 않더라도 사태 발발직후

인상된 현재 가격으로 부터는 하락하지 않고 배럴당 26-28 불선을 유지할것으로 전망되는바, 그 이유는 아래와 같음.

-원유가격은 전통적으로 산유국들이 FULL CAPACITY 의 85 퍼GTR니트를 생산하고15 퍼센트는 유휴 시설로 가동하지 않을때 일정한 가격을 유지해왔는바, 금번 사태로 일일 4.0 백만 배럴의 추가생산을 위해서는 현재 산유국 생산시설의 FULL CAPACITY 를 가동해야 하며, 이는 필연적으로가격 인상을 초래함.

-세계 석유 수요는 당분간 급격히 감소하지는 않을것으로 예측됨.

0 또한 금번 사태이전의 국제 원유 가격은 세계석유 수급사정을 감안한 정상적인가격보다 낮게 책정된 가격이므로 금번 사태가 원만히 해결되어이락. 쿠웨이트 산 원유의 공급이 재개될 경우에도 국제 원규 가격은 최소한 배럴당 20-22 불선을 넘는 선에서 유지될것으로 관측됨.

첨부: USW(F)- 1880 (6 매)

(대사 박동진- 구장)

주 미 대 사 관

보 안 통 제	외

번 호 : USW(F) -1880

수 신 : 장 관 (기협)

발 신 : 주미대사

제 목 : USW-3828 첨부 (표지제외 6매)

0032

2.

(별첨1)

02-Aug-90
10:00 A.M.

TABLE 1
ESTIMATED
OIL PRODUCTION CAPACITY AND EXCESS CAPACITY
AS OF AUGUST 2, 1990
(million of barrels per day)

Country	Maximum Sustainable Capacity	Estimated Production	Excess Max. Sustainable Capacity
OPEC Production:			
Saudi Arabia	7.9	5.6	2.3
Iran	3.2	3.2	0.0
Iraq	3.3	3.2	0.1
Kuwait	2.6	1.4	1.2
UAE	2.4	1.7	0.7
Qatar	0.5	0.4	0.1
Neutral Zone	0.6	0.3	0.3
Total Persian Gulf	20.5	15.9	4.6
Algeria	1.2	1.4	0.0
Ecuador	0.3	0.3	0.0
Gabon	0.3	0.2	0.1
Indonesia	1.4	1.4	0.0
Libya	1.6	1.3	0.3
Venezuela	2.6	2.2	0.4
Nigeria	1.8	1.7	0.1
Total Non-Persian Gulf	9.2	8.4	0.8
Total OPEC	29.7	24.3	5.4
Canada	2.0	1.9 - 2.0	0.0 - 0.1
Mexico	3.0	2.9 - 3.0	0.0 - 0.1
United States	9.4	9.3 - 9.4	0.0 - 0.1
North Sea	3.9	3.8 - 3.8	0.1 - 0.1
Other	8.6	8.4 - 8.5	0.1 - 0.2
Total Non-OPEC	26.9	26.4 -26.6	0.3 - 0.5
Total Market Economies	56.6	50.6 -50.9	5.7 - 6.0

0033

Table 3.1 Net Oil Imports Into OECD1/ Countries (1st Quarter 1990)
(Million Barrels per Day)

	Total	OECD Europe						OECD Outside Europe			
		Total	United Kingdom	France	West Germany	Italy	Other Europe2/	United States3/	Canada	Japan	Other4/
Total Net Imports...	21.279	8.235	-0.239	1.902	2.044	1.906	2.623	7.661	-0.292	5.480	0.195
Imports from OPEC5/.	16.242	6.894	.463	1.048	.766	1.373	3.244	4.580	.196	4.162	.410
Imports from Persian Gulf6/											
Total............	10.260	4.276	.332	.863	.233	.657	2.191	2.064	.101	3.540	.280
Bahrain...........	.061	.007	–	.007	–	–	–	-.001	–	.054	.001
Iran..............	1.566	1.245	.182	.203	.058	.118	.684	.000	–	.321	.000
Iraq..............	1.784	.908	.008	.138	.005	.152	.603	.577	.022	.258	.019
Kuwait............	1.193	.494	.064	.006	.021	.076	.326	.164	.016	.499	.020
U.A.E.............	1.664	.357	.013	.156	.020	.110	.058	.024	.007	1.140	.137
Qatar.............	.285	.031	–	.016	.004	–	.010	.000	–	.254	.0[illegible]
Saudi Arabia......	3.706	1.235	.064	.336	.124	.200	.510	1.380	.056	1.014	.1[illegible]
Imports from OPEC-Africa											
Total............	3.852	2.453	.108	.186	.468	.711	.980	1.328	.054	.012	.005
Algeria...........	.980	.647	.051	.067	.131	.146	.253	.335	–	.002	-.003
Gabon.............	.114	.012	–	–	–	–	.012	.085	–	.010	.006
Libya.............	1.210	1.210	.028	.058	.249	.526	.350	.000	–	–	.000
Nigeria...........	1.549	.585	.030	.062	.088	.039	.365	.908	.054	–	.002
Imports from OPEC-South America											
Total............	1.311	.171	.022	.006	.066	.005	.072	1.011	.042	.007	.080
Ecuador...........	.075	.000	–	.000	–	–	–	.052	–	–	.022
Venezuela.........	1.237	.171	.022	.006	.066	.005	.072	.959	.042	.007	.058
Imports from OPEC-Far East											
Total............	.880	.002	–	–	–	–	.002	.175	–	.657	.046
Indonesia.........	.880	.002	–	–	–	–	.002	.175	–	.657	.046

1/OECD=Organization for Economic Cooperation and Development. See Appendix A for countries in this group.
2/"Other Europe" consists of Austria, Belgium, Denmark, Finland, Greece, Iceland, Ireland, Luxembourg, the Netherlands, Norway, Portugal, Spain, Sweden, Switzerland, and Turkey.
3/U.S. geographic coverage is the 50 States and the District of Columbia.
4/"Other" consists of Australia, New Zealand, and the U.S. Territories.
5/OPEC=Organization of Petroleum Exporting Countries. See Appendix A for countries in this group.
6/The Persian Gulf countries are all members of OPEC, except for Bahrain.
Notes: o Imports are on a direct basis. o Negative numbers represent net exports. o A dash (–) indicates no trade. o Zeroes (.000) indicate net imports of less than 0.0005 million barrels per day.
Sources: See end of Section 3.

0034

Table 3.2 Net Oil Imports Into OECD1/ Countries (1989 Average)
(Million Barrels per Day)

	Total	OECD Europe						OECD Outside Europe			
		Total	United Kingdom	France	West Germany	Italy	Other Europe2/	United States3/	Canada	Japan	Other4/
Total Net Imports...	20.142	7.999	-0.197	1.711	2.112	1.716	2.657	7.202	-0.356	5.035	0.262
Imports from OPEC5/.	14.707	6.208	.342	.875	.739	1.261	2.990	4.119	.205	3.789	.387
Imports from Persian Gulf6/											
Total............	9.128	3.755	.240	.697	.216	.619	2.033	1.854	.069	3.173	.276
Bahrain...........	.049	.005	–	.002	–	.001	.002	-.001	–	.042	.003
Iran..............	1.384	1.076	.122	.158	.041	.124	.631	.000	.017	.291	.000
Iraq..............	1.580	.898	.034	.128	.009	.138	.590	.447	.013	.219	.007
Kuwait............	1.084	.452	.006	.021	.022	.093	.310	.156	–	.458	[illegible]
U.A.E.............	1.306	.214	.006	.040	.023	.085	.059	.026	–	.929	–
Qatar.............	.281	.024	–	.009	.002	.008	.004	.002	–	.250	.006
Saudi Arabia......	3.443	1.086	.072	.288	.119	.171	.437	1.224	.039	.984	.111
Imports from OPEC-Africa											
Total............	3.450	2.241	.083	.218	.436	.627	.876	1.134	.065	.016	-.007
Algeria...........	.921	.648	.039	.089	.106	.150	.263	.269	.002	.015	-.012
Gabon.............	.081	.017	–	–	–	.001	.016	.050	–	.002	.013
Libya.............	1.044	1.044	.027	.065	.235	.430	.287	.000	–	–	.000
Nigeria...........	1.404	.532	.017	.064	.095	.045	.310	.815	.064	–	-.007
Imports from OPEC-South America											
Total............	1.321	.213	.019	.012	.086	.014	.082	.947	.070	.011	.080
Ecuador...........	.111	.001	–	–	–	–	.001	.086	.001	–	.023
Venezuela.........	1.211	.212	.019	.012	.086	.014	.080	.861	.070	.011	.057
Imports from OPEC-Far East											
Total............	.857	.004	–	.000	–	.002	.001	.182	–	.631	.040
Indonesia.........	.857	.004	–	.000	–	.002	.001	.182	–	.631	.040

1/OECD=Organization for Economic Cooperation and Development. See Appendix A for countries in this group.
2/"Other Europe" consists of Austria, Belgium, Denmark, Finland, Greece, Iceland, Ireland, Luxembourg, the Netherlands, Norway, Portugal, Spain, Sweden, Switzerland, and Turkey.
3/U.S. geographic coverage is the 50 States and the District of Columbia.
4/"Other" consists of Australia, New Zealand, and the U.S. Territories.
5/OPEC=Organization of Petroleum Exporting Countries. See Appendix A for countries in this group.
6/The Persian Gulf countries are all members of OPEC, except for Bahrain.
Notes: o Imports are on a direct basis. o Negative numbers represent net exports. o A dash (–) indicates no trade. o Zeroes (.000) indicate net imports of less than 0.0005 million barrels per day.
Sources: See end of Section 3.

0035

3363-1)

DEPARTMENT OF ENERGY -- ACTION ITEMS

3 Department of Energy has taken the following actions:

o **Assist the parties in resolving their differences in order to begin production at Point Arguello (Central California Coastline)** -- Crude oil production from the Pt. Arguello offshore platform can be brought on line quickly by successfully negotiating pending permits for transporting the oil by tanker to Los Angeles, or developing existing onshore pipeline alternatives. DOE intends to work closely with the Minerals Management Service, the California Coastal Commission, the County of Santa Barbara, the U.S. Coast Guard, the Chevron Corporation, and others to help resolve outstanding problems with the permitting process and assure the earliest possible flow of oil from Pt. Arguello. Industry estimates that production from the platform could be at 75,000 barrels per day within 90 days.

o **Increase Alaskan production** -- DOE has requested the management of Alaska's oil production system to increase flow by 50,000 to 100,000 barrels per day. This level of increased production is feasible without damaging future production capabilities.

o **Increase Naval Petroleum Reserve (NPR) production** -- The Department of Energy and Chevron (the operating partner) have agreed to increase production at the Elk Hills Naval Petroleum reserve by 5,000 barrels per day by October, 1990. This is made possible by recently completed upgrades in the system.

o **Request states to increase "allowables"** -- DOE will be contacting state officials in Texas, New Mexico, Kansas, Alabama, Mississippi, and other states to urge adjustments to the allowable production levels in certain fields (such as Austin Chalk in Texas) which are under their regulatory jurisdiction. Increasing "allowables" will add a minimum of 30,000 barrels per day to the domestic supply.

o **Maximize Fuel Switching** A substantial capability for fuel switching exists in the U.S. DOE and FERC will work with state authorities to identify natural gas pipeline projects that will enable fuel switching to occur and be sustained. DOE and FERC also will work with state authorities to make sure that switching to domestic fuels is not disadvantaged by the regulatory process. DOE

(MORE)

0036

첨3-2)

believes that 100,000 barrels per day of oil could be backed out by other fuels in the short term. Over the longer term, more savings are possible.

o The Secretary of Energy also encouraged Americans to voluntarily increase energy efficiency and reduce domestic demand for oil. Practical, common sense suggestions to save energy include:

o Maintaining proper tire pressure. Up to 100,000 barrels a day of oil could be saved by the simple measure of maintaining recommended automobile tire pressure. DOE will request dealers, service facilities, and gas station operators to remind consumers of the benefits of maintaining proper tire pressure. Fleet operators will be asked to ensure tire pressure checks are part of routine maintenance.

o Observing posted speed limits. Every American can save lives, money, and energy by driving at posted speed limits. Each MPH driven above the speed limits consumes 2% more fuel than necessary. Currently, average speed on non-congested highways exceeds posted speed limits by more than 5 MPH. Voluntary compliance with posted speed limits can save at least 50,000 barrels of oil per day.

o Using the more efficient vehicle. Over half of U.S. households have two or more vehicles, one of which is an average of 5 MPG more fuel efficient than the other. If just 20% of these vehicle owners would shift driving patterns so that the more efficient vehicle was utilized for the major portion of vehicle miles traveled, 40,000 barrels of oil per day could be saved.

o Carpool/Vanpool/Public Transit. States, metropolitan areas, and employers can encourage and facilitate the use of carpools and vanpools and the use of public transit service. A 20 percent increase in car/van pool and public transit use can reduce oil consumption by 90,000 barrels per day.

o Increase Alternative Fuel Use. Current U.S. ethanol facilities are operating at 80% capacity. An increase in alternative fuel use would have the effect of offsetting crude oil use by an estimated 10,000 b/d in the near term. DOE is exploring other options to increase the use of alternative fuels over the longer term.

o The Department of Energy is also working with all federal agencies to lower Federal energy use.

-DOE-

0037

별첨4

Spot Crude Oil and Spot Unleaded Gasoline Prices (7/30-Present)

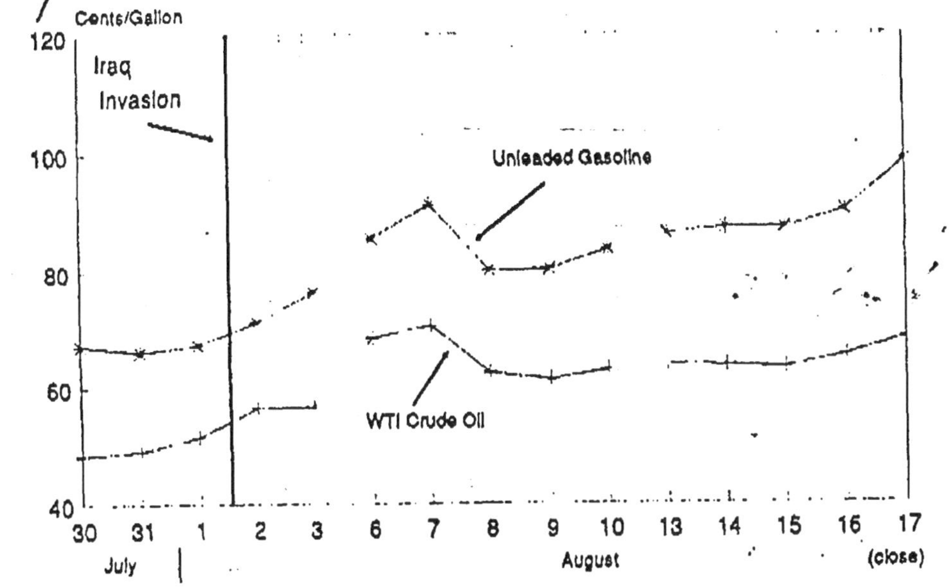

Cents/Gallon

120, 100, 80, 60, 40

Iraq Invasion

Unleaded Gasoline

WTI Crude Oil

30 31 1 2 3 6 7 8 9 10 13 14 15 16 17

July August (close)

Prices for business trading days only.

Date/Time	WTI (Cushing) Spot	WTI (Cushing) Futures (Sept.)	Unleaded (NYH) Spot	Unleaded (NYH) Futures (Sept.)	No.2 HO (NYH) Spot	No.2 HO (NYH) Futures (Sept.)	Kerojet (NYH) Spot	Retail Gasoline AAA	Retail Gasoline Lundberg	Retail Gasoline EIA
History:										
7/24	19.84	20.56	66.55	63.28	56.68	57.32			104.4	
7/30	20.24	20.21	67.15	65.88	56.20	56.93				
7/31	20.57	20.69(+0.48)	66.10	65.60(-0.28)	56.10	57.11(+0.18)				
8/1	21.59	21.54(+0.85)	67.25	64.27(+1.81)	59.83	61.19(+2.84)		107.5		
8/2	23.71	23.11(+1.57)	71.18	68.07(+3.80)	63.33	64.69(+3.50)				
8/3	23.79	24.49(+1.38)	76.45	72.18(+4.11)	65.35	66.58(+1.89)		111.5		
8/6	28.73	28.05(+3.56)	85.75	81.52(+9.34)	74.30	75.55(+8.97)		118.6		
8/7	29.60	28.31(+0.26)	91.40	82.39(+0.87)	77.90	75.14(-0.41)		120.1		
8/8	26.19	25.96(-2.35)	80.20	76.21(-6.18)	68.78	70.13(-5.01)		123.7		
8/9	25.69	25.67(-0.29)	80.40	76.42(+0.21)	68.38	69.77(-0.36)		125.3		
8/10	26.38	26.23(+0.56)	83.70	79.45(+3.03)	71.23	72.61(+2.84)		125.0	115.0	
8/13	27.10	26.77	86.55	82.80	73.80	75.05	78.05	121.6		
8/14*	26.70	26.42(+0.19)	87.50	82.73(+3.28)	71.95	72.97(+0.36)	76.95			
8/15	26.54	26.46(+0.04)	87.43	84.05(+1.32)	71.60	72.85(-0.12)	76.60	121.8		118.0
8/16	27.40	27.36(+0.90)	90.33	87.46(+3.41)	74.20	75.47(+2.62)	77.95			118.1
Daily:										
8/17 open	27.93	27.85	92.20	89.40	76.08	77.30	79.83			117.7
8/17 10:00A	27.93	27.95	92.20	90.20	76.08	77.80	79.83			
8/17 11:00A	28.03	28.15	94.53	91.90	77.40	78.35	81.28			
8/17 12:00P	28.17	28.40	94.53	92.50	77.40	78.80	81.28			
8/17 01:00P	28.42	28.40	96.03	93.70	77.75	78.90	81.63			
8/17 02:00P	28.50	28.47	97.53	94.85	79.55	80.30	83.43			
8/17 03:00P	28.57	28.45	98.53	95.60	79.20	80.40	84.20			
8/17 04:00P	28.62	28.63	98.53	95.97	79.20	80.54	84.20			
8/17 close	28.65	28.63(+1.27)	98.58	95.97(+8.51)	79.30	80.54(+5.07)	84.30			

o September Brent closed at $28.25--up $1.50 from Thursday's close.

Energy Information Administration.

* NYMEX closing prices for August 14 indicate changes from August 10 close due to an electric outage which forced an early closure of the NYMEX on Monday, August 13.

0038

원 본

외 무 부

종 별 : 지 급

번 호 : BUW-0185 일 시 : 90 0823 1050

수 신 : 장 관(기협,통일,아동)

발 신 : 주 브루나이 대사

제 목 : 석유수급및 유가동향파악

대: WBU-112

당관 김서기관이 8.21. HAMID JAFAAR 외무성 경제국부국장을 접촉 확인한바를 아래보고함

1.주재국의산유능력:일165,000배럴

2.최근의생산량:일15만배럴

3.국내석유소비량:일4,000배럴

4.수출량:146,000배럴

5.수출국별현황

-일본:총수출량의 약30

- 아세안제국:약30

한국:17-18

- 현물시장:약13,7 (일2만배럴)

-기타

6.수출시기간계약:계약기간은 연간, 가격결정은 월별기준으로함

7.이,쿠 사태에따른 증산실시여부

주재국 정부의 공식발표에 의하면 에너지 보존정책을 그대로 유지하며 증산계획이없다고함.비공식탐문에 따르면 국제시장 가격을 고려 10-12월간 (성수기)은 일16만배럴 생산도 고려중임.

(대사 허세린-국장)

경제국 2차보 아주국 통상국 동기부

PAGE 1 90.08.22 14:09 WG

외신 1과 통제관

0039

08/22/90 18:08 ☎202 797 0595 EMBASSY OF KOREA →→→ WOI 2 ▣001/010

보안 통제	외

주 미 대 사 관

번 호 : USW(F) - 1902
수 신 : 장 관 (기협, 통일)
발 신 : 주미대사
제 목 : 원유가격 (6매)

Higher Oil Prices Only Add to Fed's Pressing Dilemma

8/22 WP

By John M. Berry
Washington Post Staff Writer

Top Federal Reserve policy makers met yesterday to confront a dilemma: how to keep inflation under control and the U.S. economy out of recession with oil prices up more than $8 dollars a barrel in a month.

NEWS ANALYSIS

The problem is not just that the Iraqi invasion of Kuwait sent oil prices soaring, but that it happened at a time when the economy had already lost its wind and inflation was stubbornly high. Higher oil prices only made the Fed's dilemma more acute.

"The jump in oil is like a tax on the economy and a bubble on the inflation rate," said analyst Ray Stone of Stone & McCarthy, a financial markets research firm. "It's got to be a tough time at the Fed."

In fact, it is no less of a tough time for the U.S. economy. While there is no sign of a serious nationwide slump, some parts of the country and some industries are headed downhill; unemployment has begun to rise and higher oil prices have begun to work their way through the economy. Consumers were already spending cautiously when the invasion occurred, and some forecasters fear the new uncertainty about economic prospects will cause them to zip up their pocketbooks.

So far this month, all of the economic data have pointed to a softening of the economy. For instance, the number of payroll jobs fell in July, while retail sales rose a scant 0.1 percent and factory output was unchanged from June.

Part of the Fed's problem is that it has an admittedly powerful but ultimately quite limited tool with which to effect work—the rate at which it supplies money to the U.S. banking system. Normally, if it pours more money into the system, both short- and long-term interest rates fall. If financial markets fear that the additional money will lead to higher inflation, however, long-term interest rates—which generally are set by market forces rather than the Fed and are quite sensitive to expected inflation—could rise.

For a moment, put yourself in the shoes of Fed Chairman Alan Greenspan or one of the other key central bank officials who sat around the table in the Fed board room yesterday.

Even if you favored easing monetary policy to give a boost to the economy

See ECONOMY, F4, Col. 1

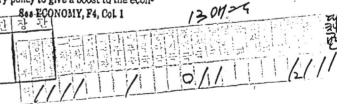

공람	국제경제국	년 월 일	담당	과장	국장	차관보	차관	장관
				홍	✓			

1902 -1

0040

Crisis Adds to Fed's Woes

ECONOMY, From F1

omy—lowering short-term interest rates by adding cash to the banking system—you might have paused. If financial markets took the move the wrong way and bid up long-term interest rates because of a fear the Fed was abandoning its effort to bring inflation under control, then easing policy might backfire. After all, the level of long-term rates is usually more important to the economy than short-term rates, most economists believe.

Suppose, on the other hand, that your principal concern is making sure that inflation does not get out of hand (several of the officials around the table yesterday have taken that position in the past on the grounds that the way to maximize long-term economic growth is to lower inflation). In that case, you did not want to pump money into the economy at a faster rate.

Nevertheless, even an anti-inflation hawk might hesitate to stand by while the economy drops into a recession if only for fear of a political backlash against the Fed that could restrict its freedom to fight inflation in the future.

Of course, Fed policy is only one of myriad influences on the economy. The economy might well move into a recession, or stay out of one, regardless of whether the central bank seeks to lower short-term interest rates.

As usual, the Fed made no announcement about any decisions it made yesterday. Stone and most financial analysts expect the Fed to lower rates slightly, though not necessarily right away.

Another aspect of the Fed's dilemma is that foreign exchange traders, focusing on the weakness in the U.S. economy, believe short-term interest rates are headed downward. Since that means a lower return on investments here, there is less demand for dollars and its value has been falling compared to the Japanese yen, German mark and several other currencies. A lower dollar can help spur U.S. exports, but it also makes imported goods more costly, which adds to inflation.

Meanwhile, with the Japanese and most West European economies growing faster than that of the United States, central banks in the other countries have been raising interest rates to keep inflation from worsening. That probably makes it less likely that long-term rates will fall significantly here short of a sharp economic slump, many analysts believe.

All in all, it probably was not much fun to sit around that Fed table yesterday. Whatever else it can or cannot do, Stone noted, "The Fed can't control oil prices."

USW(F) 1902-2

0041

NYT 8/22/90

Oil and Gas Prices Rise Slightly

Fall From Early Gain Tied to 'Conciliatory' Statement by Iraq

By MATTHEW L. WALD

Prices for oil and gasoline rose slightly yesterday after swinging sharply during the day. They surged early in the day but then fell back after a statement by President Saddam Hussein of Iraq that traders said was less aggressive than expected.

Crude oil for October delivery closed up by 12 cents a barrel, at $28.71, having bounced from $28 to $29.45. But that was placid compared with gasoline, which traded over a broad 11-cent-a-gallon range, equivalent to $4.62 a barrel. It closed at $1.0125 a gallon, up 1.01 cents, after reaching $1.065 and dipping to 95.5 cents.

Heating oil for September delivery closed at 83.71 cents a gallon, up three-quarters of a cent.

Bigger Losses in Europe

Stock prices also gyrated, with the Dow Jones industrial average dropping 52.48 points, or nearly 2 percent, to 2,603.96, after being down more than 77 points early in the day. Earlier, in Europe, with tensions heightened by a rumor, quickly denied, of a downed American fighter plane, stock markets took even bigger losses. [Pages D8 and D2.]

Crude oil moved mostly because the Iraqi statement was "somewhat conciliatory, comparatively speaking," one trader in New York said.

The market's mood is making it more volatile even if price differences from one day's close to the next is not large, some experts said.

'Gorilla on a Trampoline'

Peter C. Beutel, a trader at Merrill Lynch Futures, said the market "acted like a gorilla on a trampoline." He added that in the current atmosphere of uncertainty, speculators were afraid to sell oil short, which means to promise delivery of oil they do not have. As a result, when others who are "long" decide to take a profit by selling contracts for oil they do not need, there are no ready buyers. "So you get these quick whooshes down," he said.

After trading ended yesterday, the American Petroleum Institute, the industry's main trade association, released inventory figures that will add to the cues from which the market can choose today.

In ordinary times, the new inventory numbers would be bearish. For the week ended Friday, crude oil fell by 271,000 barrels, a barely significant amount, and remained 40.4 million barrels higher than this time last year. Gasoline stocks increased by 1.56 million barrels, after an unexpected drop of 6 million barrels the previous week. Distillate stocks also rose, by 2.27 million barrels.

But with all eyes on the Middle East, market analysts said they did not know what effect the institute's numbers would have. If Saudi Arabia or Venezuela has thus far made good on promises to increase oil production, which did not appear to be the case yesterday, the market does not appear to have taken notice. And the long-term outlook still seems grim to many experts.

"If you do a supply-demand analysis for the fourth quarter," said Philip K. Verleger Jr., a commodity economist, "even with an increase by Saudi Arabia of two million barrels a day and even if the other OPEC members go to full capacity, there is still a difference between production and consumption of two million barrels a day."

Withdrawn From Stocks

Demand is usually highest in the fourth quarter, because it is winter in the importing countries, but the excess of demand over supply in that period is usually only 500,000 barrels a day, said Mr. Verleger, who is a visiting fellow at the Institute for International Economics in Washington. The difference is withdrawn from stocks, he added.

The gasoline market, meanwhile, seems driven by demons of its own. Specialists suspect that at least part of the price run-up of the last few days is because large purchasers, from fuel distributors to service station chains, were buying supplies earlier than usual, because they thought prices would keep rising. That may have ended, with the inventories of refiners rising last week, by the American Petroleum Institute's count.

But the market for refined products is also driven by the availability of refineries, and specialists are beginning to consider more seriously the fact that nearly half of Kuwait's exports of 1.5 million barrels a day were not crude oil, but refined products, which went to Europe and the Far East.

"Imports of gasoline into Europe must be down significantly," said John H. Lichtblau of the Petroleum Industry Research Foundation in New York. That cuts European exports to the United States. American refineries meet only 94 or 95 percent of domestic demand, with the balance coming from Europe and South America.

Mr. Lichtblau said that to a small extent, the military deployment in the Persian Gulf was consuming oil from Saudi refineries that would otherwise be available for export.

While the crude market may be calmed by increased production from Saudi Arabia or Venezuela, and crude prices would be lowered if Western governments decide to release reserves from strategic stocks, none of that would make more gasoline available, analysts point out.

Others say there is no justification for the price increases. "I find it difficult to understand," said Nicholas A. Fedoruk, an energy specialist at Citizen Action, a nonprofit group in Washington. "Clearly the price of oil has leveled out; there just doesn't seem to be a reason for the price of gasoline to be increasing."

Absence of Congress Cited

He suggested that the oil companies felt freer to increase the price of gasoline now because Congress was out of session. "Maybe they think the chance of a 'windfall profits' tax is less now," he added.

Whatever the reason for the rising price of gasoline in the futures market, oil experts say that the last 20 to 30 cents of increases have not been reflected in the pump price, but will be in coming weeks unless futures prices turn around sharply.

Noting the political sensitivity of gasoline prices, Mr. Lichtblau said that "all the complaints have been that the increases at the pump have been too much, but it's the other way around."

"Prices at the retail level will be moving up steadily," he predicted.

USW(F) 1902-3 0042

Wall Street Journal 8/22/90

Tired Mammoth

Soviet Oil Industry, Mismanaged for Years, Can't Fill Iraq Gap

It's Producing Less, Not More, And Looks West for Help; Big Fields Are Overtaxed

To U.S. Firms, a New Frontier

By PETER GUMBEL and JAMES TANNER
Staff Reporters of THE WALL STREET JOURNAL

NEFTEYUGANSK, U.S.S.R. – The Mammoth oil field on the edge of this Siberian town is aptly named: Beneath the swampy surface lie some of the biggest oil reserves in the world. But even mammoths grow old and sick.

Oil production at the 20-year-old field has dropped almost 25% since hitting its peak in 1988. Alexander Gusev, the chief engineer, says raising production is out of the question. Even slowing the decline is proving troublesome because of chronic shortages of such basic equipment as pipes and valves.

Supplies of those things have dried up because of ethnic unrest in Azerbaijan, where most of them are made. "We've had problems every day," Mr. Gusev sighs. "Using old equipment means more accidents and higher repair costs."

Reserves to Be Activated

Bush plans to sign an order activating military reserve specialists, while U.S. commanders suggest they need another 30,000 troops in the Persian Gulf. Story on page A3. In related developments:

- **Most Americans in Kuwait seem to have stayed out of Iraq's hands, A3.**
- **Blacks and whites diverge on Bush's actions in the Mideast, A10.**
- **Energy agency doesn't see oil-supply disruption before next month, A10.**
- **Saudi and Iraqi pilots probe each other's defenses, A10.**
- **Egyptians fleeing Kuwait bring home nightmarish tales, A6.**
- **Yemen may have stalled the outbreak of a shooting war, A6.**

The oil patch of Western Siberia, the source of almost two-thirds of Soviet output, is in trouble. As the world's largest oil producer and a major exporter, the U.S.S.R. stands to profit handsomely from the rise in prices following Iraq's invasion of Kuwait. Every $1 increase in a barrel of crude oil means as much as $1 billion a year in additional Soviet export revenue.

Irreversible Decline

But don't count on Moscow's pumping more to capitalize on the Middle East crisis, as it did during the oil shocks of the 1970s. Although Soviet oil reserves total more than 60 billion barrels, more than double America's, many of the overtaxed Soviet fields have fallen into irreversible decline.

The reasons range from big fields reaching maturity, to inefficient extraction methods and problems with equipment. Much of the gear is outdated. A lot of money has been spent for Western equipment, but some of it sits idle, Western analysts say. Pipelines and other parts of the oil-transportation system aren't adequate, and accidents and spills are frequent.

At the same time, the cost of pumping oil from new wells is soaring, straining already strapped Soviet finances. The Kremlin, reversing its investment policy of the past 20 years, is actually cutting back capital spending on the oil industry.

While such problems mean Soviet oil won't be able to make up for the lost Iraqi and Kuwaiti supply, they do present the West with a big opportunity. The Kremlin has long insisted on developing its oil resources alone, guarding industry details like military secrets. That is starting to change as Mikhail Gorbachev opens the economy to the West. For beleaguered Siberian oil officials, the prospect of cooperation with Western companies is one bright spot on an otherwise dark horizon.

Steadily Declining Output

How dark? Last year, total Soviet energy output declined for the first time since the 1940s. Western analysts believe oil output fell 2.5%, to an average 12.1 million barrels a day.

Soviet experts say it may soon drop below 12 million barrels, to its lowest level in over a decade. But Western experts say it's already below that, and see a slippage to less than 11 million barrels a day before 1995. An even more pessimistic projection comes from a senior Estonian scientist, Mikhail B. Korchemkin, who sees daily Soviet output falling to just over 10 million barrels by 1995, and then, by 2010, to nine million.

The Soviet Union is trying to give priority to exports, which account for about a third of production and bring in much of the nation's hard currency. But it has recently cut sales to Eastern Europe to keep supplies flowing to its own energy-hungry economy and the West.

Even though Moscow has drawn down domestic inventories to try to maintain exports, those exports have fallen from the 1988 peak of 4.1 million barrels a day to an estimated 3.7 million a day last year. Of this, about 1.7 million barrels a day went to the West and two million to Eastern Europe. This year, the Soviets have cut East Europe deliveries 140,000 barrels a day.

Robert Ebel, an Ensearch Corp. executive and former U.S. intelligence expert on Soviet energy, sees Soviet oil exports falling another 400,000 barrels a day in 1990.

Although no cure-all, the Soviets' hopes for joint ventures with Western oil companies offer promise. Such ventures could give them both the technology and the capital they need.

"Tell the Americans and anyone else that they should come to us. They're welcome," says Anatoly Tyukalov, deputy head of Glavtyumenneftegaz, the body that oversees Western Siberia's oil and gas industry. "We need new technology and new equipment to get oil out more cheaply. That means we want your capital, your technology, your credits."

Western oil companies have been quick to respond. This month, 15 officials from Mr. Tyukalov's organization were flown to the U.S. by Du Pont Co.'s Conoco unit. Oil giants such as Royal Dutch/Shell Group and Amoco Corp. and oil-service firms such as Halliburton Co. are trekking to Siberia in hopes of getting access to Soviet oil through joint ventures.

So far, however, there is little to show for the flurry of activity. The talks are often laborious, Westerners complain, and many Soviet oil officials continue to harbor deep-rooted suspicion of Western motives. Rather than giving the foreigners free rein, officials want them to work on fields that are tricky and expensive to exploit.

It doesn't help that the Soviet bureaucracy in charge of oil is in a chaotic state because of the government's attempts to restructure the economy. The Oil Ministry last year merged with the Gas Ministry, its longtime rival. But the super-agency that emerged may not have long to live itself; officials say one option is to replace it with a government committee.

Moreover, since Boris Yeltsin became president of the Russian Republic in May, the question of who controls Siberian oil has been thrown into doubt. The republic's parliament recently stipulated that it must approve any natural-resources ventures negotiated by Soviet authorities. And this week, Russian officials even held out the prospect that they would be interested in joining the Organization of Petroleum Exporting Countries.

0043

This confusion is hard on foreign oil companies trying to get a Soviet foothold. Do they need separate agreements with separate republics? If they sign an agreement with the Ministry of Geology, as Texaco Inc. did recently, will it hold with the other ministries? (Texaco's agreement is to explore areas of the Timan-Pechora region, straddling the Arctic Circle, where Texaco estimates oil reserves could be more than five billion barrels.)

With perseverance, some Westerners have managed to navigate this maze. One of them is Canadian Fracmaster Ltd., a Calgary-based oil-services company with a technique to recover oil from wells damaged during drilling.

In March 1989, the company set up a joint venture with the oil-production enterprise here. The Canadian company provides most of the equipment and several oil specialists to oversee the process.

Unlike in the West, where it would normally be paid for its services on a contract basis, Fracmaster is paid according to the amount of additional oil that flows from the wells it has treated. The joint venture has treated about 100 wells and recovered about 300,000 tons of additional oil, but it is not yet profitable.

Monty Meikle, chief of technology for the venture, says work tends to be slower than in the West, with jobs that could be done in one week taking two to three. One of the biggest problems is long waits for Soviet equipment that the venture uses, such as trucks, surface rigs and fluid tanks. Still, Mr. Meikle says, "as we get to know each other, things improve and move more to our standards."

The Soviets are in dire need of such sophisticated drilling and recovery methods. For years, the government and oil workers paid scant attention to the efficiency of extraction techniques; oil was so abundant they didn't need to bother.

In the rush to pump as fast as possible, drilling was often slapdash and led to frequent damage of the wells. Poor-quality pipes often corrode or are damaged by careless workers, leading to an estimated seven million barrels of oil being spilled on Siberian soil every year.

The Soviet oil-equipment industry, too, ignored the needs of smaller fields, concentrating on providing for huge fields. Now, as some big fields reach maturity and new ones become harder to find, such neglect is returning to haunt the industry.

"Most of our sources were wrongly exploited," says Alexander Arbatov, an oil expert at the Soviet Academy of Sciences. "We have a very low technical level, and haven't improved our standards." As a result, he says, "production is falling faster than we expected."

For Prof. Arbatov and some other Soviet experts, such technical problems are merely the tip of the iceberg. They contend that the Kremlin's entire energy strategy over the past 20 years has been flawed.

Since oil was first exploited in Western Siberia in the mid-1960s, the government has poured billions of dollars into the region in order to pump as much as possible. The resulting revenues from exports, particularly following the oil price surges of the 1970s, kept the economy afloat.

Economics is dictating a drastic change of policy. When oil prices started falling in the mid-1980s, the newly appointed Mr. Gorbachev initially chose traditional methods to offset the shortfall in revenue: more money to pump more oil.

But that policy proved prohibitively expensive. According to internal government figures, the cost of extracting Soviet oil—now mostly from smaller fields, which are harder to exploit—has almost tripled since 1985. Last year, the Kremlin slammed on the brakes. Investment in the oil sector, along with capital outlays to other industries, was pared back heavily.

Critics say the move came too late. Over the years, they say, some of the huge amount invested in oil would have been better spent on other sectors of the economy, especially production of consumer goods. At the same time, heavy subsidies

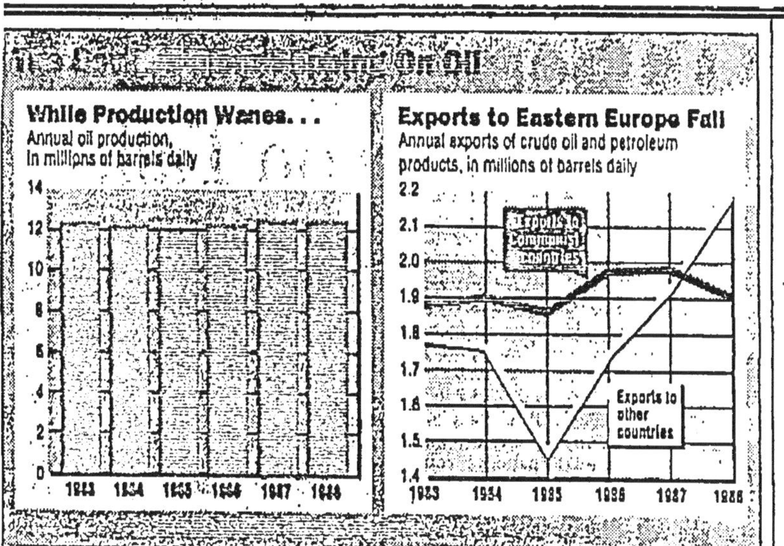

0044

on energy allowed the nation's industry to get hooked on cheap oil.

As a result, consumption surged. In all energy, the Soviet Union consumes the equivalent of nearly 28 million barrels of oil a day, more than all of Western Europe and second only to the U.S.

Alexei Makarov, director of the Institute of Energy Research at the Academy of Sciences, says the government needs to triple domestic energy prices just to bring them into line with actual costs. But such a move is politically tricky at a time of growing social unrest.

Here in Nefteyugansk, a town of 140,000 whose name means "Oil South," local officials are equally critical of past policy. Government spending in the area doubled between 1980 and 1988, but most of it went to the oil industry, not the pressing social needs of residents.

One tenth of the town's population is on the waiting list for better housing. There is a dire shortage of hospitals and schools. Oil workers here and throughout Western Siberia threatened to strike earlier this year to protest poor living conditions. They backed off after the government gave them some hard currency from oil revenues to buy imported meat.

Vladimir Solomin, deputy director of the town's oil-producing enterprise, would like his company to become independent both of Moscow and of the oil authorities in Tyumen, 600 miles to the south. "We must use the oil we extract to improve social conditions," he says. "Cooperation with foreign partners is thus very important."

Foreign oil companies are eager. With prospects rapidly shrinking elsewhere, they see the U.S.S.R. as a new frontier.

France's state-owned Elf Aquitaine announced the first major exploration and production agreement with the Soviets—although, like most agreements, it's not in Siberia, where the oil is easiest to exploit. It was to give Elf the right to drill on 13,500 square miles of territory north of the Caspian Sea near the Volga River. Or so it seemed. Elf's president said later that many details still had to be worked out.

Then, last June 2, while Mr. Gorbachev was in the U.S., Chevron Corp. signed a declaration of intent to explore and develop regions including the giant Tengiz field—the biggest discovered in the world in the past 10 years, according to Soviet authorities. Its potential reserves are estimated at 25 billion barrels, almost equal to all the proven reserves of the U.S.

Chevron can provide the equipment and the management skills the Soviets lack, says Edward B. Scott II, vice president of Chevron Overseas Petroleum Inc., who calls Soviet equipment "30 years behind us." But he says developing the field will be difficult. The Soviets have invested $1 billion so far, he says, and much more will be necessary. The field itself has high pressure, and there is a high concentration of hydrogen sulfide in the gas—a dangerous substance in an oil field if not handled correctly.

Mr. Scott says Chevron has been in "intense negotiations" for more than a year. It has brought groups of Soviet authorities, including the top official of the province, to the U.S. and taken them on tours of facilities. It brought the minister of petroleum to the U.S. But it still doesn't have a final agreement with the Soviets.

Some smaller oil companies and oil-service concerns are succeeding in carving out niches. Anglo-Suisse Inc. of Houston has formed a joint venture company with the Soviets called White Knight. It drills horizontal wells—extremely helpful in reviving oil fields thought to be worn out. It's studying the feasibility of drilling as many as 450 horizontal wells. It will share in the oil recovered.

Under a recent agreement between Texas-based Halliburton and the Soviet Ministry of Oil and Gas, a Soviet ship is sailing the Chukchi Sea collecting seismic data for future oil exploration. The data will be packaged for sale to Western oil companies.

But until more foreign oil companies come to the region, officials here admit their daily struggle with the uncertainties of the Soviet economy will continue.

One morning, Mr. Solomin drives out to the Mammoth oil field with a visitor and Mr. Gusev, the field's chief engineer. On the way, they stop to inspect a well.

The Romanian-made rig isn't moving.

"Why isn't it working?" Mr. Solomin asks.

"Repairs," Mr. Gusev replies.

Mr. Solomin, embarrassed to show off something that isn't functioning, turns to his visitor and tries to shrug it off.

"They'll be here tomorrow to fix it," he says, hopefully.

1902

0045

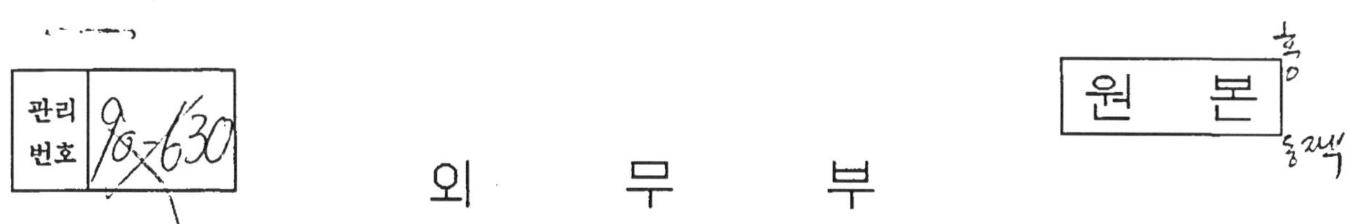

관리번호 90-630

원 본

외 무 부

종 별 :

번 호 : QTW-0109　　　　일 시 : 90 0822 1230

수 신 : 장관(기협)

발 신 : 주 카타르 대사

제 목 : 원유 안정공급 확보를 위한 교섭

대:WQT-0083

연:QTW-0091,0100

1. 표제건, 본직은 8.22 . 09:30-10:15 간 카타르석유공사 (QGPC)의 DR. JABER AL-MARRI 총재를 방문 면담하였는바 동내용 아래와 같음.

2. 면담내용

가. 동총재의 7 월방한 성과

체한중 아국의 주요정유사인 유공 및 한국가스공사측과 협의한 결과 유공측으로부터 카타르산 LNG 도입과 LNG 관련사업에 대한 적극참여언질을 받았기때문에 매우만족하고 고무되었으며 10 월중에 유공사장이 카타르를 방문하게되어 있어 구체적협력추진을 기대하고 있음.

나. 이락, 쿠웨이트 원유공급중단에 따르는 증산가능성

QGPC 는 OPEC 참가국의 협의 결과에 따라 생산쿼터가 재조정되면 현쿼터 371,000 B/D 보다 100,000 B/D 을 증산할 능력과 용의가 있음.

다. 한국에 대한 원유공급 증가 문제

(아국의 대이락 경제제재조치 내용을 설명하고 그로 인한 경제적타격 극복을 위하여 카타르원유의 안정내지 증량공급을 요청한데 대하여)

기존계약물량의 안정공급을 확약하며 유공에 대하여는 91.1 월부터 2 만 B/D 을 증량(도합 3 만 B/D)공급키로 합의한바 있음.

(OPEC 재협의에 따라 카타르의 쿼터가 상향조정될 경우 , 아국에대한 증량공급을 희망한다는 본직의 요청에 대하여)

OPEC 쿼터가 상향조정되고 한국회사측에서 요청이 있으면 호의적으로 고려될수 있음.

경제국 대책반	차관	1차보	2차보	중아국	통상국	정문국	청와대	안기부

PAGE 1　　　　90.08.22 19:26

외신 2과 통제관 DO

0046

라. 금후원유가격에 대한 의견

이락, 쿠웨이트사태로 인한 유가상승은 일시적 현상으로서 현재시장에도 충분한 물량이 있으므로 안정을 되찾을 것으로 생각하며 , 금후소비국 뿐만 아니라 산유국을 위해서도 원유가의 안정은 절대필요한것임.급격한 하락으로 인한 위험부담도 고려되어야 함.

3. 의견

금번 면담을 통해 QGPC 내지 주재국고위층(하마드 경제무역장관 및 압둘라 내무장관 면담시 얻은 감촉)의 아국에 대한 호의적인 태도는 주재국의 경제정책상 최대의 과제인 LNG 수출 및 동관련사업에 대한 아국의 부자등 참여를 기대하는대 기인하는 것이므로 금후 유공등 정유사의 적극적인 참여가 요망됨.

(대사 유내형-국장)

예고:90.12.31

PAGE 2

0047

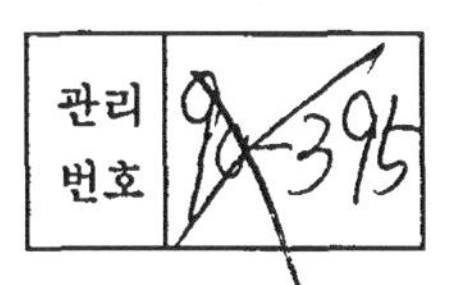

외 무 부

종 별 : 지 급

번 호 : DJW-1219 일 시 : 90 08230850

수 신 : 장관(미북,통이,기협)

발 신 : 주 인니 대사

제 목 : 이라크.쿠웨이트 사태

대:WDJ-0634

연:DJW-1210

당관 여참사관이 8.22. 주재국 최대회교단체 MUHAMMADIYAH 사무총장 RAKUMAN HARUN 가 면담내용 하기 보고함

1.OPEC 회원국중에서도 쿠웨이트가 쿼타를 무시하고 원유를 생산함으로써 여타 회원국으로부터 비판을 받아왔으며, 막대한 원유수입금으로 왕족과 일부 특권층이 부를 독점, 아랍세계 지탄을 받아 오던중 이락이 원유가 인상을 위해 쿠웨이트의 협조를 수차 요청하였으나, 쿠웨이트가 이락의 요구를 묵살함에따라 이번 사태가 발발함

2. 이락으로서는 사우디주둔 미군철수 보장없이 쿠웨이트에서의 철수는 수락할수 없으며, 미군도 쿠웨이트 원상회복없이 사우디에서 철군및 대이락해상 봉쇄를 해제할수 없어 전쟁발발 위험이 고조되고 있음. 중동에서의 전쟁은 중동전체를 폐허로 만들것임

3. 이번 사태로 중동은 분열되고 있으며, 이락을 지지하는 국가는 리비아, 수단, 튜니시아, 알제리아, 예멘등이며, 사우디를 지지하는 국가는 모로코, 시리아, 이집트, UAE, 오만, 카타르등으로 분리되고 있음

4. 미군이 사우디에 주둔, 그 영향력을 확대함에따라 이스라엘의 입지가 강화되고 있고 PLO 의 입장은 더욱 위축되고 있음. 이집트는 미, 사우디로부터의 군사적, 경제적 지원을 바탕으로 중동의 지도국 역할을 담당코저함. 요르단만이 미, 이락분쟁의 틈바구니에서 자구책에 부심하고 있음

5. 앞으로 중동사태가 평화적으로 해결되려면 이락이 쿠웨이트에서 철수하고 미군이 사우디에서 철수해야 한다는것이 아랍인들의 희망사항이지만 미, 이락의

미주국 대책반	차관	1차보	2차보	중아국	경제국	통상국	청와대	안기부

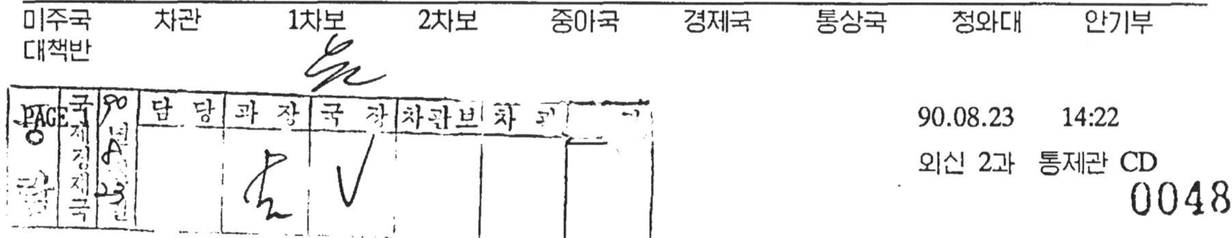

90.08.23 14:22

외신 2과 통제관 CD

0048

태도는 강경하고 특히 미국은 중동에 발판구축을 위해 노력해왔고 이번 사태가 미국세력 부식에 절호의 기회로 삼아 대중동 영향력을 확대해 나갈것이 예상되므로 전쟁이 아닌 협상에 의한 평화가 정착되어도 금후 미국은 사우디주둔 미군을 근거로 중동에서 상당한 영향력을 행사하는 교두보를 구축할것임

6. 인니는 과거 이락 원유 3 만베럴을 바타제로 도입하였으나, 사우디와는 현금거래를 해야 하므로 경제적으로 부담이 증가됨. 국제원유가격이 계속 강세를 지속할경우 선진국및 개도국의 인니산 공산품 구매력이 감소되므로 경제적으로 유익한점이 없고 일부 OPEC 회원국이 쿼타이상으로 원유를 생산하게 되면 유가 폭락의 우려도 있어 OPEC 회원국이 쿼타를 준수하여 국제유가(21 분선)를 안정시키는것이 중요과제임.끝

(대사 김재춘-국장)

예고:90.12.31 일반

PAGE 2

0049

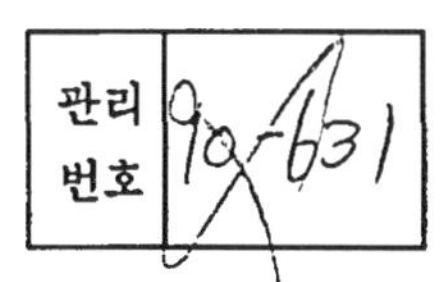

원 본

외 무 부

종 별 :

번 호 : MXW-1031 일 시 : 90 0822 1900

수 신 : 장관(기협,미중)

발 신 : 주 멕 대사

제 목 : 석유수급 및 유가동향 파악

대 WMX-0732,0714

연 MXW-0977,0960

1. 대호 당관 김서기관이 주재국 석유 수출회사(PMI) PEDRO HAAS 국제업무담당국장 접촉, 확인 사항 아래 보고함.

가. 산유국 관련사항

- 주재국 산유능력 260 만 바렐

- 최근 생산량: 260 만 바렐

- 석유소비량: 128 만 바렐

- 수출량 및 수출국별 현황

0 미국: 71 만바렐

0 스페인: 15 만

0 일본: 13 만

0 불란서: 5 만

0 이스라엘: 3 만

- 이.쿠사태 이후 10 만바렐 증산실시

나. 주재국의 유류가격 동향: 약 25 불/바렐

다. 향후 국제원유 시장에 대한 수급 및 가격전망

HAAS 국장은 차주중 미국-이라크간 무력충돌이 야기될 경우 국제 원유가는 베럴당 40-45 불선까지 치솟을 가능성이 있으나 이러한 고유가는 일시적일것이며 결국 장기적으로 는 25 불선에서 조정될 것으로 보고있음.

2. 한편 동국장에 의하면 아국 호남정유와는 과거 2 년간 거래실적이 없음을 지적, 동정유사와의 기존 1 만바렐 계약은 현재 멕시코 석유수급 사정으로보아 이행하기가

경제국 차관 1차보 2차보 미주국 안기부

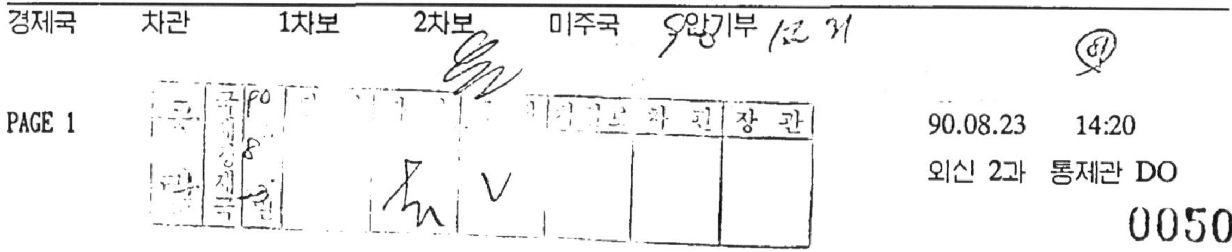

PAGE 1

90.08.23 14:20

외신 2과 통제관 DO

0050

어렵다고 말함. 그러나 동국장은 아국 극동정유사와는 이라크, 쿠바사태 발발이전부터 원유 공급계약 체결 추진해오고 있음에 비추어 동사와 9 월중 2 만벨 공급계약을 체결할 예정임을 밝힘.

3. 동국장의 발언은 멕측이 장기적이고 안정적인 멕산 원유 구매를 원하고 있음에 비추어 그간 호남정유가 멕산원유를 구매하지 않은데에 대한 불만의 표시로 감지 되었으며 이에대해 당관은 호남정유의 구매의사 표시시 호의적 고려를 요청하였음.

4. 대책 및 건의

최근 이라크-쿠웨이트 사태에 따른 원유확보 및 석유수급 안정대책상 멕시코산 원유수입이 불가피할 경우 호남, 극동정유로 하여금 멕시코 원유공급 계약체결을 적극 추진토록 유도하고 장기적 원유공급선 확보를 위하여 정제시설 및 경제성 측면에서 그간 수입을 지양해온 멕산 중질류 정제시설 확충등을 통하여 외교적 유대관계 강화목적의 정책적 원유 성격의 도입을 지양하고 COMMERICAL BASE 에 의한 거래방식 전환을 검토하여 줄것을 건의함.

(대사대리-국장)

예고 90.12.31. 까지

PAGE 2

0051

관리 번호	90-633

원 본

외 무 부

종 별 :

번 호 : DJW-1223　　　　일 시 : 90 08231430

수 신 : 장관(기협,통이)

발 신 : 주 인니 대사

제 목 : 원유 안정확보를 위한 대산유국 외교활동 강화

대:WDJ-0635

대호관련, 당관 여참사관이 8.23. 주재국 PERTAMINA 총무국장 H.BAHARUDDIN과 면담한 내용 하기보고함

1. 인니는 한국에 LNG 및 원유를 공급하고 있는 주요 에너지자원 협력대상국임.한국은 최근 인니산 원유 15-35 천베럴을 정기적으로 수입하고 있고, LNG 는 년간 200 만톤 장기공급외에 최근 90 년 50 만톤, 91 년 80 만톤을 추가도입키로 합의함

2. 인니는 추가생산을 위한 시설부자가 최소 3-4 개월 소요되며,90 년말 또는 91.1 월 증산계획을 목표로 시설확장을 하고 있으나, 막대한 부자비 충당에 어려움이 있음. 현 실정으로는 한국이 원유추가도입을요청하여도 응할수 없으며, 내년 1 월경 생산이 증가될경우 협의가 가능할것이나 과거 한국은 인니산 원유가 중동산에 비해 가격면에서 불은하다는 인식을 가지고 있었기 때문에 장기적인 거래가 성립되지 않았음

3. 중동사태가 장기화될경우, 세계유가는 금년말까지 28-38 불선에 육박할것임.사우디가 OPEC 합의를 무시하고 증산한다해도 1-1.5 백만 베렐이상증산은 어렵고, 여타 산유국 증산능력이 1 백만 베럴을 넘지 못할것으로 보아 선진공업국의 비축량을 대폭 줄이지 않는한 유가는 하락하지 않을것임

4. 사우디가 요청한 OPEC 자문회의가 8.25. 비엔나에서 개최되며, GINANDJAR 장관이 참석예정임.동회의는 인니, 사우디, 베네주엘라, 나이제리아등 일부 OPEC 국가 석유상이 참석하며, 사우디, 베네주엘라, 나이제리아가 요구하고 있는 원유증산을 자제토록 하고 유가안정을 위해 선진공업국이 비축량을 축소해줄것을 호소하게될 것임.끝

경제국 장관 차관 1차보 2차보 통상국 동자부 대책반

PAGE 1　　　　90.08.23 18:04

외신 2과 통제관 FE

0052

(대사 김재춘-국장)
예고:90.12.31 일반

PAGE 2

0053

國際原油需給 및 價格動向 速報

(8.23 公館報告 綜合)

1990.8.24.
국제경제국, 기술협력과

1. 原油需給

   o 멕시코, 이·쿠 事態 以後 10만B/D 增産實施 (PMI 國際局長)

   o 카타르, OPEC 生産쿼터 再調整時 10만B/D 增産 用意表明 (QGPC 總裁)

   o 英國, 北海油田 定期補修 日程 延期등으로 增産 展望 없음 (英國 BP社)

   o 印尼, 追加生産위한 施設投資에 3-4개월 所要(PERTAMINA 總裁)

2. 油價

   o 現物市場 動向 (단위 : $/B)

	7.31	8.7	8.10	8.17	8.22	8.23	전일대비
Dubai	17.20	25.40	22.72	26.35	31.75	32.00	0.25
Oman	17.65	25.90	23.22	26.95	32.35	32.60	0.25
Brent	19.49	29.40	25.70	28.95	32.15	32.45	0.30
WTI	20.75	29.62	26.39	27.46	31.57	31.73	0.16

   o 미국-이라크간 武力衝突時, 배럴당 40-45불선 暴騰 豫想되나 長期的으로 25불선 調整 豫想 (멕시코 石油輸出會社 國際局長)

   o 事態 長期化時, 금년말까지 28-30불선 육박할 것이며 先進工業國의 備蓄量을 大幅 줄이지 않는 한 油價下落 없을 것임 (印尼 國營會社 總務局長)

     - 사우디 1-1.5백만배럴 이상 增産難望, 여타 産油國 增産能力 1백만배럴 미만

3. 其他 關聯事項

   o 사우디 要請 OPEC 諮問會議 8.25 비엔나 開催豫定 (印尼 PERTAMINA 總務局長)

   o 멕시코 PMI, 극동과 9월중 2만B/D 供給契約 締結 豫定 (PMI 國際局長)

   o 카타르 QGPC, 油公과 91.1月부터 2만B/D 增量 供給合意 (QGPC 總裁)

앙고재	기술협력과	90년 8월 24일	담 당	과 장	국 장	차관보	차 관	장 관
			홍성화					

0054

國際原油需給 및 價格動向 速報

(8.24 公館報告 綜合)

1990.8.25.
外務部, 國際經濟局

1. 原油需給

o 베네수엘라, 美國 要請에 따라 50-60만B/D 增産計劃

- 대신 美國에 自由貿易協定締結 및 原油增産施設擴大 投資 要請中

o 이집트, 現在 增産餘力 없으며, 배럴당25불시 新規投資로 增産(약10-20만B/D)예정

o 부시대통령, 8.22 記者會見에서 향후 繼續 적정한 石油供給量 確保 可能, 現在로선 에너지 節約 措置 不必要 言及

2. 油價

o 現物市場 動向 (단위 : $/B)

	7.31	8.7	8.10	8.17	8.22	8.23	8.24	전일대비
Dubai	17.20	25.40	22.72	26.35	31.75	32.00	31.35	- 0.65
Oman	17.65	25.90	23.22	26.95	32.35	32.60	31.95	- 0.65
Brent	19.49	29.40	25.70	28.95	32.15	32.45	31.83	- 0.62
WTI	20.75	29.62	26.39	27.46	31.57	31.73	31.21	- 0.52

o 長期的으로 25불선 安定 展望되나, 그동안 事態推移 따른 心理的 要因으로 騰落現狀 豫想 (주베네주엘라 대사)

o 8.22 油價 急騰原因 分析 (美國 言論 報道綜合)

- 軍事的 緊張高潮로 戰爭勃發 可能性 우려

- 사우디 政府, 8.22 精油製品 輸出 減縮 발표 (20-30만B/D)

- 사우디·베네주엘라등의 增産 遲延

※ 需給의 不均衡보다 緊張高潮에 대한 心理的 反應

o 佛蘭西, 9.12 發表豫定인 91年度 豫算編成에서 향후 油價를 배럴당 25불 展望

3. 其他 關聯 事項

o 이집트石油公社 (EGPC)側, 약 20만톤 年內 我國供給可能 言及(주카이로총영사)

- 同 公社, 現在 GEISUM 중질유 10만-20만톤 競賣公告(入札期間 8.23-8.28間)

0055

이라크 , 쿠웨이트事態 報告

1990. 8.23

1. 當事國動向

o 이 라 크
- Saleh 國會議長이 人質들에 대해 國家別로 選別的인 釋放可能性을 示唆, 西方 協助體制를 고란시켜 보려는 의도를 보인 이외에는 特異動向 없음.

o 美 國
- Bush 大統領 記者會見 (22일)
① 이라크가 쿠웨이트撤收등 國際法을 遵守하지 않는한 協商意思가 없음.
② 豫備軍 召集令에 署名
③ 쿠웨이트 大使館 閉鎖要求 拒否

o U N
- 美國側은 『상당한 進展』이 있었다고 言及하고 있으나, 蘇聯側은 『經濟制裁 措置의 명백한 失敗』 狀況下에서만 介入이 承認되야 한다는 立場 固守

2. 主要國 反應

o 이 란 : 사우디와 UAE가 增産하면 OPEC은 油價下落이라는 중대한 위협에 直面할 것이라고 警告 (Kahyan紙 社說)

o 英 國 : 人質問題로 英國과 友邦의 페만政策은 影響받지 않을 것임 (King 國防長官)

o 사우디 : 사우디 國營販賣會社(SAMAREC)은 9월분 燈油販賣(販賣量 月2카고 水準) 中斷
. 사우디 駐屯 美軍에 대한 石油製品 供給原因

o 프랑스 : 空輸部隊 180여명의 프랑스 地上軍 UAE 派兵 宣言

o 요르단 : 西方世界가 이라크 侵攻에 대해 過剩反應 (Hussein王 記者會見, 22일)

o 蘇 聯 : UN의 대이라크 制裁案에 따르기 위해 이라크와의 모든 事業關係 中斷指示 (Ryzhkou 수상, 22일)

3. 石油市場 動向

o 26일경 페만危機에 따른 代替供給問題를 論議키 위해 사우디,인니,이란,나이제리아, 베네주엘라,알제리등 6개국 會議 開催豫定 (비엔나)

o 사우디등의 代替增産과 商業在庫 放出로 이라크.쿠웨이트 供給中斷 物量補塡 可能 (美 에너지省 次官, 22일)

o 一部 業界消息通은 이미 사우디,나이제리아,베네주엘라등이 增産에 突入한 것으로 추정

o 前日對比 : 武力衝突 危機高調로 2.80-3.68$/B 暴騰

(單位 : $/B)

	7.31	8. 7	8.10	8.17	8.21	8.22	前日對比
Dubai	17.20	25.40	22.72	26.35	28.07	31.75	3.68
Oman	17.65	25.90	23.22	26.95	28.67	32.35	3.68
Brent	19.49	29.40	25.70	28.95	29.35	32.15	2.80
W T I	20.75	29.62	26.39	27.46	28.70	31.57	2.87

0056

이라크 , 쿠웨이트事態 報告

1990. 8.21

1. 當事國動向

o 이 라 크
- 24日까지 쿠웨이트內 外國大使館의 業務를 閉鎖시키지 않는 國家의 外交官들은 一般外國人과 똑같이 取扱될 것임.
- 美國을 支援하는 國家의 外國人들은 아무도 이라크를 떠날 수 없음.
- 이라크에 抑留중인 外國人들이 軍事的 目標 및 전략요충지로 移動되었음.

o 美 國
- 페만내 軍事的 行動은 이라크군의 쿠웨이트 撤收와 쿠웨이트 政府의 回復後에나 終了될 것임.
- 이라크내 美國人들은 石油化學團地, 彈藥武器貯藏庫, 化學武器 生産團地 등으로 移動되었음.

o 쿠웨이트
- OPEC이 産油量을 增大하여 油價를 安定시키도록 促求

2. 主要國 反應

o U N : UN 安保理 상임이사국 5개국은 20일, UN 合同軍事行動을 論議하기 위해 非公式的으로 會同

o 이집트 : 이집트는 20일부로 全油種의 輸出價格을 2.25$/B 引上

o 이 란 : 사우디는 OPEC 結束力을 와해시키는 秘密去來를 中止할 것을 警告

o MEES지 (20일)
- OPEC은 대이라크 封鎖와 관련, 두가지 상반되는 危險에 直面
① 增産을 위한 共同行動을 취하는 경우, 이라크와 쿠웨이트가 生産에 復歸할때 더큰 어려움에 直面
② 增産치 않는 경우 高油價의 不安定한 供給으로 需要가 減退, '80년대 中盤과 같은 狀況 再現

3. 石油市場 動向

o 20일 油價는 전일對比 0.65$/B 上昇

(單位 : $/B)

	7.31	8. 7	8.10	8.16	8.17	8.20	前日對比
Dubai	17.20	25.40	22.72	25.03	26.35	27.00	0.65
Oman	17.65	25.90	23.22	25.63	26.95	27.60	0.65
Brent	19.49	29.40	25.70	27.42	28.95	29.30	0.35
W T I	20.75	29.62	26.39	27.46	27.46	28.66	1.20

0057

이라크 . 쿠웨이트事態 報告

1990. 8.18

1. 當事國 關聯動向

○ 이 라 크
- 17일 9,000명의 이란포로를 釋放하고 이란占領地에서 軍隊撤收 開始 發表
- 封鎖措置 以後 最初로 식품을 積載한 이라크 船舶, 17일 홍해로 進入키 위해 스웨즈 운하 通過

○ 美 國
- 부시大統領은 요르단 國王과 會談후 이라크에 대한 전면적인 海上封鎖 措置 指示
- 이라크.쿠웨이트行 貨物을 積載한 船舶에 대한 搜索.發砲 및 최소한의 필요한 武力行事 許容
- 이라크의 美.英國人 호텔集結 命令은 人質化 試圖라고 非難

2. 主要國 反應

○ U N
- UN의 對이라크 制裁强化를 위한 武力使用은 安保理의 承認이 없는한 UN 憲章을 違反한 것이라는 立場 表明
- UN安保理 特別委員會가 UN의 對이라크 封鎖案과 關聯 非公開會議 召集

○ 사우디 : 이라크 탱커(8만톤) 17일, 사우디 Yanbu港 入港 거절당함.

○ E C : 사우디에 政治.經濟.軍事的인 支援努力 示唆

○ 日 本
- 페만事態와 관련, 非戰鬪部隊 派遣檢討中임을 示唆
- 이란으로부터 4/4分期中 70만B/D 船積키로 合意 (從前보다 40만B/D 增)

○ 요르단 : 후세인 國王은 美大統領과 會談結果를 說明키 위해 이라크 訪問豫定

3. 石油市場 動向

○ OPEC 臨時總會 召集은 會員國間의 意見不一致로 早期召集 難望

○ 사우디, 나이제리아, 리비아, 베네주엘라는 이미 增産에 突入한 것으로 알려짐.

※ 國際油價 變動推移 : 前日對比 0~1.53$/B 上昇

(單位 : $/B)

	7.31	8. 7	8.10	8.15	8.16	8.17	前日對比
Dubai	17.20	25.40	22.72	24.00	25.03	26.35	1.32
Oman	17.65	25.90	23.22	24.60	25.63	26.95	1.32
Brent	19.49	29.40	26.70	26.45	27.42	28.95	1.53
W T I	20.75	29.62	26.39	26.54	27.46	27.46	0

0058

관리번호	90-632

분류번호	보존기간

발 신 전 보

900823 1850 DY

번 호 : WSB-0349 타 종별 :

수 신 : 주 수신처참조 대사. 총영사

발 신 : 장 관 (기협)

제 목 : 이라크·쿠웨이트 사태

표제사태로 인한 유가인상으로 물가상승, 국제수지악화등 국내경제에 대한 제반 심각한 영향이 우려되고 있어 국제원유수급 및 유가동향에 대한 면밀한 분석이 요구되고 있는 바, 주재국 관련부서, 연구소, 언론등과 접촉을 견지하면서 기 보고한 사항에 계속하여 아래사항에 대한 변동사항을 수시 보고 바람.

1. 산유국 해당사항
   - o 산유정책
   - o 산유량 및 유가
2. 수입국 해당사항
   - o 이라크·쿠웨이트 물량감소에 대한 확보대책 및 대응방안
   - o 원유 및 석유제품 비축현황 (물량, 지속일수등), 비축유 방출 여부 및 향후계획
   - o 주재국내 유류가격 동향
3. 공통사항
   - o 국제원유시장에 대한 수급 및 가격전망. 끝.

(국제경제국장 최 대화)

수신처 : 주사우디, 이란, UAE, 오만, 베네주엘라, 에쿠아돌, 리비아, 페루, 카타르, 이집트, 알제리, 가봉, 인니, 말련, 멕시코, 브르나이, 미국, 카나다, 영국, 프랑스, 독일, 이태리, 일본, 대만, 스페인, 소련.

안 통 제	

앙 고 재	90년 8월 23일	기술협력과	기안자 성명		과 장	심의관	국 장		차 관	장 관
			홍성화		(서명)	(서명)	전결			(서명)

외신과통제

1990. 12. 31.

④ 제2차관보: (서명)

0059

WSB-0349 외 별지참조

WSB-0349 900823 1850 DY

WIR -0286	WAE -0178	WOM -0126	WVZ -0273	WEQ -0199
WLY -0308	WPU -0364	WQT -0091	WCA -0313	WAG -0112
WGA -0126	WDJ -0667	WMA -0601	WMX -0749	WBU -0114
WUS -2801	WCN -0874	WUK -1411	WFR -1618	WGE -1219
WIT -0777	WJA -3575	WCH -0694	WSP -0423	WSV -0628

0060

원 본

외 무 부

종 별 :

번 호 : CAW-0563 일 시 : 90 0823 2030

수 신 : 장관(기협)

발 신 : 주 카이로 총영사

제 목 : 석유수급및 유가동향등 보고

1. 주재국 관련사항 (89.7-90.6말)

- 산유능력: 년43.4백만톤, 최근 89만 BPD(생산목표 87만 BPD)

- 석유소비량: 21.3백만톤(42.5만 BPD,생산량의 약 50퍼센트)

- 수출량 : 년 22.1백만톤

- 수출내역

. 기간 계약 수출분: 7.5백만톤

. SPOT MARKET: 10.5 백만톤

. 원유 시추 회사분: 5백만톤

- 수출국별 기간계약 현황

. 수출국별(88/89년 단위 백만톤):이스라어(2),이태리(1.7),싱가폴(1.1),그리스(0.85),스리랑카(0.5),한국(0.364),스페인(0.3),미국(0.26),예멘(0.24)

. 기간계약: 이스라엘, 이태리등 (물량미상)

- 주재국은 현재 증산 여력이 없으며 시추업체는원유가가 15불 이하일시 증산을위한 투자를 해오지않았으나 배럴당 25불 이상이 될경우 신규 투자를하여 원유를 증산 예정이라고 함. 다만 수개월의시일이 소요될 것으로 보임(10-20만 배럴정도)

2. 주재국은 에너지 절약 대책을 고려치 않고있음.

3. 주재국 유류 가격 동향

- 90.7말까PUIC QR불, 8.1-7: 21불, 8.8-15: 23불, 8.16-19:24.25불, 8.20-22: 26.50불, 8.23-현재: 31.65불

4. 원유수급 및 가격 전망

경제국 2차보 통상국 상공부 동자부 대책반 미주국 1차보 안기부

PAGE 1

90.08.24 00:37 DN

외신 1과 통제관

0061

- 사우디등 증산 여력이 있는 국가들도 원유증산에 다소 시일이 소요되며 걸프 사태에 따른 심리적 영향에 의한 수요 증가등으로 단기적으로 원유 공급부족 사태가예상됨.

- 이에따라 원유 가격도 상승세를 시현할 것으로 전망됨.

5. 참고사항

- 주재국 석유공사측(EGPC) 은 아국에 20만톤정도는 연내에 공급할 수 있다고함.

- 또한 공사는 현재 GEISUM 원유(중질유)10만-12만톤 을 경매 공고하였으며 입찰마감은 8.23-8.28간으로 9.3-6중에 선적이 가능하다고 함.끝.

(총영사 박동순-국장)

0062

원 본

암호수신

외 무 부

종 별 :

번 호 : UKW-1573　　　　일 시 : 90 0823 2000

수 신 : 장관(기협,통일,구일)

발 신 : 주 영 대사

제 목 : 석유수급및 유가동향 보고

대: WUK-1379

대호관련 당관 이참사관이 금 8.23.(목) 주재국 에너지부 B.MORGAN 경제및 통계담당관 및 BP 사와 접촉 파악한 내용을 아래와 같이 보고함

1. 산유국 관련사항

가. 산유능력

-주재국은 북해유전을 중심으로 석유 총매장량이 약 38 억 배럴이며 가채년수(R/P)는 5.5 년임

-전 세계 매장량(10,118 억 베럴)의 3.0 프로임

나. 최근의 생산량및 소비량(단위: 천 BD)

내용,85,86,87,88,89 년 순

생산량: 2,665 2,665 2,555 2,365 1,905

소비량: 1,630 1,645 1,610 1,690 1,730

다. 수출량및 수출국별 현황

89 년도 EC 국가. 남아공 및 동구 국가에 대해 49,165 천본의 원유를 수출하였으나 수출국별 상세 통계는 추후 입수 보고예정임

라. 이.쿠웨이트 사태이후 증산 실시 여부

87 년 이래 생산량이 점차 줄어들고, 특히 금년도 북해 유전의 정기 보수 일정이 8-9 월로 늦추어 지고 있는 점등을 감안, 현재로선 생산량이 증가될 전망은 없음

2. 이라크, 쿠웨이트로 부터의 수입물량 감소에 대한 대응방안

-주재국은 기본적으로 자국 생산량으로 국내 소비에 충당할 수 있으므로 큰문제는 없음

-다만, 급격한 국제 유가 인상등에 대비, 도입선 다변화를 통한 물량확보, 자국산

경제국 대책반　차관　1차보　2차보　구주국　중아국　통상국　청와대　동자부

PAGE 1

공람	국제경제국	90년 월 일	담 당	과 장	국 장	차관보	차 관	장 관

90.08.24　06:57

외신 2과　통제관 CW

0063

원유 수출억제, 소비자들의 자율적인 에너지 절약등이 예상됨

-EC 및 IEA 를 통한 공동 대처 방안을 추구할 것임

3. 주재국의 유류가격 동향

-영국은 산유국으로서 석유산업이 완전히 자유화 되어 있고 유가 또한 석유회사별, 지역별, 주유소별 판매가격이 자유화 되어 있음

-따라서 석유제품 판매가격은 원유가격이 오르면 즉시 제품가격에 반영이되고, 원A 가격이 하락하면 즉시 판매가격에 반영됨

-최근 유류가격 동향

이락-쿠웨이트 사태이후 석유제품별로 6.4-8.4 프로 상승

유연휘발유(갈론당) 8.2 일 2.04 파운드, 8.22 일 2.17 파운드

경유(갈론당) 8.2 일 1.72 파운드, 8.22 일 1.86 파운드

4. 향후 국제 원유시장 전망(수급및 가격전망)

가. 수급전망

-이락-쿠웨이트 공급 감소분 약 500 만 B/D 를 충당하기 위해 증산 여력이 있는 타 산유국이 생산한다해도 OPEC 자체로서는 80 프로 정도만 보전이 가능한 상태임

-소비국들이 비축유를 방출하지 않는다고 가정할때 계절적으로 성수기로 진입하는 점등이 장애 요인이 되고 있음

-KLEINWART BENSON SECURITIES(90.4 월 전망)

내용, 90,91,92,93,94 순

BRENT 유: 20 불 22 불 25 불 28 불 30 불

-영국 CBI 소속 D.MCWILLIAMS 박사 전망(90.8.20)

(1) 경제적, 군사적 교착상태가 장기화 될 경우 3-4 년간 유가는 점진적 상승 전망

(2) 군사적 충돌 발생시, 유가는 단시간에 베럴당 40 불선 도달

-서방측 군사적 승리시: 90 년대 후반기 유가, 20 불/베럴 이내 유지(실질가격 기준)

-서방측 패배시: 초기유가 40 불/베럴로 급등이후 계속 큰폭 상승

5. 기타 참고사항

주재국 외무성(J.THORNTON 에너지 담당관)측에 의하면 주재국은 상기 원유 확보및 석유 수출 안정을 위해 독자적인 해결책을 추구하기 보다 EC 차원의 공동노력과 90.8.31.(금) 파리 개최 예정인 국제에너지기구(IEA)회의등을 통해 공동대책을 모색할

PAGE 2

0064

예정이라함. 끝

(대사 오재희-국장)

원 본

외 무 부

종 별 :

번 호 : VZW-0461 일 시 : 90 0823 1800

수 신 : 장 관(기협,미남,기정,국방부)

발 신 : 주 베네수엘라 대사

제 목 : 석유 수급및 유가동향

(자응 제 40호)

대: WVZ-267

대호 관련 주재국 관련 사항을 아래 보고함.

1. 산유능력: 275만 B/D

(향후 5년간 20억불 투자, 1998년부터는 일일생산능력을 350만 B/D 로 증대시킬계획)

2. 현 생산량: 194.5만 B/D(OPEC 쿼타)

3. 국내 소비량: 30만 B/D

4. 수출량: 165만 B/D(1989-1990)

5. 수출국별 현황

- 미국 66퍼센트, 구라파 13퍼센트, 카리브지역 13퍼센트, 일본, 싱가폴등 아시아지역 7퍼센트

6. 수출시 기간계약:

- 주재국은 가격변동을 반영하는 장기공급계약을 희망하나 현재로서는 동 장기계약을 체결한 국가는 없음.

7. 중동 사태에 따른 증산실시 여부

- 미국의 요청에 따라 50-60만 B/D증산계획이나, 주재국은 이에 대한 대가로 미국이 카나다및 멕시코와 체결한 자유무역협정을 주재국과도 체결하여 줄것과 원유 증산 시설확대를 위한 투자를 하여줄 것을 요청하고 있음.

8. 향후 국제원유시장에 대한 수급및 가격전망

- 현 중동사태로 인하여 현재 약 450만 B/D 의원유량이 국제원유 시장에서 탈루되는바 OPEC회원국및 비회원국 공히 또 한차례의 석유파동은 장기적으로

경제국 2차보 미주국 안기부 국방부 통상국 대책반 통차부 1차보 차관

PAGE 1

공람	국제경제국		담 당	과 장	국 장	차관보	차 관	장 관
					✓			

90.08.24 09:52 WG

외신 1과 통제관

0066

산유국에게도 큰 경제적 충격을 가할 것으로 인식하고 있음으로 원유가의 급격한 상승을 방지하고 안정된 가격유지를 위하여 증산노력을 경주할 것임.

- 따라서 장기적으로는 원유가가 25미불선에서 안정될 것으로 보이나, 그사이에 사태의 추이에 따른 심리적 요인으로 가격의 등락현상이 있을 것으로 예상됨.

9. 원유확보및 수급안정대책

- 산유국의 생산회사와 50:50 의 합작투자 형태로 국내 정유시설을 운영하여 산유국 생산회사로 하여금 소요 원유량을 공급토록 하는것이 현재 미국, 서구등 에너지소비국들이 산유국들로부터 원유를 조달하고 있는한 형태임을 참고바람.끝.

(대사 김재훈-국장)

원 본

외 무 부

종 별 :

번 호 : USW-3876 일 시 : 90 0823 1931

수 신 : 장 관(기협)

발 신 : 주 미 대사

제 목 : 석유시장 및 가격동향

대: WUS-2801

대호 금 8.23 당지 언론 보도를 종합 보고함.

1. 유가동향

가. 원유가격은 8.22 9 푸로의 높은 상승율을 보여 금번 사태 발발 이후 최초로 30 불선을 돌파하였으며, 휘발유등의 정유제품 가격도 일제히 인상되었음.

0 원유 (뉴욕 상품시장, 10월 인도가격):

배럴당 31.22 (전일에 비해 2.51 불 상승)

0 무연 휘발유 (뉴욕 상품 시장, 9월 인도가격):

갤론당 1.04 불 (전일에 비해 2.85 센트 상승)

0 난방유 (뉴욕상품시장,9월 인도가격):

0.91 불 (전일에비해 7.64 센트 상승)

나. 당지 전문가들에 따르면 원유가격의 급등원인은 아래와 같음.

0 부쉬 행정부의 예비군 동원령, 요르단 정부의 대이락 국경폐쇄등 군사적 긴장고조로 전쟁발발 가능성에 대한 우려가 높아지고 있음.

0 사우디 정부는 8.22 자국내 주둔 미군에 대한 유류공급을 위해 다젤유등 정유제품의 수출을 일일 20-30만 배럴정도 감축할 것임을 발표하였으며, 여타 일부 산유국들도 비상사태에 대비, 정유제품을 비축하기 시작했음.

0 사우디.베네주엘라 등의 원유 증산이 예상보다 지연되고 있음.

다. 대부분의 전문가들은 사우디의 원유수출은 정유제품 수출감축과는 무관하게 계속되고 있고 정유제품 수출 감축액 (일일 약 500만불)도 세계 석유제품 시장에 큰 영향을 미칠수 있는 규모가 아니며, 사우디의 증산 원유가 곧 시장에 방출될 것임을 들어 8.22.일의 유가급등은 수급의 불균형보다는 긴장고조에 대한 심리적 반응에 의한

경제국 2차보 1차보 동자부 통상국 미주국 정문국 차관 장관

PAGE 1

공람	국제경제국 90년 월 일	담 당	과 장	국 장	차관보	차 관	장 관
				V			

90.08.24 10:04 WG

외신 1과 통제관

0068

것이라고 분석하고 있음.

2. 주재국 대책

0 부쉬 대통령은 8.22 기자회견에서 에너지 절약에 관한 질문을 받고, 절약해야할 시점이기는 하나 향후에도 계속 적절한 석유공급량을 확보할수 있으므로 현재로서는 일상생활에 급격한 변화를 가져올 조치를 취할 필요는 없다는 요지로 답변하였음.

0 일부 의원들 및 소비자 단체들은 석유 소비감축을 위한 자동차 연료효율 제고등을 내용으로하는 법률 제정을 추진하고 있으나, 행정부는 에너지 절약을 위한 새로운 입법에는 반대하고 있음.

첨부: USW(F)-1919

(대사 박동진-국장)

외 무 부

종 별 :

번 호 : DJW-1224 일 시 : 90 0823 1430

수 신 : 장관(미북,통이,기협)

발 신 : 주인니대사

제 목 : 이라크.쿠웨이트 사태

이라크.쿠웨이트 사태와 관련 주재국 KOMPAS 지와BISNIS INDONESIA 지 사설요지 하기 보고함

1. KOMPAS 지 8.21자

쿠웨이트가 유가인상에 동조하지 않은데 불만을품은 이락이 쿠웨이트를 침공함으로써 지난주세계유가는 30분선을 육박함.

세계유가상승관련,고유가상황이 장기화될 경우생산국은 경제적으로 WIND FALL 효과를보게되고,비산유국은 국가적 어려움에봉착함.

서방국가들은 원유가 생존에 주요영향을주고있어 미국이 동 사태에 즉각 개입하고있음.

가장 심한 타격을 받는국가는 비산유개도국들임.

70년대 석유파동때보다 적은 진폭의유가인상에도 불구하고 제3세계 경제가 더욱악화되고 있어 이들국가에 주는 충격은 심각함.

제3세계 국가들은 경제적 파탄으로 새로운차관도입이 어려운 실정에 유가 상승은더 큰부담을 주고있음.

멕시코,나이제리아및 인니등은원유수지가 다소 호전되는 반면 브라질은 15억불을추가로 지불해야하는 어려움이 있음.

아프리카빈곤국은 공업용부품 수입대금이 원유수입대금으로 대체되어 장기적인 공업발전을 기대하기어려 운 입장임.

한국,대만같은 중진공업국도신속한 공업발전으로 에너지 소비가 증가되고 자동차수요가 급속히 증가,유류소비가 큰부담이 될것임.

미국은 70년대 석유파동후 에너지원 개발에정진,8-10프로의 원유대체 에너지원을개발하였으며,2030년에는 미국에너지의 28프로를비원유 에너지원으로

미주국 경제국 통상국 대책반 1차보 2차보 안기부

PAGE 1

90.08.24 22:11 CT

외신 1과 통제관

0070

충당할것임.

선진국은 GNP대비 에너지 비용이 절감되고 있으며,연료절약형자동차 개발로 경제성이 높아지고 있음.

전체적으로유가인상은 산유국에 일시 유리하나,개도국및후진국 경제가 어렵게되며,개도국의 공산품에대한 선진국 구매효과가 감소됨에 따라 개도국수출에 타격을 주는점등 미묘한 이해관계가 있어 인니로서는 면밀히 분석,신중히 대처해 나가야할것임.

2. BISNIS INDONESIA 지 8.20자

이락.쿠웨이트 사태는 중동전역에 확전의위험과 인니의 경제에도 영향을 주고있음.인니는 사우디의 파병요청을 거절하고유엔결의에 따라 이락과 무역을 중단함으로써이번 사태에 중립적인 태도를 보이고있으나,수출에 상당한 손실을 감수하게됨.

이번사태는 쿠웨이트가 2천억불의 해외재산을 가지고 있는 반면 이락은 막대한대외부채 상환부담을 안고 있어 국제원유가를 25불선으로 인상을 요구한데 대해 쿠웨이트가동조하지 않음으로써 발발함.

이번사태로 OPEC의 단합이 시험대에 올랐으며,주요에너지자원공급지역인 중동에서 전쟁위험이 고조되고있음.

세계 에너지원의 보호와 유가안정을 위 해모든 국가들이 전쟁억지 노력에협조하고,선진공업국들이 이락에 경제제재를가한다면 이락에 수출하던 개도국 상품에 대한선진국의 수입문호를 더욱 개방,개도국 경제 를지원해야 할것임.끝

(대사 김재춘-국장)

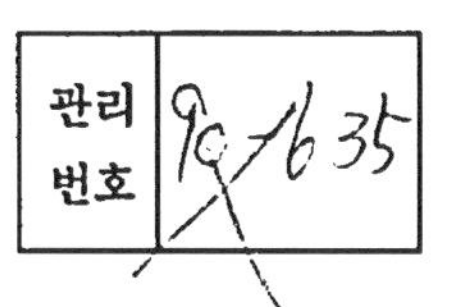

원 본

외 무 부

종 별 :

번 호 : FRW-1539 일 시 : 90 0824 1620

수 신 : 장관(기협)

발 신 : 주 불 대사

제 목 : 이라크.쿠웨이트 사태

대:WFR-1618

연:FRW-1434

1. 주재국은 GULF 사태(유가인상)의 경제전반에 대한 파급효과를 인플레 가속화, 기업생산비 증대, 금융시장 교란등으로 분석하고 이에대한 다각적인 대응방안을 모색중인 바,8.17. ROCARD 수상은 LIONEL STOLERU 기획담당장관(SECRETAIRE D'ETAT AU PLAN)을 주축으로 전문가 그룹을 결성,9 월말까지 GULF 사태의 중.단기 전망및 대책(경제. 사회분야)을 수립토록 지시하였음.

2. 또한, BEREGOVOY 경제. 재무상은 8.20. 물가안정을 정책의 최우선 과제로 내거는 한편, 공공및 민간부문 인금인상 억제, 세율인하를 통한 기업의 투자증대를 강조한바, 특히 외부적 요인(유가상승)에 의한 물가상승을 주재국 경제가 흡수해야 함을 강조하고, 생산적 투자를 위한 범국민적 소비억제를 역설하였음.

3. 상기관련, 주재국은 9.12. 경 발표예정인 91 년도 예산편성시 향후 경제를 아래와 같이 전망한 바 있음.

-원유가격:25 미불/B

-원유가 상승에 따른 추가부담:200 억 프랑(약 40 억불)

-90-91 년도 실질 경제성장률:3 프로 내외. 끝.

(대사 노영찬-국장)

예고:90.12.31. 까지

90 12 31

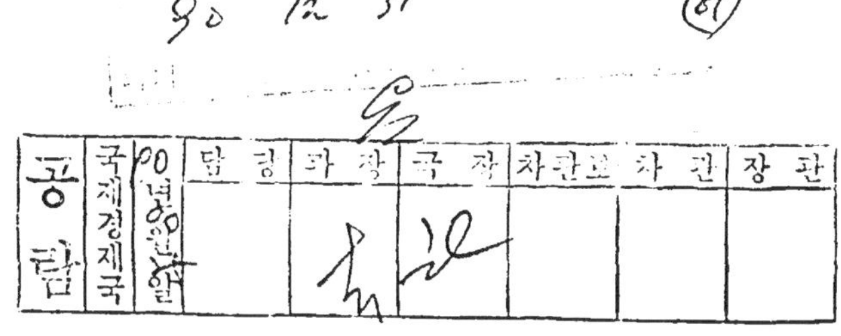

공람
국제경제국
90 년 8월 일
담 당
과 장
국 장
차관보
차 관
장 관

경제국 차관 1차보 2차보 구주국 중아국 통상국 청와대 안기부 대책반

PAGE 1 90.08.25 00:41

외신 2과 통제관 DO

0072

원 본

외 무 부

종 별 :

번 호 : USW-3889 일 시 : 90 0824 1812

수 신 : 장 관(기협)

발 신 : 주 미 대사

제 목 : 석유시장 및 가격동향(2)

표제관련 금 8.24(목) 당지 언론 보도를 종합보고함.

1. 유가 동향

가. 8.23 원유및 정유 제품가격은 지속적인 상승세를 나타내었음.

0 원유 (뉴욕 상품 시장,10월 인도가격):

배럴당 31.93 불 (전일에 비해 0.71 불 상승)

0 무연 휘발류 (뉴욕 상품 시장, 9월 인도가격):

개런당 108.55 센트 (전일에 비해 4.44 센트 상승)

0 난방유 (뉴욕 상품 시장, 9월 인도가격):

갤런당 96.3센트 (전일에 비해 5.3 센트 상승)

나. 미에너지부는 90.8. 현재의 민간 부문 원유 비축량은 379.5백만 배럴로 작년 동기에 비해 42백만 배럴이 증가하였다고 발표하였으나, 당지 전문가들은 원유 및 정유제품 가격이 계속 상승하고 있는 이유를 아래와 같이 분석하고 있음.

0 원유가격은 향후 수급 전망을 기초로하나, 현재 미국에 도입되고 있는 이유는 금번 사태 발발이전 계약분으로서 가격결정에 별다른 영향을 미치지 못함.

0 금번 사태 발발 이후 계약 체결된 원유가 실제도입되는 시기는 10월경인바, 국제원유 시장내에서는 10월경에는 공급 부족 사태가 올것이라는 우려가 높아지고 있음.

0 현재 미국내 휘발유등 정유제품의 재고는 오히려 낮은 수준인바, 미국 정유회사들이 FULL CAPACITY를 가동하고 있으므로 정유제품의 증산 가능성은 희박함.

2. 주재국 대책

금 8.24 자 WALL STREET JOURNAL 지 보도에 따르면 미에너지부는 금번 사태관련 전략 비축 석유의방출 및 더욱 적극적인 에너지 대책 실시를 원하고 있으나,

경제국 2차보 안기부 동자부 통상국 대책반 1차보 차관

PAGE 1

국	국제경제국	년 월 일	담 당	과 장	국 장	차관보	차 관	장 관

90.08.25 09:16 WG

외신 1과 통제관

0073

백악관측은 아직 심각한 원유공급 부족 사태는 도달하지 않았다고 판단, 에너지부의 건의를 거부했다함.

3. OPEC 동향

알제리는 원유 증산문제 협의를 위한 OPEC회의를 금주말 개최할 것을 제의하였는바, 현재 알제리, 베네주엘라, 인도네시아, 가봉, 이란등 6개국만 회의 개최에 찬성하였으며 사우디등 기타국가는 명확한 태도 표명을 유보하고 있음.

4. 8.24 당지 언론 보도내용 별첨 FAX 송부함.

첨부: USW(F)-1930 (6매)

(대사 박동진-국장)

주 미 대 사 관

번 호 : USW(F) - 1530
수 신 : 장 관 (기협)
발 신 : 주미대사
제 목 : USW-3889 첨부(5PH)

Shortage Fears Swell Oil Prices

Justice Intensifies Its Collusion Probe

By Thomas W. Lippman
Washington Post Staff Writer

Crude oil prices rose again yesterday, and prices for gasoline, heating oil and other fuels surged along with them to peaks that apparently guarantee a very expensive winter for consumers.

The Energy Department reported that inventories of oil and fuels increased last week, despite the cutoff of shipments from Iraq and Kuwait, but traders and analysts said the rising prices reflect a widespread belief that shortages are likely by October, when current stocks have been used.

"The stuff that's coming in now was purchased in July or earlier," said John Redpath, an oil expert at Energy Security Analysis Inc. in Washington. "But the market is trading on contracts for October, and it reflects what people believe will be the supply and demand situation that month."

On the New York Mercantile Exchange, crude oil for October delivery closed yesterday at $31.93 a barrel, up 71 cents. The price continued to rise in private trades after the closing bell, according to Platt's Oilgram News.

The November price rose $1.50—the maximum permitted by the exchange—to $30.64. Prices for delivery in every month through April also rose the maximum $1.50.

Gasoline prices are rising even faster. The closing price yesterday was $1.08.55 a gallon, up 4.44 cents from Wednesday. Before this week, unleaded gasoline had never traded for more than $1 a gallon on the New York exchange.

As retail prices continued upward, a senior Justice Department official said yesterday that the department was intensifying its investigation into possible price collusion by the oil companies.

Assistant U.S. Attorney General James Rill said he is calling in top executives of the major oil companies and independent oil marketers "on a one-by-one basis" to explain the reasons for the sharp increases in gasoline prices that followed the Aug. 2 Iraqi invasion of Kuwait.

Heating oil, which has drawn relatively little attention because the start of the heating season is still two months away, closed at just over 96 cents a gallon. A year ago, it was about 51 cents; a month ago, it was 55 cents. Fuel oil dealers acquiring supplies now for the winter season are certain to pass these prices on to their customers, industry analysts said.

The apparent anomaly of rising inventories and simultaneously rising prices is easily explained by the time lag between order and delivery, industry analysts said. The oil and refined products that filled U.S. storage tanks last week were shipped weeks ago, before the Iraqi invasion of Kuwait removed 4.45 million barrels of oil and about 600,000 barrels of gasoline a day from world markets. The prices being paid for oil and gasoline ordered today reflect expectations about the supply situation in the fall.

"The stocks arriving today are ancient history," said Peter Beutel, a trader at Merrill Lynch Energy Futures. Privately held crude oil stocks rose last week to 379.5 million barrels, about 42 million above the level of a year ago, according to the Energy Department, but Beutel said these numbers "have to be kept in perspective." He said the United States refines about 14 million barrels of oil a day, "so if you take all the stocks that they have at the refineries and the crude in the pipelines, that's only about 27 days."

"The refined product situation is actually worse than the crude situation," said Adam Sieminski of Washington Analysis Group. Despite last week's small increase, gasoline stocks are dangerously low, he said, and cannot be made up domestically because U.S. refineries are operating at full capacity.

Saudi Arabia, the world's biggest oil exporter, has pledged to increase its crude oil production by as much as 2 million barrels a day to make up some of the shortfall from Iraq and Kuwait, but apparently it has not yet done so.

Industry experts said that once the Saudi government gives the order to increase production, there still will be a time lag while sales contracts are negotiated, storage facilities are prepared and tankers are ordered.

Atlantic Richfield Co. said yesterday that the surge in spot-market gasoline prices had forced it to scrap the retail price freeze it imposed two weeks ago when all other major oil companies were raising prices in step with the market.

30 - 1

0075

Arco said its sales had increased 19 percent because its prices were lower than its competitors' by as much as 13 cents a gallon. As a result, company officials said, Arco was selling more gasoline than it can refine, so the company was forced to buy gasoline on the wholesale spot market at prices higher than it was getting at the retail pump. George Babikian, president of Arco's refining and marketing division, said the company would increase prices about 2.5 cents a gallon in areas "where Arco prices are well below their competitors."

The American Petroleum Institute, which represents the major oil companies, said last night that "the pump price for gasoline has increased by a considerably smaller amount than have the costs oil companies must pay to replenish those supplies." It said the oil companies "appreciate the patience the public is demonstrating" in the face of the price increases.

Assistant Attorney General Rill said the meetings with oil company executives, which are being held at the Justice Department, are part of an unusually wide-ranging inquiry into allegations of oil industry collusion and other anti-competitive pricing practices that was launched by the antitrust division on Aug. 6.

"We are aggressively pursuing the possibility that that kind of [anti-competitive] conduct might occur," Rill said during a briefing with reporters.

Among the areas the antitrust division is "looking at," Rill said, are allegations by independent petroleum marketers that refiners were providing gasoline to company-owned filling stations at prices substantially lower than what they were charging the independents.

He said that the oil companies so far have cooperated with the inquiry.

Stocks Slide On World Exchanges

War Fear Pushes Interest Rates, Oil Prices Higher

By Stan Hinden
Washington Post Staff Writer

Fear of war in the Middle East and widespread economic disruption yesterday slashed stock prices around the globe, pushed interest rates higher and drove oil prices to nearly $32 a barrel.

The Dow Jones industrial average, the market's most closely watched indicator, slid 76.73 points to close at 2483.42. Since Aug. 2, when the Middle East crisis began, the Dow has dropped 416 points, representing about 14 percent of its total value. The index is now at its lowest point in more than a year. [Details, Page B1.]

The vast economic trauma that could be caused by an all-out war in the Persian Gulf was clearly the concern that caused investors to push down stocks, not only in New York but in the Far East and in Europe, market analysts said. Investors clearly were concerned that rising oil prices would lead to higher inflation and help bring on a recession in the United States and elsewhere.

In Tokyo, the stock and bond markets have been particularly hard hit, with the key stock market index falling nearly 10 percent in just two days. Yesterday, it posted its fourth-worst point loss in history, helping cut its value since Aug. 1 by nearly one-fourth. This morning, reacting to the ebb and flow of Mideast news, the 225-stock Nikkei average reversed course, recouping 3 percent of its market value, only to head lower by the close of the morning session.

What worries the Japanese is that they are heavily dependent on Middle Eastern oil. Japan's economy could also be hurt because it is a heavy exporter of industrial and consumer products and services to Iraq and Kuwait.

Dismal showings in the Tokyo, Hong Kong and other Far Eastern markets spilled over to London, where stock prices fell 1.4 percent, despite a late afternoon recovery.

The nervous trading in financial markets also affected the oil sector yesterday, where the price of crude rose another 71 cents to close at $31.93. Oil prices have surged nearly 50 percent since Iraq invaded Kuwait.

The movement of oil prices, fueled by fears that a war could severely disrupt oil supplies, continued to affect U.S. Treasury bonds, with bond prices falling as oil prices rose, and vice versa. The bellwether 30-year U.S. Treasury bond dropped $7.81 per $1,000 face amount. Its yield, which moves in the opposite direction of its price, climbed to 9.13 percent from 9.05 percent.

The dollar again took it on the chin in international currency trading as traders who were worried about a U.S. economy possibly beset by war, inflation and recession, sought refuge in other currencies.

In London, the dollar dropped to a nine-year low against the British pound. The dollar also saw new lows against the German mark and the Swiss franc. In Toyko, the dollar closed at 145.88 yen, down 1.04 yen. In New York, later in the day, it fell to 146.12 yen.

Stock market analysts acknowledged yesterday that the Middle East situation made it difficult for them to devine how and when the stock market fall might end.

"All the conventional tools of market analysis are useless against the threat of military confrontation and possible economic strangulation" if oil supplies are interrupted, said Larry Wachtel, market analyst for Prudential-Bache Securities Inc.

Dean Witter Reynolds Inc.'s chief market strategist, John Connolly, in attempting to assess the damage to financial markets, said he saw a tension between two groups of investors.

USW(F)-1930-2

1930-2

0076

The pessimists, he said, expect war and fear that damage to the flow of oil would cause inflation, layoffs and a deep recession in the United States. The more optimistic investors are hoping that the United Nations-led embargo against Iraq will dampen the chances of a shooting war.

Connolly noted that large investment institutions, such as pension funds, appeared to be unloading stocks regularly and in all industries. Since the Dow closed just shy of 3000 on July 17, some stocks such as Boeing Corp., McDonald's Corp. and Woolworth Corp. have fallen 30 percent each.

Such across-the-board selling was one of the reasons that oil company stocks were dropping, he noted, even though oil prices were still rising.

Texaco fell to $60.12½, down $3.62½; Exxon was off $1.75 to $49.62½; Chevron lost $3 to $75.62½; and Mobil dropped $2.37½ to $62.87½.

Once again, the downdraft was broad-based, beyond the 30 stocks in the Dow. Declining issues overwhelmed advances by about 11 to 1 on the New York Stock Exchange, with 148 up, 1,645 down and 242 unchanged.

While the market has been hard hit, several analyst said the Dow's plunge might have been much worse, without the recently adopted New York Stock Exchange rule that curtails the use of computerized program trading when the Dow falls more than 50 points.

Under the 50-point rule, program traders can sell only when prices are rising, and can buy only when prices are falling. The effect is to slow and curb the use of the computerized programs, used by large investment institutions to profit from the differences between prices in the stock and futures markets.

OUT IN THE COLD: Top Bush aides put the freeze on the Energy Department.

Sununu and Darman seek to rein in the department, which they see as too eager to act. The White House vetoed DOE plans to pump oil from the strategic petroleum reserve, despite growing pressure with oil prices over $30 a barrel. "You want to use it when you have a situation where supply suggests it is necessary," says an administration official, "and we're not there yet."

Some department officials hoped for a high-profile announcement of major energy conservation measures, but the White House limited them to minor measures and refused to give the announcement a presidential push.

USW(F) 1130-3

0077

Five Firms Called For Questioning On Fuel-Price Rise

By PAUL M. BARRETT
Staff Reporter of THE WALL STREET JOURNAL

WASHINGTON – The Justice Department said it called in three major oil refiners and two independent gasoline marketers for questioning about the big price jump since Iraq's invasion of Kuwait.

The department said it's looking for possible price-fixing or other antitrust violations. James Rill, the department's antitrust chief, declined to identify the five companies but said more companies will be interviewed in the inquiry.

"We are getting cooperation from the oil companies," he said at a news briefing yesterday, indicating that compliance with the investigation has been voluntary.

Such confidential questioning is typical in the preliminary stages of an antitrust investigation.

At this point, the inquiry is focusing on the entire U.S. petroleum-products industry, rather than on particular companies, Mr. Rill added.

Federal officials will decide within four weeks whether to take the further step of making compulsory demands for documents from target companies or convening a grand jury to consider criminal charges, Mr. Rill said. A team of 10 Justice Department lawyers and economists are looking into the possibility of collusion by major oil companies and price-gouging by distributors and retailers, he said.

The American Automobile Association said its most recent national survey found that the average price of gasoline at the pump jumped 15% from Aug. 1, the day before the invasion, to Aug. 20. The average pump price of unleaded regular gasoline jumped to $1.237 from $1.075 over that period, the AAA reported.

State attorneys general, as well as officials from the Federal Trade Commission and U.S. Department of Energy, are working with the Justice Department. Scores of members of Congress, as well as state officials, have criticized big oil companies for recent increases in gasoline prices.

In a statement issued late yesterday, the American Petroleum Institute defended the industry's pricing. Despite the market turmoil since the Iraqi invasion, "members of the petroleum industry have been trying to act with restraint and responsibility," the trade group said. As evidence, it asserted that the 16-cent-a-gallon increase in gasoline pump prices since the invasion compares with a rise of about 25 cents a gallon for spot-market crude prices and 35 cents a gallon for spot-market gasoline prices.

"In other words, the pump price for gasoline increased by a considerably smaller amount than have the costs oil companies must pay to replenish those supplies," the statement said.

Shell Oil Co. Fire At Texas Refinery Lifts Prices Faster

By CALEB SOLOMON
Staff Reporter of THE WALL STREET JOURNAL

HOUSTON – Shell Oil Co. said a fire at its Deer Park, Texas, refinery injured two workers and closed a large portion of the plant, causing already rising gasoline prices to climb faster.

With gasoline supplies tight and the market extremely edgy because of the potential for war in the Middle East, any supply disruption, even short term, can have impact. "It's bad news," said Thomas Manning, a vice president at refining consultants Purvin & Gertz Inc.

In addition, U.S. refiners have been producing gasoline, heating oil and other petroleum products at full capacity, a situation that has sparked a flurry of accidents and could cause more. "The harder you run something, the more likely a fire is," Mr. Manning said. "They seem to run in bunches."

Indeed, Crown Central Petroleum Corp. said a critical portion of its Houston refinery developed a leak yesterday and was shut down. The petroleum products markets are so on edge that rumors flew among traders that other refineries across the country had operating difficulties.

The Shell accident, at a 215,000 barrel-a-day capacity refinery along the Houston Ship Channel, occurred in a large distillation unit. A spokesman for the company, a unit of Royal Dutch/Shell Group, said the fire started yesterday morning, but he didn't know the cause. One Shell worker was flown to a nearby hospital with first-degree and second-degree burns, and another was treated at the plant, the spokesman said.

The fire was burning as of yesterday afternoon, but Shell expected that it would burn itself out by the end of the day, the spokesman said. He said it was too early to assess how long the distillation unit, which processes 165,000 barrels a day of crude oil, would be out.

The distillation unit is the first stage in processing crude oil before sending it to other parts of the refinery. Analysts said Shell can probably continue to produce gasoline for a short time without the unit by processing so-called intermediates it has in storage through the rest of the plant.

Shell has had a number of accidents and operating problems in its refining system in the past few years. Last winter, its plants had to shut down, triggered by an extraordinary Gulf of Mexico freeze. And in May 1988, the company's Norco, La., refinery exploded, killing seven workers and injuring scores of others.

USW(F)-1130-4

0078

A2 THE WALL STREET JOURNAL FRIDAY, AUGUST 24, 1990

OPEC Ministers to Meet This Weekend

As Oil Picture Deteriorates, Some to Seek 'Blessing' To Raise Their Output

By JAMES TANNER
Staff Reporter of THE WALL STREET JOURNAL

Some OPEC oil ministers will meet in Vienna this weekend to discuss the deteriorating world oil picture.

The Organization of Petroleum Exporting Countries confirmed that Sadek Boussena, Algeria's oil minister and OPEC president, invited his fellow ministers to the Austrian capital to talk about possible responses to the recent loss of Iraqi and Kuwaiti crudes from world markets.

"There are going to be consultations among some ministers Sunday," a spokesman for OPEC said at its Vienna headquarters, "but we are not calling it a meeting."

'Very Unusual Procedure'

Whatever it's called, the session is likely to be the closest thing yet to the OPEC "blessing" that some countries with spare capacity have sought for their pledges to produce more oil. These countries have been turned down in a request for an emergency meeting of OPEC to endorse higher output quotas.

"This is a very unusual procedure," said a senior OPEC delegate from one of the countries, "but let's hope it works."

Although the promised production increases are slowly beginning, world oil prices continue to surge. Yesterday, crude oil jumped by $1.50 to $4 a barrel, pushing more crudes beyond $30, and fuels rose as much as six cents a gallon.

In U.S. oil fields, some refiners now are posting prices as high as $30.75 a barrel for West Texas Intermediate, the benchmark crude. In U.S. futures trading, the October crude contract rose 71 cents to $31.93 a barrel yesterday, while unleaded gasoline for September delivery rose 4.44 cents to nearly $1.09 a gallon.

Crude oil prices now are more than double their levels as recently as June. To calm the volatile markets, Venezuela and Saudi Arabia had been pressing for an emergency OPEC meeting to act on quotas and production levels.

That request was rejected Monday. Still, the two countries have begun to increase output toward a promised total of about 2.5 million barrels a day, with the bulk of it coming from Saudi Arabia. The United Arab Emirates could produce an additional 500,000 barrels a day. This would replace three-fourths of the four million barrels a day of Iraqi and Kuwaiti crudes removed from world markets as a result of Iraq's Aug. 2 invasion of Kuwait.

It isn't clear whether all 13 member nations will have representatives at the Vienna talks. Nor is it known whether anyone will represent Kuwait, which remains occupied by Iraqi troops.

As of late yesterday, only six ministers had confirmed they plan to attend, OPEC sources said. They are from Algeria, Venezuela, Indonesia, Nigeria, Gabon and Iran.

In Caracas, Venezuelan President Carlos Andres Perez said seven nations—the majority required to call a special meeting of all 13—had agreed to be in Vienna for the "consultative session" on possible oil production increases. He didn't list the seven.

Possible Emergency Session

The OPEC ministers cannot take official action unless they are in a regular or special conference. But Celestino Armas, the Venezuelan oil minister, said Venezuela's view is that the ministerial majority expected in Vienna could turn the talks into an emergency session at which decisions could be made. He told the Venezuelan Congress that the national oil companies already have begun pumping more, with an extra 350,000 barrels a day targeted that will be stored for eventual sale abroad.

Venezuela has been coordinating its efforts with those of Saudi Arabia for several weeks. But the attendance of Saudi Arabia in Vienna is a question mark. Hisham Nazer, the Saudi oil minister, has been critical of the lack of any official OPEC response to threatened shortages and volatile oil markets.

Yesterday, a person close to Saudi oil policies cited two objections to "this so-called meeting" in Vienna. There was no formal invitation to the oil ministers from Mr. Boussena, he said, and there is no agenda. "What we have here is an invitation to a Sunday barbecue party," he said.

Others suggested, however, that the Saudis can hardly afford to ignore the talks. "The only thing I can see [developing at Vienna] is that Venezuela, Saudi Arabia and the Emirates will be given some kind of blessing to produce more," one senior OPEC delegate said.

USW(T)-1430-5.

0079

OPEC Crude Oil Supply Declines

Knight-Ridder Financial

LONDON — The Organization of Petroleum Exporting Countries' average crude oil supply in the first three weeks of August fell 3.8 million barrels a day to 20 million b/d compared with July levels, oil industry sources said Thursday.

In the first two weeks of the month, estimated supply had averaged 20.5 million b/d, the sources added.

The figures are based on tanker-tracking information and estimates of inland consumption. The sources stressed the figures are provisional, and subject to revision.

The largest declines in average output took place in Iraqi and Kuwaiti production.

Kuwaiti supply, averaged out on a daily basis over the three weeks, was just 65,000 b/d, because the country only produced for the first two days of the month before the Iraqi invasion.

Average oil supply from Iraq over the same period fell to 1.3 million b/d from 3.2 million b/d in July, sources said. Iraqi exports dried up soon after the invasion, but included in the figures is an estimate of the country's domestic consumption of about 500,000 b/d.

Saudi Arabia's average oil supply was 5.6 million b/d, including 200,000 b/d from the Neutral Zone, down about 200,000 b/d from July.

Supply from the Neutral Zone, which should be shared equally between Saudi Arabia and Kuwait, was at 200,000 b/d, down 180,000 b/d from July. However, oil industry sources said all Neutral Zone production was now assumed to be for Saudi Arabia.

Despite the apparent cut in Saudi oil supply, oil industry sources said actual well-head output has risen recently. This production is apparently being held in storage to allow the kingdom to boost exports substantially in September, when term customers expect to receive greatly increased volumes of crude.

Mexico national pride costing U.S. extra oil

By Thaddeus Herrick
SCRIPPS HOWARD NEWS SERVICE

MEXICO CITY — With the flow of oil to the West threatened by upheaval in the Middle East, Americans may be expecting Mexico to keep their gas tanks full.

They shouldn't.

Mexico might have the largest untapped oil reserves of any nation outside the Middle East and the Soviet Union, according to the U.S. Geological Survey. Yet, by 2000, Mexico will barely be pumping enough oil to satisfy domestic demand, says Bill Orme, editor of Latin Finance, a Miami-based publication.

The problem is a mixture of nationalistic pride and economics.

Mexico's nationalized oil company, Pemex, doesn't have the resources to expand production or even do much additional exploration. Mexico's debt situation doesn't make it a prime candidate for loans, and the government is loathe to allow other nations to do the work — and share the profits.

Oil touches a profoundly nationalist nerve here. It has ever since Mexican President Lazaro Cardenas threw out the foreign companies in 1938 to cries of "The oil is ours!" Mr. Cardenas, in fact, believed Mexico's oil should benefit only Mexicans.

That thinking changed somewhat in the 1970s and early 1980s as Mexico struck it rich during the bonanza of high oil prices. But the market crashed and Mexico, which had borrowed heavily and spent wildly, found itself mired in debt.

Pemex, whose spending has dropped from $6 billion in 1981 to $1 billion today, has since neglected exploration. Meanwhile, production has fallen from 3 million barrels a day in 1982 to 2.5 million barrels a day, about half of which is sold at home.

Mexico wants to see to its needs first — and to avoid making the mistake of over-dependence on oil exports.

But that strategy may be tested as the United States and Mexico prepare to negotiate a free-trade pact.

"The Mideast crisis has pushed Mexican oil to the top of the agenda," said George Baker, a U.S. oil consultant and head of Profmex, an international consortium of academic research programs on Mexico. "And that's a very awkward place for Mexico to have it."

Mexico, which supplies the United States with about 600,000 barrels of oil a day, is nudging up its U.S. exports as best it can in response to Iraq's takeover of Kuwait.

Still, Pemex is without the resources to increase production. Nor is it likely to receive fresh loans. So, unless Mexico gets out of the oil business altogether, it may have to open up the exploration and pumping of oil to outside interests.

USW(F)-1930-6.
End

0080

국제원유수급 및 가격동향 속보

(8.24 공관보고 종합)

1990.8.25.
외무부, 국제경제국

1. 원유수급

o 베네수엘라, 미국 요청에 따라 50-60만B/D 증산계획

- 대신 미국에 자유무역협정체결 및 원유증산시설확대 투자요청중

o 이집트, 현재 증산여력 없으며, 배럴당25불시 신규투자로 증산(약10-20만B/D)예정

o 부시대통령, 8.22 기자회견에서 향후 계속 적정한 석유공급량 확보 가능, 현재로선 에너지 절약 조치 불필요 언급

2. 유가

o 현물시장 동향 (단위 : $/B)

	7.31	8.7	8.10	8.17	8.22	8.23	8.24	전일대비
Dubai	17.20	25.40	22.72	26.35	31.75	32.00	31.35	- 0.65
Oman	17.65	25.90	23.22	26.95	32.35	32.60	31.95	- 0.65
Brent	19.49	29.40	25.70	28.95	32.15	32.45	31.83	- 0.62
WIT	20.75	29.62	26.39	27.46	31.57	31.73	31.21	- 0.52

o 장기적으로 25불선 안정 전망되나, 그동안 사태추이 따른 심리적 요인으로 등락현상 예상 (주베네주엘라 대사)

o 8.22 유가 급등원인 분석 (미국 언론 보도종합)

- 군사적 긴장고조로 전쟁발발 가능성 우려

- 사우디 정부, 8.22 정유제품 수출 감축 발표 (20-30만B/D)

- 사우디·베네주엘라등의 증산 지연

※ 수급의 불균형보다 긴장고조에 대한 심리적 반응

o 불란서 9.12 발표예정인 91년도 예산편성에서 향후 유가를 배럴당 25불 전망

3. 기타 관련 사항

o 이집트석유공사 (EGPC)측, 약 20만톤 년내 아국공급가능 언급(주카이로총영사)

- 동 공사, 현재 GEISUM 중질유 10만-20만톤 경매공고(입찰기간 8.23-8.28간)

심의관: [signature]

앙고재	기술협력과	90년 8월 25일	담 당	과 장	국 장	차관보	차 관	장 관
			홍성화	[signature]	[signature]	[signature]		

0081

國際原油需給 및 價格動向 速報

(8.24 公館報告 綜合)

1990.8.25.
外務部, 國際經濟局

1. 原油需給

o 베네수엘라, 美國 要請에 따라 50-60만B/D 增産計劃

- 대신 美國에 自由貿易協定締結 및 原油增産施設擴大 投資 要請中

o 이집트, 現在 增産餘力 없으며, 배럴당25불시 新規投資로 增産(약10-20만B/D)예정

o 부시대통령, 8.22 記者會見에서 향후 繼續 적정한 石油供給量 確保 可能, 現在로선 에너지 節約 措置 不必要 言及

2. 油價

o 現物市場 動向 (단위 : $/B)

	7.31	8.7	8.10	8.17	8.22	8.23	8.24	전일대비
Dubai	17.20	25.40	22.72	26.35	31.75	32.00	31.35	- 0.65
Oman	17.65	25.90	23.22	26.95	32.35	32.60	31.95	- 0.65
Brent	19.49	29.40	25.70	28.95	32.15	32.45	31.83	- 0.62
WTI	20.75	29.62	26.39	27.46	31.57	31.73	31.21	- 0.52

o 長期的으로 25불선 安定 展望되나, 그동안 事態推移 따른 心理的 要因으로 騰落現狀 豫想 (주베네주엘라 대사)

o 8.22 油價 急騰原因 分析 (美國 言論 報道綜合)

- 軍事的 緊張高潮로 戰爭勃發 可能性 우려

- 사우디 政府, 8.22 精油製品 輸出 減縮 발표 (20-30만B/D)

- 사우디·베네주엘라등의 增産 遲延

※ 需給의 不均衡보다 緊張高潮에 대한 心理的 反應

o 佛蘭西, 9.12 發表豫定인 91年度 豫算編成에서 향후 油價를 배럴당 25불 展望

3. 其他 關聯 事項

o 이집트石油公社 (EGPC)側, 약 20만톤 年內 我國供給可能 言及(주카이로총영사)

- 同 公社, 現在 GEISUM 중질유 10만-20만톤 競賣公告(入札期間 8.23-8.28間)

0082

이라크, 쿠웨이트事態 報告

1990. 8.27

1. 當事國動向

o U. N.

- CUELLAR 事務總長, 페만危機의 平和的 解決을 위해 이라크측과의 緊急會談 提議(25일)

o 美國

- 이라크군의 無條件的 即刻撤收下에 全 UN 會員國의 討議 歡迎(백악관 代辯人)
- 對 이라크 封鎖措置의 效果를 높이기 위한 最小限의 武力만 使用할 것임(美 行政府 國家安全 고문)

o 이라크

- HUSSEIN 大統領, UN 事務總長의 페만危機 關聯 緊急會談 提議 歡迎.
- 쿠웨이트 駐在 外國公館에 閉鎖措置以後 電氣, 水道 供給 中斷
- UN 經濟封鎖以後, 食糧 및 醫藥品 不足을 막기위한 協助呼訴(이라크 적십자사)
- MUBARAK 社會勞動長官, 아프리카 7個國에 特使로 派遣

2. 主要國 反應

o 蘇 聯 : UN의 武力使用案 通過에도 불구하고 페만에서 武力使用 않을 것임(蘇聯外相)

o 프랑스 : 海軍에 이어 地上軍 兵力(대대규모) UAE에 追加派遣 豫定(프랑스 國防 長官)

o 이 란 : - 이라크 및 쿠웨이트내 外國人들이 이란 國境을 통해 대피할 수 있도록 同意. 할 것임(이란外相)
- 필리핀에 原油輸出 倍加, 4萬B/D까지 供給하기로 原則的 合意. (이란 AGAZADEH 石油相)

o 英 國 : UN 事務總長의 提議는 全體的 與件이 未成熟된 段階에서 나온 提議로서 會談成功에 懷疑的(대처首相)

3. 石油市場 動向

o OPEC 石油相會議(비엔나) - 사우디, 베네주엘라의 開催要求로 26일 11個國(이라크, 리비아 미확인)參加했으나, 이란등 高油價 支持國家들의 反對로 難航 展望

o IEA
- 原油供給 蹉跌이 10月까지 繼續될 것으로 豫想되나 深刻하게 憂慮되는 정도는 아님. (IEA 高位 관계자)
- 備蓄原油는 價格安定이 아닌 供給不足時 放出하는 것이 會員國들의 政策임

※ 石油市場은 土.日曜日 休務로 去來없음(前週 金曜日 去來動向임)

(單位 : $/B)

	7.31	8. 7	8.10	8.17	8.23	8.24	前日對比
Dubai	17.20	25.40	22.72	26.35	32.00	31.35	△0.65
Oman	17.65	25.90	23.22	26.95	32.60	31.95	△0.65
Brent	19.49	29.40	25.70	28.95	32.45	31.83	△0.62
W T I	20.75	29.62	26.39	27.46	31.73	31.21	△0.52

0083

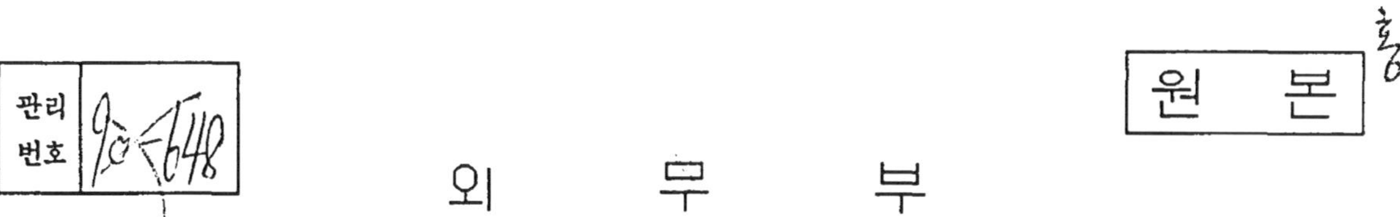

관리 번호 90-648

원 본

외 무 부

종 별 :

번 호 : PUW-0702　　　　일 시 : 90 0827 1830

수 신 : 장관(기협)

발 신 : 주 페루 대사

제 목 : 석유 수급및 유가동향보고

대:WPU-0353,0364

대호 관련 주재국 석유 수급동향을 아래와같이 보고하며, 기타 관련자료는 입수되는대로 추보예정임.

1.88 년 기준 석유 수급동향(백만 배럴)

-생산량:51.7

-소비량:51.2

-수출량:16(미국)

-수입량:15.5(에쿠아돌)

2.90.6 월 석유 수급동향

-일일 생산량:132,000 배럴

-일일 소비량:140,000 배럴

3. 주재국의 산유정책

-주재국은 국내 소비용 유류 정제를 위해 에쿠아돌로부터 경유를 수입하고 있으며, 자국산 일부 중유를 미국등에 수출하고있음. 최근 주재국 석유 국영회사PETROPERU 가 3 억불 규모의 아마존 장글지대 천연개스 개발 프로젝트 추진 예정으로 보도된바 있으며, 동지역 CAMISEA 유전지대에는 16 TRILLON 큐빅피트 의 천연가스및 9 억 7 천만 배럴의 CONDENSATE 가 매장되어 있는 것으로 알려짐.

(대사 윤태현-경제국장)

예고:90.12.31. 까지

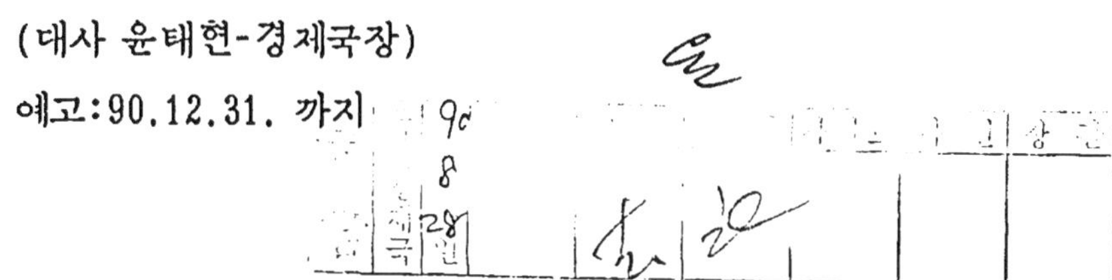

경제국　차관　2차보　동자부

90 12 31

PAGE 1　　　　90.08.28　09:37

외신 2과　통제관 CW

0084

원 본

외 무 부

종 별 :

번 호 : USW-3903 일 시 : 90 0827 1735

수 신 : 장 관(기협)

발 신 : 주 미 대사

제 목 : 석유시장 및 가격 동향 (3)

표제관련 8.25 (토)-27 (월) 당지 언론 보도를 종합 보고함.

1.유가 동향

가. 8.24 (금) 원유 및 정유제품 가격

0 원유 (뉴욕 상품시장, 10월 인도 가격)

배럴당 30.91불 (전일에 비해 1.02 불 하락)

0 휘발유 (뉴욕 상품시장,9월 인도 가격)

갤런당 104.66 센트 (전일에 비해 3.89 센트 하락)

0 난방유 (뉴욕 상품시장 , 9월 인도 가격):

갤런당 90.96 센트 (전일에 비해 5.27 센트 하락)

나.당지 전문가들은 8.24. 유가하락은 8.23.까지 유가가 급등한 반면, 주말의 OPEC 회의등으로 향후 원유시장 동향이 불확실하다는 점을 감안한 석유상들이 그간 확보했던 원유를 일부 방출했기 때문인 것으로 분석하고 있음.

2.원유 수급 전망

0 당지 전문가들은 향후 원유가 전망에 대해 의견이 엇갈리고 있는바, 원유가가 계속 상승할것으로 전망하는 전문가들은 아래와 같은 이유를 들고 있음.(

.가.이락-쿠웨이트산 원유 수입 중단분 충당 곤란

.사우디, 베네수엘라, UAE 등이 증산을 실시한다고 하더라도 이락-쿠웨이트로 부터의 원유 수입금지에 따른 공급 감소량 4.3-4.5 백만 배럴을 보전하기는 어려울것임.

.특히 사우디는 국내 주둔 미군에 대해 정유 제품을 공급해야 하므로 대폭적인 원유 수출증가가 어려움.

나.원유 시장의 낮은 가격 탄력성

경제국 2차보 동자부

PAGE 1

공람	국제경제국	90.8.28	담 당	과 장	국 장	차관보	차 관	장 관

90.08.28 09:18 WG

외신 1과 통제관

0085

.원유 시장에서의 수요, 공급은 가격 탄력성이 극히 낮아 가격급등에 따른 수요.공급의 증감을 단기간내에 기대하기가 어려움.

.특히 원유시장은 일시적인 공급 부족이 발생할 경우 장래 소요분 비축을 위한 가수요가 많으므로 2-3퍼센트 내외의 소량의 공급 감소만 으로도 가격이 급등할수 있음.

다.비축 석유 방출지연

.현재 민간 부문의 원유 비축분 및 각국 정부의전략 비축 석유 만으로도 공급 부족분을 장기간 충당할수 있기는 하나, 석유회사 및 각국정부는 향후 지속적인 원유가 인상에 대비, 비축분의 시장 방출을 서두르지 않고 있음.

라.난방유등 동계 유류 소요 증대

3.당지 언론 보도 내용 별첨 팩스 송부함.

첨부: USW(F)- 1952 (10 매)

(대사 박동진- 국장)

0086

보안 통제	引

주 미 대 사 관

번 호 : USW(F) - 1952
수 신 : 장 관 (기협)
발 신 : 주미대사
제 목 : USW - 3903 첨부 (10매)

Oil Prices Fall Back $1 a Barrel

Traders Take Profits After Sharp Increase

By THOMAS C. HAYES

Prices of crude oil fell $1.02 a barrel in the futures market yesterday, and prices for gasoline and home heating oil eased slightly. Analysts and brokers said jittery commodity traders cashed in some profits before the close of a landmark week in the oil markets.

The contract for October delivery settled yesterday at $30.91, a gain of $2.28 on the week. Alarmed by American military maneuvers and fear of fighting near the giant Middle East oilfields, traders had pushed oil prices to $31.93 on Thursday, and at one point during the day to $32.25, which equalled the highest level in the seven-year history of the New York Mercantile Exchange.

Gasoline Prices Ease

Gasoline prices ended the week at $1.05 a gallon, off 4 cents from a record close on Thursday at $1.09 a gallon on the New York Merc. Home heating oil finished the week at 91 cents a gallon, losing 5 cents yesterday, but up 10 cents for the week.

Albert Helmig, a principal with Energex, a commodity brokerage firm, said that although traders remained nervous about events in the Persian Gulf, many reduced their holdings of October contracts because of the uncertain impact of military and diplomatic activity over the weekend, as well as the unofficial meeting of the Organization of Petroleum Exporting Countries set for tomorrow in Vienna.

If Saudi Arabian oilfields are damaged, it will likely cause crude prices to soar when trading resumes Monday. But if tensions between Baghdad and the West ease, or if OPEC members agree to raise production to replace the estimated four million barrels lost from Iraq and Kuwait, prices will fall, analysts said.

Reason for Caution

"If something good happens, it would put a lot of pressure on the October contract price," Mr. Helmig said, explaining why traders are cautious, even though most continue to bet on an outbreak of war and disruption of supplies. Many European traders closed their positions yesterday since the London commodity market will be closed Monday.

"Most people in the market think this is a crucial weekend," said Robert S. Jonke, a trading manager and analyst at Cargill Investors Services, a commodity brokerage firm in New York.

"There has been no lessening of tensions, but some people wanted to take their profit and get out," said James R. Fiedler of E.D.&F. Man Inc., in New York, despite a very dangerous situation in the Persian Gulf.

Ministers from as many as 10 OPEC nations are to meet tomorrow in Vienna to discuss raising output quotas, although the role of Saudi Arabia, the group's largest producer, was unclear. Some analysts said little of consequence was expected from the meeting.

The Saudis indicated last week that they would increase output by nearly two million barrels a day next month, and other OPEC members, including Venezuela, Nigeria and the United Arab Emirates, were expected to add one million barrels to help cover the shortfall from Iraq and Kuwait.

Global demand for OPEC oil was estimated at 22 million barrels a day before the Iraqi invasion on Aug. 2. Fareed Mohamedi, senior economist at the Petroleum Finance Company in Washington, said OPEC output would rise to 22.5 million barrels a day next month if the Saudis, Venezuela, the United Arab Emirates and Nigeria succeed in raising output to their recently voiced objectives.

Doubt About Output

But many analysts doubt that those production levels will be achieved in the coming months. In that case, oil prices could resume their climb even if war is avoided.

Also, some analysts said, little of the Saudis' additional production would be available for export, since much would be diverted for Saudi and American military use.

Adam E. Sieminski of the Washington Analysis Corporation, a Washington consulting firm, said a worldwide crude oil shortage would probably would be evident as early as mid-September. He predicted heating oil shortages by November.

"Prices are going to go higher," he said. "How much higher depends on whether we have a shooting war, whether the Administration taps the Strategic Petroleum Reserve and how effective the embargo of Iraq is. The odds that we could have $35 oil, at least for a while, are pretty good."

A war would drive prices to $50 or higher, he added.

Increases by Refiners

Domestic refineries in the United States continued to increase the cash prices paid for oil delivered this week. The Mobil Corporation said yesterday that it increased its posted price at its Texas refineries by $3.25 a barrel, to $30.25 a barrel, on Thursday. The Texas Railroad Commission, which regulates the state's oil industry, estimated that posted prices at refineries would average more than $29 a barrel for the week.

Oil prices have doubled from a close of $15.30 in the futures market on June 20, and are up nearly $10 a barrel since the day before the Iraqi invasion. The Middle East events have also sent gasoline prices surging, and consumers face further increases in coming weeks, even though supplies were reported adequate as the end of the summer driving season neared.

The average price of unleaded regular gasoline at self-service pumps rose 3.7 cents since Monday, to an eight-year high of $1.27 across the nation, the American Automobile Association said yesterday.

Higher oil prices are also expected to extract a heavy toll on the nation's work force. Stephen P. A. Brown, an economist at the Federal Reserve Bank of Dallas, said that if oil prices held at $31 a barrel through 1991, the economy would lose 1.2 million jobs.

An analysis of 1989 economic data indicates the nation loses 90,000 jobs for every $1 rise in oil prices, Mr. Brown said, although the effects vary by region. For instance, in Texas 15,000 jobs are added for every $1 rise in oil prices, as the domestic oil industry increases drilling activity.

NYT 8/25

0087

Higher Oil Prices Could Inflict Long-Lasting Damage on Global Economies

By Steven Mufson
Washington Post Staff Writer

Just as the crisis in the Middle East has gun to alter the political and military map the world, so, too, does it promise to rest the economic landscape—straining untries and businesses with large nounts of debt, transferring additional ealth from oil consumers to oil producers, ifting investment from stocks to bonds id causing economic growth to slow orldwide.

And no matter how fast a resolution there is to the crisis in the Persian Gulf, most economists and business leaders beeve that the damage to the world econo-y could be long-lasting.

NEWS ANALYSIS

"When the military dust settles in the liddle East, the economic consequences ill still be with us," said Roger Altman, a artner in the New York-based Blackstone roup and a Treasury official during the arter administration. "There is no way, ven if [Iraqi President] Saddam Hussein pologizes and returns to Baghdad on his nees, that the situation will return to the ay it was. This has touched off deep wores and confirmed a lot of people's fears."

Added Altman: "This whole situation is 1 economic crisis for the [Bush] administation as well as a military crisis."

Mere uncertainty about the future has aken consumer and business confidence orldwide, throwing consumer spending nd business investment into doubt and inreasing the chances of a recession in the Inited States.

If people can't be sure what the next 24 ours will bring, much less the next year or wo, they aren't likely to make any big ommitments. The anecdotal evidence athered from around the nation is that, for ie moment, many consumers are postpong purchases of homes and cars, and busiess executives are cutting back on capital ivestments and staff sizes to prepare for arder times.

A number of polls in recent weeks show nat a majority of both consumers and executives now expect a recession.

On financial markets, many investors are onverting their holdings to cash, both to void further losses in the value of stock nd bond holdings as market prices decline, ut also to be in a good position to lock in ong-term interest rates that now are heading up.

Should a stalemate give way to fighting 1 the Middle East, uncertainty will give which occurred after the oil crisis of the early 1970s.

The effects could include a shift of billions of dollars to Saudi Arabia and other oil producers; a crippling blow for developing countries that don't produce oil; a drain of billions of dollars from consumer spending and business investment in industrialized nations to pay for steeper oil prices and higher interest rates; and a resurgence of inflation in industrialized countries, a cut in growth rates and the possible return of 1970s-style stagflation.

Perhaps the clearest manifestation of the uncertainty that has gripped the world's economy is the rapid increase in interest rates. The U.S. Treasury's 30-year bond was yielding 9.16 percent when the bond markets closed Friday in New York, up about 0.65 percentage points this month.

Similar increases have occurred in West Germany and London. In Japan, the era of 2 percent and 3 percent money has given way to a previously unheard of long-term prime interest rate of 8.5 percent.

Investment, whether in stocks, bonds or other assets, represents a commitment for the future, so the greater the uncertainty, the greater premium demanded by the investor.

"There is a cost to uncertainty," said Shafiqual Islam, an expert on international economics at the Council on Foreign Relations in New York.

"Consumer and business confidence is affected by a prolonged stalemate," he said, adding that "the cloud of uncertainty makes it difficult for people to make decisions based on a new reality."

In the developing world, a new reality that includes $30 a barrel oil would be "an unmitigated disaster," Islam said.

When the first oil crisis hit in 1973, developing nations consumed 18 percent of world's oil supplies and many were able to borrow money to cover the added costs of more expensive energy. Today, those countries consume 28 percent of the world's oil output and many already are so deeply in debt—or in default—that additional borrowing is impossible.

In addition, because developing countries haven't been able to afford investments in conservation and alternate energy technologies, their economic growth still is closely linked to oil consumption. Industrialized countries, by contrast, have lowered the

Over the next 10 years, developing countries are expected to increase oil consumption by 57 percent while industrialized countries are expected to increase oil consumption by 27 percent.

There also are indirect effects.

Increased inflation in industrialized countries will raise the cost of finished goods imported by developing countries. Higher interest rates will increase the cost of servicing foreign debt. And any world economic slowdown will lower the demand and the prices for products developing countries manufacture and grow.

Ghana is a good case in point.

In 1983, Ghana used up 90 percent of export earnings to service its foreign debt and pay its oil import bills. The country embarked on a disciplined and at times painful economic reformation, and by last year the West African nation had managed cut its oil import bill to 11 percent of exports and its debt service to just 30 percent.

But the new economic conditions could push those two numbers way up and cut earnings from cocoa, the country's main export.

Despite tough sacrifices made in the last five years, Ghanaians could wind up in the same impoverished condition they were in eight years ago.

While bad news for the world's smallest economies, the fallout Persian Gulf crisis could be bad news for the world's biggest economy—the United States.

Felix Rohatyn, an investment banker with Lazard Freres in New York, warns that the crisis could push the United States closer to recession and reveal long neglected problems in the U.S. economy.

"We are going into this with significant weaknesses in our financial system in large part due to the fact that we have been abusing our financial credit system for a decade," he said.

WP 8/26 Post

USW(F) 4093 2

0088

Rohatyn points out that while U.S. industry has become more energy efficient since the first oil crisis, the overall economy is more vulnerable because another oil price crisis would increase interest costs and reduce revenue for corporations, government and individuals who are significantly more in debt than they've ever been.

Much of the money for those debts was borrowed in anticipation of higher sales and incomes and profits that now seem uncertain.

According to Merrill Lynch, Pierce, Fenner & Smith Inc., the interest burden of U.S. businesses has risen to an average 25.7 percent of cash flow, up from 19.9 percent in 1983 and up even farther from historic averages.

"With the possibility of recession rising, long-standing questions about how well U.S. corporations can withstand the pressures of meeting their debt burdens may soon be answered," Merrill Lynch said in its weekly market commentary.

The securities house warned that "nonfinancial corporations seem ill-equipped to cope with their debt burdens in a recession, and the nondurables and trade sectors could be particularly vulnerable."

Not surprisingly, the prices plunged last week for the high-risk, high-yield junk bonds issued by companies saddled with heavy debt burdens.

Moreover, the ability of the U.S. government to respond to this economic crisis is extremely limited. The federal government has been running up the largest peacetime deficits in the nation's history, making it more difficult to pump up the economy by increasing spending further.

In other nations, the Persian Gulf crisis looms as a problem, too.

In Eastern Europe, an increase in oil prices would be a unwelcome shock for countries already struggling to adjust to life without Soviet [illegible] price increases caused by the end of other government subsidies.

Many of these countries also had counted on infusions of capital from the investors in the United States and Western Europe who may now find themselves distracted by the threat of economic slowdown and unwilling to make what are, at best, risky new long-term investments.

In Japan, stock markets have tumbled 35 percent this year, raising fears about the viability of some major investors and banks.

But most analysts said that with its continued rate of brisk economic growth, continuing trade surpluses and big petroleum reserves, Japan is relatively well-positioned to weather the crisis.

Even for some oil-producing countries, the fallout from the Persian Gulf crisis may be bad.

Mexico, for example, would receive much more revenue from oil exports. But after years of economic reforms in Mexico, oil revenue accounts for only half of Mexico's export earnings.

As a result, gains in oil income would be largely offset by decreased demand for other Mexican exports.

"Even here, the oil price increase is not a clear-cut blessing," Islam said.

Perhaps the only place where the Persian Gulf crisis is good economic news is Saudi Arabia, which through a combination of increased oil output and higher oil prices could earn an extra $11 billion this year and an additional $33 billion next year in the wake of the crisis.

Those figures are based on an assumption that the price of a 42-gallon barrel of crude oil would drop from their current levels of $31 a barrel to a more reasonable $25.

A portion of that money would flow out of the kingdom to compensate countries like Turkey or Jordan for participation in the international embargo of Iraq.

Another chunk would go toward paying part of the costs of the U.S. forces and for new military equipment.

"Along with higher revenues, Saudi Arabia will face higher expenses," said Sharif Ghalib of the Institute of International Finance in Washington. "We're talking about some very large numbers in military spending."

But much of the increased revenue would go toward reversing the decline in Saudi financial reserves, which have dwindled to about $25 billion since the kingdom began running overall trade deficits in 1982.

Those reserves would flow largely back into the banking system in London and New York, eventually providing capital to governments and businesses around the world.

But as it did in the 1970s, this process of recycling petrodollars will have a permanent and profound effect of transferring wealth to those countries which, by dint of luck or ingenuity, are able to produce more energy than they consume.

USW(F) 1952 -3

0089

Key Talks Under Way For OPEC

Iraqi Invasion Brings Anti-West Sentiment And Political Rifts

By YOUSSEF M. IBRAHIM

Special to The New York Times

VIENNA, Aug. 26 — As members of the Organization of Petroleum Exporting Countries gathered informally here today to confront some of the most crucial issues in the group's 30-year history, some predicted that a formal meeting would be announced on Monday to address questions of oil production and prices.

But regardless of the forum, a majority of OPEC members expect at least three member nations to carry out their plan to raise oil production to help meet the supply shortfall caused by Iraq's invasion of Kuwait on Aug. 2.

While there are serious differences on how to respond to the turmoil in the world petroleum markets, Saudi Arabia, the United Arab Emirates and Venezuela are pressing to increase their production substantially when the meeting ends.

There is a growing sentiment here that the member nations would be better off to permit production increases within an OPEC framework instead of allowing a free-for-all that [illegible] crisis is over. Once the Kuwait-Iraq crisis comes to an end, this logic holds, OPEC can retake control and regulate production under its quota system.

Long-Dormant Animosities

The Iraqi-Kuwaiti conflict has rekindled long-dormant animosities within OPEC that reflect the political schisms separating poor and rich countries and pro-Western and anti-Western nations.

OPEC officials from Algeria, Libya, Iran, Nigeria and Iraq, for example, argue that it is not OPEC's mission to save the West from an economic crisis caused by rapidly rising oil prices. They say the West has done little for indebted third world nations in the last decade and argue that there is enough oil in world markets to compensate for the interruption of supplies caused by the Iraqi invasion.

Delegates from Saudi Arabia, Venezuela, Kuwait, the United Arab Emirates and Qatar, however, say that unless OPEC allows members that can raise their output to do so immediately, OPEC itself will pay a high price if demand drops.

These delegates say higher oil prices will eventually create a backlash as they have done in the past, when industrialized countries countered rising prices with conservation measures that reduced oil consumption.

A number of member countries, including Indonesia, Algeria and Nigeria, seem to favor a middle ground in which OPEC would raise output to make up for only part of the shortages in the markets.

Their view is that oil prices had been quite weak for a long time earlier this year, and higher prices now are needed to compensate for the earlier losses.

A Fundamental Split

But behind the issues of output and prices is a more fundamental split along political and ideological lines.

Among the poorer, more militant members of OPEC, there is an unquestionable antipathy toward the United States and a conviction that Saudi Arabia and Venezuela, the prime advocates of higher production, are acting under strong American pressure.

"We are not here to respond to the wishes of the Americans," said an Arab delegate from one of the militant countries. "This is OPEC, and our mission is to serve the best interest of our members."

In an argument echoed by several moderate countries, including Nigeria and Indonesia, which are allies of the West, an OPEC official from Algeria said: "There is no real shortage of oil in the market. If the American and Western oil companies release their stocks of oil instead of hanging on to them to make more money, there will be no shortage."

Advocates of this view say that even if OPEC now authorized all its members with surplus capacity to produce all the oil they could, this would not amount to the full four million barrels a day missing from Kuwait and Iraq.

Among the delegates who gathered today, Kuwait's representative, Ali Khalifa al Sabah, the Finance Minister and a senior member of the Kuwaiti ruling family who has been an architect of OPEC policies for a decade, was greeted warmly by most other OPEC ministers.

So far, there has been no sign of the Iraqis, who have indicated that they would wait for the meeting to be elevated into a formal session.

The general sentiment here is that even if Iraq took part, it would not be able to prevent other OPEC members from raising output to compensate for the loss of the four million barrels of oil a day.

A Middle Ground

In pressing their case for increased production, Saudi Arabia and Venezuela concede that international oil companies, the United States, Japan and Western European countries hold large stocks of oil that could be released to help make up for the shortfall.

But they argue that these stocks are held by rich industrialized nations and that poorer third world countries, like India, Pakistan, Brazil and many African nations, which do not have stocks of oil, are experiencing a real shortage and are facing huge, untenable price increases.

One OPEC delegate, who is among those who are unable to raise production but strongly favor higher prices, advocates bargaining for a smaller increase in output by Saudi Arabia, Venezuela and the United Arab Emirates. "Perhaps something on the order of two million barrels instead of say 3.5 or so," he said.

But Saudi Arabia and Venezuela have said that under the existing OPEC agreement, which mandates the production of a total of 22.5 million barrels a day by all 13 members at a price of $21 a barrel, there is plenty of room to produce all they can now. Prices now stand at about $31 a barrel and production is substantially below 22.5 million barrels a day.

Some delegates are hoping that the talks do not raise emotions too high. Sadek Boussena, the OPEC conference president and Algeria's oil minister, said in an interview tonight on CNN: "I have big hopes that all of us will try to remain calm and stay out of matters that do not concern us."

Making a Decision

Mr. Boussena added, "I think we have to make this decision in a way that allows all OPEC members not to consider this decision as against them."

The Algerian oil minister noted [illegible] thing OPEC can remedy by itself.

He and others have said psychology and market speculation are driving prices up and that these elements have little to do with how much oil is on the market or how much production is missing from Kuwait and Iraq.

8/27 NYT

USW(F) 1952-4

0090

OPEC Begins Talks on Raising Output Aimed at Holding Down the Price of Oil

By JAMES TANNER
Staff Reporter of THE WALL STREET JOURNAL

VIENNA—OPEC's oil ministers began politically charged talks on higher output quotas to help hold down petroleum prices during the Middle East crisis.

As more ministers than had been expected arrived here over the weekend, a consensus seemed to build that the Organization of Petroleum Exporting Countries might turn what had been billed as a series of informal talks into a full-blown meeting. Such a formal meeting could officially act on proposals by some countries that they be allowed to produce more oil to replace embargoed Iraqi-Kuwaiti oil.

A previous request by Saudi Arabia and Venezuela for such an extraordinary conference, or emergency meeting, failed to receive majority approval and was rejected by Sadek Boussena, Algeria's oil minister and OPEC's president.

Even Mr. Boussena, who has insisted that the consuming nations should draw down their high oil inventories before asking OPEC to produce more, showed some signs of flexibility on the issue that has sharply divided the organization. "The only thing we have in mind is to save OPEC," he said on his arrival.

Of OPEC's 13 member nations, 11 were represented here by last night. The only absentees were the ministers from Iraq and Libya. Libya's minister is still expected.

Saudi Arabia, Venezuela and the United Arab Emirates are thought to be capable of making up three million barrels a day of the four million barrels taken out of world oil markets by the embargo. The three countries would like to get a meeting to officially approve output beyond their current quotas, though it has been clear they intend to increase production, anyway, if OPEC's clearance isn't forthcoming soon.

Iraq strongly opposes such a move by OPEC, and has been supported by several other members who argue that OPEC's late July production agreement shouldn't be altered until there is real evidence of tight supplies. Some worry that changing that agreement would appear to be bowing to U.S. wishes to hold down petroleum prices while the U.S. leads global sanctions against Iraq and Kuwait.

On Friday, oil prices eased but remained above the $30-a-barrel mark. West Texas Intermediate, the benchmark crude, fell $1.05 to $30.90, while in the international market, North Sea Brent dropped $1.20 to $31.20.

Celestino Armas, Venezuela's oil minister, renewed the call for an emergency session on his arrival. "We need to take some action [now]," said Mr. Armas, adding: "The world is waiting for OPEC."

Venezuela already is pumping more than its quota of 1.9 million barrels a day, but the additional oil is going into storage, Mr. Armas said. Other officials from Venezuela confirmed that the country's national oil company can increase output by 350,000 barrels a day within a week and by an additional 150,000 barrels a day by year end.

The UAE could exceed its quota by a similar amount, while Saudi Arabia is understood to be capable of producing as much as two million barrels a day over its quota, making up 50% of the four million barrels of oil taken out of world markets by the embargo.

Supporting the wish of those three countries to raise output is a delegation from Kuwait's government-in-exile. Heading the delegation is Ali Khalifa al-Sabah, Kuwait's finance minister and former oil minister.

Sheik Ali was the architect of Kuwait's long-standing practice of over-production. That practice particularly enraged Iraq, which contended the excess Kuwait production depressed oil prices and kept Iraq from gaining funds needed to rebuild its war-torn economy.

Sheik Ali slipped out of Kuwait the night of Iraq's invasion and has been shepherding his country's vast global investments and its oil policy from exile. He had little to say on his arrival other than to express hope for an agreement on increased quotas for "those who can produce" more.

Others backing the Saudi-Venezuela proposal are the United Arab Emirates, Ecuador and Qatar. Delegates from these countries not only support expanded output by OPEC's producers but also recommend that consuming nations draw additional supplies from their government and commercial stockpiles. That combination, they argue, would change the market psychology that has resulted in a doubling of oil prices since June.

8/27
WSJ

Oil? Nation's Utilities Are Not So Worried

By MATTHEW L. WALD

Whatever damage the run-up in oil prices inflicts on the economy as a whole, the effect on electricity bills is likely to be relatively modest. Of the fuel-consuming industries, the electric utilities have been the most successful in learning the lessons of the first two oil shocks, in the 1970's, and finding other sources.

Oil accounted for about 18 percent of the fuel used by utilities at the time of the Iranian revolution in 1979, but amounted to only an average of 5.7 percent last year, despite a vast increase in the amount of electricity generated over the last decade. Moving the electric system off oil is important because a growing share of the energy used in this country — almost 36 percent last year — is turned into electricity before it is consumed.

But the amount of oil used by utilities still varies widely from company to company, so the effect of rising oil prices on consumer bills will also vary. The Hawaiian Electric Company, for example, is nearly all oil-powered. The Long Island Lighting Company is still 63 percent oil-dependent, while the Consolidated Edison Company of New York depends on oil to generate 41 percent of its power.

A barrel of oil produces about 500 kilowatt-hours when burned. The average household uses about 500 kilowatt-hours a month. If a utility was 100 percent oil-dependent, a $20 increase in the price of a barrel of oil would raise the monthly electric bill by the same amount.

But most utilities that were heavily dependent on oil in the 1970's have weaned themselves away by converting to coal or natural gas and by purchasing or building hydroelectric capacity or nuclear reactors. In addition, experts say, few plants built in the last few years use oil.

"As the utilities began to see themselves as competitors, and wanted to portray themselves as low-cost producers, the incentives were for them to switch away from oil," said Marie Corio, president of Applied Economic Research in New York.

They accomplished this first by running their own plants in a different pattern. They used gas- or coal-fired generation first, bought power from utilities with extra coal-fired capacity next, and then rebuilt their hardware to burn fuels other than oil. This required adding anti-pollution equipment in many cases, although the biggest technical difficulty was often finding a place to store the additional coal, some experts said.

As various users now substitute gas for oil, the price of gas will rise, Dr. Corio said. This may discourage the plans of some utilities and independent power producers to build new natural gas-fired power stations.

Others are not sure the price of gas will rise. "We don't see a very direct linkage," said I. C. Bupp, a managing director of Cambridge Energy Research Associates. Even if oil gives up part of the market to gas, "there will still be gas-on-gas competition," he said.

Coal prices will not rise, because "there is so much spare capacity, nobody has to dig a new mine," said Standley H. Hoch, chairman and chief executive of General Public Utilities in New Jersey. It gets about 45 percent of its energy from coal.

Companies with excess capacity to burn coal will be in a strong position to sell power to those that use oil, said Charles B. Earle and Gary R. Licht, utility analysts at Mabon, Nugent & Company, the securities firm. They add that companies that still use oil heavily may find that after they have passed increased fuel costs to their customers, they will run into political resistance to unrelated increases. Eastern Utilities Associates, which wholesales power in New England, is in the former category, they said. Central Maine Power and Con Edison are among the latter.

Emissions Still a Big Concern

Still, the public's resistance to nuclear power and the emissions problems that arise from burning coal make it doubtful that oil will disappear in electric generation.

In addition, many utilities and independent power producers have added turbines that burn natural gas when it is available and light oil when it is not. In the Northeast, these generators have been blamed for increasing the demand for heating oil on the coldest winter days, when natural gas is in short supply, as happened last December.

Over all, however, the conversion away from oil has been dramatic.

United Illuminating, which serves the New Haven and Bridgeport areas of Connecticut, is now about 22 percent oil-dependent, down from 92 percent at the time of the Iranian revolution. That figure will fall to 11 percent by 1991, the company says, at which point, even if oil prices doubled, electric costs would go up only 9 percent.

The reasons for the switch by utilities around the country are illustrated by United Illuminating's cost structure. The fuel and operating cost per kilowatt-hour at the plant gate is 2.176 cents for Bridgeport Harbor 3, a 25-year-old plant that was converted from oil to coal in 1985. A less-efficient oil-fired plant, which was used only about 7 percent of the time last year, has a price of 5.3 cents per kilowatt-hour.

Nuclear Power Increased

United Illuminating and many other utilities also substituted uranium for oil by building nuclear plants, which last year generated 19 percent of the domestically produced electricity, up from 4.5 percent in 1973, at the time of the first oil shock. The Seabrook nuclear plant, which went into commercial operation earlier this week and of which United Illuminating owns 17.5 percent, costs the company 1.792 cents a kilowatt-hour, the utility said.

But building new nuclear plants is an option now closed, for all practical purposes, because of waste disposal problems, safety and regulatory questions, and especially cost overruns. Building Seabrook bankrupted the biggest investor, the Public Service Company of New Hampshire and required United Illuminating to seek several emergency rate increases.

The New England Electric System, another Seabrook partner, which was 78 percent oil-dependent in 1979, has since reduced its reliance. John Rowe, the chairman, said the company had adopted "a general strategy of not being caught that dependent again."

Even when oil bottomed out at around $10 a barrel in 1986, he said, the coal the company was burning in converted plants was cheaper.

"In 1990, people understand the need to burn coal, with troops in the Middle East," Mr. Rowe said. "But it isn't always obvious at other times."

USW(F)1952-6

0092

Changes in Florida

Florida Power and Light, which was 53 percent dependent on oil in 1979, completed two new nuclear plants and is now seeking other ways to curtail its oil use. It has signed long-term contracts for natural gas, and recently signed a letter of intent to buy a minority interest in a coal-fired plant in Georgia. This year, oil will make up 22 percent of its fuel, said Michael R. Bumgardner, a spokesman.

Southern California Edison was more than 40 percent dependent on oil at the time of the 1973 oil shock, said Larry Papay, a senior vice president. Now it is 4 to 5 percent dependent on the fuel. In the last 10 years, nuclear power has grown to 17 percent, from 4 percent, he said. The company also burns more coal and natural gas, and buys or generates power from solar plants, geothermal plants and windmills.

Efficiency Stressed

The company's focus is on improving efficiency, he said. "Although conservation lost some of its glamour after 1985, we have continued spending $44 million or $45 million a year" to help customers use electricity more efficiently, he said. Earlier this year, after negotiations with environmental groups and others, it raised the sum to $75 million, and will increase it again to $100 million.

Less successful in reducing imported oil is Long Island Lighting, which built a nuclear plant that would have displaced more than eight million barrels of oil a year if it had operated as its designers said it would. But the plant was abandoned by agreement with New York State because of safety concerns.

In the last 12 months, the company has been 62.5 percent dependent on oil, 13.5 percent on natural gas, 5.5 percent on nuclear power from a plant upstate and 18.5 percent on purchased power — a mix of natural gas, coal, hydroelectric power and even garbage, which is burned in a power-generating incinerator.

In July, Lilco paid an average of $15.19 a barrel for the heavy oil it uses, up from $14.49 in June. On Monday, it paid $22.50.

NYT 8/25

USW(F) 1952-7.

0093

Saudis Act To Raise Oil Production

OPEC Nations Meet Informally on Quotas

By David B. Ottaway
Washington Post Foreign Service

DHAHRAN, Saudi Arabia, AUG. 26—The Saudi government has ordered its state-owned oil company, Saudi Aramco, to begin increasing production but has yet to set any new output ceiling, according to informed oil sources.

Saudi Arabia is the largest producer among the 13 members of the Organization of Petroleum Exporting Countries (OPEC), and its decision could have a significant impact on spiraling prices. It could also help calm the unsettled world oil market, particularly if the kingdom steps up production by the extra 2 million barrels it says it is capable of pumping over its OPEC-allowed level of 5.38 million barrels a day.

The sources said the government order was issued early last week after Saudi Oil Minister Nisham Nazer publicly warned other OPEC members that if they refused to hold an emergency meeting to discuss the current crisis in the market, his government reserved the right to take immediate unilateral action.

OPEC representatives meeting informally in Vienna have so far failed to respond to calls from Saudi Arabia and Venezuela to turn the discussions into a decision-making conference. Both the Saudis and Venezuelans want OPEC members to approve increases in oil production to offset the loss of 4 million barrels a day of Iraqi and Kuwaiti oil, which has been placed under a U.N. embargo since Iraq's Aug. 2 invasion of Kuwait. Fears of a war in the Persian Gulf region and of a possible shortage of oil have driven oil prices up from about $18 a barrel before the invasion to about $30 a barrel.

OPEC bylaws require a unanimous vote by its membership for any decision on pricing and production to be binding. Delegates in Vienna said the Saudis and Venezuelans would be happy with a majority vote to raise existing quotas. Such action, however, could lead to a breakup of the 30-year-old cartel.

Nazer told a news conference Aug. 18 that "immediately means immediately" when asked how soon Saudi Arabia might take action, and he seems to have kept his word. It was not clear why the government has not made its decision public, but analysts here said it might be because the kingdom is eager to avoid further angering an already hostile Iraq.

In addition, analysts said, Saudi Arabia might not have wanted the decision made known while OPEC's informal discussions on production quotas were underway.

On the other hand, sources said, Saudi Arabia is under pressure from the Bush administration and from many Third World nations to increase production as soon as possible to help meet the needs of Iraq's and Kuwait's former customers. The Saudis already have agreed to provide the exiled Kuwaiti government with 250,000 barrels a day for the three refineries its state-owned oil company operates in Europe.

The Saudi oil minister indicated last week that his country's ability to increase production by 2 million barrels—half the Iraqi-Kuwaiti total—could combine with the United Arab Emirates' and Venezuela's ability to provide another 500,000 barrels a day each.

Those three producers alone could make up 3 million of the 4 million barrels previously pumped by Iraq and Kuwait. Nazer said he did not know where the other 1 million barrels might come from.

Oil sources here said it was uncertain how long Saudi Arabia could sustain production of an additional 2 million barrels a day, or a total of 7.4 million barrels. In 1980-81, Saudi Arabia reached a production level of more than 10 million barrels a day but subsequently shut down many of its oil fields as the worldwide demand for oil dropped sharply. As a result, Saudi Arabia had difficulty sustaining production at 6.8 million barrels a day when it tried to do so in late 1988.

Special correspondent Michael Z. Wise contributed to this story from Vienna.

W.P. 8/27/90

USW(F)1952-

0094

A Little Oil Means a Lot

Only a Small Fraction of Supply Is Shut Off, Yet It's Enough to Almost Double the Price

By MATTHEW L. WALD

The price of crude oil has nearly doubled since the beginning of July, the financial markets have plunged, and the economic future of the industrial world has been thrown into question, all because of an interruption in supplies that may turn out to be quite modest. A host who bought two cases of beer for a party and broke one bottle would face about the same degree of shortage.

Economic Analysis

Why, then, is the party turning into a riot?

Because, economists and industry executives say, both supply and demand are very slow to respond to changes in oil prices. Neither producers nor consumers of oil are prompted to make changes that would restore an equilibrium. When prices rise sharply for commodities like wheat or pork bellies, farmers quickly adjust their plans to plant fields or slaughter animals, and consumers quickly switch to other products. But in the short term, the same forces do not seem to apply in the oil market.

Hence, the loss of about 4.5 million barrels a day from the world's supply of roughly 61 million barrels a day has sent the market spinning, even though three members of the Organization of Petroleum Exporting Countries are expected to make up about three million barrels a day of the lost supply. As a result, a buyer in July who wanted a contract for delivery of oil in August paid less than $18 a barrel. Today, a buyer who wants delivery in October would pay more than $30. Many analysts predict that the price will soon rise further.

The price of crude oil can also fall sharply.

When the price turns lower, as it did in 1986, it is hardly an inducement for producers to pump less from fields that cost millions or billions of dollars to develop. Even if the price falls so low that the company no longer earns a competitive return on its capital investment, some return is better than none. If all the hardware is in place, production will continue as long as the selling price exceeds the cost of pumping an additional barrel.

Overproduction Strategy

And in the Middle East, where production costs are low, some countries have tried to maintain their income in times of declining prices by raising production. Such a strategy knocks prices even lower

An oil company could stop producing for a month to wait for higher prices. If it did so, say, for a well with a 10-year life, it would be postponing the recovery of the last barrel until the beginning of the 11th year. But commercial producers figure that a dollar in hand can be invested and is therefore worth more than a dollar earned from sales in the 11th year.

And when oil prices turn up, it takes months or years to convince companies that the change will last long enough to pay off new investments in multimillion-dollar holes in the ground.

Consumers of oil, on the other hand, hardly cut their consumption at all when the price rises, at least in the short term. Longer-term consumption can be affected through decisions like what car a family will buy next or what industrial equipment a company will order. Similarly, consumers do not use much more oil when the price declines.

A Market That Lost Its Balance

The oil market was more or less in balance until Iraq invaded Kuwait on Aug. 2 and the importing nations replied with an embargo. The amount cut off was about 4.5 million barrels a day. Saudi Arabia and Venezuela have promised to increase production by 2.5 million barrels between them, although they have not yet raised their output by much, and some traders are worried by the delay. The United Arab Emirates is expected to pump another 500,000 barrels a day.

By that reckoning, by the fourth quarter of this year, the shortfall will be about 2.5 percent.

But that is enough.

"There's a tiny spread between shortage and glut in our business, between 2 and 3 percent, that's all," said George Babikian, the president of the ARCO Products Company.

A listing of supply disruptions over the last three decades by the Energy Department found that the quadrupling of oil prices during the Arab oil embargo after the 1973 Arab-Israeli war was induced by a loss of 2.75 percent of world production.

Effect of Buying Extra Oil

Philip K. Verleger Jr., an oil and commodities expert and visiting fellow at the Institute for International Economics, said he believed that whatever the physical interruption, the effect on the market would be doubled because everyone would seek extra oil to insulate against shortage, the industrial equivalent of all motorists trying to fill the gasoline tanks of their cars. Thus, if the amount of lost supplies was about 2 percent of consumption, he said, demand would rise by 2 percent and the shortfall would be 4 percent.

(Thus far, motorists do not appear to be keeping tanks much fuller. With more than 120 million cars on the road, if everyone tried to "top off" their tanks by buying an average of five gallons extra, the transfer from storage tanks to vehicle tanks would be about 14 million barrels, or roughly double one day's consumption. The nation's 50 million trucks would also demand gasoline and diesel fuel.)

Mr. Verleger also noted that commodities are generally volatile; the price of coffee rose sevenfold during the last decade, for example, then fell back. The difference is that few industries run on coffee.

World Oil Supplies High

Early in the current crisis, there appeared to be mitigating factors for oil. Analysts pointed out, for example, that world supplies were very high. Commercial stocks were about 150 million barrels above their level of the previous year, which would imply perhaps three months of grace before stocks dipped to sub-normal levels. In addition, the United States holds 600 million barrels in a strategic reserve, or enough to make up the shortfall of 1.5 million barrels a day for 400 days; other countries also have strategic stocks.

But the stocks, commercial and strategic, are not turning out to be useful, at least not so far.

"We don't know how to use them," said Dr. Ethan Kapstein, the director of Harvard University's Economics and National Security Program.

For companies that hold extra supplies, he said, the question is, "Do you sell them and seek profits now, or do you wait for prices to go up later?"

Self-Fulfilling Expectations

The answer, as demonstrated by the marketplace, appears to be that most managers expect prices to go higher and are therefore still buying oil rather than using existing stocks. If this expectation is held widely enough, it is self-fulfilling, because it keeps the demand strong and the price up.

As the Bush Administration sees it, the strategic reserve should be saved to deal with physical shortages. Many analysts doubt that such shortages can occur in an unregulated market; oil will always be available, they say, but the price may be very high. In effect, the Administration is saying, however, that the rainy day is not here yet and that the reserve, on [illegible]

U.S.W (F) 1952-9

0095

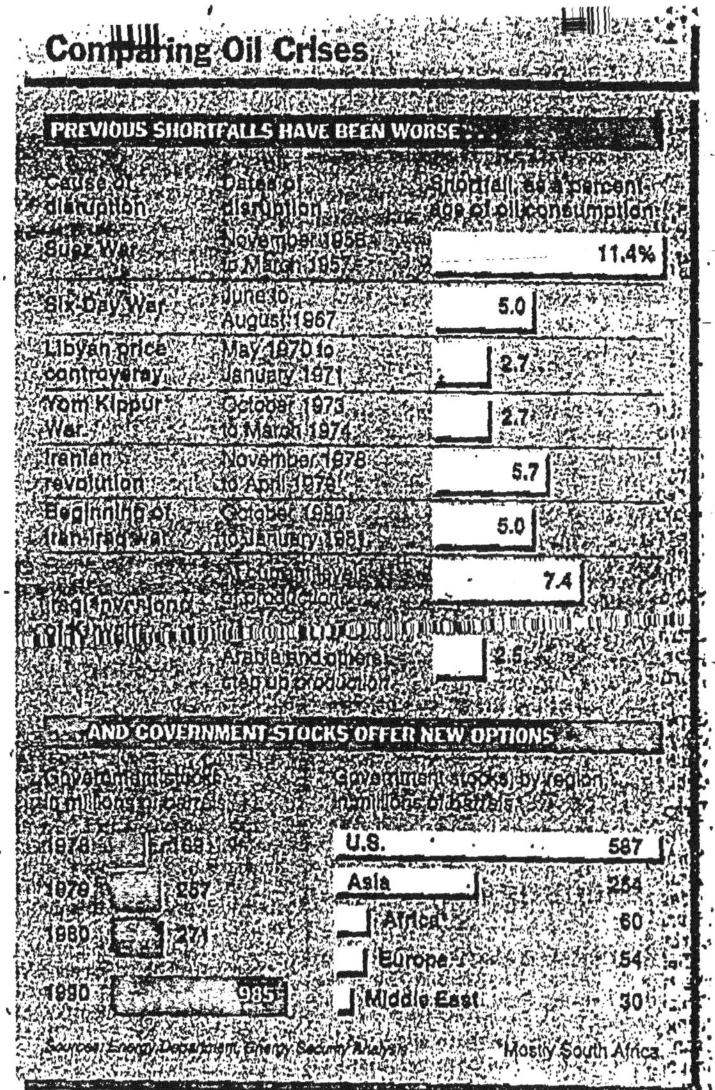

Comparing Oil Crises

PREVIOUS SHORTFALLS HAVE BEEN WORSE . . .

Cause of disruption	Dates of disruption	Shortfall, as a percentage of oil consumption
Suez War	November 1956 to March 1957	11.4%
Six-Day War	June to August 1967	5.0
Libyan price controversy	May 1970 to January 1971	2.7
Yom Kippur War	October 1973 to March 1974	2.7
Iranian revolution	November 1978 to April 1979	5.7
Beginning of Iran-Iraq war	October 1980 to January 1981	5.0
[illegible] Iraqi invasion of Kuwait [illegible]	[illegible] production	7.4
	[illegible] Arabia and others step up production	2.5

. . . AND GOVERNMENT STOCKS OFFER NEW OPTIONS

Government stocks in millions of barrels	
1978	168
1979	257
1980	271
1990	985

Government stocks by region in millions of barrels	
U.S.	587
Asia	254
Africa*	60
Europe	54
Middle East	30

Sources: Energy Department, Energy Security Analysis

*Mostly South Africa.

The New York Times

A little Oil Means a lot

2/2

billion, not counting interest, may be more useful later. This approach denies the nation the use of the reserve to stabilize the economy, Dr. Kapstein said.

In a way, the New York Mercantile Exchange is agreeing with the Administration that oil will be more expensive later, as the price is bid higher nearly every day.

Some traders doubt that the Saudis and Venezuelans will come through with much in the way of additional supplies. Another worry is that war may spread to Saudi Arabia and that its huge output may be lost. A joke among traders last week was that the weather forecast for the Middle East was 10,000 degrees and cloudy.

Some traders look ahead to the fall quarter, when Europe, Japan and the United States build stocks for the winter and when natural gas, a handy substitute in many settings, will be unavailable because of heating demands.

The markets' assessment of the chance of war is a matter of instinct and guesswork. But two structural elements of the oil market virtually assure high prices and high demand regardless of military action. One is that under the auction system represented by the open market, the price paid by the last buyer sets the price for the next buyer, and if the last buyer is desperate, the price will be high.

The other is that everyone at this party is thirsty.

"You have capital investments that require oil, the most basic of which is the automobile," said Robert Boslego, an oil consultant in Winchester, Mass. "For the person driving the car, what else is he going to put in the tank? You have no alternative. And he's not going to stay home from work because it's going to cost him an extra dollar to get there."

Mr. Boslego and Dr. Kapstein pointed out in separate interviews that thus far, the thrust of Administration policy has been to try to talk the price of gasoline down, muting the signal to consumers to conserve that would be sent by sharply higher prices.

NYT 8/27

USW(F)-152-1

End.

0096

관리 번호	90-649

	분류번호	보존기간

발 신 전 보

WAV-0880 900828 1000 FC

번 호 :

종별 : 지 급

수 신 : 주 오지리 대사. 총영사

발 신 : 장 관 (기협)

제 목 : 이라크·쿠웨이트 사태

1. 귀지발 외신에 의하면, 8.26부터 빈에서 개최된 OPEC 비공식 회의에서 회원국들은 원유증산에 원칙적으로 합의했으며, 금 8.28 전체 특별회의에서 증산여부를 확정할 예정이라 하는 바, 동 OPEC 회의결과와 향후 원유수급 및 유가에 대한 OPEC 주변 및 주재국의 전망등을 파악, 지급 보고바람.

2. 아울러, 표제사태 관련 아국의 원유수급대책등에 참고코자 하니 향후 OPEC 관련 주요동향 있을시 수시 보고 바람. 끝.

(국제경제국장 최대화)

보 안 통 제	

앙 고 재	90년 8월 28일	기안자 성명	홍석화	과 장		국 장	전결	차 관	장 관
		기술협력과	홍석화	(서명)	(서명)	전결			(서명)

외신과통제

0097

원 본

외 무 부

종 별 :

번 호 : CNW-1293 일 시 : 90 0828 1615

수 신 : 장 관(기협,미북,중근동,정일,동자부)

발 신 : 주 카나다 대사

제 목 : 주재국 원유수급 동향(자료응신 제 89 호)

1. 주재국 에네지 위원회 (NAT' ENERGY BOARD)가스 원유과장 WHITE 를 8.27.(월) 안참사관이 접촉, 파악한바에 의하면 카나다는 8 월하순 현재 89 년과 거의 같은 수준의 원유를 생산하고 있으며 금번 이락 - 쿠 사태가 아직 원유 생산 및 수출입에 별다른 영향을 미치지 않고 있으며 8.2.이락의 쿠 침공 이전에 선적된 원유가 8 월말 -9 월 중순까지 도입될 예정이라고 함.

2. 한편 8.22. 자 주재국 에네지.광물.자원부자료에 의하면, 금번 이락-쿠 사태로 주재국 원유수입의 3 프로 (약 1.7 만 B/D) 및 총 소비의 1 프로만이 영향을 받는다고 함. 또한 EPP 에너지 광물 자원장관은 지난주 카나다 정부는 우방국 협조를 통해 현사태를 타결해 나갈수 있을 것을 확신한다고 말하고, 장기적인 원유 수급 및비상사태 대비책으로서 에너지의 추가 공급원 개발, 효율성증대 및 다양화를 제시하면서 카나다의 새로운 개발은 해당지역 경제발전을 자극하고 카나다 및 여타 IEA(INT'L ENERGY AGENCY)회원국 (21 개국)에 대한 새로운 원유공급원을 제공할뿐 아니라 불안정한 원유공급 국가에 대한 의존을 감소시킬것 이라고 언급함.

3. 주재국의 원유 수급 사정은 이락-쿠웨이트 사태에도 불구하고 안정된 것으로 평가되며, 금번사태로 인해 국제원유가 상승이 지속될 경우에는 과거 저유가로 경제성이 없어 개발 포기한 OIL SAND개발을 재검토 하는 계기가 될수 있을 것으로 보임. 주재국은 서부 알버타지에 풍부한 OIL SAND자원을 보유하고 있고, 원유가가 배럴당 25 미불이상 지속될 경우 현 기술 수준으로 경제성이 있는 개발이 가능하며, 88년 이전 검토된바 있는 41 억 카불 규모의 OSLO 사업 계획 (ESSO 등 6개회사 공동주자, 개발시 8.5 만 B/D 생산가능)을 재검토하고 있는 것으로 알려졌음.끝

(대사 - 국장)

경제국 2차보 미주국 중아국 정문국 안기부 동자부 대책반 1차보

PAGE 1 90.08.29 09:33 WG

외신 1과 통제관

0098

90-679

주 중 대 사 관

중국(경)764-51 1990. 8. 28

수신 : 장관

참조 : 국제경제국장

제목 : 이라크.쿠웨이트 사태

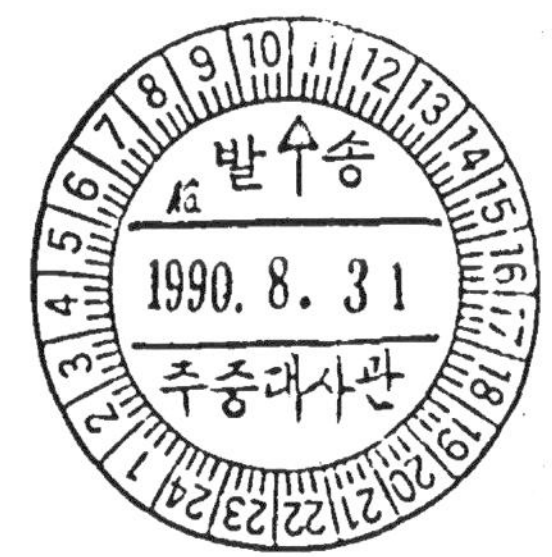

대 : WCH-0694

대호관련, 주재국 경제부 에너지위원회 등과 접촉 파악한바를 아래 보고합니다.

1. 이라크.쿠웨이트 물량감소에 대한 확보대책 및 대응방안

o 주재국은 원유의 99%를 수입에 의존하고 있는바 그중 82%를 중동지역으로부터, 나머지 18%를 나이제리아, 인도네시아 등 으로부터 수입.

o 주재국은 1일 약 42만배럴의 원유를 수입하고 있으며(90년도 원유 수입목표 2,343만 5천키로리터, 약 1억4천740만4천배럴) 그중 약 17%를 쿠웨이트로부터 수입.

o 이라크.쿠웨이트사태로 인한 쿠웨이트로 부터의 감소량 확보를 위해 중국석유 陳恩立부사장 등 3명의 "원유구매대사"를 중동 산유국으로 파견, 물량감소분 도입추진.

- 사우디아라비아 : 장기공급계약에 의한 1일 14만5천배럴의 안정공급 및 9월중 1일 200만배럴 증산시 1-2만배럴 증량공급 확약(사우디 석유차관)

- 아랍대공국 : 공급계약에 의한 1일 1만배럴의 지속공급 및 1일 80만배럴 증산여력있음으로, 필요시 증량공급 가능다짐.

- 이란 : 국영석유회사(NIOC)와 9월중 18만배럴 원유수입계약 체결 및 11월중 장기공급 계약체결 예정.

0099

- 주재국 정부의 책정 원유도입원가 US$15.46/배럴,
- 도입원유가 US$19.50배럴시 바란스
- 평균 원유도입가격 US$23/배럴로 계산, 석유제품가격 평균 21% 인상단행.
- 원유도입가격 US$24.50/배럴 초과시 재차 국내판매 가격인상 및 US$23/배럴 이하시 국내판매 가격인하 계획.

2. 원유 및 석유제품 비축현황(물량, 지속일수 등)

- 주재국은 원유의 생산, 수입, 제련 및 공급을 국영 중국석유 공사가 독점하고 있으며(88년부터 민영주유소 영업 및 일부개방 ;89년말 현재 민영주유소수 275개소, 전체주유소의 약 1/3차지) 원유 및 석유제품 비축제도는 "에너지관리법 및 시행세칙" 제5조 규정에 의해 90일분 이상을 비축토록 되어있고 이를 에너지위원회가 감독하고 있음.(별첨자료 참조)

3. 주재국내 유류가격 동향

- 주재국 경제부는 8.24. 12:00시를 기해 산업용 연료유를 제외한 석유제품에 대한 평균 21%의 가격인상을 단행했음.

제 품 명	인상후가격/리터 (NT$)	인상전가격/리터 (NT$)	인상폭(%)
Premium grade Gasoline	18.50	14.50	28
92-octane unleaded	17.50	13.5	30
95-octane unleaded	18.50	14.50	28
Two-stroke			

0100

unleaded	17.50	13.50	30
High grade			
Diesel fuel	13.00	10.00	30
Regular			
Diesel fuel	12.00	9.00	33
Aviation			
Gasoline	16.00	12.00	33
Aviation			
fuel#A1	9.50	6.70	42
Kerosene	13.0	10.50	29
Liquified			
petroleum gas	11.50/kg	9.50/kg	21
Natural gas (raw material)	7.50/입방미터	7.00/입방미터	7
Natural gas industrial use	7.50/입방미터	7.30/입방미터	3
Natural gas domestic use	7.50/입방미터	7.30/입방미터	3
Turbine fuel	12,000/킬로리터	8,500/킬로리터	41
Low-sulfur boiler oil	6,505/킬로리터	5,605/킬로리터	16

o 상기 제품가격 인상단행과 동시, 어선용 연료유, 대만전력의 발전용 연료유의 우혜가격제를 폐지하고 군용 석유제품 할인율을 과거의 50%에서 80%로 제고했음.

o 또한 동일자로 석유제품 화물세를 50%인하했음.
- 휘발유 화물세 60%에서 30%로 인하
- 경유.등유화물세 50%에서 25%로 인하

0101

4. 국제원유시장에 대한 수급 및 가격전망

가. 수급동향

o 8.28 비엔나에서 개최된 OPEC석유각료회의에서 13개 회원국 중 10개 회원국이 일산 400만배럴의 증산을 결의함으로써 이라크.쿠웨이트의 감산분을 충분히 확보, 안정적 수급과 동시 치솟던 국제원유가도 US$21-25/배럴 수준에서 안정될 것으로 전망하고 있음.

나. 가격전망

o 현재 국제원유시장의 US$32/배럴은 정상적, 장기적 유가가 아니며, 이라크.쿠웨이트사태가 평화적으로 해결될 경우 원유가격은 곧 안정될 것이나 배럴당 21-25불의 고유가 시대가 될것임.

- 장기 가격전망 1995년 : US$ 25-30/배럴
  2000년 : US$ 35-40/배럴

첨부 : 관계자료 3부

주 중 대

0102

원 본

외 무 부

종 별 :

번 호 : USW-3915 일 시 : 90 0828 1648

수 신 : 장 관(기협)

발 신 : 주 미 대사

제 목 : 석유시장 및 가격 동향 (4)

표제관련 , 8.28 (화) 당지 언론 보도를 종합 보고함.

1.유가 동향

가.8.27.(월) 원유 및 정유제품 가격은 대폭 하락하였음.

0 원유 (뉴욕 상품시장 , 10월 인도 가격):

배럴당 26.91 불 (8.24. 에 비해 4불 하락)

0 휘발유 (뉴욕 상품시장 ,9월 인도 가격):

갤런당 87.56 센트 (8.24.에 비해 17.10 센트 하락)

0 난방유 (뉴욕 상품시장, 9월 인도가격):

갤런당 78.10 센트 (8.,24. 에 비해 12.86 센트 하락)

나.당지 전문가 들은 원유가가 이처럼 급락한 이유를 아래와 같이 분석하고 있음.

0 유엔 사무총장의 중재 노력 개시등으로 금번 GZEU가 군사적 충돌없이 외교적으로 해결될수 있으리라는 낙관적인 기대 증대

0 8.27. OPEC 비공식 회의에서의 증산 실시에 관한 잠정합의 도달 (2항 참조)

다. 전문가들은 8.27. 의 원유가 급락에도 불구하고, 현재 국제 원유가격의 등락은 시장내의 실제 수요.공급에 따른 것이라기 보다는 금번 이락- 쿠웨이트 사태의 전개 방향에 대한 심리적 반응에 의해 결정되고 있기 때문에 금번 사태가 해결 되기까지는 원유가의 향배는 예측하기 어려운 것으로 평가하고 있음.

2. OPEC 동향

0 한편 8.27. OPEC 비공식 회의에서 산유국들은 이락 및 쿠웨이트로 부터의 원유 수입금지에 따른 공급 부족분 보전을 위해 아래와 같은 증산 실시계획에 잠정 합의한 것으로 알려졌음.

- 회원국에 대해 금번 사태 발발 이전에 합의된 OPEC 생산 상한선인 일일 22.5백만

경제국 2차보

PAGE 1	공람	국제경제국	90.8.29	담 당	과 장	국 장	차관보	차 관	장 관

90.08.29 09:16 WG

외신 1과 통제관

0103

배럴범위 내에서 증산 허용

- 금번 사태가 해결되어 이락 및 쿠웨이트 의 원유수출이 재개될 경우 금번 사태 전의 국별 생산쿼타를 다시 적용

- OPEC 은 서방 석유회사 및 성방국에 대해 각각 상업적 비축 원유 및 전략 비축 원유를 시장에 방출, 원유 가격 안정에 협조를 할것을 촉구

0 OPEC 에서의 잠정합의에 따라 사우디등 회원국은 아래와 같이 증산을 실시할 것으로 알려지고 있음(일일 증산량)

- 사우디: 2백만 배럴

- 베네주엘라: 50만 배럴

- UAE : 50 만 배럴

- 기타 (낭지리아, 가봉, 에쿠아돌등): 40만 배럴

3.금 8.28. 자 당지 언론 보도 내용 별첨 팩스 송부함.

첨부: USW(F)- 1964 (6 매)

(대사 박동진- 국장)

0104

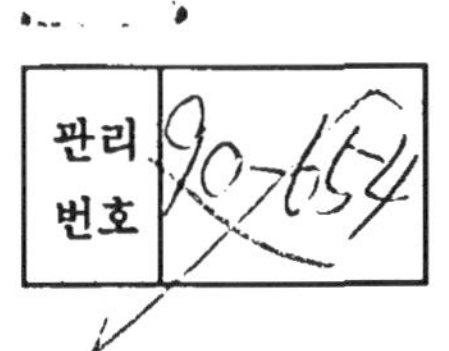

외 무 부

종 별 :

번 호 : SVW-0673 일 시 : 90 0829 0930

수 신 : 장관(중동,동구일,기협,기정)

발 신 : 주 쏘영사처장

제 목 : 이락크사태

대: WSV-628,673

당처 서참사관은 8.28 외무성 중동국 ALEXANDER HOVOZILOV 참사관을 면담, 표제관련 쏘측 입장등을 타진한바, 동인의 발언요지 아래 보고함.

-아 래-

1. 사태 해결위한 노력

-쏘측은 사태의 평화적 해결을 위한 다각적 노력을 하고 있으며 특히 이라크 지도자들에게 여러가지 채널을 통해 사태의 평화적 해결을 촉구하고 있으나 아직까지 이라크측으로 부터 긍정적인 반응이 없음.

-쏘측은 사태 해결에 있어서 유엔 안보리가 이라크에 대해 제한적인 무력개입을 하는 경우 쏘련은 이에 참여해야 하는 것을 의무(OBLIGATORZ) 적인 것으로 간주하고 있음.

2. 외국인 억류 문제

-쏘측은 이라크측에 이라크의 국제적 이미지가 더이상 훼손되는 것을 막기위해 외국인을 억류하지 말 것을 강력하게 종용하고 있음.

-쿠웨이트 거주 소련인들은 전부 귀국하였으며 이라크 주재 소련 기술자등의 가족(주로 부녀자) 950 명이 이달말까지 쏘련 특별기편으로 3 차례에 걸쳐 귀국 예정이며 제 1 진 250 명이 금 8.28 도착하였음.

3. 원유 증산문제

-쏘련은 이라크에서 '상당한 양' 의 원유를 수입해온 관계로 금번사태로 인해 새로운 경제적 문제가 야기되고 있음.

-(이라크의 물량 감산에 따른 대책을 문의한데 대해) 쏘련의 연간 원유생산은 약 6 억톤 정도이나 근년에 들어와서 시설투자등에 문제가 있어 생산이 줄어들고 있는

중아국 대책반 장관 차관 1차보 2차보 구주국 경제국 청와대 안기부

PAGE 1 90.08.29 16:16

외신 2과 통제관 BT

0105

추세로서 갑작스러운 증산은 용이하지 안을 것으로 봄.끝

(처장-국장)

90.12.31 까지

90 12 31

PAGE 2

0106

관리번호 90-656

원 본

외 무 부

종 별 :

번 호 : JAW-5243 일 시 : 90 0829 1602

수 신 : 장관(기협,통일,경일)

발 신 : 주 일 대사(경제)

제 목 : 이라크.쿠웨이트 사태

대 : WJA-3575

연 : JAW-5014

OPEC 비공식석유상회의 결과 및 최근 유가동향을 주재국 언론반응을 중심으로 하기 보고함.

1. OPEC 비공식 석유상회의

0 8.26 이래 비엔나에서 개최되고 있는 OPEC 비공식회의에서 일산400 만 베럴 증산에 대체적 으로 합의한것으로 보도됨.

0 7 월말 OPEC 총회시 생산 상한선은 2,249 만 베럴이 었으며, 이락 및 쿠웨이트 양국의 생산량이 464 만 베럴이므로 금번 400 만 베럴 증산으로 대이락 경제제재에 따른 원유 감축을 충당할수 있을것으로 보임.

0 그러나, 석유업계 전문가들은 사우디 및 UAE 등 산유국의 증산 한계가 최대 400 만 베럴이며 일부에서는 300 만 베럴로 추산하고 있으므로 금번 OPEC 비공식회의 결과가 가격 진정효과는 있으나, 이락 및 쿠웨이트산 원유 부족분을 충당하기에는 미흡하다는 견해를 피력하고 있음.

0 특히 석유의 수요기인 10-12 월 기간중 OPEC 원유공급 의존량이 2,400 만베럴에 달할것이므로, 원유부족 현상은 심화될 가능성이 있을것으로 보고있음.

2. 유가동향

0 OPEC 비공식회의 결과 27 일 뉴욕시장의 유가가 베럴당 4 달러 하락하였으며, 28 일 동경 스포트 시장에서는 중동산 두바이 원유가 전일대비 4 달러 하락한 25 달러선의 약세를 보임.

0 석유업계 전문가들은 중동사태에 따른 원유의 부기적 매입 및 원유공급 부족에 따른 심리적 불안등이 최근의 유가급등 원인이었는바, 금번회의 증산결정이 심리적

경제국 대책반	차관	1차보	2차보	아주국	경제국	통상국	청와대	안기부

PAGE 1

90.08.29 16:46

외신 2과 통제관 BT

0107

불안요인을 해소 시킴으로써 유가가 하락된것으로 판단하고 있음.

0 주재국 석유업계 전문가들은 향후 1 개월간 원유가격이 25 달러 전후가 될것이나, 원유가격은 산유국의 증산지속 여부가 관건이 될것이며, 수요기인 4/4 분기에 원유 부족현상이 심화되면, 유가상승을 피할수 없을것이라는 견해를 피력하고 있음.

3. 주재국 반응

가. OPEC 비공식 회의결과

0 통산성은 금번 OPEC 비공식 석유상회의가 원유증산에 합의한것이 원유시장 동향에 긍정적 영향을 미칠것을 기대하며 향후 사태추이를 지켜볼 필요가 있다는 신중한 자세를 피력하였음.

0 무또 통산상은 28 일 기자회견을 갖고 9.1 부터 시작하는 구주 5 개국 순방도중 IEA(국제에너지기관) 사무국장과의 회담(9.6. 파리)에서 석유공급의 불안을 해소시키고 산유국에 대해 증산을 요청할 것이라고 밝혔음.

나. 원유 비축 의무 조기완화 여부

0 통산성 및 자원에너지청은 이락 및 쿠웨이트산 원유 대체 조치가 순조롭게 진행되어 9 월중에는 비축량을 방출하지 않아도 좋을것으로 보이며 현행 82 일분의 민간 비축의무를 완화할 가능성도 있으나, 구체적인 것은 8.31 파리에서 개최되는 IEA 이사회 회의결과에 따라 결정할 것이라함. 끝

(공사 이한춘-국장)

예고:90.12.31. 까지

PAGE 2

0108

관리 번호 90-655

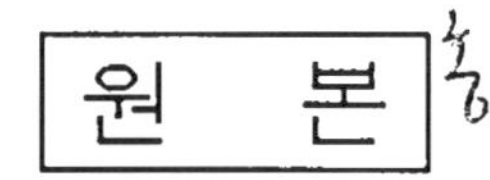
원 본

외 무 부

종 별 :

번 호 : MAW-1167 일 시 : 90 0829 1730

수 신 : 장관(기협,아동,사본:동자부장관)

발 신 : 주 말련 대사

제 목 : 이라크,쿠웨이트 사태

대: WMA-0559,0601

연: MAW-1082

1. 본직은 8.29(수) 주재국 국영 석유공사(PETRONAS) TAN SRI AZIZAN 사장을 면담, 표제 상태에 관해 의견을 교환하였음.

2. 동인은 현재의 교착 상태가 다소 장기간 지속될 것으로 전망하면서, 이경우 다소간의 원유 공급부족과 가격 상승은 피할수 없을 것이라함. 이는 증산 능력이 있는 사우디 UAE, 베네주엘라등이 최대한 증산을 하더라도 이라크, 쿠웨이트 생산분 전체를 보전할수 없기 때문이라함. 그러나 산유국, 비산유국 공히 석유 위기를 피하기 위한 다각도의 노력을 전개하고 있으므로 양차 석유 파동과 같은 위기는 피할수 있을 것으로 본다함.

3. 주재국은 연호 1 만 배럴 증산분은 필리핀및 인도에 공급하기로 하였으며, 추가의 증산은 여타 산유국의 증산 동향을 보아가면서 결정할 예정이라함. 본직은 추가 증산시 대 아국 공급에 우선적 고려를 해 줄것을 요청하였으며, 동 사장은 양국간의 긴밀한 협력관계에 비추어 최대한의 우선적 배려를 해 주겠다고약속하였음. 끝

(대사 홍순영-국장)

90.12.31 까지

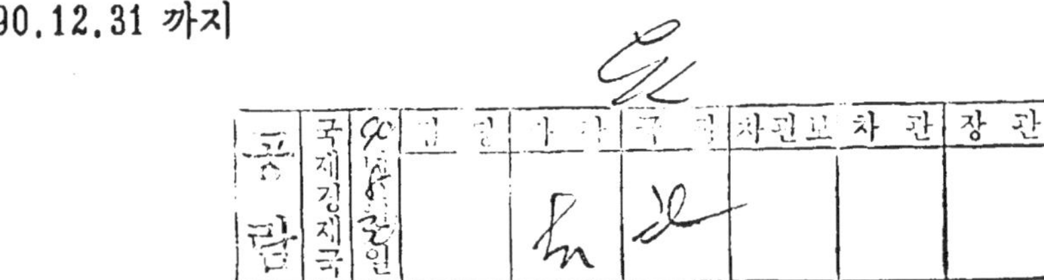

공람	국제경제국	90. 8. 31 결인	담당	과장	국장	차관보	차관	장관

90 12 31

경제국	1차보	2차보	아주국	통상국	청와대	안기부	동자부	대책반

PAGE 1

90.08.29 19:07

외신 2과 통제관 BT

0103

"에너지는 나라의 힘 아껴쓰고 비축하자"

동 력 자 원 부

W006036

원유 29210- 503-9627 1990. 8. 29.

수신 외무부 장관

제목 쿠웨이트 사태 관련 산유국 외교활동에 따른 협조

1. 금번 쿠웨이트 사태와 관련, 국내 원유수급 안정을 위한 당부의 장기안정적 원유확보 시책에 적극 호응하여 주신 귀부의 협조에 감사를 드리며, 이란, 말련, 리비아등 현지주재 아국대사들의 노고에 대해서도 감사의 뜻이 전달될 수 있도록 부탁드립니다.

아울러, 앞으로도 우리나라의 에너지 및 자원수요가 거의 해외에 의존하고 있는 점을 충분히 감안, 귀부 및 아국 현지대사관들의 협조가 절실히 요청되는 바, 당부의 에너지 자원정책이 원활히 추진될 수 있도록 배전의 협조를 거듭 당부드립니다.

2. 말레지아 주재 아국대사(홍순영 대사)의 전문보고(8.16일자)와 관련, 말레지아가 원유를 증산한다는 보도가 있어 국내정유사들의 원유도입 희망물량을 파악한 바, (주)유공이 말레지아산 원유 30천B/D 내에 최대가능한 장기계약 물량 증량을 요청하였음을 알려드리오니 동물량이 확보될 수 있도록 협조하여 주시기 바랍니다.

3. 또한, 리비아 주재 아국대사(최필립 대사)의 전문보고(8.13일자)와 관련, 양국간 공동위 합의내용의 이행을 위한 리비아산 원유 15천B/D 의 조기계약 체결이 원만히 이루어질 수 있도록 협조바라며, (주)유공이 별첨과 같이 런던 BIMC에 전문을 발송하여 동건과 관련 계약체결의사를 재차 희망한바 있음을 알려드립니다.

0110

이하 (3) 24477

원유 29210-　　　　　　　　　　　　　　　　　1990. 8. 29.

4. 이란주재 아국대사(정경일 대사)의 전문보고(8.11일자)와 관련, (주)쌍용정유가 이란 국영석유공사(NIOC)와 종전 60천B/D 의 장기계약 물량을 80천B/D 로 증량키로 합의상태에 있으며, 추후 아국 정유사들의 원유확보를 위한 제반활동시 현지대사관의 협조를 각별히 부탁드립니다.

5. 인도네시아에 대하여도 인도네시아가 원유생산을 증산한다는 보도가 있는바, 국내정유사인 (주)유공이 인도네시아 국영석유공사(Petamina)와의 30천B/D 를 비롯하여 호남(주)가 10천B/D, 극동정유가 10천B/D 등 총 50천B/D 의 장기원유 공급계약을 희망하고 있으니 동내용을 현지대사에게 통보하여 원유공급계약이 원만히 이루어질 수 있도록 협조 바랍니다.

6. 동건과 관련, 동력자원부 장관으로서 아국의 원유도입과 관련 아국의 현지대사들에게 보여준 후의에 대한 감사의 서신을 이란 및 말련등 산유국 정부의 석유상들에게 전달코자 하오니 협조하여 주시기 바랍니다.

첨부 : 동자부장관 감사서신 2통, 리비아 원유도입 관련 전문사본 1부. 끝.

동 력 자 원 부 장

0111

Unified Government Complex (Bldg. No. 4)
Kwachon427-760, Republic of Korea
TLX: MERROK K23472

MINISTRY OF ENERGY AND RESOURCES

REPUBLIC OF KOREA

August 29, 1990

H.E. Gholamreza Aghazadeh
Minister of Oil
The Islamic Republic of Iran

Your Excellency,

Upon my six months' service as the Minister of Energy and Resources, it is my great pleasure to write this letter to express my hearty thanks for your kind cooperation and continuous support extended toward the development of cooperative relations between our two countries.

Particularly, the present deplorable situation in the Middle East has aroused deep concern to all the world and came up as the most serious challenge to my job since my appointment on last March because stable security of energy sources is of prime importance and top priority of Korean Energy policy.

In this regard, I take your recent assurance of continuous supply of crude oil to my country during the visit of Korean ambassador to your office on August 11 as a firm evidence to reaffirm my highest evaluation and sincere appreciation for the truly cooperative relations so far cultivated between our two countries.

I do believe that your continuous support in this difficult time will surely be remembered by Korean people and certainly serve as another momentum to further strengthen the existing friendly ties between our two countries in the future.

Your Excellency,

Extending my hearty thanks again, I would like to kindly ask your continuous cooperation and support in the future.

Sincerely yours,

Hee-Il Lee
Minister

0112

Unified Government Complex (Bldg. No. 4)
Kwachon427-760, Republic of Korea
TLX: MERROK K23472

MINISTRY OF ENERGY AND RESOURCES

REPUBLIC OF KOREA

August 29, 1990

H.E. Datuk Dr. Hj Sulaiman Bin Haji Daud
Minister of Prime Minister's Department
Malaysia

Your Excellency,

Upon my six months' service as the Minister of Energy and Resources, it is my great pleasure to write this letter to express my hearty thanks for your kind cooperation and continuous support extended toward the development of cooperative relations between our two countries.

Particularly, the present deplorable situation in the Middle East has aroused deep concern to all the world and came up as the most serious challenge to my job since my appointment on last March because stable security of energy sources is of prime importance and top priority of Korean Energy policy.

In this regard, I take your recent assurance of continuous supply of crude oil to my country during the visit of Korean ambassador to your office on August 11 as a firm evidence to reaffirm my highest evaluation and sincere appreciation for the truly cooperative relations so far cultivated between our two countries.

I do believe that your continuous support in this difficult time will surely be remembered by Korean people and certainly serve as another momentum to further strengthen the existing friendly ties between our two countries in the future.

Your Excellency,

Extending my hearty thanks again, I would like to kindly ask your continuous cooperation and support in the future.

Sincerely yours,

Hee-Il Lee
Minister

0113

YUKONG'NOTICE'
TELEX 92920731;TO TELEX;TEXT

TO : BRINT, TRIPOLI
ATTN : MR. S. ABUSAMAHA / CRUDE OIL MANAGER

TO : BREGA DIV., LONDON
ATTN : MR. A. OMAR

PHI-0822-01 AUG 22, 1990

RE : BREGA CRUDE OIL DEAL

REFERENCE IS MADE TO YOUR TLX CD-190 DATED AUG.6 ON THE CAPTIONED SUBJECT.

IT IS REGRETTABLE TO BE INFORMED THAT YOU ARE UNABLE TO SUPPLY YOUR CRUDE OIL TO KOREAN REFINERIES AT THE MOMENT.
H/EVER, WE SINCERELY HOPE TO HAVE TERM RELATIONSHIP WITH YOUR ESTEEMED COMPANY FOR AT LEAST 15 MBD OF BREGA CRUDE OIL IN CONSIDERATION OF MUTUAL RELATIONSHIP AND ECONOMIC COOPERATION BETWEEN LIBYA AND KOREA.

WE UNDERSTAND OUR DISCUSSION ON THE CRUDE OIL CONTRACT HAS BEEN INITIATED IN THE SPIRIT OF STRENGTHENING THE CURRENT GOOD RELATIONSHIP BETWEEN TWO COUNTRIES.

WE HOPE PETROLEUM SIDE ALSO ENJOY COOPERATIVE RELATIONSHIP AS WE SEE IN OTHER INDUSTRIAL AREAS OF THE TWO NATIONS.

YOUR COOPERATION AND FAVORABLE REPLY WOULD BE HIGHLY APPRECIATED.

B/REGARDS

S. R. YU
GM/CRUDE OIL DEPT.
YUKONG LTD.
^SEND REGISTERED;CLEAR

0114

원 본

외 무 부

종 별 :

번 호 : HUW-0365 일 시 : 90 0829 0840

수 신 : 장관(경자,미북) 사본:주미대사(필)

발 신 : 주휴스턴총영사

제 목 : 석유가격및 생산동향 보고

8.2. 이락의 쿠웨이트 침공이후 미국의 석유 집산지인당지의 석유가격및 생산동향을 아래보고함.

1.베럴당 16-19 불선을 유지해오던 원유가격은 중동전발발 이후인 8.10. 베럴당 28불선으로 인상후 8.23. 32.35불로 최고가격을 형성하였으나 지난주말 부터 내림세를 보여 8.27.에는 26.90 불선으로 하락하였음.

2.텍사스주의 OIL DRILLING RIGS 는 7월말 현재 306개,8월말현재 336개로 30개 증가한반면, 미국전체는 작년 8월말 현재 858개, 최근 992 개로 34개 증가함.

그러나 이러한 증가는 석유생산 붐이 일었던 81년도의 4,500개에 비하면 미미한것임.

3.중동전 발발이후 석유가격인상에 따라 당지에서는 석유생산의 증대를 통한 경기회복을 기대하는 분위기이나 전문가들의 견해에 따르면 최근 석유가격 인상은단기적인 것이며, 미국의 석유생산 증가는 석유가격 베럴당 25불선 이상을 수년간 지속적으로 유지할경우가능시 된다함.

4.미국은 이락및 쿠웨이트를 제외한 OPEC 국가들로부터매일 2.17백만 베럴의 원유를 수KUE(총수입액의 47.9퍼로)하고있으며 국가별 수입은 아래와같음.

OPEC

사우디 17.7 퍼로, 나이지리아 15.4 베네수엘라 10.4 이락 10쿠웨이트 1.9 기타 4.4

NON-OPEC

멕시코 10.6 카나다 10 앙골라 4.6 영국 3.8 기타 11.2

(총영사 허승-국장)

경제국 미주국 2차보 동자부 통상국

PAGE 1

국	국제경제국	년	담 당	과 장	국 장	차관보	차 관	장 관

90.08.30 01:05 CT
외신 1과 통제관

0115

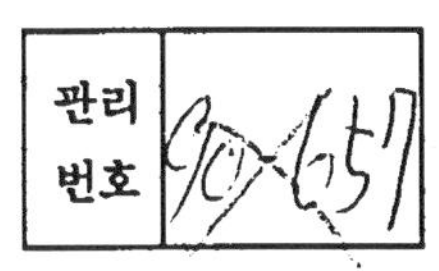

원 본

외 무 부

종 별 :

번 호 : UKW-1615　　　　　　일 시 : 90 0829 1730

수 신 : 장관(기협,통일,구일)

발 신 : 주 영 대사

제 목 : 이라크,쿠웨이트사태

대: WUK-7411

대호관련, 당관 이경우 참사관이 금 8.29(수) 오전 외무성 J.THORNTON 과학 및 에너지 담당관을 방문 파악한 내용을 아래 보고함.

아래

1. 산유국 해당사항

가. 산유정책

. 주재국은 산유국 (89 년 190 만 B/D) 이지만 국내소비량 (89 년 173 만 B/D) 을 충당하는 정도이며, 특히 북해 유전의 보수문제등으로 매년 생산량이 줄고있어 기술개선등을 통한 증산계획을 서두르고 있으나 이락사태 후에도 새로운 변화는 없음.

나. 산유량

. 주재국은 86 년 266 만 B/D 를 정점으로 매년 급격한 생산량 감소현상을 보이고 있으며, 금년 약 160 만 B/D 생산에 그치고 있음.(84 년 258 만, 85 년 265 만, 86 년 266 만, 87 년 255 만, 88 년 236 만, 89 년 190 만, 90 년 160 만)

. 주재국 산유량 감소는 북해 유전의 보수작업에 따르는 막대한 경비와 안전문제 개선을 주장하는 근로자들의 파업에 인한 것이며 당분간은 쿠웨이트 사태에도 불구하고 생산량 증가는 어려울 것임.(90.9 월부터 170-180 만 B/D 예상)

다. 유가 (북해산 BRENT 유, 바렐당)

90.8.2 미불 20.40, 90.8.4 미불 24.00, 90.8.11 미불 25.50, 90.8.16 미불 26.20, 90.8.23 미불 29.05, 90.8.25 미불 30.10, 90.8.28 미불 25.90

2. 수입국 해당사항

가. 이라크, 쿠웨이트 물량감소 대책

주재국은 산유국인 동시에 일부수입 (91.1/4 분기, 파운드 1,015 백만) 하고있으나

경제국　차관　1차보　2차보　구주국　통상국　청와대　안기부　대책반

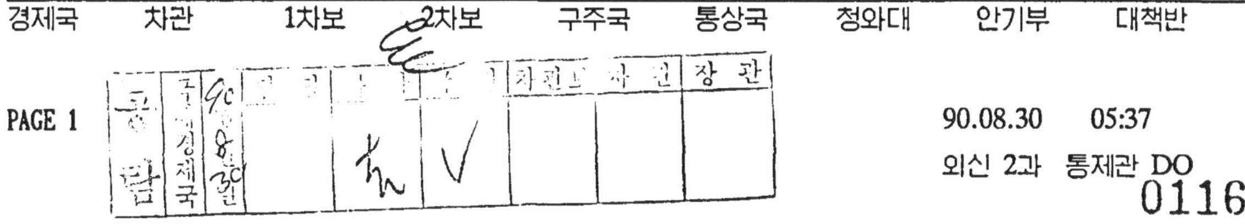

PAGE 1

90.08.30 05:37

외신 2과 통제관 DO

0116

EC 또는 국제에너지기구(IEA) 차원의 대책을 통해 이들과 공동보조를 취할것임.

나. 원유비축 현황

영국은 타 EC 국과는 달리 산유국이란 이유로 현재 76.5 일분의 비축분을 유지하고 있으며 현재로선 특별히 다른 조치는 없음.

다. 주재국내 유류가격

주재국 유가는 지역별, 주유소별 자유로 책정하고 있으며, 일률적인 통제가격이 있는것은 아니나 이락, 쿠웨이트 사태이후 현재 약 6-9 퍼센트 정도 인상된 가격으로 거래되고 있음.

3. 공동사항 (국제원유 수급, 가격전망)

이락, 쿠웨이트 사태의 급격한 진전이 없는한 단기적으로 국제 원유가의 인상이 불가피 (8.25 현재 바렐당 미불 30) 하나 앞으로의 원유가는 주로 사우디 (200 만 B/D), 베네주엘라 (50 만 B/D) 등의 증산 (약 300 만 B/D)에 힘입어 2-3 개월내 약 미불 25 선에서 안정될 것으로 전망함. 끝

(대사 오재희-국장)

예고: 90.12.31 일반

90 12 31

원 본

외 무 부

종 별 :

번 호 : USW-3928 일 시 : 90 0829 1620

수 신 : 장관(기협)

발 신 : 주미대사

제 목 : 석유시장 및 유가동향(5)

1. 유가 동향

가. 8.28(화) 원유 및 정유제품 가격

0 원유(뉴욕 상품 시장,10월 인도 가격)

: 배럴당 27.88(전일에 비해 0.97 불 상승)

0 무연 휘발유(뉴욕 상품 시장, 9월 인도 가격)

: 갤런당 88.53 센트 (전일에 비해 0.97 센트상승)

0 난방유(뉴욕 상품 시장, 9월 인도가격): 갤런당 79.52 센트 (전일에 비해 1.42 센트 상승)

나. 당지 전문가들은 8.28 의 소폭의 유가 상승에 대해 OPEC 의 증산 실시 결정발표 연기 및 석유시장자체의 적정 원유가격 도달을 위한 조정에 따른 것이라고 분석하고있음.

2. OPEC 동향

0 OPEC 은 금번 비공식회의에 불참한 이락과 리비아 대표의 입장을 고려 8.28로 예정되었던 원유 증산 실시 결정의 대외 발표를 일단 연기하였는바, 이락.리비아대표의 참석과 관계없이 금8.29일에는 발표될 것으로 관측되고 있음.

3. 8.29 자 당지 언론보도 내용을 별첨 FAX 송부함첨부: USW(F)- 1970(9매)

(대사 박동진-국장)

공람	국제경제국	90. 8. 30	담 당	과 장	국 장	차관보	차 관	장 관
				(서명)	V			

경제국 2차보

PAGE 1 90.08.30 06:02 CG

외신 1과 통제관

0118

보안 통제	최

주 미 대 사 관

번 호 : USW(F) - 1970
수 신 : 장 관 (기협)
발 신 : 주미대사
제 목 : WUS - 3928 첨부 (9 매)

Oil Prices Increase by 97¢ a Barrel

Pessimism on Iraq And OPEC Delay Cited by Traders

By THOMAS C. HAYES

Oil prices turned up yesterday, with the contract for October delivery rising 97 cents, to $27.88 a barrel, as traders searched for a new balance in the market after Monday's $4 plunge, to $26.91.

Some analysts said the optimism that swept the market on Monday about a negotiated settlement of the Iraq standoff had shifted somewhat to fear that military action would eventually be taken to force Baghdad's defeat.

They also said some traders were disappointed by the delay in an expected announcement that several members of the Organization of Petroleum Exporting Countries would produce more oil, raising the group's production ceiling to 22.5 million barrels a day.

Rise in Nervousness

The reported death of an American hostage in Iraq and a new televised appearance by President Saddam Hussein with foreign hostages added to traders' nervousness.

Spot market prices for gasoline and heating oil also posted small gains, after collapsing on Monday. The September contract for gasoline rose nearly a cent a gallon, to 88.5 cents. Heating oil added 1.4 cents, to settle at 79.30 cents a gallon.

But Monday's plunge in the crude oil markets persuaded some oil companies to lower their wholesale gasoline prices. The Phillips Petroleum Company said yesterday that it was reducing its average wholesale price 5 cents a gallon, effective today, in part because of market changes but also because of what Phillips described as its "continuing effort to show pricing moderation" during the crisis.

On Monday, Conoco Inc., a Du Pont Company unit, announced a price cut of 2 to 5 cents a gallon for its branded wholesale gasoline.

Supplies Rose Last Week

Actual daily supplies of domestic crude oil rose last week by nearly a million barrels, to 376 million, which was 11 percent more than a year ago, the American Petroleum Institute reported after the close of trading.

But gasoline supplies fell by 3 million barrels, to an average of 210.9 million a day, or nearly 8 percent below 1989 inventories.

Home heating oil and other distillates rose by 3.4 million barrels a day, a 7 percent increase over 1989.

John DiPlacido, president of Energex, a commodity firm, said Persian Gulf news during the day had little impact on oil trading at the New York Mercantile Exchange. "Traders are trying to find an area where the market will stabilize," he added. "This is still a backwash to the whole big move on the upside."

Bryan Jacoboski, an analyst at Paine Webber Inc., said Wall Street expected President Bush to assure adequate crude oil supplies as the demand for home heating oil rises. Traders say he will tap the Strategic Petroleum Reserve before the November Congressional elections.

That would keep spot oil prices from soaring above the mid-30's for long, even if war breaks out in the Middle East, he added. "There is no way, going into an election on the second Tuesday in November, that he will allow spot prices to run up," Mr. Jacoboski said.

Others said they saw little possibility of a peaceful settlement in the Middle East. Shahrokk Nikkah, a commodities trader at Prudential-Bache Securities Inc., said he had grown more pessimistic this week and concluded that oil prices would probably be pushed "substantially higher" in coming weeks.

"The moderate Arabs realize now that Mr. Hussein's ambitions just are not conducive to peace and tranquility in the region," he said. In an advisory to his clients, Mr. Nikkah wrote that a military conflict "is very likely" and forecast the failure of talks scheduled later this week between the United Nations Secretary General, Javier Perez de Cuellar, and the Iraqis.

Most analysts say that Saudi Arabia, Venezuela, the United Arab Emirates and other willing OPEC members can add three million barrels a day to world oil markets this autumn. That would leave a projected shortfall of a million barrels a day, and if President Bush does not open the Strategic Petroleum Reserve, many analysts said, the shortage will increase as winter nears.

Some new OPEC output would be lower-quality crude, meaning it would yield fewer refined products. Another complication is that fuel needs of the armed forces allied against Iraq are rising, said G. Henry Schuler, director of the energy security program at the Center for Strategic and International Studies in Washington.

"Having additional crude oil isn't enough," he added. "You've also got to have refining capacity, and we don't have any unutilized refining capacity in this country."

NYT 8/29

0119

Delay Sought In Meeting Of OPEC

Iran Wants to Consider Alternate Ways to Deal With Oil Price Crisis

By YOUSSEF M. IBRAHIM

Special to The New York Times

VIENNA, Aug. 28 — Iran's oil minister, Gholam Reza Aghazadeh, whose country said it would not support an accord proposed by a majority of the members of the Organization of Petroleum Exporting Countries to raise output, asked today that the OPEC meeting be postponed a week to consider alternative courses.

But one senior OPEC official who insisted on not being identified, said, "I think the accord we have stands and will most probably be adopted tomorrow morning."

The Iranian oil minister also suggested that a joint group of OPEC and the Paris-based International Energy Agency, which comprises 21 industrialized nations, meet to decide on joint action to be taken to tackle the oil price crisis.

[Reuters reported that Venezuela's Minister of Energy and Mines, Celestino Armas, said that he still expected the OPEC talks to end Wednesday with an accord to raise output. Mr. Armas said that OPEC would have to discuss Iran's proposal for a week's postponement to meet with the International Energy Agency, but that he did not think it would delay the accord beyond Wednesday. The I.E.A. said it would reject talks with OPEC, Reuters also reported.]

The proposal is in line with previous requests from Libya and Iran, which have both opposed any output increase from OPEC, that both oil companies and industrialized nations release their stored oil to relieve the pressure on prices and make up for any shortage of oil exports.

Shortfall Projected

Oil analysts project a shortfall of 4 million barrels a day, as a result of the embargo of Iraqi and Kuwaiti oil mandated by the United Nations after Iraq invaded Kuwait on Aug. 2. Saudi Arabia, Venezuela and the United Arab Emirates could raise their total output by 3.2 million barrels a day, but prefer to do so under what they call the OPEC umbrella, rather than on their own. Various other OPEC members together could add some 400,000 barrels.

Mr. Aqhazadeh said Western nations should first draw on oil stocks to help meet the crisis. "It is not the responsibility of OPEC only," he said. "For this reason, I cannot support an increase in production."

Several OPEC officials dismissed the proposal as "far fetched" saying it is not likely to dissuade the group's members who can increase output from doing so immediately.

Only Iraq, Iran and Libya oppose the accord, which has the support of 10 OPEC members and could be adopted by a simple majority on Wednesday.

"On the face of it, meeting with the I.E.A. may not be a bad idea," the senior OPEC official said, but he added, "This is not the time to stop everything and explore this very complicated arrangement."

8/29 NYT

WUS(F) 1970 -2

0120

WEDNESDAY, AUGUST 29, 1990

OPEC Is Seen Clearing a Boost In Oil Output

Approval Is Expected Today On Move to Offset Loss From Middle East Crisis

By JAMES TANNER
Staff Reporter of THE WALL STREET JOURNAL

VIENNA–Oil ministers meeting here delayed, probably until today, announcement of plans by the Organization of Petroleum Exporting Countries to help offset world oil losses from the Middle East crisis.

Despite opposition by Iran, a majority of OPEC's ministers agreed early yesterday to endorse production increases by any of the 13 member nations with unused capacity. That action would temporarily suspend output quotas established by the group in July, and sanction combined additional output of about three million barrels of oil a day by Saudi Arabia, Venezuela and the United Arab Emirates.

"It's an agreement to allow those who can do so to increase production on a temporary basis," Diego Tamariz, Ecuador's oil minister, said in an interview, adding: "Once the crisis is over, we will go back to the July agreement."

Though sought by the three countries, OPEC's approval of their plans to raise output doesn't change the prevailing outlook for oil supplies. That's because the nations involved previously indicated they would go ahead without OPEC sanction if necessary. So world oil markets have been operating for weeks on the assumption the added oil eventually would be coming.

The ministers held off announcing their decision so that absent representatives from Libya and Iraq could be notified that the informal talks that began Sunday had been turned into an official meeting of the organization's ministerial monitoring committee.

The output increases authorized by the meeting here won't fully replace the four million barrels a day of oil removed from world oil markets by the current embargo by consuming nations against crude from Iraq and Iraq-occupied Kuwait. As a result, OPEC also plans to call on the International Energy Agency to help replace some of the lost oil.

The Paris-based group is an organization of 21 major oil-consuming nations formed in the wake of the oil shocks of the 1970s to share supplies during shortages.

OPEC plans to ask the IEA to have its members' governments draw on oil they hold in storage and to share immediately the "present huge inventories" of petroleum owned by oil companies. OPEC's specific goal is that some of that oil be shared with developing countries that don't have such stocks.

Iran has tried to persuade OPEC to postpone any production increases until the end of September while consuming nations use up their oil stockpiles. Yesterday, Iranian oil minister Gholamreza Aghazadeh recommended that the ministerial committee meeting here be delayed for a week, "after which I will propose OPEC should meet with the IEA."

He maintained such a joint meeting would help oil-market stability immediately and in the event a Middle East war breaks out. "If we do this, we will have used the best time–a chance we should not ignore–to bring about cooperation between consumers and producers," he said.

Neither the IEA nor the other oil ministers seemed enthusiastic about Mr. Aghazadeh's suggestion. A Paris official of the IEA was quoted by the Dow Jones International Petroleum Report as saying that a meeting with OPEC "is not in the cards."

Meanwhile, several other delegates, including those from Saudi Arabia and Venezuela, were becoming irritated over the duration of the meeting. "We are preparing our departure [by noon today]," said one delegate, "and if the agreement isn't signed by then, Saudi Arabia and Venezuela will leave."

8/29 WSJ

WUS(F) 1970 -3

0121

WSJ 8/29

Gasoline Prices Aren't Expected To Fall Soon

Companies Say the Market Hasn't Yet Kept Pace With Crude Oil's Rise

By DAVID D. MEDINA And CAROLYN PHILLIPS
Staff Reporters of THE WALL STREET JOURNAL

Despite Monday's $4 a barrel plunge in crude-oil futures prices, motorists looking to pay less at the pump will likely be disappointed.

While a few oil companies—Conoco Inc. and Phillips Petroleum Co., for instance—lowered wholesale prices slightly after the sharp drop, most major oil companies said they would maintain current prices. Exxon Corp. actually raised its wholesale prices by six-tenths of a cent.

The industry has defended its wholesale pricing, saying the run-up in gasoline prices never kept pace with the meteoric 50% jump in crude prices over the past four weeks. Most oil companies say they are still trying to recoup their costs. Unleaded gasoline prices at the pump are about 18% higher since Iraq invaded Kuwait Aug. 2, according to the American Automobile Association.

William C. Wood, associate professor of economics at James Madison University in Harrisonburg, Va., and a specialist in natural resources and energy, said that had the price of crude oil dropped by $4 before the Middle East crisis, wholesale gasoline prices would have dropped, too.

"A substantial fraction of the price reflects uncertainty," he said. "It's not just how much [oil companies] have to pay. It's more how can [they protect their inventories] in the event that something unusual happens."

The oil industry has been under attack from consumers, politicians and government officials for raising gasoline prices so quickly and so steeply following the start of the Middle East crisis. Early on in the crisis, President Bush asked major oil companies to hold the line on prices. The Justice Department has since begun preliminary inquiries into the sharp rise in gasoline prices.

Conoco was first to react to the $4 a barrel drop in the price of the October crude-oil futures contract in Monday trading on the New York Mercantile Exchange. The Houston company lowered prices on its branded wholesale gasoline by two cents to five cents a gallon. It lopped an average of 10.65 cents a gallon off its unbranded wholesale gasoline.

"We try to stay as close to the market as we can," a spokesman said. Conoco is a unit of Du Pont Co., Wilmington, Del.

The futures prices took a nosedive Monday as tensions in the Middle East seemed to ease. There were indications that the

Please Turn to Page A12, Column 6

U.S. might be backing away from possible military action and was more inclined toward negotiating a resolution to the crisis. Yesterday, however, the October crude-oil contract regained 97 cents a barrel to close at $27.88.

A spokesman for Phillips said the Bartlesville, Okla.-based oil company was also responding to the market when it cut wholesale gasoline prices by 5.27 cents a gallon to 93.91 cents.

Gasoline price changes happen all along the supply chain, from refiners to wholesalers to corner stations, but are tied very closely to futures prices, which seesaw back and forth with every news report—or rumor. The volatility of the markets, where traders are focusing on the Middle East situation and on a gathering of ministers from the Organization of Petroleum Exporting Countries in Vienna, has made it tough for some oil companies to say what they'll do.

"It's very hard to project what we will do with prices," said a spokesman for Atlantic Richfield Co. in Los Angeles. "Our prices are substantially below the market [levels] and in some instances our prices at the pump may not accurately reflect the price of crude oil." Arco froze its wholesale prices for a time following the invasion, but has since raised them an average of 2.5 cents a gallon.

Exxon raised its prices by six-tenths of a cent to 87.1 cents a gallon. A spokesman said, "Exxon's prices reflect its assessment of competitive market conditions." He wouldn't elaborate.

San Francisco-based Chevron Corp. said it will maintain its prices because it hasn't recovered the cost of higher crude-oil prices. "We haven't passed on to the consumer our full amount of the raw price," a spokesman said. Amoco Corp. in Chicago and Mobil Corp. in New York will both hold tight despite the drop. "In some areas, we are selling at cost," a Mobil spokesman said.

In Houston, a Shell Oil Co. spokesman said the Royal Dutch/Shell Group unit "will be responding along with the competition."

Because so many of the major oil companies are maintaining wholesale prices, experts expect retail prices to remain about the same. "I wouldn't expect much change," said Mike Doyle, an editor at Computer Petroleum Corp., a petroleum price information service in St. Paul, Minn. The company conducts weekly surveys on gasoline prices for the American Automobile Association.

WUS(F) 1970-4

0122

Opec likely to approve output boost

8/29 Financial Times

By Steven Butler in Vienna

A SHARP increase in oil output is almost certain to be sanctioned by the Organisation of Petroleum Exporting Countries to counter the shortfall on world markets caused by the Gulf crisis.

The increase, backed by most Opec members at a meeting in Vienna yesterday, would allow members of the organisation to compensate for the loss of about 4m barrels a day of Iraqi and Kuwaiti oil exports. The agreement is likely to be endorsed this morning by 10 of Opec's 13 members.

The Opec move represents a political victory for Saudi Arabia and Venezuela which have led the campaign to restore stability to world oil markets, where prices have soared following Iraq's invasion of Kuwait.

However, North Sea Brent oil prices for October delivery fell $3.60 yesterday over Friday's close, reflecting the $4 fall in the price of crude on the New York Mercantile exchange on Monday – a holiday in the UK. In New York yesterday, oil prices were slightly firmer on the day.

The fall in North Sea prices prompted Shell UK to shelve plans to announce a further 18p increase in petrol prices.

The Opec agreement is expected to be opposed by Iraq and Libya, whose ministers were absent from Vienna, and by Iran. Mr Gholamreza Aghazadeh, the Iranian minister, last night said he would oppose an immediate increase in Opec production unless this was agreed in a joint action with the International Energy Agency, the Paris-based agency responsible for co-ordinating the response of industrialised countries to an oil supply shortfall.

Mr Aghazadeh said he would propose to other Opec members that the meeting of Opec's Ministerial Monitoring Committee, scheduled for this morning, be postponed one week. Meanwhile, Opec should propose a joint meeting with the IEA to consider a co-ordinated action involving an increase in Opec production and a release of oil stocks held in the IEA countries.

Although Mr Aghazadeh's wish for producer-consumer co-operation is widely shared among Opec members, a majority is keen to sanction an immediate increase in production. Opec observers believe oil output has already started to rise rapidly and that the agreement will merely provide political justification for it and help restore Opec credibility.

The 10 Opec members reached agreement yesterday noon when they decided to turn an informal consulation into a formal committee meeting.

Libya, however, objected from Tripoli that a meeting could not be held unless it was invited. Iraq and Libya were subsequently sent invitations to attend the session this morning, although they are thought unlikely to attend. Algeria, Nigeria, and Indonesia are understood to have been cool to the agreement on the grounds that stocks in the industrialised countries are plentiful. They backed the agreement in an evident attempt to support Opec unity.

WUS(F)1970 -5

0123

Opec meeting defies prophecies of doom

Steven Butler sees Saudi Arabia win an agreement for a rapid rise in oil production

THE Organisation of Petroleum Exporting Countries was yesterday doing all it could to make the best out of a bad situation. Amid predictions that it would see its demise as a result of the Gulf crisis, it was managing to walk, if not actually race, through a tough obstacle course.

The agreement provisionally endorsed yesterday by 10 of Opec's 13 members was a political victory for Saudi Arabia, which has lobbied hard for a rapid increase in production. Some delegates to the meeting said, however, that Saudi tactics and threats to raise output unilaterally if necessary had caused considerable friction. Opec has traditionally worked by consensus.

The agreement is aimed explicitly at promoting stability in the oil markets. In reality it will merely provide formal political sanction for an increase in Opec production which has already begun. Delegates none the less said that the agreement would bolster the organisation's credibility as a force for stability.

The last agreement signed on July 27 in Geneva, which set a production ceiling of 22.5m b/d and a target price of $21 a barrel, is to be upheld by suspending production quotas and allowing Opec production to rise toward the 22.5m b/d level.

Saudi Arabia, the United Arab Emirates, and Venezuela are expected to lift production by about 3m b/d, compared to 4m b/d of lost exports from the Gulf.

The agreement was about to be approved yesterday at midday when the 10 ministers agreed to turn an informal consultation session into a formal meeting of Opec's ministerial monitoring committee.

However, Mr Fawzi Shakshuki, the Libyan minister, who has not attended the talks, telephoned to protest at the convening of a formal meeting to which he had not been invited. The organisation subsequently telexed invitations to Libya and to Iraq, also not in attendance, and has given the ministers until this morning to arrive.

Neither minister is expected to accept the invitation, although if they come to Vienna the proceedings could become more complex.

Mr Gholamreza Aghazadeh, the Iranian minister, has been the sole member in attendance to hold out against the agreement. He has argued strongly that Opec should wait until October before raising output in order to force the industrialised countries who are members of the Paris-based International Energy Agency to co-operate in stabilising the market.

"I would like to ask the IEA to release their stocks," he said. Oil market stability "is not the responsibility of Opec only. Everybody is responsible for this matter."

The Iranian minister argued that oil supplies were plentiful. The price had been driven up by political factors and Opec should not be in the business of just sending signals to the market.

The draft agreement includes a paragraph advising the IEA to release stocks, but Mr Aghazadeh wanted stronger language and a direct request to the IEA. He also suggested that the IEA make a formal request to Opec to increase production. He said that with IEA stocks equal to about 98 days' forward consumption, agency members could release 4m b/d of crude oil for 90 days and still have a comfortable stocking level that would be reduced by only 10 days of forward cover.

The IEA governing board will meet in Paris on Friday, although it is not expected to endorse a release of government-held strategic stocks.

Many of the delegates from other Opec members were impressed by Mr Aghazadeh's arguments, although there were also accusations that Iran's stubborn refusal to back the agreement was politically motivated.

They suggested Mr Aghazadeh wanted to avoid handing an even bigger political victory to Saudi Arabia.

The steep fall in oil prices on Monday convinced many delegates that it was psychology rather than supply and demand that has driven the price so high. The Saudis have conceded this, but have argued that Opec must respond now to a potential shortage of oil in the fourth quarter.

Algeria, traditionally an ally of Iraq, was also reluctant to back the agreement. But Mr Sadek Boussena, the Algerian minister, is the Opec president and endorsed the agreement in an apparent attempt to uphold unity. Indonesia and Nigeria appear to have backed the agreement reluctantly for similar reasons.

Although Opec will emerge from the meeting divided, the fact that 10 members have endorsed the agreement is a remarkable achievement, given the political differences among them. The organisation will probably become dormant until an end to the Gulf crisis makes it politically possible to hold a meeting in which all 13 members participate.

Until then, Opec's production quota system will have no meaning. Even if all Opec countries produce at capacity, they will not be able to make up for all of the lost Iraqi and Kuwaiti production.

But at least the organisation will in the meantime have avoided destruction by agreeing to mothball itself. Eventually, members are sure to find the oil cartel useful again.

OPEC: PRODUCTION QUOTAS AND ACTUAL PRODUCTION (million barrels per day)

	Quotas* (August 1990)	Production (April-June 1990)
Algeria	0.827	0.8
Ecuador	0.273	0.3
Gabon	0.197	0.2
Indonesia	1.374	1.2
Iran	3.140	3.1
Iraq	3.140	3.1
Kuwait	1.500	1.7
Libya	1.233	1.3
Nigeria	1.611	1.7
Qatar	0.371	0.4
Saudi Arabia	5.380	5.4
UAE	1.500	2.0
Venezuela	1.945	2.0
TOTAL	22.491	23.6

* International Energy Agency estimates

WUS(F)1970-6

0124

Opec and the crisis

F T 8/29/90

IRAQ'S INVASION and attempted absorption of one member of the Organisation of Petroleum Exporting Countries and its threatening behaviour towards others, above all Saudi Arabia, could not leave the organisation unaffected. It has not done so. Opec's response – perfectly sensible, in the circumstances – is to hibernate for the duration of the emergency.

A formal meeting of the Opec Committee is to occur today, but what was agreed at the informal meeting in Vienna yesterday is likely to stand. Despite some misgivings, Opec members – apart from Iraq, Iran and Libya – will try to meet their current aggregate target of 22.5m barrels a day, despite the loss of 4m barrels a day from Iraq and Kuwait. In order to achieve this goal, they will have to ignore previously agreed ceilings for individual countries.

The main spare capacity is in Saudi Arabia, the United Arab Emirates and Venezuela, with some potential for increased supply from Libya and Nigeria. The principal actor among these countries is Saudi Arabia, which now has more than adequate cover for actions that it recognises as both inevitable and desirable. Saudi Arabia could hardly be the beneficiary of current levels of military support, without a *quid pro quo* of this kind. There are also wider interests at stake. Oil prices that are too high or unstable are damaging to producers who are in the business for the long term.

Controversial moves

None the less, these moves have proved controversial. One objection is that oil prices are still about half the peak level reached (in real terms) during the second oil shock. Oil exporters who have struggled with the debt contracted during previous periods of high prices must feel relief at the sight of prices rising again.

The level of stocks is a still wider concern. On paper, the planned increase in supply should neutralise the effects of the UN-mandated embargo on the oil exports of Iraq and Kuwait. But there might still be significant disruption, since Opec production could have been considerably higher than the ceiling.

Private stock-holders know this. They also know that the threat of war remains. They are likely, therefore, to speculate on further increases in prices. The imbalance between supply and demand (including the demand for increased stocks) could lead to rapid self-justifying price rises.

Reconsider approach

It is for this, entirely understandable, reason that Opec members wish to see members of the International Energy Agency play a greater role in stabilising the oil market. These countries must now reconsider their intellectually barren approach to the use of official stocks. The role of these stocks should not be to meet physical shortages that will, in a free market, never come. It should rather be to mitigate an inventory-driven price cycle of the kind that proved so destabilising during the last oil shock.

Meanwhile, Opec suppliers themselves could offer the increased output, on a first refusal basis, to countries outside the principal distribution channels, which were most directly dependent on oil from Iraq and Kuwait. These countries are likely to consume what they are sent. Moreover, the disruption in established patterns of distribution can be as destabilising in the short term as any shortfall in aggregate supply.

This is particularly true of the market for refined products. Yet little can be done about the difficulties in these markets. The world may well be able to manage the supply and demand for crude oil. But the loss of Kuwaiti refining capacity, on top of what was already a very tight situation, will create difficulties.

Most members of Opec are, it appears, playing a constructive role in this crisis. Given a forthcoming response from members of the IEA, severe disruption might be avoided. This is not the only interest the two groups share. The Iraqi President has invaded two Opec members and thus created two oil shocks. Opec members share with the rest of the world an interest in ensuring that he is deprived of the ability to do this a third time.

WUS(F)1990-7

0125

Japan's Contribution in Gulf Crisis Remains Vague

By URBAN C. LEHNER
Staff Reporter of THE WALL STREET JOURNAL

TOKYO—Despite pressure from Washington that Japan make a stronger commitment to U.S.-led efforts to dislodge Iraqi forces from occupied Kuwait, Tokyo is on the verge of announcing a package of measures that will leave vague the full extent of its financial contribution.

After weeks of deliberation, the government is expected to unveil the package today. A government official said it would include the dispatch of a medical team to the region and the chartering of civilian aircraft to transport nonmilitary supplies to the multinational force in the Persian Gulf. There is also a "50-50 chance" the package will include increased support for U.S. troops stationed in Japan, the official said.

But more weeks of deliberation will be needed before Japan decides how much aid it will give to Turkey, Egypt and other Middle Eastern countries whose economies have been hurt by the crisis. The official said today's measures "will most likely be announced as a first package, to be followed up later."

U.S. pressure on Japan has been intense. The Kyodo news agency quoted Tokyo officials as saying that U.S. Ambassador Michael Armacost had warned them that Japan's response will determine whether it can rise to a position of international leadership, such as permanent membership in the U.N. Security Council. Unless Japan upgraded the pace and substance of its Gulf contribution, Kyodo reported Mr. Armacost as saying, "'dangerous doubts' could arise among Americans as to who their true friends really are."

News reports have indicated that the package announced today might include as much as $35 million in emergency grants to Middle Eastern countries, with a promise of greater sums later. But a senior Finance Ministry official dismissed the reports as speculative. He said Japan would like to see a multilateral aid package for the region, with contributions from the U.S. and other countries as well as Japan, funneled through such international institutions as the World Bank and the International Monetary Fund.

"Japan should make a significant contribution, but there's a limit to what one country can do," he said.

But devising such a package could take time. The senior Finance Ministry official said Japan has just begun talking to the U.S. and European countries about it. Another Finance Ministry source said the deliberations might not be concluded until just before Prime Minister Toshiki Kaifu visits five Mideastern countries in early October.

"The Foreign Ministry wants to come up with something faster, but we'd like to study all the options," he said.

Japanese officials all say they want Japan to make a noteworthy contribution to the multinational effort. But they are clearly having difficulty reaching a consensus on how to do so. Almost every aspect of its deliberations have been dogged by controversy, from budgetary worries to concerns about violating Japan's war-renouncing constitution.

For example, the government's decision to help transport supplies to U.S. forces in Saudi Arabia had to overcome strong reservations by cargo companies. The two Japan Air Lines 747 freighters that the government is expected to charter represent 20% of JAL's cargo fleet, and the airline had deep concerns about the safety of its crews and the fate of 23 of its employees who are currently "guests" in a Baghdad hotel. The airline also successfully insisted that it not be required to carry munitions. The Transport Ministry reported asked three airlines, including JAL, and a ship-owner organization to provide cargo planes and ships to transport nonmilitary items such as water, food and medical supplies to the multinational forces in the Gulf.

The difficulties the government has faced are in part the result of bureaucratic infighting, but may also reflect a deeper public attitude. Social commentator Kazuhisa Ogawa said on Japanese television recently that Japan suffers from "a lack of a sense of being a direct participant" in the Gulf crisis.

In the short run, Japan's inability to specify its financial contribution probably won't hurt Mr. Kaifu's government domestically. For weeks, Japanese opinion makers have been saying that it isn't enough for Japan to write a check; the important thing is for it to participate in the international effort more directly. So the initial reaction to the package here is likely to emphasize Japan's direct contribution of logistical and medical support.

But if U.S. congressmen and other Americans criticize the package as inadequate, Mr. Kaifu could eventually feel political backlash from public perception of worsening U.S.-Japan relations. Already public-opinion polls in the U.S. show that large majorities of Americans don't think Japan is contributing enough in the crisis. Some Japanese fear that Japan's contributions or lack of them could become an issue in this fall's U.S. congressional campaign.

But other Japanese are defiant. Tomomitsu Oba, president of the Japan Center for International Finance and a former top Finance Ministry official, says Japan can't spend huge sums at home and abroad.

WUS(F)1990-8

0126

OPEC would hear out absentees

By Sally Jacobsen
THE ASSOCIATED PRESS

VIENNA, Austria — OPEC's oil ministers yesterday delayed formal endorsement of a plan for production increases to give more time to hear from absent members Iraq and Libya.

Iran, which has refused to back the tentative agreement, made a surprise call for a joint meeting between the cartel and nearly two dozen oil-consuming Western nations, including the United States, to discuss the oil crunch caused by the Persian Gulf crisis.

Iranian Oil Minister Gholamreza Aqazadeh said the talks should cover the current situation in the crude market and consider what would happen in the event of war in the region.

However, it was not likely that such a meeting will occur.

A majority of OPEC's members tentatively agreed early yesterday to support higher output mostly by Saudi Arabia, Venezuela and the United Arab Emirates during the military crisis in the oil-rich Gulf.

Mr. Aqazadeh refused to join 10 other ministers in the accord worked out during two days of informal consultations by the Organization of Petroleum Exporting Countries.

"I think it is a big mistake from OPEC," Mr. Aqazadeh told reporters after speaking privately with other ministers.

He said Western nations should release crude from their own stockpiles before asking OPEC to help.

"It is not the responsibility of OPEC only," he said. "For that reason, I cannot support the increase in production."

Later, he said he would ask other OPEC ministers to back his proposal for a joint session between the group and the International Energy Agency, comprised of 23 industrialized nations. But the agency indicated it would reject the proposal, saying through a spokesman that no such meeting was contemplated.

The arrangement worked out by the cartel would endorse extra pumping by countries with spare capacity to help make up part of the loss of 4 million barrels a day of Iraqi and Kuwaiti crude. An international embargo has been placed on the oil because of Iraq's Aug. 2 invasion of Kuwait.

Analysts estimate OPEC countries could fill more than 3 million barrels of the gap.

All 13 nations of the cartel agreed last month to limit production to 22.5 million barrels a day in the last half of the year. The aim was to bump prices up to a benchmark target of $21 a barrel. Prices passed $30 a barrel last week before receding this week.

Peter Bogin, associate director for oil markets at Cambridge Energy Research Associates in Paris, said the OPEC accord should help restrain prices during the crisis.

"As long as there is no military action . . . prices will be lower as a consequence," he said.

OPEC officials had expected to seal the agreement yesterday morning but postponed their talks until today after deciding to extend a formal invitation to Iraq and Libya for a meeting of the group's monitoring committee.

A Libyan delegation has been expected for several days. But Iraq strongly opposed this week's informal consultations.

Both were expected to reject any plan for higher production.

Mr. Aqazadeh said he was not alone in his opposition. "Three countries do not accept," he said, in an apparent reference to Iran, Iraq and Libya.

OPEC Secretary-General Subroto said officials were continuing their consultations. "We are trying, of course, to get everybody [in the accord]," he said.

Sources have said it appears Saudi Arabia has already stepped up production, but no details have been given. The kingdom, which pumps about a quarter of the cartel's crude, has an OPEC supply quota of 5.4 million barrels a day.

OPEC's "interim agreement" endorsing higher production was expected to insist that countries reduce pumping once the Gulf crisis is over.

It also was expected to urge consuming nations to use some of their stored oil to help cover any shortages.

0127

WUS(F) 1970-9. End.

원 본

외 무 부

종 별 :

번 호 : HUW-0367 일 시 : 90 0829 1120

수 신 : 장관(기협,미북) 사본:주미대사(필)

발 신 : 주휴스턴총영사

제 목 : 석유가격및 생산동향보고(2)

연: HUW-365

1. 8.28. 현재 원유가격은 (WEST TESAX INTERMEDIATE) 어제보다 약 1불이 높은베럴당 27.88불로 인상됨. 이는 지난 일요일 비엔나에서 개최된 OPEC 회의에서 이란을제외한 모든 참석국(이락및 리비아 불참)이 석유생산증가에 찬성하였으나 이란이 서방 국가들의 원유부족 해소를 위해 생산을 증가할수는 없다는 이유로 반대하여 합의에 이르지 못한데 기인한 것으로 평가되고있음.

2.당지 석유전문가들에 의하면 최근 이락사태로 전 세계원유시장에서 매일 4백만베럴정도의 원유부족이 초래되고있다함.

3. JAMES SCHLESINGER 전 에너지장관은 휴스턴에서 미국 뿐아니라 타국에서도 이정도의 원유부족 사태로는 각국의 비상시 대비 비축원유를 사용할 정도는 아니며 좀더 심각한 사태가 올 경우 사용하게 될것이라고 언급함.

(총영사 허승-국장)

공람	국제경제국	90.8.31	담당	과장	국장	차관보	차관	장관
					V			

경제국 2차보 미주국 통제관

PAGE 1 90.08.30 06:04 CG

외신 1과 통제관

0128

원 본

외 무 부

종 별 :

번 호 : MXW-1058　　　　　일 시 : 90 0829 1800

수 신 : 장 관(기협,미중)

발 신 : 주 멕 대사

제 목 : 원유수급 및 가격동향

1. 최근 이.쿠 사태이후 주재국 원유 수출가는 계속 상승, WEST TEXAS, BRENT 등 국제원유가에 접근하고 있으나 아라비아 경질유 가격에는 훨신미치지 못하고 있다고 8.28. 주재국 국영석유회사 PEMEX 가 발표함.

2. PEMEX 에 의하면 멕산 원유는 금주초 TEXAS, BRENT 유가보다 평균 2.5불이 낮은 배럴당 25.08불에 거래되었는바 이는 아라비아 유가에 비해 6.5불이 낮은 시세라함.

3. PEMEX 는 상기 멕산 원유가격이 국제원유 가격에 미달되는 이유로 멕산 중질류 MAYA 의 품질로 인한 COMMERCIAL VALUE 차이라고 밝히고 있음. 현재 멕산원유중 최경질류인 OLMECA 는 소량생산, 전량 미국으로 수출되고 있음.

4. 지난 8.27. 멕산원유는 미국, 유럽 및 중동시장에 배럴당 24.50불, 22.39불 28.37불로 각각 거래되었다고 PEMEX 자료는 밝히고 있음.

(대사 이복형-국장)

공람	국제경제국	8/30 국장	담당	과장	국장	차관보	차관	장관

경제국　2차보　미주국　안기부　동자부　통상국　대책반

PAGE 1　　　　　90.08.30 09:38 WG

외신 1과 통제관

0129

國際原油需給 및 價格動向 速報

1990.8.30
外務部, 國際經濟局

1. 原油需給

o OPEC 臨時 會議, 事態勃發에 따른 原油供給 不足分 保全위해 8.29 暫定的 原油增產 合意 (公館報告 및 外信綜合)

- 금번 會議에 11個國 參加 (이라크, 리비아는 不參)

- 各國 豫想 增產量 : 사우디 2백만B/D, 베네주엘라 50만B/D, UAE 50만B/D 등

o 카나다, 8.5만B/D 生產가능한 ~~Oslo~~ 신규 油田開發 事業計劃 再檢討中 (駐카나다大使報告)

o 蘇聯, 이라크產 原油輸入 中斷으로 새로운 蘇聯內 經濟的 問題 擡頭 및 施設 投資등으로 갑작스런 原油增產 困難 (蘇聯外務省 中東國 政務參事官)

2. 油價

o 現物市場 動向 (단위 : $/B)

	7.31	8.7	8.10	8.22	8.27	8.28	8.29	전일대비	8.30	8.31	9.3	9.4
Dubai	17.20	25.40	22.72	31.75	27.20	27.13	24.75	- 2.38	[illegible]	[illegible]	[illegible]	[illegible]
Oman	17.65	25.90	23.22	32.35	27.80	27.73	25.35	- 2.38	[illegible]	[illegible]	[illegible]	[illegible]
Brent	19.49	29.40	25.70	32.15	27.80	28.32	26.35	- 1.97	[illegible]	[illegible]	[illegible]	[illegible]
WTI	20.75	29.62	26.39	31.57	27.25	27.98	26.05	- 1.93	[illegible]	[illegible]	[illegible]	[illegible]

o 8.27 油價急落 原因分析 (美國 言論 報道綜合)

- 유엔사무총장 仲裁努力等 事態의 外交的 解決 期待

- OPEC 非公式會議, 暫定增產 合意 보도

※ 실제 需要供給보다 事態展開 方向에 대한 心理的 反應에 의해 決定되기 때문에 事態 解決時까지 油價향배 예측 難望.

o 향후 1개월간 油價는 25달러前後 豫想되나, 產油國 增產持續 與否가 관건이며, 盛需期인 4/4분기 原油不足 현상 심화시, 油價上昇 불가피 (일본석유업계 전문가)

3. 其他 關聯 事項

o 말련, 追加增產時 對 我國 供給에 優先的 配慮 約束 (PETRONAS 社長)

o 8.31 파리에서IEA 理事會 開催 豫定

앙고재	기순집리과	90년 8월 30일	담 당	과 장	국 장	차관보	차 관	장 관
			홍성화	[signature]	[signature]	[signature]		

0130

國際原油需給 및 價格動向 速報

1990.8.30
外務部, 國際經濟局

1. 原油需給

o OPEC 臨時 會議, 事態勃發에 따른 原油供給 不足分 保全위해 8.29 暫定的 原油增產 合意 (公館報告 및 外信綜合)

- 금번 會議에 11個國 參加 (이라크, 리비아는 不參)
- 各國 豫想 增產量 : 사우디 2백만B/D, 베네주엘라 50만B/D, UAE 50만B/D 등

o 카나다, 8.5만B/D 生產가능한 신규 油田開發 事業計劃 再檢討中 (駐카나다大使報告)

o 蘇聯, 이라크產 原油輸入 中斷으로 새로운 蘇聯內 經濟的 問題 擡頭 및 施設 投資등으로 갑작스런 原油增產 困難 (蘇聯外務省 中東局 政務參事官)

2. 油價

o 現物市場 動向 (단위 : $/B)

	7.31	8.7	8.10	8.22	8.27	8.28	8.29	전일대비
Dubai	17.20	25.40	22.72	31.75	27.20	27.13	24.75	- 2.38
Oman	17.65	25.90	23.22	32.35	27.80	27.73	25.35	- 2.38
Brent	19.49	29.40	25.70	32.15	27.80	28.32	26.35	- 1.97
WTI	20.75	29.62	26.39	31.57	27.25	27.98	26.05	- 1.93

o 8.27 油價急落 原因分析 (美國 言論 報道綜合)

- 유엔사무총장 仲裁努力等 事態의 外交的 解決 期待
- OPEC 非公式會議, 暫定增產 合意 보도

※ 실제 需要供給보다 事態展開 方向에 대한 心理的 反應에 의해 決定되기 때문에 事態 解決時까지 油價향배 예측 難望.

o 향후 1개월간 油價는 25달러前後 豫想되나, 產油國 增產持續 與否가 관건이며, 盛需期인 4/4분기 原油不足 현상 심화시, 油價上昇 불가피 (일본석유업계 전문가)

3. 其他 關聯 事項

o 말련, 追加增產時 對 我國 供給에 優先的 配慮 約束 (PETRONAS 社長)

o 8.31 파리에서IEA 理事會 開催 豫定

0131

관리 번호	90-668

원 본

외 무 부

종 별 :

번 호 : MAW-1171 일 시 : 90 0830 1120

수 신 : 장관(기협,아동,사본:동자부 장관,주 파키스탄 대사-본부 중계요)

발 신 : 주 말련 대사

제 목 : 이라크.쿠웨이트 사태: 원유확보

연:MAW-1167

대:WMA-0559,0601

1. 당지 최대 영자지 NEW STRAITS TIMES 8.30 자는 주재국 정부가 파키스탄에 원유를 공급키로 동의하였다고 보도하였음. 파키스탄은 이라크, 쿠웨이트 사태로부터 원유 부족난 타개를 위해 주재국에 90.10-91.6. 간 일산 15,000-20,000 배럴의 원유 공급을 요청하였으며, 현재 파키스탄과 PETRONAS 간에 공급량 및 가격등 조건에 관한 교섭이 진행중이라함.

2. 본직은 8.30 외무부 MAJID 정무차관보 면담 기회에 상기 내용에 관해 문의한바, 주재국은 이미 연호와 같이 인도에 원유 추가 공급을 결정하였으며 형평상 파키스탄의 요청을 거절할수 없는 실정이라함. 그러나 주재국 생산능력(최대 일산 4 만 배럴증산 가능)및 인도와의 균형을 고려할때 동 공급량은 일산 2,500-5,000 배럴 수준이 될 것이라함.

3. 당관 이준규 서기관이 8.30 접촉한 주재국 수상실 ANWAR 석유 개발과장은, 상기 파키스탄 정부의 요청을 외무부 경유 접수하여 현재 수상실및 PETRONAS에서 검토하고 있다고 확인하고, 말. 파키스탄 양국간의 외교, 통상 관계등이 종합적으로 고려되어 결정이 내려질 것이나 최대 공급량은 일산 5,000 배럴 수준에 그치게 될 것이라함. 끝

(대사 홍순영-국장)

예고:90.12.31 까지

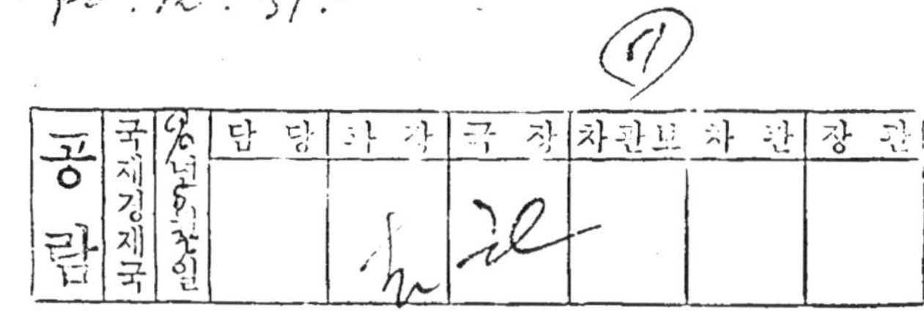

공람
국제경제국
90년 8월 31일
담 당
과 장
국 장
차관보
차 관
장 관

경제국 1차보 2차보 아주국 통상국 청와대 안기부 동자부 대책반

PAGE 1

90.08.30 13:07

외신 2과 통제관 EZ

0132

관리 번호	90-664

원 본

외 무 부

종 별 :

번 호 : FRW-1573　　　　일 시 : 90 0830 1000

수 신 : 장관(기협)

발 신 : 주 불 대사

제 목 : OECD/IEA 업무협조

연: FRW-1455

1. OECD/IEA 는 연호 이사회에 이어, 9.31. 이사회를 재개 걸프사태 관련 원유시장 동향및 대책등에 관해 협의 예정이라함.

2. 이와관련, IEA 측과 차주중 재접촉 예정인바 IEA 측이 관심을 갖고 있는아래사항에 대해 회시바람.

가. 아국의 OIL STOCK 정책및 현황

나. 아국의 원유 수입선별 도입현황

다. 걸프사태가 아국의 원유공급, 수요 및 가격에 미치는 영향및 대책.끝.

(대사 노영찬-국장)

예고:90.12.31. 까지

90 12 31

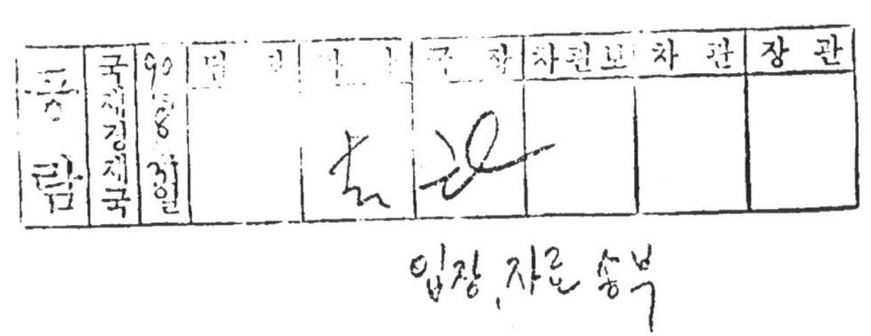

입장, 자료 송부

경제국　차관　1차보　2차보　구주국　청와대　안기부

PAGE 1　　　　90.08.30 17:20

외신 2과 통제관 BT

0133

수 : USW(F)- 1994
신 : 장 관 (기협. 미남) 발신 : 주미대사 통제 31
목 : 베네주엘라 원유사정 (1 매)

Venezuela's New Oil Prominence

By JAMES BROOKE

Special to The New York Times

LAGUNILLAS, Venezuela — The lines of oil wells that stretch across Lake Maracaibo here are pumping higher volumes of crude to help offset the shortage caused by the embargo of oil from Iraq and Kuwait.

By the end of September, an extra 350,000 barrels a day should be flowing from Venezuelan oilfields, and by the end of December nearly 500,000 more barrels a day. Two-thirds of that oil is likely to be sold to the United States, Venezuela's largest customer. Last year, Venezuela sold a million barrels a day to the United States, 18 percent of American oil imports and about half of the country's total production.

With war preparations gripping the Persian Gulf, it is no surprise that American eyes are suddenly turning to Venezuela, which likes to style itself as a "safe source" nation, unlike those in the troubled Middle East. And Venezuela holds the world's largest proven oil reserves outside the Middle East — 59 billion barrels.

"When you buy the cheap oil of the Middle East, you're not calculating the cost of defending the Middle East," said Antonio Cassella, planning manager for Petróleos de Venezuela, the state oil company, known as PDVSA.

But beyond the short-term production increases, Venezuela, one of Latin America's oldest and most stable democracies, is poised to play a newly prominent role in the United States energy scene well into the 1990's.

Moves that Venezuela is already making in that direction include a $24 billion six-year capital investment plan by PDVSA that was started months before the current Middle East troubles, and new policies to encourage foreign investment. There is also the geographical proximity to the United States.

Most of the oil will come from Maracaibo, an oil-soaked region in western Venezuela where decades of production have caused the ground to sink by as much as 15 feet.

A Four-Day Trip

An oil tanker leaving Maracaibo takes just four days to reach the East Coast of the United States. That compares with the 30 days it takes a tanker to reach the United States from Saudi Arabia, Venezuela's traditional competitor as America's top foreign supplier. That means not only lower transportation costs, but more flexibility for changing orders on short notice.

The story of Venezuela's energy exports in the 1990's will largely center on PDVSA, the fourth-largest oil company in the world, according to Petroleum Intelligence Weekly, which bases its rankings on ownership of reserves, production and refining capacity, among other factors. The company ranks behind only Aramco of Saudi Arabia, Royal/Dutch Shell of the Netherlands, and Exxon.

In contrast to widespread negative stereotypes of state companies, PDVSA is profitable and is considered to be professionally managed. But it has found itself hemmed in by production quotas.

Not known as a successful negotiator within the Arab-dominated Organization of Petroleum Exporting Countries, Venezuela has seen its quota share of OPEC production drop almost in half over 20 years, from 16 percent in 1970 to 8.6 percent today. But Venezuela was a prime engineer behind OPEC's decision to authorize its members to start pumping all they could to make up for the embargo against Iraq and Kuwait.

New Technologies a Concern

Noting that many Arab oil producers cheat on their quotas, oil company executives here had been bitter about Venezuela's regular OPEC quota of 1.945 million barrels a day.

"The question of how long our oil will last is irrelevent," said Alberto Quirós Corradi, a former president of one of PDVSA's 11 subsidiaries. "The question is: Will new technologies replace oil before we run out of oil?"

The company has invested aggressively in extending control over production, refining and marketing. It ranked as the second most profitable company in the world in 1989, after a Brazilian state mining company, according to Fortune magazine's survey of the world's 500 largest corporations. Using the same formula, profits as a percent of assets, the survey ranked the company as the most profitable oil concern in the world.

The company startled Americans by paying $700 million last November to complete its purchase of Citgo Petroleum. Through Citgo, Venezuelan oil has priority access to 8,500 affiliated gasoline stations.

More Profitable Than Pemex

When compared with Latin America's other oil-exporting giant, Petróleos Mexicanos, the contrast is striking.

Both companies had roughly similar sales volumes in 1989 — $15.2 billion for Pemex, and $13.7 billion for PDVSA. But Pemex had more than triple the labor force — 165,000 workers compared with 47,000 for PDVSA. The Venezuelan company was 8.5 times as profitable as Pemex in 1989: $2.7 billion, compared with $320 million for the Mexican company.

"For a state-run company, PDVSA is admirably run," said an American diplomat in Caracas. "There is very little smell of corruption, and they think in terms of businessmen."

Much of the profit comes from the extraordinary energy wealth of Venezuela, which is larger than Texas and Oklahoma combined.

The cost of oil exploration averages 10 cents per discovered barrel — literally pennies when compared with the $5-a-barrel average in the United States. Oil production costs here average $2.50 a barrel — less than 10 percent of the current international sales price.

Last year, the company accounted for 75 percent of Venezuela's $12 billion export earnings and for 17 percent of the nation's $79 billion gross domestic product.

In 1975, when PDVSA was formed from multinational companies, the company refined 40 percent of its product. Now it refines 80 percent.

One Soft Spot

The company's only major soft spot is domestic sales. Those operations had a $286 million loss last year. High-octane gasoline is sold here for 26 cents a gallon, cheaper than bottled water. Street riots have greeted Government efforts to raise the price, which may be the world's lowest.

Since becoming President of Venezuela last year, Carlos Andrés Pérez, has promoted a free-market economic program of less Government controls and more foreign investment.

Given PDVSA's proven track record, American suppliers, investors and importers are looking closely at the company's ambitious capital program, an expansion announced several months before the Persian Gulf crisis. About two-thirds of the expansion is to be financed by the company's cash flow.

These are some of the goals for 1995:

¶An increase in crude production potential by 30 percent, to 3.5 million barrels a day.

¶An increase in domestic refining capacity by 25 percent, to 1.5 million barrels a day.

¶A tripling of petrochemical production, to 10 million tons a year, and a doubling of natural gas production, to the equivalent of 200,000 barrels of oil a day.

Plans also call for building, with foreign participation, a $3 billion liquefied natural gas plant and increasing coal production sixfold, to 10 million tons a year.

N.Y.T. 8/30/90

0134

08/30/90 17:50 ☎202 797 0595 EMBASSY OF KOREA → 卄卌I 2 005/017

: USW(F)- 1995

: 장 관 (기협, 동일) 발신 : 주미대사

: 이락·쿠웨이트 자산동결 (1 매)

Japanese worry about how to pay their oil bills

By Robert Thomson in Tokyo

JAPANESE like to pay their bills on time, so the freeze on payments to Kuwait and Iraq has presented oil companies with a deepening dilemma on how to honour debts for oil shipped before the trade embargo.

Oil companies and trading houses, whose debts to Kuwait are reckoned to total between Y20bn (£70m) and Y30bn, would like to deposit funds into a special account with the Bank of Tokyo, but are unsure of what name to use or whether they should haggle over interest rates.

The companies are concerned that they could be sued by either Kuwait or Iraq, depending on the unravelling of the crisis, for having failed to pay debts. They also worry that they could be charged the difference between interest earned in Japan and what the eventual creditors estimate is fair compensation for the delayed payment.

An official at Cosmo Oil said that "we will probably have to put the money in a short-term account" because a fixed deposit could prove embarrassing if there is a sudden solution to the crisis.

"We really don't know who to pay the money to or what to call the account," the Cosmo official said.

Japan relies on Kuwait for about 6 per cent of oil imports, and Iran for another 6 per cent. The Ministry of International Trade and Industry has told the oil companies not to pay Iraq, but the Ministry of Finance, Bank of Tokyo and the Kuwait National Petroleum office in Tokyo have been negotiating the outstanding Kuwaiti debts.

Kuwaiti officials in Tokyo have said that they would like the account in the name of the national petroleum company, but they accept that the funds will be frozen for the time being.

They indicated that a failure to prove that payment was attempted would be a violation of contracts, which demand payment within 30 days of shipment.

F.T. 8/30/90

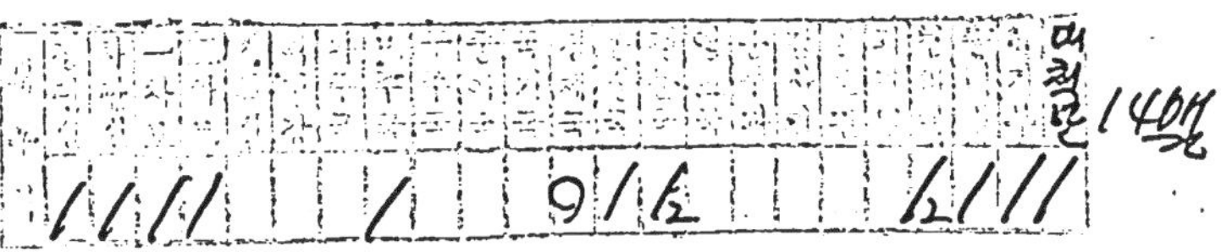

0135

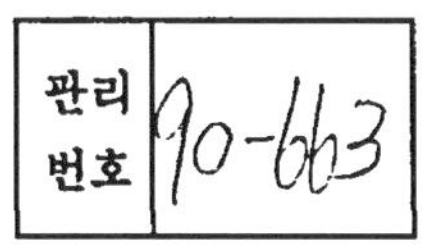

원 본

외 무 부

종 별 :

번 호 : FRW-1565　　　　일 시 : 90 0829 1630

수 신 : 장관(기협)

발 신 : 주 불 대사

제 목 : 이라크.쿠웨이트 사태

대: WFR-1539, 1434

연호 주재국의 유가 동결조치 내용 및 최근 유가 동향 아래 보고함

1. 유가 동결 조치

- 시한: 9.15.까지

- 적용범위: 휘발유, 디젤, 가정용 연료

- 시행방법:

0 유류별 CEILING PRICE 를 고시, 상한선을 넘지 못하게 통제(실제로는 유류별 상승 MARGIN 범위를 결정, 동 범위내에서 융통성 부여)

0 유류별 MARGIN: 휘발유 37/100 프랑, 디젤 42/100 프랑, 가정용 연료 27.7/100-47.4/100 프랑

0 MARGIN 산정 기준: MRAGIN 결정시한 직전 8일동안의 유가(CRUDE OIL 이 아닌고 REFINED OIL 기준)평균치 적용

기타: 전국을 8개지역으로 구분, 산간지역등은 다소 높게 책정

2. 최근 유가동향및 전망(휘발유 "SUPER" 기준)

-상기 동결조치 시행당시 1L 당 5.29 프랑(약 1.02 미불)이던 SUPER 가격이8.25. 최초로 6 프랑을 상회한바,8.25. 기준 CEILING PRICE 는 5.93-6.07 프랑(약 1.16-1.19 미불)임.

-주재국 경제전문가들은, 주재국이 CRUDE OIL 을 주로 수입하는 관계로, 급격한 유가상승은 없을것이나, 당분간 REFINED OIL 가격이 점진적으로 상승할 것으로 전망하고 있음.

-또한, 인플레에 대한 파급효과 관련,10/100 프랑 상승시 소비자 물가지수는 0.1 프로 상승할 것으로 예측함.

경제국　차관　1차보　2차보　구주국　청와대　안기부　대책반

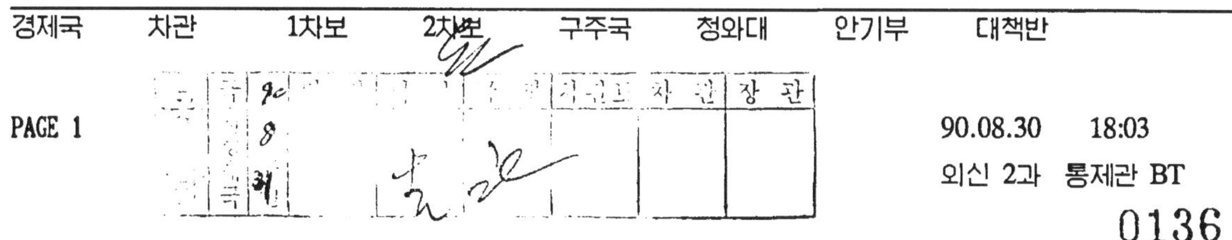

PAGE 1　　　90.08.30 18:03

외신 2과 통제관 BT

0136

3. 참고사항: 주재국 유가 구조(8.6. 현재 휘발유 가격 5.29. 프랑 기준)

-생산가:1.24 프랑(23.4 프로)

-유통마진:0.09 프랑(1.7 프로)

-세금(TVA 포함):3.96 프랑(74.9 프로). 끝.

(대사 노영찬-국장)

예고:90.12.31. 까지

원 본

외 무 부

종 별 : 지 급

번 호 : DJW-1272 일 시 : 90 0830 1430

수 신 : 장 관(기협,정일)

발 신 : 주 인니 대사

제 목 : OPEC 자문회의 결과(자료응신 제74호)

주재국 광업에너지성에 의하면, 비엔나 개최 OPEC 자문회의에 11개국(이락,리비아 제외) 대표가 참석, 4일간의 협의를 거쳐 이락.쿠웨이트 사태가 안정될때까지 잠정적으로 3.5백만 베럴의 원유증산에 합의하였다 함.

동 증산은 사우디 2백만, 베네주엘라 50만, 인니 10만 베럴, 잔여 90만 베럴은 OPEC 회원국이 분할하기로 합의하였으나, 이란은 세계 유가인상을 위해 상기 증산계획에 반대했다고 함. 끝.

(대사 김재춘-국장)

경제국 1차보 2차보 통상국 정문국 안기부 대책반 아주국 동자부

PAGE 1 90.08.30 18:08 BB

외신 1과 통제관

0138

관리 번호	90-665

원 본

외 무 부

종 별 :

번 호 : QTW-0114 일 시 : 90 0830 1220

수 신 : 장관(기협)

발 신 : 주 카타르 대사

제 목 : 원유안장공급확보

연: QTW-0109

1. 8.26-29 간 비엔나에서 개최된 OPEC 석유상회담 (주재국 SH.ABDULLAH BIN KHALIFA AL-THANI 내무장관 대리참석) 은 13 개 회원국중 이락, 리비아를 제외한 11 개국 석유상이 참석한 가운데 10 개국 (이란제외) 의 다수 찬성으로 이락, 쿠웨이트 원유수출 금지조치에 따른 공급부족량을 보충하기위하여 OPEC QUOTA 와 관계없이 잠정적으로 각각 증량 (정확한 물량은 발표치 않음) 생산키로 합의하였음.

2. 연호 보고와 같이 주재국 석유공사 (QGPC) 는 현 OPEC QUOTA(37.1만 B/D)에서 10 만 B/D 가량을 증량할 것으로 추정되는바 동사 DR. JABER AL-MARRI 총재가 8.22 본직과의 면담시 아국 정유사에 대한 증량공급 배려의사를 표시하였으므로 유공등 해당정유사로 하여금 조속교섭에 임하도록 지도함이 가하다고 사료됨.

3. 탐문한 바에 의하면 유공측은 9 월중 담당상무급을 걸프지역에 파견할 계획이라 하니 참고바람.

(대사 유내형-국장)

예고:90.12.31 일반

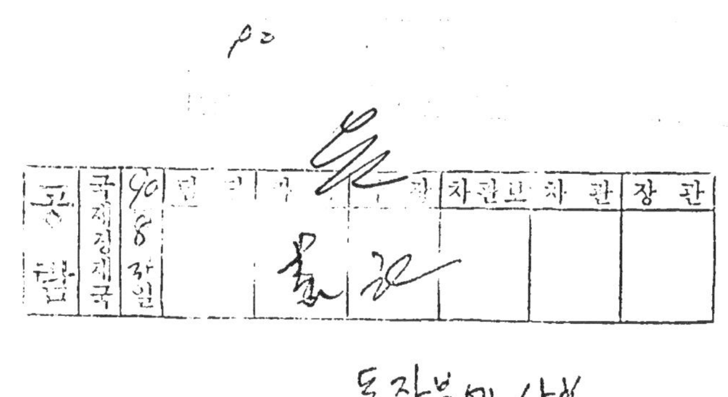

동자부에 사본

경제국	차관	1차보	2차보	중아국	청와대	안기부	대책반	동자부.

PAGE 1

90.08.30 19:17

외신 2과 통제관 BT

0139

관리번호	90-662

외 무 부

종 별 :

번 호 : FRW-1574 일 시 : 90 0830 1100

수 신 : 장관(중근동,구일,경일,사본:국방부)

발 신 : 주 불 대사

제 목 : 이라크사태(ARAFAT-ROCARD 면담)

ARAFAT PLO 의장은 8.29(수) 파리를 방문, ROCARD 수상과 면담을 가졌는바,그 상세 내용은 알려지지 않았으나, 파악된 개요를 아래 보고함.

1. ARAFAT 의장은 HUSSEIN 요르단 왕과의 협의후 제신된 것으로 보이는 아래요지의 걸프위기 해결책을 비롯한 중동지역 평화안을 불란서측에 설명함.

-봉쇄 해제

-이라크군의 쿠웨이트 철수및 걸프만 주둔군을 UN 군으로 대체

-UN 감시하, 쿠웨이트에서의 총선

2. ROCARD 수상은 UN 결의의 시행만이 걸프사태 해결 특히 억류 외국인의 무조건 석방및 이라크의 쿠웨이트 철수를 실현 시킬수 있을 것이며, 팔레스타인 문제에 대해서는 국제사회가 평화적인 해결을 위해 노력해야 한다는 불란서의 입장이 불변임을 상기 시키므로서, ARAFAT 와 의견 접근을 보지 못한 것으로 알려짐

3. 상기회담이 비록 성과가 없었으나, 불란서가 ARAFAT 를 접수, 협의한 기본 의도는 걸프사태가 협상 국면에 접어든 현시점서 주재국이 서방국중 주요한 협상 중재자로 부각 시킬수 있는 기회를 마련한것으로 분석되고 있음. 끝.

(대사 노영찬-국장)

예고:90.12.31. 까지

90 12 31

공람	국제경제국	90년 8월 31일	담 당	과 장	국 장	차관보	차 관	장 관

중아국 대책반 차관 1차보 2차보 구주국 경제국 청와대 안기부 국방부

PAGE 1

90.08.30 19:43

외신 2과 통제관 BT

0140

원 본

외 무 부

종 별 :

번 호 : AVW-1233 일 시 : 90 0829 1930

수 신 : 장관(기협,구이,동자부)

발 신 : 주 오스트리아대사

제 목 : OPEC 비공식 회의

1.지난 8.26(일) 부터 계속되고 있는 표제회의는 8.28(화) 현재까지 회원국간의의견 차이로 OPEC 원유 생산량 상향 조정에 관한 구체적인 합의 도출을 이루지 못한채, 금 8.29(수) 회의를 재개할 예정인 것으로 알려지고 있음.

2.상기 비공식 회의에서, 사우디, 베네주엘라, UAE등 전통적으로 원유시장의 안정을 중시하는 회원국은 원유 CARTEL 로서의 OPEC 기능보다 안정적인 원유 공급원으로서의 OPEC 역할이 안정적 시장확보를 위하여 더욱 바람직함을 주장하면서, OPEC 원유 증량의 필요성을 강조하였다고 함. 또한 이들은 고유가의 지속은 선진공업국의 절약 정책을 초래하게 , 선진국의 이러한 정책은 OPEC 원유에대한 수요 감소를 불러 일으킬 가능성이 크기때문에 종국적으로는 OPEC 회원국에게도 도움이 되지 않는다는 입장을 견지함.

3.상기에 대해 인도네시아, 나이제리아, 알제리아, 이란등은 사우디 등이 미국의 압력으로 증산을 주장하고 있다고 하면서, 제 3세계의 외채문제에 대하여는 큰 관심을 보이지 않고 있는 미국이 이러한 방식으로 OPEC 에 대해 증산 압력을 가하고있는 것은 오히려 역효과를 초래할 가능성이 크다고 주장하였다 함. 또한 이들은선진공업국이 원유시장 안정성을 중시 여긴다면, OPEC 원유증량 요구 보다는 현재선진 공업국 정부 및 기업이 비축하고 있는 원유를 방출하는 것이 안정적 시장 유지에 더욱 도움이 될 것이라고 지적하면서 이를 위한 IEA 측의 역할을 강조한것으로 알려짐.

4.한편 IEA 측은 상기 주장에 대해, 현 원유가 상승이 물리적 공급 부족 사태에서 기인된 것이 아니고, 전쟁발발 가능성에 대한 거래업자의 우려에서 비롯된 것이므로, 아직은 물리적 공급부족에 대비해 선진 공업국이 비축하고 있는 원유를 방출할 시기가 아니라고 함으로써, 상기 주장을 반박하였음.

5.상기와 같이 OPEC 회원국간의 의견이 대립되고 있기 때문에, 금일

경제국 구주국 동자부 2차보

PAGE 1

국	담 당	과 장	국 장	차관보	차 관	장 관
90.8.31						

90.08.30 21:08 DA

외신 1과 통제관

0141

회의에서도OPEC 생산물량 상향 조정 등 OPEC 회원국 전체를 구속하는 결정(DECISION) 이 나오기는 어려울 것으로 보이나, 사우디, 베네주엘라 등이 OPEC회의 결과와 관계없이 증산할 것임을 강력히 시사하고 있기 때문에, 선언 (DECLARATION) 등의 형태를 통하여 타협이 이루어질 수 있을것으로 OPEC 관측통들은 보고 있음.

(끝)

PAGE 2

0142

원 본

외 무 부

종 별 :

번 호 : AVW-1241 일 시 : 90 0830 1920

수 신 : 장 관(기협,구이,동자부)

발 신 : 주 오스트리아 대사

제 목 : OPEC 회의

연: AVW-1233

1.OPEC 의 10개 회원국(이라크,리비아는 대표단불파견, 이란은 대표단 파견했으나 회의 참가거부) 석유상은 90.8.29(수) 개최된 특별회의(비공식협의를 공식회의로 전환)에서,'' GULF 위기가 계속되는 동안, OPEC회원국은 수요 사정에 따라 원유 생산량을증가할 수 있다''고 결정하였음.

2. OPEC 관계관에 의하면, 상기 결정은 이라크및 쿠웨이트산 원유 금수 조치로 인한 공급부족을 보전하기 위하여, OPEC 회원국의 할당량을 상향 조정하여야 한다는 사우디,베네주엘라, UAE등의 주장과 이에 소극적인 회원국들간의 타협에 의해 성립된한시적 조치라고 함.

즉, 동 결정은 GULF 위기 기간동안 개별회원국이 스스로의 수요 판단에 따라 생산량을 자율 조정할 수 있게 함으로써 증산을 주장하는 사우디 등의 입장을 살려 줌과동시에, 동 조치의 한시성의 강조로 기존 OPEC 할당량인 일산22.5백만 배럴을 그대로 유지할 수 있게 함으로써 여타 회원국의 입장도 적절히 반영한 타협안이라고 함.

3.또한 여타 회원국이 상기 결정에 찬성한 이면에는 사우디 등의 잉여생산능력이 최대 일산350만 배럴 정도이기 때문에, 이들에게 증산을 허용한다 할지라도, 이라크와 쿠웨이트의 할당량이 일산 460만 배럴인 점을 감안한다면,이라크,쿠웨이트를 제외한 OPEC 생산 물량이 기존 OPEC 할당인 일산 22.5백만 배럴을초과할 수 없을 것이라는 현실적인 계산이 깔려있는 것으로 당지 석유업계는 보고 있음.

4.주재국 경제성,상공회의소 등 주요 경제정책 담당기관은 금번 유가상승이 현실적인 공급부족보다는 전쟁발발시 사우디산 원유 공급이 중단되는 사태가 올지도 모른다는 요인에서 비롯된것이기 때문에, OPEC 의 상기와 같은 조치로 약간의 원유가

경제국 2차보 구주국 정문국 안기부 동자부

PAGE 1

공람	국제경제국		담 당	과 장	국 장	차관보	차 관	장 관

90.08.31 08:50 ER

외신 1과 통제관

0143

하락은 예상되지만, GULF 위기가 지속되는 한 유가가 이라크-쿠웨이트 사태이전의 수준까지 하락하지는 않을 것으로 예측하고 있음.

(끝)

원 본

외 무 부

종 별 :

번 호 : MXW-1062 일 시 : 90 0830 1200

수 신 : 장 관(기협,미중)

발 신 : 주 멕 대사

제 목 : 원유 수급동향

연:MXW-1058

1. 주재국 국영석유회사 PEMEX 는 멕산유가와 WEST TEXAS, BRENT 유가와의 균형을 이루기 위하여 9.1. 부터 멕산 원유수출 가격인상을 결정하였다고 발표함.

2. 최근 이.쿠사태 이후 주재국 원유수출 가격은 지난 8월중 배럴당 약9불이 인상되었는바 9월중 유럽 및 극동지역에 대한 멕산원유 ISTHMUS 및 MAYA 의 수출가격은 배럴당 각각 25.89불 (0.9불인상) 및 20.17.불 (1.50불인상)이 될것이라함.

3. PEMEX 는 유가 인상결정이 주재국 재무성, 상공성, 멕시코은행, PEMEX 등으로 구성된 석유 대외수출 위원회에 의해 결정되었다고 밝힘.

(대사 이복형-국장)

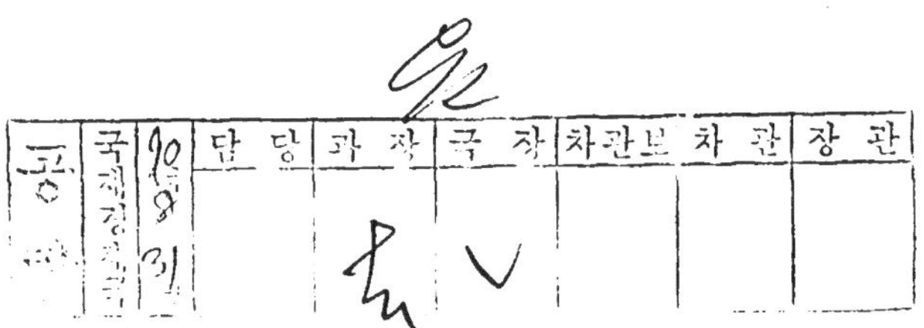

경제국 2차보 미주국 동자부

PAGE 1

90.08.31 09:08 WG

외신 1과 통제관

0145

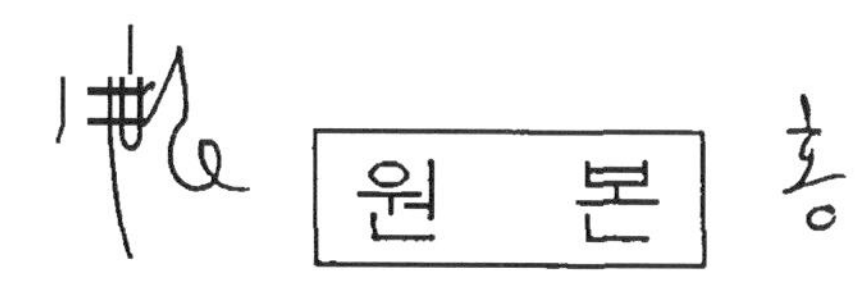

외 무 부

종 별 :

번 호 : HUW-0369 일 시 : 90 0830 1500

수 신 : 장 관(경자,미북) 사본:주미대사(필)

발 신 : 주 휴스턴 총영사

제 목 : 석유가격 동향보고(3)

1. 8.29.현재 서부텍사스 중질원유 가격은 어제보다 1.96불 하락 25.92 불로 거래됨. 이는 8.29. OPEC 비엔나회의에서 사우디등 주요 산유국들이 석유행산량을 각국이 자유로 증가시키기로 합의하여 원유 생산이 1일 300 만베럴정도 (1일 400 만베럴부족)증가하게 될것이라는 점과, 최근 사담후세인 이라크 대통령이 8.28. 인질중 여자와 어린애들을 석방하기로 결정하므로서 긴장이 완화되어 당분간 무력충돌은 없을것이라는 예측때문이라함.

2.90.1.월현재 원유 및 천연가스 매장량은 아래와 같음.

가.원유(전세계 매장량: 약 1조바렐)

1)사우디 25.5 푸로

2)이락 10.0

3)쿠웨이트 9.4

4)이란 9.3

5) ABU DHABI 92. (MIDDLE EAST 66)

6) 베네주엘라 5.8

7)소련 5.8

8)멕시코 5.6

9)미국 2.6

10)중국 2.4

기타 리리아 나이제리아 놀웨이 아러지리아 인니 인디아 카나다 이집트 영국등 순위임

나. 천연가스(전세계 매장량:약 4백만 BILLION CUBIC FEET)

1) 소련 37.6 푸로

경제국 2차보 미주국 안기부 동자부

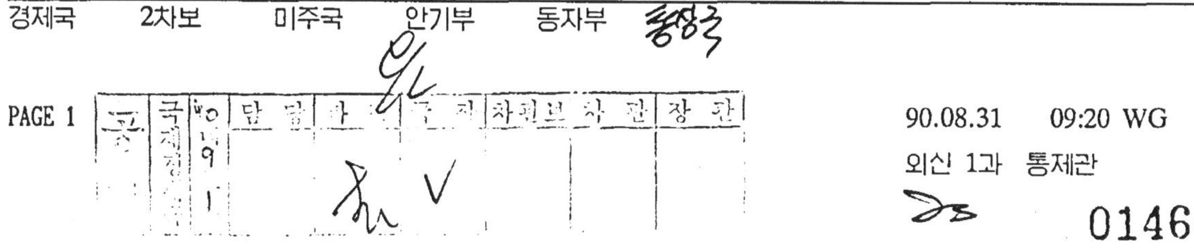

PAGE 1

90.08.31 09:20 WG

외신 1과 통제관

0146

2) 일본 12.5

3) ABU DHABI 4.6

4) 사우디 4.5

5)카탈 4.1

6)알제리아 2.9

7)베네주엘라 2.5

8)카나다 2.4

9)나이제리아 2.2

10)인니 2.2

기타 놀웨이 멕시코 네덴란드 말레시아순임.

(총영사 허승-국장)

0147

원 본

외 무 부

종 별 :

번 호 : USW-3948 일 시 : 90 0830 1812

수 신 : 장 관(기협)

발 신 : 주 미 대사

제 목 : 석유 시장 및 유가 동향(6)

표제 관련, 8.30 자 당지 언론 보도를 종합보고함.

1.유가 동향

가. 8.29 원유 및 정유 제품 가격 (뉴욕 상품 시장)

0 원유 (10월 인도 가격)

: 배럴당 25.92 불 (전일에 비해 1.96 불 하락)

0 무연 휘발유 (9월 인도 가격)

: 갤런당 84.72 센트 (전일에 비해 3.81 센트 하락)

0 난방유 (9월 인도 가격)

: 갤런당 71.64 센트 (전일에 비해 7.88 센트 하락)

나. 당지 전문가들은 8.29 의 대폭적인 유가 하락은 OPEC 의 증산 실시 계획 발표 및 후세인 대통령의 이락 소재 외국인 중 부녀자 및 미성년자 출국 허용 방침 발표등 유화적인 태도 표명에 따른것으로 분석하면서, 금번 사태가 지속되는 한유가가 배럴당 25 불 이하로 하락하지는 않을 것으로 전망하고 있음.

2. OPEC 동향

0 8.29 OPEC 은 금번 사태가 해결되기까지 회원국들에 대한 무제한 증산 실시 허용 방침을 발표하였음.

0 한편 사우디는 동 증산 허용 결정 발표 이전에 이미 일일 7.5 백만 배럴을 생산중이며, 향후일일 8 백만 배럴까지 증산계획인 것으로 알려지고 있고, 베네수엘라, UAE 및 나이지리아, 가봉, 에쿠아돌등도 즉각 증산을 실시할 것으로 관측되고 있음.

3.서방국 대처

0 국제 에너지 기구 (IEA) 는 8.31(금) 이사회를 개최, 국제 원유 시장 현황에

경제국 2차보 미주국 안기부 동자부 통상국

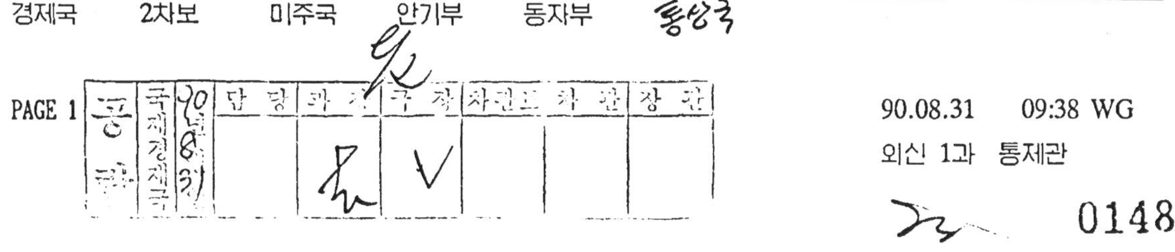

PAGE 1

90.08.31 09:38 WG

외신 1과 통제관

0148

대해 협의할 예정임.

0 OPEC 은 8.29 회원국들에 대한 증산 실시허용 결정을 발표하면서, 유가 안정을 위해 IEA 회원국들이 전략 비축 석유를 시장에 방출할 것으로 요청하였으나, 미국등 IEA 회원국들은 현재로서는 심각한 공급 부족이 없다고 판단, 즉각적인 방출 조치를 취하지는 않을것으로 관측됨.

0 당지 일부 전문가들은 그러나 난방유 수요가 증대되는 2-3개월후에는 세계 시장에서의 원유 공급량부족이 뚜렷해져 IEA 가 방출 조치를 취해야할 것으로 전망하고 있음.

4. 8.30자 당지 언론 보도 내용 별첨 FAX 송부함.

첨부: USW(F)-1997

(대사 박동진-국장0

0149

: USW(F)- 1997
: 장 관 (기협) 발신 : 주미대사 보안 통제 | 외
: USW - 3948 첨부 (10 매)

Oil Prices Plunge on OPEC Pact to Lift Output, Perception That Mideast Tensions Are Easing

By Caleb Solomon
Staff Reporter of The Wall Street Journal

HOUSTON – Crude oil prices fell sharply following an OPEC agreement to raise production and a growing perception among market participants that Middle East tensions were easing.

Ten of the 13 members of the Organization of Petroleum Exporting Countries agreed to raise output immediately to help replace the four million barrels of oil taken off the market because of the embargo of Iraqi and Kuwaiti petroleum. Market estimates varied as to how much oil OPEC could quickly put on the market.

Crude oil for October delivery fell $1.96 a barrel to $25.92 on the New York Mercantile Exchange, the lowest level in nearly three weeks. So far this week the contract has dropped about $5 a barrel, or 16%, as financial markets increasingly believe the chances for Mideast hostilities have lessened.

"The crude market weakened on perceptions of a moderating Persian Gulf crisis," said Andrew Lebow, a crude oil analyst with E.D.&F. Man International Futures Inc. He said a number of news reports pointed to the "potential for a peaceful solution."

A number of traders said Iraq's promise to release women and children held hostage, followed quickly by praise from the U.S. government for the move, was one sign of easing tensions. Market participants also pointed to reports that Iraq had made behind-the-scenes peace overtures to the U.S.

And in a market looking to go lower, even news that was several days old was cited as a factor, such as the planned meeting between the U.N. Secretary General and Iraq's foreign minister, scheduled for today.

Among OPEC members, the country that has sizable spare capacity that could ratchet up production quickly is Saudi Arabia. Traders were expecting that country to produce an extra two million barrels a day, with enough output from other OPEC nations to replace a total of three million to 3.5 million of the lost Iraqi and Kuwaiti production.

But some reports on the New York Merc said Saudi Arabia already was producing an extra two million barrels a day and could produce one million beyond that by the end of the year, for a total output as high as 8.5 million barrels daily. Some people remained skeptical, however. "They've been working on projects to upgrade production capacity, but 8.5 million is a very high number," Mr. Lebow said.

Gasoline prices also were off yesterday, in sympathy with crude declines. Gasoline for September delivery finished at 84.72 cents a gallon, down 3.51.

Heating oil fell sharply, with the Sep-

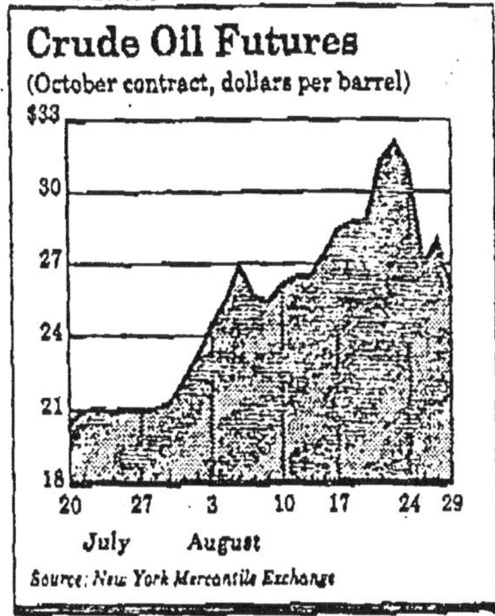

WSJ. 8/30/90

0150

08/30/90 17:52 ☎202 797 0595 EMBASSY OF KOREA →→→ WOI 2 ☑008/01

호 : USW(F)-

수신 : 장 관 발신 : 주미대사

제목 : (매)

OPEC Lifts Its Restrictions On Production

Group's Mideast Crisis Move Is Seen as Bid to Reassert Influence in Oil Markets

By JAMES TANNER
Staff Reporter of THE WALL STREET JOURNAL

VIENNA—The Organization of Petroleum Exporting Countries, in a bid to reassert its influence over oil markets, freed its members to pump to capacity during the Middle East crisis.

The suspension of production quotas had been expected and won't significantly change anticipated oil supplies for the months ahead. The few key OPEC members with substantial excess capacity had previously indicated they were going to use it with or without formal approval.

Oil Prices Continue Slide

Crude prices for October delivery fell $1.96 a barrel to $25.92 on the OPEC output pact. The contract has slipped about $6 a barrel, or 16%, so far this week. Quotes for gasoline and heating oil also declined. Story on page C12.

But in announcing the move, OPEC signaled its determination to take a bigger role in the current crisis after weeks of indecision. In an official statement issued here, the ministers said they authorized production increases to "clearly restate to the world that OPEC stands for market stability and regular supply of oil to consumers."

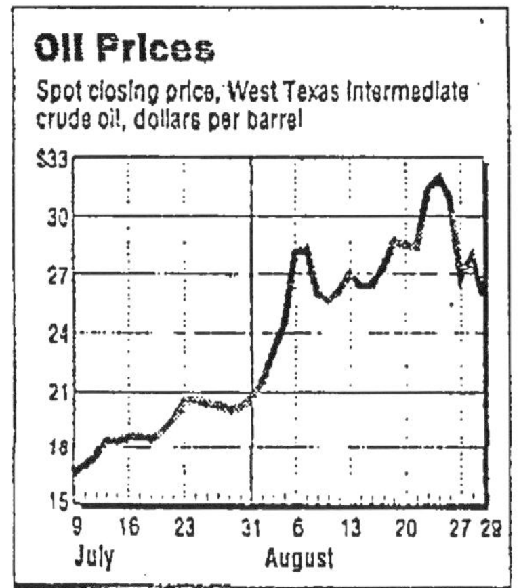

OPEC in recent years has attempted to control its production to avoid the gluts, shortages and severe price gyrations that cost its members enormous amounts of revenue and market share in the 1980s.

Consistent with that strategy, Saudi Arabia and other leading OPEC members have already begun boosting output following the price run-up caused by the global embargo against Iraqi and Kuwaiti oil. The action finally taken yesterday by a majority of the oil ministers sanctions that output surge. The ministers, who have been meeting since Sunday, reached a tentative accord earlier this week.

Crude-oil prices fell almost $2 a barrel yesterday, with traders citing the OPEC agreement and a growing perception of easing tensions in the Middle East.

Many OPEC ministers here suggested the organization passed a crucial test. There has been some question about OPEC's ability to function during this crisis, which has entangled three of its five founding members: Iraq, Kuwait and Saudi Arabia.

"OPEC has survived the most critical challenge in its history," Ginandjar Kartasasmita, Indonesia's oil minister, said in an interview.

Not all OPEC members were pleased with the outcome, however. Approval came over the objections of the ministers of Iraq and Libya, who boycotted the meeting and questioned its legitimacy. A third opponent, Gholamreza Aghazadeh, Iran's oil minister, did attend but urged that OPEC not increase output until after major oil-consuming nations have drawn down their oil inventories to help fill the supply gap.

Mr. Aghazadeh also tried to have yesterday's ministerial monitoring committee meeting postponed for a week to permit joint discussions with the Paris-based International Energy Agency. The IEA represents 21 major oil-consuming nations. The 10 other ministers rejected his proposal. Instead, they called on consuming nations to execute existing oil-sharing arrangements designed for shortages and to utilize the "present huge accumulation" of oil inventories.

Despite the OPEC request, a U.S. Energy Department spokesman in Washington argued that there is no need yet to draw on strategic reserves. That also will be the U.S. position at tomorrow's IEA governors meeting in Paris. Nevertheless, there are signs that U.S. resistance to dipping into its reserves is softening. With OPEC sanctioning more production from members that are able to increase output, the U.S. could consider a small release of oil from its reserve to help calm markets.

A majority of OPEC members have been producing at peak capacity for some time, so despite yesterday's go-ahead, only a handful can do more. These are expected to make up at least three million of the four million barrels a day formerly exported by Iraq and Kuwait. Saudi Arabia is understood to hold two-thirds, or about two million barrels, of that spare capacity.

Hisham Nazer, the Saudi oil minister, left immediately after yesterday's brief meeting and didn't outline the kingdom's production plans. OPEC sources said, however, that it is already producing more than seven million barrels a day. Its quota had been 5.4 million barrels a day.

Venezuela also is already producing more. Celestino Armas, oil minister, confirmed output recently was increased 300,000 barrels a day. A further 200,000 barrels a day will be added by the end of the year, he said.

The United Arab Emirates is pushing up output by 500,000 barrels a day. And although some of the production claims seem inflated, lesser amounts are likely to come from some other exporters. Nigeria can produce 250,000 to 250,000 barrels a day more, said its oil minister, Jibril Aminu.

Several of the oil ministers suggested that a tabulation of all the increases still leaves OPEC slightly short of its former second-half production ceiling—22.5 million barrels a day—as long as Iraqi and Kuwaiti output is choked down.

Still, Ali Khalifa al-Sabah, Kuwait's finance minister and former oil minister who represented that country here, said supplies should be ample, with oil prices dropping as a result. "There will be plenty of oil on the market, and there is definitely no reason for panic," he said.

—Alan Murray and Rose Gutfeld in Washington contributed to this article.

W.S.J. 8/30/90

USW(F)1990-2

0151

CRUDE PRICES DROP

4 Million Barrels a Day Are Added to Supply — Iran Dissents

By YOUSSEF M. IBRAHIM

Special to The New York Times

VIENNA, Aug. 29 — After weeks of deliberations, the Organization of Petroleum Exporting Countries authorized its key oil producers today to begin pumping all the oil they can immediately, averting a feared shortage that has sent prices surging on world markets.

The OPEC decision is expected to add some four million barrels a day to current world oil supplies, making up for nearly all the oil exports lost as a result of the commercial embargo imposed on Iraq and Iraqi-occupied Kuwait by the United Nations.

[Oil prices fell sharply in futures market trading in response to the OPEC decision, with the contract for October delivery down $1.96, to $25.92 a barrel, on the New York Mercantile Exchange. That brought its decline for the week to $4.99. Gasoline and heating oil also retreated. Page D1.]

Intense International Pressure

Despite the extensive haggling in the negotiations that began here Saturday, the OPEC decision had been expected in view of the intense international pressure that followed the spectacular rise in oil prices from $14 in early May to above $30 last week. Both industrialized and third world countries raised fears that recession, inflation and economic disruptions could result.

In its communiqué today, OPEC stated that it took its majority decision after reviewing these trends and worrying that instability "may well be prolonged" into the fourth quarter and perhaps throughout the first three months of next year as well.

"OPEC, as a body which is fully aware of its mandate and responsiblity to help insure an adequate global energy supply" decided to opt for higher production, it said.

Avoiding Past Experiences

Saudi, Venezeulan and other OPEC officials who voted for the decision said they were trying to avoid repeating the experience of the 1970's and 1980's when oil prices surged only to crash later with demand also falling.

The current OPEC minimum price is $21 a barrel, but most OPEC officials do not expect the market price to drop below $25, given the continuing nervousness over war. In case of war, [illegible] of the officials say, prices could go as high as $50 a barrel. At the end of July, prices were $18 a barrel, but they had begun to edge up even before Iraq invaded Kuwait on Aug. 2 and now stand at around $26.

The OPEC production decision is seen largely as a further blow to Iraq, which had hoped that an oil shortage and rising prices would eventually diminish international enthusiasm to enforce the embargo.

The boycott is primarily aimed at crippling the Baghdad regime of President Saddam Hussein economically and forcing him to pull his troops out of Kuwait. Iraq has said repeatedly over the past few days that it would view any increase in OPEC production as an "aggressive act."

Saudi Arabian officials disclosed that their country, which is OPEC's largest exporter, had already raised its output to 7.5 million barrels a day from 5.5 million — a considerly higher production level than most oil analysts had expected.

The officials said they expected to push Saudi oil output further, to exceed 8 million barrels a day by September, a 45 percent rise from the country's output in May.

In addition, a senior official from the United Arab Emirates said today that his country was immediately raising its output in "a dramatic way." The official, who insisted that he not be identified, suggested that the U.A.E. would produce more than the 600,000 barrels a day that was thought to be its maximum spare capacity, but he did not elaborate.

Ten of the 13 OPEC members supported the production decision, which was advanced largely by Saudi Arabia and Venezuela. Iran opposed it, as did Iraq and Libya, which did not attend the consultative meeting here. Even so, Iran and Libya are expected to increase their output to take advantage of the opportunity to sell more oil.

Little Choice for Some

Even though at least half OPEC's members were initially reluctant to agree to increased output, the actions of the Saudis and Venezuelans left them little choice. For days before the meeting, the two big producers had repeatedly served notice that regardless of OPEC's deliberations, they would increase output by September.

Saudi Arabia and Venezuela, which did not want to appear to be reacting to demands of the United States and other Western allies for more oil, contended that it would be best if increases happened under an OPEC "umbrella," so as to prevent a free-for-all in production. Also, they said, that would enable OPEC to return promptly to its normal output once the crisis was past.

The two big members exerted so much muscle that in the end, even members like Algeria and Indonesia, which are not capable of lifting their outputs, went along despite worries that their oil revenues would tumble as prices come down.

Varying Increases

Within OPEC, Venezuela and the United Arab Emirates are expected to raise daily output by 600,000 barrels each. Nigeria, Gabon and Ecuador are also expected to increase production immediately by varying amounts.

Together, all the other OPEC members are expected to add perhaps two million barrels in oil exports by pushing their production to the limit.

Iran, which was the prime opponent of today's agreement, argued there was enough oil on world markets to make up for the loss of Kuwaiti and Iraqi exports.

Iran's oil minister, Gholam Reza Aghazadeh, insisted yesterday without success that international oil companies and Western and industrialized governments use their commercial and strategic stocks of oil before asking OPEC to pump more crude.

Praise From Energy Group

In Paris, the International Energy Agency commended the OPEC decision. Its executive director, Helga Steeg, said that the increased production would "make an important contribution toward compensating for any shortfalls in supplies which might occur over the coming weeks following the loss of Iraqi and Kuwaiti crude."

But the I.E.A., which represents the energy interests of 21 industrialized Western countries and Japan, rejected an Iranian call that it join OPEC in an effort to remedy the supply situation, saying the idea "is not feasible, politically or economically."

Still, in a move to appease Iran, Algeria, Indonesia and others, OPEC called upon the 21 member countries of the Paris-based I.E.A. to use their strategic oil reserves and upon oil companies to draw down the "present huge accumulation of stocks" of oil they are known to be holding.

Saudi Arabia was said, however, to have repeatedly pointed out during deliberations here that consumers held considerably less oil now than they had in July, before the crisis began.

Saudi Arabia also urged that the OPEC communiqué stress that much of the new oil be directed to third world countries that have no reserves and that depended on Kuwait and Iraq for oil.

OPEC said its move was a "temporary arrangement" to deal with the Middle East crisis. Once the crisis passes, OPEC said it would return to its July 1990 agreement that set combined output for all members at 22.5 million barrels a day.

OPEC left open the possibility that production and prices, set in the July agreement at $21 a barrel, might be raised after the crisis.

USW (F) #999-3

0152

Oil Drops Nearly $2 A Barrel

By KEITH BRADSHER

Oil prices fell sharply yesterday as traders responded to the decision by the Organization of Petroleum Exporting Countries to allow an immediate increase in oil production, as well as to reduced fears of war in the Persian Gulf.

The contract for October delivery of oil fell $1.96 a barrel, to $25.92, on the New York Mercantile Exchange. So far this week, the October price for oil has plunged $4.99 a barrel.

Gasoline and heating oil prices also retreated yesterday.

The energy market has focused on diplomatic moves to ease Middle East tensions and on the OPEC decision, which is expected to add some four million barrels a day to current world oil supplies, making up for nearly all the oil exports lost as a result of the embargo imposed on Iraq and Iraqi-occupied Kuwait.

The Market's Retreat

News of the OPEC decision, reached yesterday in Vienna, drove prices down by about $1 a barrel in early trading, said Bradford H. Hughes, an energy futures trader at Cargill Investor Services.

Prices fell another dollar on reports that Saddam Hussein, Iraq's president, was taking a more conciliatory stance on his country's occupation of Kuwait, Mr. Hughes said. The Iraqi leader was reported to have offered to allow all Western men to join Western women and children in leaving Kuwait and Iraq, if the United States would guarantee that it would not attack Iraq.

But yesterday's fall in oil prices is unlikely to cause an immediate reduction in gasoline prices, refiners said. Even at $25.92 a barrel, the Chevron Corporation is still paying 17.3 cents a gallon more for oil than its average payment in July, about double the 8 to 10 cents a gallon increase in the wholesale prices it charges dealers for gasoline, said James E. Huccaby, the manager of pricing for Chevron USA.

The Amoco Corporation said the prices it charged dealers for gasoline had risen 16 cents since July 1, while oil costs had climbed 22 cents.

Gasoline and Heating Oil Fall

In futures trading yesterday, the contract for September delivery of gasoline fell 3.81 cents a gallon, to close at 84.72 cents, while the contract for September delivery of heating oil tumbled 7.58 cents, to close at 71.64 cents a gallon.

Prices of oil for delivery next year fell less sharply yesterday than the October price of oil. This is an indication that the markets are becoming less anxious and less willing to pay a premium for oil available soon, said Philip K. Verleger Jr., an energy economist at the Institute for International Economics in Washington.

"It's the first small step back toward the situation at the end of July," he said. "That'll last until the first gunshot is fired."

Chevron and the Shell Oil Company, a unit of the Royal Dutch/Shell Group, announced yesterday morning that they were immediately cutting by $3, to $26.50, the posted price they would pay for West Texas Intermediate crude oil, the American benchmark grade.

Bonner & Moore, of Houston, a consulting firm to the oil and petrochemical refining industries, said the announcement in Vienna underscored a consensus among the 10 OPEC members voting for it that they wanted to avoid a sustained surge above $30 a barrel, for fear that such prices could push the industrial nations — their largest customers — into recession.

'Possibility of a Powder Keg'

At the meeting, only Iran opposed the accord, as did Iraq and Libya, which did not attend the meeting. Iraq has said it would regard higher production by other OPEC members as an act of aggression.

"We still have the possibility of a powder keg as long as there is a heightened military presence in the Middle East," said Craig Whitley, a futures market analyst at Bonner & Moore. "We are still holding to our belief for the long term that OPEC will make up most of the shortfall in production."

Bonner & Moore forecasts that oil will cost $24 a barrel during the first half of 1991 and $22 for the second half.

Saudi Arabian officials said yesterday that they had already increased production to 7.5 million barrels a day from 5.5 million and would lift their output to 8 million barrels a day by September. Venezuela and the United Arab Emirates are also committed to raising production. Other OPEC members are expected to raise output to keep up their oil revenues, including Iran and Libya, which opposed the accord.

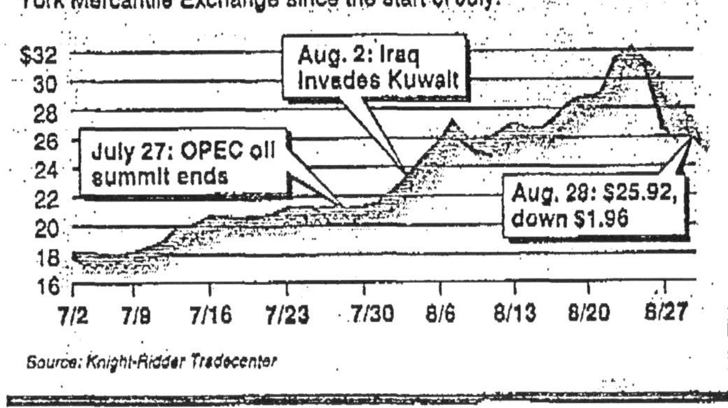

Source: Knight-Ridder Tradecenter

The New York Times

USW(F) 1990-4

Opec agrees an immediate increase in production

By Steven Butler in Vienna

AN IMMEDIATE increase in oil production was agreed yesterday by the Organisation of Petroleum Exporting Countries meeting in Vienna, in an effort to restore stability to world oil markets following the Gulf crisis. The agreement, backed by 10 of Opec's 13 members, suspends production quotas temporarily until "the present crisis is deemed to be over".

A communiqué notes, however, that the oil supply crisis could be prolonged and a number of ministers were privately pessimistic that the Gulf crisis could be resolved peacefully. Oil prices have risen sharply since Iraq invaded Kuwait, although they have eased this week on perceptions that tension is easing.

Ministers and delegates to the meeting were broadly satisfied that Opec had reacted responsibly to the Gulf crisis. Iraq, which did not attend the meeting, had earlier warned that Opec moves to lift output would be seen as an aggressive act, but these threats were ignored. Libya was also absent.

There was relief that Saudi Arabia, the United Arab Emirates and Venezuela had not been forced raise production unilaterally in violation of the Opec production agreement signed a month ago.

"I hope consumers will see that Opec is there to assure supplies to the market," said Sheikh Ali al-Khalifah al-Sabah, the Kuwaiti Finance Minister who has been a key architect of Opec strategy in recent years. "There will be plenty of oil on the market."

Opec production has already started to rise rapidly, according to oil market analysts. Venezuela and the UAE are expected to increase production by 500,000 b/d each. Mr Jibril Aminu, the Nigerian minister, said his country was prepared to lift production by over 250,000 b/d.

Saudi Arabia is understood to be preparing to increase production by over 2m b/d, to a sustainable production volume between 7.5m b/d and 8m b/d. Sustained production at this level would be higher than most outside observers have believed is possible. The Saudis are understood not to have a specific production target in mind but are prepared to respond to customer requests for additional supplies until capacity is reached.

None the less, said one minister, "Whatever we do in Opec we will not be able to compensate for the closure of Iraqi and Kuwaiti facilities."

Together the Opec countries should be able to compensate for over 80 per cent of the 4m b/d of Iraqi and Kuwaiti oil lost to the market.

The Opec ministers also called on the International Energy Agency, the Paris-based organisation responsible for co-ordinating the response of industrialised countries to an oil supply shortfall, to execute the IEA oil-sharing agreement and to release oil stocks held by consumer countries.

Mrs Helga Steeg, the IEA executive director, welcomed the Opec decision to increase production but said that the oil supply situation did not yet warrant the use of government stockpiles. She also rejected a proposal by Mr Gholamreza Aghazadeh, the Iranian oil minister, for joint IEA-Opec action as not feasible, politically or economically.

The IEA governing board meets in Paris tomorrow to review the market situation and to decide whether any action is required. Iran remained opposed to the agreement to lift production on the grounds that this should be done only in co-operation with the consuming countries. However, Opec ministers stressed yesterday that they understood the Iranian position and did not wish to isolate Iran.

The communiqué from the meeting said that additional supplies from Opec members and stock releases from consumers should be directed toward developing countries which are being hit hardest by the current crisis.

F.T. 8/30/90

OPEC Chooses Caution

OPEC NOW invites its members to increase their production and prevent disruptive oil shortages. With that, Iraq has been abandoned by its partners in the oil cartel. In terms of oil policy, the Iraqis have succeeded in achieving the opposite of their intentions. Their stated purpose in invading Kuwait was to punish it for exceeding its OPEC quota and driving world oil prices down. Now OPEC is abandoning its country-by-country quotas altogether and has left it to each member to follow its own policy.

The consensus at the OPEC meeting suggested that total production for all 13 members is to be at roughly the level set at its meeting last month—meaning that others would now increase exports to compensate for the boycott of Iraq and Kuwait. The purpose of the quota then was to reduce production and lift prices. Now it's the opposite—reasserted by the cartel in the name of stability and reliability of supply.

The principal beneficiaries in terms of dollars will obviously be the industrial democracies. But in terms of standards of living, it is the countries of the Third World that have the most at stake in this attempt to protect world markets from another enormous surge in oil prices. The OPEC communique made that point.

The great increases in oil costs during the 1970s hurt the rich countries, but they rapidly regained the lost ground. The damage has not been so easily repaired in less wealthy countries, particularly in Latin America and Africa. The oil price increases were the origin of the enormous debts that most of the Latin countries are still carrying. They borrowed desperately to protect their living standards, to a point at which the weight of the debts threatened to crush them. The effects in Africa have been even more severe, for most of those countries were poorer to begin with. Iraq has tried to portray its invasion of Kuwait as a crusade of the poor against the rich. But no countries have a greater interest in stable oil pricing than the poor ones. While that's hardly OPEC's chief reason for its decision, to its credit it acknowledges that lesson of the past decade.

W.P.

USW (F) 1990 -5

0154

OPEC Approves Higher Output

Oil Prices Drop, but There Are Signs of Supply Problems

By Thomas W. Lippman
Washington Post Staff Writer

The Organization of Petroleum Exporting Countries yesterday ratified an increase in production to make up for oil lost to world markets because of the Persian Gulf crisis. Oil prices immediately dropped to their lowest point in nearly three weeks.

There are signs, however, that the loss of supplies from Iraq and Kuwait is disrupting the flow of crude oil and that refined products—especially jet fuel—are being squeezed in some places. The Pentagon, in particular, was reporting problems in ensuring supplies of the vital fuel.

While the OPEC production increase was targeted for developing countries, several that depended on Iraqi or Kuwaiti crude are scrambling for oil—a quest complicated in some places by their lack of hard currency to pay for it. Others that have ample sources of supply are also struggling to pay the higher costs.

The Defense Department, which is consuming vast quantities of jet fuel for the airlift of troops and equipment to Saudi Arabia, said yesterday that it has been unable to find suppliers for all the fuel it needs. Kuwait was the U.S. military's principal supplier of aircraft fuel for the western Pacific region, including Japan and the Philippines, Pentagon officials said.

Frank Burkacki, a spokesman for the Defense Fuel Supply Center in Alexandria, said the center sought bids on Aug. 23 for the supply of 1.1 million barrels of jet fuel for delivery in the first three weeks of September, but received bids for only 845,000 barrels.

In addition, he said, the department has sought new bids on 3.5 million barrels to be delivered Oct. 1 through Dec. 31 because that contract had been awarded to the Kuwaitis. "They were unable to deliver," he said.

One well-informed official said the Pentagon's supply problem was compounded by a decision last spring to save money by letting its normal fuel inventories dwindle. Now the military has to replenish those supplies as well as find fuel for "Operation Desert Shield," he said.

Spokesmen for several major U.S. oil companies said they are fulfilling their contracts to supply fuel to airlines but the tight market created by military demand made it difficult to serve new customers or commit themselves beyond the expiration of current agreements. Some reports said that airlines throughout Asia are short of fuel because Kuwait's refineries are not delivering and Saudi Arabia's output has been diverted to the mammoth military operation there.

According to the American Petroleum Institute, the oil industry trade association, U.S. commercial stocks of jet fuel totaled 43.2 million barrels last week, an increase over the previous week and over the same week a year ago. But traders and analysts said the figure is deceiving because it includes supplies snapped up by some airlines that feared a shortage.

"Some airlines are building inventory because of fear," said John Armbrust, a Washington-based jet fuel trader. He said that in a normal market, the 4.6 million barrels sought by the Pentagon "is not a lot, but in a panic market, it causes panic buying."

He identified United Airlines as an "aggressive" buyer of jet fuel to be held in storage. United declined to comment.

The price of crude oil for October delivery closed at $25.92 a barrel yesterday in trading on the New York Mercantile Exchange—the lowest since Aug. 9. A week ago, before diplomatic initiatives eased fears of war in the Persian Gulf region, the price approached $32.

Venezuela, Saudi Arabia and the United Arab Emirates had announced they would increase production no matter what OPEC did, but the resolution approved yesterday keeps them within an ostensible framework of agreement with their OPEC partners. Iraq did not attend the meeting.

The effect of the resolution is to authorize members to exceed production ceilings agreed to at an OPEC meeting in July thought at the time to satisfy Iraq's demand for reduced production and higher prices. That agreement was shattered by Iraq's invasion of Kuwait, but the resolution adopted yesterday said the July agreement will take effect again when "the present crisis is deemed to be over."

The July agreement, adopted at a time when the world oil price was about $18 a barrel, set a target price of $21. The resolution adopted yesterday did not set any specific price or any specific production targets.

Kuwait and Iraq between them

continued #2

USW(F) 1999 -6

0155

3/2 OPEC Approves...

had been exporting 4.3 million barrels of oil a day, 9 percent of the non-Communist world's production. Reporters in Vienna said they were told that Saudi Arabia alone is expected to increase its output by nearly 3 million barrels a day by the end of the year.

Anxious to defuse charges that they are being manipulated by the United States, the OPEC ministers specified that their resolution was aimed at helping poor and developing countries that have been hit hard by the oil crisis.

"The additional supplies of oil from OPEC member countries and the release of stocks by consumers should be primarily directed toward the countries of the Third World which are those that will be most immediately and adversely affected by any supply disruption," the resolution said.

Some of these countries, including all the nations of Central America, say they have sufficient oil sources of supplies but cannot pay the higher price caused by the crisis. Others were dependent on imports from Iraq or Kuwait and have to find new supplies—supplies that may not be compatible with the specifications of their refineries.

Brazil has been especially hard hit because it obtained much of its oil from Iraq in barter arrangements, mostly for weapons.

Japan, which before the crisis was obtaining 4.7 percent of its imported oil from Iraq and 9.1 percent from Kuwait, and Western European countries, which obtained 17 percent of their imports from the two, seem affluent enough to buy elsewhere at market prices, passing the cost along to prosperous consumers.

Their situation is similar to that of the United States, which had been receiving about 9 percent of its imports from Iraq and Kuwait, according to Energy Department figures.

The burden is greater for countries like the Philippines, Bangladesh, South Korea and Taiwan, which were heavily dependent on Iraqi and Kuwaiti oil. They are negotiating for additional supplies from Iran, Saudi Arabia, Indonesia, Malaysia and China.

Special correspondent Michael Z. Wise contributed to this article from Vienna.

OPEC To Allow Output Hikes

From Wire Reports

VIENNA, Austria — The Organization of Petroleum Exporting Countries reached an accord Wednesday to permit members to raise oil production above their quotas and help ensure supplies during the Persian Gulf crisis.

A statement agreed by a majority of the 13 members of OPEC said the group "stands for market stability and regular supply of oil to consumers."

The cartel's Market Monitoring Committee decided that members could increase production "in accordance with need," freeing major producers to increase output and ease shortages caused by the embargo on oil from Iraq and Kuwait.

Iraq and Libya did not send their ministers to the talks.

Iran expressed reservations, saying it wanted OPEC to wait before raising production in order to reduce the huge stocks of petroleum on world markets.

The OPEC statement called on the West's energy watchdog, the 21-nation International Energy Agency, whose board of governors meets in Paris Friday, to activate an agreement which permits it to order consumer nations to share oil and draw down stocks.

Western industry sources said Saudi Arabia could provide 2 million extra barrels a day fairly soon.

Gulf sources suggest that well before the end of the year Saudi Arabia could boost output to 8.5 million barrels daily, compared with its OPEC quota of 5.4 million.

The industry expected Venezuela to be able to add 350,000 barrels now and 150,000 more by year-end, with the United Arab Emirates able to add 500,000 above its quota.

JoC 8/30/90

USW (F) 1990 -7

0156

호 : USW(F)-
수 신 : 장 관
발 신 : 주미대사
제 목 :
(매)

Jessica Tuchman Mathews

The Era of Cheap Energy Is Over

Laboratory rats, scientists say, are capable of one-trial learning. If the reward is sweet enough or the punishment harsh enough, they can learn a complex lesson in one encounter. Not so, it seems, for Americans and energy.

Our attitude toward the central commodity of modern economies can be roughly summarized this way:

While energy is cheap, use all you can. Respond in a crisis. When those measures work, abandon them. Return to the old ways, and forget the long term. Never on any account take command of energy availability by managing demand through price or policy. Leave that, by default, to OPEC. Instead, wait until supply gets tight again and foreigners raise the price. Then pay them what we might have paid to ourselves.

We've ridden this roller coaster up and down the energy price-and-demand-curve twice already; after the 1973 embargo and again after the '79-'80 price increase. Both times we've absorbed staggering economic shocks without ever seriously reexamining the notion that there is nothing we can do about energy other than respond to crises caused by others. Our unwillingness to act on energy is an inexplicable and hideously costly national blind spot.

Our third ride up the coaster began in 1986, when oil prices fell sharply. While other countries raised taxes to keep their energy-use trends constant, we prepared to enjoy another binge. Energy use, which had been declining in relation to GNP, took off again and has grown steadily ever since.

After the 1973 embargo, there was talk of invading Saudi Arabia. Rapid deployment forces for use in the Middle East were proposed and funded. Over the ensuing years, administrations proved willing to spend vast amounts of political capital accommodating Iran and Saudi Arabia with controversial arms sales. Now we are again poised on the brink of war and economic turmoil.

Yet never in all of this have we connected energy self-reliance with national security. At his most recent press conference, the president's flip response left little doubt of his views.

Q: We haven't really heard you call upon Americans to conserve as part of this crisis.

A: I call upon Americans to conserve.

Q: Will you elaborate?

A: No."

On second thought, he added, "We are doing everything we can to guarantee . . . that there will be an adequate supply of hydrocarbons."

The president's mind was clearly on the immediate crisis, but in the broader sense nothing could be further from the truth.

Insofar as the United States has had a national energy policy, it has focused single-mindedly on energy supply, whereas adequate energy is equally a matter of supply and demand. Our assumption has been that we need all the energy we can get. The truth is that energy demand is far more malleable than are the ineluctable geological limits of fossil-fuel supply.

We've nearly used up the U.S. oil resource. Production in the continental United States peaked in 1970 and has been declining for 20 years despite large price increases and intense exploration. In 1988 Alaskan production, too, passed its peak. North America holds 4 percent of the world's proven oil reserves. Iraq, Kuwait and Saudi Arabia together own 44 percent. OPEC as a whole holds 75 percent. Nothing the United States can do on the supply side—including drilling every drop of expensive and environmentally risky offshore oil—can even slightly alter these numbers.

There is, however, much we can do. Step 1, without which nothing else follows, is to recognize that the era of cheap energy is over. That means using taxes to price energy commensurate with its value. The small price increases caused by the Middle East crisis are no reason not to act. The real price of gasoline is still less than it has been for 40 years. The price swings we will see in the coming weeks are irrelevant to the underlying need to set oil prices on a slow but steady long term incline. The prices of other forms of energy will follow. Taxes should be designed with the costs of air pollution and the eventual need to slow greenhouse warming in mind.

Step 2 is to recognize that the value of a barrel of oil not burned because of cost-competitive efficiency improvements is actually greater than the value of a barrel burned, because it performs the same services but produces no pollution. From this insight many changes flow. Federal law should require state regulators to allow utilities the same profit on each kilowatt hour they save as on every kilowatt hour they generate. This simple regulatory change will unleash a vigorous new industry of mining waste in the electric sector.

In transportation, we need cars whose mileage is not equal to but better than anyone else's, because our population density is so low and our suburbs enshrine a heavy reliance on the automobile for years to come. Today Detroit is way behind. But this can be changed through a combination of innovative price and regulatory signals. In residential and commercial buildings, too, energy demand can be dramatically cut.

Step 3 is to get serious about developing new efficiency technologies and alternative energy sources. Nuclear energy should remain an option, but only after we have a hardheaded answer to the question of why a technology that has been commercialized for decades, which should be mature, should still require the lion's share of public R&D funds. Dollar for dollar, solar technologies and hydrogen as a replacement for gasoline show greater promise, as do energy storage technologies and other new opportunities.

Presidents Reagan and Bush have given us 10 years of non-leadership and worse on energy. But it must be said that leaders need followers, and so far we Americans have punished any politician with the courage to say out loud that energy prices are too low. We are properly consumed right now with resolving the immediate crisis, but five years from now what will most matter to us is not the fate of Saddam Hussein or the house of Saud, but whether three oil crises were enough to learn the energy lesson.

The writer is vice president of the World Resources Institute.

W.P. 8/30/90

USW(F) 1999-8

0157

: USW(F)-

: 장 관 발신 : 주미대사

보안
통제

(매)

Strategic Oil Reserve Still Growing

Bush's Decision Not to Tap Supply Appears to Pay Off—for Now

By Thomas W. Lippman
Washington Post Staff Writer

Four weeks after Iraq's invasion of Kuwait touched off the biggest oil crisis in a decade, the Bush administration is holding firm in its decision not to sell oil from the Energy Department's Strategic Petroleum Reserve.

In fact, the reserve is growing. A shipment due this week of oil purchased before the invasion will bring the total amount of government-owned oil stored in Louisiana salt caverns to just over 590 million barrels, according to Energy Department officials. That is about a 65-day supply at current import rates.

It is a measure of the wide range of oil prices in the 14 years since the reserve was created that the average price of those 590 million barrels was $27.26 a barrel—within a dollar of the opening price in yesterday's trading in New York. In the early 1980s, the Energy Department, like everyone else, was paying more than $30 a barrel. Early this year, the price was about $16. In the interim, the price was everywhere in between.

As crude oil prices doubled in about six weeks and retail gasoline prices went up about 20 percent, the administration resisted strong appeals from influential members of Congress, consumer groups and some independent energy analysts to open the reserve.

The policy gamble appears to have paid off, as prices have retreated sharply from last week's peak and the Organization of Petroleum Exporting Countries has ratified a decision by Saudi Arabia and some other members to increase production to compensate for the 4.3 million barrels of oil a day lost to world markets by the shutdown of Iraqi and Kuwaiti production. Commercially owned stocks of crude oil in the United States rose by 1 million barrels last week, according to the American Petroleum Institute.

As a result, pressure to open the reserve has eased, and the Energy Department still has an untouched

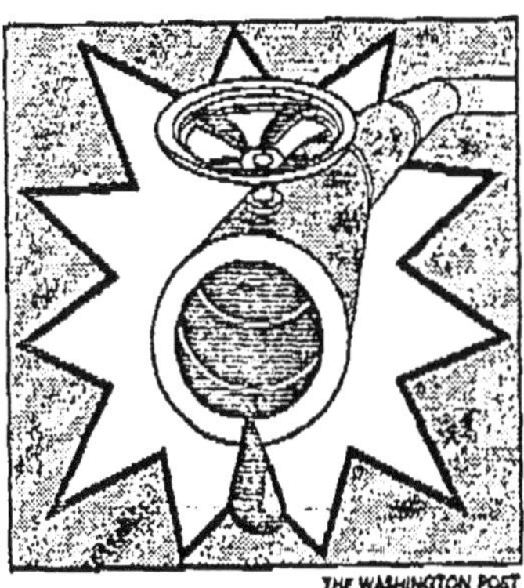
THE WASHINGTON POST

590 million-barrel ace in the hole to play if President Bush declares an energy emergency later this year.

Energy Department officials have told Congress that the president would consider putting some of the reserve oil on the market in an emergency, but they did not define "emergency." Many oil analysts, however, said that the mere existence of the reserve exerted a moderating influence on oil markets, preventing the panic buying that marked the oil crises of the 1970s.

Between them, Kuwait and Iraq supplied about 9 percent of the oil produced in the non-communist world, according to the Energy Department, and 8.7 percent of the roughly 9 million barrels a day that the United States imports, according the American Petroleum Institute.

The overnight removal of that oil from the supply stream sent prices spiraling upward, even though crude oil inventories were high, because traders and refiners feared they would not be able to get replacement oil when current stocks were used up. A barrel of crude oil that cost about $16 on the New York futures market in June cost nearly $32 last week.

Advocates of opening the reserve said it was created to help the United States cope with just such a crisis. They argued that the Energy Department could put 1 million barrels a day up for bid for three months, earning revenue and calming the oil markets while leaving most of the reserve intact.

Powerful members of Congress, including Senate Energy and Commerce Committee Chairman J. Bennett Johnston (D-La.) and Rep. Philip R. Sharp (D-Ind.), chairman of the House energy and power subcommittee, urged that the reserve be opened. But the Energy Department said no real supply crisis existed, and has refused to open the reserve as a means to hold down prices.

"We haven't seen anyone who disagrees with our calculations that there is no true supply-demand price increase. It's just the psychology of the market," said Deputy Energy Secretary W. Henson Moore. "We are looking at the true supply numbers."

Petroleum stocks in the United States, Japan and Europe are "500 million barrels above normal for this time of year," according to the Energy Department's "situation analysis report" of Aug. 14.

With oil flowing freely, even at much higher prices than last spring, President Bush accepted the Energy Department's argument that no attempt by the government to influence the market was justified and it was not necessary to dip into the government-owned reserve, administration officials said.

Some analysts have argued that this position cannot be maintained beyond October, when inventories dwindle and demand for heating oil begins to rise. For example, Arnold E. Safer, president of the Energy Futures Group in Bethesda, has calculated that no more than 200 million barrels of oil from commercially held stocks will be "immediately available" by then.

A supply reduction of 3 million barrels a day for 90 days "would exceed this quantity, clearly indicating the need for governmental release of strategic reserves of pehaps as much as 1 million barrels a day over the next 90 days," according to Safer.

Congress is expected to act next month on a bill that would increase the maximum size of the reserve from 750 million to 1 billion barrels.

W.P. 8/30/90

1λ(ω) 1∽) 1990 -9

0158

(F)-

관

발신 : 주미대사

보안 통제

(매)

본 전문의 누락부분은 (10page) 재송 요청중이므로 추후 재배부 하겠습니다. 통제관 :

IEA Would OK Use of Stocks In Oil Shortage

Knight-Ridder Financial

PARIS — The International Energy Agency is ready to declare this week that its member governments will release oil from their strategic stocks if supply shortages warrant such a move, IEA sources said.

Under current market conditions the IEA's governing board, due to meet here Friday, will not decide any immediate release, the sources predicted.

But a declaration, to be issued after the meeting, would aim to respond positively to an agreement in Vienna by 10 members of the Organization of Petroleum Exporting Countries to hike their oil output, they said.

The 10 OPEC members agreed Wednesday to permit cartel members to raise oil production above their quotas. This frees Saudi Arabia and Venezuela to increase production and help see that the embargo on oil from Iraq and Iraqi-held Kuwait does not create shortages and send prices sky-high.

Iraq and Libya boycotted the ministerial meeting at which the plan was discussed. Iran supported the arrangement, though objecting to the insufficient emphasis on the need for consumer stock releases.

IEA officials said the agency remained opposed to using strategic government stocks to massage market prices, despite a 1984 pact among the 21 member governments that envisaged doing that.

The consensus is that strategic stocks should be held back for meeting serious shortages that could still emerge if the Persian Gulf crisis drags on or escalates, they said.

Agency calculations indicate supplies, including oil company and floating OPEC stocks, should be adequate through to the end of October, they said.

But by November and December, with seasonal winter demand building up, serious supply shortages look probable. At that point government stock releases may be unavoidable, one source said.

JSC
8/30/90

USW(F) 3999-14. End

0159

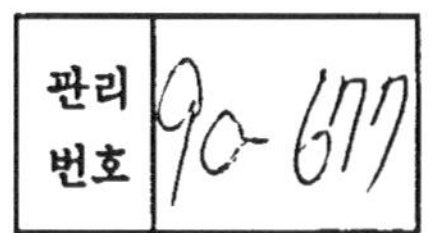

외 무 부

종 별 :

번 호 : JAW-5298 일 시 : 90 0831 1813

수 신 : 장관(중근동,아일,정일,경일)

발 신 : 주 일 대사(일정)

제 목 : 일정부 중동지원책

연 : JAW-5255

1. 일정부 관방장관은 8.30. 연호 다국적군 지원을 위한 수송, 물자, 의료 및 자금협력의 방법으로 10 억불을 금년도 예산에서 지출하기로 결정했다고 발표하였음.

2. 동 금액은 당초 지원책 발표시에는 금액 결정이 되지않은 상태에서 향후검토키로 한것이나, 8.29 카이후 수상이 연호 일본의 지원책을 발표한 직후 이를 서둘러 밝힌것은 미국측을 크게 의식한 카이후 수상의 정치적 결정으로 보여짐.

- 일 외무성에 의하면 당초 미측은 20-30 억불의 지원을 요청하였다고 하나, 90 년도 일정부의 예비비 총액이 3,500 억엥임에 비추어 금번 일정부의 10 억불(1,500 억엔)지원 금액규모는 금년 일정부의 예산에 상당한 부담으로 작용할것으로 보인다고함. 끝

(공사 김병연-국장)

90.12.31. 까지

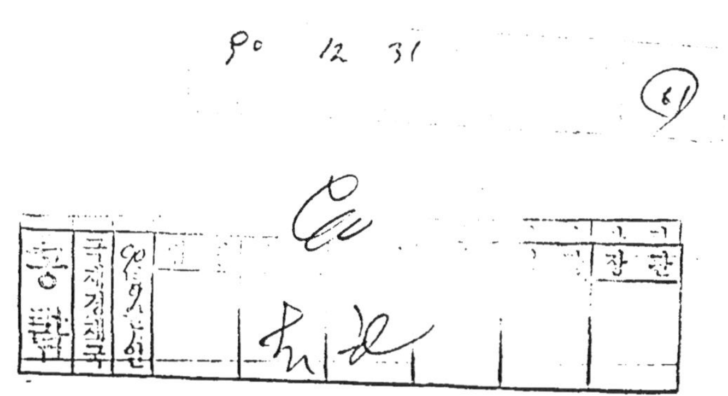

중아국 차관 1차보 2차보 아주국 경제국 정문국 청와대 안기부

PAGE 1

90.08.31 18:52

외신 2과 통제관 BT

0160

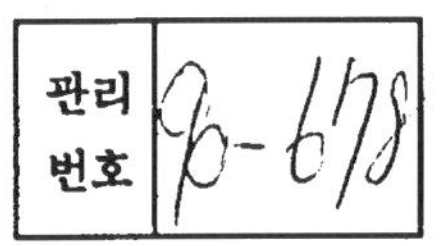

원 본

외 무 부

종 별 :

번 호 : SPW-0501 일 시 : 90 0831 1100

수 신 : 장관(기협, 구이)

발 신 : 주 스페인 대사

제 목 : 이라크.쿠웨이트 사태

대: WSP-0423

대호 다음과같이 조사 보고함.

1. 이라크. 쿠웨이트 물량감소에 대한 확보대책및 대응방안

가. 1989 년도 양국의 대주재국 원유공급량및 주재국의 전체수입량 대비

이라크:528 만톤(10.6 프로)

쿠웨이트:10 만톤(0.2 프로)

나. 확보대책

-멕시코:일당 15 만-18 만 배럴 대주재국 추가공급 약속(8.13)

-베네주엘라:5 억불규모 장기 공급계약 협의중(9.15. 양국간 혼성위에서 구체협의 예정)

1989 년도 멕시코, 베네주엘라의 대주재국 원유공급량은 각각 1 천만톤(주재국 전체수입량의 20.4 프로)및 5.7 만톤(주재국 전체수입량의 0.1 프로)임

다. 대응방안

-주재국 정부는 상기 원유확보대책과 병행하여 유류소비 절감대책을 수립, 분쟁사태 진전상황을 보아가면서 단계적 실시방안을 검토중임.

-동방안에는 차량 홀.짝수 운행, 냉방기 온도조절 , 차량시속 80 킬로 감속운행(8.31. 국제 에너지위원회에 제안 예정), 주유소 제한 운영등이 포함되여있음

2. 원유및 석유제품 비축현황, 비축유 방출여부및 향후계획

-주재국은 90 일분 원유(1,200 만톤 추정)를 비축하고 있다고 발표되였으며아직 동비축분을 방출하지않고 8.2. 분쟁발생이후 고가의 원유를 계속 도입하고 있는바 이러한 방침은 전쟁발발등 극한 상황 발생시까지 계속될것으로 전망함.

3. 주재국내 유류가격 동향

경제국 1차보 2차보 구주국 중아국 청와대 안기부 대책반

PAGE 1

국제경제국	90년 월 일	담 당	과 장	국 장	차관보	차 관	장 관

90.08.31 18:58

외신 2과 통제관 BT

0161

-7.10. 이후 주재국 정부는 석유시판 가격을 2 주단위로 조정(SPOT 가격, EC 가솔린가격, 분배비용등을 고려, 시판최고가격을 지정함) 시행하고 있는바 원유가격의 일시 하락에도 불구하고 시판가격은 계속 상승 추세임.

-슈퍼가격 변동추세

일자, 리터당최고가격, 시판가격(순서임)

7.10., 80.8 페세타,80 페세타

7.25., 81.3, 80

8.7., 83.3, 82

8.21., 86.1, 84

9.4., 91.8, --

4. 국제원유시장에 대한 수급및 가격 전망

-주재국은 소유원유의 97 프로를 도입(1989 년도 5 천만톤), 그중 75 프로를 내수에 충당하고 (전체 에너지 소비량의 53.54 프로를 차지함) 25 프로를 수출함.

-상기와 같이 주재국은 이락. 쿠웨이트 도입분을 멕시코.베네주엘라 추가도입으로 대체충당및 국내 소비절약을 통해 소요원유 물량확보에는 차질이 없는것으로 전망함.

-다만, 전세계 원유생산, 매장량의 상당부분을 차지하느 분쟁지역 사태가 계속 악화되여 국제원유가격이 장기간 고가로 지속될경우(언론은 전문가 전망으로 배럴당 40-50 불까지 가능하다고 보도), 주재국으로서도 향후 고인프레, 성장율저하등 과거 두차례와같은 석유파동(경기침체)가 도래하지 않을까 우려하고 있음.

(대사-국장)

예고 1990.12.31 일반

PAGE 2

0162

원 본

외 무 부

종 별 :

번 호 : USW-3983 일 시 : 90 0831 1757

수 신 : 장 관(기협)

발 신 : 주 미 대사

제 목 : 석유시장 및 유가동향(7)

표제관련, 8.31(금) 자 당지 언론 보도를 종합 보고함.

1. 유가 동향

가. 8.30 원유 및 정유 제품 가격 (뉴욕 상품 시장)

0 원유 (10월 인도가격)

:배럴당 26.77 불 (전일 대비 0.85 불상승)

0 휘발류 (9월 인도가격)

:갤런당 89.07 센트 (전일대비 4.35 센트 상승)

0 난방유(9월 인도가격)

:갤런당 75.54 센트 (전일대비 3.90 센트 상승)

나. 당지 전문가들은 8.30 정유제품 가격의 상승율이 원유가격 상승율보다 높은점을 지적하면서, 이락-쿠웨이트 사태가 장기화 될수록 정유제품의 부족 현상이 심화될것이라고 전망하고 있는바, 그이유는 아래와 같음.

0 일일 63만-80만 배럴에 달했던 이락-쿠웨이트로부터의 정유제품 공급 중단

0 페르시아만 지역에서의 군사작전으로 인해 제트 연료, 등유, 난방유등 정유제품의 시장 공급량이 일일 50만 배럴 감소

0 서방국의 정유 시설은 현재 완전 가동 중인바추가 생산 능력이 없음.

0 이락-쿠웨이트산 원유는 다량의 고급 정유제품 생산에 적합한 경질유였으나 기타 OPEC 국가가 증산 예정인 원유는 고급 정유제품 생산비율이 낮은 중질유임.

0 서방국가의 전략 비축분은 정유 제품은 없고 원유뿐임.

0 겨울철에는 휘발유.난방유등 정유제품에 대한 수요가 증대됨.

다. IEA 의 한 석유전문가는 향후 세계 석유시장의 수급 전망에 대해 언급, 현재로서는 산유국의 증산 실시 및 석유회사의 비축분 사용등을 통해 공급 부족량이

경제국 2차보 미주국 동자부

PAGE 1

90.09.01 09:32 WG

외신 1과 통제관

0163

10 만 배럴에 불과하다고 평가하고 (수급 상황은 별첨 FAX 참조)동 공급 부족량은 10월 중 20만 배럴로, 12월중50만 배럴로 증가될것이며, 공급부족량이 50만배럴 이상에 달할 경우 IEA 회원국은 전략비축 석유를 방출해야할 것이라고 전망하였음.

2. 주재국 대책

0 부쉬 대통령은 8.30 금번 중동사태에 대한 기자회견에서 미국은 현재 세계 원유 수급 상황을 비교적 안정적이라고 평가하고 있으며 심각한 수급불균형이 도래하리라고는 예측하지 않는다고 발언하였음.

3. 금 8.31 당지 언론 보도 내용을 별첨 FAX송부함.

첨부: USW(F)-2014 (11 매)

(대사 박동진-국장)

주 미 대 사 관

보안 통제 : 외

번호 : USW(F) - 2014

수신 : 장관(기협)

발신 : 주미대사

제목 : USW - 3983 첨부 (1매)

Renewed Jitters Boost Prices Of Oil, Products

Concern Is Solution for Gulf Won't Be Found in Time To Avoid Tight Supplies

By ALLANNA SULLIVAN
Staff Reporter of THE WALL STREET JOURNAL

Oil prices rose on renewed jitters that a solution to the Persian Gulf crisis might not be found quickly enough to prevent a tight supply situation, climbing 85 cents a barrel to $26.77.

Traders late yesterday said they perceived that peace initiatives by the U.N. seemed destined to produce little progress.

Product prices moved upward more quickly than crude prices because market participants are finally realizing that if and when a shortage as a result of the embargo of Iraqi-Kuwaiti crudes arises, it will likely hit the products sector first. "We are consuming products faster than we are producing them," said Ted Eck, economist for Amoco Corp. "There are no refined products in the strategic petroleum reserve, just crude."

Gasoline futures prices for September delivery rose 4.35 cents a gallon to 89.07 cents, while heating oil for the same month climbed by 3.90 cents to 75.54 cents.

Capital Flows Out of Mideast

The Gulf crisis leads wealthy individuals from the Mideast to buy billions of dollars of relatively stable Western currencies and to sell less-liquid securities and local investments, according to international bankers. Story on page C1.
In other developments:

- **Americans working in Saudi Arabia get by with relative calm, A8.**
- **China has a chance to reassert its role in international politics, A8.**

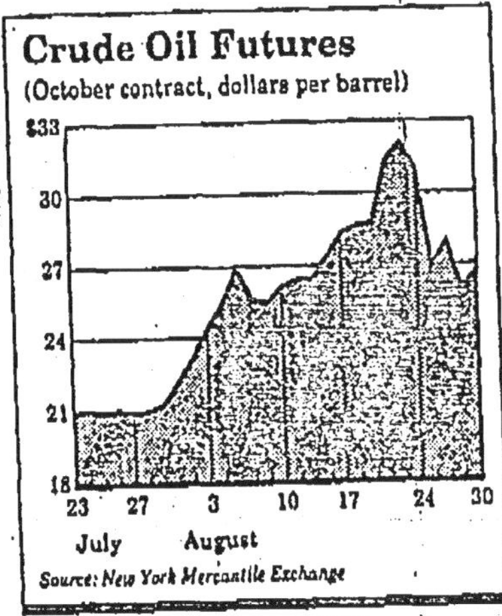

Indeed analysts and industry executives are becoming increasingly concerned that the longer the crisis persists, the more difficult it will be to replace dwindling product supplies. Under the best of situations, refining capacity in the U.S. can barely meet the needs of consumers. Mr. Eck added that world-wide the war has already knocked out 600,000 barrels a day of refining capacity in Kuwait, where several sophisticated facilities capable of putting out high-quality refined products have been closed down.

Members of the Organization of Petroleum Exporting Countries Wednesday promised to increase their output by at least three million barrels daily to make up for the Iraq-Kuwait shortfall. But at least for the short term, markets will remain short of one million barrels of daily production.

Remarks made by Sun Co. Chairman Robert McClements to analysts yesterday did little to allay fears. He told the gathering that the additional production brought on line by global producers during the crisis would be of lesser quality than crude that has been previously available. These crudes, he explained, will yield less gasoline and other refined products.

In addition, reports that oil workers in Brazil were threatening to strike sparked buying in the gasoline pit. Brazil exports gasoline to U.S. markets. Also perceived as bullish were reports by Dow Jones International Petroleum Report that Yemen, a small Middle Eastern producer, would be unable to export any oil in September because it needed to use all of its oil internally. Yemen feeds some of its refineries with Iraqi crude.

WSJ 8/31

0165

AUG.31 '90 18:■ KOREAN EMBASSY WASHINGTON DC P.06

주 미 대 사 관

보안	
통제	

번호 : USW(F) -

수신 : 장관(

발신 : 주미대사

제목 :

Wholesale Gasoline Price Soars

By KEITH BRADSHER

Wholesale gasoline prices surged yesterday, reflecting traders' concerns about low supplies and strong demand. Crude oil prices also rose, with the contract for October delivery up 85 cents a barrel, or 3.3 percent, to $26.77 on the New York Mercantile Exchange.

Also unsettling the markets were remarks by Saddam Hussein, Iraq's President, yesterday and late Wednesday. Traders feared that war remained a possibility in the Middle East.

Even small news items, like reports of large gasoline contract purchases by an unidentified Wall Street brokerage house at midday, produced large price swings in tense trading, said Michael Wilner, the president of Hilltop Trading Company Inc., an independent trading and brokerage firm on the floor of the New York Mercantile Exchange.

'Getting Battle Weary'

"The main thing that's happening in these energy markets is that people are incredibly, incredibly nervous, and the activity is absolutely frenetic," he said, adding, "Judgments tend to be a little less than keen right now, because people are getting battle weary."

Trading of gasoline, heating oil and other petroleum products was particularly heavy on the eve of the expiration of some futures contracts today. Traders who had committed to delivering oil scrambled to find cargos to meet these contracts. Large oil companies are holding most of the available stocks and are selling little, Mr. Wilner said.

The gasoline contract for September delivery rose 4.35 cents a gallon, or 5.1 percent, to close at 89.07 cents. The contract for September delivery of heating oil increased 3.9 cents, or 5.4 percent, to close at 75.54 cents a gallon.

Traders and analysts said there were widespread concerns about possible shortages of refinery capacity. Kuwait and Iraq, which exported fourmillion barrels of oil exports a day before a United Nations embargo was imposed, sent out 630,000 to 800,000 barrels of that as refined products.

Although the Organization of Petroleum Exporting Countries authorized all production necessary to stabilize energy markets on Wednesday, a move that could lead to an extra four million barrels a day, almost all of that will be shipped as crude for lack of extra refinery capacity, said Fareed Mohamedi, an economist at the Petroleum Finance Company in Washington.

"I think that'll result in stock drawdowns," he said.

Another factor is that Kuwaiti and Iraqi oilfields produce a lighter oil that, when refined, yields a higher proportion of gasoline than oil from most other countries.

Military activities in the Persian Gulf and reduced refinery production there could trim exports of such petroleum products as jet fuel, household kerosene and home heating oil by 500,000 barrels a day, Bernard J. Picchi, an oil industry analyst at Salomon Brothers in New York, said. A lack of refinery capacity will become "particularly noticeable" as winter approaches, with shortages possibly resulting, and gasoline and heating oil prices almost certainly rising, he said.

The Strategic Petroleum Reserve, a Government emergency stockpile, consists of crude oil, not petroleum products, Mr. Picchi added.

Down to 210 Million Barrels

But some experts contended yesterday that enough refinery capacity could be found. William D. Hermann, the chief economist of the Chevron Corporation, said that while refineries in the United States were already very busy, there was extra capacity elsewhere.

Some of the 120 older, mostly small refineries in the United States that have been closed in the last 10 years could probably be reopened if needed, he said.

The American Petroleum Institute estimated Tuesday that the nation's gasoline stocks were down to 210 million barrels, not far above the 200 million barrel minimum that oil companies try to have on hand for routine operations. A three-week moving average shows American demand for gasoline set a new record last week, and demand will probably be strong over the Labor Day weekend, said Robert S. Jonke, an energy futures trader at Cargill Investor Services.

NYT - 8/31/90

2014 -2

0166

AUG.31 '90 18:0▬ REAN EMBASSY WASHINGTON DC P.003

주 미 대 사 관

보안 통제

번호 : USW(F) -

수신 : 장관(

발신 : 주미대사

제목 :

Oil Shortage Is Seen by Year-End

By STEVEN GREENHOUSE

Special to The New York Times

PARIS, Aug. 30 — Officials at the International Energy Agency, which represents 21 oil-consuming nations, predict that a substantial oil shortage will develop late this year. At present, however, daily worldwide demand for oil is only slightly greater than supply, despite the embargo on Iraqi and Kuwaiti crude.

As the agency's governing board prepared for a meeting on Friday, an official said the worldwide shortage in September would be only 100,000 barrels a day, despite the loss of some 4.3 million barrels a day from Iraq and Kuwait.

As a result, a senior agency official predicted in an interview, the United States, West Germany, Japan and other members of the agency at Friday's meeting would probably postpone any decision to begin drawing oil from their government-controlled strategic reserves, saying only that they will act at the appropriate time.

Known as Consumers' Club

Industrialized oil-consuming nations formed the agency in 1974 to help protect against oil shocks. The agency has worked to develop policies, like increasing strategic reserves and putting in place emergency conservation programs, to help cope with an oil crisis. It has also encouraged alternative energy forms like coal and nuclear power.

The agency — often called the oil consumers club — includes the United States, Canada, Japan, most Western European nations, Australia and New Zealand. The group, which acts by consensus and is charged with coordinating the industrialized world's response to an energy crisis, is highly regarded for the work it does in monitoring oil supply and demand.

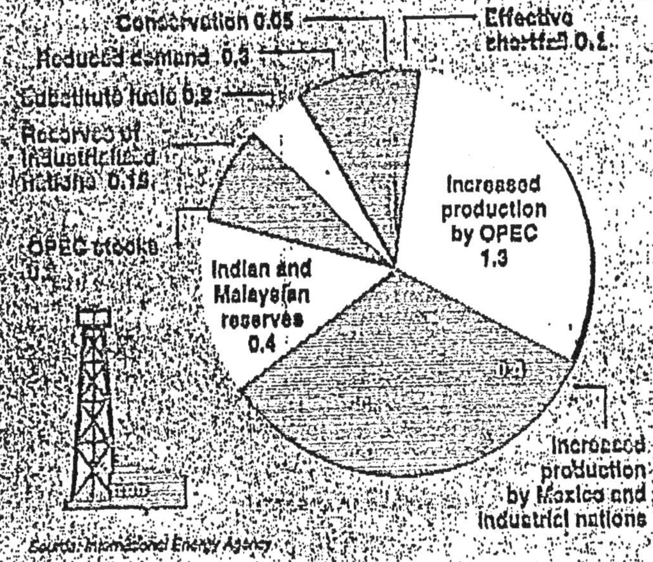

The New York Times

Agency officials said a serious shortage had not yet developed because oil companies had drawn down their petroleum stocks, production had increased in some countries and demand had dropped modestly.

But a senior agency economist said that — despite Wednesday's decision by the Organization of Petroleum Exporting Countries to allow members who can produce more oil to begin pumping immediately, the worldwide shortage could rise to 200,000 barr a day in October and to more th 500,000 barrels a day in December demand swells with cold weather a as oil companies and some countri feel they should stop drawing dov their stocks.

OPEC officials said their acti would replace nearly all the oil l

Continued on Page D4

NYT 8/31/90

2014 —3

0167

AUG.31 '90 09 KOREAN EMBASSY WASHINGTON DC P.

Substantial Oil Shortage Seen by Year-E

Continued From First Business Page

from Iraq and Kuwait, but agency officials expect the move to add only four million barrels a day.

"A shortage of 100,000 barrels a day is manageable, but uncomfortable, but a shortage of 500,000 barrels a day is unmanageable," said an agency official. "If it gets up above that level, then the shoe really starts to pinch." Member governments might then decide to draw down their strategic reserves, agency officials say.

Many oil experts and economists have criticized the agency's members for their refusal so far to tap their emergency reserves. They say such a move would have gone far to hold down oil prices, forestalling damage to the world's economic growth.

But agency officials say that the United States and other leading agency members contend that the reserves should be drawn down only when there is a serious shortage. "The philosophy, particularly among the major holders of emergency stocks, is to look at the situation in terms of physical volume, rather than influencing the market," said an agency economist.

Peter Bogin, a Paris-based oil economist with Cambridge Energy Research Associates, agrees with the I.E.A. that a significant shortage will develop by late fall. "In the November-December period things will start to get a little more hairy," he said. "Even with the OPEC decision, you're still not going to get the full four million barrels a day, and the quality of the replacement oil is not as good as the missing Iraqi and Kuwaiti oil."

Saudi Arabian officials said they had increased production to 7.5 million barrels a day, from 5.5 million, and would lift their output to 8 million by September; Venezuela plans to increase its output by some 500,000 barrels a day. But much of the Saudi oil is medium and heavy, and the Venezuelan oil is also heavy. This, oil experts say, will mean a shortage of light oil and its derivatives — kerosene, airplane fuel and gasoline — and possibly an excess of heavy products, like sludgy oil derivatives used for paving roads.

Agency officials calculate a 100,000-barrel daily shortfall in September, given a 4.3-million-barrel Iraqi-Kuwait loss, in the following way:

¶Oil companies will draw down their stocks by about one million barrels a day, and OPEC natio[ns] duce their stocks on the sea[s] 200,000 barrels.

¶OPEC is expected to [in]creased daily production b[y] ... lion barrels by late Septem[ber] ... ico by 100,000 barrels a day a[nd] ... trialized nations by 300,000.

¶Non-OPEC non-indu[strialized] countries like Malaysia and ... expected to draw down their ... by some 600,000 barrels a day.

¶Demand will be redu[ced by] 150,000 barrels a day as the i[ndustri]alized countries stop buildi[ng] strategic reserves, by 200,000 ... a day as power plans switch t[o substi]tute fuels from oil and by 300,... rels a day as a result of hig[her] prices.

¶Government-encouraged [conser]vation could pare demand by ... 50,000 barrels a day.

Robert Mabro, director of t[he Ox]ford Institute for Energy Re[search] said the agency's scenario m[ay be] overly optimistic. He que[stioned] whether oil companies would b[e will]ing to draw down their comm[ercial] stocks to the extent the agency sees. He also said that even i[f they] did, they would ultimately move [to re]build those stocks, which cou[ld in]crease daily demand, and thus ... vate the supply imbalance.

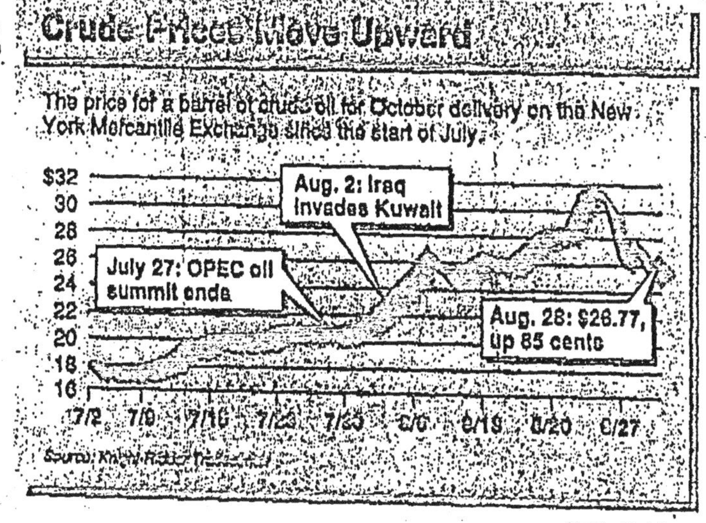

The New York Times

2014 -4

0168

AUG.31 '90 18: KOREAN EMBASSY WASHINGTON DC P.005

주 미 대 사 관

보안	
통제	

번호 : USW(F) -

수신 : 장관

발신 : 주미대사

제목 :

WT 8/31/90

Bush sees stability in world oil market

FROM COMBINED DISPATCHES

President Bush said yesterday the United States expects no "major imbalances" in the oil markets from the Persian Gulf supply cutoff stemming from Iraq's invasion of Kuwait.

"At the present time we don't anticipate major imbalances in the oil market," Mr. Bush told a news conference.

The Iraqi invasion Aug. 2 ignited a swift rise in the nation's oil prices, with fears of a broader military conflict raising the U.S. benchmark price last week to a seven-year high of $32.35 a barrel, from $21.55 the day before the invasion.

On the New York Mercantile Exchange oil futures rose yesterday. Light sweet crude for October delivery closed at $26.77 a barrel, up 85 cents, after dropping nearly $2 Wednesday.

The president praised the Organization of Petroleum Exporting Countries for increasing its oil production to make up for some of the 4 million barrels a day previously produced by Kuwait and Iraq.

"We are pleased with OPEC's decision to help take up the slack in crude-oil production and although we're in what I would see as a transition period, the situation appears manageable," Mr. Bush said.

see OIL, page C7

OIL

From page C1

The president also said the U.S. government-owned Strategic Petroleum Reserve, which holds nearly 600 million barrels of oil in deep caverns in Texas and Louisiana, has been tested and would be available "if it is truly needed."

"Right now the situation, I would say, is relatively stable," he said.

Texas energy regulators yesterday voted in an emergency session to allow maximum output from most of the state's oil wells starting tomorrow — a move that will boost output by 20,000 to 30,000 barrels per day to help ease shortfalls caused by the Mideast crisis.

The Texas Railroad Commission, which regulates the state's energy industry, lifted production limits after deciding that increased output would not cause long-term damage to oilfields.

The commission approved the increase at the request of the federal government, which is attempting to boost domestic energy production to reduce the effects of the world embargo on oil from Kuwait and

The state currently pro[...] about 1.7 million barrels per d[...]

"Every little bit helps," co[...] sion chairman Kent Hance sai[...]

Mr. Hance said he expect[...] United States to face an oil cru[...] 90 days if the Gulf crisis do[...] end.

Meanwhile, Venezuela order[...] state-owned oil monopoly Petr[...] de Venezuela (PDVSA) to start[...] ing extra petroleum on the m[...] company President Arturo [...] Pietri said yesterday.

He said PDVSA was order[...] begin selling oil above the cou[...] OPEC quota of 1.94 million ba[...] per day.

At a ceremony to celebrate t[...] monopoly's 15th anniversary, he [...] gested Venezuelan oil could sup[...] Middle Eastern sources.

"Industrialized nations will [...] tolerate again a growing de[...] dence on Middle East oil," he sa[...]

Mr. Sosa Pietri said Brazil [...] Spain will each receive 50,000 [...] rels per day of Venezuela's [...] tional crude, while India woul[...] ceive 10,000 barrels per day an[...] United States would get 200,000 [...] rels.

2014 .

0169

AUG.31 '90 18:1 · KOREAN EMBASSY WASHINGTON DC

P.006

번호 : USW(F) -

수신 : 장관

발신 : 주미대사

제목 :

Effect of Gulf crisis 'could be devastating'

By Paul Betts, Aerospace Correspondent

AN EXTENDED period of high crude oil prices caused by the Gulf crisis could have a "devastating" impact on the commercial aerospace industry with the potential loss of more than $380bn of business over the next 20 years.

Mr Lou Harrington, general manager of the McDonnell Douglas MD-11 and DC-10 commercial aircraft programme, warned yesterday at a Financial Times aerospace conference that a $50-a-barrel crude oil price over a protracted period would reduce demand for commercial jet aircraft by more than 45 per cent between now and 2010.

McDonnell Douglas is currently forecasting, on the assumption of world economic growth based on a $18 a barrel crude oil price, a total of 14,078 new passenger aircraft deliveries during the next 20 years worth a total of $843.7bn

However, he believed, like other aerospace executives, that there was a low risk that oil prices would remain at such significantly high levels for an extended period. If they stayed high for a temporary period, demand for new aircraft was expected to decline by a much lower rate of around 10-15 per cent. This would still be significant but not devastating, he said.

Mr Frank Turner, the director of civil engines at Rolls-Royce, said the whole industry was concerned by the situation in the Gulf and the long-term effect on oil prices. But he argued that the experience of the 1973 and 1979 oil shocks was that short-term dramatic increases in oil prices served only to delay growth in air travel and did not undermine the underlying growth trend.

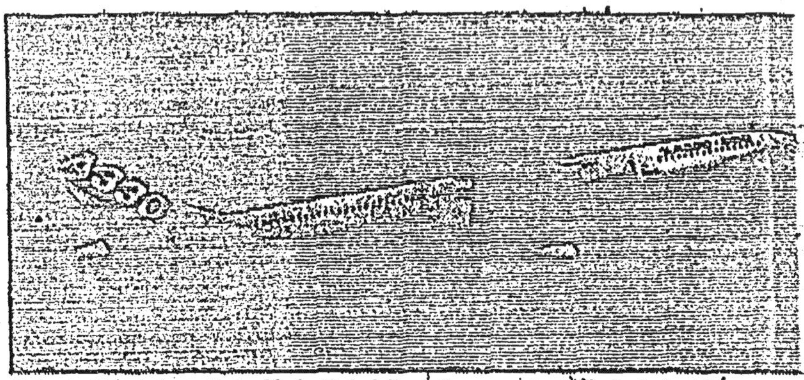

Airbus's A330 twin-engine wide-bodied airliner: faces a potentially turbulent future

Rolls-Royce is predicting a $1.6bn market for civil engines and spares over the next 15 years. "Although there may well be perturbations emanating from the current crisis, we remain optimistic that this market is still there, with an underlying trend towards fewer, larger engines per aircraft," Mr Turner said.

Mr Chris Longridge, vice-president of sales of Boeing's commercial aircraft group, broadly agreed with the McDonnell Douglas forecasts of the possible impact of higher oil prices on the commercial jet aircraft business. But he also suggested it was unlikely oil prices would remain at excessive levels for a long period.

He said Boeing was still forecasting a total of $626bn worth of new aircraft deliveries between now and 2005. For aircraft manufacturers, he argued that the most pressing problem was to catch up with the growth in demand for new aircraft from airline companies.

The three large airframe manufacturers – Boeing, Airbus Industrie and McDonnell Douglas – had a combined order backlog of $175bn. Boeing, the biggest of the three, had a backlog of $91bn.

Mr Longridge said all Boeing's production lines were full and the company was investing to boost production rates to meet demand. After delivering

CONFERENCE

AEROSPACE

284 aircraft last year, Boeing expected to deliver 351 aircraft this year. The rate was expected to increase to 419 aircraft deliveries next year.

"By mid-1991, we will be producing aircraft at a rate of 38 per month," the Boeing executive said, adding that if longer-term economic conditions remained favourable the company could be producing

0170

more than 500 aircraft a year by the middle of the decade.

He disclosed that Boeing was considering the development of an even larger Boeing 747 jumbo airliner with a maximum gross weight of more than 1m lb carrying up to 600 passengers as far as 8,000 nautical miles.

However, the industry is still waiting for Boeing to launch its 767-X, a 350-seat twin-engine wide-body aircraft which will compete against the Airbus A330 and the McDonnell Douglas MD-11 trijet.

"We are working very closely with several airlines to finalise the aircraft's configuration and will start major assembly in 1992 with certification and delivery in 1995," Mr Longridge said. Boeing is studying new technological innovations for the new wide-body aircraft including the possibility of a folding wingtip to give the aircraft more flexibility on the ground to park at airport terminal bays.

But Boeing is facing stiff competition from both Airbus and McDonnell Douglas in this market. Indeed, Boeing is trailing its two competitors in this field.

McDonnell Douglas expects to complete the certification of the MD-11 next October and start delivering the first aircraft to customers before the end of the year. McDonnell Douglas is also expected to launch a stretched version of the trijet early next year and is talking with Japanese partners to take a large risk-sharing interest in the project, known as the MD-12X, which will involve the development of a new wing.

The European Airbus consortium is also expected to unveil more details at the Farnborough Air Show next week of a stretched version of its A330 wide-body twin engine airliner.

Wide-body aircraft are expected to account for an increasingly large proportion of the commercial aircraft business in coming years. Just as the three leading airframe manufacturers are vying for a big slice of this market, the three big aero-engine makers are battling for a share of this business by offering new, more powerful engines to power this new generation of aircraft.

Rolls-Royce is competing in this market with its Trent engine against General Electric's new GE90 big thrust engine programme and Pratt & Whitney's PW4000 series.

But Mr Arthur Wegner, president of Pratt & Whitney, asked yesterday whether there was room in the market for three or more competitors developing separate products for the same market. "How big will the market actually be and how many winners, how many losers, will emerge?" he asked.

2 of 2

2014 — 7

0171

Flood of Ship Surcharges Appears To Recede

CONTINUED FROM PAGE 1A

charges are now $40 a TEU and $80 an FEU.

• Also effective Sept. 15, south European traffic served by the South Europe USA Rate Agreement and its sister conference will get fuel surcharges of $120 a TEU and $180 an FEU.

To the Far East

• The Transpacific Westbound Rate Agreement had scheduled an increase from $64 a TEU and $80 an FEU to $176 a TEU and $220 an FEU by Sept. 7. The group is already moving to adjust those charges downward.

• The Asia North America Eastbound Rate Agreement scheduled a series of fuel surcharge increases. For a 40-foot box, the group's typical equipment size, the surcharge will go up from $55 to $330-$370, depending on height, by Sept. 10. That would build to $605 to $680 by Oct. 1 and $880 by Nov. 1.

To Africa

• Effective Sept. 23, the U.S/Southern Africa Conference will put in a new charge amounting to 5% of the base freight rate. The American West African Freight Conference also plans new charges of $120 a TEU and $200 an FEU eastbound and $240 a TEU and $400 an FEU westbound effective Sept. 13.

• The U.S. Eastern Mediterranean-North Africa Rate Agreement will charge $300 a TEU and $600 an FEU, effective Sept. 6, with additional increases to $500 a TEU and $800 an FEU. Currently the charges are $175 a TEU and $315 an FEU.

• The Mediterranean Pacific Coast Conference has scheduled a new surcharge of $70 a TEU and $130 an FEU for Sept. 10.

To Australia and Indian Ocean

• The U.S. Atlantic and Gulf to Australia New Zealand Conference and the Pacific Coast/Australia-New Zealand Tariff Bureau will charge 2.62% of the freight bill for shipments to Australia and 3.55 % for moves to New Zealand, effective Sept. 16.

• The Indian, Pakistan, Bangladesh, Ceylon & Burma Outward Freight Conference and its sister conference moving goods back announced surcharges of $220 a TEU and $350 an FEU, effective Sept. 21.

To South America

• The Inter-American Freight Conference said goods from Brazil will be charged 17% of the freight bill, and goods moving to Brazil will be charged 11% of the freight bill, effective Sept. 1. Those charges were 9% and 3.5%, respectively.

• The U.S.-Colombia Conference will charge $9.50 a ton, with a $180 minimum, effective Sept. 9. On Oct. 8 that charge is slated to increase to $15 a ton with a $250 minimum.

• U.S. Atlantic Gulf-Venezuela Freight Conference plans an increase from $60 to $120 a TEU and $100 to $200 an FEU, effective Sept. 9.

• The U.S. Ecuador Freight Association will start charging $90 a TEU and $120 an FEU, effective Sept. 9.

• The U.S.-West Coast of South America Conference plans new surcharges of $100 a TEU and $150 an FEU, effective Sept. 13. Those surcharges are cleared to double Sept. 14.

7 0

2014 -9

0172

AUG.31 '90 18:1 REAN EMBASSY WASHINGTON DC 주미대사관

P.010

보안 통제

번호 : USW(F)

수신 : 장관

발신 : 주미대사

제목 :

JOC 8/31/90

Big Railroads Plan Broad Rate Increases

By GEOFFREY BROWN
Journal of Commerce Staff

WASHINGTON — Most major railroads announced plans to increase freight rates by about 4% due to the recent surge in diesel fuel prices brought on by the confrontation in the Persian Gulf.

But the increases are being taken independently, unlike in 1975 when the nation's rail carriers collectively filed for a fuel surcharge tariff, said John Dobrzynski, the Chicago Board of Trade's transportation manager.

CSX Transportation Inc., for example, is seeking from the Interstate Commerce Commission a 4% increase on all traffic except coal and recyclables such as scrap aluminum, effective Oct. 1.

Consolidated Rail Corp. said it expects to implement a 4% rate increase on most joint-line traffic, effective Oct. 1.

- Trucking rate bureaus apply for fuel surcharges to aid companies. Story, Page 2B.
- Truckers attack third-party transportation companies for refusing to accept fuel surcharges. Story, Page 2B.

Norfolk Southern Corp. reported plans for an across-the-board rate increase of 4% on all joint and single-line traffic except coal, coke, iron ore and contract rates, effective Oct. 1.

Union Pacific Railroad Co. said it will seek an across-the-board increase of 4% on all joint-line traffic except for contract rates, effective Oct. 1.

Companies that ship products not subject to government regulation have been notified by Union Pacific that a 4% rate increase will take effect Sept. 15.

John Bromley, a Union Pacif-

SEE BIG, PAGE 10A

1 of 2

2014 — 10

0173

Big Railroads Plan Broad Rate Increases

CONTINUED FROM PAGE 1A

ic spokesman, said the rate increase is intended to cover higher health, welfare and labor costs as well as rising diesel prices and therefore would not be rescinded if the threat of war in the Middle East evaporated.

He added that fuel price increases stemming from the Middle East conflict will cost Union Pacific more than $15 million in August and September.

Burlington Northern Railroad Co. also said it no longer could absorb increased diesel costs and other expenses, such as the workplace injury costs paid under the Federal Employers' Liability Act.

Burlington Northern said it plans to raise joint-line freight rates by an average of 4%. A spokesman said it was also looking into increasing rates for traffic that moves only on Burlington Northern track.

Atchison, Topeka & Santa Fe Railway Co. said it is seeking a 4% rate increase on all joint and single-line regulated traffic, effective Sept. 14. Santa Fe also plans to impose a 2.5% fuel surcharge on deregulated joint-line traffic, effective Sept. 22.

Last week, the Santa Fe imposed a 2.5% fuel surcharge on intermodal traffic and carload deregulated traffic originating and terminating on its line.

Illinois Central Railroad Co. said it intends to publish a selective rate increase of 4% on all joint-line traffic, except intermodal and contract traffic, effective Oct. 1.

Unlike the trucking industry, which must provide seven days' notice to raise rates, railroads must notify the ICC 20 days prior to raising their rates.

In addition, because Canadian carriers must give 30 days' public notice before raising their rates, to accommodate joint-line rates and for the sake of uniformity, Union Pacific has adopted the 30-day standard throughout its system.

The ICC said that as of Thursday no railroads had filed for rate increases. Railroads can request special permission to file for a rate increase on less than 20 days' notice, a spokesman for the commission said.

Fuel represents about 7% of operating costs for railroads, but comprises only about 20% of the operating costs of some trucking companies.

Soo Line Railroad Co. said it is seeking rate increases on intermodal traffic averaging from 2.5% to 4% effective in the near future. Some increases are also expected for joint-line traffic.

Southern Pacific Transportation Co. also announced a 4% rate increase on most regulated and deregulated railroad shipments.

Philip Baumel, an Iowa State University transportation economist, said it's uncertain whether the higher rates will stick.

"Grain bins are nearly empty, so it's unlikely there will be much distressed selling of this year's (grain) harvest, plus exports are likely to be down somewhat," he said.

"The rail lines with no direct barge alternative will probably have the best luck in being able to hold the rate increases," he added.

2 of 2

2014. 11. End.

0174

원 본

외 무 부

종 별 :

번 호 : HUW-0372 일 시 : 90 0831 1630

수 신 : 장 관 (경자,미북,정일) 사본: 주미대사 (필)

발 신 : 주 휴스턴 총영사

제 목 : 석유동향 보고 (4)

1. 8.30. 현재 서부텍사스 중질원유 10월 인도가격은 어제보다 85센트상승, 베럴당 26.77불로 거래됨.

2. 부시대통령은 8.30. 미국내 석유생산업자들에게 이락및 쿠웨이트로부터 공급받아온 1일 70만베럴 부족해소를 위해 향후 90일간 석유생산 증가를 요청하였음. 텍사스주는 최근까지 1일 170만베렐을 생산해 왔는바 석유업자들은 대통령의 요청에 따라 1일 2만베럴을 증산할 것으로 보인다함. 텍사스주는 현재의 시설을 100프로 가동할경우 1일 3만베럴 증산이 가능하나 업자들은 단기적 수요충족을 위해 증산하는 것이장기적으로 손해이기 때문에 증산을 기피하는 경향을 보이고 있다함.

3. MICHAEL MCELWRATH 미에너지성 부차관보는 미국이 현재의 석유생산시설을 모두 가동하는등 가능한 모든조치를 취할 경우 연말까지 1일 25만베럴 증산이 가능할 것이라고 언급함.

(총영사 허승-국장)

경제국 미주국 정문국 2차보 동자부

PAGE 1

90.09.01 09:50 FC

외신 1과 통제관

0175

정 리 보 존 문 서 목 록					
기록물종류	일반공문서철	등록번호	2021010196	등록일자	2021-01-27
분류번호	763.5	국가코드	XF	보존기간	영구
명 칭	걸프사태 : 국제원유 수급 동향, 1990-91. 전6권				
생 산 과	기술협력과	생산년도	1990~1991	담당그룹	
권 차 명	V.3 1990.9-12월				
내용목차	* 국제원유 수급 및 유가전망, 원유 안정확보를 위한 대산유국 외교활동 강화 등				

0001

관리 번호 90-671

분류번호 | 보존기간

발 신 전 보

번 호 : WFR-1678 900901 1108 FC 종별 :

수 신 : 주 불 대사. 총영사

발 신 : 장 관 (기협)

제 목 : 이라크·쿠웨이트 사태

대 : FRW - 1573

대호 IEA측 관심사항에 대한 자료를 다음 통보함

1. 아국의 oil stock 정책 및 현황

o 정책

- 정부비축량, 현재 60일분 확보 목표

- 민간 정유사에 대해서는 현재 비축의무가 없으나, 향후 비축 의무 부과 방안 검토중

o 정부비축현황 : 39,800천 배럴

- 원유 38,000천 배럴, 제품 1,800천 배럴

2. 아국의 원유수입선별 도입현황 (90년 상반기, 단위 천B/D)

o 오만 (211), 이란 (104), UAE (163), 사우디(50), 쿠웨이트(70), 이라크(39), 카타르(24), 중립지대(37), 말련(83), 브루나이(33), 중국(30), 인니(43), 호주(4), 에쿠아돌(6), 멕시코(3), 카나다(13), 이집트(7), 알제리(8) : 총 928

/계속...

90. 12. 31

①조기2차관보: ②아중동국장:

앙 고 재	90년 9월 1일	기술협력과	기안자 성명		과 장	심의관	국 장		차 관	장 관
			홍석화		(서명)	(서명)	전결			(서명)

보안 통제

외신과통제

0002

3. 걸프사태가 아국의 원유수급 및 가격에 미치는 영향 및 대책

가. 영향

o 원유수급

- 이라크·쿠웨이트로부터의 장기도입물량 중단

· 이라크 20천B/D, 쿠웨이트 55천B/D

- 단기적으로는 정부비축량, 도입선 전환, 현물시장 확보등으로 수급대처 가능

o 유가

- 국제 유가인상으로 국내유가인상 압박

· 국제원유가 1$ 상승시 국내유가 5%, 도매물가 0.44% P 소비자 물가 0.07% P 상승요인

- 금년내에는 석유사업기금 (1조6천억원) 및 관세율 조정 (10%→1%)등을 통해 국내 유가 인상없이 대처 방침이나 내년에는 인상 불가피

나. 대책

o 우선 이라크·쿠웨이트산 원유도입 부족 물량 대체 확보

- 기개발 해외유전 원유도입, 사우디, 멕시코, 이란 원유 증량 도입 추진등

o 에너지 소비절약

o 원유도입선 다변화 : 현재 중동지역으로부터 75% 이상 도입

o 장기 계약 도입 확대

o 원유 및 가스개발참여 확대

o 대체 에너지 개발등을 통한 석유의존도 완화

(국제경제국장 최대화)

0003

관리 번호	90-674

	분류번호	보존기간

발 신 전 보

번 호 : WIR-0298 900901 1109 FC 종별 :

수 신 : 주 이란 대사. 총영사

발 신 : 장 관 (기협)

제 목 : 원유도입 교섭

대 : IRW - 0438, 0457

연 : WIR - 0266

1. 대호 관련, 쌍용정유(주)가 이란 국영석유공사 (NIOC)와 종전 60천B/D의 장기계약물량을 80천B/D로 증량키 위해 교섭중인 바, 동 교섭을 지원하고 결과 보고 바람.

2. 대호 주재국 아가자데 석유상의 대 아국 원유공급에 대한 협조용의 표명관련, 이 희일 동자부장관이 아가자제 석유상에게 보내는 협조요청 서한을 차파편 송부예정이니, 적의 전달 바람. 끝.

(국제경제국장 최대화)

1990. 12. 31. 에 예고문에 의거 일반문서로 재분류됨 (인)

제12차관보실
아중동국장:

	보 안 통 제

앙 고 재	90년 9월 1일	기술협력과	기안자 성 명		과 장	심의관	국 장		차 관	장 관
			홍성화		(서명)	(서명)	전결			(서명)

외신과통제

0004

관리 번호	90-613

	분류번호	보존기간

발 신 전 보

WLY-0325 900901 1109 FC

번 호 : 종별 :

수 신 : 주 리비아 대사. 총영사

발 신 : 장 관 (기협)

제 목 : 원유도입 교섭

대 : LYW - 0500

1. 대호 관련, 유공(주)는 8.22 런던 DIMC 에 양국간 공동위 합의사항인 원유 15천B/D 도입계약 체결을 재차 희망하는 전문을 발송하였는 바, 귀관에서도 동 도입계약이 조속 체결될 수 있도록 주재국 정부측과 계속 교섭하고 결과 보고 바람.

2. DIMC측은 8.6자 유공(주)앞 전문으로 15천B/D 공급이 현재로선 불가능함을 통보하여온 바 있음을 참고 바람. 끝.

(국제경제국장 최대화)

90. 12. 31 (인)

제12차관보: 아국동국장

보 안 통 제	

앙 고 재	90년 9월 6일	기술협력과	기안자 성 명		과 장	심의관	국 장		차 관	장 관
			홍석화		(서명)	(서명)	전결			(서명)

외신과통제

0005

관리 번호	90-675

	분류번호	보존기간

발 신 전 보

번 호 : WMA-0642 900901 1109 FC 종별 :

수 신 : 주 말레이지아 대사. 총영사

발 신 : 장 관 (기협)

제 목 : 원유도입 교섭

대 : MAW - 1072(1), 1167(2)

연 : WMA - 0559

1. 연호 관련, 유공(주)는 현재 말련 국영석유공사 Petronas와 30천B/D 이내 최대 가능한 장기계약 증량 도입을 교섭중에 있는 바, 대호(2), 주재국의 추가 증산 계획있을시 가능한 한 유공에 대해 증량공급이 이루어질 수 있도록 측면 지원 바람.

2. 대호(1) Sulaiman 장관의 아국에 대한 호의적 고려 검토 언급 관련, 이 희일 동자부장관이 Sulaiman 장관 앞으로 보내는 협조요청 서한을 차파편 송부 예정이니 적의 전달 바람. 끝.

(국제경제국장 최대화)

90. 12. 31

제2차관보:
아주국장: 아주국장:

보 안 통 제	

앙 고 재	90년 9월 1일	기술협력과	기안자 성 명		과 장	심의관	국 장		차 관	장 관
			홍성화				전결			

외신과통제

0006

관리번호	90-672

	분류번호	보존기간

발 신 전 보

번 호 : WDJ-0711 900901 1110 FC 종별 :

수 신 : 주 인니 대사. 총영사

발 신 : 장 관 (기협)

제 목 : 원유도입 고섭

연 : WDJ - 0635

대 : DJW - 1272

1. 대호 인니의 원유증산 관련, 국내 정유사들이 아래와 같이 주재국 국영석유회사 (Petamina)와 장기 원유공급계약을 고섭중에 있는 바, 동 고섭이 원만히 이루어 질 수 있도록 측면 지원하고, 결과 보고 바람.

- 유공(주) : 30천B/D
- 호남(주) : 10천B/D
- 극동정유 : 10천B/D

2. 아측은 9.7-8간 서울에서 개최예정인 한.인니 자원협력위에서도 인니측의 상기 원유공급 협조를 요청할 예정인 바, 참고 바람. 끝.

(국제경제국장 최대화)

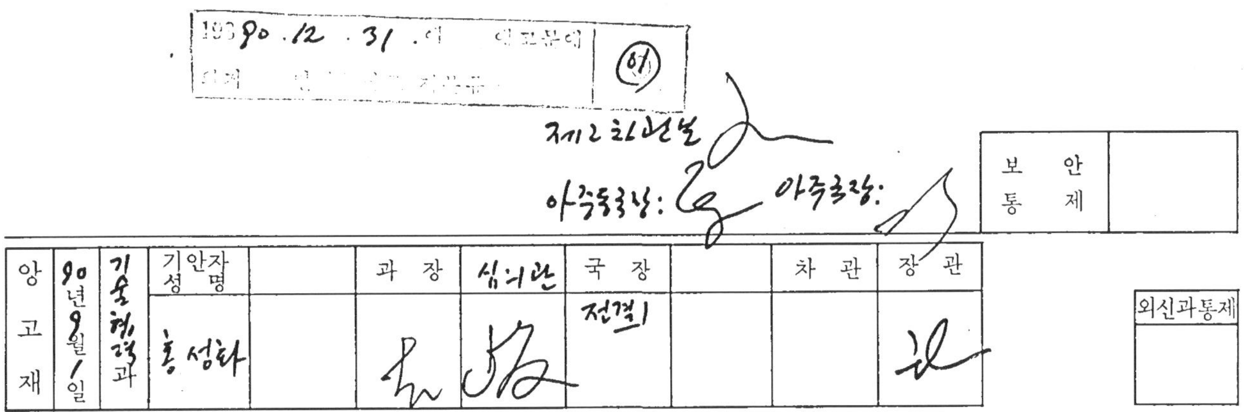

앙고재	90년 9월 1일	기술협력과	기안자 성명		과 장	심의관	국 장		차 관	장 관
			홍성화				전결			

보안통제	

외신과통제

0007

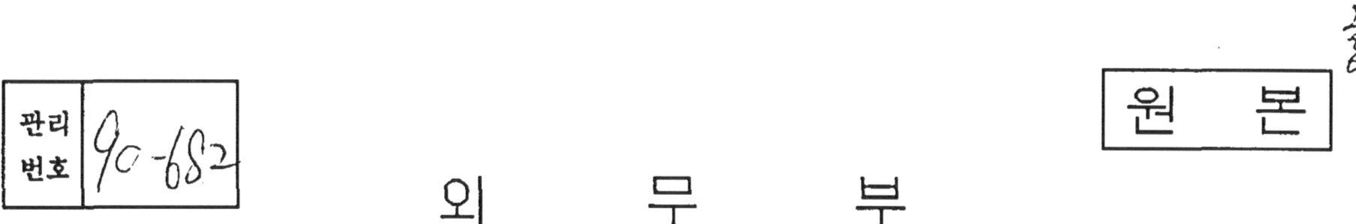

외 무 부

종 별 :

번 호 : IRW-0497 일 시 : 90 0902 1400

수 신 : 장관(기협)

발 신 : 주 이란 대사

제 목 : 원유도입교섭

대:WIR-0298

1. 대호 쌍용의 20,000 BPD 석유공급증량과관련 9.1 현재 런던에 체재중인 HEDAJATZADEH 차관과 통화하고 석유부의 요청에따라 동일 AGAZADEH 장관앞 본직서한을 발송하였음. 9.1 저녁 MR. YARJANI 원유판매공사 수출국장은 본직에게 전화로 쌍용은 오랜고객인점에 비추어 쌍용이 원한다면 90,000 BPD 까지의 원유공급(따라서 30,000 BPD 증량)도 제공할것이라는 뜻의 TELEX 를 쌍용에 타전하였다고 알려왔음.

2. 한편 당관은 선경구룹의 유공요청에따라 20,000-30,000 BPD 원유공급 장기계약을 교섭중이며 9.2 석유장관, 차관및 상기 MR.YARJANI 수출국장으로부터 동의통보를 받았기 참고로 보고함. 끝

(대사정경일-국장)

예고:90.12.31 까지

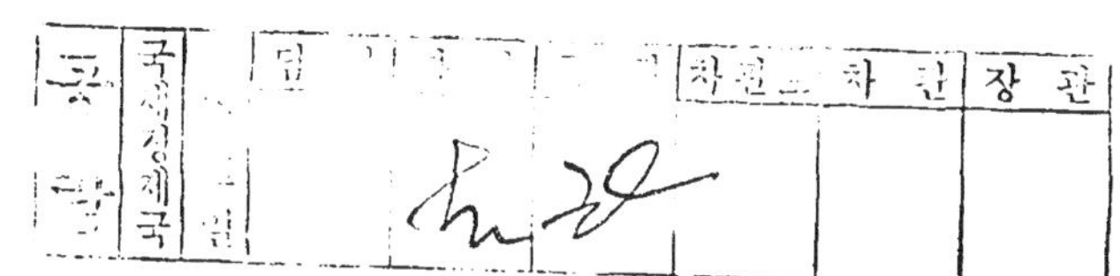

경제국 차관 2차보 중아국 동자부 대책반

PAGE 1 90.09.03 07:27

외신 2과 통제관 CW

0008

관리번호	90-686

원 본

외 무 부

종 별 :

번 호 : DJW-1296 일 시 : 90 0903 1200

수 신 : 장관(기협)

발 신 : 주 인니 대사

제 목 : 원유도입 교섭

연: DJW-1223

대: WDJ-0711

대호 관련, 9.3. 당관 여참사관이 광업에너지성 MARZUAN 오일가스청장 보좌관 및 PERTAMINA BAHARUDIN 총무국장과 면담한 내용 하기 보고함.

1. MARZUAN 보좌관:

OPEC 임시회의 결과를 대통령에게 보고중에 있으며, OPEC 추가쿼타(잠정 10 만 B/D) 증산문제는 확정된 것이 아님. 여타 OPEC 국가들의 증산 추이를 보아가면서 대통령이 신중히 결정하게될것임.

금번 제 12 차 한. 인니 자원협력회의에서 충분한 협의가 있을 것으로 예상되나, 현재로서는 추가 공급은 어려울 것임.

2. BAHARUDIN 총무국장:

OPEC 추가 쿼타가 확정되더라도 실질 증산시기는 내년 1 월이후가 될것이며 증산문제는 OPEC 단합과 관련 매우 예민한 사항임.

한국에 추가 공급하는 문제는 제 12 차 한. 인니 자원협력위에서 협의, 호의적으로 검토될수 있으나, 한국측에 만족할만한 량을 공급하기는 어려울것임.

참고로 동인이 대외석유 판매에 상당한 영향력을 가진 인사인 만큼 서울에서접촉을 강화하는 것이 바람직 함. 끝.

(대사 김재춘-국장)

예고:90.12.31. 까지

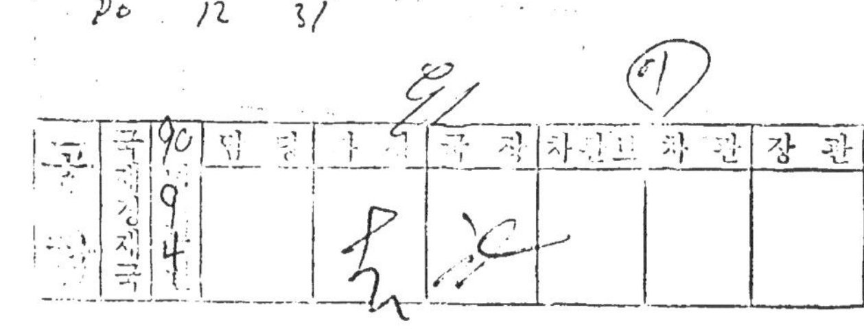

경제국 1차보 2차보 아주국 청와대 안기부 동자부

PAGE 1

90.09.03 17:53

외신 2과 통제관 BT

0003

4U030

기 안 용 지

분류기호 문서번호	기협 20635-	(전화 :)	시 행 상 특별취급	
보존기간	영구·준영구. 10. 5. 3. 1.	장 관		
수 신 처 보존기간				
시행일자	1990.9.3.			

보조기관	국장	전결	협조기관		문 서 통 제
	과장				
기안책임자	홍성화				발 송 인

경 유 수 신 참 조	주 이란대사	발신명의	
제 목	원유 도입 교섭		

연 : WIR - 0298

연호 이 희일 동자부장관의 Aghazadeh장관 앞 서한을 별첨 송부합니다.

첨부 : 상기 서한 원본 및 사본 1부. 끝.

0010

1505-25(2-1) 일(1)갑 190㎜×268㎜ 인쇄용지 2급 60g/㎡
85. 9. 9. 승인 "내가아낀 종이 한장 늘어나는 나라살림" 가 40-41 1990. 2. 10.

30009

기 안 용 지

분류기호 문서번호	기협 20635-	(전화 :)	시 행 상 특별취급	
보존기간	영구·준영구. 10. 5. 3. 1.	장 관		
수 신 처 보존기간				
시행일자	1990.9.3.			

보조기관	국장	전결	협조기관		문서통제
	과장				검열 1990. 9. 04 통제관
기안책임자	홍 성화				발 송 인

경 유 수 신 참 조	주 말레이지아 대사	발신명의	
제 목	원유 도입 교섭		

연 : WMA - 0642

연호 이희일 동자부 장관의 Sulaiman 장관 앞 서한을 별첨 송부합니다.

첨부 : 상기 서한원본 및 사본 1부. 끝.

0011

1505-25(2-1) 일(1)갑
85. 9. 9. 승인 "내가아낀 종이 한장 늘어나는 나라살림"

190㎜×268㎜ 인쇄용지 2급 60g/㎡
가 40-41 1990. 2. 10.

관리 번호	90-685

원 본

외 무 부

종 별 :

번 호 : MAW-1215 일 시 : 90 0903 1730

수 신 : 장관(기협,아동,사본:동자부 장관)

발 신 : 주 말련 대사

제 목 : 원유도입 교섭

대:WMA-0642

연:MAW-1167

1. 대호관련, 본직은 9.3(월) 주재국 석유공사(PETRONAS) TAN SRI AZIZAN 사장을 접촉, 유공의 증량 도입문제에 관한 특별 고려를 요청하였음. 본직은 특히 금번 마하틸 수상 방한에 제하여 대 아국 원유 증량 공급은 매우 훌륭한 우호적 제스쳐가 될수 있음을 지적하였음.

2. 동인은 상기 추가도입 요청은 금번 이라크, 쿠웨이트 사태와는 별도로 그 이전부터 추진되던 것으로 안다하고, 현재 주재국의 생산 능력상 우선 당장 증량공급은 확답할수 없으나 그 가능성을 신중히 검토해 보겠다하 하였음을 우선보고함. 끝

(대사 홍순영-국장)

91.12.31 까지

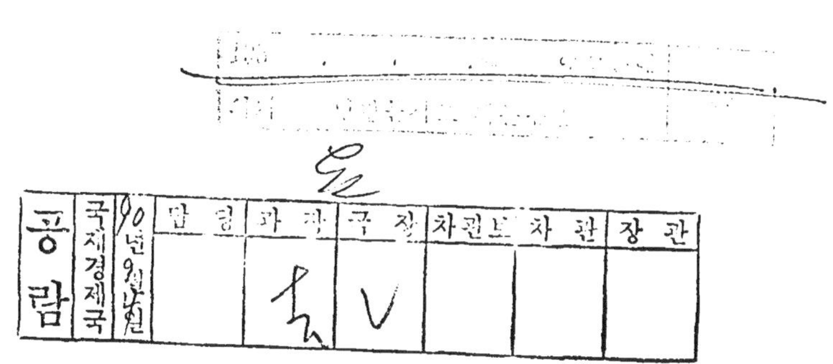

경제국 1차보 2차보 아주국 청와대 안기부 동자부

PAGE 1 90.09.03 19:58

외신 2과 통제관 BT

0012

원 본

외 무 부

종 별 :

번 호 : MAW-1221 일 시 : 90 0903 1800

수 신 : 장관(기협,아동,사본:동자부 장관)

발 신 : 주 말련 대사

제 목 : 이락,쿠웨이트 사태(원유 확보)

1. 주재국은 9.12 자로 소비자 유류가를 약 3 프로인상한바, 동 내역은 아래와 같음

- 고급 휘발류:리터당 1.02 마불에서 1.05 마불로
- 보통 휘발류:리터당 95 센트에서 98 센타로
- 디젤:리터당 54 센트에서 56.1 센트로
- 등유:리터당 59.3 센트에서 62.1 센트로(환율:1미불:2.68 마불)

2. 한편, 9.3 당지 BUSINESS TIMES 는 주재국은 금번 사태로 인한 국제유가 상승에 힘입어 금년도에 예상을 웃도는 두자리 숫자의 경제성장을 기록할 것으로 예측된다고 보도함.즉, 당초 배럴당 16.50 미불을 기초로 9 프로 경제성장을 계획하였으나, 유가가 30미불이 될 경우 10.2 프로의 성장을, 35 미불이 될 경우 10.7 프로의 고도 성장을 달성할수 있을 것이라함. 단, 주재국정부는 그러한 성장률 초과 달성과 함께 높아질 인플레율(4.3 프로에서 4.8 프로로 높아질 예정)에 대해 우려하고 있음.끝

(대사 홍순영-국장)

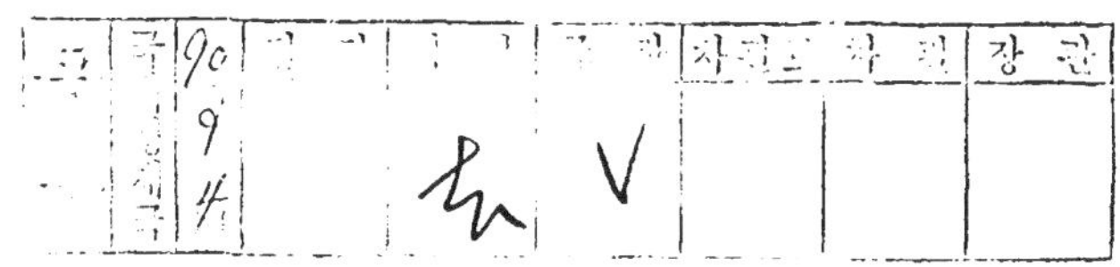

경제국 2차보 아주국 안기부 동자부 통상국 미주국

PAGE 1

90.09.03 22:44 DP

외신 1과 통제관

0013

원 본

외 무 부

종 별 :

번 호 : NJW-0711 일 시 : 90 0903 1200

수 신 : 장 관(기협,아프일)

발 신 : 주 나이제리아 대사

제 목 : 경제정세(자료응신 88호)

1.주재국 석유부 소식통에 의하면 주재국은 작주의 OPEC 합의에 따라 원유생산을 1.861 MBD(OPEC 쿼타는 1.611)로 증산 결정하였고 동조치는 중동사태가 지속되는한 계속 될 것이라함.

2.주재국 중앙은행 발표에 의하면 90년 전반기중 원유수출 증가로 인하여 국제수지 흑자가 87억 나이라,수출입은 406억 나이라(작년동기비 50.9프로증)및 310억 나이라, 무역흑자 96억 나이라로 잠정 집계되었다함.

(대사 오채기-국장)

						차관보	차 관	장 관

경제국 1차보 2차보 중아국 정문국 안기부

PAGE 1

90.09.03 22:45 DP

외신 1과 통제관

0014

원 본

외 무 부

종 별 :

번 호 : SBW-0780 일 시 : 90 0903 1400

수 신 : 장 관(기협,동자부,기정)

발 신 : 주 사우디 대사

제 목 : 주재국 산유동향

1.9.2 REUTER 통신은 주재국 DAHRAN 발 8.31 현재 사우디의 산유량이 평소보다 200만 베럴이 증대된 일산 740만 베럴에 이르고 있으며, UAE가 일산 50만 베럴, 베네주엘라가 일산 30만베럴, 멕시코가 일산 10만베럴, 기타 OPEC 회원국이 일산 20만베럴, 알라스카 유전이 일산 5만베럴 정도를 추가 생산하고 있다고 주재국소식통을 인용, 보도함.

2.상기 보도관련, 당관이 접촉한 주재국 석유광물부나 ARAMCO 측은 사우디가이미 증산을 개시한 사실을 확인하고 있으나 주재국의 구체적인 산유량에 대해서는 언급을 피하고 있음. 동건 상세 파악 되는대로 추보 위계임.

(대사 주병국-국장)

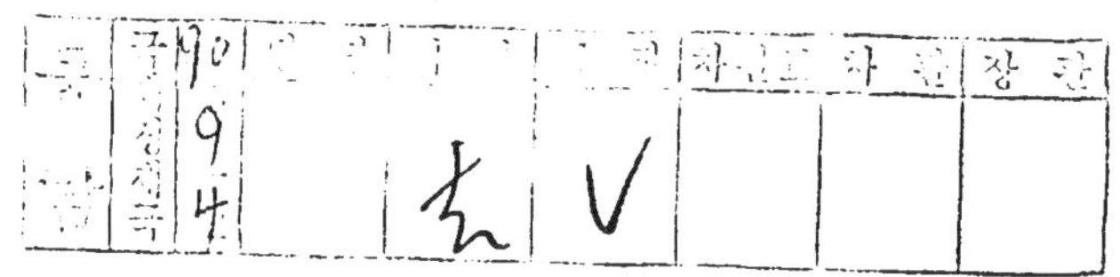

경제국 1차보 2차보 중아국 정문국 안기부 동자부 대책반

PAGE 1

90.09.03 22:52 DA

외신 1과 통제관

0015

홍

외 무 부

종 별 :

번 호 : SUW-0232 일 시 : 90 0903 1330

수 신 : 장 관(미중,경이,정일)

발 신 : 주 수리남 대사

제 목 : 주재국 원유상황보고(자료응신 90-49)

1.당지 주유소에는 위발류 공급이 부족, 주유소마다 자동차 행열이 2,3백미터씩이나 줄지어 있는 실정임.

2.주재국에는 TEXCO, ESSO, SHELL 등 3개의 원유회사가 공급하고 있으며 지난 중동사태 이후 원유감산으로 인한 유가인상을 주재국 정부측에 통보하였으나 회답이 없자 체불된 원유값등을 독촉하면서 지난주부터 휘발류 공급을 지연시키고 있음.

3.현재 정부측에서는 상기 원유회사측과 협상중에 있으며, 유가는 (15-2-,50 설도있음)인상 결정, 다음주부터는 정상적으로 공급이 가능할 것으로 예상됨.

4.주재국 SURINAME STATE OIL CO. 는 현재 일산 4,000베렐에서 6,500베럴로 원유증산을 위하여 ABN BANK (홀랜드)1,500만불 차관협정을 체결하였음을 보도하였음.끝.

(대사 김교식-미주국장)

기헙

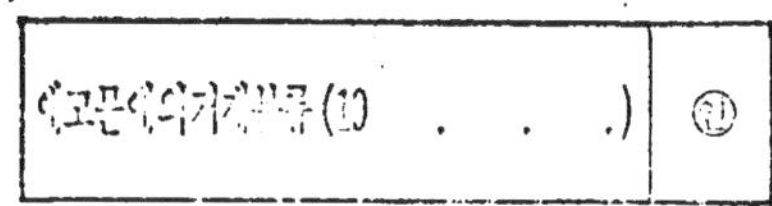
(고문서에의거재분류(19 . . .)) ⓘ

공람	국제경제국	90.9.4일	담당	과장	국장	차관보	차관	장관
				(서명)	V			

미주국 1차보 2차보 경제국 정문국 안기부 동자부 통상국

PAGE 1 90.09.04 09:21 WG

외신 1과 통제관

0016

원 본

외 무 부

종 별 :

번 호 : JAW-5349 일 시 : 90 0904 1714

수 신 : 장관(기협,통일,경일,통이)

발 신 : 주일대사(경제)

제 목 : 주재국 석유제품 가격 동향

주재국 통산성은 9.3 석유제품 가격인상을시장동향에 따라 연동제로 허용한다는방침을밝혔는바, 상기 방침내용과 주재국 유가 및석유제품 가격 동향을 하기 보고함.

1. 통산성의 기본방침

0 무또 통산상은 최근 일본의 주요 석유회사들의도입원유가 상승으로 인한 석유제품 가격 인상움직임과 관련, 원유 및 석유제품 조달 비용상승분을 반영하되 석유제품 가격 인상을최소한으로 억제하고, 국제 원유시장 동향에편승한 가격 인상방지를 목적으로 하기 방침을석유회사들에 통보하였음.

가) 원유도입 비용 상승분을 가능한한 기업노력으로 흡수토록함.

나) 석유제품 상승폭은 도입비용 상승을반영하되 필요한 최소한도로 억제함.

다) 9월 이후 매월 유가도입 비용의 변동내요을자원에네르기청에 보고토록함.

0 금번 통산성의 방침은 주요석유 회사들의원유가 상승을 반영하여 9월 중순부터휘발유,등유 및 경유 제품 가격을 리터당 10엥 인상움직임에 대한것임.

0 통산성은 석유제품의 국내가격은 기본적으로원유 수급상황을 반영한 시장원리에 입각하여석유회사들이 자주적 판단에 의하여 결정토록한다는 입장에는 변함이 없으나, 불안정한국제원유시장 동향에 편승한 석유제품 가격인상을 불허한다는 입장을 밝혔음.

2. 도입원유가 상승

0 UAE 아부다비 국영 석유회사는 9.3. 8월분 대일원유 도입가격을 7월에 비해 베럴당10.55달러(65퍼센트) 인상된 27달러로일본석유업계에 통고하였으며, 동 가격은85.12이래 4년 8개월만에 최고 가격임.

0 일본이 주요 산유국들로부터 직접 도입한 8월분원유가격은 배럴당 평균 약 10단러인상되었으며, 국내 석유회사들의 정제비용은리터당 10엥 인상 효과를 가져옴.

경제국 경제국 통상국 통상국 2차보

PAGE 1

공람	국제경제국	90.9.6	담당	과장	국장	차관보	차관	장관

90.09.05 00:29 CT

외신 1과 통제관

0017

3. LPG 도입가 상승

0 사우디는 9월분 LPG 대일 수출가격 대폭인상을 통보하였는바, 프로판 가스는 8월에 비해64퍼센트가 인상된 톤당 165.88달러, 부탄가스의경우 163.61달러로 알려짐.

0 사우디는 일본의 최대 LPG 수입선으로총수입량중 약 40퍼센트가 사우디산이며,UAE 도사우디의 결정에 따라 대일 LPG 수출 가격을인상할 것으로 알려짐.끝

(공사 이한춘-국장)

원 본

외 무 부

종 별 :

번 호 : UKW-1655 일 시 : 90 0904 1640

수 신 : 장 관 (기협,통일)

발 신 : 주 영 대사

제 목 : 석유수급및 유가동향

대: WUK-1379

당지 국립 경제사회연구소(NIDSR)는 90. 3/4분기 보고서에서 최근 이라크.쿠웨이트 사태로 유가가 금년 하반기중 25달러선을 유지하고 1991년에는 20-22달러선에서 변동될 것이며 유가가 25프로 인상될때 선진7개국(G7)의 경제에 미치는 영향은 물가상승율 0.25-0.5프로, GNP 0.25 프로 감소효과를 가져올 것으로 전망하였음.끝

(대사 오재희-국장)

공람	국제경제국	90.9.6	담 당	과 장	국 장	차관보	차 관	장 관
					V			

경제국 통상국

PAGE 1

90.09.05 08:20 FC

외신 1과 통제관

0019

원 본

외 무 부

종 별 :

번 호 : SBW-0783 일 시 : 90 0904 1100

수 신 : 장 관(기협,동자부)

발 신 : 주 사우디 대사

제 목 : 주재국 산유동향

연: SBW-780

1.9.3 MIDDLE EAST ECONOMIC SURVEY 지 (NICOSIA 에서 발간)는 주재국의 9월중 일일평균 산유량이 OPEC 쿼타를 227만베럴 초과한 765만베럴 (사우디 ARAMCO: 750 만베럴, 중립지대: 15만베럴)에 달할것이며, 사우디 ARAMCO 는 4/4분기중 북반구의 원유수요가 커질경우 단기적으로 일산 800-85만 베럴까지 산유량을 증대시킬수 있을 것이라고 보도함.

2.또한 동지는 주재국이 원유증산분을 판매하는데 있어 이라크, 쿠웨이트산 원유의 공급중단으로 어려움을 격고있는 터키, 브라질, 필리핀, 인도, 파키스탄, 방글라데시, 한국, 대만등 개도국에 우선권을 줄것이라고 보도함.

3.한편, 아국 정유회사들은 최근 타결된 장기공급 계약에 따라 9월부터 사우디 ARAMCO로부터 일일 105,000베럴 (쌍용6만, 유공4만5천베럴)을 금년 9월부터 도입하고 있음을 참고바람.

(대사 주병국-국장)

국제경제국	담 당	과 장	국 장	차관보	차 관	장 관
90.9.6			V			

경제국 2차보 중아국 통상국 동자부

PAGE 1

90.09.05 09:01 CT

외신 1과 통제관

0020

원 본

외 무 부

종 별 :

번 호 : USW-4002 일 시 : 90 0904 1815

수 신 : 장 관(기협)

발 신 : 주 미 대사

제 목 : 석유시장 및 유가동향(8)

표제 관련, 9.1 (토)-3 (월) 당지 언론 보도를 종합 보고함.

1. 유가 동향

가. 8.31 원유 및 정유제품 가격 (뉴욕 상품 시장)

0 원유 (10월 인도가격)

: 배럴당 27.32 불 (전일대비 0.55 불 상승)

0 휘발유 (9월 인도가격)

: 갤런당 96.07 센트 (전일비 7.25 센트 상승)

0 난방유 (9월 인도가격)

:갤런당 75.89센트 (전일대비 3.90 센트 상승)

나. 9.3 원유 가격 (런던 국제 석유 시장)

0 원유 (북해 BRENT 원유,10월 인도가격)

: 배럴당 28.55 불 (전일대비 1.80 불 상승)

0 뉴욕 상품 시장은 9.3. 노동절 휴무.

다. 당지 전문가들은 8.30 이후 유가 상승은 중동사태의 외교적 해결전망이 불투명해진데 대한원유 시장의 심리적 반응으로 분석하고 있음.

2. IEA 동향

0 8.31 IEA 는 이사회를 개최, 현세계 원유시장은 OPEC 원유증산 실시, 일일30 만 배럴에 달하는 석유회사의 상업 비축분 사용 및 가격인상에 따른 공급 감소등으로 대체적인 수급 균형을 이루고 있다고 평가하고, 동수급 상황에 비추어 즉각적인 전략 비축분 사용은 불필요하다고 결정하였음.

0 IEA 는 다만 향후 수개월 내에 원유 공급부족 상황이 심각해질 경우 전략 비축 원유 방출등 비상조치를 검토하기로 했다고 발표하였음.

경제국 2차보 미주국 안기부 동자부 통상국

PAGE 1

공람	국제경제국	년 월 일	담 당	과 장	국 장	차관보	차 관	장 관
					V			

90.09.05 09:42 WG

외신 1과 통제관

0021

3. 미국내 원유 증산

0 에너지부 발표에 따르면 미국은 알라스카주, 텍사스주에서의 원유 추가 생산등을 통해 4/4 분기까지는 일일 25만-26만 배럴의 증산이 가능할것이라 함.

4. 상기 언론 보도 내용 별첨 FAX (USW(F)-2067)송부함.

(대사 박동진-국장)

09/04/90 18:02 ☎202 797 0595 EMBASSY OF KOREA →→→ 001 2 ☑001/012

주 미 대 사 관

보안 통제: 외

번호 : USW(F) - 2067
수신 : 장관 (기협)
발신 : 주미대사
제목 : USW - 4002 첨부 (12 매)

Newsclippings
Econ Section

IEA optimistic on oil supply outlook

By Steven Butler in Paris

THE International Energy Agency yesterday declared oil markets well supplied and decided against immediate measures to counteract the loss of Kuwaiti and Iraqi oil exports of 4.3m barrels a day.

But the IEA, responsible for co-ordinating emergency responses to an oil shortfall for 21 industrialised countries, said it was ready to respond if the situation deteriorated.

"We are prepared and able to act if the need arises," said Mrs Helga Steeg, IEA executive director, after a meeting of the IEA governing board.

She rejected suggestions that the IEA should intervene to calm markets by releasing strategic stocks, arguing this could undermine IEA credibility if done prematurely.

Mr Ulrich Engelmann, chairman of the governing board, said: "In global terms, the situation is calm."

Following a decision by the Organisation of Petroleum Exporting Countries this week to increase production, the IEA expects no crude oil supply difficulties in September or October. But it cautioned that the onset of winter would bring tighter supplies, as the ability of oil companies to draw on stocks declines.

Mrs Steeg said companies had co-operated so far by drawing on stocks in August at a rate of 300,000 b/d. She said the companies' stock draw would be "substantially higher" in September and October.

The IEA expects tighter markets in some refined products, but said it was too early to assess how serious this would be. Although the IEA stressed its readiness to act by encouraging demand restraint or releasing strategic stocks, it said the situation was too complex to outline situations that would trigger a response.

Mrs Steeg rejected a view expressed by some US officials that strategic stocks would be used only when fuel could not be obtained regardless of price.

France yesterday said it would begin negotiations to join the IEA. France stayed out of the IEA when it was set up in 1974 because it was seen as a weapon to break Opec.

● British Petroleum yesterday rounded off a week of price increases by other UK oil companies by adding 6.4p to a gallon of petrol, taking the price at the pump for its leaded petrol to 224.1p, writes David Thomas, Resources Editor. The RAC motoring organisation said it had asked the European Commission to investigate the latest round of price rises.

FT
9.1.90

2067-1

0023

	분류번호	보존기간

발 신 전 보

번 호 : WJA-3757 외 별지참조 종별 : 긴급

900905 1340

수 신 : 주 수신처 참조 대사. 총영사

발 신 : 장 관 (기협)

제 목 : 중동원유 의존도

국별 중동지역 원유의존도를 파악코자 하니 최근1-2년간 주재국의 원유 총수입량 (B/D) 및 중동지역 국가로 부터의 수입량 (국별구분)을 긴급 보고 바람. 끝.

(국제경제국장 최 대 화)

수신처 : 주일본, 싱가폴, 자유중국, 태국, 호주, 뉴질랜드, 불란서, 서독, 벨기에, 오지리, 덴마크, 스페인, 아일랜드, 네덜란드, [illegible], 스웨덴, 폴투갈, [illegible], 그리스, 핀랜드, 브라질 대사

주홍콩총영사

	보 안 통 제	

앙 고 재	90년 9월 5일	기술협력과	기안자 성명		과 장		국 장		차 관	장 관
			홍성화		(서명)	(서명)	전결			(서명)

외신과통제

0024

WJA-3757 900905 1340 FC

WSG -0631 WCH -0728 WTH -1111 WAU -0633 WNZ -0266
WFR -1696 WGE -1289 WBB -0625 WAV -0911 WDE -0295
WSP -0440 WID -0289 WHO -0252 WSD -0458 WPO -0257
WGR -0305 WFN -0255 WBR -0386 WHK -1095

0025

駐 日 大 使 館

(Page 1 -- 1)

JAW(F) : 日時 :

受 信 : 長 官 (기협)

発 信 : 駐日大使 (경제) '90 9 - -5 18 :50

"긴급"

題 目 일본의 중동산 원유수입 통계

대 : WJA-3757

대호, 일본의 중동산 원유수입 통계를 별첨 송부합니다.

중동산 원유 수입 현황

단위 : 킬로리터(%)

구 분	88년(수입비중)	89년(수입비중)	90.1-6간수입비중
총수입	193,850,626(100)	209,691,714(100)	100(380만B/D)
대중동 수입총계	130,955,904(68.4)	148,968,603(71.3)	71.8
국 별			
UAE	37,814,090(20.0)	42,769,706(21.3)	20.6
사우디	27,942,198(14.4)	27,391,379(13.4)	16.9
이 란	10,969,650(5.9)	16,991,191(8.5)	7.4
쿠웨이트	8,124,435(3.5)	9,670,111(4.9)	5.9
이라크	9,966,344(5.0)	12,578,259(6.1)	5.8
카타르	10,254,838(5.8)	12,359,277(5.2)	5.6
오 만	17,097,657(8.3)	14,782,928(6.6)	5.1
중립지대	8,199,714(4.9)	11,558,792(5.2)	4.4
북예멘	586,978(0.5)	866,960(0.2)	

상황실

배부처	장관실	차관실	一차보	二차보	기획실	의전장	아주국	미주국	구주국	중아국	국기국	경제국	통상국	정문국	영교국	총무과	감사관	공보관	외연원	청와대	총리실	안기부	동자부
	/	/		/		/						O								/		/	/

0026

관리 번호	90-694

원 본

외 무 부

종 별 : 지 급

번 호 : MAW-1240 일 시 : 90 0905 1600

수 신 : 장관(기협,아동,사본:동자부장관)

발 신 : 주 말련 대사

제 목 : 원유 도입 교섭

대:WMA-0642

연:MAW-1215

1. 본직은 9.5(수) 주재국 외무부 ISMAIL 경제차관보를 면담(이준규 서기관배석), 대호 유공의 원유증량 도입 추진 현황을 설명하고, 주재국 정부의 각별한 고려를 요청하였음(요청 공한 수교)

2. 동 차관보는 이를 핫싼 외무장관및 마하틸 수상에게도 보고하겠다하고, 내주로 예정된 마하틸 수상의 방한등 양국간의 긴밀한 관계에 비추어 아국의 요청은 말련의 증산 여력이 미치는 범위에서 가급적 긍정적 방향으로 검토할수 있도록 노력하겠다함. 끝

(대사 홍순영-국장)

90.12.31 까지

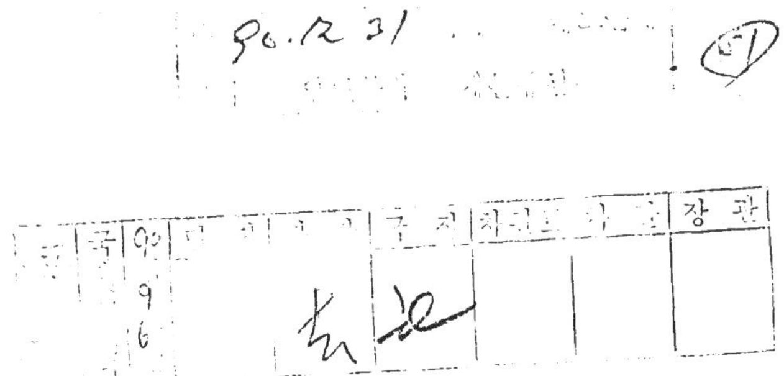

경제국 1차보 2차보 아주국 청와대 안기부 동자부

90.09.05 18:00

외신 2과 통제관 EZ

0027

관리 번호	90-693

원 본

외 무 부

종 별 : 지 급

번 호 : DJW-1316 일 시 : 90 0905 1540

수 신 : 장관(기협)

발 신 : 주 인니 대사

제 목 : 원유도입 교섭

대:WDJ-0711

연:DJW-1311

1. 본직은 대호 관련, 9.5. GINANDJAR 광업에너지성 장관을 면담하고, 주재국으로부터의 50 천 B/D 원유 추가도입 문제를 교섭하고, 장관의 각별한 협조를 요성하였음.

2. 동 장관은 아국입장을 충분히 이해하며, 주재국은 금후 7.5 천-10 천 B/D 의 원유를 추가 생산할 계획이나, 추가생산 시설기간이 최소 5 주정도 소요된다고 하면서 아국의 추가 물량공급에 대해서는 이번 제 12 차 한. 인니 자원협력회의에서 충분히 협의할 예정이라고 호의적인 반응을 보였음. 끝.

(대사 김재춘-국장)

예고:90.12.31. 일반

90 12 31

경제국 2차보 아주국

PAGE 1 90.09.05 19:01

외신 2과 통제관 EZ

0028

관리번호	90-695

원 본

외 무 부

종 별 :

번 호 : IRW-0503 일 시 : 90 0905 1030

수 신 : 장관(기협,중근동,상공부,동자부)

발 신 : 주 이란 대사

제 목 : 이란원유동향

대: WIR-0286.0276

1. 주재국상유정책:3.1-3.7 백만 B/D (4.5 백만 B/D 증산계획)

가. 산유정책

-주재국의 산유기본정책은 OPEC 내에서의 협력으로 합의된 생산을 통한 고가정책(증산, 저유가정책반대)고수, 현생산능력은 3.1 백만 B/D 증산계획중

-OPEC 내 증산가능국가및 생산량

사우디 2,000 천 B/D, UAE, 베네주엘라 500 천 B/D, 이란 400 천 B/D(시설파괴로 현실적으로 가능한지는 의문)

나. 주요수출국및 가격조건

-과거 서구와 아세아지역수출비율을 3:1 로 하였으나 이를 1:1 로 조정하기로확정, 따라서 아세아수출량이 1 백만 B/D

-극동지역: 일본(700 천 B/D), 한국(100 천 B/D)

-계약조건

아국쌍용, 대량물량도입 일본가격과 SPOT 시장가격을 기준으로 신규도입희망자에게는 양가격차이 1 불 20 전 을 양분하여 BUYER 가 PREMIUM 으로 60 센트를 부담케함.

기본적으로 장기계약선호 90 12 31.

2. 아국의 대주재국 언유확보방안

가. 이란과같은 안정적 공급원과 정부차원에서 장기유류공급협정

-아국의 유류저장시설을 이란이 무상으로 사용케하므로써 아국은 별도재원 사용없는 물리적인비상유류확보

-이란은 필요시 극동지역으로 공급하는 유류를 한국으로부터 단기간내에

경제국 2차보 중아국 청와대 안기부 상공부 동자부

PAGE 1 90.09.05 17:16

외신 2과 통제관 BT

0029

공급할수있으며, 이란 한국간 수송을 비수요기를 이용한 자국선사용으로 비용절감.

나. 주재국으로부터 직도입

-쌍용정유:20,000-30,000B/D 추가(현 60,000 B/D)

-선경(유공 신규직도입추진

물량:20,000-30,000B/D

가격협의중

-이란산 GAS 도입추진

현재 일부한국업체가 일본상사를통해 이란산 GAS 수입

장기적 에너지확보책으로 직수입추진

-아국기업이 일본상사로부터 PREMIUM 을내고 도입(극동정유 40,000 B/D) 하는 비정상적형태를 없애고 국내신규도입희망 상사의 물량을통합 대표상사나 정부가 도입가격, 조건등을 교섭할경우, 상대적으로 많은 물량구매의 이점으로 유리한계약가능

3. 주재국이 보는 유가전망

가. 현 쿠웨이트 사태가 관건

-전쟁발발시, 이른바 정치심리 유가 30 불을 상회

-현상태계속시 21 불-25 불선

나. 사우디등 산유국의 증산과 유가

-사우디의 200 만 B/D 증산의 상당분이 주둔미군의 소요로전용

-주요국은 사우디와같은 불안지역보다는 이란과같은 안정적지역으로부터의 공급확보경쟁으로 유가의 점진적상승은 필연적임.

다. 금년하반기 계절적인 유가수요증가시 23 불선 가격형성전망

4.(참고)일본의 대이란 원유도입현황

-일일평균총도입량:3,610 천 B/D

-이란원유도입

90.1-8 월: 290 천-300 천 B/D

90.9 월중 600 천 B/D.. 기존:300 천 B/D

-SPOT MARKET 추가:300 천 B/D..90.10-12 월:(396)00-700 천 B/D

이란 LIGHT OMAN 프러스 0.35불 (전회대비 0.6불 상승)

이란 HEAVY DUBAI 프러스 0.25 불(전회대비 1.40 불 상승). 끝

PAGE 2

0030

예고:90.12.31 까지

91 12 31

PAGE 3

0031

원 본

외 무 부

종 별 : 긴 급

번 호 : THW-1414 일 시 : 90 0905 1800

수 신 : 장 관 (기협)

발 신 : 주 태 국 대사

제 목 : 중동원유 의존도

대 : WTH-1111

1. 태국의 88,89년도 원유 총수입량은 각각 54.92백만 배럴(15만 B/D) 및 74.18백만배럴 (20만 B/D) 임.

2. 중동지역으로 부터의 수입량은 다음과 같음.

가. 88년

0 중동지역 합계 : 35.04 백만 배럴 (9.6만 B/D)

0 국별 : UAE (14.6 백만), 사우디(6.18백만), 쿠웨이트(5.26백만), 오만(4.6백만) 등

나. 89년

0 중동지역 합계 : 49.08 백만 배럴(14만 B/D)

0 국 별 : UAE(16.28 백만), 사우디 (11.61백만), 쿠웨이트(6.77백만), 오만(3.43백만), 이락(2.59백만), 이란(1.76 백만) 등

(대사 정주년-국장)

공람	국제경제국	90 [illegible] 6일			국			장 관

경제국 상황실

PAGE 1

90.09.05 21:13 DA

외신 1과 통제관

0032

원 본

외 무 부

종 별 : 긴 급

번 호 : SGW-0561 일 시 : 90 0905 1900

수 신 : 장 관(기협,아동)

발 신 : 주 싱가폴 대사

제 목 : 중동원유 의존도

대: WSG-0631

1. 대호 주재국의 88년, 89년 원유수입 총량은 각각 257 백만배럴 (704천 B/D), 275 백만배럴 (753천 B/D) 이며 이중 중동지역 국가로부터의 수입량은 159 백만배럴 (61.8 프로), 201 백만배럴 (73프로)임.

2. 국별, 년도별 수입량은 다음과같음. (단위: 천배럴)

(국별, 1988년, 1989년 순임)

사우디: 72,560. 104,363.

UAE: 37,385. 44,465.

이란: 25,487. 21,217.

쿠웨이트: 4,158. 9,432.

오만: 1,925. 8,765.

카탈: 14,122. 5,379.

이집트: 1,333. 4,135.

예멘: 1,625. 3,041.

바레인: 277. --.

소계 (중동지역): 158,872. 200,797.

말련: 47,154. 38,718.

중공: 37,759. 26,454.

호주: 6,195. 4.487.

브루나이: 6,046. 3,349.

파키스탄: --. 741.

총계: 257,000. 275,000.

196,662

공람	국제경제국	90.9.6일	담당	과장	국장	차관보	차관	장관
					V			

경제국 아주국

상황실

PAGE 1

90.09.05 21:51 DA

외신 1과 통제관

0033

원 본

외 무 부

종 별 : 지 급

번 호 : HKW-2245 일 시 : 90 0905 2000

수 신 : 장 관(기협,아이)

발 신 : 주 홍콩 총영사

제 목 : 중동원유 의존도

대: WHK-1095

1. 홍콩 통계국에 의하면 홍콩은 원유(CRUDE OIL)를 수입하지 않고 있으며 (정제소 없음), 휘발유, 등유등 석유제품(OIL PRODUCTS) 만을 수입하고 있다함.

2. 참고로 홍콩은 89년 전체 석유제품 수입의 70프로 이상을 싱가폴로부터 수입하였으며, 중동의 U.A.E 및 (사우디로 부터는 약 4프로 수입함. (상세사항 FAX HKW(F)-113참조). 끝.

(부총영사-과장)

공람	국제경제국	90 년 9 월 6 일	담 당	과 장	국 장	차관보	차 관	장 관
					V			

경제국 아주국 상황실

PAGE 1 90.09.05 21:52 DA

외신 1과 통제관

0034

(기협, 아이)

대: WHK-1095

Table 6(C) Quantity of imports of oil products by source and of re-exports of oil products by destination for 1989

	Aviation gasoline and aviation kerosene (kilolitre)	Motor gasoline (kilolitre)	Kerosene (kilolitre)	Gas oil, diesel oil and naphtha (tonne)	Fuel oil (tonne)	LPG (tonne)
A. Imports by source						
China	171 862 (8)	39 056 (9)	47 620 (86)	617 020 (20)	216 071 (7)	8 400 (4)
Singapore	1 661 034 (82)	344 595 (80)	7 418 (13)	1 966 133 (63)	2 223 604 (77)	40 277 (20)
Japan	127 162 (6)	45 125 (11)	0	228 189 (7)	198 067 (7)	4 341 (2)
U. Urab Emirates	0	0	0	154 111 (5)	0	0
Philippines	0	0	0	0	0	134 856 (66)
Saudi Arabia	42 888 (2)	0	0	65 697 (2)	40 977 (1)	0
Taiwan	0	0	0	0	130 754 (5)	0
Others	29 408 (1)	272 (#)	45 (#)	85 634 (3)	73 302 (3)	16 826 (8)
Total imports	2 032 354	429 048	55 083	3 116 784	2 882 775	204 700
B. Re-exports by destination						
China	5 (#)	99 494 (85)	8 133 (35)	1 201 591 (98)	735 482 (82)	21 919 (79)
Macau	0	17 629 (15)	3 308 (14)	24 781 (2)	135 419 (15)	5 998 (21)
Singapore	31 792 (100)	54 (#)	0	134 (#)	95 (#)	0
Japan	0	0	11 670 (50)	0	22 984 (3)	0
Others	0	0	0	80 (#)	0	0
Total re-exports	31 797	117 177	23 111	1 226 586	893 980	27 917
C. Retained imports	2 000 557	311 871	31 972	1 890 198	1 988 795	176 783

Figures in brackets denote percentage shares against the corresponding total.

Less than 0.5%

상황

배부처	장관실	차관실	一차보	二차보	기획실	의전장	아주국	미주국	구주국	중아국	국기국	경제국	통상국	정문국	영교국	총무과	감사관	공보관	외연원	청와대	총리실
							/					O									

0035

원 본

외 무 부

종 별 : 긴 급

번 호 : DEW-0368 일 시 : 90 0905 1700

수 신 : 장관(기협)

발 신 : 주 덴마크 대사

제 목 : 중동석유 의존도

대: WDE-0295

1. 대호 아래 보고함.

가. 88년도(환율 미화 1불당 6.73크로너)

1) 총수입량: 4,477,615톤, 3,245,232천크로너(482,203천불)

2) 중동지역

- 사우디: 167,256톤, 111,476천 크로너(16,546천불)

- 쿠웨이트: 2,798,980톤, 2,023,311천크로너 (300,640천불)

나. 89년도 (환율 미화 1불당 6.89크로너)

1) 총수입량: 4,096,741 톤, 3,762,448천 크로너(546,073천미불)

2)중동지역

- 사우디: 112,098톤, 101,783천 크로너 (14,772천 미불) 2,903,079

- 쿠웨이트: 2,790,981톤, 2,453,314천 크로너 (356,068천미불)

2. 주재국은 72년 북해 유전의 최초개발 이후 현재 연간 생산량 550만톤 (89년도), 수출 238만톤 (89년도)에 달하는 서구 3대 산유국이며, 현재 생산량은 국내수요의 80 퍼센트를 자체 조달할수 있고 주재국은 향후 2-3년내 수요전량의 자체조달이 가능할 것으로 전망하고 있음을 참고로 첨언함. 끝.

(대사 장선섭-국장)

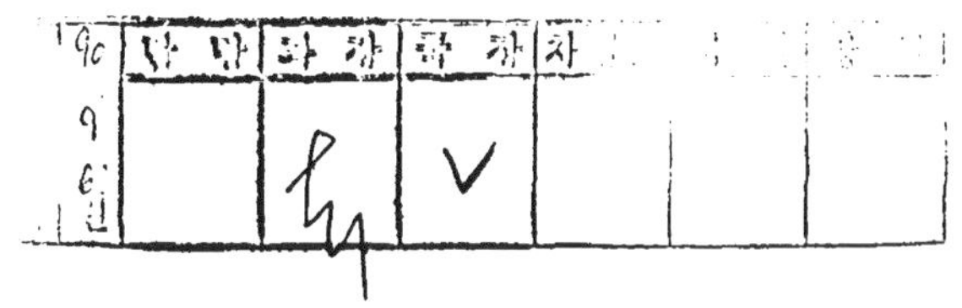

경제국

PAGE 1

90.09.06 04:30 DA

외신 1과 통제관

0036

원 본

외 무 부

종 별 : 긴 급

번 호 : SDW-0845 일 시 : 90 0905 1500

수 신 : 장관(기협,구이)

발 신 : 주 스웨덴 대사

제 목 : 중동원유 의존도

대: WSD-0458

대호 주재국의 중동원유 의존도를 아래 보고함.

1.'89년도 (1-12월)

0 총 수입량: 15,552 천톤

0 중동 도입량: 2,265,286 톤(14.56 퍼센트)

- 국별: UAW 274,610 톤, 오만 256,789 톤, 사우디263,385 톤, 이락 268,939 톤,이란 1,201,563 톤

2.'90년도 (1-5월)

0 총 수입량: 7,217 천톤

0 중동 도입량: 1,016 천톤 (14 퍼센트)

- 국별: 사우디 300 만톤, 이란 716 천톤

3. 참고로, 주재국은 원유의 약 50 퍼센트를 노르웨이로 부터 수입하고 있으며('89년도 도입량 7,153,201톤), 중동원유 의존도는 상기와 같이 크지않음. 끝

(대사 최동진-국장)

공람	국제경제국	'90.9.6	담 당	과 장	국 장	차관보	차 관	장 관
					V			

경제국 구주국

PAGE 1

90.09.06 04:30 DA

외신 1과 통제관

0037

원 본

외 무 부

종 별 : 긴 급

번 호 : FRW-1618 일 시 : 90 0905 1920

수 신 : 장 관 (기협,구일)

발 신 : 주 불 대사

제 목 : 중동 원유 의존도

대: WFR-1696

불란서의 1989년도 국별 원유 의존도 아래보고함.

1.총수입량: 69.7 MT(백만톤)

2.지역별 의존도

가.중동: 30.6 MT(43.3 프로) (이하단위 퍼센트)

-사우디(18.7), 이란(11), 이라크(8.1), 에미레이트(2.8), 두바이(1.1), 시리아(1.1)

나.북아프리카: 6.6 MT(9.3)

- 알제리아(3.7), 리비아(3.5)

다.서구: 14.2 MT(16)

- 노르웨이(11.3), 영국(4)

라.여타 아프리카: 10.1 MT(14.3)

- 나이제리아(4.5), 가봉(4.4),카메룬(3.1)

마.기타 지역: 8.2 MT(11.6)

- 소련(7.2),멕시코(3.7),베네수엘라(0.7)

2.참고사항

가.89년중 쿠웨이트로 부터 원유도입 실적 없음.

나.중동원유 의존도 감소및 수입지역 다변화 노력지속

.중동지역 원유 의존도 감소: 79년 74프로, 89년 43프로

.서구지역 원유 의존도 증가: 78년 3프로, 89년 16프로. 끝.

(대사 노영찬-국장)

경제국 구주국

PAGE 1

공람 | 차관보 | 차 관 | 장 관

90.09.06 04:34 DA

외신 1과 통제관

0038

원 본

외 무 부

종 별 : 긴 급

번 호 : HOW-0367 일 시 : 90 0905 1700

수 신 : 장 관(기협)

발 신 : 주 화란 대사

제 목 : 중동원유 의존도

대: WHO-0252

대호, 주재국의 원유수입현황을 아래 보고함.

1. 총 수입량

0 1988년도: 51,394 백만 KG, 11,043 백만길다(약5,556 백만 미불)

0 1989년도: 51,475 백만 KG, 14,277 백만길다(약6,734 백만 미불)

2. 중동지역 국가로부터의 수입

0 1988년도: 총 25,483 백만 KG, 약 2,596 백만미불

- 시리아 62 백만 KG, 10 백만 길다(약 5백만미불)
- 이락 1,894 백만 KG, 396 백만 길다(약 200백만 미불)
- 이란 10,354 백만 KG, 2,091 백만 길다(약1,050 백만 미불)
- 사우디 6,549 백만 KG, 1,367 백만 길다(약 685백만 미불)
- 쿠웨이트 6,254 백만 KG, 1,239 백만 길다(약620 백만 미불)
- U.A.E 354 백만 KG, 67 백만 길다(약 34백만 미불)
- 오만 16 백만 KG, 3 백만 길다(약 1.5백만 미불)

0 1989년도: 총 29,042백만 KG, 약 3,848 백만미불 56.4%

- 이락 4,866 백만 KG, 1,364 백만 길다(약 680백만 미불)
- 이란 8,312 백만 KG, 2,222 백만 길다(약 1,110백만 미불)
- 사우디 8,748 백만 KG, 2,273 백만 길다(약1,136 백만 미불)
- 쿠웨이트 6,522 백만 KG, 1,688 백만 길다(약843 백만 미불)
- U.A.E. 594 백만 KG, 159 백만 길다 (약 79백만 미불). 끝.

(대사 최상섭-국장)

경제국

PAGE 1

90.09.06 08:27 WH

외신 1과 통제관

0039

원 본

외 무 부

종 별 : 지 급

번 호 : USW-4028 일 시 : 90 0905 1756

수 신 : 장관(기협)

발 신 : 주미대사

제 목 : 석유시장 및 유가 동향(9)

표제 관련 9.4-5 당지 언론 보도를 종합 보고함.

1.유가 동향

가. 9.4 원유 및 정유 제품 가격(뉴욕 상품 시장)

0 원유(LIGHT SWEET CRUDE, 10월 인도 가격)

:배럴당 29.12(전일 대비 6.6 프로- 1.80불 상승)

0 휘발유(9월 인도 가격-)

: 갤런당 94.52 센트(전일 대비 9.7 프로- 8.34 센트상승)

0 난방유(10월 인도 가격)

:갤런당 82.39 센트(전일 대비 5.83 센트 상승)

나.유가 상승 원인

0 유엔 사무총장의 대이락 중재 노력 실패등에따른 중동 위기의 장기화 전망 팽배와 이에 따른석유 시장내의 불확실성 고조

0쿠웨이트의 대단위 정유소 손실에 따른 정유 시설부족 현상(원유 공급은 여타 수출국이 증산하여해결 가능하나, 정유 시설 부족은 단기간에 해결곤란)

2.중장기 유가 전망

0중동 전쟁 발발등 특별한 상황 변화가 없다면유가는 현재의 상승된 가격 수준(23-30불)에서보합세를 보일것으로 전망

0 유류 소비가 급증하는 겨울철에 접어들면 유가 상승이 있을것으로 예측

0 그러나, 여타 수출국의 증산 매문에 유가가 최고32 불을 초과하게 되지는 않을것으로 전망됨.

3.상기 언론 보도 내용 별첨 FAX 송부함.

첨부: USW(F)-2082 . 끝.

경제국

PAGE 1

공람	국제경제국	10년 9월 6일	담 당	과 장	국 장	차관보	차 관	장 관
					V			

90.09.06 08:40 CT

외신 1과 통제관

0040

09/05/90 18:14 ☎202 797 0595 EMBASSY OF KOREA ---→ WOI 2

주 미 대 사 관

보안 통제	협

번호 : USW(F) - 2082

수신 : 장관 (기협)

발신 : 주미대사

제목 : USW - 4028 첨부 (17매)

Oil Prices Turn Up, Rising 6.6%

Events Suggesting Mideast Stalemate Worry Investors

By MATTHEW L. WALD

Oil prices jumped 6.6 percent in New York yesterday, but traders cited no compelling reason, except an attitude of general pessimism about the Persian Gulf, and Monday's price rise in London when the New York market was closed for Labor Day.

Some analysts cited the failure over the weekend of negotiations between the United Nations Secretary General, Javier Pérez de Cuéllar, and the Iraqi Foreign Minister, Tariq Aziz, to produce movement toward resolving the five-week-old crisis.

Light sweet crude for October delivery closed on the New York Mercantile Exchange at $29.12, up $1.80 from Friday's close, to the highest level since Aug. 24. "This market is still searching for an equilibrium price," said Andrew Lebow, a futures trader at E.D.&F. Man International. "In getting there, it has been subject to these wide emotional swings."

Markets Made Skittish

Two news items during the day made the market more skittish: The United States Navy said it boarded an Iraqi-flag tanker headed home with Sri Lankan tea, and Reuters reported that Iraq had repudiated an announcement by the Palestine Liberation Organization that Iraq would make peace in exchange for a small slice of Kuwaiti territory and other concessions.

"The market heard that and got spooked even higher," said one trader, who said that his firm's rules did not allow him to be identified. If Iraq was backing away from a proposed settlement, the trader said, it indicated that the Iraqi President, Saddam Hussein, "does not have his back to the wall." That, he said, suggests that the crisis will drag on.

At Temple, Barker & Sloane Inc., a consulting firm based in Lexington, Mass., Paul E. Mawn, an oil consultant, said prices were rising because "the only thing the oil industry can't stand is uncertainty."

Potential for a Spark

The Persian Gulf is at a stalemate, with the potential for an electric spark," he said. "You have a very volatile situation."

Some analysts said the price of oil was depressed on Friday in the expectation that the United Nations Secretary General would make progress in his visit to Baghdad. An analyst at one oil company said: "When he got there, they found out they were miles apart and they had nothing to talk about. And today, nothing has been positive. It is an emotional type of market, and it doesn't take much to trigger it in one direction or the other."

At Purvin & Gertz, a Houston consulting firm, Ken Miller, who follows the oil market, said, "Delays in getting the hostages out, fear of military action, anything of that nature tends to make the market do radical things."

But the prices are still far short of where they would be in a war, oil experts say. Mr. Lebow of Man International said the lack of diplomatic progress might suggest that a military solution was more likely. He added: "But I don't think the market really believes that, either. Most people don't believe a military conflict is coming any time soon."

Gasoline was up even more sharply than crude oil. Unleaded regular, for delivery next month, closed at 94.62 cents a gallon, up 8.34 cents a gallon, the equivalent of $3.50 a barrel.

Gasoline is in tighter supply than crude oil for two reasons. Consuming companies that want to increase inventory because they are nervous about future prices have strongly increased orders, and refining capacity is in short supply. Prices are up sharply in Europe, and traders said that cargoes from the Gulf Coast were going to Europe instead of New York, thus dragging up the New York price.

Traders often base decisions o[n in]ventory figures. But the Ameri[can] Petroleum Institute, which usu[ally] releases inventory numbers after [the] market closes on Tuesdays, said y[es]terday that its weekly figures wou[ld] be late because of Labor Day.

Heating oil prices were also [up] sharply, by 5.83 cents, to 82.39 cent[s] for October delivery.

With continuing concern about [a] crisis that drags on into the winter when demand for many products [is] higher, both heating oil and gasolin[e] rose by their allowable limits, 4 cent[s] a gallon, for the next four months

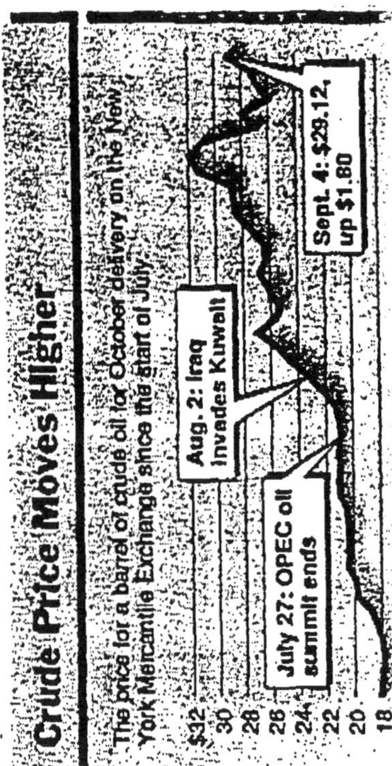

NYT 9/5/90

Newsclippings Econ. Section I

0041

09/05/90 18:15 ☎202 797 0595 EMBASSY OF KOREA →→→ WOI 2

WP 9/5/90

0042

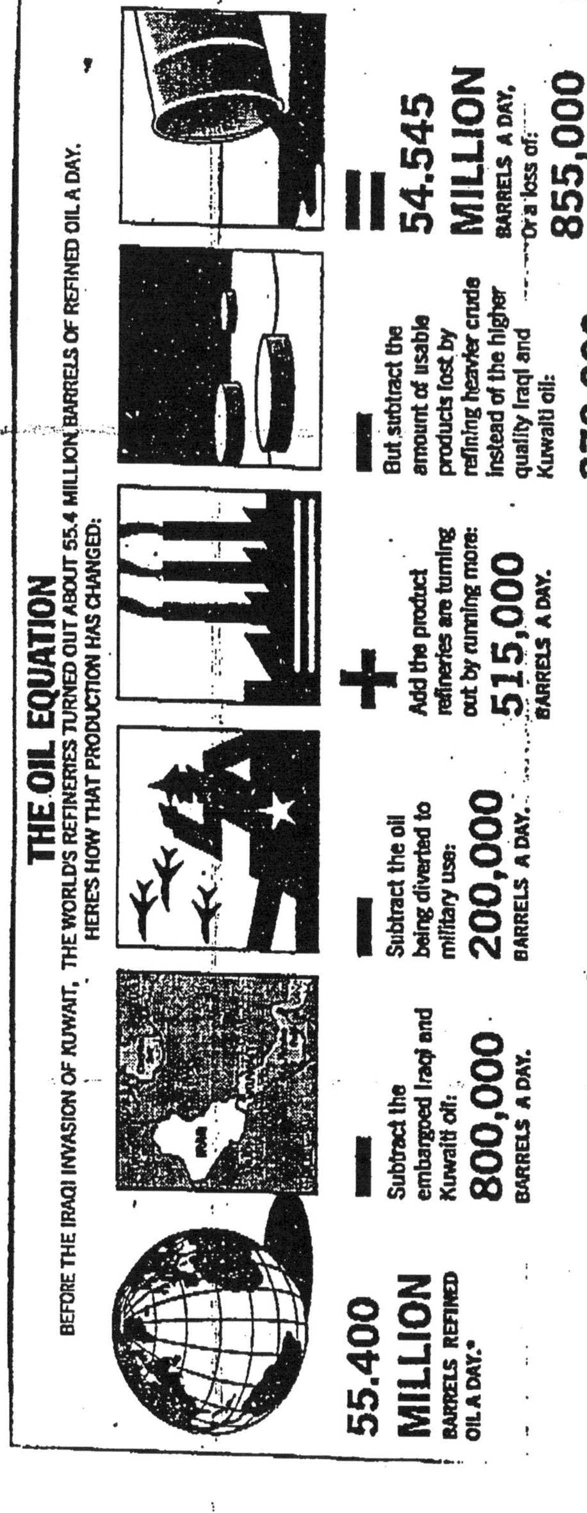

THE OIL EQUATION

BEFORE THE IRAQI INVASION OF KUWAIT, THE WORLD'S REFINERIES TURNED OUT ABOUT 55.4 MILLION BARRELS OF REFINED OIL A DAY. HERE'S HOW THAT PRODUCTION HAS CHANGED:

55.400 MILLION BARRELS REFINED OIL A DAY.*

− Subtract the embargoed Iraqi and Kuwaiti oil: **800,000** BARRELS A DAY.

− Subtract the oil being diverted to military use: **200,000** BARRELS A DAY.

+ Add the product refineries are turning out by running more: **515,000** BARRELS A DAY.

− But subtract the amount of usable products lost by refining heavier crude instead of the higher quality Iraqi and Kuwaiti oil: **370,000** BARRELS A DAY.

= **54.545 MILLION** BARRELS A DAY, Or a loss of: **855,000** BARRELS A DAY.

*World 1989 production, excluding China and the U.S.S.R.
SOURCES: American Petroleum Institute, Kidder Peabody & Co.

2082-2

REUTER

Officer guards Saudi Arabia's Ras Tanura refinery, one of world's largest.

Squeeze on Refineries May Lead to Shortages

Industry Changes Leave U.S. Vulnerable

By Thomas W. Lippman and Mark Potts
Washington Post Staff Writers

The threat of a worldwide crude oil shortage has receded, but consumers and businesses in the United States and Asia appear to be facing another painful side effect of the Persian Gulf crisis: shortages of gasoline and other fuels because of a lack of refineries to turn the oil into usable products.

Kuwait's huge, sophisticated refineries provided gasoline and diesel fuel for the U.S. military in the Pacific and for commercial users throughout Asia. With those refineries out of business and Saudi Arabia diverting fuel from commercial markets to the immense military buildup there, many oil industry experts believe fuel shortages are likely even if supplies of crude oil are adequate.

The United States is especially vulnerable because more than 100 refineries have closed in this country for economic and environmental reasons in the past decade, while no new ones have been built. The refineries that remain are operating very close—dangerously close, some experts believe—to full capacity.

Fear of such shortages is the reason prices of gasoline and jet fuel keep rising, analysts said. While crude oil prices are not as volatile as they were in the initial days of the crisis, they continue to fluctuate. Yesterday, crude oil contracts in New York were up $1.80 a barrel over Friday, closing at $29.12.

Most world attention since Iraq invaded Kuwait has focused on the availability of crude oil. But industry officials say the refining capacity problem preceded the current crisis and has its roots in the economics of the oil industry over the past 10 years—a period in which more than 100 U.S. refineries have shut down, reducing the nation's refinery capacity to 15.5 million barrels a day from 18 million in 1981. Total world refining capacity, outside the Soviet Union and China, is 55.4 million barrels a day, according to the American Petroleum Institute.

Refiners here and overseas are scrambling to increase their output.

The Ashland Oil Co. refinery in Canton, Ohio, for example, was scheduled to shut down in mid-October for routine maintenance, putting its 66,000 barrels a day of capacity out of commission for four weeks. But now the Ashland,

2082 3

0043

Ky., company is considering a plan to perform only essential repairs and return the refinery to service in a much shorter time, perhaps 10 days.

Houston-based Coastal Corp., meanwhile, is accelerating the reopening of a 50-year-old refinery on the Caribbean island of Aruba that it bought last year. And Saudi Arabia has increased the output of its refinery at Ras Tanura, on the Persian Gulf, by nearly one-third, even though the former operating level was more efficient.

Some tightness in the market has already developed. The Department of Defense has reported difficulty in obtaining enough jet fuel to support the airlift of troops and equipment to Saudi Arabia. Some U.S. airlines are reportedly stockpiling jet fuel. Analysts say that jet fuel and diesel oil are in short supply throughout Asia, which was heavily dependent on supplies from Kuwait.

"We're starting from a tight situation," said the chief executive of one major oil company. "I'm not saying it's the end of the world or anything, but it's going to stay tight."

"OPEC production does not solve the refinery problem," said Theodore Eck, chief economist for Amoco Corp., referring to last week's agreement by the Organization of Petroleum Exporting Countries to allow its members to increase oil production to make up for the loss of Iraqi and Kuwaiti output. "The bottleneck could well be the refinery problem."

U.S. refineries were running almost at full bore even before Iraq invaded Kuwait, and have continued to do so. In the week that ended Aug. 24, capacity utilization at American refineries was 96 percent—the highest figure industry officials can remember, and a level some experts consider dangerous.

"Whenever the utilization is above 85 percent, the situation becomes literally explosive," according to Peter Beutel, an oil expert at Merrill Lynch & Co.

The embargo on imports from Iraq and Kuwait applies to refined petroleum products as well as crude oil, removing about 1.5 percent of the world's refining capacity, according to one estimate. Other oil-producing countries are making up for most of the lost crude, but it is more difficult to replace the missing refining capacity.

The world has become more dependent in recent years on refining capacity in the Middle East that now is endangered by the crisis there.

ago refined all its own oil, now imports about 11 percent of its refined petroleum products, mostly from Europe and the Caribbean, but also from the Middle East.

"I believe that the most immediate concern here is for [petroleum] products," said Ernie W. Stamper, vice president for administration at Ashland's refining division. "Crude oil is a secondary concern. The crude oil shortage is out there, but it looms in the more distant future."

Many oil industry officials and analysts believe that the tight refining situation could easily result in spot shortages of products—especially if there is a significant refinery fire or accident in the United States, of which there have been several already this year.

"If people are worried about any one thing that I see in the industry, they're worried about product supplies," Eck said. "By the time the first snow falls, that could be a pretty big problem."

"Refineries are running flat out. If we were to have a major disruption—heaven forbid, a fire or a major disruption at a plant—it would produce some problems," said Scott Lovejoy, executive director of the American Independent Refiners Association, a trade group. "Any protracted disruption would be very serious."

"Are you worried about a tight gasoline market? You ought to be," said William Randol, an oil industry analyst at First Boston Corp. in New York. "Depending on how long this thing goes on, we could see gasoline supplies be very tight." For that reason, many Wall Street analysts are recommending that their clients buy stocks in oil refining companies, such as Ashland, because their profits will rise as demand drives up prices.

Not everybody is so pessimistic about fuel supplies. "I wouldn't characterize it as an alarm," said Will Price, president of Chevron USA, the refining and marketing arm of San Francisco-based Chevron Corp., the nation's largest refiner. "In our forecasting, we do not visualize any ratcheting up of prices due to refining capacity."

"The refinery utilization rates are high, but they're in the low 90s [percent], and they're probably sustainable," said Ron Jones, director of refining for the American Petroleum Institute, a Washington-based industry association.

Other experts argue that higher petroleum prices will reduce demand enough to keep it within the capacity of the world's refining sys-

2082-4

0044

fall more heavily on developing countries, which cannot afford to compete with the United States, Japan and Europe for available supplies.

U.S. capacity, meanwhile, is likely to fall further in the next few years, experts say, because of tighter regulations on gasoline quality and refinery pollution. Not a single full-scale refinery has been built in the United States in nearly two decades, and industrial officials and analysts say environmental and economic constraints will continue the drought for the foreseeable future.

Overseas refinery construction, on the other hand, has been robust in recent years because of looser environmental regulations and the desire by oil-producing companies to cut out the middle man and refine their own oil. The effect of that was to increase U.S. dependence not only on imported crude oil but on imported gasoline, jet fuel and heating oil as well.

Analysts at Kidder, Peabody & Co. have calculated the worldwide net loss of refinery output since the Aug. 2 invasion at 855,000 barrels a day: 800,000 in Kuwait and Iraq shut down because of the embargo, 200,000 in Saudi Arabia diverted from commercial markets to military use, and 370,000 in reduced output elsewhere from using lower-quality replacement crude oils, partially offset by a 515,000 barrel increase in output at operating refineries.

That is a shortfall of only 1.5 percent. But analysts say that what matters is not the total but the availability of the "last barrel" needed by a consumer. If the U.S. Air Force and a commercial airline in Southeast Asia are both shopping for jet fuel, for instance, they are going to bid up the price and probably buy more than they need for immediate use. Crude oil output can be increased with relative ease, but refinery expansion requires time and money.

Another problem is that much of the crude oil that OPEC members have promised to produce to make up the loss of Iraqi and Kuwaiti crude is of poorer quality than the oil that was removed from the market. As a result, it takes more oil—and more expensive processing—for a refinery to make gasoline and other fuels.

For this reason, some experts say, some of the additional OPEC production is having trouble finding buyers, despite the shortfall in world oil supplies. Venezuela, for example, produces heavy, high-sulfur crude—closer in composition to asphalt than gasoline—that most refineries in this hemisphere cannot break down into light fuels such as gasoline and jet fuel. The products most easily made from such heavy crude are industrial fuel oils, for which there is less demand.

While refineries in the United States and Asia are running at near-maximum capacity, there is surplus capacity in some other parts of the world, notably Europe and the Caribbean. But experts say the extra refining capacity is limited and, in any case, those plants don't make the kinds of products—principally high-quality unleaded gasoline—needed by the United States. Arnold Safer, a former Exxon Corp. executive who now is president of the Energy Futures Group in Bethesda, estimates that it would cost $8.6 billion and take 20 years to upgrade Caribbean refineries to U.S. standards.

"There is idle refining capacity not in this country but in other parts of the world, but that idle refining capacity is not designed to supply the needs for products that we have," Lovejoy said.

3/3

2082-5

0045

WT 9/5/9

Oil price rise hits world economies

By Lauren Weiner
THE WASHINGTON TIMES

As the price of crude oil soars and a trade embargo against Iraq and Kuwait bites, the Persian Gulf crisis is also beginning to hit the global economy, affecting everything from the Japanese construction industry to Irish beef sales.

A spokesman at the Jordanian Embassy in Washington said obeying the United Nations embargo imposed on Iraq and Kuwait Aug. 6 will cost Jordan $2 billion by the end of this year, or half its annual gross domestic product.

Egypt said the crisis could cost it $2 billion in 1991.

Experts said Brazil could lose a comparable sum by participating in the embargo because it is both highly dependent on Iraqi oil and one of Iraq's major trading partners, supplying arms, manufactured goods and frozen chicken to the Middle Eastern country.

Ireland's observance of the U.N. embargo has sent the Irish cattle industry into a tailspin. Ireland earned some $135 million a year from beef sales to Iraq, its fourth most important customer in an industry that brings 10 percent of total Irish export earnings.

Canadian wheat and grain sales, which constituted most of its $258 million in exports to Iraq last year, were halted as soon as sanctions were announced, and ships bearing the wheat and grain have yet to find alternative customers.

Even countries with healthy economies to cushion the ill effects of an oil crisis stand to lose billions. Japanese construction firms were active in Iraq, for example, and Japan may never see repayment of some $4.7 billion Iraq owes for plant and equipment purchases.

Egypt's losses come mostly in wages sent home by more than 1 million Egyptian workers in Iraq and Kuwait. Similarly, the economy of the Philippines will lose some $1 billion sent home yearly by the 75,000 Filipino workers in the two Middle Eastern countries.

Pakistan, with 100,000 nationals working in the two countries at the time of the invasion, also will be severely hurt.

Speakers at a U.N. conference on the world's 41 least developed countries voiced concern yesterday that the Gulf crisis would cut the "peace dividend" emerging from reduced military spending by the superpowers.

The United States, fearing Third World nations especially hurt by the loss of trade might be tempted to violate the embargo, has begun a fund-raising drive to aid poor countries and keep them involved in the campaign against Iraqi President Saddam Hussein.

Treasury Secretary Nicholas Brady, in Paris yesterday seeking a French commitment of funds, will go from there to London, South Korea and Japan, among other stops. Tonight, Secretary of State James A. Baker III will embark on a similar fund-raising mission.

President Bush yesterday announced the United States would forgive Egypt's $7 billion military debt, a reward for its heavy commitment of troops to Saudi Arabia.

Washington's mood of forgiveness "will probably not spill over to other countries, such as those in Latin America," said John Williamson of the Institute for International Economics.

Mr. Williamson said the debts of most Third World countries may weigh even more heavily if the crisis wears on for months, bringing on a global recession and higher interest rates.

The crisis comes at a particularly crucial time for the countries of Central and Eastern Europe as the cash-poor former Soviet clients attempt to switch from communist to free-market economies.

2082-6

0046

09/05/90 18:20 ☎202 797 0595 EMBASSY OF KOREA → WOI 2

Failure of U.N. chief, Iraqi to reach accord sends crude prices up

By Penny Britell
REUTERS NEWS AGENCY

NEW YORK — Crude oil prices in New York staged their strongest advance in more than a week yesterday, boosted by renewed concerns about the Mideast crisis.

October crude oil futures jumped $1.80 to $29.12 a barrel — the highest close since Aug. 24 and the largest gain since Aug. 23.

"The major bullish factor was the collapse of talks between U.N. Secretary-General Javier Perez de Cuellar and Iraqi Foreign Minister Tariq Aziz this weekend," said Andrew Lebow of E.D. and F. Man International Futures Inc.

"U.S. crude prices were also catching up to Europe," Mr. Lebow added. Crude oil price gains matched overseas gains Monday, when U.S. markets were closed for the Labor Day holiday.

"The market is where it should be," said Mari Buglass, an analyst with Shearson Lehman Hutton in London.

October gasoline rose 8.34 cents to 94.52 cents a gallon, with October heating oil gaining 5.83 cents to 82.39 cents.

Traders said crude oil futures were mainly catching up with gains posted in European and Asian cash markets Monday, when U.S. futures markets shut for the holiday.

But prices also rose on belief there will be no near-term solution to the Persian Gulf crisis sparked by Iraq's Aug. 2 invasion of Kuwait, analysts said.

"Even though there is no news out, it [trading] is still on the Gulf crisis," said one trader, who described early business as stormy.

Analysts predict energy prices, which gained sharply after Baghdad's invasion, will settle into a steadier trading pattern short-term and then rise as winter approaches.

"The market seems to be settling into a cyclic range of $23 to $30 per barrel for crude, and in the absence of military action this situation could persist for some weeks," said London-based analyst Geoff Pyne of UBS Phillips and Drew.

Mr. Buglass said technical charts pointed to possible further gains — even if war does not break out in the Gulf. But the analyst thought it unlikely the market would test recent highs of $32 now that some producer nations are pumping [extra] oil to make up for the absence of I[raqi] and Kuwaiti exports.

But as winter nears, demand is li[kely] to pick up.

"During the fourth quarter the ma[rket] will gradually tighten, so the underl[ying] pressure on prices remains upwa[rd]," Mr. Pyne said.

And Mehdi Varzi of brokerage K[lein]wort Benson says a tightening of supp[ly] is likely to push oil prices back over [$30] per barrel during the fourth quarter.

He called on the International En[ergy] Agency to release strategic reserve[s of] oil stocks from its member countrie[s to] alleviate potential shortages.

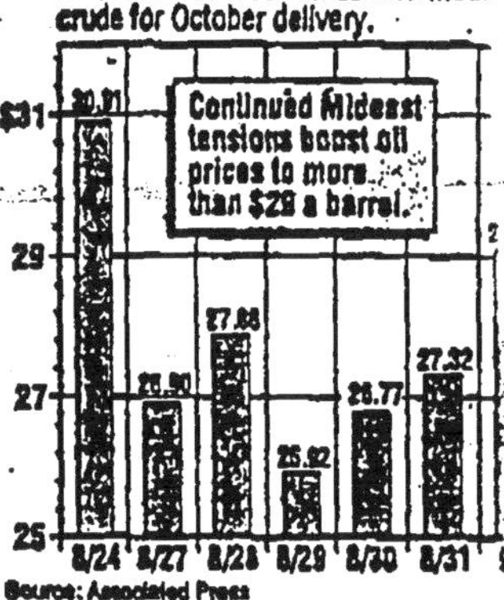

Chart by Paul Compton / The Washington [Times]

WT 9/5

2082-7

0047

Little guys cut gas prices to get buyers

By Todd Smith
THE WASHINGTON TIMES

Small independent marketers of gasoline are realizing they hurt themselves by jacking up prices in the past few weeks and have begun scaling them down to win back the customers they lost.

Crown, Getty, Merit, Hess, East Coast Oil and Steuart Petroleum Co. — stations that once prided themselves and profited by undercutting the major brands down the street — discovered that the unrest in the worldwide oil market since the Persian Gulf crisis erupted pushed their prices higher than the competition's.

Last week, these gasoline marketers started aiming toward pre-crisis levels. While still higher than they were before Iraq invaded Kuwait, the independents' prices are lower than the $1.20 average of Washington's major stations.

Since the independents don't pump their own crude from the ground, they have to buy refined products and crude oil through an increasingly volatile New York Mercantile Exchange. In passing the increases on to the consumer, they concede, they have alienated their customer base.

"We have had a 55 percent drop in volume since the developments in the Middle East have escalated," said John C. Johnson, chief executive officer of the Steuart Petroleum Co. of Washington, which has 87 stations from Jacksonville, Fla., to Baltimore.

"We have decided we must lower the prices in order to keep the customers we had before this whole thing happened."

He said customers started abandoning Steuart's pumps after he raised the price of regular unleaded to $1.23 a gallon, three cents higher than the major oil company average of $1.20 for the Washington area. Last week, he dropped it back to $1.17 and has seen an immediate resurgence of customer support.

It was the first time in the company's 85-year history that its prices were higher than those of the major oil companies, he said.

Analysts said the move to lower prices would help the independents in the short term, but they cautioned that if the oil-price crisis persists, these companies will have to rethink their pricing strategies or take a big hit in the bottom line.

"The smaller stations will do better at first, but since they are tied to the spot market, we do not know how long they can afford to do this, nor do we know how long [crude] prices will remain elevated," said John Hilton, an oil expert with Argus Research in New York.

Steve Mottus, an analyst with Legg Mason Wood Walker of Baltimore, said the overall implications of these pricing strategies remain to be seen.

"They are trying to win back some market share from the majors," Mr. Mottus said, adding, "While they are trying to keep their customers, the price situation both at the pump and in the crude market are still very uncertain. ... These companies could be hurting themselves."

Richmond-based East Coast Oil Co., which operates 42 gas stations in Virginia, had raised prices by as much as 12 cents to $1.24 for a gallon of regular unleaded. President John Steele said he immediately saw a drop in customer traffic at his stations.

"We've been in discount gas retailing for 50 years and we have always priced below the majors," he declared. "But over the last month, costs went up so much the consumers were hurt at the pump.

"The consumers were mad. They were negative. They thought someone was doing something illegal," he said. As a result, he rolled back prices nine cents a gallon last Thursday to $1.15. "Customers immediately started coming back."

Crown Central Petroleum Corp. of Baltimore, one of the largest independent marketers in the area, has rolled prices back from $1.15, still below the area average, to $1.13. That's 10 cents above Crown's July price.

"Being the smaller merchan[ts] ... are followers [behind major oil c[om]panies] as opposed to a leader," Paul Ebner, general manage[r of] marketing and support service[s at] Crown. "We establish our prices [rel]ative to our primary competit[ors] however, we are forced to buy o[n the] spot market."

He said that while the comp[any] has had good reaction from cust[om]ers, there is some unrest among b[uy]ers of the mid- and high-gr[ade] blends.

"We lost our customers on high and middle gasolines, but ti[me] again prices in the worldwide market are higher than they ha[ve] been in recent memory," Mr. Ebn[er] said. He added, "It's difficult to p[re]dict what will happen, but I hope [we] have seen the marketplace peak. We are still in an uneasy situation."

The story is the same at Hess a[nd] Merit. Representatives of both sa[id] they have lowered prices because t[oo] many customers were staying aw[ay].

Greg Marshall, manager of t[he] Merit station at 1739 New Jers[ey] Ave. NW, said he was forced to rai[se] prices to $1.19 a gallon but cut ba[ck] to $1.159 in recent days. "We s[aw] people leaving. We lost our custom[er] base, so we really had no choice."

His price was $1.09 before t[he] Gulf situation sent gas prices spir[al]ing, and as low as 99 cents a gall[on] in early July.

At a Getty station at 5930 Gree[n]belt Road in Greenbelt, manag[er] Rusty Kerber said he saw day-to-d[ay] sales slump when prices peaked [at] $1.199 a gallon, so he peeled his pric[e] back to $1.16. "We had to to keep th[e] customers rolling in," he sai[d]. "Lower prices are definitely gettin[g] more of our customers back."

WT 9/5/[90]

2082-8

0048

New Heavy Oil Supplies Could Prove Costly

By DAVID BIRD
Knight-Ridder Financial

NEW YORK — Increased volumes of heavy crude oil, particularly from Venezuela, may cause problems for less-sophisticated refineries and lead to costlier petroleum products later this year, executives at smaller U.S. refineries said.

Many older U.S. refineries could handle the types of heavy Kuwaiti and Iraqi oil lost to the market but will have difficulty processing the even thicker oil expected from Venezuela.

Refiners said this could add about 2.5 cents a gallon to the cost of making light products, such as gasoline, later this year. Another likely effect is very high stocks of heavy products such as residual fuel oil.

"A lot of the smaller refineries can't make good use of the heavy oil," said a supply executive at one such company.

"Your Exxons and Shells and big companies have invested in more sophisticated equipment over the years, so they can handle it. What's going to happen is refiners who can run heavy oil will run heavy oil and they'll get it for a decent price. But those of us who can't will have to pay higher prices and look for the lighter stuff."

Larger refiners with massive cash resources began making investments to upgrade machinery to process heavy oil in the last decade, officials said.

"Light crude volumes have been expected to taper off and the heavy stuff has been seen as the crude of the future. But there are greater amounts than some people expected and it's a lot sludgier," one refiner said. "Some people are going to have a real problem with it, and for quite a while, if the situation in the (Persian) Gulf isn't resolved" quickly, he said.

At least 2.5 million barrels of heavy oil is expected from Saudi Arabia and Venezuela, as a result of an Organization of Petroleum Exporting Countries agreement last week to lift output restraints until the gulf crisis ends.

Celestino Armas, Venezuelan oil minister, who told Knight-Ridder Financial News at the Vienna OPEC talks he will imminently increase supplies of oil to the market, has only more heavy oil to sell.

Mr. Armas also indicated his concern with the quality of the new oil coming to the market. He said he favored cooperation with consumer countries, which would result in the release of light crude oil from strategic reserves, "to balance the global quality of the energy supply," he said.

Venezuela has indicated it may try to switch supplies to its own refineries, using its heaviest oil for domestic consumption and releasing lighter grades to the market, IEA officials said.

Venezuela, a major supplier of gasoline to the United States, may use a lot of the heavy oil in their own refinery network, supply officials said. But some are concerned.

"Venezuela has come to us looking to buy some light crude oil," said a supply executive at a major U.S. company. "That's a little worrying, since we're looking to them for more oil."

Officials at the Paris-based International Energy Agency expressed concern last week that releases of government stockpiles may be necessary in the fourth quarter, as shortages of light refined products — gasoline and naphtha — are likely to develop at that time, because of the predominance of heavy oil in the market. In particular, IEA officials said, Venezuelan oil with an American Petroleum Institute gravity of 22 degrees may be too heavy for some refiners to handle.

2082-9

0049

09/05/90 18:23 ☎202 797 0595 EMBASSY OF KOREA --→ WOI 2

No Panacea

Petroleum Reserve Has Lots of Oil, but Using It Could Be a Challenge

Many Refineries Can't Handle 'Sour' Crude; Distribution Might Bring Bottlenecks

A New Game for Speculators

By CALEB SOLOMON and ROSE GUTFELD
Staff Reporters of THE WALL STREET JOURNAL

BRYAN MOUND, Texas—In early May, as Phillips Petroleum Co. moved a tanker-load of oil into a pipeline near here, a dock employee scrawled an identifying label: "5-2-90 Basra." It said. Iraqi crude.

Iraq might not be pleased with the disposition of that shipment, but the U.S. is. Today it sits in a huge underground cavern here, part of America's 590-million-barrel insurance policy in a global crisis Iraq brought on.

U.S. policy makers take comfort in the confidence that if the crisis worsens and world oil supplies contract, this Strategic Petroleum Reserve can be summoned at the stroke of a presidential pen; its crude oil can be quickly and smoothly distributed, refined and put to use fueling everything from cars to home furnaces to factories.

Or at least that's the theory.

In practice, getting SPR oil into the hands of consumers would be a formidable challenge. While strategists often talk of the petroleum reserve as if it could be turned on like a water tap, the reality is a vast and enormously complex system. Nobody says the reserve wouldn't work, but the current crisis is raising a host of practical questions about how fast and reliably it could deliver.

Strategic Petroleum Reserve oil, some of it in storage for 13 years, has been withdrawn and sold only once. That was a 10-week, million-barrel test auction begun in late in 1985 conducted under non-stressful conditions. This worries oil executives such as Leighton Steward, chairman of Louisiana Land & Exploration Co. "If you had a potential weapon you could use—that's what the SPR is, a weapon—you wouldn't go to battle with it never tested," he says. Before there's any turn for the worse in the Persian Gulf, he and others suggest, maybe the government should tap into the SPR to "get out the bugs."

Among the bugs they see are these:

—Two-thirds of petroleum-reserve oil is the wrong kind for many U.S. refineries. It is "sour" crude containing so much sulfur that if those plants tried to turn it into gasoline they could be ruined.

—Equipment and physical problems have dogged the reserve since it was hastily set up in the mid-1970s. At one site, certain pipes have corroded and ruptured. Another $90 million facility may collapse inward as soon as oil is withdrawn.

—If the SPR is opened, anyone with enough money will be able to buy its oil, including speculators who could hoard it, defeating the reserve's purpose.

—Up to 10% of the oil can be allocated any way the Energy Department sees fit, a rule that could spur a political free-for-all.

—U.S. law says only American-flag tankers can move the oil about the country. So heavy drawdowns could mean a distribution bottleneck.

Officials of the Strategic Petroleum Reserve express confidence that they could handle such problems. Although "it's predictable we'll have some operational difficulties," says the reserve's director, John Bartholomew, "the SPR stands at its highest state of readiness ever." He says it has been "exercised" more than 25 times in the past decade. But Randy Suhl, a crude oil analyst for Lyondell Petrochemical Co. in Houston, says, "The question is whether they can pump it at the rate they say they can."

At the moment, officials ranging from Washington politicians to Middle East oil ministers are debating whether or when the ocean of oil buried in the SPR ought to be tapped. The Iraq-Kuwait crisis and world embargo has sidelined four million barrels of daily oil production, and while other producers promise to fill most of that gap, the SPR could eliminate the rest. It could also offset any spot shortages in the coming heating season, and some experts say that release of even small amounts of reserve oil would calm the volatile petroleum markets. But so far the free-market-oriented Bush administration isn't buying these arguments.

The idea of a strategic oil reserve first popped up before World War I when Winston Churchill converted the British navy to oil from coal. But he never set one up, and neither did the U.S. until after the 1973-74 Arab oil embargo. Congress authorized the SPR a year later.

The government began pumping oil into it in 1977, but it took another oil crunch to spur serious buying. In 1981, with prices soaring to more than $40 a barrel, SPR purchases hit a one-year record of 122.5 million barrels. Unfortunately, in that

scramble the government boug
the most affordable oil, and tha
was the lowest grade.

Now the SPR is heavy on "so
which is harder to process than
"sweet." It also yields less per
the most popular products, suc
octane gasoline. In fact, about
reserve is sour Mexican crude
that was bought for special rea
billion oil purchase in the early
part of a financial rescue of t
try.

Many large refineries, such a
huge facility in Texas City, Texas
cess both sweet and sour crudes
ers can't; a Marathon Oil refine
same city demands almost ex
sweet crude. So do numerous oth
oil refineries from Odessa, Tex
Dorado, Ark. Overall, about ha
million barrel-a-day refining ca
the Gulf Coast and 50% of Midwe
ity isn't suited to sour crude, says
Manning of Purvin & Gertz Inc.,
dustry consultant.

"I've only found three crude
SPR] we could even run," says a
official of the Indiana Farm Bure
erative. (The reserve contains eig
of crude in all.) He fears supply p
for his 21,000 barrel-a-day, 1940-vi
finery. "The metallurgy of our
quires a sweet crude. In a short ti
crude] would eat up the plant,"
The co-op supplies 50% of the fuel
Indiana farmers.

Mr. Bartholomew, the director
petroleum reserve, concedes that s
fineries can't handle sour crude.
notes that many are changing equ
and also says that the SPR would
the only source of oil, even in a
gency. "Sometimes [refiners] th
SPR should be the answer for an
he complains.

SPR oil is stored in Texas and
ana in five giant salt domes and o
doned salt mine. A typical cavern
200 feet in diameter and 2,000 feet
taller than the World Trade Center
York. At the facility here in Bryan
50 miles south of Houston, 20 caver
been hollowed out of a 10-mile-de
formation far below the marshy
Engineers make the caverns by dr
hole and pouring in fresh water, th
solving some of the salt, and then
ing the process to enlarge the cav
unlike fresh water, doesn't dissolve
walls.

To retrieve stored oil, fresh
would be pumped in through a pipe
to the bottom of the cavern. T
which is lighter than water, would
the top and be piped away. At
Mound, it could be pumped 46 mi
terminal on the Houston Ship Cha
four miles back to the Phillips doc
rently, this site, like the rest of th
leum reserve, is on "Alert Level T
poised to withdraw oil, says Neil P
Department of Energy site mana
works beautifully," he declares.

WSJ 2082-10

0050

Apparently not all SPR sites are in such fine fettle. A facility in Calcasieu Parish, La., was developed in such a hurry that its three caverns are too close to each other and to the edge of the salt dome. The first time water is pumped in to extract oil is also expected to be the last. Though officials say the oil will come out, they predict the walls will collapse behind it. The Energy Department has been hoping to move the oil elsewhere but can't until 1992.

In fact, structural integrity is a long-term problem for most of the other SPR caverns. Every time fresh water is pumped in, it will dissolve more of their walls, too. By contrast, commercial salt dome facilities that regularly move oil in and out use brine, which doesn't eat away the salt walls. But that is expensive and requires huge brine storage capacity. While not an impediment to the immediate use of the SPR, the fact that most caverns can only be emptied about five times is one reason officials have been reluctant to conduct a sustained test of the system.

SPR employees are often waging war on corrosion. At Weeks Island, La., the government pressed an old salt mine into service instead of carving out a salt dome. Pumps and other equipment there are deep in the mine, where salt and flooding are threats, rather than above ground. A backup system is planned for 1991.

At a site in Cameron Parish, La., pipe used to carry off brine formed as the caverns are created has corroded and ruptured. The General Accounting Office of Congress contends these failures "may be the forerunners of similar problems at other sites."

The SPR's Mr. Bartholomew, acknowledging the need to constantly inspect and repair pipes and pumps, says part of the problem was the "mad rush" to store oil in the early days. "Pipelines were built and protective measures were made later," he says. But corrosion is a common problem in the Oil Patch, he says, and "I'm not aware of any corrosion that will prevent a full-scale drawdown of the SPR."

If the U.S. did draw down the oil, who would get it? Energy Department rules permit anyone—including traders and speculators—to bid for SPR oil so long as they can demonstrate financial responsibility. That would probably mean a certified check, a cashier's check or a letter of credit for 5% of the potential contract amount. The buyer isn't even required to refine the oil. Says Cambridge Energy Research Associates: "SPR oil might just go from salt domes to steel tanks."

"There is essentially no restriction on buyers," agrees Mr. Bartholomew. "Our job is to get the oil out." But he doubts traders would bid if the SPR were tapped. "They can [buy oil] any day they want to," he says, and storing oil adds a carrying cost. Any such trader would be "running a great deal of risk," he says. If speculation did become a problem, presumably the Energy Department could halt it by changing the rules.

Others worry about politicians, not speculators. Under existing rules, the Energy Department can allocate 10% of SPR oil any way it wants. This could pit one part of the country (and its politicians) against another in a scramble for favors. "It could be a problem," says an Energy Department spokesman, "given the large number of potential recipients who all believe in good conscience that they are deserving of it."

Bharat Patel, for instance. He is an official of the New Jersey Board of Public Utilities, and he recently traveled to Houston from Newark for a briefing on the SPR. People in the Northeast "are the ones who will suffer the inordinate price hike" in an oil shortage, he said, asking repeatedly about the 10% special allocation. He finally concluded that "we don't know how it works and neither do the feds."

Pumping the oil and selling it aren't the only challenges; scheduling and loading tankers and moving crude through an intertwined pipeline system could prove daunting for oil buyers. For instance, two oil pipelines initially hooked to the SPR have since become natural-gas pipelines, making it more difficult to reach the Midwest and other points north. And there is no good way to get SPR crude from the Gulf Coast to the West Coast except for the Panama Canal. "It's a really complex network of distribution," says Margaret Felts, a California energy consultant. "You can only move the oil so fast."

The 1985 test of the SPR required only two tankers. In an emergency, most transportation experts say, there might not be enough qualified ships to transfer oil around the U.S. Under a 1920s law called the Jones Act, only U.S.-flagged vessels can operate from one U.S. port to another. Last winter, that kept some badly needed heating oil from getting to the Northeast from Gulf Coast refineries.

The Energy Department says it has an agreement with the Maritime Administration that oil shippers can obtain waivers of the Jones Act within 48 hours. The key would be the extent of SPR use. At 500,000 barrels a day, "there should be enough U.S.-flagged ships," says an Energy Department official. "At one million it starts to get fuzzy. ... At three million there

A final question is whether leum reserve, meant to provid curity, is itself secure. The GA greater vigilance against sabo a 1987 drill in which make-bel ists damaged or destroyed SPR stations, pipeline valves, an em erations center and a bridge. had easily obtained blueprints, e data and diagrams from a local Worse, defenders took 53 "ca 50% from friendly fire.

SPR officials won't say what they're adding in the current co with a nation known for its t rorism. But their concern with evident to a would-be visitor to Mound salt domes, who, after r an unmarked road, is forced to crawl and weave between con riers to get to the gate—only to away by armed guards.

So SPR officials are annoye cism such as the GAO's. In the the mock terrorists "didn't get t fence line," boasts Paul Plaisanc ergy Department manager in leans. Besides, he complains, " mortar attacks against us. Tha War III. I'm not sure the SPR able to defend against World W

2082-11

0051

WSJ 9/5/90

Oil Appetite Grows as Users Top Off Tanks

Unleaded Gasoline Jumps 8.34 Cents to 94.52 Cents; Crude Oil Rises by $1.80

By JAMES TANNER
Staff Reporter of THE WALL STREET JOURNAL

The world's appetite for petroleum seems to be rising on fears of a Middle East war, despite already sharply higher prices and sluggish economies.

People and companies concerned about potential shortages are suddenly "topping off" their tanks, oil economists say. That is putting more upward pressure on prices, the economists add. Also, if there are going to be any oil shortages from the Middle East crisis, such buying could trigger them prematurely.

Consumers aren't using more oil, just purchasing it now and storing it instead of buying it later when they normally would need it. Such demand is "borrowed" from future months and simply moves fuel out of primary commercial inventories and into so-called secondary and tertiary storage. Many European apartment dwellers are filling their fuel oil tanks in these final days of summer, for example, rather than waiting for winter to approach.

'An Acceleration of Demands'

"Nothing is really changing, except whose tank holds the oil," said Paul Mlotok, an oil economist with Morgan Stanley Group. However, "an acceleration of demands on commercial inventories could cause an apparent tightening of supplies and a rise in price faster than would occur otherwise," he says.

Fuel and crude oil prices, paced by gasoline, surged again yesterday. In U.S. futures trading, unleaded gasoline for October delivery jumped 8.34 cents a gallon to settle at 94.52 cents. Heating oil rose 5.63 cents a gallon to 82.39 cents. October crude oil, similar to West Texas Intermediate, increased $1.80 a barrel to settle at $29.12. Also, several refiners raised their field postings for the benchmark WTI crude by $1.75 to $27.50.

The trend in demand is similar to one that developed during the 1979 Iranian revolution. Large volumes of oil were closed down then, similar in size to the 4.3 million barrels a day that Iraq and Kuwait exported before global sanctions were imposed. In 1979, oil demand was artificially stimulated by precautionary inventory building—some called it hoarding—and surged to nearly 52 million barrels a day as prices doubled.

Petroleum Demand

Petroleum demand only recently has again reached the 1979 level. Many estimates for current demand range from 52 million to 53 million barrels a day.

Demand normally begins to rise at this time of year, hitting its annual peak during the fourth and first quarters. But there is evidence that demand is suddenly spurting well ahead of this time a year ago. In the four weeks through Aug. 24, U.S. petroleum demand is estimated to have averaged 16.2 million barrels a day, up nearly 6% from the year-earlier period.

Many oil forecasters are drawing up new demand projections for the third quarter—even though it is two-thirds over. These replace some predictions made only a month ago to take into account the unexpected surge.

The International Energy Agency will report this week that its new estimate for third-quarter demand has been revised upward by 500,000 barrels a day from its forecast of 52.6 million barrels a day made a month ago. On the other hand, the Paris agency will revise its estimated demand for the fourth quarter downward by 800,000 barrels a day from the month-earlier forecast of 55.3 million barrels a day.

"There has been movement of demand forward from the fourth quarter to the third," said an IEA official.

Withdrawals from commercial inventories and higher production by the Organization of Petroleum Exporting Countries are expected to provide adequate supplies through October. The IEA's new figures would suggest that chances of any real tightening of supplies should ease later in the year because of the anticipated slackening of fourth-quarter demand.

Nonetheless, IEA officials are concerned that supplies could become tight during the winter months. At that time, inventories will be drawn down and demand will be at its seasonal highest. Inventories "don't have infinite staying power," said an IEA official. One potential offset to that scenario is an actual weakening of consumption brought on by what would then be months of high petroleum prices.

For next year's first and second quarters, the IEA will report new demand estimates of 54.3 million and 51.4 million barrels a day, respectively. These are down 1.2 million and one million barrels a day, respectively, from the IEA forecasts made a month ago.

2082-12

0052

Threatened Saudi oil province given economic boost

By Lara Marlowe in Dhahran

ONE IRONY of the Gulf crisis is that it has stimulated industry and local business in the region most threatened by Iraqi aggression – Saudi Arabia's Eastern Province.

With 53 of Saudi Arabia's 58 oilfields, the petrochemical city of Jubail and a host of manufacturers and trading companies, the Eastern Province is the epicentre of the Saudi economy.

The government-owned Saudi Arabian Oil Company (Saudi Aramco) is the mainstay of the kingdom's wealth. If Aramco sneezes, the old adage goes, the whole country catches cold.

Now Aramco has increased its production by 2m barrels per day and is rapidly accelerating its 10-year expansion programme. Also Jubail's 15 petrochemical companies – all in their second or third phases of their own expansion programme – plan to double their capacity over the next 15 months.

"You might think construction in Jubail would stop because of the threat of war," one western businessman said. "But they are going ahead. They may even end up with some surplus capacity." Jubail-produced aromatics and methanol are in big demand on the world market. The Saudi Government owns majority shares in Jubail's 15 companies.

The Saudi government has sought western participation in the creation of the industrial cities of Jubail and Yanbu over the past decade. Royal Dutch Shell, Exxon, Mobil and Mitsubishi are a few of the companies which have invested.

British companies have not invested directly in Jubail but have done a lot of trade behind the scenes in, for example, pumps and valves. A 15-man energy industry council delegation is still scheduled to visit Jubail on a selling mission at the beginning of October.

Yanbu, on the Red Sea coast, would be less at risk in the event of war, but Jubail is home to a naval base and is only 120 miles from the Kuwaiti border. Although new investors have shown little interest since the beginning of the Gulf crisis, it does not seem to worry the Saudis. "If you have a goose laying golden eggs, you aren't eager to sell it," a western businessman said.

Over the past 12 months Aramco began opening new flow lines, installing new well heads, demothballing gas oil separating plant (GOSP) and injecting water into all the wells to bring oil to the surface. These measures will have to be stepped up if the company is to sustain and further increase its rate of nearly 7.4m barrels per day.

Five new light crude oil fields discovered over the past two years in the Central Province have yet to begin pumping and exploration continues.

In Dhahran, there are rumours that Aramco may reduce the price of Arabian heavy crude which it produces most easily. There is also talk of using the IPSA pipeline through Saudi Arabia – formerly used by Iraq – to pump Aramco oil, doubling pipeline capacity.

A number of western companies with franchise or joint venture operations here stand to benefit from the mini-boom. Colgate Palmolive of the US, for example, began producing everything from toothpaste to soap with the Saudia Olayan company this year. Olayan holds the Coca Cola licence and appears to have beat the Gossaibi company – the bottler of Pepsi Cola – to the US troops market. The Irish company Mastock's joint venture with al Marai provides the Eastern Province with milk, butter, cheese and yoghurt.

The situation is not without its problems. Up to one half of the Saudi labour force are expatriates and many have fled. Morning newspapers are filled with job offers.

FT 9/5/90

2082-13

0053

Tax on Energy Still Considered By Democrats

Negotiators in Budget Talks Discuss Two Alternatives Despite Higher Oil Price

By JEFFREY H. BIRNBAUM
Staff Reporter of THE WALL STREET JOURNAL

WASHINGTON—Despite the sharp run-up in oil prices, Democratic negotiators for this week's budget talks are still considering proposing a tax on energy consumption.

Congressional aides say higher oil prices have made an energy tax a somewhat less likely component of a deficit-reduction package than it was prior to the Iraqi standoff. But the tax-increase idea is still very much alive, they add, and is under active discussion in at least two forms.

The first plan would impose a tax on energy only when the price of oil dropped below some threshold amount, certainly below the nearly $30-a-barrel level at which it stands today. The rate of the tax would either be a set amount or would vary with the price of oil—the lower the price, the higher the tax.

The second plan would impose only a tiny tax on energy initially, but would increase over time. This start-small, grow-big proposal would have the advantage of bringing in increasing amounts of revenue in the coming years, an outcome that fits well with the negotiators' hopes of agreeing to a relatively compact tax increase for the first year that grows substantially over five years.

The Democrats intend to devise their own deficit-reduction package in private discussions before the full budget summit reconvenes on Friday and over the weekend at Andrews Air Force Base near here. Aides say the Bush administration has made clear that it believes that it is the Democrats' turn to make a proposal; the Republicans tentatively agreed to one just as the talks closed down early last month.

The energy tax is being discussed by Democrats as potentially one of the fundamental parts of a tax-increase package that could be as large as $25 billion in the first year, but probably would be smaller, perhaps $18 billion.

Other likely components, aides say, would be an increase in the top personal income tax rate to at least 33% from the current 28%, which Democratic budget-writers have been pushing for some time, along with an increase in "sin" taxes on alcoholic beverages and tobacco, a tax on various luxury items and the adoption of a variety of fees that were proposed by President Bush in his own tax-increase proposals issued early this year as part of his fiscal 1991 budget plan.

At least initially, the Democrats aren't likely to propose a cut in the tax on capital gains, which is one of the president's most coveted tax proposals.

The tax-increase package tentatively adopted by Republican negotiators last month would sharply increase taxes on alcoholic beverages, limit the deductibility of tax payments to state and local governments and cut the capital gains tax.

Democrats are continuing to discuss the energy tax under the banner of energy conservation. Increasing the cost of fuels is one way to discourage their use.

But the variable form of the tax could turn controversial if it became yet another gimmick to mask the deficit problem. It could, for instance, allow budget negotiators to claim substantial reductions in the deficit in future years that might not really occur.

Bush administration officials, who have also discussed a variable energy tax, warn that it would be difficult to accurately forecast the revenues that would be generated by a levy that rose and fell with the price of oil because oil prices are so tough to predict. But by simply assuming that the U.S. prevailed against Iraq and oil prices fell sharply, budget negotiators could project a huge windfall from such a tax in the future.

WSJ
9/5/90 2082-14

0054

Keep Working to Cut the Deficit

Board of Contributors

The pace of economic growth has slowed over the pa 12 months, but we still have an unemployment rate belo 5.5% and a capacity utilization rate of more than 83%.

By Martin Feldstein

Now, just as the key administration and congressional budget negotiators are heading for seclusion to shape a final deficit-reduction package, political forces are gathering on Capitol Hill to jettison deficit reduction completely. The advocates of abandoning deficit reduction argue that the slowdown of economic activity that has already occurred and the risk of even greater weakness in the future make it inappropriate to reduce overall demand further by cutting government spending and raising taxes. I believe that argument is incorrect.

The economic slowdown doesn't mean we should abandon deficit reduction, but we should alter the pace of its introduction. A reliable multiyear program of deficit reduction is now more important than ever.

The economic argument against deficit reduction in a slow economy is only an excuse for some members of Congress. There are Democrats who don't want a budget deal because they think that President Bush has not endorsed a tax increase publicly enough and loudly enough. There are Republicans who are so opposed to any tax increase under any circumstances—for either political or economic reasons—that they welcome the chance to scuttle the whole deficit-reduction process. And some members of Congress simply don't want to vote for either higher taxes or reduced benefits in an election year.

Labor and Product Markets

But the economic argument against deficit reduction in the current economic circumstances is a serious one that deserves a response. The key fact is that achieving substantial deficit reduction would raise economic growth over the next three years and beyond and is compatible with continued expansion in the nearer term. Even with our relatively weak economy, Congress should therefore enact a package of $50 billion of deficit reductions for fiscal 1991 and $500 billion of deficit reductions over the next five years.

It is true that the pace of economic growth has slowed over the past 12 months, but we still have an unemployment rate below 5.5% and a capacity utilization rate of more than 83%. Both of these measures reflect relatively tight labor and product markets. Unemployment is lower now than it was for any year from 1974 to 1987. And capacity utilization has been as high as it is today in only six of the past 20 years. The recent slow rate of expansion reflects the Federal Reserve's policy of limiting demand to bring down the rate of inflation. The roughly 1.5% rate of increase during the past six months has been in line with the Fed's implicit goal for the current year.

The rise in the price of oil will reduce growth during the coming year but is not likely to push the economy into recession. The current oil price hike is much smaller than the increases of the 1970s, and the economy starts from a much more modest overall rate of inflation. Unlike the 1970s, the Fed is not tightening credit in response to the current rise in oil prices. If the Fed sticks to its goal of keeping overall nominal gross national product rising at about 6% over the coming year, the oil price rise is likely to mean only about a 0.5% decline in next year's growth and a temporary 0.5% rise in the price level. Real GNP and employment should continue to expand.

The current expansion is, however, a lopsided one in which output and employment in construction and in many manufacturing industries are stagnant or declining. These interest-sensitive industries are the ones that would be particularly helped by the fall in interest rates that would follow a substantial reduction in the budget deficit.

The simplistic Keynesian analysis that argues against deficit reduction ignores the favorable effect of deficit reduction on interest rates and interest-sensitive spending. Instead it reckons that a package of spending cuts and taxes aimed at slicing $50 billion from the 1991 deficit would simply cut real GNP by nearly as much, dragging real growth to zero or even into a slight decline.

But the Keynesian direct impact on GNP of higher taxes and reduced government outlays is only part of the story. A cut in current and future budget deficits would mean lower interest rates and therefore more spending on construction, business investment and other interest-sensitive goods. Even without help from the Fed, medium-term and long-term interest rates would fall as financial-market participants recognize that less government borrowing means a reduced demand for funds both now and in the future. Anc Greenspan signaled in testimony this summer that the Fed would a assist that decline in rates by incr the money supply more rapidly and c the short-term money market rate.

The increase in spending on in sensitive goods and on construction not only help those industries but, f economy as a whole, could fully off even more than offset the contracti effects of the other spending cuts th sult from higher taxes and reduced g ment outlays. Lower interest rates also help to make the dollar more cor tive, giving a boost to our export making domestic products more cor tive with imports. If interest rates dr enough in response to the budget pac total demand and real GNP cou higher in 1991 than they would have without a cut in the deficit.

The size of the interest-rate declin reflect the market's expectations c magnitude of deficit reduction ove next several years. The bigger the cu tive reduction in the deficit is expec be, the greater will be the fall in in rates. It's important therefore to e deficit package that specifies credibl cit reductions over the five-year budg rizon.

The best way to make those ou deficit reductions credible to a fina market that has become skeptical years of phony budget projections have a first-year deficit reduction tl both substantial and real. Scaling bac 1991 reduction from $50 billion and accounting gimmicks and temp changes to meet the target would r the credibility of the entire package. $50 billion deficit reduction for 1991 a explicitly articulated set of deficit tions for the following four years bring interest rates down sharply.

Timing is important in the pacing first year of the deficit-reduction pac Experience shows that lower interest and a lower dollar expand demand o ter a delay of about six months. It that long for the fall in interest rates

WSJ 9/5/90

2082-15

0055

WSJ 9/5/90

translated into new housing starts, increased production of investment goods and increased orders for exports. In contrast, reductions in government spending and hikes in taxes on households drain demand from the economy immediately.

It would be best therefore if the magnitude of the deficit reduction increased during the year, starting at less than a $50 billion annual rate in the first few months and rising to more than a $50 billion annual rate by the end of the fiscal year. That should be easy enough to engineer by legislating that the excise-tax increases and some of the other changes begin part-way through the fiscal year.

Although the economic debate about cutting the deficit now may focus on the impact on overall demand and economic activity during the coming year, the real reason for deficit reduction is its favorable effect over the years ahead. Shrinking the budget deficit by $500 billion over the next five years will give us a balanced budget by mid-decade and will add more than a trillion dollars to the nation's capital stock by the end of the decade. That means a stronger economy and a higher standard of living.

Risk of Recession

A political decision to postpone deficit reduction for yet another year would run the risk that the financial-market participants will give up hope of ever seeing a fall in government borrowing. They may well conclude that if President Bush's willingness to cut defense outlays and raise taxes is not enough to get a budget deal, nothing ever will be. If the hope of deficit reduction is lost, the result could be a sharp rise in long-term interest rates and a collapse of interest-sensitive spending and of exports. Abandoning the process of deficit reduction at this time thus runs the serious risk of pushing the economy into a recession induced by higher interest rates.

It would, of course, have been better to start cutting the deficit several years ago when the economy was growing much more rapidly. The increase in capital formation and the reduction in interest rates that would have followed an earlier deficit reduction would have given us higher productivity and a stronger economy today. But we cannot turn back the clock. We can only hope that common sense will prevail before time runs out.

Mr. Feldstein, former chairman of the president's Council of Economic Advisers, is a professor of economics at Harvard.

2/2

Western Oil Firms Invited To Bid for Soviet Tracts

By a WALL STREET JOURNAL *Staff Reporter*

The Soviet Union said it is inviting Western oil companies to bid for rights to explore for and produce oil and gas in two regions in the Republic of Turkmen.

The areas cover about 90,000 square kilometers in the South Caspian and Amu-Daria Oil and Gas Provinces. The Soviet Ministry of Geology rated the areas as "highly prospective," and said there is existing major hydrocarbon production in the area.

In a statement, the Ministry of Geology and the government of the Republic of Turkmen said invitations to bid will be made available in November and December during a visit to the U.S. by Soviet oil and gas officials. They said they will then provide prospective bidders details on the potential of the areas.

The Soviet statement said that small tract competitive bidding will be used to select participating companies, similar to the bidding format used in the U.S. and some other countries. In the past, Western oil companies have negotiated directly with government agencies for the possibility of joint ventures in large areas.

2082-16

0056

JoC 9/5/90

Hussein Is the Fed's Best Friend

By H. ERICH HEINEMANN

Robert Bork remarked ruefully the other day that "it took Saddam Hussein to get Judge David Souter off the front pages" of the nation's newspapers. Mr. Bork, whose own failed quest for the Supreme Court was a cause celebre two years ago, was concerned with potential opposition to Judge Souter, President Bush's first nominee to the high court. However, his comment applies equally to any number of other Washington players who are thankful to be temporarily out of the limelight.

Consider for a moment the problems facing Federal Reserve Chairman Alan Greenspan. On Labor Day 1990, the traditional kickoff for the midterm election this fall, the economy is sliding inexorably into recession. While some Wall Street analysts — notably those who didn't see the slump coming — have tried to pin the downturn on the shock of soaring energy costs, this doesn't have much credibility at either end of Pennsylvania Avenue.

Three years of tight money, not three weeks of higher oil prices, were the primary cause of the 1990-91 recession. At this point, there is nothing that Mr. Greenspan can do to duck responsibility as the current slowdown gradually cumulates into a full-fledged recession.

Investors can look forward to substantial political fallout from the downturn. The U.S. Chamber of Commerce, which often reflects views of the White House political staff, is now forecasting a recession for the first time since 1981. "The sad state of the American economy," the U.S. Chamber said in a recent commentary, "is the direct consequence of misguided economic policy."

The U.S. Chamber report continued: "Although Congress and the administration must share substantially in the blame — they have increased the tax burden, allowed federal spending, once again, to get out of hand and piled on excessive new regulations — the greatest responsibility for the looming recession lies at the doorstep of the Federal Reserve Board."

Recession may be only part of the Fed's problem. It's only a matter of time until somebody in Washington figures out that the Fed is responsible for a big slice of blame for the collapse of the nation's S&Ls, which ultimately will cost taxpayers hundreds of billions of dollars.

In the mid-1980s, the Fed poured vast quantities of unneeded money into the U.S. economy. Velocity, the ratio of national income to the money supply, fell like a rock. Lenders, including S&L managers, of course, had to scramble to invest these funds. Under such circumstances, it's hardly surprising that the rush to get this excess money to work resulted in billions in bad loans.

In the three years from 1984 through 1986, Federal Reserve officials added to total reserves in U.S. banks by an average of more than $500 million a month. Bank reserves are under the direct control of the Fed. They largely determine the level of bank deposits and thus total bank lending. As such, bank reserves represent the high-powered money that provides fuel for economic activity.

"I'd like to apply for a non-performing loan."

Keep in mind that the effective reserve requirement in the U.S. banking system is less than 2%. This means that every dollar of additional bank reserves the Fed pumps into the money market will ultimately result in more than $50 of new loans and investments in the credit system. No wonder bankers had so much trouble finding good lending opportunities in this period.

Mr. Greenspan has, of course, reversed the easy money approach of his predecessor, Paul A. Volcker. The Fed's tight-fisted policy of the past three years — bank reserves have risen at an average of less than $10 million a month — has plainly thrown a wet blanket over the growth of spending, employment and income.

This means that while the cost of energy and energy-related products and services surely will jump during the second half of 1990, the ripple effects of this surge will be limited in both size and duration. The additional amounts consumers spend for oil won't be available for other goods and services.

This is the good news. The bad news is that the recession is likely to be deeper and longer than would otherwise have been the case. Still, it should not even remotely resemble a collapse. Indeed, there's a good case that in economic terms the price of oil has been, and continues to be, too low.

Since the 1940s, oil prices have increased about 4.5 times, while the overall price level is up roughly 5.5 times. Thus on a relative basis, the price of crude is lower today than it was 40 years ago. This suggests there's room for oil prices to increase considerably without fundamental damage to the real productive potential of the economy.

Nonetheless, a substantial decline in business activity is now in the cards. I believe this decline will be associated with a large increase in the already lopsided Democratic majorities in Congress. If the U.S. Chamber's rancorous attack on the Fed is any guide, then Mr. Greenspan is likely to be the political fall guy for Republican losses this fall.

Mr. Greenspan's tenure at the Fed is at risk. His term as chairman has less than a year to run. Were President Bush to appoint a high-profile individual to fill the vacant post of Fed vice chairman, Mr. Greenspan would become an instant lame duck.

In effect, the White House is in a position to force Mr. Greenspan to resign at any time. This would be extremely unlikely so long as the Persian Gulf crisis continues. Even so, the risk remains. At the moment, Saddam Hussein may be Alan Greenspan's best friend.

H. Erich Heinemann is the chief economist of Ladenburg, Thalmann & Co., investment bankers in New York.

0057

2082-17

원 본

외 무 부

종 별 :

번 호 : HUW-0376 일 시 : 90 0905 0910

수 신 : 장 관(경과,미북,정일)

발 신 : 주 휴스턴 총영사

제 목 : 석유가격및 생산동향보고(5)

연: HUW-372

1. 연호 8.31.현재 서부텍사스 중질원유 10월 인도가격은 어제보다 55센트 상승, 베럴당 27.32 불로 거래됨. 9.3. 노동절 3일 연휴로 새로운 가격은 9.4.에 형성될 것임.

2. OPEC 국가들의 비엔나 증산 합의이후 각국은 석유 증산을 시작하였으며 최대의 산유국인 사우디의 경우 금주중 자국의 1일생산 쿼타 5.8백만 베럴보다 1.2백만베럴을 초과 7백만 베럴생산이 예상된다함.

(이락사태이후 세계 원유시장에서 1일 3-4백만 베럴이 부족해왔음.)

(총영사 허승-국장)

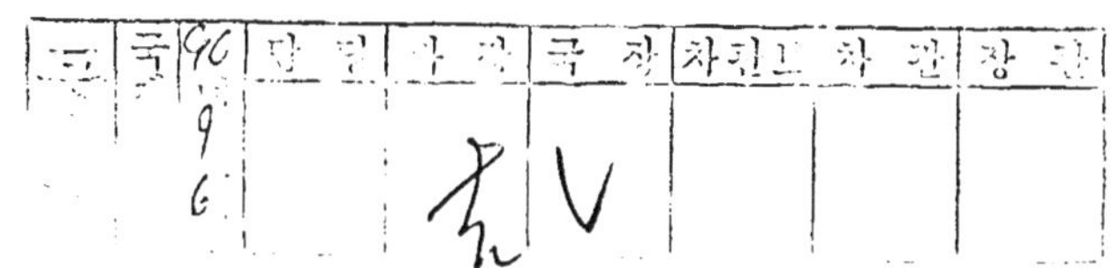

경제국 1차보 2차보 미주국 안기부 동자부

PAGE 1

90.09.06 09:12 WG

외신 1과 통제관

0058

원 본

외 무 부

종 별 :

번 호 : HUW-0380　　　　일 시 : 90 0905 1540

수 신 : 장 관(경자,미북,정일)

발 신 : 주 휴스턴 총영사

제 목 : 석유가격 동향보고(6)

1.9.4.현재 서부 텍사스 중질원유 10월 인도가격은 8.31.보다 약 2불이 상승 베럴당 29.31불로 거래됨.

2.이는 케야르 유엔사무총장의 교섭실패 및 유조선의 해상운송 보험료 인상등에 주로 기인한다함.

(총영사 허승-국장)

경제국　1차보　2차보　미주국　정문국　안기부　동자부

PAGE 1

90.09.06　10:57 WG

외신 1과　통제관

0059

원 본

외 무 부

종 별 :

번 호 : GEW-1506 일 시 : 90 0905 1800

수 신 : 장 관(기협)

발 신 : 주 독 대사

제 목 : 중동 원유 의존도

대: WGE-1289

대호 주재국의 원유 수입량 관계사항 아래보고함

(단위 : 백만톤)

1.총수입량

1988년 72.0

1989년 66.4

2.중동지역 국가로부터의 수입량(국별 1988년 1989 년 순임)

리비아 11.2 11.0

사우디 4.7 5.2

알제리 5.5 4.0

시리아 1.1 2.4

이란 2,6 2.1

UAE 0.3 1.0

이락크 1.4 0.9

쿠웨이트 0.1 0.7

이집트 0.2 0.7

(대사 신동원-국장)

경제국

PAGE 1 90.09.06 09:46 WG

외신 1과 통제관

0060

國際原油需給 및 價格動向 速報

(公館 報告 綜合)

1990.9.6.
外務部, 國際經濟局

1. 原油需給

o 8.31 현재 世界 原油增産量 : 315만B/D (9.2 로이터통신, 사우디 소식통 인용 보도)

- 사우디 200만B/D, UAE 50만B/D, 베네주엘라 30만B/D, 멕시코10만B/D 기타 OPEC 회원국 20만B/D, 알라스카유전 5만B/D

o 나이지리아, OPEC 合意따라 25만B/D 增産決定 (나이지리아 석유부 소식통)

2. 油價動向

o 現物市場 動向 (단위 : $/B)

	7.31	8.7	8.22	8.27	8.29	9.4	9.5	전일대비
Dubai	17.20	25.40	31.75	27.20	24.75	26.73	27.40	0.67
Oman	17.65	25.90	32.35	27.80	25.35	27.33	28.00	0.67
Brent	19.49	29.40	32.15	27.80	26.35	30.88	31.75	0.87
WTI	20.75	29.62	31.57	27.25	26.05	29.27	29.85	0.62

o 사우디의 200B/D 增産의 상당분이 주둔 美軍所有로 轉用되고, 輸入國들이 사우디와 같은 불안지역 보다 安定的 地域으로부터의 供給確保 競爭으로 油價의 漸進的 上昇 必然的 (주이란대사 보고)

3. 其他 關聯 事項

o '89년도 國別 中東原油 依存度 (公館報告 綜合)

- 한국74.8%, 싱가폴73%, 일본71.3%, 태국70%, 불란서43.3%, 이태리36.1%, 미국25.7%, 스웨덴14.6%, 서독10.2%

- 대만 60.8% ('88)

o 이란, 對我國 原油增量 供給 同意 (주이란대사 보고)

- 쌍용 3만B/D, 유공 2-3만B/D

o 印尼 및 말련, 對 我國 原油增量 供給 要請에 대해 가능한 범위내에서 好意的 檢討 노력 표명 (주인니, 말련 대사 보고)

공람	기술협력과	90년 9월 6일	담 당	과 장	국 장	차관보	차 관	장 관
			홍석화	(서명)	(서명)			

0061

원 본

외 무 부

종 별 : 지 급

번 호 : FNW-0259 일 시 : 90 0906 0930

수 신 : 장 관(기협,구이)

발 신 : 주 핀랜드 대사

제 목 : 중동원유 의존도

대: WFN-0255

1. 주재국의 최근년도 원유 도입량 아래 보고함.

가.87년: 총수입 10,685천톤 (사우디 1,116천톤, 소련 8,557천톤, 영국 1,012천톤)

나.88년:총수입 8,937천톤 (사우디 560천톤, 소련 8,377천톤)

89년:총수입 8,832천톤 (사우디 430천톤, 소련 8,273천톤, 영국 129천톤)

2.한편 주재국의 88년도 총소요 에너지중 60프로를 국외로부터 도입 충당하였는바, 그주요 수입대상국은 소련 (84프로), 서전 (6프로), 폴란드 (4프로), 사우디 (3프로)였으며

총수입 에너지중 원유 (CRUDE OIL 및 NGL) 의 비중은 50프로였음을 참고바람.끝

(대사 최상진-국장)

공람	국제경제국		담 당	과 장	국 장	차관보	차 관	장 관
					V			

경제국 구주국

PAGE 1

90.09.06 16:56 WG

외신 1과 통제관

0062

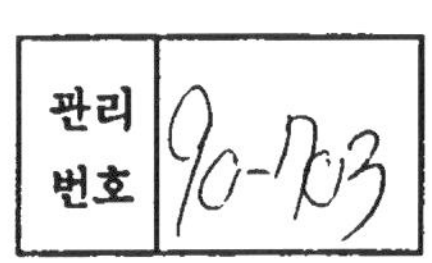

원 본

외 무 부

종 별 :

번 호 : MAW-1271 일 시 : 90 0906 1730

수 신 : 장관(기협,아동,사본:동자부 장관)

발 신 : 주 말련 대사

제 목 : 원유 도입교섭

대:WMA-0642

연:MAW-1240

1. 대호 동자부 장관 서한을 본직의 서한 첨부 9.6(목) SULAIMAN 장관실에 전달하였음 (동 장관 지방 출장중)

2. 당관은 대호 유공의 증량 요청이 최대한 받아들여 질수 있도록 주재국 수상실을 비롯한 관계기관을 계속 접촉중임.끝

(대사 홍순영-국장)

90.12.31 까지

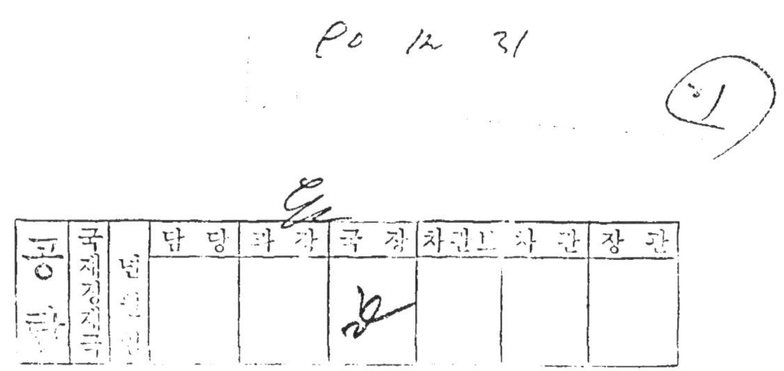

경제국 2차보 아주국 동자부

90.09.06 18:58

외신 2과 통제관 BT

0063

원 본

외 무 부

종 별 :

번 호 : AUW-0689 일 시 : 90 0906 1600

수 신 : 장 관(기협,아동)

발 신 : 주호주대사

제 목 : 중동 원유의존도

대: WAU-0633

1. 대호, 주재국이 최근 (88/89년도) 원유총수입량은 262,000 B/D 규모임.

0 동 수입량은 총소비량 (667,000 B/D) 의 39 임.

0 주재국의 경우 원유수입량은 최근 분기별 변화가 많은바, 89년도 1/4분기의 경우 거의 100 자급자족 상황이었으며, 현재는 82 자급하고 있음.

(약 20 의 수입원유는 정유후 다시 아태지역 도서국가에 재 수출 또는 원조로 사용)

2. 중동국가로부터의 수입량(141,540 B/D) 은 아래와 같음.(전채 수입량의 54점유, 기타수입원은 싱가폴, 인니, 말련 순으로 동남아 국가)

0 UAE (61,900), 사우디 (52,320), 쿠웨이트 (14,110),카타르(6,500), 바레인(2,690), 오만(2,380), 예멘(1,300), 시리아 (340).

0 기타 이집트, 알제리로부터 극소량 수입.끝.

(대사 이창수-국장)

경 제 국	90	담 당	과 장	국 장	차관보	차 관	장 관
람	9 / 7			V			

경제국 아주국

PAGE 1

90.09.06 20:41 CG

외신 1과 통제관

0064

원 본

외 무 부

종 별 :

번 호 : CHW-1395 일 시 : 90 0906 1600

수 신 : 장관(기협)

발 신 : 주중대사

제 목 : 중동원유 의존도

대 WJA-3757

대호 관련 주재국의 88,89년도 90-1,5 현재 원유·수입 현황은 다음과 같음.

1.88년도 원유 수입 실적

1)총수입량:19,952,497. M/T

2) 총수입액:2,242,562.천미불

3)중동지역수입량:14,047,278. M/T(70.40퍼센트)

4)중동지역 수힙액:1,549,653.천미불(69.10퍼센트)

5)국별 수입량(M/T), 수입액(천미불)내역

- 이란:263,857 29,390
- 쿠위이트:3,948,752 437,635
- 리비아:119,224 16,550
- 오만:1,533,414 171,548
- 카타르:148,160 17,665
- 사우디:8,033,871 876,865

2.1989 원유 수입 실적

1)총수입량 21,388,499 M/T

2) 총수입금액:2,600,680천 미불

3)중동지역수입량:14,210,071. M/T(66.43 퍼센트)

4)중동지역수입금액:1,680,691.천미불(64.62펀센트)

5)국별수입액(M/T), 수입액(천미불)내역

- 이라크:729,918 84,921
- 쿠웨이트:3,485,093 404,270

경제국

PAGE 1

국	90.9.7	담 당	과 장	국 장	차관보	차 관	장 관
국제경제국				V			

90.09.06 21:06 CG

외신 1과 통제관

0065

- 사우디:8,797,623 1,044,269

- 아랍에미리트:1,099,960 133,577

- 예멘:97,477 13,654

3.1990년 1.-5.월말 현재 수입실적

1)총수입량:9,105,362. M/T

2) 총수입액:1,188,705천불

3)중동지역 수입량:7,033,889. M/T(77.25 퍼센트)

4)중동지역 수입액:902,511천불(75.92퍼센트)

5)국별수입량(M/T), 수입액(천미불)내역

- 이라크:245,814 32,869

- 쿠웨이트:1,781,135 220,832

- 오만:811,585 106,980

- 카타르:93,935 13,357

- 사우디:3,080,172 388,065

- 아랍에미리트:924,115 125,514

- 예멘:97,133 14,894

끝.

(대사 한철수-국장).

원 본

외 무 부

종 별 :

번 호 : GRW-0442 일 시 : 90 0906 1610

수 신 : 장 관(기협)

발 신 : 주 희랍 대사

제 목 : 중동원유 의존도

대: WGR-305

대호 주재국의 88년도 및 89년도 원유수입량 및 중동지역 국별수입량을 아래 보고함.

-아 래-

구분 1988년도 1989년도(1-11월)순임

총수입량 4,200백만 KG 5,817 백만 KG

중동지역수입량 3,103백만 KG 5,289 백만KG 사우디 175 585

이란 131 2,516

이락 360 158

이집트 136 -

쿠웨이트 445 297

리비아 1,364 1,272

알제리 126 -

오만 366 -

튀니지 - 461

(대사 박남균-국장)

공람	국제경제국	90년 9월 7일	담당	과장	국장	차관보	차관	장관
					V			

경제국

PAGE 1

90.09.06 22:34 CG

외신 1과 통제관

0067

원 본

외 무 부

종 별 :

번 호 : SPW-0519　　　　일 시 : 90 0906 1700

수 신 : 장관(기협 구이)

발 신 : 주스페인대사

제 목 : 중동원유 의존도

대: WSP-0440

대호 지시에 따라 주재국의 대중동 원유수입량및 총수입량을 다음과 같이 조사보고함.(단위:톤,괄호안은 총수입량에 대한 백분율임)

국명, 1989년도, 1990년 1월-6월간 (순서임)

이란, 6,313,832(12.7) , 370,621(2.9)

이락 , 5,285,785(10.6) , 2,057,827(16.1)

→ 리비아 , 4,272,887(8.6) , 1,372,092(10.7)

사우디 , 3,152,179(6.3) , 681,581(5.3) ,

→ 알제리아 ,1,878,968(3.8) , 303,754(2.3)

→ 이집트 , 790,652(1.6) , 121,967 (0.9)

두바이 , 438,971(0.9) , 273,793(2.1)

아부다비 , 373,062(0.7) , 452,354(3.5)

시리아 ,. 237,038(0.5) , -

→ 튜니지아 , 202,659(0.4), -

쿠웨이트 , 105,444(0.2), -

중동지역합계 , 23,051,477(46.2) , 5,633,989(44.1)　15,906,311

주재국 총수입량 , 49,848,430(100) , 12,781,840(100)

(대사-국장)

16,696,963

공람	국제경제국	90 9 12	담 당	과 장	국 장	차관보	차 관	장 관
					V			

경제국　　구주국

PAGE 1　　　　90.09.07　00:55 CG

외신 1과 통제관

0068

관리번호	90-700

원 본

외 무 부

종 별 :

번 호 : BUW-0207　　　　일 시 : 90 0906 1715

수 신 : 장관(기협,통일,아동)

발 신 : 주 브루나이 대사

제 목 :

대:WBU-114

연:BUW-180

1. 본직은 9.5. BRUNEI SHELL 의 GEORGE INNES 사장을 세리아 소재 본사로 방문 지속적 원유공급에 사의를 표하고 증산수출 가능성 타진한바 동사장은 현재 증산계획은 없고 대한 원유수출은 유공과 호남정유와의 계약분을 계약대로 수출이행 예정이라말함.

2. 주재국의 국내유류가격은 현가격유지 (정부보조) 예정이며 수출가격은 국제시세에 의한다함. 끝

(대사허세린-국장)

90. 12. 31

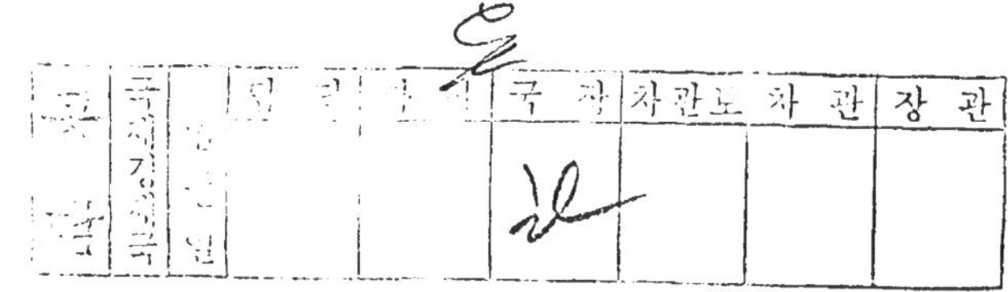

경제국　2차보　아주국　통상국

PAGE 1　　　　90.09.07 00:22

외신 2과 통제관 EZ

0063

원 본

외 무 부

종 별 : 긴 급

번 호 : BBW-0689 일 시 : 90 0906 1720

수 신 : 장 관(기협)

발 신 : 주벨기에대사

제 목 : 중동 원유 의존도

대: WBB-0625

대호, 벨지움의 88,89년 원유 총수입량 및 중동지역 각국으로 부터의 수입량을아래 보고함.(자료 : 경제부).

년도 구분 단위(천 MT) 단위 (B/D) 순

1988 총수입 23,423 462,043

사우디 3,610 71,211

쿠웨이트 -- --

이란 5,623 110,919

이라크 1,798 35,467

카타르 -- --

기타 중동지역 579 11,421

(알제리 419 8,265)

(리비아 1,639 32,331)

1989 총수입 24,798 489,166

사우디 2,765 54,542

쿠웨이트 -- -- 이란 8,575 169,151

이라크 2,288 45,133

카타르 -- --

기타 중동지역 614 12,112

(알제리 593 11,698)

(리비아 1,379 27,202).끝

(대사 정우영-국장)

국	국제경제국		담 당	과 장	국 장	차관보	차 관	장 관
					V			

경제국

PAGE 1 90.09.07 00:21 CG

외신 1과 통제관

0070

외 무 부

종 별 :

번 호 : NDW-1230 일 시 : 90 0906 1730

수 신 : 장관(아서,중근동,통일,정일,기정) 사본:사본처참조

발 신 : 주인도대사

제 목 : 중동사태 인도동향 (자료응신90-174)

기협 미사용

연: NDW-1207

1. 원유수급

9.5 인도정부는 UAE 로부터 500천톤의 원유를 9월 및 10월중에 도입, 바레인으로부터 150천톤의 석유(KEROSENE) 도입계약을 체결하였다고 밝힌 것으로 보도됨.

2. 석유제품에 대한 SURCHARGE 부과 구상

0 인도정부는 중동사태에 의한 외환부담에 대처하기 위해 수입 및 국내생산 원유에 대해, 우선 3-4개월 시한으로 SURCHARGE 를 부과하고 그 연장여부에 대해서는 추후 검토하는 방안을 고려하고있음.

0 원유가격의 배럴당 1불 상승은 400천만 루피(약230백만불)의 추가부담이 발생하며 현재 약1,600천만 루피(약 920백만불)의 부담이 예상되고있는데 이에 대한 대처방안으로 정부 재정긴축을 통한 가격인상 요인 흡수 또는 SURCHARGE 부과 등이 될 수있는데 다소 가격상승을 감수하더라도 SURCHARGE 부과하는 방향으로 의견이 모여지고있는 것으로 보도됨.

(대사 김태지-국장)

수신처: 상공부,동장부,산업연구원,대한상의,무역협회,전경련,중소기업중앙회.

아주국 2차보 중아국 통상국 정문국 안기부 상공부 동자부 산업연
KOTRA . 대한상의. 전경련. 중소기업중앙회.

PAGE 1 90.09.07 00:29 CG

외신 1과 통제관

0071

원 본

외 무 부

종 별 :

번 호 : IDW-0292 일 시 : 90 0905 1600

수 신 : 장 관 (기협) 사본: 주아일랜드대사

발 신 : 주 아일랜드 대사대리

제 목 : 중동석유 의존도

대: WID-0289

1. 주재국은 수입원유의 대부분을 영국북해산으로 충당하고 있으며 중동지역으로부터의 수입량은 무시할 정도라함.

2. 수입량 및 국가는 아래와 같음.

년도 수입량 도입국가

88 161백만 미불 영국(100퍼센트)

89 233백만 미불 영국(93퍼센트) 및 쏘련(7퍼센트).끝.

(대사대리 유영방-국장)

공람	국제경제국	90.9.10	담당	과장	국장	차관보	차관	장관
					V			

경제국 구주국 (대사)

PAGE 1 90.09.07 02:54 FC

외신 1과 통제관

0072

원 본

외 무 부

종 별 : 긴 급

번 호 : POW-0465 일 시 : 90 0906 1900

수 신 : 장관(기협,구이)

발 신 : 주폴부갈대사대리

제 목 : 원유 의존도

대: WPO-0257

대호 아래 보고함

1.주재국의 윤유 총수입량(단위-톤)

88년 7,947,544

89년 9,823,383

90.7월 5,562,3602.국가별 수입량(단위-톤)(88,89,90.7월 순임)

이락 1,313,451 1,155,860 657,820

사우디 1,301,043 945,565 676,435

이집트 648,744 872,314 492,179

아랍에미레이트 208,874 1,065,153 221,426

이란 130,360 615,932 375,819

터키 132,136 0 0

리비아 60,341 77,726 236,238

알제리아 708,658 554,023 542,906

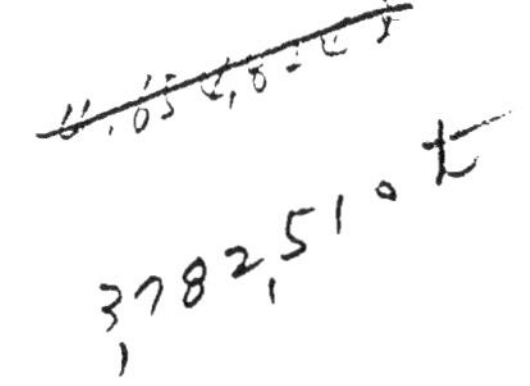

3.주재국의 주요 원유 도입국은 나이지리아(90.7월까지 최근 3년간 전체 도입원유량에 대한비율:22-25프로),사우디(10-16프로),이락(11-15프로),아제리아(7-12프로),아랍에미레이트(2-10프로),영국(5-9프로),이집트,멕시코,놀웨이,앙골라,인니,소련 등으로 원유수입선이 다양하여, 현 중동사태 관련, 이라크산원유를 도입하지 않아도 현재로서 큰 문제점이 없는 것으로 파악됨.끝

(대사대리 주철기-국장)

경제국 구주국

PAGE 1

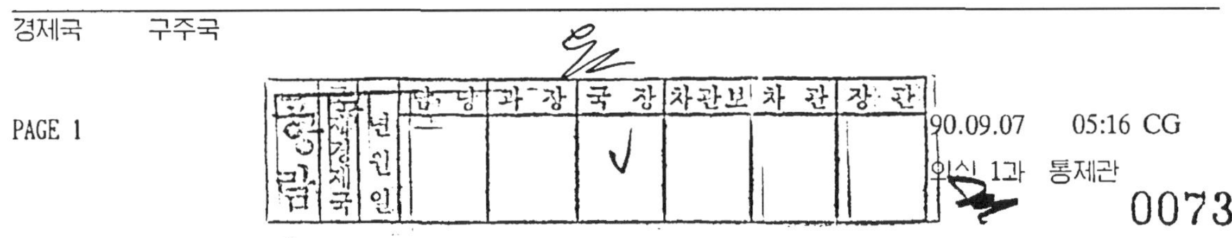

90.09.07 05:16 CG

외신 1과 통제관

0073

관리번호	90-701

원 본

외 무 부

종 별 :

번 호 : FRW-1625 일 시 : 90 0906 1820

수 신 : 장관(기협)

발 신 : 주 불 대사

제 목 : OECD/IEA 이사회

연:FRW-1455,1573

대:WFR-1678

1. 걸프사태와관련 당지 OECD/IEA 의 이사회(8.31)개최 결과 아래 보고함.

가. 석유시장의 현황, 단기 전망

-8 월말경의 부족량이 상업용 비축분 방출로 보충되어 오일시장에 대한 공급이 양호

-9,10 월중 원유부족분이 상업용 비축량의 방출, 산유국의 석유증산 및 고유가에 따른 수요 감소로 적적히 보전될수 있음.

-그러나 겨울에는 계절적 수요증대와 상업용 비축분 방출의 점진적 감소로 인해 시장 상황이 긴장될것이며 혹한과 산업용 정유시설의 완전 가동으로 인한 석유 시장의 긴장이 예상됨.

나. 회의 결론

-단기적 수요, 공급 상황은 높은 비축 수준과 증산으로 인해 MANAGEABLE 함.

-사태의 불확실성과 난방계절에 들어서면서 일어나는 수급의 불균형 가능성에 비추어 회원국 정부간에 정부 통제하의 비축분의 상호 조정 사용 또는 필요시의 수요 억제등을 포함한 상호 협력 조치 필요

- 사무국은 상황을 면밀히 MONITOR 하고 예상 부족분 보충을 위한 상호 조정된 대책의 수립준비

-회원국 정부는 각기 석유 공급 증대를 위한 노력을 강화하고, 석유회사 및 소비자가 비정상적 구매를 삼가토록하고 유리한 비축상황을 이용, 이득을 추구치 말도록 촉구

- 에너지의 효율적 사용, 보존, 다양화, 국내생산 및 R AND D 를 증진시키기 위한

경제국 차관 1차보 2차보 구주국 청와대 안기부

PAGE 1 90.09.07 06:02

외신 2과 통제관 EZ

0074

정책을 통해 장기 에너지 안전대책을 강화해야 하며, 이와 관련 효과적인 에너지 안전 전략을 발전시킬 목적으로 비회원국과의 접촉을 확대해 나감.

-9 월중 이사회 재개최(긴급사태가 발생치 않으면 9.28 개최)

2. 상기 이사회에 제출된 IEA 사무국 보고서는 차파편 송부함.

3. 한편 IEA 비회원국인 프랑스는 동기구 가입을 위해 IEA 측과 교섭을 진행중이라함. 끝

(대사노영찬-국장)

예고:90.12.31 까지

PAGE 2

0075

외 무 부

종 별 :

번 호 : HUW-0384 일 시 : 90 0906 1615

수 신 : 장관(경자,미북,정일) 사본:주미대사(필)

발 신 : 주휴스턴총영사

제 목 : 석유가격및 생산동향보고(7)

1. 9.5. 현재 서부텍사스주 중질원유 10월 인도가격은 이락대통령이 TV 를 통해 아랍국 가들에게 대서방 성전을 촉구한이후 어제보다 46센트 상승 베럴당 29.77불로 거래됨

2.미 에너지성 관리들은 9.5. 9월중 세계의 원유공급은 절절할것으로 예상되나 진정한 평가는 HEATING SEASON 이 도래했을때 가능할 것이라고 언급함.

(총영사 허승-국장)

공람	국제경제국	90.9.7	담당	과장	국장	차관보	차관	장관
					V			

경제국 2차보 미주국 정문국

PAGE 1

90.09.07 06:34 CG

외신 1과 통제관

0076

원 본

외 무 부

종 별 : 긴 급

번 호 : BRW-0540 일 시 : 90 0906 1900

수 신 : 장 관(기협,중근동)

발 신 : 주 브라질 대사

제 목 : 중동원유 의존도

대: WBR-0386

연: BRW-0466,0499

대호건 아래 보고함

1.최근 1-2년간 원유총수입량

- 88년도: 일일 63.9만배럴(국내생산량은 일일57.6만 배럴)

- 89년도: 일일 59.2만 배럴(국내생산량은 일일61.6만 배럴)

2.대 이라크 원유도입금지 조치전 일일원유도입현황

- 이라크 : 16만 배럴

- 쿠웨이트: 3만 배럴

- 사우디 : 14만 배럴

- 이란 : 10만 배럴

- 현물시장: 6만 배럴

- 기타국가: 6만배럴

계: 55만 배럴

끝

(대사 김기수-국장)

경제국 중아국

PAGE 1

90.09.07 08:31 CT

외신 1과 통제관

0077

원 본

외 무 부

종 별 :

번 호 : USW-4049 일 시 : 90 0906 1817

수 신 : 장관(기협)

발 신 : 주미대사

제 목 : 석유 시장 및 유가 동향(10)

표제 관련, 9.6 당지 언론 보도를 종합 보고함.

1.유가 동향

가. 9.5 원유 및 정유 제품 가격(뉴욕 상품 시장)

0 원유(LIGHT SWEET CRUDE, 10월 인도 가격)

-베럴당 29.77 불(전일 대비 65 센트 상승)

0 휘발유

-개런당 92.27 센트(전일 대비 2.25 센트 하락)

-휘발유값 하락의 원인: 9.4 의 대폭 상승(8.34센트)의 반작용으로 다소 하락한것으로 분석됨.

나.유가 상승 원인 분석 및 전망

0 현재의 석유 공급은 실수요를 충족시키기에충분

0 고읍이 충분함에도 불구하고 유가가 상승되고있는것은 심리적 요인 즉 소비자및 중간 유통과정에서의 ''사재기''에 따른것으로 분석(특히일본등 극동 지역 국가들의 사재기도 유가 상승에영향하고 있는것으로 관측)

0 다만, 겨울철 성수기가 시작되는 11월 중순경에는실질적인 공급 부족 현상이 일어날것으로 전망

2.한편 JOHN EASTON 미 에너지부 국제및 에너지위기 담당 차관보는 9.5 미하원 정부 운영위에서최근의 에네지 위기에 대해 증언한바 그 발언 요지아래임.

가. 석유 수급 전망

0 향후 석유 수급에는 큰 문제가 없을것으로전망

0 쿠웨이트, 이락산 석유 금수분은 여타 산유국의잉여 생산 능력 활용및 IEA 가맹국의비축분 활용에 의해 상쇄 가능한것으로분석

경제국

PAGE 1

공람	국제경제국	90년 9월 7일	담당	과장	국장	차관보	차관	장관
					V			

90.09.07 08:41 CT

외신 1과 통제관

0078

나.에너지의 대응 조치 계획(CONTINGENEY PLANNING)

0 단기 조치: 전략 비축분(STRATEGIC PETROLEUMRESERVE) 사용 방법및 시기 판단

0 중기 조치: 석유 증산

0 장기 조치: 에너지 절약 및 대체 에너지(GAS및 COAL 등) 사용 증가

3.상기 언론 보도 내용및 EASTON 차관보 발언내용 별첨 FAX 송부함.

첨부: USW(F)-2096

(대사 박동진-국장)

USW(F) - 2096.
: 장 관 (기협) 발신 : 주미대사
: 주미대사 (14 매)

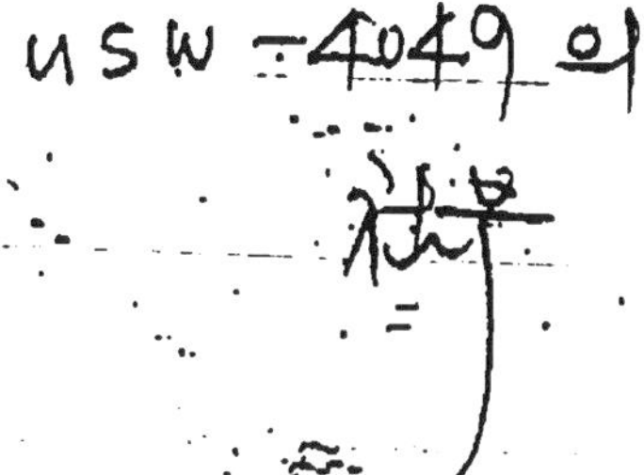

Prices of Oil Rise Again Amid Signs of Hoarding

By JOHN HOLUSHA

Oil prices rose again yesterday on fears of looming shortages and signs of hoarding by distributors and retail consumers of gasoline and home heating oil.

On the New York Mercantile Exchange, light sweet crude for October delivery rose 65 cents, to $29.77 a barrel. Unleaded gasoline declined by 2.25 cents a gallon, to 92.27 cents, but analysts said that this was a technical adjustment to the sharp increase of 8.34 cents on Tuesday.

Oil company spokesmen said they were reluctant to report on speculative demand for gasoline because a rush by motorists to fill tanks could cause shortages by itself. But some said it appeared that some distributors and motorists were trying to hedge against possibly higher prices.

Controls Imposed by Texaco

"It appears to be happening all through the distribution chain; wholesalers, retailers and customers are topping off their tanks in anticipation of higher prices," said Paul Weeditz, a spokesman for Texaco Inc. "We have had spot outages at some terminals." He added that the company had imposed a system of controls limiting the amount distributors can withdraw each day to prevent runs on storage terminals and shortages.

"Yes, people are filling their tanks," said Deborah Urso, a spokesman for the Mobil Oil Company. "They are filling up because they are nervous about price."

Sales made directly to gasoline stations are following normal patterns, but intermediate buyers, called jobbers, have been increasing their demand, said James Huccaby, a manager of supply for the Chevron Corporation. "We do not know if they are keeping it in their tanks or selling to other accounts on an unbranded basis. But jobber demand is up."

A rush by motorists to fill their tanks could cause shortages because of the sheer number of cars on the road, oil industry officials said. "There are 140 million vehicles on the road," said Cyrus Tahmassebi, chief economist for Ashland Oil Inc. "If each one of them starts carrying five more gallons, that is a tremendous amount of gasoline; almost [illegible] barrels."

Current supplies of crude oil and refined products appear to be adequate, according to figures released yesterday by the American Petroleum Institute. Gasoline inventories, for example, remained virtually unchanged during the week ended Aug. 31 at 210.5 million barrels compared to 210.9 million in the previous week.

But the loss of 4.3 million barrels a day of exports from Iraq and Kuwait could start producing shortages as early as November, according to the International Energy Agency, a monitoring agency for the industrialized nations.

The agency said stocks on hand appeared adequate to meet demand for now, but colder weather could bring regional shortages. The agency said the 24 countries represented had stocks adequate for 98 days of consumption on July 1, two days better than a year ago.

Demand in the fourth quarter will be 1.25 million barrels a day higher than the third quarter because of weather, estimated Mehdi Varzi, an oil analyst with Kleinwort Grievson Securities in London. In trading there, the benchmark Brent crude closed at $30.95 a barrel, up 80 cents on the day.

Buying From Far East Cited

The higher prices, he said, were being driven by buying from the Far East. "Underlying all this is fear that war will break out in the Persian Gulf and Far Eastern customers will suffer, so they need to retain a higher level of stocks than other areas of the world," he added.

Similarly, an analyst in New York, who declined to be quoted by name, said war fears were also propelling prices upward. "People are reluctant to let go of the barrel they have," he added. "If war breaks out, they may be better off with that barrel."

Yesterday, President Saddam Hussein of Iraq made one of his most inflammatory statments to date, calling for Arabs to unite in a holy war against United States forces in Saudia Arabia and to depose King Fahd of Saudi Arabia. Shortly before Iraq invaded Kuwait, touching off the current crisis, oil was selling for about $21 a barrel.

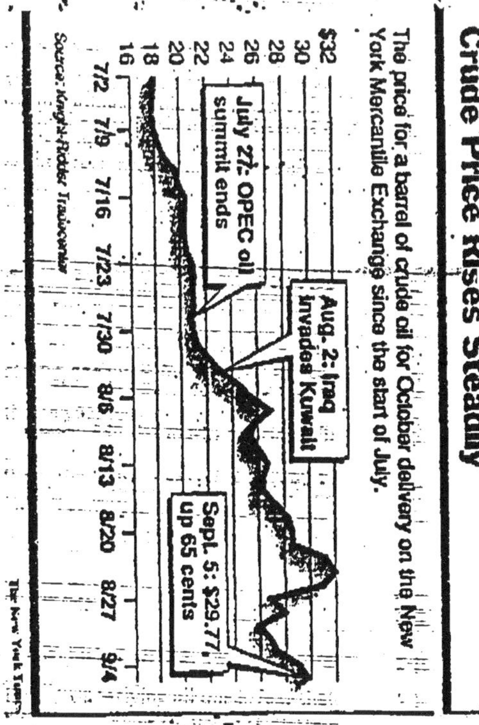

N.Y.T. 9/6/90

0080

09/06/90 17:36 ☎202 797 0595 EMBASSY OF KOREA →→→ WOI 002/02

USW(F)-

수 신 : 장 관

발신 : 주미대사

제 목 :

(매)

Supplies of Oil Start to Shrink, Firming Prices

Inventories Sufficient Now, But Consumer Shortages Seen by Mid-November

By JAMES TANNER

Staff Reporter of THE WALL STREET JOURNAL

World oil inventories are beginning to shrink as a result of the Middle East crisis, suggesting tight supplies may lie ahead at the consumer level.

While more than enough oil is available now, shortages could develop by the last half of the fourth quarter, John Easton Jr., an assistant energy secretary, told a House committee yesterday.

Whether oil supplies become that tight or not, the mere prospect of such a development is keeping prices firm. Petroleum prices rose again yesterday, though traders attributed the increases more to tough talk by President George Bush and Iraq's Saddam Hussein than to fundamental supply and demand factors.

North Sea crudes increased between 65 and 95 cents a barrel. U.S. refiners raised field postings for West Texas Intermediate, the American benchmark crude, 75 cents to $28.25 a barrel. In U.S. futures trading, the price of a similar crude for October delivery was up 65 cents to settle at $29.77 a barrel. Though the futures price of October gasoline fell 2.25 cents a gallon to 92.27 cents, traders had expected a correction in the wake of Tuesday's big run-up of more than eight cents a gallon.

Above-ground stores of crude oil and petroleum products—enough to be considered a surplus before Iraq's Aug. 2 invasion of Kuwait—still are relatively high. They have provided a comfortable cushion for the world's fuel users, despite the loss to oil markets of 4.3 million barrels a day that Iraq and Kuwait had exported before the global embargo.

But they aren't expected to remain at such levels much longer. Inventories are coming down, oil analysts say, because petroleum demand has risen beyond seasonal expectations on war fears, and because of the time it is taking for promised supply increases to reach the market. Several producers with idle capacity, including leading members of the Organization of Petroleum Exporting Countries, are increasing output sufficiently to replace the bulk of the missing Iraqi oil. But production technicalities and shipping delays will delay the effect on oil markets by several weeks.

As a result, "We are beginning to see the initial evidence of some drawdowns" in oil inventories, said John Redpath, an analyst with Energy Security Analysis, which tracks world oil supplies.

Though petroleum products generally had been considered to be in balance before the Iraqis occupied Kuwait, there was a surplus of crude oil. The crude "overhang," as the glut was known in the industry, was estimated to be 100 million to 300 million barrels.

Washington-based Energy Security Analysis set the crude surplus at the lower end of the range. In late July, according to its estimates, crude oil accounted for 1.56 billion barrels of the total petroleum inventories of 2.8 billion barrels.

"Since then, it's very conceivable we have used 60 million barrels of the overhang" of 100 million barrels, Mr. Redpath, the analyst, said.

The International Energy Agency estimates that inventories have been drawn down steadily since the Middle East crisis developed but at rates averaging only about 300,000 barrels a day. However, the Paris-based agency reported yesterday that it expects a "large" drawdown in commercial inventories this month, before the effect of the OPEC output increases becomes significant. Some International Energy Agency officials have estimated that this month's withdrawals could exceed one million barrels a day.

The U.S. had been expected to be relatively immune to the inventory reductions for a while, because it had been receiving only modest amounts of Iraqi and Kuwaiti oil. But yesterday, signs emerged that the U.S. already is affected. According to the American Petroleum Institute's weekly report, U.S. crude oil inventories dropped 4.4 million barrels last week to 372.2 million.

Because oil companies have the inventories from which they can draw supplies as needed, the world oil market "is generally well supplied," according to the International Energy Agency's monthly oil report yesterday. But the International Energy Agency forecasts that supplies will become "increasingly tighter" during the peak-demand winter months.

In testimony before the House Government Operations Committee yesterday, Mr. Easton, the Energy Department official, agreed. He said that while the current oil supply is more than adequate, shortages could develop before year end. He said the Energy Department is "readying" the 590 million-barrel Strategic Petroleum Reserve for use "when the conditions o[f] the statute and public policy require it."

So far, the Bush administration has refrained from drawing on the reserve the government has built up to protect the country from an oil emergency. But Mr. Easton insisted that the government stands ready to tap into it. "We are prepared to use it in concert with our allies at the time we see significant supply interruption," he told the House committee.

Mr. Easton also predicted that by December, through heightened U.S. production efforts, "We will have been able to secure out of Alaska alone an additional 250,000 barrels [of oil] a day."

—*Hilary Stout contributed to this article.*

W.S.J. 9/6/90

2096-2

0081

N.Y.T. 9/6/90

End-of-Year Shortage of Oil Forecast

U.S. Expecting Jump In Cost of Home Heat

By NATHANIEL C. NASH

Special to The New York Times

WASHINGTON, Sept. 5 — Despite efforts by oil-producing countries to increase their production of crude oil, shortages are likely to develop by the end of the year, causing prices of home heating oil to soar, a Bush Administration official acknowledged today.

John J. Easton Jr., Assistant Energy Secretary, told the House Government Operations Committee that the cumulative effect of a shortfall of a million barrels a day in lost production in Kuwait and Iraq could begin to create serious shortages of both crude oil and refined products like heating oil.

Mr. Easton also defended the Administration's decision not to tap the Strategic Petroleum Reserve. He said that there was no shortage of crude oil now and that the main reason for rising gasoline prices was a near-record demand during the heavy summer traveling season and the loss of refining capacity in Kuwait.

Prices Increase Again

Oil prices rose again today, with light sweet crude for October delivery increasing by 65 cents, to $29.77 a barrel, on the New York Mercantile Exchange. [Page D7.]

"Worldwide, the amount of oil held in commercial stocks is more than sufficient to meet near-term demand," Mr. Easton said. "But we've got to be concerned about the availability of product during the fourth quarter, as demand for winter heating oil starts to rise."

Mr. Easton said the loss of exports from Iraq and Kuwait was about 4.3 million barrels a day, of which about 3.3 million would be made up by the additional output agreed to by Saudi Arabia and other oil producers.

Private Economists Pessimistic

While he suggested that over time key areas of the country could find heating oil in short supply, private economists painted a much grimmer picture. "We are convinced that the usable commercial crude oil stocks will be depleted by the end of October," said Edward N. Krapels, president of Energy Security Analysis in Washington, a consulting firm that tracks the price of oil.

Mr. Krapels added that the daily shortfall in production could easily reach two million barrels, pushing the price of oil to $40 a barrel.

That prediction is significantly larger than the one made by the 21-nation International Energy Agency, which estimated last month that oil-producing countries could make up for all but 500,000 barrels of the loss from Iraq and Kuwait.

Mr. Easton, as one of the first representatives of the Bush Administration to testify on the energy supply situation since Congress returned from its August vacation, encountered a host of worried lawmakers, who expressed frustration over the rising cost of gasoline, accused the oil industry of price gouging and criticized the Administration for refusing to tap the nation's 560-million-barrel reserve to ease rising prices. Most members of Congress have supported Mr. Bush's actions.

"Despite urging from many in Congress, the Administration refused to ease the pain of consumer price increases by drawing down the Strategic Petroleum Reserve, which could have prevented both a shortfall and Wall Street speculation about it," said John Conyers Jr., Democrat of Michigan and chairman of the committee.

"The U.S. is being held hostage, not by Saddam Hussein, but at the gas pump," said Chuck Douglas, Republican of New Hampshire.

Collusion Issue Played Down

Mr. Easton also tried to play down questions about collusion by the oil industry to push prices up. "I don't think we have enough empirical evidence at this point to make statements like that," he said.

The members of the panel pressed him on how the Administration was planning to address the problem of the country's growing dependence on imported oil. While he said the first priority would be to promote a more efficient use of fuel, Mr. Easton added that the Administration was looking at a series of tax breaks to promote production, as well as efforts to open up drilling in new areas.

But he declined repeatedly to be specific, saying that more than 700 proposals had been submitted to the Energy Department, which will propose a policy to the President by the end of the year. He added that the President would make his recommendations to Congress by early next year.

2096-3

0082

Oil supply adequate, feds say, but cold weather's on its way

By Todd Smith
THE WASHINGTON TIMES

Energy Department officials told Congress yesterday world oil supplies are adequate this month but could tighten by the end of the year when the heating season begins.

Despite record-high inventories and commitments by OPEC producers to make up much of the Iraqi-Kuwaiti production, both government and private analysts said in a hearing on the economic impact of the Persian Gulf crisis that they expect a world shortage to develop by late November or early December.

But the Bush administration sees no need to release oil from the 590-million-barrel Strategic Petroleum Reserve to keep down prices, said John Easton, assistant secretary for international affairs and energy emergencies.

It will do so only in coordination with U.S. allies that, like Japan and West Germany, have their own stockpiles.

"Worldwide, the amount of oil held in commercial stocks is more than sufficient to meet near-term demand," Mr. Easton told a House Government Operations Committee hearing — the first look into the economic impact of the Persian Gulf crisis since Congress' summer recess.

The 21-nation International Energy Agency estimates a shortage of 500,000 barrels a day could develop by December. But private analysts say the shortage could be worse because demand for oil is expected to increase by several million barrels a day with cold weather.

Legislators at the hearing urged the Bush administration to adopt a wide-ranging energy policy that would ensure adequate oil supplies, the production of higher refinery capacity and further development of alternative fuels to wean United States consumers off foreign oil dependence.

"The fundamental issues raised for this country by the Iraqi invasion will not be solved by military force alone, but by the development of a comprehensive energy policy," said Rep. John Conyers Jr. of Michigan, chairman of the House Committee on Government Operations.

"In the short term, the question this country faces is: How will we handle a major international shortfall in oil production, and how will American consumers be protected? In the long term, the question is how to reduce our dangerous reliance on an unstable energy supply?"

Crude oil and gasoline prices reached five- and ten-year highs respectively in the weeks following the Iraqi invasion. West Texas Intermediate jumped over the $30-a-barrel level for the first time since 1985. Regular unleaded gasoline soared to $1.06 a gallon on the New York Mercantile Exchange, the highest price since 1982.

Mr. Easton said that U.S. refineries are operating at virtually full capacity as a result of the Middle East conflict, a trend that could lead to an even tighter fuel market this winter.

The Energy Department is assessing how and when to tap the Strategic Petroleum Reserve and has also submitted to the White House, a balanced plan of increasing oil production, fuel-switching, and reduction in consumption, he said.

"These options include increasing existing production from Alaska's North Slope; increasing production from the Naval Petroleum Reserves; and increasing production in states that regulate production," Mr. Easton said.

Several congressmen expressed concern that 100 refineries in the U.S. have closed for economic or environmental reasons over the last 10 years.

Consumer advocate Ralph Nader blasted the administration and the Department of Energy for not doing enough to promote conservation and energy efficiency in the past few years.

"The 1975 Fuel Efficiency Act has not been upgraded," said Mr. Nader. "It's doubtful whether it's even being met now. The lack of responsibility of Congress to tame gas-guzzling practices is evident."

He said Congress should push back the national speed limit to 55 mph and mandate the production of cars that can travel 45 miles on a gallon of gas by 2001.

Other legislators urged the development of alternative-fuel vehicles and renewable energy sources. Some criticized oil companies, renewing the argument of price gouging, collusion and anti-trust legislation.

"I want to hear why prices can go up within 48 hours of the invasion, but they can't come down when oil prices drop," said Rep. Chuck Douglas, New Hampshire Republican.

"There's no question that people are taking advantage of this crisis," said Rep. Christopher Shays, Connecticut Republican.

William O'Keefe, chief operating officer of the American Petroleum Institute, told the committee it is not unusual for gasoline prices to respond immediately to world events.

"In a competitive market," he said, "selling prices must reflect today's supply/demand conditions, including perceptions of what the future holds."

Higher prices have brought a wave of consumer outrage over the last few weeks, which has attracted the attention of federal and state officials.

In the past month, government officials have launched investigations into the pricing policies of American refiners. Two weeks ago, the National Association of Attorneys General drew up a 15-point plan seeking to give states more power to punish refiners found guilty of price fixing.

Energy Department officials met yesterday with the Justice Department, which had summoned major oil companies to answer questions about gasoline prices, in an effort to get to the bottom of the price crisis, Mr. Easton said.

Also, Maryland Comptroller Louis Goldstein said yesterday oil companies in his state have changed their pricing system since the Iraqi invasion, and that independent gasoline distributors are being hurt.

Mr. Goldstein said he sent a questionnaire to the state's 239 distributors about their companies policies, and will give the results to Attorney General J. Joseph Curran Jr.

W.T.
9/6/90

2096-4

0083

Effect of Fall in Soviet Oil Output

Decline Amplifies Impact of Crisis

By MATTHEW L. WALD

Independent of the Iraq crisis, which has taken some 4.6 million barrels of oil a day off the world market, oil production in the Soviet Union has fallen by more than half a million barrels a day since last year, and it is likely to continue declining, according to analysts in the United States and Europe.

In a roundabout way this is amplifying the effect of the Mideast crisis on some importing nations, and even on the price of gasoline in the United States, experts say, because the regional markets for crude and products are interconnected.

Soviet production is running lower by 500,000 to 600,000 barrels a day, or 4 to 5 percent, and exports are down about 250,000 barrels a day, according to the International Energy Agency, a monitoring agency for the industrialized nations; some put the export decline higher. Part of the shortfall is made up by declining demand in the Soviet Union itself, which is in the grip of economic problems.

Halt in Sales of Iraqi Oil

In addition, early this year Moscow stopped its worldwide marketing of Iraqi oil, which it had received in exchange for arms shipments, according to experts. Experts say Iraq produced that oil, estimated at 145,000 to 200,000 barrels a day last year, outside its quota set by the Organization of Petroleum Exporting Countries, and its loss further reduces world supplies.

The Soviet Union's own exports will average about 3.3 million barrels a day this year, down from 3.7 million barrels a day last year, according to Robert E. Ebel, the vice president for international affairs of the Enserch Corporation of Dallas. Mr. Ebel, a former Government intelligence officer, said that in 1988 exports reached 4.1 million barrels a day.

Eastern European countries that took about half the Soviet exports, paying for them through barter or in currencies that are not freely exchangeable on world markets, have borne the brunt of the export cuts, according to Western experts. Some of that crude was refined and sold to Western countries. They were also major users and processors of Iraqi oil, generally acquired by barter.

There is also some reduction in sales of Soviet crude to Western European countries that paid in hard currency, but Soviet oil income could is up sharply.

The Soviet Union is the world's biggest oil producer, but as an exporter it trails Saudi Arabia, the world's largest, which had an OPEC quota of *5.38 million barrels under the last* agreement before the Iraqi invasion of Kuwait on Aug. 2. But it is ahead of Iraq, which had a quota of 3.14 million barrels, and Kuwait, which had a quota of 1.5 million. The United Nations-led embargo has denied world markets the 4.6 million barrels a day from Iraq and Kuwait, but OPEC has authorized other members to produce more oil to try to make up the loss.

The United States is the second-largest producer, with about 8.5 million barrels a day of crude oil and condensates, but it also the world's largest importer, buying about the same amount it produces, in normal times.

Compared with these numbers, the Soviet declines are small, but they come at a time of tightness in the market.

The Iraqi barter with the Soviet Union ended early this year, months before the invasion of Kuwait. Robert Mabro, director of the Oxford Institute for Energy Studies, said that the Iraqis had been paying for "arms, flour, tractors, whatever," and that none of the oil actually went to the Soviet Union; it was simply sold or re-bartered. Western experts are not sure why the barter stopped; one suggested that it was for a debt that had been paid off.

With demand heightened by tourism and other factors, Eastern European countries like Yugoslavia and Bulgaria, which were large users of Iraqi oil either through direct barter or through the Soviet Union, are importing refined products, adding to the pressure on Western European refineries, according to Western experts. And oil traders in New York say that demand for gasoline in Europe is so strong now that some cargoes have gone from the Gulf Coast of the United States to northwestern Europe, opposite the normal flow, driving up prices in the United States.

Diversion to India

Moscow was also channeling 90,000 barrels a day of Iraqi oil to India, and is reportedly making that up from domestic production. With that diversion and the general decline in Soviet output, deliveries to Eastern Europe are down by 30 percent, by some estimates.

Soviet officials have told the former members of the Soviet bloc that they will demand payment for oil in hard currency beginning next year, and have reportedly asked for cash even sooner from some countries. But Western analysts doubt that the countries can meet the deadline.

The main reason for the decline in Soviet production is a decision early last year to decrease investment in the oil industry, in favor of investment in areas that could put products *for consumers on store shelves.*

"If perestroika means anything, it means cuts in energy and military capital expenditures," said one analyst based in Paris, who said he could not be publicly identified.

The oil and gas sector had soaked up 70 percent of the new investment capital available in the late 1980's, according to Thane Gustafson, a professor of government at Georgetown University and an expert on the Soviet oil industry. When production began to drop in 1985, he said, "their response was to throw money at the problem. But this time they've decided explicitly not to do it again. The Soviets have said 'no,' they will let oil output fall."

Ethnic unrest and a general breakdown of the Soviet economy are adding to production problems, experts say, but have not been as important as the lack of investment.

Mehdi Varzi, an oil expert at Kleinwort Grieveson Securities, in London, pointed out that Soviet production peaked in 1988, before the unrest in Azerbaijan, site of much of the oil service industry, and before the restiveness of other republics and the general breakdown of the economy.

"They really haven't undertaken the necessary measures in maintenance, well workovers, replacement of equipment and so forth, what is normally called good industry practice," Mr. Varzi said.

Claim by Republics

A "wild card" for future oil production, according to Mr. Gustafson, is that some constituent republics have asserted a claim to their mineral resources.

The Soviet Ministry of Geology and the government of the Turkmen republic made a joint announcement earlier this week that they would open about 90,000 square kilometers, or 56,250 square miles, to exploration by Western companies. This was the first joint announcement between the national government and a republic, Professor Gustafson said. About 85 percent of existing production is in the Russian republic, however.

Soviet and American oil production is declining at roughly the same rate. But oil companies in the United States say that Soviet geology offers far more promising possibilities than does that of the United States. "They have not developed a technical base for drilling deep for oil," said Mr. Ebel of the Enserch Corporation.

N.Y.T. 9/6/90

2096-45

0084

09/06/90 17:40 ☎202 797 0595 EMBASSY OF KOREA →→→ WOI 006/02

: 장 관. 발신 : 주미대사

(메)

Hobart Rowen

The Gulf Crisis: No Excuse . . .

If President Bush and Democratic leaders give up too easily on their earlier target of slicing $50 billion off next year's budget deficit and $500 billion over a five-year period, Saddam Hussein will have chalked up another hostage victory. The conventional wisdom in Washington, since the onset of the Persian Gulf crisis a month ago, is that the budget "summit" process that resumed this week will do well to find $25 billion in savings.

Political experts and commentators were too quick to bury the prospect of a peace dividend. It can't be denied that Saddam's invasion and annexation of Kuwait, followed by a huge American military commitment to defend Saudi Arabia, altered the economic landscape.

Sen. Sam Nunn (D-Ga.) estimates that a full year's cost of the troop buildup in Saudi Arabia, plus the economic aid to be given to friendly nations suffering because they've joined in the

A "real world" deficit figure for next year, short of actual war, is $400 billion.

blockade of Iraq, will come to $50 billion. And that assumes no shooting: If war breaks out, the military costs alone will run to about $1 billion a day—four to five times the financial cost of Vietnam.

But facing this reality makes it all the more imperative that the budget-summit exercise be carried through, not dropped as "too hard." Of course, attention must be focused more intensively on cutting non-defense spending programs and on raising taxes.

It goes without saying that the Pentagon's needs for the Persian Gulf have to be met fully. But that shouldn't give Defense Secretary Dick Cheney carte blanche—as much as he'd like it—to continue wasteful, pseudo-sophisticated systems, mostly designed to level the Evil Empire.

The best guess at the moment is that the deficit for fiscal 1991 will run around $300 billion, including the true costs of paying off the savings and loan obligations to depositors. But that figure is understated by about $100 billion, because of the still-permitted use of Social Security and other trust-fund surpluses to pay ordinary bills.

So a "real world" deficit figure for next year—again, short of actual war with Saddam—is $400 billion. A deficit-cutting exercise should look at a $50 billion reduction for fiscal 1991 as a minimum. Uncle Sam is so short of cash that Secretary of State James A. Baker III and Treasury Secretary Nicholas Brady this week are going hat in hand to the Gulf, Europe and Asia to demand that our allies share the monetary burden of the confrontation with Saddam. In principle, this is wholly justified, and especially relevant to wealthy countries such as West Germany, Japan, Taiwan and Korea. They have no armed forces standing shoulder to shoulder with Americans on the front line in Saudi Arabia.

However, the real need for America to beg for financial support in this circumstance tells us dramatically that the excesses and failures of economic-policy making of the decade of the '80s have finally caught up with us: Uncle Sam is broke. We not only don't have the money with which to match our leadership in the necessary business of crushing Saddam, we don't have the money to rebuild our educational system and our roads and bridges and to pay other bills on the home front.

Worse, the nation appears to be heading into a real recession for part of this year and calendar 1991. This will boost expenditures for unemployment insurance and reduce normal tax revenues. Brady told reporters at the start of the Persian Gulf crisis early in August that inflation resulting from higher oil prices would cut the sputtering economic growth rate, then around one percent, about in half.

Many business economists are even more pessimistic. They think that government data lag behind actual results and that the economy already is in a recession, with many commercial banks and corporations facing a true crisis.

There is too much at stake, given what may be a long-term commitment in the Persian Gulf, to allow the budget to soar out of control. An extension of the deficit in these boxcar numbers means that we must continue to depend on imported capital—a dependency even more serious than that relating to oil, especially at a time when it appears that Japanese will have more difficulty in finding the multibillions they have been pumping into Treasury obligations.

To a major extent, we can and should reduce our dependency on petroleum. But when we borrow foreign capital to finance the deficit, we transfer our wealth abroad on a near-permanent basis, as interest costs multiply over the years.

Given the problems in the banking and financial community, a majority at the Federal Reserve Board knows they can't tolerate a deep or extended recession. In this situation, the economy desperately needs the lubrication of lower interest rates. Normally, the Fed is willing to accept slower growth than is really healthy for the economy—say, around the 2 percent level—so long as it keeps inflation under control.

But Brady's 0.5 percent real economic growth projection is too close to zero for comfort. To give the Fed the opportunity to move promptly and dramatically enough to cut interest rates, the budget summit must do its part.

W.P. 9/6/9

2096-6

0085

09/06/90 17:41 ☎202 797 0595 EMBASSY OF KOREA →→→ WOI 007/0

DER NO. 173 • WASHINGTON, D.C. THURSDAY, SEPTEMBER 6, 1990

...scheduled for Oct. 10, before Glenn's Governmental Affairs Committee.□

International Finance

MEXICO TO SEEK FUNDS INCREASE FROM IFC, FINANCE UNDERSECRETARY SAYS

MEXICO CITY—(By a BNA Special Correspondent)—Mexico, which received more International Finance Corporation investment than any other country in 1989-90, will push for significant increases in funds during the Sept. 24-27 IFC meeting in Washington, D.C, Finance Undersecretary Angel Gurria said at an IFC press conference Sept. 5.

Gurria noted that the European Development Bank was set up with $12 billion in capital, 7 percent of which will be channeled to the private sector. He said countries that already have market economies deserve much more but declined to say how much capital Mexico will seek. The point is to make more money available to developing economies, he said, adding that the developing world should start negotiations by asking for twice what it has received in the past.

The IFC is a multilateral development affiliate of the World Bank with equity capital provided by its 135 member countries in both the developed and developing worlds.

IFC spokesman Mark Kirk later said Germany and Mexico are expected to lobby hard to increase the IFC's capital at the meeting later this month. "The United States is footdragging," he said, adding that the U.S. Treasury Department is against increasing the IFC's capital.

Kirk said that the IFC wants to increase investment in Latin America by 12 percent per year. The region currently represents 48 percent of the IFC portfolio, he said.

Mexico topped the list of all countries getting IFC investment with more than $200 million in the year that ended June 30, 1990. Investments were in the fields of petrochemicals, manufacturing, and restructuring of credit. It also handled a debt swap that the Mexican Banco Serfin used to exchange currency for the foreign-exchange risk associated with a 40 million deutschemark loan and thus gain access to additional German loans.

Second place in IFC loans went to India which received $147 million.

...said Mexico's private sector, which had b[...] from the IFC in financial restructuring following t[...] 1982 peso devaluation, is in good financial conditi[...] with "a spirit of growth, change and expansion."

A press release distributed in Mexico quoted him saying, "Business opportunities Mexico offers [...] enormous. This has allowed the IFC to carry out m[...] operations in this country than in any other during last year. The Mexican economic opening and t[...] opportunities that the government of President (C[...]los) Salinas de Gortari has opened for the priv[...] sector in Mexico mean that the future perspectiv[...] are even more brilliant."

IFC Vice President Richard Frank called Mexico [...] model economy and said IFC will continue to he[...] finance privatization of state-owned companies. [...] also acknowledged that the IFC is involved in t[...] pending privatization of Sicartsa, the state-own[...] steel company, and is very interested in the repriva[...]zation of the telephone company and domestic bank[...]

Frank said that he expected Mexico to again sta[...] out this year in terms of economic recovery a[...] foreign investment.

IFC officials, who were to leave Mexico Sept. [...] embargoed the contents of their annual report un[...] Sept. 11 when it will have been presented in Londo[...] Paris; Frankfurt; Washington, D.C.; Tokyo; and Ho[...] Kong. They said the IFC was paying tribute to Mexi[...] as a model country climbing out of its economic cri[...] by unveiling the report here.□

Energy

NATIONAL ENERGY STRATEGY WILL FOCUS ON EFFICIENCY, PRODUCTION, DOE SAYS

Assistant Energy Secretary for International A[...]fairs John J. Easton Jr. told Congress Sept. 5 that t[...] Bush administration's forthcoming National Ener[...] Strategy—with a focus on energy efficiency and [...]mestic production—will set the energy policy o[...] different course from the Reagan years.

Easton made his comments at a House Governm[...] Operations Committee hearing at which he fielded t[...] hours of questions on the National Energy Strate[...] which will be presented to the president in Decem[...] and is expected to be ready for Congress' consid[...]ation by the following spring. Easton also answe[...] questions on price gouging by oil companies, the S[...]

0086

tegic Petroleum Reserves, and the expected home heating fuel market for this winter.

In 14 months of meetings with energy industry representatives, environmentalists, and consumer advocates, Easton said the most commonly heard themes to emerge concerned energy efficiency, security, environmental, and technology.

In the interim, the DOE has sought to reinstitute tax incentives to spur domestic production, develop environmentally safer energy technologies, and increase oil reserves.

Current Energy Supplies

Easton told the committee that current oil supplies on the world market have been sufficient to meet short-term requirements, though at higher prices. He said the shutdown of Iraqi and Kuwaiti oil came a time when world oil stocks were at high levels.

Long-term supplies are harder to estimate, Easton said, but they may be supplemented by increased production outside of Iraq and Kuwait. The administration has urged Organization of Petroleum Exporting Countries and non-OPEC countries to increase their production.

In response to a question on a Western hemispheric energy coalition, Energy Information Agency Administrator Calvin Kent said that increased production in Venezuela and Mexico is a good bet for the long term, but that those countries could use investment from U.S. companies to increase development technologies. He added that this may not be in the interest of some sectors of domestic energy producers. "We've got loads and loads of coal," he said.

Easton said that the DOE nearly has completed a Western Hemisphere study and that it will be delivered to Congress in the near future.

Strategic Petroleum Reserves

Easton said the United States is readying its oil reserves, but would not release the SPR without coordination with the International Energy Agency, which met Aug. 31. He said that IEA member countries have more than one billion barrels of government-controlled petroleum inventories.

The United States holds 590 million barrels of crude oil in its reserves, which Easton said can be drawn at a maximum average rate of 3.5 million barrels per day for 90 days or 3 million barrels per day for six months.

Rep. Frank Horton (R-NY), the committee's ranking minority member, said in his opening statement that the IEA has recommended that members use their reserves at the same time.

Committee Chairman John Conyers (D-Mich) said he believed that Energy Secretary James Watkins preferred releasing the SPR in August, but was overruled by Office of Management and Budget Director Richard Darman and Chief of Staff John Sununu.

Conyers requested the Energy Information Agency to assess how much withholding the reserves cost consumers at the pump. "By some estimates the current (gas price) increase could cost consumers $25 billion, boost inflation more than half a percentage point, shave the nation's growth rate and output one percentage point," he said. "I believe the American people have a right to know whether a different policy could save them billions of dollars."

The DOE has been assessing use of the SPR, "but we must carefully weigh many factors in considering a proper response to a disruption, and not just react to volatile price changes in the petroleum marketplace," Easton said.

Easton did say that the department may use the reserves in the winter if there is a home heating oil crisis, but again emphasized that they would coordinate with allies beforehand.

The administration had been increasing its reserve supplies until the Aug. 2 invasion, Easton said.

Price Gouging

Accusations of price gouging by oil companies at the onset of the crises was a "rush to judgment" by those who did not understand the workings of the petroleum market, American Petroleum Institute President William O'Keefe told the committee.

Indeed, the oil companies acted with restraint, O'Keefe said. He said that while spot crude prices were up 29 cents a gallon by Aug. 23, major oil companies, which provide about one-half of the nation's gasoline supplies, raised their wholesale prices by an average of 20 cents.

Nevertheless, both Republican and Democratic members repeatedly questioned whether supply and demand justified the price increases. Some suggested collusion on the part of the oil companies. "I just don't believe this is the perfect market where things adjust well," Rep. Christopher Shays (R-Conn) said.

Easton said the Energy Information Agency is examining the price increases, and will issue a report as early as next month. But he added, "with any disturbance of the international petroleum market, it is not unusual for prices of crude oil to rise quickly on the spot and futures markets ... as long as this uncertainty persists, so will price volatility."

Energy Strategies

The DOE has been working to "remove barriers" to domestic production, switch to cleaner and more efficient fuels, and reduce energy consumption, Easton said. This has included discussion among federal, state, and industry officials on increasing existing production in Alaska, the Naval Petroleum Reserves, and in states that regulate production. "We estimate that these efforts could increase domestic supplies by about 250,000 barrels a day by December," he said.

He said a meeting is scheduled Oct. 2 among federal, state, and industry officials to consider options to ameliorate home heating fuel costs this winter.

Several committee members said they were concerned about the nation's refinery capacity. EIA Administrator Kent said that this summer capacity has been utilized to the maximum because of an abnormally high use of oil during the summer vacations

0148-8155/90/$00.50

0087

coupled with a desire to stock home heating fuel. "As soon as the driving season ends, it will ease capacity," he said.

Although the department's suggestion for a national energy strategy will not be presented to the president until December, Easton said that in the meantime the DOE has recommended tax incentives for domestic production, which he said were removed in the 1986 Tax Reform Act.

The department also has been forwarding the clean-coal technology program. Between private and public contributions that program receives $7.5 billion in funding, but Easton said he fears elements of the Clean Air Bill, which is now in conference, may limit that program.

Easton also said that his department is encouraging research and development of renewables, a point which Rep. Mike Synar (D-Okla) contested. Synar read figures, which showed that the DOE budget for renewables has decreased dramatically during the eighties. Easton responded that some of the figures compared levels from the Carter years. "You should compare us with Reagan," he said. "Bush has recommended many increases."

Consumer advocate Ralph Nader agreed backhandedly that Bush initiatives reach further than those of his predecessor. "I do think they're going to come out with a slightly better policy than Reagan's 'see no gouge, hear no rip-off' policy," he said. "There's no where to go but up."

Nader recommended that the government change its procurement standards by purchasing only energy efficient vehicles as well as changing government building lighting, furnaces, and other appliances to more efficient types. "You've got a gigantically powerful consumer here," Nader said of the government.

Nader also said that with the record profits automobile industry made during the eighties, they should have been required to invest in development of more efficient, and safe vehicles.

Economic Effects

U.S. consumers paid about $63 million more per day for gasoline on Aug. 10 than on July 31, three days before the Iraqi invasion, Victor Rezendes, an energy development specialist with the General Accounting Office, told the committee.

He said the higher costs will not only spread to other industries, such as agriculture and airlines, but if sustained over a long time will touch all sectors of the economy by raising inflation and unemployment, and lowering output.☐

Auto Sales

BIG THREE CAR, TRUCK SALES DOWN SUBSTANTIALLY IN AUGUST

DETROIT—(By a BNA Staff Correspondent)—Big Three sales of domestically made cars and light trucks were down substantially in August as consumers expressed uncertainty over the Middle East oil crisis, automakers reported Sept. 5.

Sales of domestically made cars at GM were dov 18.7 percent—from 296,482 deliveries last year 241,014 this year. Light truck sales fell from 166,3 units last year to 140,025 this year, or 15.8 percent.

At Ford Motor Co., domestically made cars dropp a sharp 26.8 percent—from 209,951 deliveries la August to 153,604 this year. Light truck sales were o 7.1 percent. The automaker sold 126,433 units la year, compared with 117,440 this year.

Chrysler Corp. fared the worst of its traditional U. rivals. Sales of domestically made cars fell 32.2 pe cent in August—from 90,345 last year to 61,207. D mestic light truck sales were equally weak. Tl number of units delivered dropped from 33,052 la August to 23,072, or 30.1 percent.

Layoffs

The current layoff picture is mixed. At GM, 30,2 workers were indefinitely idled as of Aug. 1—the mo recent figures available—compared with 45,200 l year. There were 33,300 workers on temporary fu lough through Aug. 1, down from the 39,500 recorde last year.

No new down time was scheduled for any G plants.

At Ford as of Aug. 26, 653 workers were indefinitel idled, compared with 616 last year. As of Sept. 3, 3,42 workers were on temporary furlough, compared wi 4,371 last Sept. 4.

The automobile assembly portion of Ford's Kans City, Mo., plant will be down for one week beginni Sept. 10, affecting 2,300 workers. The automaker Louisville, Ky., truck facility will also be closed du ing the same period, temporarily idling 1,900 worke

As of Sept. 4, 5,761 Chrysler workers were indef nitely idled, compared with 3,223 for the same peri last year. About 4,636 workers were temporarily la off, compared with 3,196 through last Sept. 4.

There were no new temporary layoffs scheduled.

Pontiac Plant Closing

A local union official said that GM plans to close i Pontiac, Mich., engine plant, indefinitely idling 2,2 workers.

GM officials would neither confirm nor deny r ports that the automaker is poised to shutter t engine plant by next spring.

But a GM spokesman suggested that any such clo ing, should it occur, could be linked to continu consumer skittishness about the Iraq-Kuwait oil crisi The 2.5-liter, four-cylinder engine built in Pontiac not as powerful or fuel-efficient as other GM mode analysts say.

"Whatever action will be taken, local [United Au Workers Local 653] officials have known about it f quite some time," said GM spokesman John Macia "They make a 4-cylinder engine there, and with wha going on in the Middle East, it wouldn't be surprisi But nothing is confirmed yet," he said.

Two years ago, GM angered UAW officials by definitely idling another Pontiac plant—the Fl

0148-8155/90/$00.50

7591-9

0088

STATEMENT OF

JOHN J. EASTON, JR.

ASSISTANT SECRETARY

INTERNATIONAL AFFAIRS AND ENERGY EMERGENCIES

U.S. DEPARTMENT OF ENERGY

BEFORE THE

COMMITTEE ON GOVERNMENT OPERATIONS

U.S. HOUSE OF REPRESENTATIVES

SEPTEMBER 5, 1990

2096 - 10

0089

Mr. Chairman and members of the Committee, I am pleased to be here today to discuss the current situation in the petroleum market and to bring you up to date on what the Department of Energy is doing in response to developments in the Middle East. I want to discuss two main points:

- o the current supply of oil on the world oil market;
- o what the Department of Energy is doing to address potential supply problems.

Current oil supplies on the world market have been sufficient to meet short-term requirements, albeit at higher prices. The shut-off of Iraqi and Kuwaiti oil took place coincidentally at a time when world oil stocks were at very high levels. In the United States, crude oil stocks are still higher than the average range of crude oil stocks during the last three years. Worldwide, the amount of oil held in commercial stocks is more than sufficient to meet near-term demand.

We estimate that, with time, the excess production capacity outside of Iraq and Kuwait could nearly equal the current loss of exports from those two countries, if this capacity were to be fully utilized. It is, however, not clear how much of this excess capacity can be sustained over the long term. The

2096 -11

0090

Administration has urged countries with excess production capacity to increase their oil production. Certain OPEC countries have announced production increases and some non-OPEC countries are preparing to add to their current production.

In addition, there are over one billion barrels of government-controlled and strategic petroleum inventories held by member nations of the International Energy Agency. The U.S. Strategic Petroleum Reserve holds almost 590 million barrels of crude oil, which can be drawn down at a maximum average rate of 3.5 million barrels per day for 90 days, and a maximum average rate of 3 million barrels per day for six months.

Now I'd like to discuss what the Department of Energy is doing to address the domestic energy consequences of the United Nations sanctions against Iraq. We are developing response options for the short-term, medium-term, and long-term. First, our short-term options include a full assessment of how and when we might use the Strategic Petroleum Reserve. We are gathering data on a daily basis from industry, from the intelligence community, and from state and local officials on supply, prices, demand and stock activities. We must carefully weigh many factors in considering a proper response to a disruption, and not just react to volatile price changes in the petroleum marketplace.

Secondly, we have announced a balanced plan of increasing oil

2096-12

0091

production, fuel-switching, and reduction in consumption. The Department of Energy (DOE) has been working with other Federal agencies to remove regulatory barriers to the movement or production of energy supplies. For example, DOE worked initially with the Department of Treasury to ensure that oil en route to the United States from Iraq and Kuwait -- and already purchased and paid for by U.S. companies -- would be allowed to enter the country, thereby obviating possible localized supply problems. The Department has also held discussions with Federal, state and industry officials to explore options to promote domestic crude oil production, while at the same time protecting the environment. These options include increasing existing production from Alaska's North Slope; increasing production from the Naval Petroleum Reserves; and increasing production in states that regulate production. We estimate that these efforts could increase domestic supplies by about 250,000 barrels a day by December, 1990.

Thirdly, in line with the President's request that Americans conserve energy, DOE is encouraging domestic energy conservation and fuel switching by consumers. This initiative includes helping utilities and industry switch from petroleum to domestic fuels, like natural gas and coal. We will remind private citizens, through a national public information campaign, that they can save a significant amount of oil by taking four simple measures: maintaining proper tire pressure; obeying speed limits;

2096-13

0092

using the most fuel efficient car in the household; and car pooling. Such measures could save consumers money and conserve oil at the same time without discomfort or loss of mobility. Smarter use of energy can be a win-win strategy for the consumer as well as the country as a whole. Collectively, these domestic production and conservation measures could offset much of the oil that the United States had been importing from Iraq and Kuwait.

With respect to medium-term options, the Department is in the process of evaluating additional measures that could be taken in the next 12 to 24 months. These, too, would be a balanced approach of energy production, reduction in demand, and fuel-switching.

We stand ready to draw on our Strategic Petroleum Reserve to redress any severe oil supply disruption. Immediately after the Iraqi invasion of Kuwait, the SPR was placed in a status of increased readiness for drawdown, and detailed plans for the deployment of the Reserve inventory are ready to be implemented, if so directed by the President. We have also temporarily suspended further oil purchases for the Reserve, thus removing from world oil demand approximately 40-50,000 barrels per day. Furthermore, the Administration is actively working with our partners in the International Energy Agency to ensure that our respective actions in response to the events in the Persian Gulf are well coordinated. This will improve the effectiveness of all

2096-14

0093

of our responses.

The appropriate use of the Strategic Petroleum Reserve (SPR) and our membership in the International Energy Agency are key ingredients in our contingency planning. Before the Congress recessed, we received a temporary extension in the provisions of the Energy Policy and Conservation Act (EPCA) which authorize the SPR and permit full involvement by U.S. industry in the Agreement on an International Energy Program. These authorities will expire on September 15, 1990. We urge the Congress to extend these authorities as soon as possible. The Administration has put forward a creative and workable set of amendments to the EPCA to permit cost-effective approaches to SPR financing and to streamline some important aspects of the drawdown process. Congress should enact these amendments, while avoiding a time-consuming and costly debate about proposals for expanding the SPR beyond 750 million barrels and for requiring regional and refined product storage.

I want to say a brief word about the recent gasoline price increases. With any disturbance of the international petroleum market, it is not unusual for prices of crude oil to rise quickly on the spot and futures markets. Such price increases have been reflected in varying amounts in retail gasoline prices. Prices are going up in real terms, because oil from the Persian Gulf is usually priced at the time of delivery to the markets, not upon

2096-15

0094

loading into transport vessels. It is difficult to predict future price movements because those movements depend on the market's perception of future crude oil supply availability. That perception, in turn, is influenced by individual judgments about the likelihood of further losses of oil supplies in the future.

In short, price volatility occurs because it is unclear how long any losses of oil supplies will last, or how readily the market will be able to absorb such losses. So long as this uncertainty persists, so will price volatility.

Whatever its cause, the Department is quite concerned about the rapid run up in prices of petroleum products. We are gathering information on the commercial oil market to track any sharp fluctuations in the marketplace and will provide data analyses to the Department of Justice, Congress, and the American people. If tensions ease in the Middle East, we can expect prices to become more stable, to the relief of suppliers and consumers alike.

Finally, the Iraqi invasion points to the need for long-term solutions to energy issues. In July 1989, the President directed Secretary Watkins to lead the development of a comprehensive National Energy Strategy. The principal objective of this strategy is to reduce our dependence and that of our Allies on unstable supplies of oil, and to do this in a way which is

2096 -16

0095

7

economically and environmentally beneficial to the United States. We are well along in completing this task, and will make a report to the President in December, as scheduled.

This concludes my testimony, Mr. Chairman. I would be happy to answer questions that you or members of the Committee may have.

2096 - 17

0096

원 본

외 무 부

종 별 : 긴 급

번 호 : NZW-0233 일 시 : 90 0907 1800

수 신 : 장 관(기협)

발 신 : 주 뉴질랜드 대사

제 목 : 주재국의 중독석유 의존도

대: WNZ-0266

1. 대호 관련, 주재국의 원유 수입량을 아래와 같이 보고함.

가.총원유 수입량 (1톤-8.1 배럴)

- 1988:2,483.21천톤 (약 5만 5천 B/D)

- 1989: 3,043.00 천톤 (약 6만 7천 B/D)

나.중동지역 원유수입 의존도 (1989년도)

- 사우디: 1,541천톤(50.6)

- UAE: 698 천톤(23.0)

- 알제리: 320천톤(10.5)

2. 주재국의 석유 자급률은 55-60 정도이며, 수입석유의 약 84는 중동 지역의 사우디, UAE, 알제리등으로 부터 수입하고 있으나, 1989년도중 이라크와 쿠웨이트로부터는 석유를 직접 수입하지 않았음. 석유 수입의 나머지 16 는 호주, 인도네시아등 아주지역 국가들로부터 수입하고 있음.

(대사 서경석 국장)

경제국

PAGE 1

90.09.07 18:09

외신 1과 통제관

0097

國際原油需給 및 價格動向 速報

(公館 報告 綜合)

1990.9.7.
外務部, 國際經濟局

1. 原油需給

o 사우디, 9월중 OPEC 쿼다 (538만
(Middle East Economic Survey 보
- 4/4 분기중 북반구 原油需要增
- 原油 增産分은 한국, 대만, 브
방글라데시등 開途國에 우선

9.7.	9.10	
26.26	27.03	Dubai
27.25	27.63	Oman
31.85	30.85	Brent
30.19	30.80	WTI

o 미국, 알라스카주 및 텍사스주
增産 가능 (미 에너지부 발표)

o IEA, 8.31 현단계에서 즉각적인
- OPEC 增産실시, 石油會社의 商業在庫分 사용 및 價格引上에 따른 需要
減少등으로 대체적 需給 均衡 평가

2. 油價動向

o 現物市場 動向 (단위 : $/B)

	7.31	8.7	8.22	8.27	8.29	9.5	9.6	전일대비
Dubai	17.20	25.40	31.75	27.20	24.75	27.40	28.23	0.83
Oman	17.65	25.90	32.35	27.80	25.35	28.00	28.83	0.83
Brent	19.49	29.40	32.15	27.80	26.35	31.75	33.36	1.61
WTI	20.75	29.62	31.57	27.25	26.05	29.85	31.60	1.75

o 최근 油價上昇 인인 (미국 언론 보도종합)
- 유엔 사무총장의 대 이라크 仲裁努力 失敗에 따른 中東危機의 長期化 전망
및 불확실성 고조
- 쿠웨이트 精油供給中斷, 사우디 精油의 駐屯 美軍用으로의 轉用 및 世界
精油施設不足 (精油施設 不足은 短期的 해결 곤란)

3. 其他 關聯 事項

o 쌍용 및 유공, 최근 타결된 사우디 ARAMCO 와의 長期 供給契約에 따라
금년 9월부터 각각 6만B/D, 4.5만B/D 原油導入 (주사우디 대사 보고)

공람	기술협력과	90년 9월 7일	담당	과장	국장	차관보	차관	장관
			홍석화		[signature]	[signature]		

0098

국별 중동 석유 의존도

국명	GNP (단위:10억불)	중동석유의존도	무역수지 ('89년도, 단위:억불)		
			수출	수입	수지
싱가폴	28.9 ('89)	~~60.4% ('86)~~ 73% ('89)	447	497	- 50
자유중국	150.2 ('89)	60.8% ('88)	661	525	- 136
홍콩	54.7 ('88)	미 파악 X	731	722	+ 9
태국	56.9 ('88)	~~47.6% ('87)~~ 70% ('89)	201	255	- 54
한국	210.1 ('89)	72.7% ('89)	624	615	+ 9
일본	2833.7 ('89)	~~69.7%~~ ('89) 71.3%	2,742	2,101	+ 641

경제기획원 조사통계국 자료관리과 (720-2788)
에너지 연구원 정보분석실 부경진 차장 245-0106-8

0099

국별 중동 석유 의존도

(90년 1/4분기)

(단위 : 만B/D)

국 명	총 수입	OPEC	Gulf 국가 (사우디,바레인, 이란 이라크,쿠웨이트,UAE 카타르)	Gulf 국가 점유비율
프랑스	190	104	86	45.3%
서 독	204	76.6	23	11.3%
이태리	190	137	65	34.2%
미 국	766	458	206	26.9%
일 본	548	416	354	64.6%
기타OECD 유럽국가	422	324	219	51.9%

(미국 Energy Information Agency 자료)

※ 기타 OECD 유럽국가

오지리, 벨기에, 덴마크, 필랜드, 그리스, 아이슬랜드, 아일랜드,

룩셈부르크, 네덜란드, 노르웨이, 스페인, 스웨덴, 스위스, 터키, 폴투갈

※ 아국의 중동원유의존도 (90년 1/4분기) : 75.4% (64만 B/D)

- Gulf 국가 : 53.4% (45만 B/D)

· 오만 : 22% (19만 B/D)

0100

국별 중동 원유 의존도 ('89)

(단위 : 백만배럴)

국 명	총 수입량	중동지역수입량	점유 비율	비 고
한 국	296	222	75%	
일 본	1,319	937	71%	
싱가폴	275	201	73%	
대 만	156	103	66%	
태 국	74	49	66%	
불란서	509	223	44%	
서 독	485	95	20%	
벨기에	179	103	58%	
스페인	364	122	34%	
화 란	376	212	56%	
폴투갈	72	34	47%	
스웨덴	114	17	15%	
덴마크	30	21	70%	북해산유국으로 국내수요 80%를 자체 조달
그리스	42	26	62%	
핀랜드	64	3	5%	
호 주	96	52	54%	원유총소비량의 39%를 수입

0101

외 무 부

종 별 :

번 호 : JAW-5419 일 시 : 90 0907 1823

수 신 : 장관(경일,기협,통이,아일)

발 신 : 주 일대사(경제)

제 목 : 중동사태의 일본경제에의 영향

1. 최근 중동사태에 따른 유가상승이 일본경제에 미칠 영향과 관련, 주재국 연구기관의 분석결과를 아래 요약 보고함.

0 본격적인 원유가격 상승영향은 금년 3/4분기 이후로서, 90년도 일본경제에의영향은 적을것으로 예측 (실질 경제성장율 4퍼센트 달성 가능)

0 91년도는 금융긴축 및 유가상승으로 경제상황의 악화가 예상되는 미국의 대일압력 요인등으로 내년도 일본경제의 실질 성장율은 3.5-4.0 퍼센트로 전망

0 원유가격은 점차 안정세를 보여 향후 바렐당 25불대가 될것으로 예상

0 유가상승의 금년도 도매물가 및 소비자 물가에의 상승효과는 각각 0.3-0.6 퍼센트 및 0.3 퍼센트 이내가 될것이며, 90년도 경제 성장율에는 0.1퍼센트 정도의 감소 효과

2. 연이나, 미국경제에의 영향은 심각할 것이며, 향후 경기가 후퇴 국면이 될 가능성도 있음을 전망하고 있음.

0 90년도 실질경제 성장율은 0.2-0.3 퍼센트 저하되어 1.1 퍼센트의 성장에 그칠것으로 예측

0 인플레율은 0.5-0.6 퍼센트 상승

3. 상기 예측은 이라크- 쿠웨이트 사태 발발후 일본내 최초의 계량적, 종합적분석으로서 동경은행, 후지은행등 주재국 주요 금융기관 등이 9.5 발표 하였음.

끝

(공사 이한춘-국장)

공람	국제경제국	90.9.10	담당	과장	국장	차관보	차관	장관
				(서명)	V			

경제국 2차보 아주국 중아국 경제국 통상국 정문국 안기부 동기부

PAGE 1 90.09.07 22:23 DA

외신 1과 통제관

0102

원 본

외 무 부

종 별 :

번 호 : UKW-1678 일 시 : 90 0907 1430

수 신 : 장 관(기협,통일,구일)

발 신 : 주 영 대사

제 목 : 유가동향 보고

1.금 9.7(금) 자 당지 FINANCIAL TIMES 등은 계속된 GULF 사태의 불안으로 인해 9.6 북해산 BRENT 유가 8.25 이래 다시 바렐당 31 불 (10월배달분)로 인상되었다고 보도하였음

2.한편 당지 B.P. 측에서도 9.6 처음으로 시중 고급휘발류가 갈론당 2.30 파운드를 기록하고 당분간은 더 이상될 가능성이 있음을 시사하고 있으며, 90.8월중 신규 자동차 판매 (등록기준)도 전년대비 13.5 프로가 감소되었다고 함.끝

(대사 오재희-국장)

공람	국	담당	과장	국장	차관보	차관	장관
		9/10		V			

경제국 2차보 중아국 통상국 안기부 구주국 통진부

PAGE 1

90.09.08 09:35 WG

외신 1과 통제관

0103

원 본

외 무 부

종 별 :

번 호 : HUW-0387 일 시 : 90 0907 1640

수 신 : 장 관(경자,미북,정일) 사본:주미대사(필)

발 신 : 주 휴스턴 총영사

제 목 : 석유가격및 생산동향(8)

1. 9.6.현재 서부텍사스 중질유 10월 인도가격은 어제보다 1.66불이 상승, 베럴당 31.43 불로 거래됨.동가격은 이락의 쿠웨이트 침공후 최고가격이는 8.23.의 32.35 불보다 92 센트 낮은가격임.

2.전문가들은 사우디등 OPEC 국들의 증산결정이후에도 석유가가 계속 상승되는 이유를 이해할수 없다 하며 주로 심리적요인에 기인하는 것으로 평가된다함.

3.최근 한 미국인이 쿠웨이트에서 이라크군의 총격에의해 사살된 사건, 사담후세인 대통령의 두번째 성전촉구, 지난 수요일 미에너지성 차관보가 의회에서 금년말경 원유부족이 예상된다고 증언한 점등이 석유가 상승에 작용한 것으로 보임.

(총영사 허승-국장)

경제국 1차보 2차보 미주국 정문국 동자부

PAGE 1 90.09.08 10:52 WG

외신 1과 통제관

0104

원 본

외 무 부

종 별 :

번 호 : USW-4084 일 시 : 90 0907 1924

수 신 : 장 관(기협)

발 신 : 주 미 대사

제 목 : 석유 시장및 유가 동향(11)

표제 관련, 9.7 당지 언론 보도 종합 보고함.

1.유가 동향

가. 9.6 원유 및 정유 제품 가격 (뉴욕 상품 시장,10월 인도 가격)

0 원유

- 배럴당 31.43불(전일 대비 1.68 불 상승)

0 휘발유

- 갤런당 95.07 센트(전일 대비 2.8 센트 상승)

0 난방유

- 갤런당 88.24 센트(전일 대비 4.87 센트 상승)

나.유가 상승 원인 분석및 전망

0 당지 전문가들은 9.6 유가 상승원인을 아래 분석하고 있음.

- 중동 사태의 외교적 해결을 위한 진전 결여

- 동절기 유류 제품 수요 증대 전망

- 9.5 하원 정부위에서 EASTON 에너지부 차관보가 동절기 중 유류 공급 부족 현상이 있을지도 모른다고 증언한 사실

0 한편 대부분의 전문가들은 중동 사태 해결 방향 및 원유 수급 전망의 불확실성으로 현재 석유시장이 매우 불안정한 사태에 있으며, 이에 따라 유가도 당분간 등락을 거듭할 것이라고 전망하고있음.

3.금 9.7자 언론 보도 내용 별첨 FAX 송부함.

첨부: USW(F)-2116

(대사 박동진- 국장)

공람	국제경제국	90 9 10	담당	과장	국장	차관보	차관	장관
				(서명)	V			

경제국 2차보 통상국 미주국 동자부 안기부

PAGE 1

90.09.08 09:05 WG

외신 1과 통제관

0105

호 : USW(F) - 2116
신 : 장관 (기협)
발 : 주미대사
제목 : USW - 4084 첨부 (5 매)

WT 9/7/90

Barrel of oil tops $30 for second time

By Dirk Beveridge
THE ASSOCIATED PRESS

NEW YORK — Oil prices soared over $30 a barrel yesterday, reaching that plateau for the second time since the Persian Gulf crisis as traders bet that supply shortages will develop.

Light sweet crude rose throughout a hectic day of trading on the New York Mercantile Exchange, closing up $1.66 at $31.43 per barrel for October contracts. At its peak Thursday, oil traded at $31.58.

"The U.S. Energy Department testified yesterday to Congress that they thought there'd be a shortage of oil this winter," said Philip L. Dodge, an analyst with Nomura Securities International Inc. "That was enough to move the markets. Also, there's no sign of peace breaking out in the gulf."

Oil futures had last traded above $30 per barrel on Aug. 22-24, at one point matching the all-time Merc high of $32.35. Before that surge, the Merc had not seen $30 crude since November 1985.

The stock market dived sharply yesterday in the face of rising oil prices, with the Dow Jones industrial average falling 31.93 points to 2,596.29.

Unleaded gasoline futures also traded higher, up 2.8 cents to 95.07 cents per gallon for October delivery. Analysts partially attributed the increase to a realization that increased crude output by Saudi Arabia and Venezuela will not accommodate most U.S. refineries because it is a more difficult oil to refine.

Even though those nations are exceeding temporarily their OPEC production limits to make up for the shortfall caused by the boycott of Iraqi and Kuwaiti oil, petroleum experts fear that refinery capacity in Kuwait cannot be replaced quickly.

"Gasoline is the item to worry about," Mr. Dodge said. "It was in relatively short supply going into the crisis. Also, the oil that replaces the Iraqi crude has a lower yield of gasoline. The excess oil that's being made up by the Saudis and the Venezuelans is sour, heavy crude, which is not something the U.S. refineries like to run through their systems."

Domestic refinery operators prefer light sweet crude, which has less sulfur and costs less to refine.

The petroleum markets opened strong on news that an American citizen had been shot in the hand by an Iraqi police officer in Kuwait. The continued tensions in the Middle East kept oil high all day.

...pings
...ection I

0106

Oil Price Back Above $30 a Barrel

Supply Concerns Are Being Felt

By Mark Potts
Washington Post Staff Writer

Oil prices, which many analysts expected to drop significantly once members of OPEC began making up for oil lost in the embargo of Iraq and Kuwait, are continuing to move stubbornly upward, and many experts now believe they will stay higher for some time.

The prices are being pushed up by newfound concerns that a long-term standoff is developing between the United States and Iraq, worries about winter supplies of heating oil and simple market speculation by oil buyers and users, many of whom are said to be stockpiling supplies of crude oil and petroleum products to guard against future price increases or supply shortages.

The price of a contract for a benchmark barrel of crude oil rose $1.66 yesterday, to $31.43, on the New York Mercantile Exchange—the highest price since oil peaked at $32.35 a barrel two weeks ago. The current price is almost twice as high as the price of crude oil in early July.

Prices of oil products also rose sharply yesterday, with unleaded gasoline contracts rising 2.80 cents to 95.07 cents a gallon on the New York Merc and heating oil contracts rising 4.87 cents to 88.24 cents on the exchange.

Analysts said the price increases reflect deep-seated concern about future supplies of both crude and petroleum products and the absence of favorable news from the Middle East.

"The price run-up originally was based on psychology and insecurity. Now the price run-up is based a little bit on considerations of supply," said Roger Gale, president of Washington International Energy Group, a consulting firm. "If the situation doesn't get any worse, we'll stay in the low $30-a-barrel range."

"I think the crisis is beginning to bite," said Arnold Safer, president of Energy Futures Group, a consulting firm in Washington. "The expectations of a prolonged stalemate, on the political side, on the military side, are beginning to settle on the market."

Analysts said the prospect of a stalemate was pushing prices higher by fueling concern that oil supplies would remain tight for the foreseeable future, that high-quality Iraqi and Kuwaiti crude oil would continue to be replaced by lower quality crudes, and that the world would have no excess production capacity to handle additional shortfalls.

"People are starting to talk about $35-, $40-, $50-a-barrel crude. My numbers would project the market to about $36. And that's presuming no shooting," said Michael McDermott, an oil trader for PaineWebber Inc. in New York.

"With a shooting war you could go substantially higher. If we stay in a stalemated condition, I think we're going to work gradually higher for the rest of the year."

Other analysts, however, said they continue to believe that prices will recede somewhat.

"I don't think we've moved permanently into $30 oil," said Paul Mlotok, an oil-industry analyst for Morgan Stanley & Co. in New York.

WP 9/7

2116 — 2

0107

Crude Up By $1.66, To $31.43

Price for Barrel Near Post-Invasion Peak

By MATTHEW L. WALD

Crude oil jumped to more than $31 a barrel yesterday, nearing its highest price since the Persian Gulf crisis began when Iraq invaded Kuwait in early August.

The price of a barrel of light, sweet crude climbed by $1.66, to $31.43, in trading on the New York Mercantile Exchange yesterday in contracts for October delivery. That was just 50 cents below its post-invasion peak of $31.93 on Aug. 23.

Analysts said that the day's news from the Middle East was mild but that the market was particularly volatile.

"It takes less and less to move the market more and more," said Robin West, president of the Petroleum Finance Company, a Washington-based consulting firm.

Uncertainty of Traders Cited

He attributed the market's jump to the uncertainty of buyers and sellers about how to interpret unfamiliar events. "People don't understand what the implications of war are and they don't understand what the implications of peace are," he said. "The easiest reaction is to panic."

Robert P. Boslego, an oil analyst in Lexington, Mass., said, "The market as a whole is very unclear as to what the equilibrium price really should be, and it is fishing, so to speak."

Several analysts described a market that is setting itself up for the possibility of a fast slide. The inventory levels of producers and refiners indicate that users farther down the distribution chain, from industrial companies to distributors to retailers, have bought extra supplies in anticipation of shortages or price rises. If those companies judge that the crisis is waning and that they should use up those extra stockpiles, their purchases would drop and prices would fall, even if consumption did not change.

That was not the assessment of buyers yesterday, however, as the crude oil price approached its post-invasion high.

Bad News Emphasized

The bad news cited by traders included the report overnight that an American had been shot in the hand by Iraqi troops in Kuwait; Saddam Hussein's call on Wednesday for a holy war, the second by the Iraq President since the invasion, and Congressional testimony, also on Wednesday, by an Assistant Energy Secretary predicting shortages by the end of the year, an expectation that had been raised earlier by private analysts.

Based on that news, however, John H. Lichtblau of the Petroleum Industry Research Foundation in New York, said, "I can't figure out why prices are near $32."

"Volatility is part of the game,"

said Mr. Lichtblau of yesterday's 5.6 percent oil price rise. "Everybody is sort of tense, in continuous fear that there will be a war starting at any moment," he added. "But the traders don't know anything about the world situation that everybody else doesn't know."

Pushed upward by crude, the price of gasoline rose to 95.07 cents a gallon, up 2.8 cents, for October delivery, and the price of heating oil was 88.24 cents a gallon, up 4.87 cents, also for October delivery.

Crude oil contracts for November and December delivery also rose beyond $31 a barrel.

"It's just the same old story," said one broker on the floor who asked not to be identified; "more expectations of increased hostilities."

Self-Reinforcing Expectations

At Ashland Oil Inc., a refining company, Cyrus Tahmassebi, the chief economist, said that price changes reflected daily mood changes in the market about the likelihood of war, but that some expectations were self-reinforcing. For example, he added, if the market believed that shortages were likely, "then everyone wants to stock up with inventories, and that could cause even more tightness in the market."

Mr. Tahmassebi said that the short-term price trend would be higher.

Mr. Lichtblau suggested, however, that "if there is any kind of calming statement, I think you would see prices come down again." He said the loss of Iraqi and Kuwaiti crude to world markets — a total of about 4.5 million barrels a day — pushed the price of a barrel of crude to about $27 in New York, and that the rest of the increase, more than $4, was because of the fear of war.

Others attributed even more of the elevated cost to the war fear. Vahan Zanoyan, of the Petroleum Finance Company, said he expected production by the Organization of Petroleum Exporting Countries to be the same by the middle of this month as it was before Iraq invaded Kuwait on Aug. 2 because of extra production by Saudi Arabia, Venezuela and others.

Not a Permanent Dent

In that case, he added, the invasion did not represent a permanent dent in supplies, but a one-time loss that he put at about 100 million barrels. But when the crisis began, he pointed out, crude stocks around the world stood about 250 million barrels higher than at the same time the previous year, indicating the loss could be absorbed easily.

Mr. West predicted that even if war came, the results were likely to resemble those of the "tanker war" that began in 1982, when Iran and Iraq bombed each other's tankers and export facilities. The main Saudi terminal on the Persian Gulf, Ras Tanura, is probably out of reach of the Iraqis, he said, and crude oil, as was discovered in 1982, is harder to ignite than many people imagine. "These facilities are harder to hit and easier to repair than people think," he added.

But Mr. Boslego said that if shortages developed, then oil was "still undervalued, relative to the kind of price we would need to seriously affect demand." If a reduction in OPEC output has to be made up by consumers going without, he added, "a pretty substantial increase in price will be required to balance the market."

NYT 9/7

2116-3

0108

Oil Prices Jump Amid Pessimism On Gulf Crisis

Fear of Winter Shortages Also Helps Some Crudes Rise Beyond $31 a Barrel

By JAMES TANNER
Staff Reporter of THE WALL STREET JOURNAL

World oil prices surged again on panic and some speculative buying that began in Asia and Europe and spread to the U.S.

The price increase, sparked by growing pessimism over the Persian Gulf crisis and the petroleum supply outlook for winter, bounced some crude prices beyond $31 a barrel. The higher prices helped some oil company stocks but contributed to declines in U.S. stock and bond markets.

The steep rise in petroleum prices—more than $1 a barrel for most crudes—came even as some small oil exporters planned to try to follow leading members of the Organization of Petroleum Exporting Countries in raising output. Trinidad, Malaysia and others were said yesterday to be among those planning to increase output, to add to the higher volumes already being produced by Saudi Arabia, Venezuela and some other OPEC nations.

Also yesterday, Mexico said its extra 100,000 barrels a day of oil exports will continue until the end of the year, rather than the end of this month as originally pledged.

However, most non-OPEC oil producers already are believed to be running flat out. There is considerable skepticism whether any of them can produce much more oil, even in modest increments. Also, there is doubt the new OPEC supplies can replace all the oil lost from the embargo against Iraq—or can reach the oil market in time to fill the gap left by the 4.3 million barrels a day of former Iraqi and Kuwaiti exports.

"Temporarily, there is a lag between the cutoffs [of Iraqi and Kuwaiti oil] and the increased production," said Roger W. Gale, president of the Washington International Energy Group, a consulting firm. That gap is going to be showing up, he said, in reductions in volume in the oil market, where demand already is rising seasonally.

The main concern among energy watchdogs for major oil-consuming nations, such as the Paris-based International Energy Agency and the U.S. Department of Energy, is that the biggest potential for tight supplies, and possibly shortages, will be during the winter peak-use period. It could start as early as November as the heating-oil season gets under way in colder climates.

Heating oil, in fact, set yesterday's pricing pace. In heavy U.S. futures trading, heating oil for October delivery rose 4.87 cents a gallon to settle at 86.24 cents. Unleaded gasoline for October delivery settled at 95.07 cents, up 2.8 cents a gallon.

The crude traded on the New York Mercantile Exchange, which is similar to the benchmark West Texas Intermediate, jumped $1.66 a barrel to settle at $31.43 for October delivery.

Another wave of higher price postings swept through the oil fields, meanwhile, with refiners generally raising the prices they pay for West Texas Intermediate by $1.75 a barrel, to as much as $30.

The gains in U.S. prices followed jumps in Asia and Europe. Spot prices of Europe's North Sea crudes were up by $1 to $1.20 a barrel. Some trading officials said this underscores a shift from U.S. pricing leadership.

"The driving force in the markets today is in Europe and in the Far East," said Peter Gignoux, London-based manager of the Shearson Lehman Hutton international energy desk. He said strong European currencies and a weak U.S. dollar—the currency used to price and pay for oil—make up one reason. Another, he said, is that European and Asian buyers expect supply disruptions by the fourth quarter.

Many traders expressed surprise, nevertheless, at the high levels oil prices are again reaching. Some look for a major pullback, possibly as soon as today, similar to the $4-a-barrel drop that followed the August price surge kicked off by Iraq's invasion of Kuwait and the resulting U.S.-

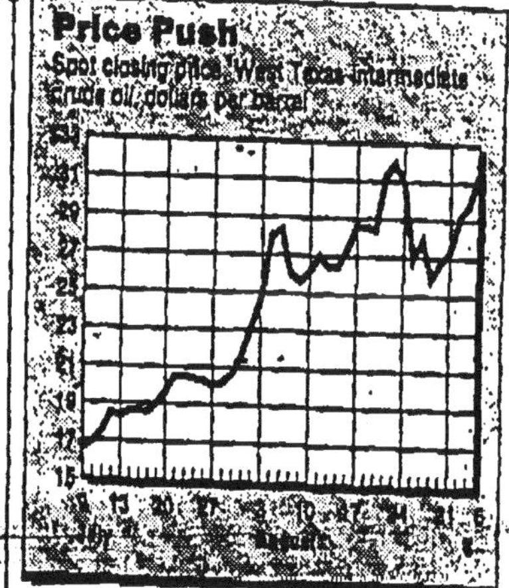

Iraq armed faceoff in the Gulf region.

Price corrections are sure to come if supplies prove adequate after all the talk of possible shortages. And the higher prices are helping to bring on new supplies. Mexico will continue its increased oil exports for the remainder of the year "to take advantage of rising prices," Petroleos de Mexicanos said in its announcement yesterday.

Charles A. Gargano, U.S. ambassador to Trinidad, said in an interview that Trinidad is considering a 5% to 10% increase in its production of some 150,000 barrels a day after his request to government oil authorities.

"We have asked all our friends who are oil producers to help out the situation now," he said.

WSJ
9/7/90

2116-4

0109

Learning the True Cost of Oi

By RICHARD L. LAWSON

The father of free market economics, Adam Smith, once said that the true cost of anything is the toil and trouble of acquiring it.

We now are bitterly learning, once again, the true cost of imported oil. The true cost of imported oil is not the market price, even if it eventually goes to $35 or $40 a barrel, as it may, or even $100. The true cost of imported oil is having the United States and the world economy held in thrall by a thug like Saddam Hussein.

The true cost of imported oil is thousands of American troops put in harm's way in the desert, facing an unprincipled foe armed with weapons bought with our money and that of the other industrialized nations. Those U.S. troops are supported by $8 billion aircraft carriers, $3 billion battleships, $1 billion cruisers and tens of billions of dollars in other military material. We spent $60 billion equipping, supplying and providing bases for the Rapid Deployment Force we sent to Saudi Arabia, and that does not include the cost of the operation itself.

The true cost of imported oil involves forcing President Bush and our allies into the untenable position of strangling our own economies by mounting an embargo against Saddam Hussein in an attempt to force him to withdraw from the sovereign Kuwaiti territory he usurped.

Even in the absence of acts of war, the true cost to America of imported oil under "business as usual" conditions includes saddling presidents with the need to twist and bend foreign policy and economic policy to compensate for energy dependence.

Sadly, we can reflect on the current situation in the Middle East and know that it has happened before. We lost good men in the Persian Gulf in the tension-filled months of 1987 and 1988. That time, Iran was the chief culprit threatening disruption of the passage of oil and Saddam Hussein was, strangely enough, our "friend."

The first time the oil weapon came to our attention was during the oil embargo of 1973. When that disruption led to gas lines and a five-fold run-up in the price of oil, President Nixon initiated a program called Project Independence. The objective was to create an "energy free" America by reducing and ultimately eliminating our dependence on imported oil.

However, the gas lines went away and public interest waned. When public interest waned, political interest waned. Project Independence was dismissed as a naive attempt to achieve an impossible, and much too costly, objective.

The Iranian Revolution fomented a second crisis in 1979. The world's economies shook again, and there were efforts by the government at new action. Once again, as people adjusted to the aftershocks of the surprise, the market price of oil overshadowed the true cost of oil. The politics of the moment and the economics of the next quarter's bottom line took hold. We learned to live with the results of oil at about nine times the pre-1973 price.

The focus was lost and today took charge of tomorrow.

We must regain control of tomorrow. As Saddam Hussein is teaching us anew, oil and its control represent power.

That power is largely concentrated in the hands of the few Middle East nations that control nearly two-thirds of world oil reserves. The United States, the first oil superpower, now can produce barely half its needs, and at present rates of production it has about 10 years of reserves remaining.

Clearly, we cannot produce our way out of dependence on imported oil. We discovered that as far back as 1974. We must take those steps necessary to reduce our dependence on imported oil instead.

We must develop a national energy strategy, and its first objective must be to stop and then reverse the rise in dependence on imported oil. Our efforts should be oriented to reducing imported oil dependence to 30% of our total requirements. The strategy should encourage our allies to do the same to the maximum degree possible.

We do have alternatives to oil, and chief among them is coal. The United States has 268 billion tons of recoverable coal reserves, the energy equivalent of 1 trillion barrels of oil, more than the world's present proved reserves.

Coal is a key part, but only one part, of an effective national energy strategy. The strategy should use all domestic resources and rationalize them to ensure the highest long-term use of each.

It should foster conservation; increase domestic production of oil and natural gas; increase coal use in all possible applications; restore nuclear power at the earliest possible time; deploy alternative fuels, particularly methanol from natural gas; reduce imported oil demand in transportation by appropriate electrification of railroads and cars, and in other ways; deploy clean coal technology; encourage new fuel forms; and attack rising world imported-oil demand with an energy "Marshall Plan" to export coal and clean coal technology to energy-dependent nations.

Such a plan would be costly, and would require some adjustment in our lives and in our economy. It is that cost that caused us to shy away from taking extreme measures in the past.

However, if we remain dependent on imported oil, it will be at the cost of repeated shocks to our economy as the masters of oil grow ever more able to manipulate the world price. It will be at the cost of maintaining the defense forces necessary to protect our interests in the Middle East. It will be at the cost of our foreign policy independence in the world. And, most importantly, it will be at the cost of human life placed in harm's way in far off places because we couldn't bring ourselves to act coherently in our national interest.

Richard L. Lawson is president of the National Coal Association.

2116-5. End

0110

관리번호	90-708

원 본

외 무 부

종 별 :

번 호 : PUW-0746　　　　일 시 : 90 0907 1730

수 신 : 장관(기협,미남)

발 신 : 주 페루 대사

제 목 : 주재국 산유정책

대:WPU-0364

연:PUW-0702

1. 대호 주재국 산유정책 파악 관련 SANCHEZ 동자부 장관및 OCHOA 석유국장을 접촉 입수한 내용을 아래 보고하며, 관련자료는 차파편 송부예정임.

가. 현재 주재국 산유량은(90.6 일일생산량 기준)미국회사인 OCCIDENTAL 이전체 생산량의 약 50 프로인 64,100 배럴, 자국회사가 69,2000 배럴을 생산하고있음.

나. 주재국 석유채굴 가능 지역은 60 개 광구로 구분되어 있으며, 국영회사인 PETROPERU 및 V.G 회사가 3 개광구에서 탐사작업 중이며, 외국회사로는 MOBIL(4 개광구), PETROMINEROS(1 개광구), OCCIDENTAL(2 개광구)이 탐사 계획 실시중임.특히 OCCIDENTAL 사는 제 36 광구 개발을 위해 아국 금성사, 베네주엘라 마라벤회사및 대만의 1 개 회사와 협의중인것으로 알고있다함.

다. 신정부는 외국회사들이 합작또는 단독 투자형식으로 유전을 개발하는것을 적극 환영하고 있다하며, 아국정부가 관련 업체로 하여금 현지를 직접 답사 유전탐사 가능성을 조사토록 권유함.

라. 이라크, 쿠웨이트 사태이후 브라질, 멕시코등 많은 국가들이 페루 유전탐사 계획에 관심을 보이고 있는가운데, 프랑스 국영회사인 CFP TOTAL 사 조사단이 9.9 당지 도착예정이라함.

2. 당관은 그동안 당지 언론매체를 통해 경제성이 확실한것으로 보도된바있는 연호 CAMISEA 유전지대에 대한 프로젝트등 관련 자료 입수 노력중인바, 구득되는대로 추보예정임.

(대사 윤태현-경제국장)

예고:90.12.31. 까지

경제국　차관　2차보　미주국

PAGE 1　　　　90.09.08 10:35

외신 2과 통제관 FE

0111

원 본

외 무 부

종 별 :

번 호 : AVW-1289 일 시 : 90 0907 2000

수 신 : 장관(기협,구이,동자부)

발 신 : 주오스트리아대사

제 목 : 오스트리아의 원유 수입선

대: WAV-0911

1. 주재국의 87-90.5.간 수입선별 원유 수입량은 다음과 같음.(단위: 천톤, 괄호는 총수입중 차지하는 비율)

수입선, 87년, 88년, 89년, 90(1-5월) 순임

리비아, 1,741.4(27.9), 1,774.2(31.5), 1,065.2(17.9),686.9(26.4)

알제리아, 633.0(10.2), 739.5(13.1), 1,631.60(27.6),565=8(21.8)

나이제리아, 548.5(8.8), 210.6(3.7), 394.8(6.6), 256.5(9.9)

소련, 556.2(8.9), 999.1(17.7), 576.6(9.7), 251.2(9.7)

에집트, 70.9(1.1), --, 432.7(7.3), 222.1(8.5)

이란, 294.3(4.7), 517.20(9.2), 816.5(13.7), 179.5(6.9)

사우디, 250.3(4.0), 180.7(3.2), 136.5(2.3), 155.1(6.0)

예멘, --, 124.8(2.2), 253.8(4.3), 128.2(4.9)

튀니지아, 67.7(1.1), --, 79.9(1.3), 80.9(3.1)

멕시코, 350.4(5.6), 225.9(4.0), 235.36(4.0), 69.9(2.7)

쿠웨이트, --, 182.9(3.2), 96.19(1.6), --

이라크, 756.5(12.1), 348.1(6.2), --, 1.7(0.1)

기타, 936.6(15.0), 327.8(5.8), 224.65(3,8), --

계, 6,232.8(100), 5,630.8(100), 5,943.8(100), 2,597.8(100)

2.경제성 관계관에 의하면, 매년 원유수요량의 80퍼센트 이상을 수입에 의존하고있는 오스트리아는, 안정적인 물량 확보를 위하여 1973년제1차 OIL SHOCK 이후, 수입 선 다변화 정책을 추구, 특정 국가에 대한 수입 의존도가 과도하게 되지 않도록 유의하고 있다함.

경제국 2차보 구주국 동자부

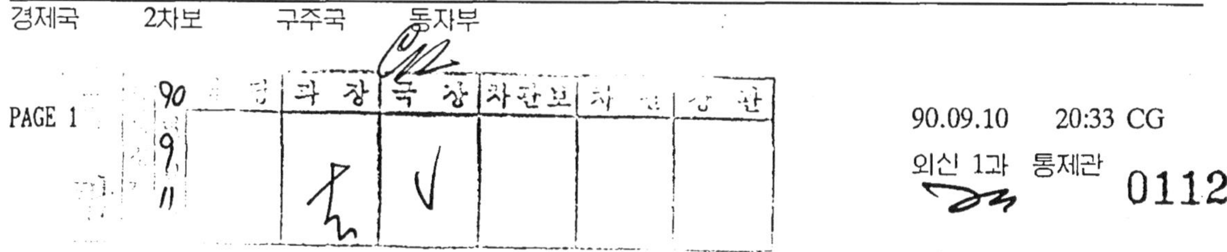

PAGE 1
90
9
11
과 장
국 장
차관보
차 관
장 관

90.09.10 20:33 CG

외신 1과 통제관

0112

3.또한 동 관계관은 금번 GULF 사태와관련, 쿠웨이트 및 이라크로 부터의 수입량이 극히 미미하기 때문에, 오스트리아는 지금까지 물량확보에는 전혀 지장이 없었으며, 앞으로도 당분간은 물량 확보에 큰 문제가 없을 것으로본다고 하였음.

4.최근 주재국 유가가 유종에 따라 5-10퍼센트 인상되었는데, 이는 주재국 유류업체가 경제성의 주선으로 소비자 대표에게 국제원유가인상 등으로 국내 유가 인상이 불가피함을 유류업계대표가 설명, 소비자 대표가 이를 양승함으로써 결정되었다고상기 관계관은 부언하였음.

(끝)

"에너지는 나라의 힘 아껴쓰고 비축하자"

동 력 자 원 부

원유 29210-6385 503-9627 1990. 9. 10.

수신 외무부 장관

제목 OECD/IEA 업무협조 관련 회신

1. 귀부 FRW-1573호('90.8.30)와 관련입니다.

2. 위호 관련, 주한 프랑스 대사로 부터 우리나라의 석유비축등 석유관련 현황 자료 요청건에 대하여 아래와 같이 회신합니다.

= 아 래 =

가. 우리나라의 석유비축 정책 및 현황

ㅇ 기본목표 : 정부비축 및 민간재고 지속일수 90일분 수준 확보

ㅇ 현비축량 : 74.7백만바렐 (정부 39.8백만바렐, 민간 34.9백만바렐)

나. 우리나아의 원유도입 현황

ㅇ '90.1-6 도입실적 : 167,951천바렐

ㅇ 도 입 선

- 중 동 : 오만, UAE, 이란, 사우디, 카타르

- 동 남 아 : 말련, 인니, 브루네이, 중국, 호주

- 미주.아프리카 : 에쿠아돌, 멕시코, 카나다, 알제리, 이집트

다. 페만사태로 인하여 원유도입에 미치는 영향 및 대책

(영향) 이라크.쿠웨이트로 부터의 원유도입 감소물량 : 109천B/D

('90 상반기 기준)

원유가 상승에 따른 수입부담 가중

0114

총 25795

원유 29210- 1990. 9. 10.

(대책) 현물보다 장기계약 물량 증량. 끝.

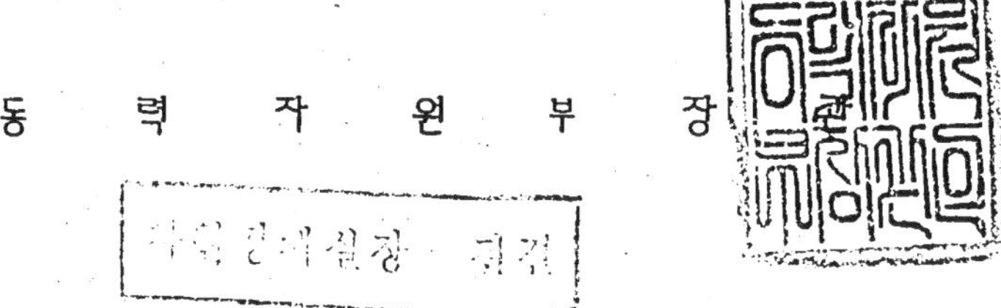

동 력 자 원 부 장

0115

원 본

외 무 부

종 별 :

번 호 : USW-4102 일 시 : 90 0910 1914

수 신 : 장 관(기협)

발 신 : 주 미 대사

제 목 : 석유시장 및 유가 동향(12)

표제 관련 9.8(토)-10(월) 당지 언론 종합 보고함.

1. 유가동향

가. 9.7(금) 원유및 정유제품 가격 (뉴욕 상품 시장, 10월 인도가격)

0 원유: 배럴당 30.04 (전일대비 1.39불 하락)

0 휘발유: 갤런당 93.06 센트 (전일대비 2.01 센트 하락)

0 난방유: 갤런당 83.98 센트 (전일대비 4.26센트)

나. 9.7 유가 하락은 이락에서의 쿠데타 발생에 따른 후세인 대통령 실각 루머에인한 것으로 분석되고 있음.

2. 석유시장 동향

0 90.7월까지 23백만 배럴에 달했던 OPEC의 일일 원유 생산량은 8월중 이락 및 쿠웨이트로부터의 원유 수입금지로 인해 19.7백만 배럴로 감소하였으나, 사우디등의 증산 실시로 9월중에는 21.5백만, 10월중에는 최대한 22백만 배럴에 달할수 있을 것으로 전망됨.

0 OPEC 이 일일 22백만 배럴의 원유를 생산할 경우에도 이는 OPEC 원유에 대한 세계수요인 일일 23백만 배럴에 미치지 못하며, 따라서 당분간 불안정한 유가 변동 및 석유회사 비축분사용 계속이 불가피할 것으로 예상됨.

0 특히 석유회사 비축분의 사용 규모는 8월중에는 일일 30만 배럴로 추산되고 있으나 9월중 일일 1백만배럴로 증가할 것으로 예상되며 4/4 분기에는 일일 2.1 백만배럴에 달할 것으로 전망됨.

3. 9.8-10. 당지 언론 보도 내용 별첨 FAX USW(F)-2153 (8 매) 송부함.

(대사 박동진-국장)

경제국 2차보 미주국 안기부 동자부

PAGE 1

90.09.11 09:33 WG

외신 1과 통제관

0116

How OPEC's Post-Crisis Oil Production Is Rebounding

(In millions of barrels a day)

COUNTRY	OPEC QUOTA	JULY[1]	AUGUST[1]	SEPTEMBER[2]
Saudi Arabia	5.380	5.3	5.5	7.2
Iran	3.140	3.0	3.3	3.2
Iraq	3.140	3.1	0.9	0.4
United Arab Emirates	1.500	2.0	1.6	2.1
Kuwait	1.500	1.6	0.0	0.0
Neutral Zone[3]	—	0.3	0.2	0.3
Qatar	0.371	0.4	0.4	0.4
Nigeria	1.611	1.7	1.8	1.9
Libya	1.233	1.3	1.3	1.4
Algeria	0.827	0.8	0.8	0.8
Gabon	0.197	0.3	0.3	0.3
Venezuela	1.945	2.0	2.0	2.8
Ecuador	0.273	0.3	0.3	0.3
Indonesia	1.374	1.3	1.3	1.3
Total[4]	22.491	23.2	19.7	21.9

[1]Estimates by International Energy Agency [2]Industry estimates
[3]Neutral Zone, where output was shared by Saudi Arabia and Kuwait prior to the embargo against Iraqi and Kuwaiti oil [4]Totals may not add due to rounding

OPEC Production Rises, but Reaching Pre-Crisis Levels Could Take Awhile

By James Tanner
Staff Reporter of The Wall Street Journal

Oil production by the Organization of Petroleum Exporting Countries is rebounding after the August plunge caused by the Mideast crisis.

Leading producers are starting to make good on promises to pump more crude to replace embargoed Iraqi and Kuwaiti oil, according to those who monitor OPEC output. They said, however, that total OPEC production probably won't reach pre-crisis levels of more than 23 million barrels a day until late in the year, if then.

An anticipated gap in total crude oil supplies this month, caused by the six-week shipping lag for Middle East oil to reach world markets, isn't expected to be a large problem, industry analysts said. Crude inventories, particularly in the U.S., are high. If tight supplies or shortages do appear, they'll probably involve only some refined products and some regions, the analysts said.

"There could be product imbalances," said Cristina Haus, who monitors OPEC production for Washington-based Energy Security Analysis. "There will be no problem in crude oil." In addition to an increase of as much as two million barrels a day in crude oil produced by Saudi Arabia, she said she foresees the September output increase by the United Arab Emirates to be more than the generally estimated 500,000 barrels a day.

She placed total OPEC September production as high as 21.9 million barrels a day.

"We are seeing a steady rise for September," added Conrad Gerber, president of Petro-Logistics Ltd. of Geneva, who also tracks OPEC output. He estimated total September OPEC output should be at least 21.5 million barrels a day, and said "it could hit 22 million barrels a day for October." He maintained, however, "that is the maximum."

Whatever the September level, it will show a sharp rise from last month. For August, according to the figures released last week by the International Energy Agency, OPEC production dropped to the year's low of 19.7 million barrels a day from more than 23 million barrels a day in the preceding months.

The September increase will fall short of meeting demand for OPEC oil, estimated by energy economists at around 23 million barrels a day for the remainder of the year. That suggests pricing volatility and big draws of inventories—or "stocks"—even after the additional crude begins reaching the Western oil-consuming nations.

Oil prices, which have climbed nearly 50% since Iraq invaded Kuwait, fell Friday on profit-taking. In U.S. futures trading, October crude dropped $1.39 to $30.04 a barrel, leaving it up $2.72 a barrel for the holiday-shortened week. The biggest gain

Continued From Page A2

of the week, $1.66 a barrel on Thursday, came the day after the weekly report of the American Petroleum Institute. That report showed U.S. crude inventories declined 4.4 million barrels the preceding week.

World-wide inventory reductions averaged some 300,000 barrels a day last month, according to the Paris-based IEA, the energy watchdog agency for the Western oil-consuming nations. For September, IEA and industry officials anticipate bigger withdrawals, probably as much as one million barrels a day and reaching higher amounts as winter nears.

"There could be something like a 2.1 million [barrels-per-day] stock draw over the fourth quarter," said Roger Benedict, an editor with Energy Information Ltd., which provides analysis of oil industry news. "The real crunch could be from November on," he added. "A lot depends on how cold the winter is."

Petroleum inventories were exceptionally high when the Middle East crisis began. Supplies of petroleum products were considered in balance; there was a glut of crude in onshore storage and at sea. As late as Aug. 31, according to the American Petroleum Institute, U.S. crude inventories still stood at 372.2 million barrels, or 11% higher than the year-earlier level of 335.8 million.

Oil companies would like to avoid drawing down stocks further because of the uncertainties, but won't have much choice as demand peaks seasonally in the winter months.

The losses in OPEC's August output weren't fully reflected in world oil markets last month. That's because tankers carrying oil from Iraq and Kuwait still were at sea long after the embargo closed off all exports from those countries. Although estimates vary, Iraq's output for last month averaged nearly one million barrels a day. That was one-third the 3.1 million barrels a day it produced in July. Its September output is estimated at only about 400,000 barrels a day, or just enough for domestic use.

The impact now is more evident. According to Roy Mason, publisher of England-based Oil Afloat, there were some 440 million barrels of oil in tankers at sea on Aug. 5, three days after the Mideast crisis began. By Aug. 20, according to his latest estimate, oil at sea had been drained down to 370 million barrels.

"It has taken this long to see the effect of the cutoff" of Iraqi and Kuwaiti oil, said Mr. Mason. As a result, before volumes of oil at sea begin rebuilding, "it's almost inevitable that onshore stocks [inventories] will start falling."

외신 -2

0117

Stephen Kroninger

Energy Tax: Still on the Table

By Leon Panetta

WASHINGTON

Until this weekend, the budget summit between the White House and Congress has been a high-stakes game of political hide-and-seek, with each party trying to avoid blame for the tough choices that must be made. Now the eleventh hour has arrived.

The President, to his credit, has acknowledged the need to reach an agreement and to include taxes, entitlement and budget reforms and defense and discretionary savings in that agreement. Those tough choices require bold bipartisan leadership, to produce not policies that slide by our fiscal and energy problems but policies that directly confront those problems.

The Middle East crisis has made our already worrisome economic and fiscal problems worse. But perhaps the threat of war, stagflation and the prospect of $300 billion budget deficits will shock us into action, as political business as usual during the late 1980's did not.

The new demonstration of our energy vulnerability, after a decade of wasted opportunity, at least makes clear the direction in which policy should move. The American people are economic hostages to Middle East dictators, who produce oil shocks, and to Government budget deficits, which produce high interest rates.

We desperately need both a fiscal policy of assured long-term deficit reduction and an energy policy of assured incentives for conservation. A phased-in energy tax should be the centerpiece of a five-year deficit reduction plan, which would also include other savings and revenues.

The tax should begin at low levels, and increase over several years. In anticipation of increased energy prices, businesses and families will begin to conserve energy now. Similarly, the certainty of lower future deficits will lead to lower long-term interest rates now, reducing the likelihood or severity of recession and stimulating investment, economic growth and job creation.

> The core of a five-year plan to cut the deficit by $500 billion.

A phased-in energy tax also fits our fiscal dilemma. The weakness of the economy means that deficit reduction may have to be "back-loaded" — adjusted from the contemplated $50 billion in fiscal year 1991, but increased enough in later years to keep a five-year total of at least $500 billion.

We should not play Russian roulette with the economy in an attempt to reach an arbitrary figure for 1991. It is just as obvious, however, that we must not back away from our responsibility to reduce deficits now. Nothing could be more damaging to our Government's credibility, and more likely to raise interest rates and destabilize financial markets, than a collapse of U.S. economic policy at a time of crisis.

Obviously, an energy tax alone will not solve the budget crisis. The Middle East confrontation has not resurrected the cold war, so we should still pursue long-term defense reductions, particularly in European-based forces and in defense weaponry dedicated to a Soviet threat that has largely disappeared — while enhancing our capacity to deal with the Saddam Husseins of the world.

We must also pursue restraint in the growth of entitlement programs and low-priority discretionary spending, while recognizing that new funding is required in a number of areas, such as education, health and research, for an efficient economy and just society.

And we must adjust any fiscal package to make sure it is equitable — a problem that energy taxes bring sharply into focus. If we enact an energy tax, it must be accompanied by tax and other measures to ease the impact on those least able to pay. We should avoid the kinds of policies that led in the 1980's to a shift of income from lower- and middle-income families to the wealthy.

The President has set the right guideposts. His biggest problem has been not with Democrats but with some Republicans, who have consistently undermined him by criticizing his decisions, leaking his budget proposals to the press and threatening to oppose a final budget agreement.

At this time of crisis, the nation cannot afford delay or partisanship. And it cannot afford avoidance of responsibility by our political leaders. In the long run, the deficit and our dependence on oil pose a greater threat to our economy than Saddam Hussein. They, too, must be confronted head on. □

Leon Panetta, Democrat of California, is the chairman of the House Budget Committee.

NYT 9/9/91

0118

: 장 관 발신 : 주미대사 | 봉— | |

: (매)

Either Force Oil Prices Down . . .

By Joseph Stanislaw and Daniel Yergin

CAMBRIDGE, Mass.

With oil prices pushing past $30 a barrel, the economy either in recession or on the brink and with growing predictions of shortages of home heating oil in November, the case for tapping the Strategic Petroleum Reserve is becoming very strong. Unfortunately, the Bush Administration continues to resist the idea, preferring to hold the 600 million barrels exclusively for "physical" shortages.

The Administration also fears that the symbolic shock of opening the reserves would send the oil market into panic. It worries about establishing the precedent of using the reserves to calm oil prices: it does not want to put the Government in business of managing prices. And it does not want to provide any reasons for exporting nations not to raise production or to eliminate the incentive for domestic production and conservation.

While these are all sound reasons, they do not begin to match the case for tapping the reserves.

The oil market is currently walking a high wire, highly susceptible to the state of panic the Administration is trying to avoid. Traders are nervous not only about a possible gulf war but also about the approach of winter, when demand for oil rises and ability to switch to natural gas diminishes.

Markets — financial as well as oil — are indicating that they expect the consuming nations to fall off the oil trapeze in October or November. As soon as shooting looks imminent — or it appears that supply will not match demand — the price will really take off, to $40 a barrel and beyond.

The idea of using the S.P.R. only to avert a physical shortage ignores economic reality. A "shortage" at $20 a barrel will disappear at $40 a barrel, as the world economy crashes and consumers cut back sharply on purchases. The fundamental rationale of the international energy emergency system established in the 1970's was to protect economic growth.

Moreover, a persistence of sharply higher prices will threaten the Administration's geopolitical objectives. Consumer complaints about gasoline and heating oil prices will send political shock waves that will erode the national consensus on the gulf intervention. Worse, severe inflationary and recessionary effects around the world eventually will raise questions, as Saddam Hussein is hoping, about the costs of the embargo. This could undermine the even more remarkable international consensus that has been forged.

If geopolitical reasoning isn't enough, simple arithmetic should convince us to open the reserves. On paper, we seem to have enough supplies to replace the four million barrels a day lost in the embargo of Iraq (perhaps with an assist from reduced consumption). But to get that extra oil into the market requires a lot more than the flick of a switch.

Some of the facilities in the exporting countries have been idled for 10 years. Inevitably, there are going to be engineering problems, and, possibly, accidents. Thus, it will be months before the additional suppplies can be brought to the market.

In addition, there can always be further, unforseeable pressures in the market: everything from declining Soviet exports to hurricanes in the Gulf of Mexico. The system is very taut. There is no security margin, except for the emergency stocks.

Panic takes a very specific form in the oil market. It always involves the hasty and fevered building of inventories that drives up price. The slightest uncertainty can set the process in motion, sending prices through the roof.

But the process also works in reverse. The best antidote to an upward spiral is the fear among buyers that the oil they are contracting to buy at $40 a barrel will bring $30 a barrel when they sell it two months hence. That's how the S.P.R. can cleverly be used now.

The Administraion could simply announce that the S.P.R. has been activated, run modest demonstration sales and respond to needs as they emerge. Such steps — combined with increasing domestic production and conservation — would send a powerful, calming message to markets and governments around the world.

Of course, there are problems with the S.P.R. Much of the oil has a high-sulfur content, which makes it unsuitable for some domestic refineries. But the same is true of most of the additional oil supplies from Venezuela and Saudi Arabia, which the Administration is counting on to calm the markets and assure supplies this winter.

The real value of the reserves would be to counteract the inherent tendency to panic. Using it for this purpose would establish a new credibility, showing the markets not only that the S.P.R. exists but that it is going to be part of the energy equation. □

Joseph Stanislaw is managing director, and Daniel Yergin is president, of Cambridge Energy Research Associates, a consulting firm.

N.Y.T. 9/10/90

2153-4

0119

... Or Tax Excess Profits

By Silvio O. Conte

An energy levy that doesn't hurt.

WASHINGTON

Has the recent rise in oil prices ruled out a hike in energy taxes? Not necessarily. While higher prices make it harder to tax consumers — a regressive way to go anyway — there is an alternative that is pro-consumer and appropriate under today's circumstances: the windfall-profits tax.

For weeks now, we have been reaching into our wallets to pay much higher prices for gasoline — and, soon, for heating oil — even though it should have been months before those higher prices reached consumers. We have seen it time and time again: retail energy prices respond immediately to price increases but very slowly to price decreases. There are only two words to describe the process: price gouging.

As the price of imported oil escalates, the windfall to domestic producers of oil grows and grows. The artificially inflated world price of oil increases the price that domestic producers can charge, even though the cost of production remains the same.

This windfall is direct profit to oil companies, and the amount can be substantial. According to one recent estimate, a rise in oil prices of $7 a barrel would increase the value of U.S. oil production by $21 billion a year. That's gravy on the plates of Big Oil at the expense of American consumers.

We should skim a bit off the top to help reduce the Federal deficit and protect consumers from having to bear the brunt of deficit reduction. That is one of the benefits of the windfall-profits tax. It is an excise tax that does not get passed through to the consumer. Because the price of oil is determined on the world market, it would not be economical for oil companies to raise the price of domestic oil to recover the tax. They would have no market for their oil.

Based on recent history, the windfall-profits tax is a proven revenue raiser. Between 1980 and 1988, the original windfall profits tax generated approximately $80 billion in gross Federal revenues.

Preliminary estimates indicate that several billion dollars in new Federal revenues could be raised from a windfall profits tax. True, when and if the price of crude oil falls back below a certain level, revenues would decline. However, even a short-term leveling off of the current upsurge could generate substantial revenues. Some could even be directed to programs aimed at protecting low-income consumers; heating assistance and weatherization, for instance.

In our free enterprise system, profits in the regular course of business are expected and encouraged. Windfall profits generated by an international crisis and price gouging at the expense of consumers are intolerable and should be taxed. ◻

Silvio O. Conte, Republican of Massachusetts, is a member of the House Appropriations Committee.

N.Y.T

2155 — 5

0120

Oil Security

How Japan Became So Energy-Efficient: It Leaned on Industry

Conservation Experts Patrol Plants, Keep Lights Low, Idle Machines Turned Off

Consumers Are Less Diligent

By CLAY CHANDLER
And MARCUS W. BRAUCHLI
Staff Reporters of THE WALL STREET JOURNAL

KIMITSU, Japan—Add energy conservation to the proliferating measures of Japanese superiority.

Perched atop a 12-story cooling tank at this sprawling seaside steelworks, Takeo Harada waxes rhapsodic about his favorite topic: saving energy.

"In Japan, we love spending money on contraptions like this," shouts the 30-year-old engineer, gesturing proudly at a tangle of pipes and turbines. The object of his affection is a "coke dry quencher," a $5.6 million apparatus that helped his company, Nippon Steel Corp., slash the energy required to produce a ton of steel nearly 25%. At a plant using 1% of the energy consumed in Japan—enough to power a city of two million—such savings matter.

Devoted to the Cause

Like most Japanese manufacturers, Nippon Steel pursues energy conservation with near-religious devotion. The enthusiasm at the Kimitsu plant goes a long way toward explaining why this resource-poor country has the world's most fuel-efficient economy—and why Japan is the industrialized nation least likely to be knocked for a loop by a short-term surge in oil prices stemming from the Persian Gulf crisis.

No country was harder hit than Japan by the oil shocks of 1973 and 1979. And no country subsequently insulated itself better from the vagaries of world oil markets. Some experts contend that if the rest of the industrialized world had worked equally hard over the past decade to reduce dependence on foreign oil, the U.S. might not have found it necessary to send troops to the Mideast and the global economy might not face such a recession threat.

How did Japan get so energy-efficient? Can the rest of the world learn from it?

"The lessons for America are so simple they're almost banal," says Richard Samuels, a specialist on Japanese energy policy at Massachusetts Institute of Technology. "Oil is a nonrenewable resource. It's possible to reduce consumption, but first you have to decide you really want to."

Government's Role

Japan really wanted to. But will alone wasn't enough. The production engineers at the Kimitsu Steel Works and thousands of other Japanese factories didn't collectively decide, in reaction to enormous popular pressure, to push energy conservation. Instead, the government spurred their enthusiasm through a carefully coordinated, long-range program that continues even today. One clear lesson to learn from Japan is that forcing core industries to become more energy-efficient is one thing that government *can* do well.

A second lesson is that government has a hard time forcing individuals to be energy-efficient. Not that Japan didn't try. During the 1979 oil crisis, then-Prime Minister Masayoshi Ohira tried to set an example by arriving at a cabinet meeting sporting a tacky short-sleeved suit coat; if others would adopt the "safari look," he said, the country could stop wasting energy on air conditioning. The safari look didn't catch on.

Japanese consumers aren't helping much to save energy today, either. Now wealthier, they are demanding more appliances; Japanese households have, on the average, two TV sets, a refrigerator and an air conditioner. On weekends, Tokyo's expressways are jammed with vacationers creeping toward the beaches in big, gas-thirsty 4x4s. Ice-cold air floods from the doors of department stores to the sweltering sidewalks in Ginza, the Tokyo retailing district. Neon signs of cabarets, bars and pachinko parlors glitter all night.

Industry Keeps Up the Effort

This relative complacency was spawned in part by several years of cheap oil, and Japan's energy demand has grown 5% in each of the past three years. Japanese industrial companies, however, have continued to become more energy-efficient, so much so that some see little room for improvement if further efforts are needed.

Tokyo Electric Power Co. switched to nuclear power and slashed its dependence on oil by two-thirds. Asahi Glass Co. rebuilt its kilns and modified production processes to cut energy use 40% in a decade. A municipal train system in northern Japan recycles heat generated by its engines to run air conditioning. Japanese plant equipment, generally newer and more efficient than that in U.S. factories, increases Japan's relative energy efficiency.

Yet 20 years ago, even before the 1973 oil embargo, Japan's economy was the world's most energy-efficient: It consumed less than two-thirds as much energy, after adjustment for differences in economic size, as did the U.S. In part, Japan's lower consumption was, and is, attributable to its geographical compactness, population density and superb public transportation.

Since then, all the major industrialized countries have improved energy-efficiency by roughly a quarter. But Japan has improved by a third, even though it was already more efficient and additional gains were more difficult. Moreover, Japan, unlike other countries, has focused on reducing its dependence on oil, almost all of which must be imported. Between the 1973 oil crisis and 1987, Japan's economic output more than doubled, yet its oil imports fell 25%. (U.S. reliance on foreign oil during the same period actually increased, from 36% to 43% of total oil usage.)

Diversification Moves

And Japan has diversified its oil suppliers. In 1973, it imported nearly two-thirds of its oil from four countries in the politically volatile Mideast—Saudi Arabia, Iran, the United Arab Emirates and Kuwait. By the end of the 1980s, Japan had doubled the number of its main Mideast oil suppliers. Until Iraq's invasion of Kuwait, Tokyo carefully maintained close diplomatic ties to most Persian Gulf nations; during the eight-year Iraq-Iran war, Japanese aid flowed to both sides—and oil flowed from both to Japan. In addition, Japan is buying more and more oil from other producers, such as China.

But what really sets Japan apart from other oil-consuming countries is its patient pursuit of energy conservation and diversification throughout the 1980s, even after oil prices plunged. The U.S., more sensitive to market signals, didn't. The contrast is a classic illustration of what Ronald Morse, an energy specialist at the Economic Strategy Institute in Washington, calls the two countries' "different philosophies" about conserving energy.

"The Japanese are doing what we started during the Carter administration. The difference is just that they continued what we abandoned," Mr. Morse says. "Japan is concerned about economic vulnerability; so, it tries to insulate itself from injury from other nations." He adds:

"In the U.S., the whole thrust has been to deregulate and to keep the price of energy cheap. But that means that sometimes we have to use military might to keep the sources of cheap energy open."

With peace-minded Japan ruling out military intervention, the country emphasizes conservation. And those efforts begin where it matters most—in manufacturing, which consumes half of Japan's energy.

213 —6

0121

MITI's Muscle

This concentration plays to a crucial Japanese strength: bureaucratic management of industry. Mr. Morse credits Japan's Ministry of International Trade and Industry for much of its success in conserving energy. "This is one area where you can say that the controls the Japanese government has over the market really worked," he says.

MITI's energy controls are characteristically thorough. Since the 1979 oil shock, MITI officials have kept close watch on the energy consumption of 5,000 factories. Designated factories have to appoint from one to as many as 10 energy-conservation engineers to monitor fuel efficiency on the shop floor. Before the engineers can start work, they must pass an examination so strict that most of them spend more than a year preparing for it—and even then eight out of 10 flunk. Those who pass keep daily tabs on their factory's energy use and regularly report on progress to MITI. Failing to meet targets incurs no sanctions, but the fear of antagonizing MITI's powerful bureaucrats ensures cooperation.

MITI also openly urged companies to rely less on oil and more on coal and natural gas—both obtainable in politically stable nations. Nippon Steel's Kimitsu plant, for example, converted its blast furnaces to coal in the early 1980s and slashed oil's share of its energy supply to almost zero from about 20%. Further savings were achieved from the coke dry quencher, which recycles hot gas that used to escape as molten iron ore cooled.

Moreover, MITI lets Japanese energy suppliers, including oil and gas companies and electric utilities, keep their prices—and profits—high, provided the windfalls are channeled into energy research. That amounts to an energy tax, some say, but the artificially high cost of petroleum products hastens the transition to new energy sources. In 1987, MITI funneled more than 117 billion yen ($830 million) of such profits into energy research—more than to all other ministry projects combined—and that doesn't count the billions MITI forced utilities to spend on similar projects.

As a result, Japan now has the world's best technology for solar cells, storage and transport of liquid natural gas, and generators producing electricity from gasified coal and sea water. "Sure, a lot of this research is risky," Mr. Morse concedes. But, he adds, "relatively speaking, the projects didn't cost all that much, and probably at least 60% of them have been effective. And now that investment's paying off."

Even nuclear power has helped, despite often-emotional opposition in the only country to suffer from nuclear weapons. Before the first oil shock, Japan had virtually no nuclear-power capacity; today, it has 38 operating nuclear facilities, which supply about 9% of its total energy. The government wants to nearly double that by the end of the decade. Thanks to the government push to rely more on coal, natural gas and nuclear power, oil's share of Japan's total energy demand fell to about [illegible]% from 77.4% between 1973 and 1987.

Not all of Japan's energy management has been orchestrated by bureaucrats. Once the program was under way, even companies whose factories weren't supervised discovered that less dependence on energy meant less vulnerability to oil shocks and price surges.

At Hino Motors Ltd., Japan's biggest maker of medium and heavy trucks, the results were stunning. Switches were added to machine tools so they wouldn't idle when not in use. Machining oil was recycled. Heat-treatment rooms were insulated. Shop lighting and air conditioning were reduced. The upshot after a year: a 10% to 15% energy saving.

Japan has benefited, too, from industrial modernization. Since the late 1970s, the country has shifted from heavy manufacturing to cleaner, more fuel-efficient industries such as consumer electronics and financial services. That restructuring—Japanese pundits describe it as the change from a ju-ko-cho-dai (heavy, thick, long, big) to a kei-haku-tan-sho (light, thin, short, small) economy—was under way before the oil shocks; high energy prices merely accelerated it.

By 1985, for example, Japan's aluminum-smelting industry had all but disappeared—only a single smelter is still working in Japan—because it couldn't compete with hydroelectric-powered smelters in Canada, the U.S. and Brazil. Some manufacturers are taking advantage of those cheaper energy sources by moving production closer to them. Oji Paper Co. cut its energy costs almost 60% by shifting some paper-making operations to Canada.

However, keeping energy-conservation gains already achieved isn't easy. At Hino Motors, executives say energy use is rising again because tight labor conditions are forcing its factories to rely more heavily on machinery.

With the Iraqi invasion, the government has had a fresh reason to promote conservation. Hallways in government office buildings are dark again, and government offices are uncomfortably warm. MITI has asked drivers not to go faster than 50 miles an hour and to keep their air conditioning at 28 degrees Celsius.

However, many energy experts here admit to doubting that such symbolic measures have much effect on consumption nationwide. "We all think we're rich now," says Kenji Mogami, a MITI official. "It's difficult to get people who think they're rich to make sacrifices."

And it's more difficult to get people who already have made sacrifices to bite the bullet even harder. At Sumitomo Chemical Co., stringent measures cut energy consumption sharply in an industry in which most products require oil to produce; today, the company relies on petroleum for only half its products.

"We and the Japanese petrochemical industry as a whole did a great deal to rationalize our process already," complains Shoji Morimoto, an executive vice president at Sumitomo Chemical.

Thus, Japan may not be able to keep improving its energy conservation. "We will have more difficulty in the future," says Shijuro Ogata, deputy governor of the government-run Japan Development Bank. "There is much less room for Japan to conserve further."

0122

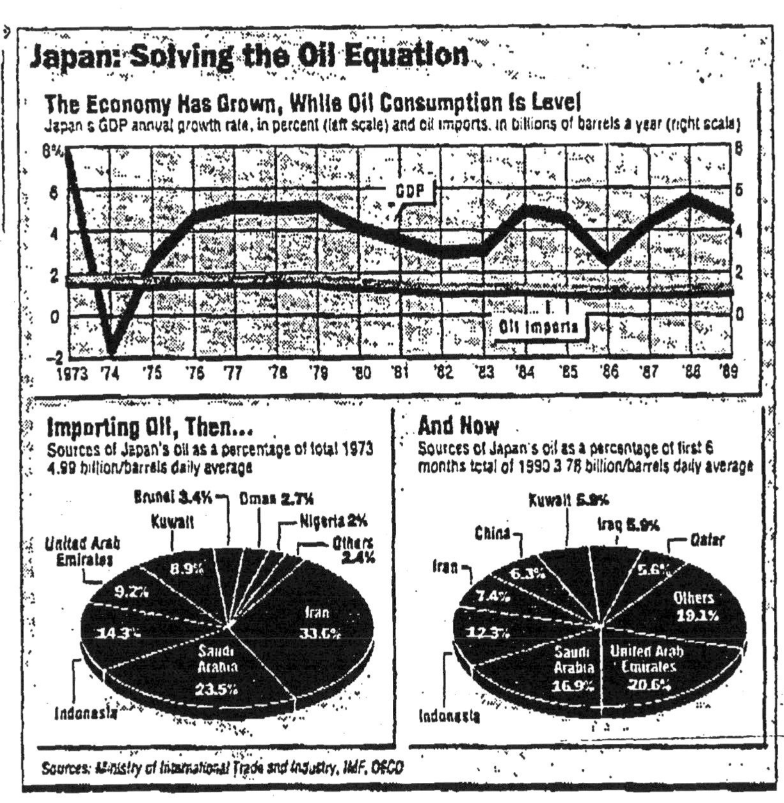
Japan: Solving the Oil Equation
The Economy Has Grown, While Oil Consumption Is Level
Japan's GDP annual growth rate, in percent (left scale) and oil imports, in billions of barrels a year (right scale)
8%
6
4
2
0
-2
8
6
4
2
0
GDP
Oil imports
1973
'74
'75
'76
'77
'78
'79
'80
'81
'82
'83
'84
'85
'86
'87
'88
'89
Importing Oil, Then...
Sources of Japan's oil as a percentage of total 1973
4.99 billion/barrels daily average
Brunei 3.4%
Oman 2.7%
Kuwait
Nigeria 2%
Others 2.4%
United Arab Emirates
8.9%
9.2%
14.3%
Iran 33.6%
Saudi Arabia 23.5%
Indonesia
And Now
Sources of Japan's oil as a percentage of first 6
months total of 1990 3.78 billion/barrels daily average
Kuwait 5.9%
China
Iraq 5.9%
Qatar
Iran
6.3%
5.6%
7.4%
Others 19.1%
12.3%
Saudi Arabia 16.9%
United Arab Emirates 20.6%
Indonesia
Sources: Ministry of International Trade and Industry, IMF, OECD

-9. End.

0123

관리번호	90-714

원 본

외 무 부

종 별 :

번 호 : MAW-1313 일 시 : 90 0911 0830

수 신 : 장관(기협,아동,사본:동자부 장관,주 말련 대사)

발 신 : 주 말련 대사 대리

제 목 : 원유도입교섭

연:MAW-1167(1),1171(2),1240(3),1271(4)

대:WMA-0642

1. 당관 이준규 서기관은 9.10 주재국 수상실 ANWAR AJI 석유 개발과장을 면담, 아국의 원유 증량공급 요처에 대한 진전 상황을 문의한바, 동인 언급 요지아래와 같음.

가. 아국 정부의 연호(3) 주재국 외무부를 통한 요청은 즉각 수상비서실 및PETRONAS 등 관계기관에 전달되어 검토되고 있음.

나. 금번 마하틸 수상 방한시 아측으로 부터 동 문제 제기시 수상은 호의적고려를 약속할 것으로 봄.

다. 수상 귀국후 9.19(수)의 정례 각의에 동 문제가 상정되어 결정이 내려질 것으로 예상됨.

라. 현재 말련의 석유 생산능력이 거의 한계에 달해 있으므로 아국에 대한 대폭 증량은 어려울 것으로 보나, 양국간의 긴밀한 관계에 비추어 아국의 요청은최대한 호의적으로 수용하자는 것이 말련 정부내의 분위기임.

2. 한편 주재국은 연호(1)과 같이 필리핀및 인도에 각각 일 5 천 배럴씩 원유를 증량공급키로 결정한바 있으며, 연호(2) 파키스탄의 요청에 대해서는 우선 호의적 검토 결정만 내려 놓고 공급량에 대해 교섭하고 있으나, 원유는 5 천 배럴 이하 수준이되고 기타 휘발류, 디젤등 석유 제품을 추가 공급하는 방향으로 검토되고 있다함. 끝

(대사대리 김경준-국장)

공	국제경제		담 당	과 장	국 장	차관보	차 관	장 관
					V			

경제국 2차보 아주국 아주국 동자부

PAGE 1 90.09.11 10:08

외신 2과 통제관 FE

0124

관리 번호 90-718

원 본

외 무 부

종 별 :

번 호 : LYW-0563　　　　일 시 : 90 0911 1400

수 신 : 장관(기협,마그)

발 신 : 주 리비아 대사

제 목 : 원유 도입 교섭

대:WLY-0325

본직은 90.9.10. 주재국 수상실(SIRT 소재) 로 MUNTASSER 수상을 방문하고 대호 원유 도입과 관련, 걸프 사태후 리비아측이 기존 태도를 변경, 아국에 공급할 원유가 없다는 입장을 취하고 있어 양국 공동위 합의 사항인 원유 15 천 B/D 도입이 추진되지 못하고 있음을 설명한바, 동수상은 리비아가 원유 판매시장의 다변화를 추구하는 정책에 하등의 변화가 없으므로 대한 원유공급을 거부했을리 없다고 하면서 경위를 파악해 보겠다고 말하였음. 끝

(대사 최필립-국장)

예고: 90.12.31. 까지

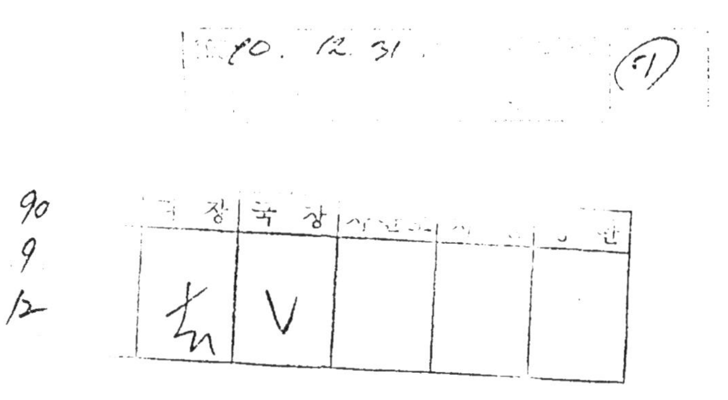

경제국　중아국　동자부

PAGE 1　　　　90.09.11　21:11

외신 2과　통제관 EZ

0125

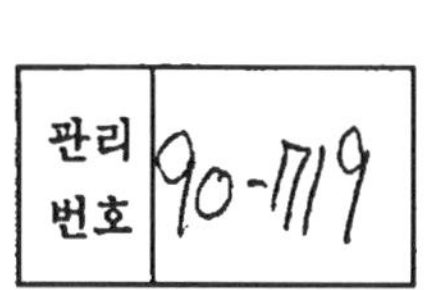

원 본

외 무 부

종 별 :

번 호 : LYW-0564 일 시 : 90 0911 1400

수 신 : 장관(기협,마그,기정)

발 신 : 주 리비아 대사

제 목 : 원유 도입 교섭

대:WLY-0325

연:LYW-0563

본직은 금 9.11. 주재국 SHAKSHOUKI 석유장관을 방문, 걸프 사태후 리비아측 입장 변화로 양국 공동위 합의 사항인 15 천B/D 원유도입 건이 추진되지 못하고 있는듯한 실정을 설명한데 대하여 동장관은 다음과 같이 언급하였음

1. 런에서 BIMC 와 유공간에 가격협상이 진행중인 것으로 알고 있음. 리비아가 시장 다변화를 위해 한국진출을 희망하는 입장에 변화가 없으며 이는 세계 석유시장의 변화와 무관함. 갈프지역 사태로 원유 시장의 앞날을 예측키 곤란한데 반해 리비아는 갈프사태 때문에 하등의 영향을 받지 않고 있음. 리비아는 분쟁 위험이 전혀 없는 곳이니 한국의 원유 공급원 다변화 시책에 리비아가 포함될뿐 아니라 그양을 늘리는 것이 원유 수급 안전책에도 도움이 될것임.2. BIMC 와 한국 유공 실무진이 리비아 정부의 상기 기본정책을 잘 이해하지 못하고 목전의 이익만을 생각했을지 모르나 리비아는 걸프사태를 이용할 의사가 전혀 없으며 금일중으로 BIMC 에 지시 가격 협상을 조속히 종결짓도록 하겠음. 다만 유공이 희망하는 항공유는 현재로선 공급 능력이 없음

3. 리비아는 한국에 거의 100 프로의 무역적자 인바 동 무역 불균형 해소를위해 한국측이 적극 노력해 주기를 희망하며 가장 용이한 적자 해소 방안이 원유 도입 이므로 한국이 15 천 B/D 도입을 시발로 도입 규모를 확대해 주기 바람

4. 유전 개발건 추진을 위해 한국측이 9.9. 까지 리비아를 방문토록 요청하였으나 한국측 사정으로 지연되고 있는바 한국측이 조속히 리비아를 방문,10 월 안으로 계약을 종결짓기 바람

5. 리비아는 한국과 같이 장래가 밝은 신흥공업국과 경제관계를 확대해 가기를

경제국 중아국 안기부 동자부

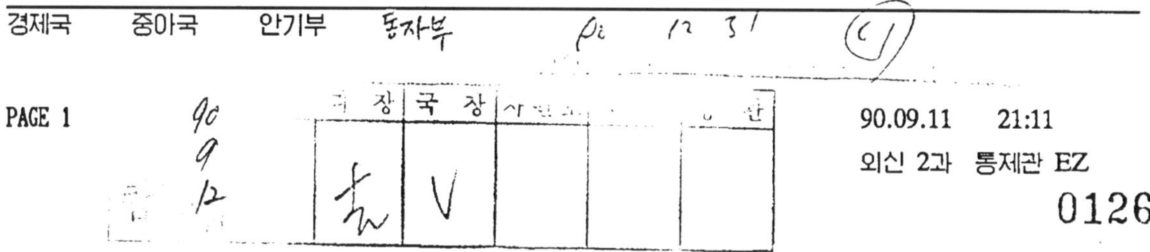

PAGE 1

90.09.11 21:11

외신 2과 통제관 EZ

0126

희망하고 있으며, 이러한 연유에서 라스라누프 폴리에틸렌(1.2 억규모)공장 시공업체로 선정하였고 MLITA 발전소 건설도 현대와 계약 추진중에 있음을 이해해 주기 바람. 끝

(대사 최필립-국장)

예고: 90.12.31. 까지

0127

원 본

외 무 부

종 별 :

번 호 : HUW-0390 일 시 : 90 0911 1000

수 신 : 장관(정자,미북,정일) 사본:주미대사(필)

발 신 : 주 휴스턴총영사

제 목 : 석유가및 생산동향(9)

1. 9.7. 현재 서부텍사스 중질유 10월 인도가격은 1.39불이 하락, 베럴당 30.04불로 거래됨

2. 이는 주중 석유가격이 계속 상승한데 대한 반작용및 이락이 인질중 부녀자와어린이들을 석방하고, 이락 선박에 미군의 검문에 순응하도록 지시하는등 사담 대통령이 강경노선에서 후퇴할 것이라는 소문등에 기인한다 함.

(총영사 허승-국장)

90
9
12

과 장	국 장	차관보	차 관	장 관
	V			

경제국 미주국 정문국 동자부 대책반

PAGE 1

90.09.12 05:58 DA

외신 1과 통제관

0128

원 본

외 무 부

종 별 :

번 호 : HUW-0393 일 시 : 90 0911 1420

수 신 : 장 관 (경자,미북,정일) 사본: 주미대사(직송필)

발 신 : 주 휴스턴 총영사

제 목 : 석유가격및 생산동향(10)

1. 9.10.현재 서부텍사스 중질유 10월 인도가격은 1.26불이 상승, 베럴당 31.30불에 거래됨.

2. 이는 이락이 쿠웨이트 국민들에게 모든 화기(무기)를 반납하라고 지시한 것,이락군대가 요르단쪽으로 이동하였다는 소문등에 기인한다함.

(총영사 허승-국장)

90.9.12	과 장	국 장	차관보	차 관	장 관
		V			

경제국 2차보 미주국 정문국 안기부

PAGE 1

90.09.12 08:40 FC

외신 1과 통제관

0129

원 본

외 무 부

종 별 :

번 호 : USW-4121 일 시 : 90 0911 1802

수 신 : 장 관(기협)

발 신 : 주 미 대사

제 목 : 석유시장 및 유가동향(13)

표제 관련, 9.11(화) 당지 언론 보도내용을 종합보고함.

1. 유가동향

가. 9.10(월) 원유및 정유 제품 가격 (뉴욕 상품시장,10월 인도가격)

0 원유: 배럴당 31.30 불 (전일대비 1.26 불상승)

0휘발유: 갤런당 94.72센트 (전일대비 1.66 센트상승)

0 난방유:갤런당 85.89센트 (전일대비 1.91 센트상승)

나. 9.10 유가 상승은 석유시장내의 루머와 투기에 인한 것으로 분석되고 있음.

2. 석유 수급 전망

0 C.KENT 에너지부 에너지 정보국장은 9.10(월)하원 에너지 상업위의 에너지.동력 소위 청문회에서 4/4 분기 중 세계 원유 공급 부족량은 일일1 백만 배럴에 달할 것으로 추정되나, 유가 인상에따른 수요 감퇴로 큰 문제는 없을 것이라고 발언하였음.

0 동인은 그러나 휘발유,난방유등 정유 제품공급량은 이번 겨울에 이상한파가 없고, 미국내 정유시설의 현 가동률 (약 96 푸로)을 계속 유지할수 있으며 중동사태의 확산으로 원유 공급에 큰 차질이 없을 것을 가정할 경우에 한해 수요를 충족시킬수 있을 것으로 전망된다고 하면서, 이상한파가 닥치거나 정유 시설의 환정 가동에 차질이 있을경우 정유 제품의 지역적인 부족 현상이 나타날수있다고 언급하였음.

3. 9.11 자 당지 언론 보도 내용 별첨 팩시 (USW(F)-2171 (8 매) 송부함.

(대사 박동진-국장)

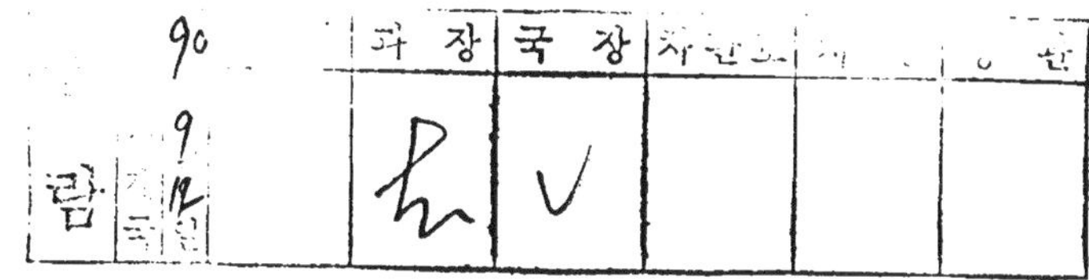

90.9.12	과 장	국 장			
람					

경제국 2차보 미주국 안기부 동자부

PAGE 1

90.09.12 09:24 WG

외신 1과 통제관

0130

주 미 대 사 관

통제 31

번 호 : USW(F) - 2177
수 신 : 장 관 (기협)
발 신 : 주미대사
제 목 : USW - 4121 첨부 (8 12H)

Price of Oil Surges 6% In Minutes

Unexplained Buying Near Trading's End Puts Crude at $31.30

By MATTHEW L. WALD

In a stampede that not even floor traders could explain, the price of oil rose nearly 6 percent yesterday in the last 10 minutes of trading on the New York Mercantile Exchange.

Meanwhile, a senior oil statistician at the Energy Department, in testimony before a House subcommittee, raised the possibility of gasoline shortages later this year.

On the Merc, crude oil contracts for October delivery went from $29.85 a barrel at 3 P.M. to $31.60 at 3:10. The "settlement" price, which takes into account several trades near the close, was $31.30, up $1.26 for the day.

Other Markets Affected

Oil's bouncing price was felt in other markets: Stock prices ended lower after a rally was cut short, prices of Treasury securities moved lower and gold prices tumbled in trading that was completed before the oil-price runup.

Earlier in the day, crude traded as low as $28.35, following the pattern of trading in London, where the market was apparently reassured by the weekend meeting between Presidents Bush and Mikhail S. Gorbachev. The trading range yesterday was thus $3.25, or more than 10 percent.

"There was no news, no rumors, but everybody started buying," said James Fielder, a broker at E.D.& F. Man International, describing the spasm at the close.

Bandwagon Buying

"Everybody saw everybody else buying," said a trader at Geldermann, Mitchell Barber, "and everyone figured that everyone else knew what was going on. Everyone jumped on the bandwagon."

Traders said that the market was now in an unstable configuration that would allow price movements, once begun, to march ahead quickly.

Christian D. Gohler, a trader at Merrill Lynch Futures, said that the "locals," or speculative traders, had taken "short" positions, promising to sell oil they did not actually have in the hope prices would fall. When prices began rising, they started buying to cover themselves and limit their losses, he said.

In addition, many buyers had left "stop" orders, to buy a specified number of contracts if the price got to $30.50, or $31, or $31.50, said Mr. Fielder. As prices rose to those levels, more buyers came into the market, he said. And with prices rising, anyone who held a "long" position, obligating another market participant to provide the oil, was reluctant to sell because the price was rising.

Yesterday's movement illustrates the extent to which the commodity market is a financial creature, rather than a place to trade real, or "wet," barrels. Price movements drew momentum not from any changing supply or demand for oil, but from the buy and sell orders of those seeking cash returns on oil contracts.

The heating oil and unleaded gasoline contracts took their cues from the crude market. Some contracts had fallen by their daily allowable limit by mid-day, but were up at the close. Gasoline ended at 94.72 cents, up 1.66 cents, and heating oil finished at 85.89 cents, up 1.91 cents, both for October delivery.

In his testimony yesterday morning, the Administrator of the Energy Information Administration, a part of the Energy Department, raised the possibility of "localized shortages" of gasoline later this year.

The official, Calvin A. Kent, pointed out that gasoline stocks are near minimum operating levels. He said that while stocks "should be adequate to see us through the fourth quarter," that "does not preclude the possibility of some localized shortages."

Given a normal winter, no unusual refinery problems and no unusual building of inventories by consumers, supplies should be adequate, he said, if various producers are able to increase their production.

But military activity in the Persian Gulf is raising demand for jet fuel by about 300,000 barrels a day, "and problems could develop later in the winter" in the market for that fuel, Dr. Kent said.

While Saudi Arabia has pledged to supply fuel for the armed forces of other countries that have come to its aid, they have done this by reducing deliveries to other countries.

Dr. Kent said the Energy Department had projected a shortfall of 1 million barrels of oil a day in the fourth quarter, which, he said, "can be handled" by "conservation, both here and abroad," brought on by higher prices.

9/11 NYT

0131

관 발신 : 주미대사 (매)

Refined Products, Not Crude, At the Heart of This Oil Crisis

By ABUDI ZEIN
Knight-Ridder Financial

TOKYO — The realization that the current oil crisis is about petroleum products, not crude oil, is starting to seep into traders' consciousness, focusing attention on refinery operations rather than crude production.

Crude oil prices are still hostage to statements by potential war parties in the Persian Gulf. The perception that tension was increasing drove West Texas Intermediate futures prices above $30 a barrel last week.

But outside the political considerations, it's the fundamentals of the refined products market, not crude oil, that are driving prices.

The best example for the distortions in the global oil market is the shifting pattern of jet fuel trading.

The past week saw Japanese trading houses trying to buy jet fuel cargoes on the U.S. Gulf Coast for shipment to Japan about three months earlier than last year's jet fuel trade started, traders said.

More unusual was the export of U.S. jet fuel to Europe and the Mediterranean, a reversal of the usual pattern. Jet fuel on the U.S. Gulf was $30 a metric ton (9 cents a gallon) cheaper than cargoes in the Mediterranean, and $36 a ton cheaper than jet fuel in northwest Europe, traders calculate.

While major oil companies were busy taking advantage of the cross-Atlantic price spread to realize some quick profits, Japanese buyers were examining the possibility of buying jet fuel in the eastern Mediterranean, where prices are $26 a ton cheaper than in Japan.

In Singapore, the traditional supplier of jet fuel for Japan, prices are being buoyed by strong demand from the Indian sub-continent. Singapore jet fuel is $12 a ton cheaper than delivered Japan prices, but there are no cargoes to be had, industry sources say.

Outside the political considerations, it's the fundamentals of the refined products market, not crude oil, that are driving prices.

Singapore traders expect prices to go up later and are keeping cargoes in storage as long as possible, or are offering them to the Indian Oil Co.

Two factors are responsible for the global scramble for jet fuel: The loss of 800,000 barrels a day of Kuwaiti refining capacity, and the strong demand for jet fuel by the armed forces in the Persian Gulf.

For the moment, jet fuel is the most visibly affected product. Others are likely to follow. Already, there are fears in the United States that Japanese buying interest could soak up heating oil supplies and lead to a shortage in the winter.

These fears seem overblown, industry sources in Tokyo say. Japan imported about 4 million barrels of gasoil, or distillate fuel oil, from the United States last year.

The quantity is not likely to be much higher this year, they say. Through July, Japan imported about 2.5 million barrels of gasoil from the United States.

Europe also is unlikely to draw gasoil cargoes across the Atlantic, traders say. German consumers bought heating oil in June when prices were low. They are now abstaining from the market, which has bloated stocks and forced Rotterdam traders to think about exports, not imports.

Another factor to consider is high gasoil stocks. U.S. refiners have 9 million barrels more in their tanks than the average at the beginning of the heating season.

A bigger concern for the U.S. oil industry is gasoline. Refinery-held stocks of gasoline in the United States are close to the level the Department of Energy has identified as likely to trigger shortages. Gasoline imports are declining as European refiners struggle with increased supplies of heavy crude that yield less gasoline.

9/11/90

2171 -2

09/11/90 17:29 ☎202 797 0595 EMBASSY OF KOREA

0132

A lot of ifs in feds' oil-supply prediction

FROM COMBINED DISPATCHES

Energy Department officials cautiously predicted yesterday that fuel oil supplies will be adequate this winter — but only if the weather isn't severe, if refineries avoid operating problems and if Mideast developments don't disrupt oil shipments further.

Several congressmen complained that the assessment was based on "rosy assumptions" and suggested that it provides little comfort to Americans relying on oil to heat homes and factories.

"There now is a very small margin of safety," said Rep. Philip Sharp, Indiana Democrat and chairman of the House energy and power subcommittee. The Energy Department "tends to underestimate what can go wrong," he complained.

Meanwhile, oil prices shook off big losses in early trading on futures markets yesterday to close sharply higher.

Analysts said the explosive rally, which lifted oil prices by more than $1 in the final minutes of the day, was ignited by reports that Iraq ordered Kuwaitis to hand over firearms and on rumors that Iraqi troops were moving toward Jordan.

The key U.S. grade of crude for October delivery closed with a gain of $1.26 at $31.30 a barrel on the New York Mercantile Exchange.

Earlier, oil plummeted by a substantial $1.69 on selling fanned by a joint statement by Soviet President Mikhail Gorbachev and President Bush urging that Iraq withdraw its troops from Kuwait, which eased fears of a Persian Gulf confrontation.

Calvin A. Kent, head of the department's Energy Information Administration, told Mr. Sharp's subcommittee that the supply of refined petroleum products — gasoline, heating oil and jet fuel — will be tight, with refineries producing near their capacities.

But he said U.S. petroleum stocks "appear adequate." The agency estimated that while the worldwide crude oil shortage is expected to still be about 1 million barrels a day during the last three months of the year, "the shortage can be handled" as higher prices dampen demand.

But Mr. Kent said significant supply problems could emerge if developments in the Mideast further reduce supplies or if the winter is abnormally cold. Operational problems at refineries, which have been running at better than 96 percent of capacity, and extensive hoarding could cause localized shortages, he suggested.

Mr. Sharp and several other congressmen reiterated their call for President Bush to release oil from the Strategic Petroleum Reserve. The president should consider "at least a modest" drawdown of the 590 million-barrel reserve "to get confidence up and hopefully force prices down," Mr. Sharp said.

The Bush administration has said tapping the reserve is not needed now. Energy Department officials said last week the reserves will be used if there are "significant supply interruptions."

09/11/90 17:30 ☎202 797 0595 EMBASSY OF KOREA

0133

0134

Rising U.S. rig count reflects higher prices

By Laura Tolley
THE ASSOCIATED PRESS

HOUSTON — The Middle East crisis finally has made its way to the domestic oil patch, according to a widely watched index of drilling activity reported yesterday.

The rig count — the number of working oil and natural gas exploration rigs in the United States — soared by 27 this week to 1,039, the second-highest total this year, Baker Hughes Inc. said.

"I think this is the beginning of the reflection of the higher [oil] prices," said Ike Kerridge, a vice president at Houston-based Baker Hughes, an oil toolmaker that has tracked the count since 1940.

"This is up more than I would have expected for the seasonal pattern. I probably would have expected an increase of about 12," Mr. Kerridge said. The same week last year, the count rose 14 to 950.

The count reflects the number of rotary rigs exploring for oil or gas. It has shown some gains since Iraq's invasion of Kuwait last month and the resulting boost in oil prices. Last week, the count increased by 10 to 1,012.

But until yesterday, Mr. Kerridge had attributed most of improvement to traditional seasonal increases. The oil patch has been suspicious of the Persian Gulf crisis, and some drilling companies stung by the oil bust in the 1980s have been hesitant about adding dollars for oil exploration, fearing any price increase is only temporary.

At the height of the oil boom in December 1981, the rig count reached a peak of 4,500. But oil prices tumbled, and the rig count followed — hitting a low of 663 in the summer of 1986.

"Some of us remember the pain we had to go through in 1986," said Don Covey, president of the exploration and production division of Mitchell Energy & Development Corp., an independent oil company near Houston. "We don't want to get caught in that trap again."

But rising oil prices have had some positive impact on Mitchell's drilling plans, Mr. Covey said. The additional revenue from production has allowed Mitchell to finance two drilling projects on its own, rather than with a partner as previously planned.

"We welcome the good news and hope to see increased activity," said Bob Palmer, president of Rowan Drilling Inc., a Houston firm that specializes in offshore drilling.

"What we have been seeing with the worldwide oil situation has pushed major oil companies to award more [oil drilling] contracts. However, I think this is a temporary situation and it would not push someone to jack exploration by 30 percent," Mr. Palmer said.

Jesse Koontz, vice president of economic analysis with Grace Energy Corp., one of the nation's largest land-drilling firms, said the full impact of the Persian Gulf Crisis is yet to surface in domestic drilling.

"There's more lag time when you're considering exploration and drilling," Mr. Koontz said. "Before rigs are booked, you have to win the contract and draw up a budget. Logistically, a lot of steps are taken before wells are built, because it is such a major investment."

He continued, "Worldwide, the pricing picture [of crude oil] has totally changed. Oil prices probably will not sink below $20 a barrel, so it should translate into more drilling. ... The real boost is yet to come; it should really surface in about three months."

Mr. Palmer also said regulations on domestic offshore drilling have forced many American oil companies to increase exploration in foreign countries.

"Laws have caused people to wonder if they want to continue drilling in the United States. ... For many, overseas offers the most profitable route to take," Mr. Palmer said. "Until political battles are solved here, I don't see a massive drilling movement."

What will happen to the rig count the rest of the year will depend on oil prices, Mr. Kerridge said. "If people think this is temporary, I don't think you'll see a prolonged increase," he said.

If higher oil prices persist, Mr. Covey said his company probably will have more money budgeted next year for drilling.

Dale Steffes, an independent oil analyst in Houston, said he expects the rig count to show better-than-average gains because he believes oil prices will remain in the upper-$20-per-barrel range for the rest of the year.

"So the producers will have extra cash flow. A lot of the majors [oil companies] will not be as quick to put it back in drilling," Mr. Steffes said. "But the independents, the minute they get their bank notes caught up, they're going to pump the extra back into drilling — that's their nature. You give them some extra money, and that's what they're going to do."

According to yesterday's rig count, Texas was the big gainer this week, with its count climbing by 11.

• *Staff writer Todd Smith contributed to this report in Washington.*

THE SEARCH FOR OIL

U.S. oil and gas exploration is increasing again.

Number of active rigs searching for oil and gas this year, monthly highs from weekly counts through July, and recent weekly counts.

1,150 / 1,100 / 1,050 / 1,000 / 950 / 900 / 850

Jan. / Feb. / March / April / May / June / July / Aug. 6 / Aug. 13 / Aug. 20 / Aug. 27 / Sept. 3 / Sept. 10

Source: Baker Hughes Inc., Houston

Chart by Paul Compton / The Washington Times

Prices Encourage Search for Oil, but Labor Is Short

By THOMAS C. HAYES

Special to The New York Times

DALLAS, Sept. 10 — With crude oil shortages looming for the first time in 11 years, one hope of Americans — consumers and officials alike — is for greater domestic production. And with prices surging past $30 a barrel, the stage would seem to be set for the comeback of the declining domestic oil industry.

But if the stage is set, some of the production troupe is missing — the $8-an-hour roughnecks who man the rigs, as well as some of the engineers, geologists and geophysicists who find the oil and map out the drilling plans. There are already spot shortages of oilfield workers in South Texas and southeastern Oklahoma, the hottest areas for drilling at present. And should the domestic industry try to put more rigs into place to halt the nation's decline in oil output over the next few years, executives say, it will face serious delays for want of both workers and professional staff.

The labor shortage was apparent in the limited pool of rig workers before the Persian Gulf crisis erupted last month, and industry executives and experts say it can only worsen in the months ahead. For one thing, companies are cautious after their experience of a decade ago. Many geared up then for a new domestic oil boom, only to slash payrolls and abandon equipment to rust when the Organization of Petroleum Exporting Countries sent oil prices tumbling from $27 a barrel to below $10 in 1986.

"We've been a very depressed industry," said John G. Nikkel, president of the Unit Corporation, a drilling and production company in Tulsa, Okla. "Getting qualified, skilled people in the right spot, at the right time, is going to be a significant problem for us."

Most of the major oil companies, as well as hundreds of independent producers, hold mineral rights to large proven reserves. But to tap those reserves, they turn to drilling companies that hire workers for 30 days at a time.

After the collapse four years ago, many of these workers found jobs elsewhere, whether driving trucks or working in convenience stores, and many are not eager to return to the oilfields.

The Houston-based Anadarko Petroleum Corporation, for example, had to delay a drilling program in Kansas because payroll cuts among drillers had reduced the number of specialists it needed for the deep wells it planned.

Speaking of one drilling contractor Anadarko uses, Paul Taylor, a company spokesman, said: "There used to be crews in every office that knew this technique. Now there are only two. So, you wait."

Drillers in southeast Oklahoma's Arkoma Basin and in the Austin Chalk range of South Texas also turned down bids from major oil companies to sink new wells because they could not find enough rig workers.

After 40 years in the oil business, James E. Russell, an independent driller in Abilene, Tex., who operates in Texas, Oklahoma and Kansas, is drilling with 15 rigs, down from 50 during the boom years and is cautious about expanding.

'A Lot of Interviewing'

"If we thought the price would stay up to $25 or more for an extended period, naturally we would work into it," he said. "Most people think this could just be a spike in price, and then fall back down."

Earl Ritchie, vice president of Maxus Energy's exploration unit for North America, said Maxus had been able to hire petroleum engineers and other oilfield brainpower, mostly by luring them from other companies. But he said it was becoming harder to find good job candidates. "It takes a lot of interviewing now," Mr. Ritchie said. "I don't think a lot of the people who have gotten out of the industry are going to come back."

Given the nation's production and consumption figures, this points to a serious problem. The domestic oil industry's output fell to an average of 7.3 million barrels daily in the first seven months of this year, from an average of 9 million barrels a day in 1985. In the same seven months, the nation's consumers — chemical manufacturers, utilities, car drivers, homeowners and others — used an average of 17 million barrels a day.

The shortfall was made up by imports, which averaged 8.5 million barrels a day in the period, and by a slight drawing down of existing crude stocks. But the Persian Gulf crisis has led many to fear that the country is depending on imports from an insecure source. Still, the industry feels there is too much uncertainty in that area to conclude that it is time to sink expensive new wells.

If the industry believed oil prices would hold above $25 a barrel in the coming years, it would be worth putting hundreds of rigs into exploratory drilling, as well as stepping up output in producing fields.

Analysts say that if drilling was expanded to 2,000 rigs, from the 1,000 now operating, the slide in output would be halted, and production of natural gas, which is far more plentiful, would be sharply raised. But acute personnel shortages are likely to delay drillers before the count reaches as far as 1,300.

More than 200,000 rig workers and other oilfield service employees abandoned the drilling business in the last seven years, according to the Bureau of Labor Statistics. Their total employment peaked at 434,500 in 1982 during the waning months of a 10-year boom during which the Organization of Petroleum Exporting Countries pushed oil prices higher than $39 a barrel from less than $4 in 1972.

One producer in the aging fields of East Texas, T. D. Howell, kept all 18 of his rigs during the four lean years and kept an average of 12 of them active during that period. His drilling and production companies have increased the payroll to 418, from 250 in the early 1980's. He was able to do that because as a unusually conservative businessman, he had no debt to repay during the downturn.

A School for Roughnecks

"One of my fears is the potential pirating of our employees," he said. "If we tried to kick off another couple of rigs now, I don't know where we would get the personnel. Our rig rate has to go up so we can pay more."

One potential source of workers is a school for roughnecks that Texas A & M University reopened in July for the first time in four years at an extension center in Abilene. But its costs — $2,200 a person for room, board and instruction — kept enrollment down to a dozen men for its first two five-week sessions, despite hundreds of callers.

"Most of the guys seeking to become rig hands don't have much savings," said Will McNair, the program director. "We approached the oil industry for help and they said, 'We don't have the money, but we need the people.'"

In two dozen recent interviews, analysts, academics and executives of drilling companies and independent producers said the tight market for rig crews would sweep the entire oil and gas industry next year if drilling activity rose.

That, in turn, would lead to higher the offer of higher wages to attract a new generation of workers, and would force drilling costs higher — perhaps pushing rig rates up to $7,000 a day from the present average of $5,000.

Geologists as Consultants

George S. Dotson, president of the international drilling unit of Helmerich & Payne Inc., in Tulsa, predicted that higher oil prices would cure recruitment worries.

"If I had a 25 percent increase in wages across the board, we would be able to attract good people into the business," he said. "They won't be as effective while we train, but we'll be able to man the rigs."

There are also concerns about pro-

5/7

2171-5 NYT 9/11/90

ɔetroleum engineers, geologists and ;eophysicists.

Fred A. Dix, executive director of he American Association of Petroeum Geologists, based in Tulsa, said nany geologists laid off in 1986 and .987 have tried to get by financially is consultants to independent proucers. Others took jobs with ground vater companies or government igencies.

"There is no shortage of profesional geologists right now to handle in accelerated domestic drilling program," Mr. Dix said. "The immediite supply is very good, but as older eople move out of the profession, here aren't going to be enough 'ounger ones to replace them."

Jeed for a Policy

Collegiate membership in the eologists' association plunged to 300 ist year from a peak of more than ,000 in 1985. And the number of raduate and undergraduate stuents in petroleum engineering najors fell last year to 2,000, down rom 11,500 in 1982, when oil prices veraged $31.22 a barrel and the rig ount was more than 3,100.

Moreover, the squeeze on bank oans, capital and oilfield drilling quipment that began after the debale in 1986 will also contribute to a onger wait for more domestically umped oil.

"The whole industry has been sayig we need an energy policy just for ie very reason of what is coming up efore us right now," said Dillard S. lammett, a vice president and direcor of the Energy Service Company, n oilfield service company based in Jallas. "Experienced rig workers ave been in short supply for the last ix to eight months."

But some players are ready to respond to casting calls from the indus-y. Sam Wade, a 40-year-old geohysicist in Dallas who quit his job in ffshore exploration at ARCO in 1985 mid a huge layoff program, says he s eager to return to the oil business, ven though the three video franchise tores he and his wife bought before e left ARCO have prospered.

Another hopeful sign is at Texas & M, where the petroleum engieering department registered its iggest freshman class in five years ist month, with more than 300 enterig students, compared with 46 last ear. Starting salaries for those who eceived bachelor's degrees last May veraged $37,500, while those with naster's degrees were paid an averge of $39,500.

And Harry E. Wingfield, a 19-yearld farm boy from Jasper, Tex., dug ito his savings to attend the Abilene oughneck school. "A derrick man as lots of responsibility," he said. "I 'ant to see the oilfield part of the 'orld, make some money and go to ollege later on."

21/2

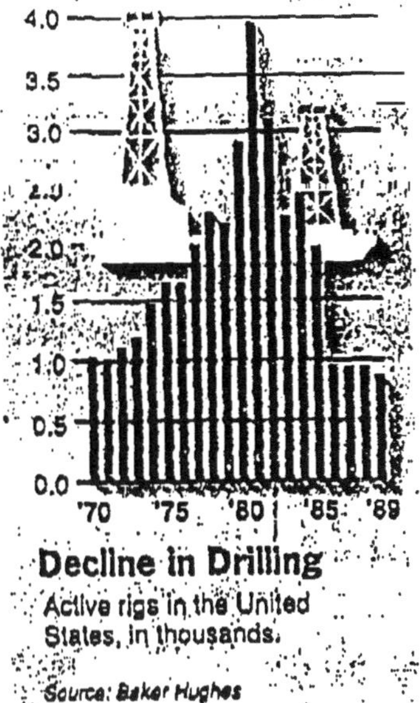
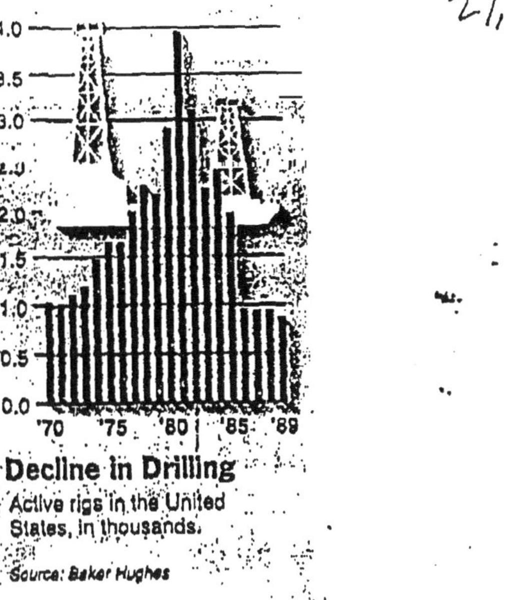

Decline in Drilling

Active rigs in the United States, in thousands.

Source: Baker Hughes

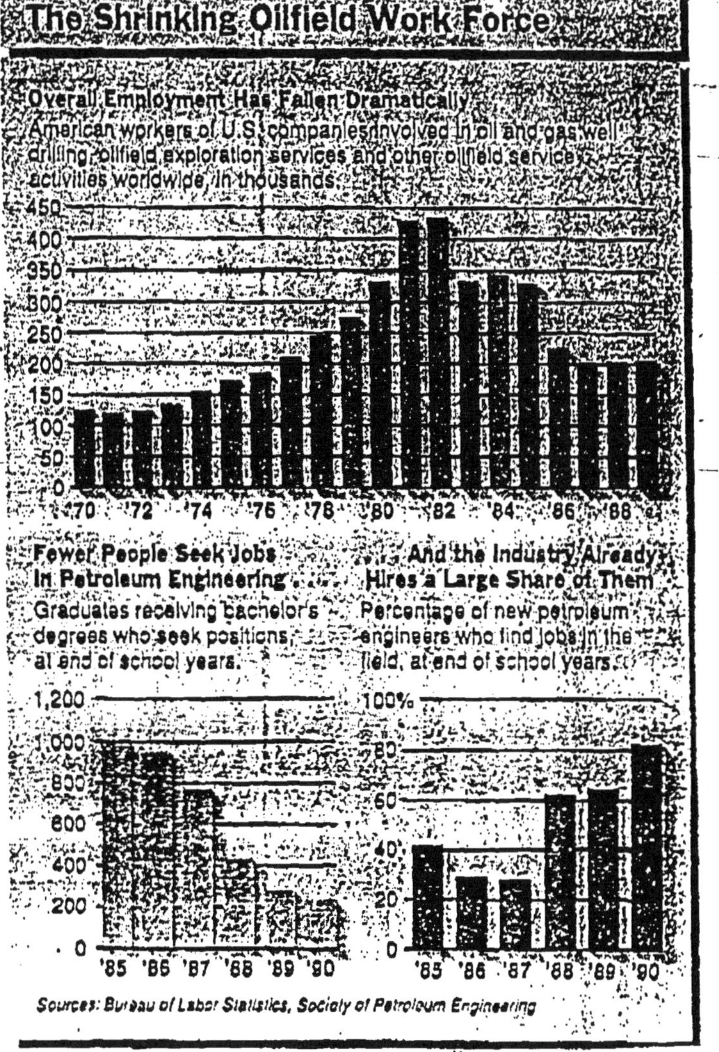

2171-6

08/11/90 17:35 ☎202 797 0595 EMBASSY OF KOREA 009

0136

6-11.12

0137

Iraq Offers Free Oil to Nations That Run Embargo

By JOSEPH B. TREASTER

Special to The New York Times

AMMAN, Jordan, Sept. 10 — In a gesture aimed at breaking the trade embargo, President Saddam Hussein of Iraq offered today to give oil to developing countries free of charge.

In a message read by a television announcer, Mr. Hussein said he believed that the doubling of oil prices to $30 a barrel as a result of the Persian Gulf crisis had hit the developing countries especially hard, and he added that he wanted to provide relief.

"We are your brothers," Mr. Hussein said. "And together with you we face one fate, and therefore we declare now that we are prepared to supply third world countries with their needs of Iraqi oil free of charge."

He said that because of the embargo, Iraq would be unable to deliver the oil and that the other countries would have to send ships to pick it up.

A Doubtful Proposition

Despite the pinch of rising oil prices, it seems doubtful that any developing country would take up Mr. Hussein's offer and run the risk of losing vessels to the armada of international warships that has quarantined Iraq. Insurance companies have stopped issuing coverage for ships destined for Iraq and almost all the sea traffic has halted.

In his brief television message, the latest of what has been a series of statements to the world, Mr. Hussein contended that his proposal would not violate the embargo because the oil was a gift and "does not involve any buying or selling."

The United Nations resolution imposing the embargo, however, makes no mention of the cost of goods, but merely prohibits their transport from or entry into Iraq.

In Baghdad today, thousands of Iraqis took part in protest demonstrations outside the United States and British embassies that were certainly approved if not fully inspired by the Government.

The protesters burned effigies of President Bush and Prime Minister Margaret Thatcher of Britain and carried signs expressing defiance of the economic blockade.

"No surrender even if we starve to death," read one sign. "The economic blockade will fail, and Iraq will triumph," read another.

In London, British diplomats announced that the United States and Britain planned to charter another Iraqi Airways jet to fly British and American women and children from Baghdad to London, as part of an exodus that began more than a week ago.

After holding thousands of Europeans and Asians hostage for nearly a month, Mr. Hussein decreed last week that women and children could leave Iraq but that most men would have to stay behind as human shields to deter an attack by the allied forces in Saudi Arabia and nearby waters.

After several delays, groups of mostly women and children have started to depart from Baghdad. The latest group of women and children, a total of 438 people, including 165 Americans and 186 Britons, landed in London on Sunday.

Boycott Beginning to Be Felt

Mr. Hussein has tried several maneuvers to circumvent the embargo, which has been in effect a little more than a month and is beginning to be felt in Bagdhad, according to reports from travelers and diplomats. Bread, rice, sugar and other basic foods are being rationed, and many restaurants have either closed or begun offering limited meals.

Last week, the Ambassadors of Pakistan, India, Sri Lanka and Bangladesh were summoned to the Foreign Ministry in Baghdad and told that the Government could no longer provide food for the tens of thousands of Asian citizens working in Iraq.

Instead, Mr. Hussein urged that the Asian countries confront the embargo by trying to ship food to Iraq for their own people.

Last week, he said in another television message, also read by an announcer, that children in Iraq were dying because of shortages of milk and medicines. The Iraqi leader has made prominent use of the fate of children, both Iraqi and foreign, in his public comments. Diplomats in Iraq said they had seen no evidence that Iraqi youngsters were being deprived of milk.

Milk Can Be Found

A woman shopping in a neighborhood grocery store in Baghdad last week said that milk and some European-made baby foods were not available in all stores, but that with persistence they could be found.

In his television message, Mr. Hussein said the developing countries need not pledge support for Iraq to get free oil.

"This decision," he said, "was made irrespective of the stands you have taken toward the current crisis because we are understanding of your attitudes, and we do understand that there are differences of views and positions."

"We can only get angry," he added, "when the imperialist countries try to impose their position on us because of their lack of respect for third world peoples and because they don't think we are equal to them."

NYT 9/11/90

Saddam offers free oil to poor nations

By Andrew Borowiec
THE WASHINGTON TIMES

BAGHDAD, Iraq — President Saddam Hussein yesterday offered free oil to poor countries willing to run the U.S.-led blockade of Iraq, as the increasingly isolated nation suffered widespread shortages of wheat, rice, sugar, powdered milk and medicine.

While Iraqi airwaves carried the offer of free oil, Saddam Hussein sent thousands of demonstrators to the U.S. Embassy and hauled off several more Westerners to serve as "human shields" at strategic sites.

"We hereby declare that we are prepared to supply all Third World countries with oil free of charge in accordance with the needs of each country," the Iraqi strongman said in a televised message read by his spokesman. "We are brothers to you. We share the same destiny."

He said his offer would not violate U.N. sanctions because no payment would be required.

In Washington, the Bush administration insisted that even free oil would violate the sanctions enacted after Baghdad's Aug. 2 invasion and subsequent annexation of Kuwait.

"The sanctions clearly cover the oil — at any cost," the White House said in a statement.

In Paris, site of a U.N. conference on the Least Developed Countries, Mr. Hussein's offer was greeted with surprise and derision by representatives from the world's 41 poorest nations.

"He doesn't mean it. It is propaganda," said Botswana representative F.G. Mogae. "Did Saddam Hussein not know before that we needed countries, he should not have attacked [Kuwait] in the first place."

Thomas Cherry, the delegate from Haiti, wondered how the oil would bypass the U.S.-led armada in the Persian Gulf.

"How do you get there? The Americans are there," Mr. Cherry said. "He is squeezed by the blockade. Does he want only sympathy, or is he going to ask, 'What goods do you have to offer?' "

In Baghdad, some 4,000 demonstrators chanted, "Bush, you will gain nothing," as they filed past the compound of 45 embassies, egged on by organizers.

They burned two U.S. flags, two effigies of President Bush and one of "Uncle Sam." Many dutifully carried portraits of Saddam Hussein and placards with slogans such as "We Want Peace. Go Home Americans."

The demonstration was supervised by the army and the ruling Baath Party.

The Westerners taken from the Melia Mansour Hotel to unknown destinations included French and British subjects. There was no specific information about Americans. U.S. officials said four Americans were held at the prison-hotel yesterday, including one woman who has opted to stay with her hostage husband.

In the incongruous Iraqi jargon, those taken to serve as human shields against attack are "very special guests," compared to "special guests" at hotels used as staging areas for transfer and mere "guests" who are prevented from leaving the country.

There was no specific information on the number of Westerners at the Melia Mansour Hotel, which stands near the bank of the Tigris River a short distance from the Information Ministry. Its "special guests" are not allowed to leave their rooms except for meals and a trip to the swimming pool once a day.

As far as the men held at strategic sites are concerned, diplomatic sources said merely they are being held "in acceptable conditions by Iraqi standards." They include at least 47 Americans seized in Kuwait.

Official frustration was obvious after Sunday's superpower summit in which Mr. Bush and Soviet President Mikhail Gorbachev reiterated their commitment to obtain Iraq's withdrawal from Kuwait.

The meeting was reported in the controlled press here as a summit at which "the Palestinian question was ignored." The Iraqi news agency said merely that "the big powers to... were motivated by direct material gains, electoral calculations and severe internal problems."

There was no further explanation.

Chief government spokesman ...Al-Hadhiti reiterated the daily line that "Iraq is known for its peace policies. It has not committed any aggression against any country in the world. It is the United States which has committed aggression against many countries."

He described the United Nations sanctions against Iraq as inspired by Washington, adding: "The United States has made so much fuss about the merger of Kuwait with Iraq, as if it were a 52nd American state."

Little was known here about Iraq's future strategy in the face of superpower and international determination to tighten the economic noose around the country.

Iraqis reported widespread shortages of wheat, powdered milk, sugar, rice and pharmaceutical supplies. The army has priority over almost eveything.

Near the center of Baghdad, several thousand Indians have been herded into a makeshift camp without any food supplies from the Iraqi authorities for the past 20 days. The Indian Embassy here has been giving them the daily equivalent of 30 cents per person — enough to buy some bread, a handful of rice, and tea.

An Indian Embassy official bitterly complained that the Iraqi government has completely ignored the plight of an estimated 500,000 Third World citizens wanting to leave, while giving priority for propaganda reasons to Western women and children, traveling with toys and at least in one case a pet.

Newsmen were informed about the demonstration outside the U.S. Embassy well before it started, to ensure maximum coverage. Demonstrators were brought by bus and trucks to an assembly point in well-disciplined ranks about one-half mile from the compound.

It was a mixture of workers, the unemployed from Baghdad slums, Baath Party members and women office employees. Some women had been issued black, ankle-length chadors for the occasion. Several discarded the garments quickly, complaining of the heat.

Officials with green armbands made sure the march was orderly and without incident. It lasted hardly more than 20 minutes. Some girls giggled at the sight of television cameras. All expressions of hostility, including the flag-burning, were carried out with considerable merriment.

WT 9/11/90 2171 -8 End

09/11/90 17:38 202 797 0595 EMBASSY OF KOREA 011

0138

45203

기 안 용 지

분류기호 문서번호	기협 20635-	(전화 :)	시 행 상 특별취급	
보존기간	영구·준영구. 10. 5. 3. 1.	장 관		
수 신 처 보존기간				
시행일자	1990.9.12.			

보조기관		협조기관		문 서 통 제
국장	전결			1990. 9. 15 통 제 관
과장				
기안책임자	홍성화			발 송 인

경 유 수 신 참 조	동력자원부 장관	발신명의		발송 1990. 9. 15
제 목	이라크 .쿠웨이트 사태			

주 이태리 대사관에서 보고하여온 표제사태 관련 이태리의 원유 수급 대책등을 별첨 송부하오니 업무에 참고하시기 바랍니다.

첨부 : 상기 공문 1부. 끝.

0139

1505-25(2-1) 일(1)갑 190㎜×268㎜ 인쇄용지 2급 60g/㎡
85. 9. 9. 승인 "내가아낀 종이 한장 늘어나는 나라살림" 가 40-41 1990. 2. 10.

주 이 태 리 대 사 관

1990. 9. 6.

주이(경)760-382

수 신 : 장 관

참 조 : 국제경제국장

제 목 : 이라크,쿠웨이트 사태

대:WIT-0777

대호 관련 조사 내용 아래 보고함

1. 이라크,쿠웨이트 물량감소에 대한 확보대책 및 대응방안
   - o 현사태가 과거 석유파동시와 비교시 국제 석유생산분포및 각국의 석유에 대한 에너지 의존도등에 있어서 과거와 크게 다르며, 최근 OPEC회원국도 공급량을 확대키로 합의함은 물론 각국이 충분한 량을 비축하고 있어 주재국도 현재로서는 별다른 대응방안을 마련치 않고 있음. (비상시는 IAEA 대책 발효 예정)
   - o 주재국은 총수요의 약10%를 이라크,쿠웨이트에 의존하고 있으나 부족분은 주요구매업체인 이태리 석유공사(ENI)가 여타 공급국으로부터의 수입량을 증가시킴으로서 문제해결이 가능하다함

50115

0140

2. 원유및 석유제품 비축 현황

o 법정비축량은 90일분 16백만톤이나 주재국은 현재 120일분 23백만톤을 비축하고 있는 상태임. 따라서 현재로선 비축유를 방출하지 않고 있으며 당분간은 방출계획도 없다함.

3. 주재국내 유류가격

o 주재국의 유가는 EC 주요 5개국(영,불,독,벨,화란)의 유가를 참조 결정됨으로 최근 국제 석유가 상승에 따라 주제국 유가도 인상되어야 하나 주재국 정부는 유가인상으로 인한 인플레 영향등을 억제키위해 지난 9.1 각의에서 인상분은 세수입 감소로 흡수하면서 자동차용 휘발유, 디젤유에 대해선 9월중 가격 동결 조치를 취하였으며 그외 난방유등은 소폭 인상하였음

o 90년도 주요 석유제품별 세포함 소비가격, 제조세, 부가가치세는 별첨 5항과 같음

4. 국제원유시장에 대한 수급및 가격전망

o 당분간 국제공급에 큰타격은 없을 것으로 보며 총수요도 전년 수준정도가 될 것으로 보아 현사태가 악화되지 않는한 국제원유시장에 수급상 큰 문제는 없을 것으로 보며 가격도 현재수준이 지속될 것으로 봄.

0141

5. 90년도 주요 석유제품별 가격동향

가. 슈퍼휘발유(보통휘발유)

(단위:리라, 현재 미화 1불=1150리라)

시행일자	리터당소비가격(세포함)	제 조 세	부가가치세(19%)
1.13	1,425(1,375)	871.67(871.67)	227.52(219.54)
1.20	" (")	861.78(좌동)	" (")
3.10	" (")	870.21(")	" (")
7.22	1,485(1,435)	920.63(")	237.10(229.12)
7.27	" (")	905.03(")	" (")
8. 9	1,510(1,460)	" (")	241.09(233.11)
8.16	1,550(1,500)	" (")	247.48(239.50)
9. 1	1,550(")	862.57(")	" (")

0142

나. 자동차 디젤유 (난방디젤유)

시행일자	리터당소비가격	제 조 세	부가가치세
1.20	930(871)	432.18(432.18)	148.49(139.07)
1.27	" (856)	443.23(좌 동)	" (136.67)
2. 3	" (862)	457.81(")	" (137.63)
2. 8	" (847)	" (")	" (135.24)
2.17	916(")	" (")	146.25(")
3.10	" (862)	470.56(")	" (137.63)
4. 4	" (879)	484.93(")	" (140.34)
4.26	" (866)	" (")	" (138.27)
5.19	910(873)	490.67(")	145.29(139.39)
5.31	" (861)	" (")	" (137.47)
6.14	" (850)	" (")	" (135.71)
6.22	905(860)	499.24(")	144.50(137.31)
7.22	960(915)	545.46(")	153.28(146.09)
7.27	" (922)	535.20(")	" (147.21)
8. 9	980(957)	" (")	156.47(152.80)
8.16	1,019(980)	" (")	162.70(156.47)
9. 1	" (1,008)	503.95(")	" (160.94)

0143

다. 난방석유(fluid 유)

시행일자	리터당소비가격	제 조 세	부가가치세
2. 3	669(519)	245.57(202.98)	106.82(82.87)
2. 8	654(506)	" (")	104.42(80.79)
2.17	" (")	" (")	" (")
3.10	" (511)	" (207.56)	" (81.59)
3.15	" (500)	" (")	" (79.83)
4. 4	" (506)	" (212.72)	" (80.79)
4.26	641(487)	" (")	102.34(77.76)
5.19	" (489)	" (214.79)	" (78.08)
5.23	" (510)	" (232.29)	" (81.43)
5.31	629(")	" (")	100.43(")
6.14	618(492)	" (")	98.67(78.55)
6.22	628(496)	254.14(235.37)	100.27(79.19)
7.22	" (524)	" (258.98)	" (83.66)
7.27	647(530)	" (255.29)	103.30(84.62)
8. 9	682(557)	" (")	108.89(88.93)
8.16	705(582)	" (")	112.56(92.92)
9. 1	733(600)	222.89(244.06)	117.03(95.80)

주 이 태 리 대 사

0144

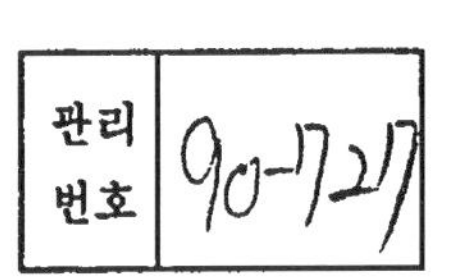

관리번호 90-7217

원 본

외 무 부

종 별 :

번 호 : LYW-0567 일 시 : 90 0912 1300

수 신 : 장관(기협,마그)

발 신 : 주 리비아 대사

제 목 : 원유 도입 교섭

연:LYW-0564

주재국측은 연호에 따라 런던 BIMC 로 하여금 가격, 선적시기등 제반 조건에 대한 유공측의 입장을 조속 타진, 원유 판매 문제를 신속히 종결짓도록 지시하였다고 하니 유공으로 하여금 신속히 응신토록 조치 바람. 끝

(대사 최필립-국장)

예고 90.12.31. 까지

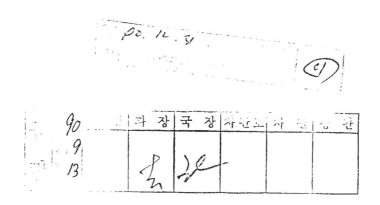

90.12.31

90.9.13	과 장	국 장	차관보	차 관	장 관
	(서명)	(서명)			

경제국 중아국 동자부

PAGE 1

90.09.13 01:45

외신 2과 통제관 CW

0145

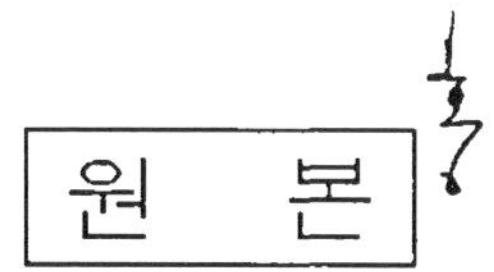

외 무 부

종 별 :

번 호 : HUW-0394 일 시 : 90 0912 1000

수 신 : 장관(기정,중근동,미북,정일)사본:주미대사(필)

발 신 : 주휴스턴총영사

제 목 : 석유가및 생산동향(11)

1.9.11.현재 서부텍사스 중질유 10월인도가격은 어제보다54센트 하락 베럴당 30.76불에 거래됨.

2.이는 미국무부가 이락군이 요르단및 사우디쪽으로 이동중이라는 소문을 부인한데 기인한다함.

3.한편 PETE WILLIAMS 미국방부 대변인은 이락군의군사행동이 시리아및 터키국경에서 증가되고있으나적대행위가 임박한 기미는 보이지않는다고 언급함.

(총영사 허승-국장)

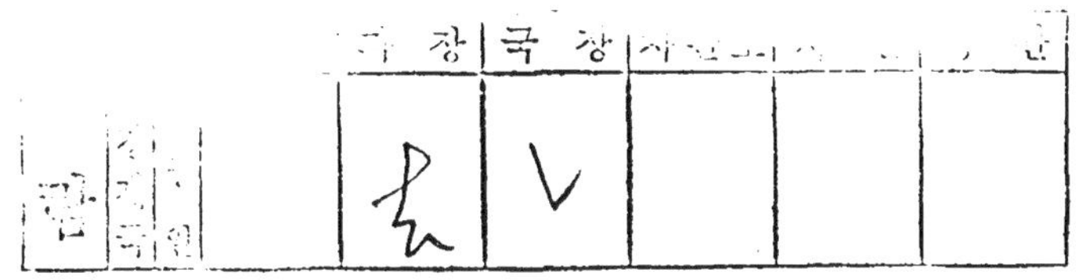

경제국 미주국 중아국 정문국 그차관 통상부

PAGE 1

90.09.13 02:03 CT

외신 1과 통제관

0146

원 본

외 무 부

종 별 :

번 호 : USW-4148 일 시 : 90 0912 1806

수 신 : 장 관(기협)

발 신 : 주 미 대사

제 목 : 석유시장 및 유가 동향 (14)

표제 관련, 9.12(수) 당지 언론 보도내용을 종합보고함.

1. 유가 동향

가. 9.11(화) 원유 및 정유 제품 가격 (뉴욕 상품시장, 10월 인도가격)

0 원유: 배럴당 30.76 불 (전일대비 0.54 불 하락)

0 휘발유: 갤런당 93 센트 (전일대비 1.12 센트하락)

0 난방유: 갤론당 83.03 센트 (전일대비 2.86 센트하락)

나. 전문가들은 현재 석유회사 등 많은 대규모 석유 구매자가 유가 불안에 따라 석유시장내의 매매에 참가하지 않고 있으며 따라서 원유 매매량이 격감한 대신 유가는 급격한 등락을 거듭하고 있다고 분석하고 있음.

2. 미국의 에너지 대책

0 부쉬 대통령은 9.11 상하원 합동회의 연설에서 미의회가 미국의 해외 석유의존도를 줄이기 위한 국내 에너지 생산장려 및 에너지 절약 조치를 입법화할 것을 촉구하였음.

0 부쉬 대통령은 금주중 석유 생산에 대한 세제혜택 부여를 포함한 일련의 에너지 대책을 발표할 예정이나, 의회는 재정적자 감축을 위해 세금감면 조치등을 반대하고 있어 실시 여부는 불투명한 것으로 관측됨.

0 상기 에너지 대책은 아래 조치들을 포함하고 있는 것으로 알려지고 있음.

- 유휴 원유 생산시설 가동 등 원유 생산에 대한세금 감면
- 대체에너지 개발 투자 에 대한 세금 감면
- 알라스카주 유전의 채굴 허가 절차 단축
- 천연개스등 석유대체 에너지 사용촉구
- 저옥탄가 휘발유 사용 촉구

경제국 2차보 미주국 안기부 동자부

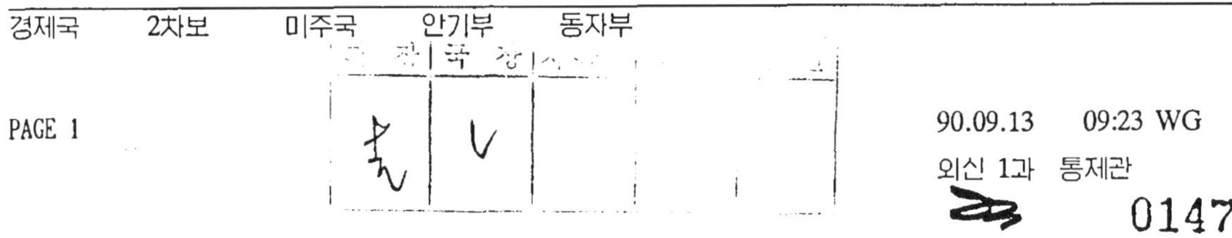

PAGE 1

90.09.13 09:23 WG

외신 1과 통제관

0147

- 연방 정부건물의 에너지 사용 효율 증대 및 에너지 사용 감축
3. 9.12 자 당지 언론보도 내용 별첨 팩시 송부함
첨부: USW(F)-2189 (4 매)
(대사 박동진-국장)

주 미 대 사 관

번호 : 2189

수신 : 장관(기협)

발신 : 주미대사

제목 : USW-4148 첨부(4매)

Oil Prices Decline Slightly

Small Rise Reported In U.S. Stockpiles

By KEITH BRADSHER

Crude oil prices retreated slightly yesterday but remained above $30 a barrel in futures trading on the New York Mercantile Exchange.

Light, sweet crude for October delivery fell 54 cents a barrel, to $30.76. Gasoline for October delivery dropped 1.12 cents, to 93.6 cents a gallon, while the heating oil contract was down 2.86 cents, to 83.03 cents a gallon.

After trading ended, the American Petroleum Institute, the Washington trade group, announced that the nation's stocks of oil and gasoline had risen modestly last week from the week before, while the combined stock of heating oil and diesel fuel jumped sharply.

Late Surge on Monday

Prices for oil and petroleum products had risen steeply in the last minutes of trading on Monday, closing at a "settlement" price of $31.30. Yesterday, the oil contract opened down $1.20, and it climbed slowly through the day before falling at the close.

Many large participants in the energy market, like the big oil companies, have cut back on trading because of uncertainty about the direction of prices, making the market vulnerable to sudden swings in price, said Michael Wilner, the president of *the Hilltop Trading* Company, an independent trading and brokerage firm on the floor of the Merc. "The currents are swirling around so much that a lot of people are getting out of the market," he said.

Light trading yesterday reflected an absence of news about the Persian Gulf crisis, said Robert S. Jonke, an energy futures trader at Cargill Investor Services. "There really hasn't been anything fresh," he said. "We're still waiting for something to happen to shake things up."

Gasoline inventories rose to 211.1 million barrels last week from 210.5 million barrels the week before, as imports increased sharply, the petroleum institute said. But Heather P. Rowland, a senior vice president at Petroleum Industry Research Associates, a New York consulting firm, said the increase was insignificant.

Refinery Capacity

"You're still uncomfortably close to what is seen as the minimum operating level" of about 205 million barrels, she said.

Gasoline stocks were at 218.4 million barrels in the first week of September last year. Some traders and oil industry analysts have warned that shortages could result from a lack of refinery capacity.

Kuwait and Iraq used to refine about a quarter of their oil production before shipping it, but a United Nations embargo imposed on Aug. 6 in reaction to the Iraqi invasion of Kuwait has shut off almost of their exports. Other oil-producing nations have agreed to increase crude production but have little extra refinery capacity.

The American Petroleum Institute said yesterday that refineries in the United States were operating at 93.5 percent of capacity last week, compared with 92 percent in the previous week and a year ago.

The nation's supply of heating oil and diesel fuel, which are similar to petroleum products and counted together by the petroleum institute, rose to 131.7 million barrels last week from 126.7 million the week before.

"We are going into the heating season," Ms. Rowland said. "It's the sort of thing you'd expect to see."

Heating oil inventories remained well above the 119.5 million barrels in stock a year ago.

Crude oil stocks, which were unusually high over the summer, partly because of refinery bottlenecks, rose to 374.3 million barrels last week from 372.2 million barrels the week before. A year ago the nation had stockpiles of 338.6 million barrels, the petroleum institute said.

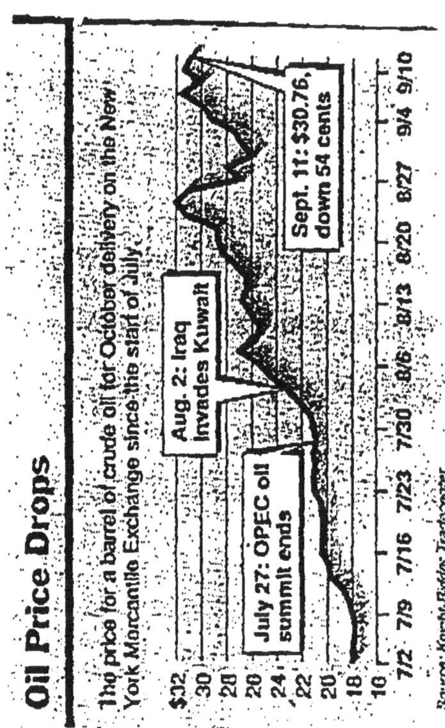

NYT 9/12/90

0149

President Calls For Tax Incentives To Boost Energy

By Rose Gutfeld
Staff Reporter of The Wall Street Journal

WASHINGTON—President Bush called for tax incentives to encourage domestic energy production, but many of his likely proposals face a hard sell in Congress and probably wouldn't produce much oil anytime soon.

In a nationally televised speech focusing on the Persian Gulf crisis, the president said, "The Congress should, this month, enact measures to increase domestic energy production and energy conservation in order to reduce dependence on foreign oil." Listing "our energy dependence" among factors determining "whether we can help our friends and stand up to our foes," he vowed that "Americans must never again enter any crisis—economic or military—with an excessive dependence on foreign oil."

The Bush administration is expected to release this week a series of specific proposals that were produced by the Energy Department and approved by the White House economic policy committee. Department officials have said the package will be longer-term and more controversial than an earlier package, which included calls for Americans to inflate their car tires more fully and increase car-pooling, and was roundly dismissed as inadequate by conservation groups.

The new proposals drawn up by the department include a tax credit designed to encourage efforts to recover hard-to-get oil from existing fields, and an extension and reshaping of a tax credit for investments in renewable energy projects such as solar power. The administration also will repropose various tax incentives for oil drilling that were included in the president's budget proposal last January. These include changes that would reduce the burden of the alternative minimum tax on producers.

Any of these revenue-losing measures, however, would face an uphill battle in Congress at a time the lawmakers are trying to rein in a budget deficit that is spiraling out of control. The tax changes in the January budget were estimated to cost $300 million in the fiscal year starting Oct. 1.

The president also may urge various federal agencies to expedite the permitting process required for certain oil drilling projects in the Beaufort Sea near Alaska and renew his call for Congress to allow oil drilling in the Arctic Natural Wildlife Refuge in Alaska. In his speech, the president urged Congress "to accelerate the development of Alaskan energy resources, without damage to wildlife." Environmentalists are already vigorously attacking proposals to open up the refuge, however.

In addition, the administration may seek to speed up its consideration of proposed pipeline projects designed to bring natural gas into California for use in projects designed to recover hard-to-get oil. Actual production from such projects would be some time off, though, according to agency officials.

Among steps proposed by the Energy Department to encourage conservation are calls for Americans to use gasoline with lower-octane ratings. Octane measures the anti-knock capacity of gasoline.

The president also called for efforts to increase fuel-switching. Higher oil prices are already persuading industries with dual-fuel capacity to switch to natural gas from oil. Energy Department officials have looked at ways to remove barriers, such as transportation problems, that could inhibit further switching.

In addition, the president may issue an executive order calling for increased energy efficiency and reduced energy consumption in federal buildings, and the Bush administration may urge people to tune up oil burners and replace them as needed.

9/12 WSJ

2189-2

0150

Market Place | Floyd Norris

A Dire Forecast On Oil Supplies

NOT all oil is created equal, and that fact could prove to be a key factor in the problems world economies will face if the stalemate in the Middle East lasts through the winter.

The lost oil from Iraq and Kuwait is of a much higher quality than the additional production that is likely to come from a number of other sources. So more of the new oil will be needed to produce the same amount of gasoline and home heating oil.

That fact is leading at least one Wall Street oil analyst, Frederick P. Leuffer of C. J. Lawrence, Morgan Grenfell, to expect even higher oil prices unless a settlement in the Middle East is negotiated soon. "The severe supply-demand imbalance would likely push oil prices to $35 a barrel or higher," he said yesterday.

• • •

Because of the difference in quality, making up the resulting supply shortage will require far more than the 4.2 million barrels a day being lost from the two Middle East countries.

In all, the replacement oil, from such countries as Saudi Arabia, Nigeria and Venezuela, is likely to produce about 8.5 percent less gasoline and home heating oil per barrel, Mr. Leuffer said. That means that more than an additional 500,000 barrels a day are needed, he estimates.

That plays an important part in Mr. Leuffer's estimate that even with additional production from a variety of sources, the world will need to draw down inventories of crude oil and products by 1.4 million to 2.5 million barrels a day in the final three months of this year, assuming that the embargo against Kuwaiti and Iraqi oil remains in force. In the first quarter of next year, when winter weather is normally more severe, he estimated the needed inventory drawdown at 1.8 million to 2.9 million barrels a day.

That is a direr forecast than the consensus, in part because Mr. Leuffer believes it will be difficult to get additional oil production from Alaska, where he thinks that no more than an extra 100,000 barrels a day will be produced, far below the 250,000-barrel-figure mentioned in Congressional testimony by a Federal energy official.

He also puts less stock than many in conservation as a means of reducing demand for oil because governments from Washington to Tokyo have been putting pressure on oil companies to restrain gasoline price increases, thus delaying conservation responses that follow higher prices. He also estimates that an additional 500,000 barrels a day of oil products will be consumed by the military buildup in the Persian Gulf.

> One analyst sees $35-a-barrel oil if the crisis continues, and recommends oil stocks.

Mr. Leuffer calculates that if his estimates are correct, world inventories by the end of next March would be cut to their lowest levels since 1979. Companies, he predicts, are likely to run out of oil supplies needed for operations, which would force countries to tap official reserves, like the United States Strategic Petroleum Reserve.

Even with that, oil prices would probably rise, which is a major reason that Mr. Leuffer forecasts that $35 oil is likely, assuming no negotiated settlement.

So far, the consensus of Wall Street on the current crisis — as shown by price movements — has been that it is unlikely to endure for long. While oil for October delivery closed yesterday at $30.76 a barrel, oil for delivery in January, the height of winter, was priced at only $28.05 a barrel in New York Mercantile Exchange trading. The gasoline spread is even larger, with wholesale gasoline for October delivery trading at 93.6 cents a gallon, 14.5 cents more than gasoline for January delivery. Mr. Leuffer estimates that current share prices for oil companies reflect an anticipated $25 oil price. "Portfolio managers simply do not believe this will last very long," he said.

• • •

If the Middle East crisis was to end with a negotiated settlement that lifted the embargo, oil and gasoline prices would likely fall, as would oil company share prices. But Mr. Leuffer thinks that the other options — war or stalemate — are much more likely and is recommending oil stocks. He has buy recommendations on Exxon, Texaco, Kerr-McGee, Occidental, Pennzoil, Unocal and USX. He also likes Crown Central, a refiner.

Refiners could end up being major beneficiaries of any shortage. "What we see is a shortage of oil, but an even greater shortage of products," Mr. Leuffer said, adding that refineries were already operating near capacity before the crisis began. "That will ultimately boost refining margins."

One thing that could go wrong with bullish forecasts for oil company shares is Government action. A windfall profits tax could slash profits for oil producers, although it is hard to imagine President Bush, a former oilman himself, making such a proposal.

But Mr. Bush did not shy away from putting pressure on oil companies not to increase gasoline prices, and Mr. Leuffer says that retail gasoline prices are still about 9 cents a gallon less than the price of crude would suggest they should be.

2189 -3

NYT 9/12/90

0151

Oil Analysts Urge Release of Strategic Reserves

By ARTHUR GOTTSCHALK
Journal of Commerce Staff

NEW YORK — Many energy analysts are urging the U.S. government to release crude oil from the U.S. Strategic Petroleum Reserve.

Ever since Iraq's invasion of Kuwait on Aug. 2, pressure has been growing for release of stocks from the 580 million barrel reserve, to ease price shocks from the disruption of Middle East oil supplies.

So far, the Bush administration has resisted. It notes that several oil producers, among them Saudi Arabia, the United Arab Emirates, and Venezuela, are increasing production to make up for the 4 million barrel-a-day shortfall caused by the Persian Gulf crisis.

The real test will come, oil industry watchers say, when the home heating oil season begins later this year.

"The president should not wait for heating oil to skyrocket," says Sarah Emerson, vice president of Energy Security Analysis Inc., Washington, D.C.

"The government should begin a moderate drawdown starting in October, and the intention to use the stocks should be announced as as soon as possible," she adds. She notes that the reserve has 200 days' worth of oil at a drawdown pace of 3 million barrels a day.

"Fourth quarter inventory accumulation will likely add as much as 2 million barrels a day to global crude demand," contends Arnold Safer, president of Energy Futures Group, Bethesda, Md. He doesn't expect offsetting production increases.

The only source for increased supplies, Mr. Safer says, would be a drawdown of stocks held in government and private hands. But drawing commercial stocks into world oil markets at a time of increased demand would only send prices higher, Mr. Safer continues.

"The only way to overcome this shortage psychology is to release oil from government-held strategic stocks, to generate a temporary surplus in the market, drive prices down, and thereby entice private sector inventory holders to sell excess stocks," Mr. Safer says.

Without a release of around 1 million b/d sometime in October, oil prices will continue to climb, perhaps to $40 or $50 a barrel, Mr. Safer says.

But, Mr. Safer adds, a large release at a time of apparent shortage or at the outbreak of hostilities would add fuel to the upward price spiral.

"Is it better to wait for these events, hoping they do not occur, or is it better to adopt a more pro-active posture which would lean against current expectations in a somewhat calmer atmosphere?" he asks.

Larry Goldstein, president of the Petroleum Industry Research Foundation, New York, also thinks President Bush should immediately release SPR stocks to protect the economy from oil price shocks.

"But you've got to realize what immediately means in this context," Mr. Goldstein says. "The oil might not reach the market for 30 days from the time of release."

But at least one analyst, Henry Schuler of the Center for International and Strategic Studies, Washington D.C., does not believe the SPR should be released to control prices.

it will, we would do well to hold onto the stockpile for a real emergency," he says. "We should hold onto them until we really need them, not use them just to keep prices down."

"Even if we were to end it quickly, by military means," Mr. Schuler argues, "it would be crippling to the oil flow. We would face catastrophic consequences in oil markets and throughout the Middle East."

The Bush administration, in resisting calls for a drawdown, adds that any stock release would have to be coordinated with U.S. allies, like Japan and West Germany, that have their own reserves.

JoC 9/12/90

0152

원 본

외 무 부

종 별 :

번 호 : HUW-0396　　　　　　　　일 시 : 90 0913 1630

수 신 : 장 관(경자,중근동,미북,정일) 사본:주미대사(필)

발 신 : 주 휴스턴 총영사

제 목 : 석유가및 생산동향(12)

1. 9.12.현재 서부텍사스 중질유 10월 인도가격은 어제보다 21센트 상승, 베럴당 30.97불에 거래됨.

2.이는 이란의 지도자 KHAMENIE 가 9.12. 이스람 각국에게 미국을 중동지역에서 축출하기 위한 대미 성전을 호소한데 기인한다함.

(총영사 허승-국장)

국	90 9 15	담 당	과 장	국 장	차관보	차 관
				V		

경제국　2차보　미주국　중아국　정문국　안기부　동자부

PAGE 1　　　　　　　　　　90.09.14 09:28 WG

외신 1과 통제관

0153

원 본

외 무 부

종 별 :

번 호 : USW-4169 일 시 : 90 0913 1845

수 신 : 장 관(기협)

발 신 : 주 미 대사

제 목 : 석유 시장및 유가 동향(15)

표제 관련 9.13 당지 언론 보도 내용을 종합 보고함.

1. 9.12 원유 및 정유 제품 가격 (뉴욕 상품 시장,10월 인도 가격)

0 원유: 배럴당 30.97불 (전일 대비 0.21 불 상승)

0 휘발유: 갤런당 93.84 센트 (전일 대비 0.24센트상승)

0 난방유: 갤런당 82.59 센트 (전일 대비 0.44 센트상승)

2.금 9.13 WATKINS 에너지 장관은 상원 에너지.천연 자원 위에서 세계 석유 시장 현황 및 미국의 대책에 관해 증언하였는바, 주요 내용은 아래임.

가.원유 및 현황

0 세계 원유 시장은 현재로서는 비교적 안정적이나 향후 공급 전망은 불확실함.

0 현재 미국등 IEA 회원국의 전략 비축분은 10억배럴을 상회하는바, 필요한 경우 미국은 일일 3.5 백만배럴, 기타 IEA 회원국은 일일 2.0 백만 배럴을 사용할수 있음. 다만 세계석유 시장의 성격상 한 회원국이 전략 비축분을 방출할 경우 다른 국가들도 혜택을 받게 되므로 전략 비축분 사용은 회원국간의 조정을 거쳐 공동으로 책임져야할것임.

0 휘발유 비축분은 필요량에 비추어 여유는 없으나 부족하지는 않은바 (STOCKS ARE TIGHT, BUT ADEQUATE),추가 정유 시설의 부재 및 증산 원유가 이락-쿠웨이트 산원유보다 저질이라는점이 우려되고 있음.

나.미국의 대책

0 에너지부는 금 9.13 원유 증산, 에너지 사용 효율증대 및 에너지 절약을 위한 중기 대책을 발표하였는바, 주요 내용은 아래임.

- 알라스카 및 캘리포니아주 유전 개발을 위한 행정절차 완화

- 천연 가스 수송 파이프 라인 건설 촉진

경제국

PAGE 1 90.09.14 09:41 WG

외신 1과 통제관

0154

- 에너지 재생 시설에 대한 기술 지원

- 연방 정부 차량의 대체 연료 사용 추진

- 석유 사용 화력 발전의 최소화

- 저 옥탄가 휘발유 사용 권장

- 석유 사용 난방 장치의 정비및 교체

- 전기등 에너지 절약 권장

3. 한편 WATKINS 장관은 전략 비축 원유 사용에 관한 행정부 계획에 대한 질문을 받고, 9월말경에야 금번 중동 사태가 세계 원유 수급에미치는 영향을 충분히 평가할 수 있으며, 9.26-29간 개최되는 IEA 이사회에서 각종 자료를 검토, 전략 비축 원유 사용 문제를 협의할것이라고 답변하였음.

4. 9.13자 당지 언론 보도 내용및 WATKINS 에너지 장관의 발언 내용을 별첨 FAX 송부함.

첨부: USW(F)-2208

(대사 박동진-국장)

PAGE 2

0155

원 본

외 무 부

종 별 :

번 호 : HUW-0397 일 시 : 90 0914 1530

수 신 : 장 관 (경자,중근동,미북,정일) 사본: 주미대사(필)

발 신 : 주 휴스턴 총영사

제 목 : 석유가및 생산동향(13)

1. 9.13.현재 서부텍사스 중질원유 10월 인도가격은 10센트상승 베럴당 31.07불에 거래됨

2. 부시행정부는 91년까지 1일 55,000베럴의 원유를 증산예정이며 94년까지 1일 60만베럴의 원유증산계획을 수립중이라함. 석유증산을 장려하기 위해 석유및 천연가스 생산업자들에게 조세혜택을 부여할 예정이며 알라스카및 북극지역에 매장되어있는 KHTFKR및 천연가스 생산을 증가시킬 예정이라함.

3. 현재 미국의 비상원유는 텍사스및 루이지아나지역 소금산(암벽)에 약 6억베럴이 비축되어 있는바 미상.하양원의 에너지위원회는 9.12. 비축원유 한도량을 7억5천만베럴에서 10억베럴로 증가시키기로 합의했다함.

(총영사 허승-국장)

경제국 1차보 2차보 미주국 중아국 정문국 안기부 동자부

PAGE 1

90.09.15 06:14 FC

외신 1과 통제관

0156

원 본

외 무 부

종 별 :

번 호 : USW-4179　　　　　　일 시 : 90 0914 1810

수 신 : 장 관(기협)

발 신 : 주 미 대사

제 목 : 석유시장 및 유가동향(16)

1. 표제관련, 9.14(금) 당지 언론 보도내용 아래보고함.

0 9.13(목) 원유 및 정유 제품 가격(뉴욕상품 시장,10월 인도가격)

- 원유:배럴당 31.07 (전일대비 0.10 불 상승)

- 휘발유: 갤런당 93.36 센트 (전일대비 0.48센트 하락)

- 난방유:갤런당 83.48 센트(전일대비 0.89 센트상승)

2. 상기 언론보도 내용 별첨 FAX 송부함.

첨부: USW(F)-2230 (4 매)

(대사 박동진-국장)

공람	국제경제국	일		과장	국장	차관보	차관	장관
					V			

경제국

PAGE 1

90.09.15 09:06 WG

외신 1과 통제관

0157

주 미 대 사 관

보안	
통제	

번호 : USW(F) - 2230

수신 : 장관 (기협)

발신 : 주미대사

제목 : USW - 4179 첨부 (4매)

N/T 9/14/90

Price of Oil Rises Amid Nervousness

Mideast Uncertainties Said to Make Traders Wary of Big Positions

By Reuters

Persistent nervousness over the Middle East crisis and its effect on energy supplies pushed oil prices slightly higher yesterday.

Many investors hovered at the sidelines, unsure how long the standoff could last and unwilling to take on big positions amid such uncertainty, analysts said.

"It's really a market that people are afraid of," said Tom Bentz, director of trading for United Energy Inc.

Crude oil for October delivery on the New York Mercantile Exchange rose 10 cents, to $31.07 a barrel, after swinging in a 60-cent range. That contract is now just 86 cents below its highest level since Iraq invaded Kuwait on Aug. 2.

A High for London Contract

In London, October futures for the world benchmark Brent blend reached a record contract high of $31.25 a barrel on the International Petroleum Exchange. The exchange said it was the highest price since the contract began selling in 1988.

The nervous tone of the world's crude oil markets was underpinned by a steady stream of ominous statements about the Middle East crisis.

Iraq accused the United States of seeking an excuse to attack it and said it would hold President Bush responsible for any strike. And Washington has informed Baghdad that it knows pro-Iraqi terrorist groups are preparing to attack United States and allied targets, the Iraqi press agency reported.

"As time goes on, it seems more and more people think the only solution is some type of military action," said Craig Whitley, futures analyst at Booner & Moore in Houston. A crude oil price of "$32 or $33 is not out of the question," he said.

Traders said they disbelieved Teheran's pledge that it would not break an economic embargo against Baghdad by swapping food and medicine for Iraqi oil.

Washington said there was no evidence that Iran or Romania had broken the embargo, but oil traders remained skeptical.

'I Wouldn't Count on Iran'

"I wouldn't count on Iran to abide by any United Nations embargo at all," one oil broker said.

Contracts for petroleum products were mixed as market players unraveled spreads, selling gasoline and buying heating oil, traders said.

The unleaded gasoline contract for October delivery fell 0.48 cent, to 93.36 cents a gallon.

Traders said gasoline prices were also under pressure from Wednesday's Energy Department inventory data, which showed stocks rose by 1.6 million barrels in the week to Sept. 7. The American Petroleum Institute said Tuesday that gasoline inventories rose by 650,000 barrels.

Heating oil for delivery next month rose 0.89 cent, to 83.48 cents a gallon, on supply concerns ahead of winter, traders said.

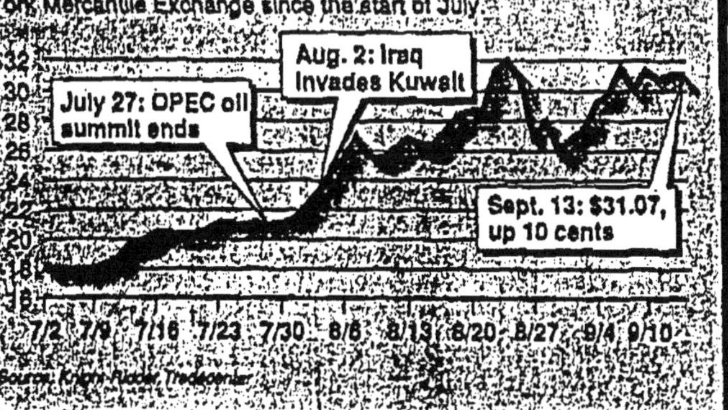

The New York Times

0158

U.S. Says It May Tap Oil Reserve

Risk of Shortage Seen In Next Few Weeks

By ROBERT D. HERSHEY Jr.

Special to The New York Times

WASHINGTON, Sept. 13 — The Bush Administration, confronting what it believes will be the maximum risk of an oil shortage over the next several weeks, seemed less confident today that it could avoid drawing on the nation's strategic reserve, a move that would almost certainly push prices down as the additional oil is auctioned into the market.

"We view the current market as relatively stable, but uncertain about future supply," Energy Secretary James D. Watkins told a Senate panel today. "Should the situation warrant it, we are prepared to implement a coordinated drawdown of the more than one billion barrels in strategic stocks" held by the United States and other members of the International Energy Agency, a Paris-based group whose member countries have agreed to build stocks and to share oil in a crisis.

Secretary Watkins insisted that the United States would not move unilaterally without the agreement of the agency, which is scheduled to meet in two weeks. The world will have an average of 3.5 million barrels of oil a day less this month than it had before the Iraqi invasion of Kuwait in August, which could produce a shortage.

Rise in Output Expected

But as more and more countries increase their production, this shortfall is expected to contract to less than two million barrels a day in October and to a million or less by March.

The Administration has repeatedly contended that the reserve should be tapped only in the case of shortages, resisting the pleas of those including Senator Bill Bradley, Democrat of New Jersey, who believe it should be tapped immediately to counter price increases. The reserve, the filling of which stopped shortly after the invasion of Kuwait to keep as much supply as possible in the markets, cannot be turned on and off, officials said.

At the same time, the Administration reaffirmed its opposition to a bill that would force auto makers to raise fuel economy in their fleets by an additional 40 percent over the decade to 40.2 miles a gallon by 2001.

Supporters of that measure, promoted by Senator Richard H. Bryan, a Nevada Democrat, complained that this showed that the Bush Administration had yet to get serious about energy conservation despite the urgency implicit in the President's address on the Persian Gulf situation Tuesday night.

"I am clearly disappointed," said William A. Nitze, president of the Alliance to Save Energy, a coalition of business, government, environmental and consumer leaders seeking improved energy efficiency. He referred both to the continued opposition to the Bryan bill and to a package of conservation and supply-enhancing measures disclosed by the Administration today.

The new measures, supplementing a list put forward in mid-August, consist mainly of hortatory items to reduce demand and raise supplies.

The conservation, or efficiency initiatives are aimed at saving an estimated 530,000 barrels a day by the end of 1991. This includes 120,000 barrels from "better driving techniques," 90,000 from car-pooling, 75,000 from more efficient utility and industrial use and 50,000 each from proper tire inflation, use of lower octane gasoline and compliance with speed limits. Previously, the Administration had projected savings of 100,000 if tires were inflated to manufacturer's specification.

Meeting in Boston

Secretary Watkins cut short his appearance before the Senate Energy Committee to fly to Boston to announce the introduction of a public service campaign before a convention of the National Association of Broadcasters, which is being enlisted to promote it. [Page D8.]

The supply-enhancing measures, totaling a hoped-for 607,000 barrels a day by the end of this year include 200,000 barrels a day of additional production from Alaska and various other efforts involving the extraction of heavy oil, state authorizations for faster pumping of wells, fuel switching, gasohol use and tax incentives.

Another critic, Edwin S. Rothschild, director of energy policy for Citizen Action, complained that the Administration is giving "lip service to conservation but policy initiatives to production."

In testimony today, Deputy Energy Secretary W. Henson Moore said he was not sure what Mr. Bush meant Tuesday night in asking Congress to pass conservation measures since those announced by the Administration today required no such approval from Congress.

After the Administration abandoned its longstanding opposition to expanding the reserve, House and Senate conferees agreed late Wednesday — and the House passed overwhelmingly today — a bill to expand the reserve to a billion barrels. The reserve, currently authorized to rise to 750 million barrels, now holds 590 million barrels at a half-dozen sites along the Gulf Coast in Louisiana and Texas.

Mr. Moore said the Administration's opposition to expansion had become politically futile but that it had not changed its view that a larger reserve would not provide enough additional security to be worth its cost.

Refined Products Added

The bill increasing the reserve also requires that 10 percent of the reserve, now confined to crude oil, consist of refined products like gasoline.

This reflected doubts, shared by the Administration, about the industry's ability to process crude that might be drawn from the existing reserve, much of which is high-sulfur "sour" Mexican oil, which few refineries can handle. Moreover, much of the new crude coming on line to replace Iraqi and Kuwait oil is of relatively low quality. "We are very concerned about the ability of refiners to continue operating at near maximum capacity for an extended period," Mr. Watkins said today.

Yet another provision of the bill authorizes the Administration to conduct a major test of the existing reserve, drawing up to five million barrels to make sure the reserve can be tapped smoothly at high rates for sustained periods.

The Administration called today's list of initiatives, most of which have been informally discussed before, "medium-term" measures that can be put in place pending its much-heralded 18-month effort to fashion a long-term national energy strategy to be completed this winter.

NYT 9/14/90

2230-2

0159

Watkins expects oil shortfall, but says it can be 'managed'

THE ASSOCIATED PRESS

The Bush administration unveiled a revised program yesterday to ease the shortfall in oil, but Energy Secretary James Watkins said worldwide shortages could linger near 1 million barrels a day through the winter.

Mr. Watkins said he believed the shortfall can be "managed" through conservation efforts and additional domestic production.

He left open the possibility of drawing oil from the Strategic Petroleum Reserve if conservation and increased production efforts fall short of expectations. But he reiterated it was too soon to use the reserve, which holds nearly 600 million barrels.

"That's a cherished reserve that has a finite life... and we don't want to use it too early," Mr. Watkins told the Senate Energy and Natural Resource Committee. He said he was "comfortable" that the department would be ready to take oil from the reserve in short notice if needed.

The department outlined a revised combined program of energy conservation and oil production measures that officials said was aimed at cutting the oil supply shortfall in the United States by about 1.1 million barrels a day.

The new program, including a radio advertising campaign urging conservation, came amid increasing criticism that the administration's efforts to ease the country's reliance on foreign oil have been more rhetoric than substance.

"The president should give more than a speech. He should give us a program," Sen. Paul Simon, Illinois Democrat, said Wednesday in response to Mr. Bush's call for increased energy conservation in light of the Persian Gulf crisis.

Mr. Watkins rejected such criticism, saying the administration's efforts to increase production and get Americans to conserve oil are "substantive. ... We do not think they are trivial."

Much of the department's program announced yesterday mirrored the response plan announced shortly after the Mideast crisis developed, including calls on motorists to conserve fuel by properly inflating tires and various measures to expand production from existing domestic oil fields.

But Mr. Watkins said as much as 165,000 barrels of day also could be saved by fuel switching and urged that regulatory and other barriers be eased to promote switching.

The plan also included tax incentives for oil and gas production, expanded production from Alaska and opening the Arctic National Wildlife Refuge for oil exploration — all proposals announced previously.

WT

9/14/90

2230 -3

0160

Ad blitz launched to fight oil shortage

By Todd Smith
THE WASHINGTON TIMES

The Bush administration yesterday launched an advertising blitz telling Americans they could fight oil shortages and high gas prices by conserving, while advising Congress there is no sign of price gouging by the oil industry and that gas prices are "not unreasonable."

The slogan for the yearlong campaign, "Do Your Part, Drive Smart," tells consumers they can save more than 7 million gallons of gasoline a day if they keep their tires properly inflated, drive slower and join car pools.

"The president has called upon Americans to do their part 'to conserve,'" Energy Secretary James D. Watkins said in Boston yesterday afternoon. "Our intention is to give people simple steps they can take immediately and have direct impact on fuel savings."

Appearing in Washington during a morning session of the Senate Energy and Natural Resources Committee, Mr. Watkins was asked repeatedly about gas prices.

Sen. Kent Conrad, North Dakota Democrat, warned him that "there will be a tremendous outrage [by the public] if we see a surge in profits for the oil companies" when they next release quarterly financial statements.

Mr. Watkins told the senators that oil companies' gasoline pricing "is working very well and is rather typical of the supply and demand situation." He said he considered recent price rises "not unreasonable."

He acknowledged that initial increases at the pump were greater than the early rises in oil prices. But, he said, *in recent weeks retail increases have* "lagged about 4 cents a gallon" behind the spot crude oil market.

Americans on average are paying 22 cents a gallon more for unleaded gasoline today than before Aug. 2, while the spot price for crude is 26 cents a gallon higher,

government and industry officials report.

Mr. Watkins promised his department would keep an eye on the profit reports. But he told the committee he does not favor legislation outlawing price gouging because such a law would require a "massive bureaucracy" to ensure adequate monitoring.

The new public-awareness campaign, which includes six radio ads and will eventually include a print and outdoor advertising package, was sponsored by the Energy Department and the Ad Council, a private, non-profit group that creates public-service ads.

Much of the program incorporates the response plan announced shortly after the Mideast crisis developed, including the tire-inflation advice and various measures to expand production from existing domestic oil fields.

But the department also urged an easing of regulatory barriers to promote fuel-switching by utilities, called on industry to increase energy conservation efforts and asked Congress to enact tax incentives to promote production of hard-to-recover oil.

It reiterated the call for expanded oil development in Alaska, including exploratory drilling in the Arctic National Wildlife Refuge.

Transportation Secretary Samuel Skinner endorsed the ad campaign at the National Association of Broadcasters convention in Boston where it was formally unveiled yesterday.

"We can make major strides in reducing U.S. dependence on foreign oil by focusing on transportation, since transportation alone consumes about 63 percent of all petroleum used in the United States," Mr. Skinner said. "Every American is asking, 'What can I do to help?'"

He urged consumers to use the lowest octane level needed for their cars, to combine trips when traveling and to drive slower.

"Together by following these simple steps, we can cut smog and acid rain and we can cut our dependence on foreign oil," said Michael Deland, White House environmental adviser.

At the Senate committee hearing, Mr. Watkins also said worldwide crude supplies could be short nearly 1 million barrels a day through the winter if current problems persist in the global oil market.

It is likely, however, that the Energy Department would take oil from the Strategic Petroleum Reserve on short notice if needed, he said. Mr. Watkins added that any shortfall can be "managed" through conservation efforts and additional domestic production.

But he said now is too soon to use the reserve, which holds nearly 600 million barrels.

"That's a cherished reserve that has a finite life . . . and we don't want to use it too early," Mr. Watkins said.

The House yesterday overwhelmingly approved a four-year extension of the president's authority to maintain the reserve and to increase the amount of oil that can be stockpiled. The authorization is to expire Saturday.

When the Senate also approves it, the bill will go to the president for his signature.

Environmentalists and some members of Congress say the administration has been slow in developing an energy plan and is giving only scant emphasis to energy conservation, while emphasizing expanded drilling, possibly in environmentally sensitive areas.

• *This article is based in part on wire service reports.*

2230 -4. End

WT
9/14/90

0161

원 본

외 무 부

종 별 :

번 호 : CNW-1374 일 시 : 90 0914 1200

수 신 : 장 관(기협,미북,정일,동자부)

발 신 : 주 카나다 대사

제 목 : 원유수급 동향(자료응신 제 92 호)

1. 주재국 에너지 광업 자원부 BOOTH 국제원유 시장과장 및 CASAUBON 원유 담당관을 9.13.(목)안참사관이 면담, 파악한 국제원유 수급 및 가격동향을 아래와 같이 보고함. (관련자료 금주정파편 송부)

가. 원유 수급 전망

1) 90. 3/4 분기

- 이락크의 쿠웨이트 침공이후 자유 세계의 원유수요는 52.8 백만 B/D (OECD : 37.8 백만 B/D, 비OECD : 15 백만 B/D) 로 전망됨.

- 원유 공급은 OPEC (쿠.이락크 제외) 쿼타량 19.7 백만 B/D 및 비 OPEC 공급량 30.4 백만 B/D 로서 총 50.1 백만 B/D 로 전망되며 부족분 2.7 백만 B/D 은 OPEC 증산 1.4 백만 B/D, 비 OPEC 증산 0.1 백만 B/D, 비축원유 1.2 백만 B/D 로 충당, 3/4분기원유 수급은 안정적 인것으로 평가됨.

2) 90. 4/4 분기

- 원유 수요는 원유가격 상승으로 인한 수요감소 (OPEC 경우 70 만 B/D 감수 추정)를 감안하더라도 동절기 난방용 유류 수요증가 및 심리적요인에 의한 소비자의 비축용 수요증가로 3/4 분기대비 3 백만 B/D 가 증가, 총 수요는 54.1 백만 B/D 에 달할 것으로 예측됨.

- 공급은 OPEC 쿼타량 17.9 백만 B.D 및 비 OPEC 공급량 30.8 백만 B/D, 합계 48.7 백만 B/D 로 전망되며, 부족분 5.4 백만 B/D 는 OPEC 증산 3.2 백만 B/D. 비 OPEC증산 0.1B/D 및 비축분 2.1 백만 B/D 로 충당될 것으로 전망.

- 91. 1/4 분기 경우 90.4/4 분기와 유사하되 부족분 5.3백만 B/D 로 전망.

3) 분석

- 90 년 상반기의 배럴당 20 불 미만의 낮은 원유가는 각국의 원유 비축량 증가에

경제국 2차보 미주국 정문국 안기부 동자부

PAGE 1

90.09.15 09:18 WG

외신 1과 통제관

0162

크게 기여하였으며, 90.10 월 까지의 국제원유 수급은 안정적일 것으로 평가되나, 11 월 부터는 동절기수요 증가라는 계절적 요인과 비축량 사용이 한계 (CRITICAL LEVEL) 에 도달하여 국제원유 수급사정은 어려운 국면으로 접어들 것으로 전망됨.

- 또한 추가 공급된 원유는 대부분 중질유로서 각국이 가동중인 정유시설에 부적합한 경우가 상당수 있으며 중질유 처리시 고급 정제유 보다는 저급 정제유 생산 비율이 높아져 고급유의 공급이 감소되는 점과, 사우디에 파견된 외국군에 대한 고급 정제유 공급 증가도 국제석유 생산물수급에 영향을 미칠 것으로 보임.

나. 원유가격

- 돌발적 사태 변화가 없는한 90.10 월말 까지는 WTI 가격 기준 배럴당 30 - 31미불을 중심으로 소폭 변동할 것으로 전망되나 중동전쟁발발 경우 50 불 까지 폭등도 가능할 것으로 보며, 사태해결시에는 21 불선으로 하락할 것으로 분석됨.

- 금번 사태가 원만히 해결된다는 가정하에서 5년 - 10 년의 중장기 국제원유가격 전망으로는 22불 - 26 불 (90 년 불변가격)까지 점차 상승할 것으로 전망됨. 사우디등 OPEC 국이 여타국의 신규유전 또는 대체 에너지 개발을 추진하지 못하도록 유가상승을 억제할 것으로 봄.

다. 이란-이라크 화해 영향

- 90.9.12. 이란 KHAMENEI 가 발표한 대 이라크 식료품.의약품 공급 및 이라크 원유 도입 계획은 이락크산 원유를 이란 국내용으로 사용하고 국내에서 사용하던 이란산 원유를 해외수출 할수도 있을 것이나 이란-이라크간의 송유관이없고 해상운송시 해상 봉쇄가 가능하다는 점과앞으로 이란이 희망하는 원유증산을 위해서는 미국등 서방 선진국의 도움없이는 불가능하다는 점을 고려할때 이라크 원유의 세계시장 공급은 현실성이 없는 것으로 봄.

라. 카나다 유류가격 동향

- 지난 8.1. - 8.31. 기간중 카나다산 경질유 가격 (CANADIAN LIGHT PAR) 은 리터당 5.3 센트 (배럴당 약8.5 불) 상승하였으나 전국 평균 휘발유 판매가격은 7.31.일리터당 57.8 센트에서 8.28. 리터당 57.3 센트로 오히려 0.5 센트 소폭 하락함.

2. 한편 9.13. 당지 언론 보도에 의하면 79 년발견된 이래 MOBIL OIL CANADA 등 4 개 회사가 공동 개발을 추진해온 52 억 카불 규모의 HIBERNIA해상 유전 개발 사업에 대한 연방정부 당국의 재정 지원이 수일내 결정될 것으로 알려졌는바, 뉴

펀드라니드주의 ST.JOHN'S 동남방 310 KM 의 대서양에 위치한 동 유전은 매장량이 9 억 배럴로 추정되며, 9 월하순 개회되는 의회의 승인절차를 거쳐 금년 가을 착공될 경우 96 년부터 20 년간 일산 11만 B/D 규모의 원유생산이 가능할 것으로 전망되고 있음.끝

(대사 - 국장)

0164

관리번호	90-739

원 본

외 무 부

종 별 :

번 호 : LYW-0573 일 시 : 90 0916 1330

수 신 : 장관(기협,마그,동자부)

발 신 : 주 리비아 대사

제 목 : 원유 구매

연:LYW-0567

리비아 BIMC 는 SHAKSHOUKI 석유장관 지시에 의해 유공에게 4/4 분기 부터 15,000B/D 공급할수 있음을 알리는 동시에 한국측의 구매 희망 여부를 알려달라는 전보를 9.13. 발송 하였다고함

리비아측은 4/4 분기 활당 계획은 늦어도 9.20. 까지 확정되야 하는 만큼, 한국측의 확답이 시급하다고함.

중동 사태로 원유시장 변동이 예측 불허 상태임을 감안하여 조속 결말 있기를 바람. 끝

(대사 최필립-국장)

예고 90.12.31. 까지

90. 12. 31

경제국 중아국 동자부

PAGE 1

90.09.16 21:04

외신 2과 통제관 EZ

0165

원 본

외 무 부

종 별 :

번 호 : USW-4218 일 시 : 90 0917 1833

수 신 : 장 관(기협)

발 신 : 주 미 대사

제 목 : 석유시장 및 유가동향(17)

1. 9.14(금) 원유 및 정유 제품가격 (뉴욕 상품 시장,10월 인도가격)

- 원유:배럴당 31.76불 (전일대비 0.69불상승)

- 휘발유:갤런당 90.36 센트 (전일대비 3센트하락)

- 난방유:갤런당 82.79센트 (전일대비 0.69센트하락)

2. 9.15(토)-17(월)간 당지 언론보도 내용 별첨 FAX 송부함.

첨부: USW(F)-2244(6 매)

(대사 박동진-국장)

공람	국제경제국	90.9.18	담 당	과 장	국 장	차관보	차 관	장 관
					✓			

경제국 2차보 통상국

PAGE 1 90.09.18 09:52 WG

외신 1과 통제관

0166

주 미 대 사 관

번호 : USW(F) - 2244

수신 : 장관 (기협)

발신 : 주미대사

제목 : USW - 4218 첨부 (6매)

보안 통제 : 최

All Oil Exporters Gain, But Not Like Saudis

By KEITH BRADSHER

Higher oil prices are helping all of the world's oil exporters, but the biggest beneficiary is Saudi Arabia, which is using the additional income to subsidize countries taking economic and military measures against Iraq and to pay for a large military buildup of its own.

Saudi Arabia's oil income should nearly double this month, according to one analyst's conservative estimate. It should be able to collect an average of $24.50 a barrel in September, about $6 a barrel more than it would have received without the Iraqi invasion of Kuwait, said the analyst, Fareed S. Mohamedi of the Petroleum Finance Company, a consulting firm in Washington.

That means an extra $880 million this month alone for the 4.9 million barrels a day the Saudis had been exporting before the invasion. That oil would have been worth only $2.7 billion. In addition, the country will take in a total of $1.6 billion for the additional 2.2 million barrels a day that it is now able to sell to help make up for the loss of output resulting from the embargo on Iraqi and Kuwaiti oil.

Altogether, Saudi oil exports for this month should increase by at least $2.6 billion, to $5.2 billion, as a direct result of the Iraqi occupation of Kuwait, Mr. Mohamedi figures. He added that his formula assumed that even without the invasion an agreement by the Organization of Petroleum Exporting Countries on July 27 to curb oil output and raise prices would have pushed the country's oil revenues up this month to $2.7 billion, from $2.3 billion in July.

The additional revenues should cover Saudi expenses related to the tensions in the Persian Gulf, said Jean R. AbiNader, the president of the National U.S.-Arab Chamber of Commerce.

These include $400 million to $500 million a month that the Saudi Government has committed as subsidies for the American military forces there; a similar amount that it has pledged in support to countries like Jordan, Egypt and Turkey, which have lost export revenues as a result of the embargo on trade with Iraq; about $750 million a month in extra operational expenses for the Saudi military, and up to $20 billion in extra

But the military buildup could distort Saudi investment patterns in ways that could hurt the country's long-term development, Mr. AbiNader said. The war economy means that investing money in building warehouses, for example, may seem more profitable than building a dress factory, he said.

Still, the Saudis will be the principal beneficiaries from higher oil prices, said Larry Goldstein, the president of the Petroleum Industry Research Foundation, a nonprofit group based in New York that is supported by oil industry contributions.

In contrast, the exiled Government of Kuwait will be forced to draw upon its estimated $100 billion in foreign investment to fulfill its pledge of $5 billion to be equally divided between the United States and countries affected by the embargo. The United Arab Emirates has also agreed to make financial contributions, although the amount has not been disclosed

Largest Share to Saudis

Because of the higher oil prices since the invasion, total OPEC revenues from August through January are likely to increase by $20 billion, to $90 billion. Of the $20 billion, the Saudi Government will collect $15 billion because it is able to increase production much more than any other country, Mr. Goldstein said. By comparison, Venezuela, the United Arab Emirates, Nigeria and Iran together should gain $10.5 billion to $12 billion in additional revenues, while Iraq and Kuwait will forfeit $13 billion in combined revenues if the embargo on their exports is maintained.

Some experts contend that the main benefit to producers will come from higher prices rather than from a rise in production. They argue that the invasion is having a much larger effect on oil prices than people like Mr. Mohamedi estimate.

"I think all the countries that can maintain exports will benefit handsomely," said Philip K. Verleger Jr., an economist at the Institute for International Economics in Washington.

Large oil exporters that do not belong to OPEC include Mexico, Norway, Britain and the Soviet Union.

The Iraqi invasion is also likely to bring long-term benefits to oil producers that are far from the Middle East and need foreign investment to develop large but untapped oil and natural gas reserves. Indonesia, Mexico and Venezuela fall into this category, Mr. Mohamedi said, explaining, "They can say, 'It's insecure over there, come to us.'"

NYT 9/15/90

Newsclippings Econ. Section I

0167

Crude Price Continues Upward

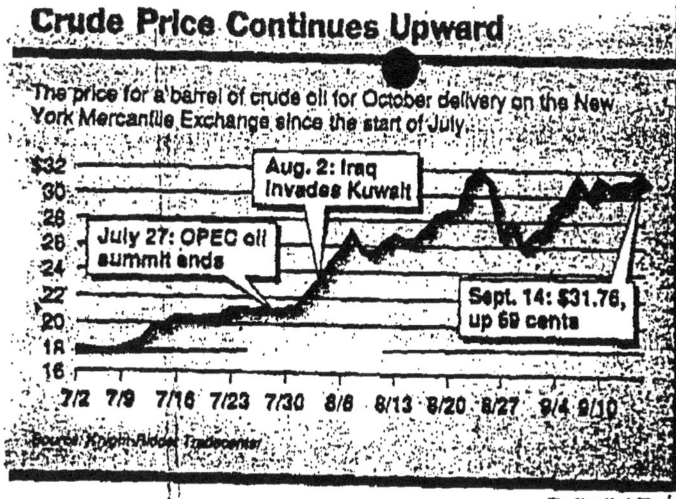

The New York Times

NYT 9/15/90

Oil Nears Highest Price Since Invasion by Iraq

By MATTHEW L. WALD

Oil prices rose further yesterday, and now stand at their second-highest level since the Iraqi invasion. On the New York Mercantile Exchange, light sweet crude for October delivery ended the week at $31.76 a barrel, up 69 cents for the day and $1.72 for the week.

Since Aug. 1, the day before the invasion of Kuwait, the price is up by 43.7 percent. It reached its post-invasion peak of $31.93 on Aug. 23.

The increase came despite a comment from President Bush at an impromptu news conference that oil supplies were adequate and prices were too high.

Product prices fell, with gasoline for October delivery off 3 cents, to 90.36 cents a gallon, and heating oil down 0.69 cent, to 82.79 cents a gallon.

The Energy Department estimated yesterday that higher oil prices and a sluggish economy could push domestic demand lower by 500,000 to 700,000 barrels a day in the fourth quarter. Gasoline consumption could fall by 140,000 barrels a day in the fourth quarter and the first quarter of next year, compared with periods a year ago, said the department. Those drops would represent a decline of about 2 percent.

International oil experts said supplies were rising from Saudi Arabia, Venezuela and elsewhere. But the Oil & Gas Journal, a trade publication, reported that further production declines were likely in this country.

Traders pointed yesterday to scattered unfavorable news. The United States Navy fired a warning shot across the bow of an Iraqi ship that American and Australian sailors then boarded, and Iraqi soldiers in Kuwait City broke into several embassies. Robert E. Martini, a trader at Cargill Investor Services, also cited an announcement by British Petroleum that a pipeline under the North Sea that normally carries 420,000 barrels a day from the Ninian field would be limited to 350,000 barrels a day for about a week, until mechanical problems could be corrected.

Mr. Martini said price rises were being limited by clients who had placed standing orders with their brokers to sell at prices in the current range. Many people, he said, have contracts that entitle them to buy more oil than they need, at prices below current ones. "They are looking to take profits," he said.

The President, speaking at the news conference, said speculators were causing higher prices. "The market should not be going for higher prices," he said. "In other words, it's speculation; it's futures speculation."

As for increasing supplies, Robert P. Boslego, a consultant in Winchester, Mass., said that short-term tanker charters from the Middle East and globally were up about 30 percent over early August. These charters represent only a fraction of the total tanker traffic, but accurately forecast the direction of the shipping trend, he said.

At Cambridge Energy Research Associates, Daniel Yergin, the president, said Venezuela had already increased its production by 200,000 to 250,000 barrels a day. "It's not something that happens overnight," he said. "It takes several months and a lot of effort." In Venezuela's case, this often means firing up equipment that injects steam into one end of an oilfield, pushing the oil toward wells at the opposite end.

Venezuela Sells Stored Oil

Vahan Zanoyan, an expert at the Petroleum Finance Company, a Washington consulting firm, said that Venezuela, in addition to sharply increasing production, had sold large amounts of oil from storage.

Additional supplies are dribbling in from elsewhere. The Petroleum Minister of Gabon, Jean Ping, said yesterday that his country had raised production to 80,000 barrels above its former OPEC quota, The Associated Press reported, and would raise it an additional [illegible]

2244 — 2

0168

Jack Anderson and Dale Van Atta

Lots of Energy in the U.S.A.

George Bush is prepared to spill American blood on the hot desert sands to safeguard a world economy that still runs on oil. He must stop Saddam Hussein, who hopes to control the flow of [illegible] of the Persian Gulf region by c[illegible]st or intimidation. This would permit him to set the world price.

The full destructive impact of another oil price explosion can be described simply: it would slam the brakes on the world economy, creating incalculable misery and mischief.

Clearly, it would be unconscionable to allow a ruthless megalomaniac such as Saddam to manipulate the world economy. Yet his coming was as visible as a sandstorm whirling on a desert horizon.

Our political leaders have known all along that the Persian Gulf was a powder keg that could blow the world economy apart. They were aware that some hothead from the dunes one day would ignite the combustibles. They anticipated that it would likely take American military forces to protect this volatile area.

Yet, our political leaders allowed this calamity to develop undeterred. They permitted our dependence on Persian Gulf oil to relentlessly increase. They failed to develop synthetic fuels or stimulate conservation programs. They hesitated to take the steps needed for damage control in case Persian Gulf oil should be cut off.

As a result of that neglect, oil is still the stuff that turns the wheels of industry, runs automobiles and heats homes. Before 1970, those people had been able to build on a foundation of low-cost energy. The supply expanded to meet any need and could be counted on. Easy, confident access to oil has produced the greatest improvement in living standards ever experienced.

Then came the oil price explosion of the early 1970s. The oil cartel, formally known as the Organization of Petroleum Exporting Countries, inflicted severe damage upon the world economy. It has amounted to a looting of the industrial world by inherently weak sheikdoms with bloated treasuries and tiny populations.

Why did our leaders allow this to happen? The oil sheiks formed an alliance with pressure groups that had a vested interest in high oil prices. Major oil companies, international banks and multinational corporations happily embraced the oil cartel. Together they mobilized to keep the price of crude in orbit.

Our leaders have had two decades to recover, but instead American dependence has become a debilitating addiction. Even as the oil flows in and the cash drains out, the United States is an energy paradise in its own right with the potential of thumbing its nose at the Persian Gulf. America produces 50 percent more natural gas than all the rest of the world combined. It also has the world's largest repository of coal.

This energy abundance should be siphoned into our automobiles, homes and factories to end the oil addiction. Compressed natural gas engines have already been developed that can make automobiles run. Equipment to convert an auto engine from gasoline to natural gas could be produced for a few hundr[ed] dollars per vehicle.

All Congress has to do is pass simple law requiring all automobiles convert to natural gas within a reaso[nable] time period. Here is what th[is] conversion would accomplish:

- It would eliminate the need to ri[sk] American lives to protect the Persi[an] Gulf.
- It would wipe out the trade deficit.
- It would help clear up smog in Amer[i]ca's cities.
- It would reduce the cost of energ[y]. Natural gas is almost 50 percent cheap[er] than oil.

There is a rub—the politics of oil. T[o] protect their profits, most oil companie[s] invest heavily in politicians, and tha[t] money can be decisive in an election.

0163

Kicking America's Oil Habit

We've Got the Technology—What We Need Is the Willpower

WP 91.1.19

By Curtis Moore and S. David Freeman

THAT RACKET you hear from the Middle East is opportunity knocking. It's telling us that when it comes to energy policy, the moral equivalent of war is vastly preferable to the real thing.

Before we can capitalize on that opportunity, however, we have to dispel two dangerously common misconceptions. One was voiced last Tuesday night by Rep. Richard Gephardt in delivering the Democratic Party's reply to President Bush's nationwide address. "For a decade," Gephardt said, "America has been left with no real energy policy at all."

Nothing could be farther from the truth. The nation *has* a clear policy, the vigorous and consistent pursuit of which has inexorably impelled us in the direction of war. Put simply, it calls for the United States to intentionally increase its reliance on Mideast oil and, when necessary, wage war to keep cheap oil flowing. Marines now swelter in the blistering heat of Saudi Arabia in large part because of what may be called "The Stockman Doctrine," after David Stockman, who became Ronald Reagan's first director of the Office of Management and Budget. In the Fall 1978 issue of The Public Interest, Stockman pilloried the energy self-sufficiency proposals of the Nixon-Ford-Carter administrations as "cramped, inward looking" strategies based on "Chicken Little logic." Calling for a strategy of "reliance on the world market for energy," he dismissed fears of OPEC extortion as "economic mythology." Avoiding dangers, he argued, requires "only two policies—strategic reserves and strategic forces."

To this day, the Stockman cheap-oil strategy remains the nation's real energy policy. For example, President Bush last Tuesday called on Congress to "enact measures to increase . . . energy conservation." Yet his administration continues to oppose a Senate bill to boost the mileage standard for cars (from the current 27.5 mpg to 34 mpg in 1995 and 40 mpg by 2001), a bill which could completely eliminate oil imports from the Persian Gulf by saving 2.8 million barrels of oil per day.

Bush also called for enactment of "fuel switching"—presumably a reference to his widely publicized "clean fuels" proposal of 1989 which would have converted 9 million cars in our dirtiest cities to cleaner fuels such as electricity, ethanol, methanol and natural gas—all available from domestic sources. But in back-room meetings with Senate negotiators over amendments to the federal Clean Air Act, White House aides abandoned the clean fuels program, agreeing instead to continue reliance on "reformulated" gasoline—and the so-called free market in oil.

Therein lies the second dangerous misconception of the current Gulf debate: that the global oil trade is a classic free market. It isn't. About 75 percent of the world's oil is controlled by the OPEC cartel, many of whose members are, at best, uneasy allies of the United States and, at worst, outright enemies. The hand on the pump is not Adam Smith's: It is Saddam Hussein's, Moammar Gadhafi's or Ayatollah Ali Khamenei's.

How Petroleum Makes Policy

The Stockman-free market doctrine has obliged the United States to surrender something vastly more important than money: independence. Moreover, the determined pursuit of our present policy—burn imported oil and fight to get it—effectively dictates many other policies:

■ *National security.* Oil imports from the Middle East, which were about 6 percent of our total energy supply in 1973, stood at 12 percent in 1989. Thus we are twice as dependent on Persian Gulf oil (relatively and absolutely) as in 1973. True, the U.S. has 600 million barrels of oil stored in the Strategic Petroleum Reserve—but that's only enough to replace a complete loss of OPEC oil for about 10 months. As a result, massive military might is required to maintain the steady flow of oil. To be sure, there are excellent moral reasons for our military presence in the Gulf. But the fact remains that as long as imported oil remains the lifeblood of U.S. cars and trucks, we will be at grave risk.

■ *National industrialization.* Investing in fuels rather than fuel efficiency is implicitly a decision to direct capital and profits towards coal, oil and gas companies rather than to industries that manufacture energy-efficient capital goods. Worse yet, much of the money goes overseas: Cumulative U.S. payments for oil imports between 1970 and 1989 totaled $1.1 trillion in 1989 dollars—roughly three years of U.S. defense spending.

■ *National public works and transportation.* A decision to rely on oil and the automobile is a commitment to continued dependence on streets, highways and bridges, rather than rails and rehabilitated housing and neighborhoods. Urban growth and government spending become caught in a vicious cycle: Worn-out highways must be repaired because so many people commute from suburbs that were built around the roads. With no money available to rehabilitate urban housing or construct urban transit, workers have only one way to commute—in a car.

Energy Agenda for the 1990s

If we are ever to free ourselves from the threat of buying foreign oil with American blood, we must set achievable goals and then pursue them with the same conviction we brought to putting a man on moon. In that case, we made the commitment, then we figured out how. In the case of energy, however, we already know what to do.

Curtis Moore, former counsel to the U.S. Senate Committee on Environment and Public Works, is an environmental analyst. S. David Freeman, formerly head of the Tennessee Valley Authority and energy adviser to Presidents Nixon, Ford and Carter, is general manager of the Sacramento Municipal Utility District.

1/2

2244-4

0170

At the outset, a rational energy policy must acknowledge something that Americans seem to have forgotten: "Government" is not a dirty word. It is, after all, government which is protecting the Mideast oil lifeline; government which fills the Strategic Petroleum Reserves; and government which in the '70s mandated the policies of conservation and fuel efficiency that have (so far) cushioned the impact of the Iraqi invasion.

Whatever the policy, the first two priorities must be cars and power plants. Cars because they burn roughly half the nation's oil, creating about half the air pollution [see box]; utilities because they consume about 33 percent of the energy and because they are notably inefficient.

There are those—including President Bush—who say the answer to America's voracious appetite is to feed it more oil by opening reserves in Alaska, California and elsewhere. Such a strategy ignores both reality and recent experience. Nor can it provide for our long-range security. The reason is simple: The world may not be running out of oil, but the United States is.

The federal government collects data on oil already discovered (called "reserves") and oil which might be found ("resources"). According to optimistic estimates of both, we now have a 25-year supply at current rates of consumption—less if the price falls again. Yet even when prices were high, production was steadily declining. Our cheap and easy oil has long since been found and burned; America is punctured by 600,000 wells compared to 6,000 in the Middle East. According to World Oil, a trade magazine, three-fourths of the world's dry holes last year were drilled in the United States. The number in Iraq: zero.

What about Alaska? Between the last oil crisis and this one, most of the North Slope oil was burned. Pressure is mounting to open up the Alaskan wilderness. How much oil is there? No one is sure. The most optimistic estimates put it at 29 billion barrels, though according to the U.S. Geological Survey, there's only a 5-percent chance of resources that large. But even assuming that we have that much—and that it would be economically and environmentally possible to get every last hypothetical drop out of the frigid ground—it could fuel the nation for only five years. A more likely outcome is a six- to 12-month supply (again assuming that prices stay high enough to make drilling cost-effective), after which we'd still have only one place to turn—OPEC.

Thus, the first goal has to be to get off of oil—from any source. The United States should commit itself to a 50-percent reduction in oil consumption by the year 2000. That is roughly the share of U.S. oil that would be imported by the turn of the century. Drastic changes are also needed in our use of coal, the chief producer of greenhouse gases and acid rain and a major factor in smog formation. A sensible target is a 50-percent reduction by 2020—by which time most U.S. power plants will have reached the end of their [illegible]

[illegible] sive expansion of atomic power with current technologies; and new, supposedly "meltdown-proof" designs could not make a significant contribution before the next century, if even then.)

Does that kind of reduction sound alarmingly drastic? It shouldn't. It's not only possible, but can be accomplished with existing technologies and policies that Americans have already shown themselves willing to accept.

Among the proven options is cogeneration, which involves putting the heat that would otherwise be wasted to some use: warming homes, offices and apartments or even running manufacturing processes. Sweden relies heavily on cogeneration; and Japan has emphasized similar efficiencies, with the result that their firms produce 11 percent more electricity—and twice as much steel—per unit of fuel consumed than we do.

Moreover, we have achieved extraordinary energy savings before, thanks to policies implemented during the administrations of Nixon, Ford and especially Carter. Automobile efficiency standards doubled the mileage of new American cars; insulation standards drove down the household consumption of energy; and energy pricing policies and government funding programs spurred development of highly efficient, promising new technologies.

One result was that there is a vast array of energy-saving techniques and new fuels waiting to be deployed. For example, huge trough-like mirrors capture and convert enough solar heat to produce electricity for 300,000 homes in Southern California. Solar-voltaic technology is within reach of competing with coal-, oil- and natural gas-fired plants. What is needed now is not more research, but purchase orders.

Electric cars and vans are ready to hit the street, but they can't compete with gasoline, which is cheaper than bottled water. Ironically, the government put an electric car on the moon, but the Big Three can't put one on the Great American Road. Ethanol can power homes and cars. Light bulbs, refrigerators, furnaces—all are now two to 10 times as efficient as they were in 1973.

Having coasted for 10 years on the momentum of these and other efforts, it's time to put the pedal to the metal. Some suggest that we start by taxing crude oil or gasoline, citing studies such as the EPA's recent finding that a $1.24 increase in the pump price of gas would cut consumption roughly 24 percent—yielding a $24-billion annual saving. But taxes are a tool, not a policy. First we need the plans for a new house, then perhaps a hammer to build it.

What could be achieved? Based on a 1988 staff analysis by the Office of Technology Assessment, an aggressive conservation program might resemble the following:

Action: Equip new cars with existing technologies ranging from four-valves-per cylinder to sleeker designs that catch less wind. These could boost average mileage to 43.8 miles per gallon, according to a study conducted by the [illegible] profit research group based in Washington. Then mandate other state-of-the art technologies to boost mileage or require non-polluting fuels. (General Motors has designed one electric car prototype and begun work on a second.)

Result: Automotive gasoline consumption is cut by 75 percent, oil imports by 50—about $30 billion a year at present prices. As an added bonus, carbon dioxide, the most difficult of pollutants to control, would drop by 50 percent or more.

Action: Put federal limits on carbon dioxide emissions equivalent to a coal-fired powerplant operating at 75-percent efficiency (the current average is about 35 percent). Utilities could switch to cleaner fuels, upgrade to improve efficiency or replace plants with new, cleaner-burning systems. Powerplants in Europe regularly achieve efficiencies of 90 percent by utilizing heat instead of wasting it, and California now generates 17 percent of its electricity from alternate fuels—up 11-fold since 1977.

Result: Utility fuel consumption declines by up to 50 percent.

Action: Require that when furnaces, air conditioners, hot-water heaters or refrigerators are replaced, the new units must be the most efficient available. Many local building codes already require replacement toilets to be water savers—the same could be done for furnaces. Or try the British Columbia approach: The state pays the salesperson a bounty for each high-efficiency appliance sold.

Result: Assuming continued population growth, total household energy consumption is capped at 1985 levels.

Pay Now or Pay Later

Some would say that such a program would be the end of consumer freedom of choice. They confuse change with sacrifice. It was a change to develop a vaccine for polio, and it no doubt had a grievous effect on manufacturers of iron lungs. But certainly it was no sacrifice. What Americans want isn't a gasoline-fueled car. What they want—and will pay for—is convenient, safe and comfortable travel.

Others will say that such a program would deal a devastating blow to the U.S. economy. Yet somehow the Japanese, German, Swedish and other economies already do quite well using roughly one-half as much energy per capita as the United States. To think that the technological genius of a nation capable of building a warplane invisible to radar and a submarine silent as a winter's night cannot build efficient cars and buildings is an insult to America.

In truth, the war to free America from oil—and Iraq—needn't have been fought in Kuwait. The weapons to win were developed years ago in our laboratories and proving grounds. What we need are leaders with the courage to deploy them.

5-7772

2/2

0171

FEARING OUTCRY, BIG OIL COMPANIES WILL TRIM PROFITS

PRICE OF GAS RESTRAINED

More Money to Be Set Aside for Future Expenses and Expected Legal Claims

By THOMAS C. HAYES

Fearful of public and Congressional outcry over the large profits that many oil companies are likely to report for the fiscal quarter that ends in two weeks, industry executives are trying to find ways to hold down those profits.

Their strategy takes two tacks. One is to hold down the increases in the retail price of gasoline. That may be news to motorists who have seen gas prices rise an average of 23 cents a gallon since the Iraqi invasion of Kuwait last month, but oil industry executives say a 36-cent-a-gallon increase would have been needed to offset the sharp increase in crude oil prices, which have nearly doubled this summer.

The oil companies' second strategy for reducing profits is to increase the amount of money they set aside, or hold in reserve, for future environmental expenses, for refinery and chemical-plant maintenance programs and for potential legal claims. Such a step is commonplace in the industry and conforms with accounting standards.

In trying to hold down profits, the oil industry is heeding the advice of the White House and senior Republicans in Congress.

Calls For Restraint

In a speech on Aug. 8, President Bush urged the oil companies to show restraint in raising gasoline prices. The next day, Senator Bob Dole of Kansas, the minority leader, sent a telegram to the chief executives of 11 major oil companies, warning that if gasoline price increases were not checked, the outcry would be overwhelming.

"I can assure you that it will be very difficult to stop legislation controlling the prices of petroleum products or taxing profits resulting from these increases should not action be taken by the oil industry," he said in the telegram.

The industry is anxious to avoid a replay of the 1970's, when angry consumers and legislators pilloried Big Oil as oil prices and company profits soared. A windfall profit tax took several billion dollars away from oil companies before crude oil prices plunged below $10 after 1985. Bryan Jacoboski, an [illegible] utives suppose now that "the best way to avoid any windfall profit tax is not to report any windfall profits."

One warning of potential backlash came Thursday, when Senator Kent Conrad, a North Dakota Democrat, told Energy Secretary James D. Watkins, "There will be universal outrage" if reports of soaring oil profits appear.

Mr. Watkins replied that antitrust officials in the Justice Department were the Administration's first line of defense against profiteering. He also said oil companies that engaged in the practice would be "hammered" by the Administration.

Senator Conrad said in an interview Friday: "If there is a significant surge in profits, we all know there will be a public reaction. I'm not engaged in oil-industry bashing. I am trying to understand what the President means when he says we will not allow profiteering. Where is the plan?"

Nonetheless, profit increases of more than 40 percent from those reported in the comparable fiscal quarter last year seem certain for at least four major oil companies, and many others are expected to show profits of close to 20 percent, Wall Street securities analysts say. In general, oil companies that will profit the most are those that produce a great deal of crude oil and thus will benefit from the near-doubling of crude oil prices.

"It's a great time to be a producer of oil, but it's a bad time to be a retail seller of gasoline," Mr. Jacoboski said.

Holding down prices at the gas pump could also help the larger oil companies in the future because smaller competitors might be squeezed out of gasoline retailing.

Smaller Company Hurt

One independent company, the East Coast Oil Corporation, which is based in Richmond and has 42 gas stations in Virginia, has had its daily sales volume reduced by 20 percent in the last month because its price are now a few pennies a gallon higher than nearby stations operated by major oil companies like Texaco and Mobil.

East Coast's president, John M. Steele, said he would have to sell the gas at a loss of a few pennies a gallon to match the major companies' prices. As it is, at an average price of $1.20 a gallon, he said he was making two-tenths of a cent a gallon in profit, before taxes and expenses. In early July, when he sold the same gasoline for 85 cents a gallon, three cents below the competing large oil companies, his operating profit was eight cents a gallon.

The oil companies' strategy of building up reserves to pay for future expenses is not uncommon.

"It's kind of a well-established tradition in the oil industry that any time your company realizes extraordinary earnings that you try to develop some extraordinary pocket to deeply hide those earnings," said Bernard J. Picchi, an analyst at Salomon Brothers. "Environmental charges have been the favorite in the last two years. I expect we will see more of them, and a lot more settlements of long-standing legal disputes."

Staying attuned to Congress has taken on a fresh urgency for oil executives, who see in the Persian Gulf crisis an opportunity to reclaim some of the political ground lost after the disastrous Exxon Valdez oil spill in Alaska

The blockade against Iraq and Kuwait crude has dramatically underscored the decline of the nation's oil production, which has fallen to about seven million barrels a day. The United States, which consumes about 16 million barrels a day, has become more dependent on low-cost crude imports. Daily crude imports were nearly eight million barrels a day before the Iraqi invasion on Aug. 2.

The oil industry wants Congress to back new tax credits that would reduce drilling expenses in the United States. It also wants to explore and produce oil in the Arctic National Wildlife Refuge in Alaska and the coastal waters near Southern California, the Carolinas and Florida.

Steps to Cut Profits

In examples of how oil companies are trying to curtail profits, ARCO and Oryx Energy announced steps last week that will bite into their third-quarter earnings. ARCO settled a long-running pricing dispute over Alaskan crude oil last week, agreeing to pay $287 million to Alaska's government.

Oryx, the nation's largest independent oil producer, said it had taken out new loans of nearly $1 billion, sharply raising its interest expense, to acquire 17 percent of its stock, held by the Pew family charitable trusts, for $968 million.

The oil industry is far from monolithic, as the plight of the independent gasoline marketers suggests. Many major oil companies, including Exxon, Mobil, Amoco and Texaco, are called "integrated" because they operate in virtually all phases of the industry: exploration, production, refining, transportation, service-station retailing and petrochemical manufacturing.

The jump in oil prices this quarter will benefit exploration and production units because each barrel will bring in sharply higher revenues, while the costs to find and pump the oil have not changed. Most refineries also should show higher profits because gasoline demand was strong during the quarter, plant operations were close to capacity and wholesale gasoline prices rose sharply.

On the other hand, petrochemical and gasoline marketing operations were squeezed. Petrochemical units were hurt because demand for products slowed while costs for crude oil, the major raw material for making plastics and other products, soared. And gasoline marketing divisions were unable to recover higher costs for wholesale gasoline deliveries because of the major oil companies' response to the President's call to keep retail prices in check.

2244-6. End

NYT 9/14/90

0172

원 본

외 무 부

종 별 :

번 호 : HUW-0400 일 시 : 90 0917 1620

수 신 : 장 관(경자,중근동,미북,정일)사본:주미대사(필)

발 신 : 주 휴스턴 총영사

제 목 : 석유가및 생산동향(14)

1.9.14.현재 서부텍사스 중질유 10월 인도가격은 어제보다 69센트 상승, 베럴당 31.76불에 거래됨

2.이는 이라크군대의 주쿠웨이트 프랑사대사 관저난입, 미국해군의 이라크 원유수송선에 대한 경고사격등 전쟁의 위험이 커지고있는데 기인한다함.

3.텍사스주의 OIL DRILLING RIGS 수는 작년 9월중순 현재 297개, 9.17.현재 349개로 52개 증가하였고, 미국전체는 작년 9월중순 현재 965개, 9.17.현재 1,060개로 95개 증가함.

(총영사 허승-국장)

공람	국제경제국	90.9.18	담당	과장	국장	차관보	차관	장관
					V			

경제국 2차보 미주국 중아국 정문국 안기부

PAGE 1

90.09.18 09:45 WG

외신 1과 통제관

0173

외 무 부

종 별 :

번 호 : IRW-0535 일 시 : 90 0916 1600

수 신 : 장관(중근동,통일,동자부) 기협

발 신 : 주 이란 대사

제 목 : 주재국 석유장관면담

금 9.15(토) 주재국 AGAZADEH 석유장관과 1630-1750 간 면담하였음. 요지아래 보고함 (전해진 참사관 배석).

1. 동자부장관 서한전달

석유장관은 동자부장관의 서한에 사의를 표하고, 한국에대한 원유공급확보에관한 자신의 약속을 다시한번 다짐함.

2. 쌍용, 선경의 원유도입

석유장관은 아국기업의 원유도입과 관련 자신의 견해를 동자부장관에 전달해줄것을 요청하면서, 쌍용, 선경의 요청에대한 언급에앞서 다음과같은 일반적 전망을 하였음.

-금번 중동사태는 악화될 가능성이 큼

-악화된 상황하에서 사우디, 오만, UAE, 카탈로부터의 원유는 미국등 이른바걸프만 평화군 파견국에 우선적으로 공급될것이며, 기타지역은 FORCE MAJUERE 조항의 적용으로 공급을 중단될것임.

-이란은 이러한 구속을 받지 않을것이므로 중동지역에서는 가장 안전한 원유 공급원이 될것임.

-태국, 비율빈, 대만등은 이와같은 전망을 염두에두고 각료를 이란에 파견, 원유도입을 추진하였으며 이들은 이란이 제시한가격(8.25 일)(DUBAI 프러스 0.25, OMAN 프러스 0.35 와 SPOT MARKET 차이의 반을 도입국이 부담)에 만족을 표시하였음.

-한국의경우 한국과 현시점에서 합의된 원유도입량은 앞으로 페만전쟁을 포함한 어떤사태하에서도 공급을 이행할것임.

가. 쌍용

쌍용의 원유 추가도입 희망에 대하여는 즉각 동의 회신을 발송하였음. 최근 쌍용이 사우디로부터 6 만 B/D 원유도입계약을 체결하였다는 소식을 듣고있음. 쌍용이 오랜

중아국 2차보 경제국 통상국 동자부

PAGE 1

공람	국제경제국	90년 9월 18일	담 당	과 장	국 장	차관보	차 관	장 관

90.09.18 14:27

외신 2과 통제관 EZ

0174

파트너인 이란에서가 아닌 불안전공급원으로 부터 원유를 도입하려고하는 의도를 이해할수없음. 앞으로 페만사태가 악화되고 그때가서 쌍용이 이란으로부터 원유를 도입하려고 할경우 이란은 이에 응하지 않을것임(본직은 쌍용의 사우디로부터의 원유도입은 공급원 다변화 방안의 일환일것이라고 설명함)

나. 선경

지난 9.4 유공관계자와 석유부 실무진간의 회담내용을 보고받았음(본직의 선경이 도입가격에대한 장관의 특별배려를 간곡히 요청한데대해) 선경은 쌍용과같은 오랜고객이 아니며, 일본상사와 같이 많은 물량을 도입하는것도 아니기 때문에 처음부터 일본상사가 도입하는 가격과 동일한 가격을 적용할수는 없음(본직은 일본상사가 이란으로 도입한원유를 한국상사에 전매할경우, 도입가격과 동일한 가격에서 실질적인 거래를하고, 다만 금융알선에서 이윤이 발생하는것으로 알기때문에 이란으로부터 도입하는 원유가격에 PREMIUM 을 붙일경우 도입의 실익이없다고 설명함)

문제는 추후 본인(장관)과 대사간에 다시 협의하기로 하고 일단 도입가격을 제외한 모든 절차에 관하여서는 양측실무진이 합의를 보도록 할것을 요청함(본직은 이에동의하고 장관과 본직간에 협의할 가격 RANGE 에 대하여문의) 선경의 도입가격은 도입시 PREMIUM 을 낸다고 하드라도 3 개월후에는 동 PREMIUM 이 ZARO 가 되도록 할것이며, 일본상사 도입가격도 각사간에 다소 차이가 있으므로 추후 협의를 통해 가격을 정하자고함.

IRW-0536 호 계속

외 무 부

암호수신

종 별 :

번 호 : IRW-0536 일 시 : 90 0916 1600

수 신 : 장관(중근동,통일,동자부) 기협

발 신 : 주 이란 대사

제 목 : IRW-0535 호의 계속

3. BIPC(과거 IJPC) BIPC 중 처음 시작하는 OLEFIN 은 LUMUS 사와 대림간에 구체적인 협조가 진행되고 있는것으로 알려, OLEFIN 과 직결되는 POLIMOR(HDPE,LDPE,P.P)는 이란측으로서는 대림이 맡아줄것을 희망하였으나, 대림이 이에 소극적인 태도임. 한편 선경은 선경이 경험을 갖고있는 AROMATIC 에의 참여만을 상정하고 있다고 알고있음(본직은 선경이 첫째 FINANCING 의무를 부담하지않고, 둘째수의 계약일경우 POLIMOR 에 UC 로 참가하는 가능성도 있다는 의견을 선경 관계자로부터 들었다고 알리면서 AORMATIC 에 선경이 참여를 원할경우 이란측으로부터 어느정도의 가능성을 보장받을수 있는지를 문의함) 선경이 POLIMOR 참여조건으로 제시한 두가지를 검토하여 회답을 주겠으며, 이란측의 기본적입장은 선경의 AROMATIC 참여를 환영하는것임.

4. 양국간 경협위개최 제 4 차 회의는 서울에서 금년 11 월중순경 개최(제 3차회의는 1989.12 예정이었으나 아측사정으로 1990.2 월로 연기)되기를 희망하여 동회의시 원유장기 공급에관한 기본양해각서, 상기 한국기업의 BIPC 참여계약서명등을 할수있도록 할것을 제의함(본직은 장관희망을 본부에 전달하겠다고 약속)

5. 금반 면담에서 포함된 BIPC 및 원유도입과관련한 석유장관의 의견은 해당기업이 참고하여야할 내용이라고 판단됨. 본보고내용의 진전상황을 추보하겠으며, 경협위개최 시기에관한 본부방침회시바람. 주재국이 전적인 관주도경제체제인관계로 아국기업과의 문제라할지라도 본직을 불러 협의하는것이 관행임을 참고로 알림.

(대사 정경일-국장

배용검토

공람	국제경제국	90년 9월 18일	담 당	과 장	국 장	차관보	차 관	장 관
				(서명)	(서명)			

중아국 2차보 경제국 통상국 동자부

PAGE 1 90.09.18 14:27

외신 2과 통제관 EZ

0176

원 본

외 무 부

종 별 :

번 호 : HUW-0401 일 시 : 90 0918 1630

수 신 : 장 관(경자,중근동,미북,정일) 사본:주미대사(필)

발 신 : 주 휴스턴 총영사

제 목 : 석유가 및 생산동향(15)

1.9.17.현재 서부텍사스 중질유 10월인도 가격은 어제보다 1.87불이 상승, 베럴당 33.63불에 거래됨.동가격은 83년도이래 최고의 가격이라하며 이락사태 발발전인 6주전가격의 2배라함.

2.금번 가격상승은 우랄산맥으로부터 발틱해로 연결되는 소련 송유관의 MAINTENANCE 에 문제가 생겨 원유수출에 지장을 초래하고 있다는 미확인 소문에 기인한다함.

(총영사 허승-국장)

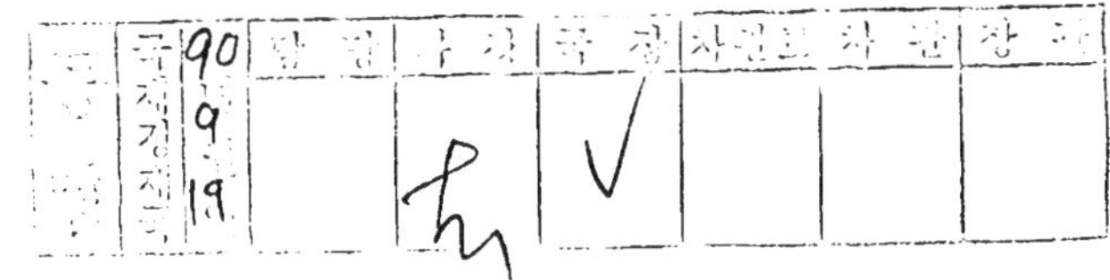

경제국 2차보 미주국 중아국 정문국 안기부 대책반

PAGE 1

90.09.19 09:50 WG

외신 1과 통제관

0177

원 본

외 무 부

종 별 :

번 호 : USW-4242 일 시 : 90 0918 1924

수 신 : 장 관(기협)

발 신 : 주 미 대사

제 목 : 석유 시장 및 유가 동향(18)

표제 관련 금 9.18 당지 언론 보도 내용을 종합보고함.

1.유가 동향

가. 9.7 원유 및 정유 제품 가격 (뉴욕 상품 시장,10월 인도 가격)

0 원유: 배럴당 33.63불 (전일 대비 1.87 불 상승)

0 휘발유: 갤런당 91.67 센트 (전일 대비 1.31 센트)

0 난방유: 갤런당 85.31 센트 (전일 대비 2.52 센트)

나. 9.17 의 원유 가격은 83.8 배럴당 32.20불을 기록한 이후 가장 높은 가격인바, 당지 전문가들은 이러한 유가 급등의 직접적인 원인으로 아래 사항을 거론하고 있음.

0 중동 지역의 긴장 고조

- 이락 군의 일부 서방국 대사관 침입 및 해당국의 이락 외교관 추방 조치

- 프랑스의 중동 파병 결정

- 이락 상공 봉쇄 논의

0 소련의 일부 소유 시설 고장에 관한 루머

다.그러나 전문가들은 금번 중동 사태 발발 직후 최최의 유가 앙등이 심리적인 반응에 의한것과는 달리 최근의 유가 인상은 사태의 장기화에 따른 원유 공급 부족 전망에 입각한 것이라고 관측하고있음. 특히 일부 전문가들은 사태 발생전 해상수송 중이던 원유로 인해 이락- 쿠웨이트산 원유 수입 금지의 충격이 당장 나타나지 않았으나 사태 가장기화 됨에 따라 대부분의 해상 수송 원유가 이미 소진되었으며 산유국들이 증산 중인 원유는 소비국에 도착되기 까지 수개월이 소요되는점을 지적, 10월중에는 원유 공급 부족 현상이 심화될것으로 예측하고 있음.

2.전략 비축 석유 사용 문제

0 부쉬 행정부는 지금까지 심각한 원유 공급 부족이 발생하지 않았다는점과 전략

경제국 미주국

PAGE 1

공람	국제경제국	담 당	과 장	국 장	차관보	차 관	장 관
				V			

90.09.19 10:41 WG

외신 1과 통제관

0178

비축 원유의 방출은 인위적인 가격 변동을 통해 시장질서를 교란한다는 점을들어 전략 비축 원유의 방출을 꾸준히 반대해 왔으나 최근에는 다소 신축적인 입장을 보이고 있음.

0 부쉬 행정분의 이러한 태도 변화는 아래 사항에 기인하는 것으로 관측되고 있음.

- 의회 및 소비자 단체등 미국 조야에서는 유가가 계속 배럴당 30불을 상회하고 있고, 10월중에는 원유 공급 부족 현상이 현실화할 것이라는 예상을 들어 전략 비축 원유의 방출을 강력히 요구하고 있음.

- 정치적으로도 11월중에는 중간 선거가 실시되고, 유가가 계속 앙등할 경우 부쉬 행정부의 중동 사태정책에 대한 국민 지지도도 하락될 것으로 예상됨.

0 다만 부쉬 행정부는 미국이 독자적으로 전략 비축원유를 방출할 경우 여타 소비국들이 자체 보유 비축원유를 사용하지 않고도 유가 인하 효과를 FREE-RIDE 할것을 우려하고 있는바, 9.28 개최예정인 IEA 이사회에서 전략 비축 원유의 공동 방출 문제가 집중 협의될 것으로 예상됨.

3. 9.18 당지 언론 보도 내용 별첨 FAX 송부함.

첨부: USW(F)- 2268

(대사 박동진-국장)

09/18/90 18:53 ☎202 797 0595 EMBASSY OF KOREA --- WOI 001/0

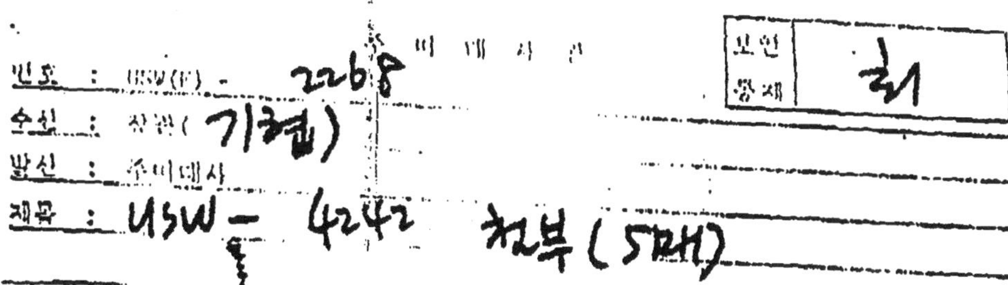

번호 : USW(F) - 2268 미 대 사 관
수신 : 장관 (기협)
발신 : 주미대사
제목 : USW - 4242 첨부 (5매)

보안 통제: 회

Pressure Is Mounting to Tap U.S. Oil Stockp

By NATHANIEL C. NASH

Special to The New York Times

WASHINGTON, Sept. 17 — After weeks of resisting calls to use the nation's Strategic Petroleum Reserve to soften the impact of soaring oil prices, the Administration is feeling growing pressure from both Congress and its own ranks to change its strategy. And events could conspire to hasten a decision that Republicans could find politically advantageous.

The White House has said it will consider using the reserve to compensate for crude oil shortages but will oppose using it to manipulate oil prices. However, Administration officials now say that supply disruptions expected in October could bring about a decision by the President to tap the oil stockpiles, a move that would almost certainly produce a drop in prices.

"We know a supply interruption is coming, and that it is going to hit sometime between the middle of September and the beginning of October," said W. Henson Moore, Deputy Secretary of Energy in a telephone interview on Friday. He said using the reserve was "under consideration by the Administration every day," adding, "It could change any day."

Indeed, drawing reserves from the petroleum stockpile of almost 600 million barrels of oil could serve both the policy and political goals of the Administration. The White House could legitimately say a decision to release oil in the reserve is a response to the loss of 4.3 million barrels a day of oil production by Iraq and Kuwait, a shortage with an impact that is only beginning to be felt here. The drop in prices from such a move would conveniently come weeks before the November election.

Prices of crude oil have risen sharply since Iraq invaded Kuwait and are almost certain to continue rising. Some members of Congress, both Democrats and Republicans, including Bob Dole, the Republican Party's leader in the Senate, have urged the White House to use the petroleum reserve to cushion the effect on the consumer.

Some political strategists are concerned that the high ratings the President has received for opposing President Saddam Hussein's seizure of Kuwait could evaporate if the public faces soaring prices for gasoline and heating oil.

"We have invested millions of taxpayer dollars in the oil reserves to make certain America would be protected from tyrants like Saddam Hussein who would use the oil lifeline to threaten our security," Senator Dole said last month, adding that the President "should strongly consider opening the taps."

But using the reserve as a way to orchestrate the price of world oil and gasoline goes against the free market instincts of the Bush Administration.

An often-heard refrain is that the President is not going to tap the reserves "just because the price of gasoline goes up 10 cents."

One official noted that oil-producing states would not necessarily favor a drop in oil prices, and that one of them, Texas, has broad representation in the Bush Administration.

Moreover, officials have repeatedly referred to restrictions that limit the stockpile's use to times of "severe energy supply disruption of significant scope and duration" that could have "a major adverse impact on national safety or national security."

But Administration officials say privately that the thinking may be changing. For one thing, the White House sees an imminent shortage coming. At the time of the Iraqi invasion, several weeks of oil shipments from Iraq and Kuwait were at sea, and they have yet to be delivered.

But once those shipments are delivered, the impact will begin to be felt. Mr. Moore, the Deputy Energy Secretary, said October was likely to be the hardest month, since new production from Saudi Arabia and other countries would take several months to reach refineries.

There may be other reasons for a new willingness by the Administration to tap the reserves. One Government official, who spoke on the condition of not being identified, said that a primary reason for resisting use of the reserve was to bring pressure on Saudi Arabia and other countries to increase their production.

"If we had tapped the S.P.R. we would have lost a big bargaining chip with the Saudis," said the official, adding that "now you are likely to see renewed pressure" on those in the Administration who did not want to use the reserves to rethink the hesitance.

A major consideration in using the nation's crude oil stockpiles would be to coordinate with Japan and Germany and other members of the International Energy Agency, which together have more than 400 million barrels of crude oil stockpiles.

Want to Act With Others

Bush Administration officials do not want the United States alone to release supplies and essentially give other countries a free ride on lower petroleum prices at its own expense.

Officials of the International agency met two weeks ago and "the prognosis the group did, showing a manageable situation in September and October, was valid then and is considered still 'alive,'" the official said. But he added that the mood could be changing in the United States because "there have been two weeks in which people have reflected intensely on the evolving situation."

Another meeting of the agency is scheduled for Sept. 28 in Paris.

Apart from an overt policy of tapping the reserves, the Administration might find other ways to bring some of the stockpile into the market. Legislation that passed Congress on Thursday gives the Administration permission to draw up to five million barrels from the reserves as a test.

But Mr. Moore and others warned that flooding the market with crude oil might not be the answer, and that the real cause of rising prices in the wake of the Iraqi invasion was insufficient refining capacity for gasoline and heating oil.

Thus the country could have unlimited supplies of oil and still suffer shortages if the nation's refineries cannot keep up with demand.

NYT 9/18/9

배부처	장관실	차관실	一차보	二차보	기획실	외정실	아주국	미주국	구주국	중아국	국기국	경제국	통상국	정문국	영교국	총무과	감사관

0180

Oil Prices Climb on War Fears

$1.87-a-Barrel Jump Puts Crude at $33.63, A Seven-Year High

By KEITH BRADSHER

Crude oil prices climbed yesterday on renewed concerns about a possible war in the Middle East, hitting a seven-year high in futures trading on the New York Mercantile Exchange.

Light sweet crude for October delivery rose $1.87 a barrel, or 5.9 percent, to settle at $33.63. The jump followed a $1.72-a-barrel increase last week in the benchmark contract for such oil.

As the price keeps rising, the Administration is feeling growing pressure from both Congress and within its own ranks to end its resistance and tap the nation's Strategic Petroleum Reserve. [Page D8.]

Alarmed by French Move

Traders were alarmed by the announcement on Saturday that France, which had close relations with Iraq through most of the 1980's, would send 4,000 troops to join the multinational force in Saudi Arabia, said Michael Wilner, the president of the Hilltop Trading Company, an independent trading and brokerage firm.

"The overall tone of the political situation is that there's less and less talk of peace," said Christian D. Gohler, an energy futures trader and vice president at Merrill Lynch Futures Inc. "By the end of the week we could certainly see $35, and in a few weeks, potentially we could see $40" a barrel, he added.

Prices also rose yesterday because speculators became convinced that the market had established a clear pattern of steady increases and rushed to invest, Mr. Wilner said, adding, "There's nothing that brings participants into the market like a clearly trending market."

Oilfields Could Be Destroyed

A war in the Persian Gulf could destroy many oilfields and disrupt the supply of crude. Traders expect prices for the remaining supplies to soar if war breaks out because such a conflict probably would not reduce worldwide demand for oil and the military operations might even increase demand.

Michael Libbey, a spokesman for the [illegible] Corporation, said the price of [illegible] make gasoline had risen by 29 cents a gallon since Aug. 1 while the company had raised the wholesale gasoline price that it charges service stations by 19 cents a gallon. "We cannot absorb higher raw material costs indefinitely," he added. "Eventually, prices will have to rise."

The main reason prices have not risen further, and might continue to stay below $40, is that oil companies have large stockpiles of crude, Mr. Gohler said. These stocks accumulated during the summer partly because of production problems at refineries, and remained unusually high in the United States in the first week of September, the American Petroleum Institute said last Tuesday.

Trading was frantic in the closing minutes yesterday, with the October contract climbing 55 cents in the last five minutes, said Robert S. Jonke, an energy futures trader at Cargill Investor Services. "It seemed everyone was scared," he added.

Many traders wanted to buy oil yesterday but delayed doing so in hopes that prices would fall, and were forced to buy at the end of the day when the hoped-for decline never came, Mr. Gohler said.

Rises at Beginning of Week

Yesterday's trading reflected a recent tendency of the oil markets to rise early in the week as bullish traders accumulated contracts, and then fall late in the week as traders sold those contracts to avoid holding large positions over the weekend, Mr. Wilner said. "Two days is a long time if a news item hits and you can't get into the market," he added.

A rumor of pipeline problems that might depress Soviet exports helped push up prices in early trading. The rumor was later denied.

Gasoline for October delivery climbed 1.31 cents, or 1.4 percent, to 91.67 cents a gallon, while the heating oil contract was up 2.52 cents, or 3 percent, to 85.31 cents a gallon.

Product prices showed more modest percentage increases than crude oil prices because they depend more on domestic stockpiles and refinery capacity than crude oil prices, traders said.

The settlement price yesterday of the October contract exceeded the previous record of $32.20 a barrel, set in August 1983, and was the highest level since the Merc began the trading of oil futures contracts on March 30, 1983.

The benchmark light sweet crude includes 10 grades of oil that are easily refined because they are less dense and have less sulfur than other grades.

Spot and official Government prices for oil before then are not directly comparable because they do not reflect the variety of blends allowed for delivery under the Merc contract, or the types of delivery allowed. Official prices ranged as high as $41 a barrel in 1981, although some countries undercut their posted prices so as to increase sales.

But after adjusting for inflation, crude oil is much less expensive now than it was in 1983.

NYT
9/18/90

2268-2

Crude Futures Soar Past $33 a Barrel to Record On War Jitters, Possible Supply Disruptions

By CAROLYN PHILLIPS
Staff Reporter of THE WALL STREET JOURNAL

Propelled by a weekend of events pointing to the likelihood of war in the Middle East and possible supply disruptions, crude oil futures prices soared past the $33 a barrel mark, setting record highs on the New York Mercantile Exchange.

"This market doesn't want to go down," said Nauman Barakat, vice president, energy futures, at Merrill Lynch Consumer Markets. "Even when there is bearish news, the market seems to be almost immune to it," he said.

But the past few days have brought little in the way of bearish news to test his theory, he concedes. On Sunday, the United Nations Security Council unanimously condemned Iraq's raids against French, Canadian, Dutch and Belgian embassy compounds in Kuwait and several countries made moves to expel Iraqi diplomats in retaliation. Talk of an air traffic embargo has intensified. President Bush's appearance on Iraqi television Sunday was met with strong anti-U.S. sentiment that many analysts said left little room for a nonmilitary resolution of the crisis spawned by Iraq's Aug. 2 invasion of Kuwait.

When crude oil futures traders started factoring in the weekend's events yesterday, they annihilated the high of $32.35 for crude contracts in the seven-year history of the New York Merc. The October crude contract settled $1.87 a barrel higher at $33.63, erasing the previous high set in August 1983.

The weekend's bullish headlines were aided considerably by word from President Bush yesterday that he wanted to increase the size of the nation's Strategic Petroleum Reserve but had no immediate plans to tap into it to ease a tightness of crude supplies.

Also on the supply side, traders attributed part of the sharp gain to news that the Soviet port of Ventspils would undergo two to four weeks of long-delayed maintenance starting Saturday. Some 290,000 barrels of crude oil is exported from there each day. It was unclear whether that production will be totally curtailed or simply cut back during the repairs.

The New York Merc trading patterns were echoed in London where the November contract for Brent, a widely traded benchmark crude, jumped to $33.00 a barrel. In Europe as well as in the U.S., trading was light. Analysts say sellers are scarce in this market where so many indicators suggest prices could go higher. "Any dips in the market bring out a lot of buyers," Mr. Barakat said.

The strength in crude carried over into gasoline and heating oil. Gasoline, which has shown slower gains than crude recently, added 1.31 cents to the October contract to settle at 91.67 cents a gallon. The October contract for heating oil, boosted in part by a huge storage tank fire in Texas over the weekend, picked up 2.52 cents a gallon to finish at 85.31 cents. Outer months of crude, gasoline and heating oil contracts all closed higher, as well.

9/18 WSJ

Oil Futures Hit $33.63 A Barrel

9/18 WP

From News Services

Crude oil futures prices zoomed to record levels yesterday amid reports that the Soviet Union was cutting back deliveries to the West and on continued concern over the situation in the Middle East.

On the New York Mercantile Exchange, a barrel of oil for delivery in October ended the day up $1.87 at $33.63 a barrel, breaching the Merc's record $32.35 trading price of Aug. 2, 1983.

But stock prices, which recently have sunk with every increase in oil prices, shrugged off yesterday's news. The Dow Jones industrials finished the day up 3 points in light trading.

Mary Haskins of PaineWebber Inc. in New York said she had been told by one oil trading company that its supply of crude to be delivered through the Soviet's Ural pipeline had been cut. Her colleague Michael McDermott said his industry sources were reporting that some big oil companies were out buying North Sea crude to make up for the loss of Soviet oil.

There was no Soviet confirmation of delivery problems to Western Europe.

Contracts for unleaded gasoline for October delivery ended the day up 1.31 cents at 91.67 cents a gallon, while home heating oil was up 2.52 cents to 85.31 cents a gallon.

2268-3

0182

Oil shortfall pushes prices up

By Richard Gourlay in London

WORLD oil prices rose close to an eight-year high yesterday as traders said underlying shortages of immediately available crude oil were becoming increasingly apparent because of the Gulf crisis.

The November futures price for the benchmark North Sea Brent crude rose $1.50 a barrel to $32.25, while on the New York Mercantile Exchange the November contract for the US benchmark West Texas Intermediate gained nearly a dollar by midday to $32.10.

Traders said further price rises towards $34 a barrel were likely as fears grew that Saudi Arabia would not be able to increase its production enough to compensate for lost output from Iraq and Kuwait.

"Nobody can come up with any reason to explain why the market should not go higher," said one trader.

Crude prices rose initially on rumours that the Soviet Union, the world's largest producer of oil and natural gas, had suffered damage to one of its pipelines carrying crude oil from the Urals.

Soviet officials denied any knowledge of supply problems but traders said the incident underlined the fragile balance between supply and demand. A fundamental tightness in the oil markets was beginning to become more important than reaction to political developments as the main spur for higher prices, traders said.

Saudi Arabia has been increasing its export of crude by running down stocks held in floating storage tankers. However, the new oil Saudi Arabia will pump is likely to be a heavier crude, from which refineries will be able to extract relatively less of the high value gasoline, kerosene and naphtha products that the world most urgently requires.

The immediate shortage was highlighted by a Brent cargo for immediate delivery to a refinery which traded at a $3 premium to the November contract.

The oil markets also began to take on board planned production shutdowns in the North Sea starting in November which will add to the shortage of crude oil. The Brent field is due to be fitted with extra safety valves and the Forties Field is to undergo routine maintenance.

Traders say any disruption in supplies in the US that added to demand for oil now destined for the European market would give a further sharp shock to world oil prices.

FT

9/18/90

2268 -4

0183

Oil Profit Prospects: Dim to Brilliant

By THOMAS C. HAYES

With crude oil prices surging above $30 a barrel, Amerada Hess could see its profits triple in this quarter, according to Wall Street estimates, while those of Mobil Oil are likely to rise only 13 percent.

The sharp difference reflects the companies' mix of businesses. Companies like Amerada Hess that are big producers of crude oil will show the biggest gains — unless they can reduce the increases through accounting ploys or by moving big costs onto the books for the quarter. The smallest gains will be recorded by companies like Mobil that are big gasoline marketers and chemical producers and must buy a considerable amount of crude oil in addition to what they produce.

Independent gasoline retailers could see declines in profits, and some small retailers may even post deep losses because the increases in gasoline prices at the pump, about 23 cents a gallon, have not kept pace with the prices of crude oil or wholesale gasoline. Wholesale prices have increased an average of 36 cents.

Still, the major oil companies that are integrated in various aspects of the oil business — crude oil production, refining, petrochemicals and gasoline marketing — are all expected to show gains.

Bryan Jacoboski, an oil analyst for Paine Webber Inc., is forecasting quarterly earnings increases of more than 40 percent above the level a year ago for the British Petroleum Company, the Phillips Petroleum Company and the Unocal Corporation; about 20 percent for the Amoco Corporation, the Chevron Corporation and Texaco Inc., and between 13 and 15 percent for the Exxon Corporation and ARCO.

Before the Mideast crisis erupted six weeks ago, he had expected that oil prices would not exceed $20 a barrel in the quarter and that large producers like Exxon, Mobil, Texaco, Chevron and ARCO would see no year-to-year improvement in profits in the quarter.

Many analysts now expect prices to average at least $25 a barrel for the quarter, a 41 percent jump from the average price of $17.75 a barrel that the nation's refiners paid for all grades of domestic crude a year earlier. Light sweet crude oil reached a seven-year high yesterday on the New York Mercantile Exchange, rising $1.87 a barrel, or 5.9 percent, to settle at $33.83.

With prices at this level, Mr. Jacoboski and most industry analysts say, the high oil revenues will more than overcome the financial setbacks in gasoline marketing, as well as narrower profits from chemical operations, for most of the major oil companies.

In his analysis, Mr. Jacoboski estimated that sharply higher oil prices would enable the Amerada Hess Corporation, the nation's 15th-largest oil company, to report a tripling of profits in the quarter, to $2.40 a share, compared with 77 cents a share, unless the company takes substantial write-offs. Before the Iraq invasion on Aug. 2, Mr. Jacoboski had forecast that Amerada's profits would increase by 30 percent, to $1 a share.

He pointed to several factors that are sharply raising the company's revenues. Early in July, with oil prices at about $18 a barrel, Amerada decided to purchase large volumes of crude oil at that price for deliveries it is now taking at its refineries. Also, Amerada uses the first-in, first-out method of determining the value of its crude-oil inventories at the end of each quarter, and that will contribute to the expected profit rise.

Another factor is that Amerada is a large refiner along the Atlantic Coast, but not a large gasoline retailer. Rather, it mostly sells gasoline in the wholesale market, where prices have risen in line with those of crude oil, to retailers.

"Anyone producing crude makes more money," said Warren M. Shimmerlik, an oil analyst at County NatWest in New York. "And the refining business, which traditionally does not do well when crude prices go up, is doing well because of the concerns about product supplies."

Most oil giants like Exxon, Mobil, Texaco, Chevron and Amoco have lost money at the gas pump, or made little profit there, since the crisis erupted. That is because they held down the increases in pump prices in a move calculated to win favor with Congress, consumers and President Bush.

Exxon, Mobil, ARCO and the Shell Oil Company will also report lower profits in their chemical units, where a slump in demand prevented them from passing along higher costs caused by rising crude prices. Crude oil is the main raw material in chemical manufacturing.

ARCO's gain would have been much higher if the company had not lost millions of dollars by restraining prices in the first three weeks after the Iraq invasion. ARCO, the largest gasoline retailer in California before the crisis, ended the practice after it ran out of gasoline at several locations, particularly in Arizona.

ARCO could afford the losses because unlike other large oil companies, it exclusively supplies its refineries with crude oil from its own production unit. Even the largest gasoline retailers, like Shell and Chevron, must buy crude oil on the wholesale market to feed their refineries.

ARCO also reduced its profits in the quarter by agreeing to pay $287 million to the Alaskan government to settle a longstanding legal dispute over the value of oil produced from ARCO's wells in Prudhoe Bay.

British Petroleum provides a rough gauge of how much profit ARCO could have recorded in the period. Mr. Jacoboski forecasts an increase of 52 percent for the company, to $1.25 a share. British Petroleum, which like ARCO derives much of its production from Prudhoe Bay oilfields, is benefiting from sharp reductions in debt payments as well as higher crude oil prices, he said.

Profits at Phillips Petroleum will increase 43 percent, to 60 cents a share, because Phillips is getting higher prices for propane, butane and other natural-gas liquids, the Paine Webber analyst said. Phillips is the nation's largest producer of natural-gas liquids.

But in the long run, high oil prices could prove damaging for the industry. Above $40 a barrel, political pressure and an urgency to find substitute fuels could prove damaging to oil companies' prospects for steadily increasing earnings.

George F. Friesen, an analyst at Deutsche Bank Capital in New York, said, "The assumption is that higher oil prices are always beneficial to oil company earnings, but that assumption is incorrect after a certain point because a lot of the increase could be taxed."

He added, "After you are over $30, you enter a danger zone." He said the prospect that Congress would reenact a windfall profit tax becomes more likely for every dollar a barrel oil prices exceed $30, although, he added, President Bush would likely attempt to veto such a tax.

Analysts said oil executives would also attempt to mute new calls in Congress for a windfall profit tax by employing accounting devices that would lower profit levels for the quarter. These include special charges against income for anticipated environmental expenses, refinery maintenance, legal claims and other unusual items.

"The companies that are likely to report real strong earnings — and most of them should — will work hard to find ways to tuck those earnings away somewhere," said Mr. Shimmerlik of County NatWest. "In general, of course, things are going fundamentally quite well."

2268-5. End

0184

외 무 부

종 별 :

번 호 : JAW-5677 일 시 : 90 0920 1806

수 신 : 장관(경기,기협,통이,아일)

발 신 : 주일대사(경제)

제 목 : IMF 의 세계경제전망

국제통화기금(IMF) 은 이라크의 쿠웨이트침공으로 인한 석유가격 인상후 국제기관으로서는최초로 금년 및 내년의 세계경제 전망을 9.19.발표하였는바, 요지하기 보고함.(아사히 9.20. 석간)

1. 석유가격

0 석유가격은 내년도에는 하락예상

-금번 석유위기의 영향은 한정적으로서 70년대의석유위기만큼 심하지 않음.

2. 세계경제 성장

0 내년도 세계경제는 2 프로대 성장예상

0 선진국간 경제성장 격차 확대예상

-일, 서독, 프랑스는 비교적 높은 성장 예상되나,미, 영, 카나다는 1 프로대 성장예상

0 경제개혁으로 인한 혼란상태에 석유가격상승까지 겹진 쏘련, 동구는 금년은 4.6 프로마이너스 성장, 내년은 2.7 프로 마이너스 성장 예상

3. 국제수지

0 금년은 일본의 흑자와 미국의 적자 축소예상

0 현 환율에 변동없을 경우, 내년은 일본의흑자와 미국의 적자 모두 확대 예상.끝

(공사이한춘-국장)

국	90 9 21						
		담 당	과 장	국 장	차관보	차 관	장 관

경제국 아주국 경제국 통상국

PAGE 1

90.09.20 21:44 CT

외신 1과 통제관

0185

홍

외 무 부

종 별 :

번 호 : USW-4297 일 시 : 90 0920 1905

수 신 : 장관(경일, 기협, 경기,통일,통기)

발 신 : 주미대사

제 목 : IMF 세계 경제 보고서

1. 9.19 IMF 는 90년도 WORLD ECONOMIC OUTLOOK 보고서를 발표하였는바, 주요내용은 아래와같음.

가. 최근 중동 사태에 따른 유가 인상으로 세계경제는 실업율 증가, 인플레율 상승등 성장이 둔화될것이나, 금번 유가 인상의 충격은 과거 1,2차 석유위기보다는 심각 하지 않을 것이므로 미국을 비롯한 주요국 경제가 경기 후퇴(RECESSION)에 접어들 지는 않을 것임.,

나. 원유 가격은 90년 4/4 분기중 배럴당 26불,91년 4/4 분기까지는 배럴당 21불을 유지할 것으로 전망되며, 이경우 세계 경제 성장율은 89년의3 푸로에서 90년에는2 푸로로 감소할것이나 91 년에는 다시 2.5 푸로로 증가할것임.

다. 90-91년 주요국별 경제성장율 전망은 아래와같음.(90년, 91년 순, 퍼센트)

0 선진국: 2.6, 2.4

- 미국: 1.3, 1.7

- 일본: 5.1, 3.7

- 서독: 3.9, 3.3

0 개도국: 2.2, 4.2

- 아시아국가: 90-91년중 5 푸로 내외(아시아지역 개도국은 수출증진에 힘입어 90년대초반 가장 활발한 경제 성장을 시현할것임.)

- 동구권 및 중남미 국가: 90년중 경제안정화계획 및 인플레이션 억제를 위한 긴축 정책으로 마이너스 성장을 기록할 것으로 예상되나, 이러한 정책들이 성공할 경우 91년에는 높은 성장율을 기록할 것으로 전망.

라. 한편 선진국의 인플레이션율은 유가 인상의여파로 89년의 4.8 푸로에서 90년에는 0.25-0.5 푸로정도 증가할것이나 91년에는 다시 4.3 푸로로 감소할것임.

경제국 ③ 2차보 통상국 ② 안기부 경기원

PAGE 1

공람	국제경제국	90.9.21	담당	과장	국장	차관보	차관	장관

90.09.21 09:47 BX

외신 1과 통제관

0186

2. 동보고서는 특히 아시아 지역의 4개 신흥 공업국에 관하여 언급, 이들 국가들의 경상 수지흑자가내수 증가 및 해외 수요 감퇴에 따른 수출 부진으로 감소해 나갈것이라고 전망하고 있음.

3. 상기 보고서는 10월초 입수 가능한바, 9.19자 IMF 보도자료 및 9.20 당지 언론 보도 내용 별첨 FAX 송부함.

첨부: USW(F)-2313 (10 매)

(대사 박동진-국장)

PAGE 2

0187

IMF Forecasts Growth, Despite Oil Price Rises

By RICHARD LAWRENCE
Journal of Commerce Staff

WASHINGTON — Higher economic growth worldwide and in the United States is projected by the International Monetary Fund's staff, despite the recent surge in oil prices.

The staff, in its semiannual World Economic Outlook released Wednesday, also suggested that inflation in the United States and the other industrial nations, as a group, will remain in 1991 at about this year's rates.

The U.S. international payments deficit on current account next year may increase slightly, but decline in terms of U.S. gross national product, according to the report.

Separately, Alan Greenspan, the Federal Reserve Board chairman, told a congressional panel that while the chances of a U.S. recession have "clearly risen," partly because of higher oil prices, the economy may improve after the oil price "shock" is absorbed.

The IMF staff, in its projections, assumed that oil prices the rest of this year will average $26 a barrel and by late next year fall to $21 a barrel.

IMF economists said this projection was based on two different scenarios — a resolution by next spring of the present Mideast crisis or, if a military-political standoff continues, more oil output by Saudi Arabia, Venezuela and the United Arab Emirates to offset a lack of supplies from Kuwait and Iraq.

The $21 a barrel price, an IMF analyst noted, was the Organization of Petroleum Exporting Countries' target price just before Iraq's invasion of Kuwait. Moreover, he said, current market prices for forward delivery of oil by late 1991 jibe with the $21 a barrel assumption.

The global economy, the IMF staff said, should grow by 2% this year and by 2.5% in 1991, after adjusting for inflation. The pickup in growth mainly will be in the developing countries, primarily in Latin America and Eastern Europe, it estimated.

The staff put U.S. economic growth this year at 1.3% and growth next year at 1.7%. Relatively low interest rates, a cheap dollar and the projected fall in oil prices were cited as factors for this increase.

Before the recent oil price rise, the IMF staff had projected 1.5% U.S. economic growth this year and 2.4% in 1991.

Economic growth in both Japan and West Germany, currently the two fastest growing industrial nations, will slow in 1991, the IMF staff suggested. Japan's output may decline from a projected 5.1% this year to 3.7%, while West Germany's is expected to slip from 3.9% to 3.3%.

The growth rate this year for the industrial nations as a whole is estimated at 2.6% this year and 2.4% in 1991. Inflation in these countries will average about 4% this year and next, according to IMF projections.

The developing nations' economic growth this year is forecast at 2.7%, down from last year, mainly because of contracting economies in Latin America and Eastern Europe.

Next year, however, these economies may recover so that growth in the countries as a whole will jump to 4.2%, the IMF staff indicated. It also suggested a very sharp downturn in inflation next year in both Latin America and Eastern Europe.

Developing countries' total foreign debt is expected to hit $1.35 trillion by the end of 1991, up 9% from the end of 1989.

DoC 9/20/90

0188

By CLYDE H. FARNSWORTH

Special to The New York Times

WASHINGTON, Sept. 19 — Despite oil price increases stemming from the Middle East crisis, the United States will avoid a recession next year and experience even faster growth than in 1990, the International Monetary Fund said today.

The global lending agency, in its first assessment of the impact of oil price rises since Iraq's invasion of Kuwait Aug. 2, concluded that the United States will not exprience the growth contractions of the rest of the world, but that most other countries will also avoid an actual economic decline.

The upbeat analysis of the I.M.F. staff is in line with projections of Bush Administration economists, but counters forecasts of many private economists who, citing rising inflation, a fall-off in real estate values and weak consumption, see a decline ahead for the United States.

Recession Is Expected

In its Blue Chip Economic Indicators letter for September, a compilation of opinion of 50 prominent economists, the I.M.F. noted that the "majority of the panel now expects recession to start this year or next."

The I.M.F. projections appeared today in its World Economic Outlook, a publication prepared for the joint annual meeting here next week of the I.M.F. and its sister lending agency, the World Bank.

While higher oil prices will cause somewhat weaker economic growth and higher inflation than would have otherwise been the case, the impact will be "much less" than in the 1970's, the last time oil prices surged dramatically, said Jacob A. Frenkel, the I.M.F.'s director of research.

Oil prices have about doubled since July to around $35 a barrel. In the mid-1970's, prices quadrupled.

I.M.F. economists said they based their forecasts on the "plausible" scenario that oil prices will average $26 a barrel for the remainder of 1990 before dropping to $21 a barrel by the fourth quarter of 1991. The $21 figure is a reference price set by the Organization of Petroleum Exporting Countries before the Iraqi invasion.

The projections assume that most of the four million barrels a day in production missing from Iraq and Kuwait will be gradually offset by increased supplies, as currently promised, from Saudi Arabia, the United Arab Emirates and Venezuela.

"If you had increased production of the order of four million barrels a day by these countries," said Ernesto Hernandez-Cato, a senior adviser in the I.M.F.'s research department, "the crude demand/supply situation would be restored to an approximate balance that would not be inconsistent with the price in the range of $21 to $25 a day."

Moderating oil prices will help in avoiding recession.

The reasons cited for the improving prospects in the United States are the diminishing impact of oil price increases, lower interest rates expected to arrest the declines in housing and consumer durable purchases and a depreciating dollar, which should help performance of American exports next year.

But American growth is likely to be sluggish, with the economy growing by only 1.7 percent next year, compared with 1.3 this year.

Although the economic growth rat[illegible]ermany and Japan are seen fall[illegible]ext year, their actual rates will still be substantially ahead of the United States. The I.M.F. sees growth tapering off in Germany from 3.9 percent to 3.3 percent and in Japan from 5.1 percent to 3.7 percent.

The unification of East Germany with West Germany is expected to result in a "temporary fall in output and employment," the I.M.F. report said. At the same time, Germany will become an even bigger importer, especially of investment goods, to restructure the East German economy.

For the short term, the I.M.F. said, there is likely to be "upward pressure" on prices, interest rates and the value of the Deutsche mark. But "over time, the short-run aggregate demand effects of unification would gradually be offset by the increase in productive capacity," causing interest rate and price pressures to subside, the report added.

2413 — 2

09/20/90 18:24 ☎202 797 0595 EMBASSY OF KOREA 002

0189

IMF: Gulf Crisis Not Likely To Cause a World Recession

Appraisal Assumes Major Oil Price Declines

By Hobart Rowen
Washington Post Staff Writer

The Persian Gulf oil crisis will weaken the global economy over the next year, boosting unemployment and inflation rates slightly, but it is not likely to tip the world into a recession, the International Monetary Fund said yesterday.

This optimistic appraisal, issued prior to the annual meeting of the World Bank and IMF here next week, is based on the assumption that the price of oil—at $33.18 yesterday—will come down to $26 a barrel in the last quarter of this year, then decline to $21 by the fourth quarter of 1991.

By the end of next year, the IMF said, the price of oil is likely to be back where it was before the crisis and then continue to be level in real terms, that is, adjusted for inflation. The net damage, according to the IMF's annual World Economic Outlook, might be a half-point annual loss in the real growth rates of major industrial countries and a quarter- to half-point rise in the inflation indexes.

The agency said that Third World countries, taken as a whole, will actually benefit slightly from the oil price increase because there are several large oil-exporting countries among them. But a senior official warned that the IMF might seek to borrow from those Third World countries enjoying that profit and lend the money at below-market rates to others hard hit by the rise in prices.

Countries feeling the impact of higher oil should allow the price increase to be passed on to business and consumers and make no attempt to ease monetary policy, the agency said, to avoid inflation.

The report warned labor unions not to try to offset higher prices through "an escalation of wages and a subsequent wage-price spiral." Because an increase in oil prices involves a decline in national income, "real wages as well as profits will unavoidably be lower than they would have been otherwise," the report said.

Jacob Frenkel, director of research for the IMF, acknowledged that the continuing uncertainties relating to the Persian Gulf crisis could result in a much higher price of oil, upsetting the optimistic economic projections.

But if the IMF's expectations are realized, global economic growth would drop from 3 percent in 1989 to 2 percent this year, then recover to 2.5 percent in 1991. In the United States, real gross national product would fall from 2.5 percent last year to 1.3 percent this year and recover to 1.7 percent in 1991.

The prospective slight improve-

See WORLD BANK, E4, Col. 1

IMF Report Says World Recession Is Not Likely

WORLD BANK, From E1

ment in the U.S. economy next year was attributed to not only the assumed fall in oil prices in 1991, but also the recent decline of the dollar IMF officials said may trigger a resumption of larger exports next year.

Frenkel, responding to a number of questions implying skepticism, defended the projections as within reason and noted that even if oil prices were to settle at around current levels, the impact would be much less than during the oil "shocks" of the 1970s. Oil prices quadrupled in 1973-74, then tripled in 1979-80.

Ernesto Hernandez-Cata, a senior IMF adviser in charge of developing the oil projections, said he "did a lot of praying" while working them out. He acknowledged that actual oil prices "will depend on the military and political outcome" in the Persian Gulf, and added that the IMF did not pretend to have expertise in those areas.

Hernandez-Cata said, "The situation is at risk, but the [IMF] scenario is plausible" and consistent with a political settlement next spring. It is also consistent, he said, with a stalemate in the Persian Gulf that nevertheless allows Saudi Arabia and other countries to boost crude oil output by about 4 million barrels a day.

2313 -3

0190

IMF warns against oil subsidies

By Stephen Fidler, Euromarkets Correspondent, in Washington

ANY ATTEMPT to soften the blow of higher oil prices would be counter-productive and their impact should be passed straight through to consumers, the International Monetary Fund said yesterday.

In its most important regular assessment of the world economy, the World Economic Outlook, the Fund urged western governments to learn the lessons of the 1970s. There should be no attempts to subsidise oil prices to western consumers or ease the impact by loosening monetary policy.

The Fund said that relaxing monetary policy would lead to pressures that "would evolve into an inflationary process of increasing severity."

Mr Jacob Frenkel, chief IMF economist, said the impact of higher oil prices would be less severe than in the two oil shocks of the 1970s. Assuming no war broke out, the absolute increase in oil prices looked likely to be less than on either occasion. The industrialised countries had weaned themselves away from oil as a result of conservation measures introduced since the 1970s.

He cited three reasons which should stop governments subsidising oil prices:

o subsidies would worsen fiscal deficits and add an additional burden to government budgets;

o market intervention would lead to pressures that would one day burst, and also lead to a misallocation of resources;

o subsidies would run counter to conservation efforts, which have already helped industrialised countries cope with higher oil prices.

The report predicts a modest slowdown in growth in the industrialised countries and a rise in inflation because of higher oil prices.

But the impact on east Europe is expected to be especially severe. These countries are highly dependent on oil as a source of energy, and are already suffering the impact of economic reform and the ending of subsidies on energy exports from the Soviet Union.

The report comes as a senior monetary official in Washington outlined details of IMF proposals to soften the blow of higher oil prices on some developing countries.

These would provide for interest rate concessions on IMF credits for those countries hit worst by the Gulf crisis outside the Middle East.

The idea, according to the official, would be for countries benefiting directly from higher oil prices to establish a fund to subsidise interest payments to these countries. The poorest countries already have access to subsidised Fund credits, but richer countries, such as Philippines, India, Brazil and Jamaica, did not.

The proposal is likely to be considered when the finance ministers and central bank governors of the Group of Seven industrialised countries meet in Washington at the weekend. The meeting precedes the annual meetings of the IMF and World bank.

However, the official said it was not felt that a special oil facility was needed and there was sufficient flexibility within current rules to accommodate increased borrowings from needy countries.

Reinforcing the analysis of the World Economic Outlook, the official said industrialised countries should leave their targets for nominal growth in gross domestic product unchanged. A rise in oil prices would therefore mean that higher inflation would be offset by lower growth. However, this would lead to improved prospects for growth in the medium term.

He described the current rise in oil prices as a "small oil shock without recycling," in a reference to the recycling of Opec oil surpluses that commercial banks undertook in the 1970s.

IMF WORLD ECONOMIC OUTLOOK

Higher oil prices expected to hit grow

tephen Fidler, Euromarkets Correspondent, in Washington

HIGHER oil prices will intensify the expected slowdown of world economic growth, according to the International Monetary Fund.

Output is expected to expand 2 per cent this year and pick up slightly to 2.4 per cent in 1991, according to the Fund's World Economic Outlook, published today.

The Fund has lowered its expectations for growth since it last published its economic forecasts in the spring, largely because of higher oil prices. The new projections - which assume no war in the Gulf - are based on oil prices averaging $26 a barrel for the rest of this year, gradually declining to $21 by the end of next year.

The growth expectations compare with 3 per cent world output growth in 1989 and 4.1 per cent in 1988.

The forecasts show the output growth in the industrialised countries being trimmed to 2.6 per cent this year and 2.4 per cent next.

The Fund expects significantly lower growth in North America and the UK, but economic expansion remaining relatively strong in Japan and Germany.

Inflation in the industrial countries will also pick up to an average 4.8 per cent this year, before slipping to 4.3 per cent in 1991. Inflation averaged 4.4 per cent in these countries last year and 3.3 per cent in 1988.

In the developing countries, the revision has been sharper - growth will slow to 2.2 per cent this year before picking up to 4.2 per cent next.

If the oil price rise is larger, the Fund projects even higher inflation and even lower output and employment. Assuming a price of about $33 for the fourth quarter of 1990 - close to current oil market levels - and an average of almost $30 for next year, inflation in industrialised countries would rise above 5 per cent this year and stay at a similar level in 1991.

Output growth in the industrialised countries would slow to roughly 2.4 per cent this year and below 2 per cent next year. These higher prices would benefit output slightly in Britain and Canada, but further contract it in the other five countries of the Group of Seven.

IMF officials point out, however, that its projections do not take into account factors such as economic confidence. These would be likely to intensify the economic impact of higher and higher oil prices.

F.T.
2313 -4 9/20/90

09/20/90 18:30 ☎202 797 0595 EMBASSY OF KOREA ⊡001

0191

US spending cuts and tax rises urged

By Peter Riddell, US Editor in Washington

HIGHER taxes as well as cuts in spending will have to form part of any package to reduce the US budget deficit, the IMF argues in its analysis of the outlook for individual countries.

The report repeatedly emphasises the need for wide-ranging fiscal action in the US to help raise national saving and "set the stage for a decline in interest rates and for exchange rate adjustments conducive to a reduced external deficit."

"To be consistent with the economy's need for saving, the long-term objective of the fiscal plan should be to balance the operational budget – the unified budget balance less the balance (surplus) of the social security trust fund.

"A decision to pare the size of the cut to be implemented out of concern that a large fiscal cut should trigger a recession would risk damaging credibility of the multi-year package that the budget summit is seeking, and thus keep interest rates from declining and raise the medium- term cost of fiscal adjustment."

The IMF economists note that Federal Reserve monetary policy has helped to avoid both a recession and a significant acceleration of inflation. But inflation has been stabilised at a relatively high rate.

"A sharp tightening of monetary policy aimed at a quick reduction of inflation could precipitate a recession – particularly in a situation where relatively high levels of corporate and household debt and the fragility of certain financial institutions raise the economy's vulnerability to high interest rates."

In relation to the UK, the IMF economists argue that the growth of demand is again proving to be more robust than expected.

"Moreover, the resistance of employers to wage demands, a crucial element in the restoration of sound economic conditions, has been weakened by favourable trends in industrial input prices."

Underlying earnings growth has risen and, with productivity falling, unit wage costs have risen at just over 10 per cent a year in the first quarter of 1990.

"On balance, these developments suggest that the process of adjustment will be protracted and will require maintenance of a stringent monetary policy for longer than previously thought."

"Although the continuation of a sizeable inflation differential with the core European Monetary System countries will tend to complicate the entry of the UK into the exchange rate mechanism, a widespread expectation that this will occur soon seems to have underpinned confidence in the pound sterling despite a continuing large external deficit."

On Japan, the report says that the pace of structural reform in areas such as land management and distribution must be intensified, both to improve economic efficiency and the welfare of the Japanese population, and to resolve trade disputes with Japan's trading partners.

F.T.
9/20/90

2313 –5

0192

09/20/90 18:33 ☎202 797 0595 EMBASSY OF KOREA

INTERNATIONAL MONETARY FUND

EMBARGOED
NOT FOR RELEASE BEFORE 6:00 P.M.
WEDNESDAY, SEPTEMBER 19, 1990
WASHINGTON TIME.

WORLD ECONOMIC OUTLOOK

(PRESS SUMMARY)

LIMITED IMPACT OF OIL RISE ON ECONOMIC GROWTH, INFLATION

IMF urges steadiness in fiscal and monetary policies

Higher oil prices will weaken world economic output slightly in 1990-91 and cause inflationary pressures to increase, but the impact of the latest "oil shock" is expected to be less severe than earlier ones in the 1970's, according to the latest projections contained in the World Economic Outlook of the International Monetary Fund.

The updated projections show real GDP growth for the world economy averaging 2 percent in 1990 and 2 1/2 percent in 1991, with industrial countries growing 2 1/2 percent in both years. Developing countries may grow by 2 1/4 percent in 1990 and 4-1/4 percent in 1991, but this masks wide differences among the oil-exporting developing countries, whose growth is projected to be 3 1/2 percent in 1990, and oil-importing countries, whose growth is only expected to be 1 3/4 percent in 1990 due not only to the oil price rise, but also to somewhat lower levels of economic growth in the industrial countries.

The new projections assume that the price of oil will average $26 per barrel for the rest of 1990 and come down gradually to the OPEC reference price of $21 per barrel by the fourth quarter of 1991. This would represent an annual average increase in the price of oil of 20 percent in 1990 and a further increase of 10 1/2 percent in 1991. The projections are based on the assumptions of constant real exchange rates at the August 1990 level, a slight decline in non-fuel commodity prices in 1991, and a U.S. dollar LIBOR interest rate at a constant 8 percent.

Consumer price inflation in the industrial countries may be about 1/4 to 1/2 of a percentage point higher in 1990 (4 3/4 percent) compared with 1989, reflecting the higher oil prices, but declining somewhat in 1991 (to 4 1/4 percent). In the developing countries, already high rates of inflation are expected to persist in 1990, but could decline sharply in 1991 assuming that current stabilization efforts in the high inflation countries are sustained.

The continuing uncertainties surrounding the political and military situation in the Middle East suggest that the economic consequences of events there could be more serious than shown in the projections. However, appropriate economic policy responses could potentially reduce

External Relations Department ◦ Washington, D.C. 20431 ◦ Telephone 202-623-7100

uncertainties. The report says that the experience of previous oil shocks indicates that attempts to limit the pass-through of oil price increases to domestic energy prices would be counterproductive. Oil subsidies would have negative effects on the fiscal position while resorting to domestic price controls would distort the functioning of the markets and give rise to shortages of oil products.

In the longer run, any attempts to keep domestic oil prices below world prices would hinder conservation and discourage development of new sources of energy. Similarly, attempts to mitigate the adverse short-run economic effects on output and employment by easing monetary policy would increase price pressures which would evolve into an inflationary process. Further escalation of inflation and expectations of inflation would ultimately require a sharp tightening of monetary conditions, resulting in high interest rates and lower output and employment. These policy considerations are valid for both the industrial and the developing countries. In those developing countries where incomes policies in the form of wage indexation, public sector wage policies or other mechanisms are prevalent, it will be important to ensure that a one-time increase in domestic prices stemming from the rise in oil costs is not translated into an escalation of wages and a subsequent wage/price spiral. Inasmuch as the increase in oil prices involves a decline in national income, both producers and consumers must clearly understand that real wages as well as profits will unavoidably be lower than they would have been otherwise, the report says.

The updated projections confirm a trend toward a slower growth rate in the world economy after several years of high levels of resource utilization. Industrial countries had grown by an average of almost 4 percent in 1988-89. In 1990-91, North America, the United Kingdom, and a number of smaller industrial countries are expected to experience relatively slow growth, in contrast with Japan and Germany where relatively high growth will be driven by increased domestic demand and investment.

Contrasts in the growth rates of the developing countries will be sharper. The Asian region is expected to experience continued high rates of growth, exceeding 5 percent in 1990-91, while in the developing countries of Europe and the Western Hemisphere output is projected to decline in 1990 as those countries pursue stabilization and anti-inflation financial policies in the face of average inflation in excess of 100 percent, compared with slightly more than 10 percent in other developing countries. Growth is expected to increase and inflation to be reduced substantially in 1991 if recently adopted stabilization programs are sustained.

From 1986 to 1989 there was a substantial reduction in the current account surplus of Japan and a reduction in the current account deficit of the United States. The external imbalance of these two countries is projected to narrow further in 1990-91 and average 1 3/4 percent of GNP. The Federal Republic of Germany would experience a reduction

2313 - 17

08/20/90 18:33 ☎202 797 0595 EMBASSY OF KOREA 004

0194

equivalent to one percent of GNP in its current account surplus to 3 1/4 percent in 1990 and 2 1/4 percent in 1991, as national savings are redirected toward investments associated with reunification. The current account deficit of the United Kingdom would decline due to a contraction of domestic demand and Canada's would increase slightly. Australia, Finland, Greece, New Zealand, Spain and Sweden would continue to post deficits; while Belgium, the Netherlands, and Switzerland would have substantial surpluses. The trade deficit of the industrial countries as a group is projected to narrow to US$28 billion in 1991, a decrease of US$12 billion from 1989.

The current account deficit of the developing countries is estimated to have risen to US$16 billion in 1989, or 1 3/4 percent of exports of goods and services. The deficit is expected to decline to US$5 billion in 1990 and then widen to US$11 billion or about one percent of exports by 1991, mainly due to a deterioration of the trade balance. The four newly industrializing countries of Asia will continue to reduce their current account surpluses as their merchandise imports respond to strong domestic demand, while the growth in their exports is expected to slow due to weaker external demand. The external accounts of several Eastern European countries will improve in 1990 reflecting declining imports and strong export growth related to weak domestic demand and improved access to foreign markets. However, in 1991 the sharp declines in output are expected to be arrested, leading to a deterioration of their current account position due to the short-term effects of trade liberalization and higher investment demand associated with the economic transformations in these countries, as well as a deterioration of their terms of trade with the Soviet Union.

The financing of the current account deficit of the developing countries will require net external borrowing to rise from US$32 billion in 1989 to US$42 billion in 1991, nearly all of it representing official flows.

Total external debt of developing countries is projected to increase by 9 percent in 1990-91 and reach US$1,354 billion at the end of 1991, while commercial bank debt is expected to fall to US$518 billion. The Western Hemisphere is the only region where external debt will remain broadly unchanged (at US$415 billion), while debt of other regions is projected to increase by about 13 percent. The share of total debt owed to official creditors will rise to 45 percent by the end of 1991, reflecting their large contributions to new financing of indebted countries and to debt-reduction operations with the commercial banks, including market-based debt conversions.

The strengthened debt strategy has continued to produce results. Costa Rica, Mexico, and the Philippines have concluded financing packages including debt and debt-service reductions. Venezuela and Morocco have reached agreements with their commercial bank creditors providing debt and debt-service reductions, while Uruguay and Jamaica have obtained various waivers for debt buyback operations. Some

0195

indebted countries --Chile, Mexico, and Venezuela-- have been able to attract external financing on a limited basis, on the strength of successful economic policies. Nevertheless, the number of debt-reduction agreements is still limited because of the prolonged and complex negotiation process, the divergence of interests among creditors, and uncertainties about the sustainability of adjustment efforts by debtors. A number of countries have introduced stabilization programs and signalled their intentions to reach agreement with their external creditors, but have encountered difficulties in the negotiations and experienced a substantial accumulation of external payments arrears.

Previous World Economic Outlook reports have identified three basic components for sustained growth in the industrial countries over the medium term: a monetary policy aimed at controlling inflation with an eventual goal of price stability; a fiscal policy fostering an adequate level of national saving and a rate of capital formation that ensures satisfactory growth; and structural policies designed to increase efficiency, particularly in the form of trade liberalization. While major political and economic events have occurred over the past year, these do not alter, and indeed increase the urgency of implementing the overall strategy required to achieve sustained growth in the world economy.

Action to raise the savings rate in the industrial world over the medium-term has become of paramount importance given the worldwide rise in the demand for investment and the low level of global saving. The most effective way to achieve a substantial increase in national saving is to speed up fiscal consolidation and cut the absorption of saving by governments, the report said. The rise in interest rates over the past year appears to reflect expectations of higher inflation in the future as well as high demand for saving. In this respect, the report points out that the experience of the 1970s shows that there is no lasting trade-off between inflation and growth, and that a relaxation of monetary policy would not yield a lasting reduction in interest rates nor a lasting improvement in employment. From a policy perspective, the issue is how to ensure that external adjustment among the major industrial countries is consistent with the goal of increasing global saving. In this connection, external adjustment should involve primarily policies aimed at raising saving in the deficit countries rather than reducing saving in the surplus countries.

Over the medium term, the global economic environment is expected to be slightly more favorable for the developing countries than in 1990-91. A positive outcome of the Uruguay Round of trade negotiations would increase world trade, which together with an improvement in the terms of trade of the developing countries would help to lift growth. The strongest economic performance in the first half of the 1990s is once again projected for the Asian developing countries on the basis of a continued strong expansion of exports. The Western Hemisphere developing countries are expected to match the Asian growth rate after

0196

1992, although with lower export growth. A recovery is also projected for the developing countries in Europe, reflecting efficiency gains in the context of market-oriented reforms. Projections for Africa show a slight increase in overall growth, but per capita income growth will remain weak.

0197

이첩

원 본

외 무 부

종 별 :

번 호 : USW-4362 일 시 : 90 0926 1724

수 신 : 장 관(기협)

발 신 : 주 미 대사

제 목 : 에너지 관련 자료 요청

당지 의회 산하 기구 CRS 의 요청인바, 90,91년도 아국 원유 수급 계획 (총량및 증가율)을 지급 회보 바람

(공사 손명현-국장)

공람	국제경제국	9월 27일	담 당	과 장	국 장	차관보	차 관	장 관
				(서명)	(서명)			

경제국

PAGE 1

90.09.27 09:28 WG

외신 1과 통제관

0198

	분류번호	보존기간

발 신 전 보

번 호 : WUS-3194 900927 1822 DQ 종별 : 지 급

수 신 : 주 미 대사. 총영사

발 신 : 장 관 (기협)

제 목 : 에너지관련자료

대 : USW - 4362

1. 대호 90년도 아국원유 수입계획은 3억 1,400만 베렐 임.
   (89년도 수입량 : 2억 9,641만 배럴)

2. 91년도 수급계획은 금년 12월에나 수립될 예정이나 90년대비 약 6-7% 정도증가 예상됨. 끝.

(국제경제국장 최 대 화)

보 안 통 제	

앙 고 재	90년 9월 27일	기술협력과	기안자 성 명		과 장		국 장		차 관	장 관
			홍성화				전결			

외신과통제

0199

이해

관리번호	90-492

외 무 부

종 별 :

번 호 : GHW-~~0456~~ 546　　　　일 시 : 90 1109 0830

수 신 : 장관(아프일,경이,기재,정일,기정)

발 신 : 주 가나 대사

제 목 : 정세보고(자료응신 제 49호)

주재국은 11.3 일자로 휘발유가격을 갤론(4.5 리터)당 999 세디(1 불 340 세디)로 인상하는등 각종 석유제품가격을 약 70% 인상하였는바, 이와 관련된 주재국 제반 정세를 아래 보고함

1.90 년중 휘발유가격 인상 경과 및 이유

-1.11.:360 세디(인상전 275 세디)-예산 편성시의 배럴당 18 불에서 23 불로 재조정

-4.2:400 세디:가격 재조정

-9.3:600 세디:걸프만 사태로 국제원유가 인상

-11.3:999 세디:국제 원유가 인상 및 석유소비 억제

2. 인상배경

가. 관계당국의 상기 인상사유와는 달리 내면적인 이유에 대해서는 각종 의견이 있음.

-당초 지식층이 반대하던 라이베리아사태 파견군 ECOMOG 의 비용충당

-91 년 주재국 개최예정의 비동맹외상회의 경비충당등

-IMF 및 세계은행이 촉구하는 외채상환 비용

나. 그러나 당관의 탐문에 의하면, 주재국 정부가 시행해왔던 보조금제도가 여타 각분야에는 거의 폐지되었으나 석유에 대해서는 계속 보조금이 부여되던 것을 동 재정부담을 없애기 위해 금번 걸프만 태를 기회로 동 보조금을 중지하고 석유제품 생산가를 그대로 시중가격으로 반영함에 따라 인상하게 되었다는 것임. 또한 관계 소식통에 의하면, 년말 또는 내년초에 재차 유가인상이 있을 가능성도 있다함.

3. 시민반응　　　　검토필(1990.12.31.) ㊞

지난 9.3 인상시는 불만이 있으도 순응하는 경향이었으나, 금번 인상에 대해서는

중아국　차관　1차보　2차보　기획실　경제국　정문국　안기부

PAGE 1

공람	국제경제국	90년 11월 12일	담당	과장	국장	차관보	차관	장관
						CONFIDENTIAL		

90.11.10　08:32

외신 2과　통제관 DO

0200

불만의 목소리가 상당히 높으며 다소간 어수선한 분위기임.특히 일반시민들이 사용하는 등유의 경우 약 80%가 인상되었으며, 상기 유류인상이 기타 제반물가 인상을 유발시켜 서민생활에 큰 영향을 줄것으로 판단됨.

4. 아국 수산업체 영향 및 대책

-수산업체의 경우 연초 갤런당 330 세디에서,9 월초 500 세디, 금번에 850 세디로 인상됨에 따라 지난 9 월의 인상충격에서 채 벗어나지 못한 상태에서 재차 금번의 705 추가 인상으로 큰 충격을 받고있음. 선박용 기름에 대해 면세혜택을 주는 국제관례를 무시하고 주재국 당국이 톤당 640 불로 고시하였다함(아비장 면세가 : 톤당 356 불)

-수산업체는 내수판매용 생선가격 인상방안, 아비쟝에서 급유하는 방안(왕복유가, 항만사용료 감안시 실익 별무)을 강구하는 한편, 주재국 당국에 선박용 유류에 대한 면세혜택조치를 건의키로 하고 동건의가 관철되지 않을 경우에는 조업중단 또는 폐업을 고려하고 있음. 끝.

(대사 오정일-국장)

예고:91.6.30 일반.

PAGE 2

0201

한국일보
90.12.12.

OPEC 오늘 빈서 「年末회의」

「油價폭락」 對應방안 첨예對立

“페灣 평화적해결땐 20弗이하로 急落”

사우디 “이라크견제” 增産고수

「쿼타中斷」 연장싸고 舌戰예상

0202

석유수출기구(OPEC)총회가 12일 빈에서 열린다. 이번 회의는 매년 개최되는 절규적인 연말회의지만 「때가 때인 만큼」 전 세계의 관심을 집중시키고 있다.

OPEC 연말회의는 회원국들이모여 다음해 석유생산량과 가격등을 논의하는 차원이었지만 올해는 사정이 완전히 틀리다.

5개월째 지속되고있는 페르시아灣 사태가 평화적인 해결기미를 보이고 있는 가운데 열리는 이번 총회는모순된 두가지 이슈를 동시에 다루어야만 한다. 페灣위기가 완전 해소될때까지 회원국의 산유량쿼타및 유가상한규정 적용을 중단하는 문제와 앞으로의 유가폭락에 대한 대응방안마련이 그것이다.

이중 전자에 대해서는 별다른 이견없이 합의할 것이 거의 확실시 되고 있으나 문제는 유가폭락에 대한 대책이다.

이번 회의에는 지난8월말의 OPEC긴급각료 감시위원회에 불참했던 이라크도 참가하며 사우디는 사상유례없는 대규모의 대표단을 보내고 있다.

이라크가 OPEC 산유국들의 자유로운 증산을 결정한 8월말 회의를 「그동안명백한 위법」이라고 비난해온데 반해 사우디는 대폭적인 증산과 함께 대규모의 다목적군을 주둔시키고 있어 양측간의 舌戰은 불보듯 뻔하다.

그러나 회원국의 산유량쿼타및 유가상한 규정적용 중단문제는 이번회의에서도 계속 연장될 정도로 보인다. 현재 전세계적인 석유 수급상황과 국제정세등을로보아 별다른 대안이 없기 때문이다.

다만 그동안 유가급등으로 인해 이라크를 제외한 OPEC회원국들은 약 4백여달러이상의 초과수입을 올렸기 때문에 앞으로 페灣사태 해결후 생산협정을개정할때 이라크측에 상당한 배려를 해야할것으로 예측되고 있다.

하지만 향후 유가폭락대책에 대해서는 첨예한 의견대립을 보이고 있다.

페灣사태 발발후 한때 배럴당 40달러선을 넘었던 유가는 현재 30달러를 밑돌고 있지만 앞으로 더욱 크게 떨어질게 거의 확실시 되고있다.

11월중 OPEC의 1일생산량은 2천3백만배럴에 달해 7월의 생산량 쿼타에 비해 50만배럴정도가 많아 이라크와 쿠웨이트의 제재조치에 따른 부족분을 완전히 메우고 있다.

현재도 석유는 공급과잉상태다. 美에너지부는 「더이상의 추가적인증산은 필요없다. 세계전체로 보아 현재의 공급량은 수요를 하루에 약 10만배럴이상 웃돌고 있다. 전쟁이 일어나지 않을 경우 내년 3월에는 공급이 1백만배럴정도 초과할 것이다」고 밝히고있다.

국제에너지기구(IEA)도 지난 10일 파리에서회의를갖고 내년도 선진국들의 석유수요가 떨어질것이라고 예측했다. 이 기구는 경제협력개발기구(OECD)의 석유비축분이 지난10월1일 4억7천7백만톤(98일분)에 달해 81년이후 최고수준에 달했다고 밝혔다.

지난주 멕시코에서 회담을 가졌던 非OPEC 산유국들도 유가급락의 우려를 표시했다. 이 자리에 함께한 OPEC 사무총장은 페灣사태가 평화적으로 해결되고 이라크와 쿠웨이트가 본격 원유수출을 재개할 경우 유가는 20달러 밑으로 떨어질 것이라고 우려했다.

관계자들은 페灣사태 해결후 이라크는 5개월내에, 쿠웨이트는 1년이내에 종전수준을 회복할 것으로 내다보고 있다.

이를 입증하듯 미국의 월스트리트 저널紙는 10일 전문가들을 인용, 페灣위기가사라질 경우 유가는 배럴당 현재보다 35~45% 떨어진 15달러선, 경우에 따라서는 10달러선까지 폭락할지도 모른다고 예상했다.

이에 가장 다급한 쪽은 OPEC이지만 내부의 의견차가 심해 뚜렷한 대응방안을 내놓지 못하고 있는 것이다.

생산능력의 한계를 느끼고있는 이란과 인도네시아, 리비아와 분쟁종결후 국내경제회복을위해 외화가 절대필요한 이라크는 이번총회에서 페灣사태 종결후 지난7월에 체결했던 생산협정으로의 복귀를 강력히 주장할 것으로 보인다.

그러나 현재 생산량을 크게 늘리고 있는 사우디와 베네수엘라, 아랍에미리트등은 한꺼번에 생산량을 대폭 줄이는것은 기술적으로 무리가 많다고 반발하고 있다. 더욱이 사우디로서는 분쟁종결후에도 이라크를 견제해야만돼 의도적으로도 유가를 낮출수밖에 없다는 분석이다. 때문에 이번 총회에서도「가격파」와「증산파」간의 간격은 결코 좁혀지지 않을 것으로 전망되고 있다.

OPEC는 또한 이번 페灣사태의 교훈으로 소비국들과의 유가안정을위한 공동회의개최를 강력희망하고 있으나 이 문제 역시 소비국들이 회의적이기때문에 별다른 결실을 이루지 못할것으로 보인다.

결국 이번 총회는 산적한 문제에도 불구, 별다른 결의도없이 지난 이란·이라크간 전쟁때처럼 회원국들간의 분쟁이 있더라도 회의는 열린다는 최소한의 단합을 외부에 보여주는 「송년파티」의 수준을 벗어나지 못할것이라는 분석이 일반적이다. 【李相湖기자】

◇OPEC주요국 증산현황

(1일생산량·단위 1천배럴)

국명	현행 생산쿼타	11월의 생산량	증산율(%)
사우디	5,380	8,000	48·7
아랍에미리트	1,500	2,280	52·0
베네수엘라	1,945	2,325	19·5
이란	3,140	3,200	1·9
나이지리아	1,611	1,900	17·9
리비아	1,233	1,500	21·6
이라크	3,140	450	-85·6
쿠웨이트	1,500	250	-83·3

◇페灣사태이후 처음으로 13개 전회원국이 참가하는 OPEC총회가 12일 빈에서 개최된다. 사진은 지난7월 87차 OPEC석유장관회의 폐막후 기자회견을 하고 있는 사데크·무세나의장 모습.

한국일보

90.12.13.

"각국 비축분 사용안해 油價파동"

【빈AP=聯合】 사데크·부세나 OPEC(석유수출국기구)의장은 12일 페르시아灣 위기가 일단 종식되면 현재의 과도한 원유생산은 전세계에 석유 과다 현상을 초래, 시장을 일대 혼란에 빠뜨릴 수 있을 것이라고 경고했다。

알제리 광업장관이기도 한 부세나 의장은 이날개최된 OPEC 동계 각료회의 기조 연설을통해 석유 소비국들이 자국의 비축량을 늘리기 위해 원유시장에 나돌고있는 잉여 석유를 사용하고있다고 신랄히 비난했다。

그는 또 페르시아灣위기가 평화적으로 해결될 경우 전세계는 석유로 뒤덮일것이며 우리는 향후10여년간 혼란의 시대에 직면하게 될것이라고 말했다。

그는 이어 만약 세계 석유 소비국들이 금수조치를 당하고 있는 이라크 및 쿠웨이트産 석유 부족분을 보전키 위해 자국 비축분 가운데 일부를 사용했더라면 최근과같은 유가 파동은 피할 수 있었을 것이라고 주장했다。

부세나의장은 『그러나 이들 소비국들이 아직도 자국의 비축분 사용과 같은 조치들을 채택하려 들지않고 있으며 오히려 OPEC로 하여금 최고한도의 생산을 하도록 부추기고 있다』고 지적했다.

0203

이혀

원 본

외 무 부

종 별 :

번 호 : MXW-1460 일 시 : 90 1218 1540

수 신 : 장 관(기협,미중)

발 신 : 주 멕시코 대사

제 목 : 91년도 멕시코 원유 생산계획

1. 주재국 국영석유회사 PEMEX 는 91년도 사업계획서를 발표, 국제 원유시장에서 의존 재강화 및 그간 주재국이 체결한 원유공급계약 이행을 위해서 내년도 멕산원유 수급 상국내 수요보다도 국제 수출에 우선순위를 둘것이라고 밝혔는바, 동 사업 계획상 원유수급 현황은 아래와 같음.

0 91년도 총 원유생산 목표액: 267만 B/D (연간 총생산액: 977백만 B)

0 수출액: 136만 B/D (연간 총수출액:496백만 B, 생산량의 51퍼센트)

0 국내 수요 충당액: 131만 B/D

2. 주재국의 원유수출은 82년 이후 계속 총생산액의 50퍼센트 이상을 점유하고 있는바, 최근 이라크 사태로 인하여 일일 10만 배럴 증산수출하고 있으며 금년 8월-11월간 평균수출액은 135.5만 B/D 로서 총생산액 (250만B/D) 의 54.2퍼센트에 해당됨.

3. 11월중 주재국 원유수출 가격은 평균 배럴당 19.63불로 평균 127만 B/D 를 수출하였으며 (당초90년 계획상 평균수출 유가 13불, 평균수출예상액 123만 B/D) 이라크 사태 발발 이전멕시코의 석유 수출가격은 배럴당 14.77불, 평균수출액 122만 B/D 에 대비, 지난 8-11월중평균 수출 가격은 28.14불, 평균 수출액은 135.5만B/D 로 집계되고 있음.

4. 한편, PEMEX 비공식 통계에 의하면 금년말 주재국 석유수출에 따른 수입은 90억불을 상회할것이라 하며 (전년대비 54.2퍼센트 증가) 이는 주재국 재정 적자 해소에 크게 기여할 것이라함.

(대사 이복형-국장)

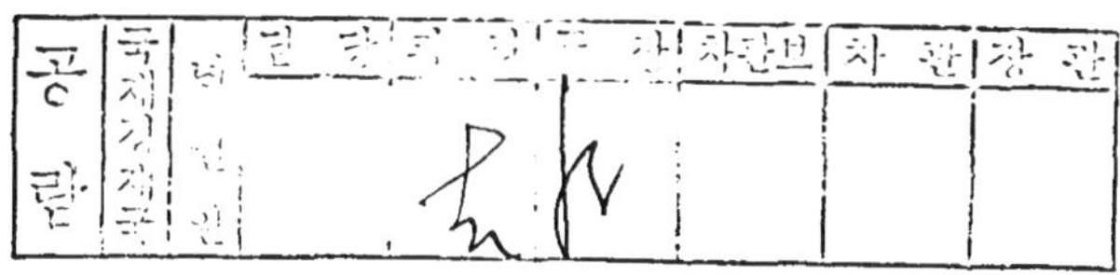

경제국 미주국

PAGE 1 90.12.19 09:13 WG

외신 1과 통제관

0204

걸 프 사 태 정 세 〈126〉

(12.20. 15:00 현재)

중동아프리카국
중 근 동 과

1. 美, 91.1.15. 開戰하긴 힘들듯

체니 美 國防長官은 걸프灣에 增派된 美軍이 유엔 安保理의 武力使用 決議案이 設定한 이라크軍의 撤收 最終 時限인 91.1.15. 까지 武力 攻擊 態勢를 갖추지 못할것 같다고 示唆함.

- o 체니 장관, 향후 수주일간 사우디 도착 예정인 추가 병력들이 동 시한까지 전투태세 돌입이 불가함을 표명.
- o 캘빈 월러 사우디 주둔 미군 사령관, 만사가 완벽히 진행 된다면 1월 15일과 2월 중순 사이 작전 준비를 갖출수 있을 것이라며, 지상군의 배치 완료 까지는 적대행위가 불가하다는 입장을 표명

2. 이라크, 接境 兵力 增强

이라크는 쿠웨이트에서의 軍事力을 强化하기 위해 쿠웨이트 및 南部 이라크의 兵力 規模를 51만명으로 增强해 놓고 있다 함.

- o 이라크 석유장관, 국민들에게 공격에 대비한 유류부품 비축을 지시
- o 후세인 대통령, 팔레스타인 문제가 해결될 경우 쿠웨이트 문제를 양보할 용의가 있음을 시사 함으로서, 화.전 양면책 구사

3. 主要 關聯 動向

〈미 국〉

- o 걸프 위기가 종결 되더라도 호르므즈 해협 개방 유지등을 위해 해군력은 걸프만내 계속 주둔 예정
- o 백악관 대변인, 베이커-후세인 직접회담 일자에 대해 미.이라크간 새로운 접촉 사실이 없음을 표명

〈소 련〉

- o 인도양 함대 사령관, 걸프 위기에 무력 공격은 세계대전으로 비화될 우려가 있으므로 외교적 해결책이 모색 되어야 함을 시사

〈기 타〉

- o 파키스탄, 이란, 터어키 3개국 외무장관, 걸프사태 관련 91.1.5. 이스라마바드에서 회담 개최 예정

4. 僑民 撤收 動向

- o 이라크 총723명중 철수인원 603명, 잔류 120명
  - 철수인원 전일과 동일

0205

외교문서 비밀해제: 걸프 사태 26

걸프 사태 국제원유 수급 동향 1

초판인쇄 2024년 03월 15일
초판발행 2024년 03월 15일

지은이 한국학술정보(주)
펴낸이 채종준
펴낸곳 한국학술정보(주)
주 소 경기도 파주시 회동길 230(문발동)
전 화 031-908-3181(대표)
팩 스 031-908-3189
홈페이지 http://ebook.kstudy.com
E-mail 출판사업부 publish@kstudy.com
등 록 제일산-115호(2000. 6. 19)

ISBN 979-11-6983-986-0 94340
979-11-6983-960-0 94340 (set)